D0667743

WINSTON
AND
CLEMENTINE

WINSTON
AND
CLEMENTINE

*The Triumphs and Tragedies
of the Churchills*

RICHARD HOUGH

BANTAM BOOKS
TORONTO • NEW YORK • LONDON • SYDNEY • AUCKLAND

WINSTON & CLEMENTINE

The Publishers have made every attempt to contact the owners of the photographs appearing in this book. In the few instances where they have been unsuccessful they invite the copyright holders to contact them direct.

A BANTAM BOOK 0 553 40162 9

Originally published in Great Britain by Bantam Press, a division of Transworld Publishers Ltd.

PRINTING HISTORY
Bantam Press edition published 1990
Bantam edition with published 1991

This book is set in 10.5 on 12pt Times by Falcon Typographic Art Ltd., Edinburgh & London

Bantam Books are published by Transworld Publishers Ltd., 61–63 Uxbridge Road, Ealing, London W5 5SA, in Australia by Transworld Publishers (Australia) Pty. Ltd., 15–23 Helles Avenue, Moorebank, NSW 2170, and in New Zealand by Transworld Publishers (N.Z.) Ltd., Cnr. Moselle and Waipareira Avenues, Henderson, Auckland.

Made and printed in Great Britain by Cox & Wyman, Reading, Berks.

Acknowledgements

The author wishes to thank Mr Winston S. Churchill MP, Mr Peregrine Churchill, and other members of the family for their kindness, helpfulness, and tangible assistance during the writing of this book.

Other political and personal reminiscences have been provided by too many people to list here, and I hope they will accept a collective acknowledgment of my gratitude.

No fewer than nine of my earlier books have featured Churchill in a major naval role, including *Former Naval Person: Churchill & the Wars at Sea*, and I have thus been able in part to draw on research and interviews conducted as long ago as the early 1960s. Many of the people involved, including Professor A. J. Marder, Rear-Admiral Edward Dannreuther, Admiral Sir William Tennant, and Admiral of the Fleet Earl Mountbatten of Burma, have long since died, but I do not forget their posthumous contribution.

R. H.
November 1989

Contents

Some of the People
Involved in Their Lives

Aitken, Max (first Baron Beaverbrook) (1879–1964) Canadian financier and newspaper proprietor. Owner of *Daily Express*. Minister for aircraft production, 1940–1941, Minister for Supply, 1941–1942.

Amery, Julian (1919–   ) Son of below. War correspondent Spain, 1938–1939. Special missions in Middle East and southeast Europe, 1939–1944, and China, 1945. MP Preston North, 1950–1966, presently MP Brighton Pavilion.

Amery, Leo (1873–1955) At Harrow with Winston. War correspondent South Africa, 1899. War Cabinet, 1917. First Lord of the Admiralty, 1922. Secretary of State for India, 1940–1945.

Asquith, Herbert Henry (first Earl of Oxford) (1852–1928) Liberal Prime Minister, 1908–1916.

Asquith, Margot, Countess of Oxford (1864–1945) Second wife of Herbert Asquith.

Balfour, Arthur James (first Earl) (1848–1930) Friend and associate of Lord Randolph. Conservative Prime Minister, 1902–1905. Succeeded Winston as First Lord of the Admiralty, 1915.

Balsan, Jacques (1892–1956) Wealthy French patron of the arts.

See Marlborough.

Barnes, Major-General Sir Reginald, DSO (1871–1946) Fellow officer and friend of Winston in the Army.

Baruch, Bernard (1870–1965) President Wilson's Chairman War Industries Board, 1918, when became close friend and confederate of Winston.

Battenberg, Prince Louis of Admiral His Serene Highness. Later first Marquis of Milford Haven (1854–1921), First Sea Lord, 1912–1914, with Winston as First Lord. An efficient adminstrator whose German origins told against him. *See* Mountbatten.

Beatty, David, Admiral of the Fleet, DSO (first Earl) (1871–1936) With Winston at Omdurman, and his Naval Secretary, 1911. Commanded Battle Cruisers and Grand Fleet, 1913–1919. First Sea Lord, 1919–1927.

Beaverbrook, Lord see Aitken.

"Bendor" see Westminster.

Berry, William (first Viscount Camrose) (1879–1954) Editor in Chief *Daily Telegraph*, 1928–1954, *Sunday Times*, 1915–1936. Close friend and ally of Winston.

Birkenhead (first Earl) *see* Smith, F. E.

Blandford, George see Marlborough, eighth Duke of.

Blood, General Sir Bindon (1842–1940) Served Zulu, Afghan,

Egyptian, Malakand wars. Soldier patron of Winston.

Boothby, Sir Robert (later Lord Boothby) (1900–1986) Principal private secretary to Winston, 1926–1929, and close friend thereafter.

Brabazon, Colonel John (1843–1922) Winston's friend and supporter. CO 4th Hussars.

Bracken, Brendan (first Viscount) (1901–1958) Irish Conservative MP and close friend and associate of Winston, to whom PPS, 1940–1941. Wide business and City associations.

Brooke, General Alan (later Field Marshal and first Viscount Alanbrooke "Brookie") (1883–1963) Commander in Chief Home Forces, 1940–1941. Chief of Imperial General Staff, 1941–1946. Could stand up to Winston, who continued to admire him nevertheless.

Campbell-Bannerman, Sir Henry (1836–1908) Liberal leader House of Commons, 1899, denounced conduct of South African War. Prime Minister, 1905–1908.

Carson, Sir Edward (1854–1935) Outstanding Irish advocate. MP Dublin University, 1892–1918. As leader of Irish Unionists, insured exclusion of Ulster from southern Ireland. Close associate of Winston's.

Cassel, Sir Ernest (1852–1921) German-born financier and international banker. Friend and associate of Lord Randolph and Winston.

Chamberlain, Austen (1865–1937) Liberal Unionist MP Foreign Secretary, 1924–1929. Half brother to Neville Chamberlain.

Chamberlain, Neville (1869–1940) Prime Minister, 1937–1940. Promoter of appeasement towards German expansionism, and political foe of Winston.

Cockran, Bourke (1854–1923) Formidable American lawyer and politician. Democrat Member of Congress for New York. Friend and admirer of Winston.

Colville, Sir John "Jock" (1915–1988) Diplomat turned private secretary successively to Neville Chamberlain, Winston, and Clement Attlee – and Winston again, 1951–1955. Also close adviser to Clementine, especially after Winston's death.

Cooper, Alfred Duff (first Viscount Norwich) DSO (1890–1954) Soldier Great War. Conservative MP and statesman. Secretary of State for War, then First Lord of the Admiralty, 1937, resigning over Chamberlain's appeasement, 1938. Ambassador to France, 1944–1947. Married to Lady Diana Cooper (Manners).

Cromer, first Earl (Evelyn Baring, of Baring bankers) (1841–1917) Consul-General in Egypt, 1883–1907.

Curzon, George Nathaniel (first Marquis) (1859–1925) Viceroy of India, 1899–1905. Foreign Secretary, 1919–1924.

Eden, Anthony (first Earl of Avon) (1897–1977) Foreign Minister, 1935–1938, resigned in protest over appeasement. Secretary of State for War, 1940. Foreign Minister, 1940–1945. Succeeded Winston as Prime Minister, 1955. Married (two) Jack Churchill's only daughter Clarissa, 1952.

Everest, Mrs Elizabeth ("Woom") (1833–1895) Beloved nursemaid to Winston and Jack.

Fisher, John Arbuthnot "Jacky" Admiral of the Fleet, Lord

(1841–1920) Highly controversial reformer of the Royal Navy. First Sea Lord, 1904–1910, 1914–1915. Mercurial friend and ally to Winston. Loved by Edward VII, distrusted by George V. Margot Asquith, Clementine Churchill, and many others.

French, Field-Marshal Sir John (first Earl of Ypres) (1852–1925) Commander in Chief British Expeditionary Forces in France, 1914–1915. Friend and admirer of Winston.

Grey, Sir Edward (first Viscount Grey of Falloden) (1862–1933) Liberal MP and statesman. Exceptionally able Foreign Secretary, 1905–1916. Close friend of Winston and Clementine.

Guest, Frederick "Freddy" (1875–1937) and *Ivor* (1873–1939) Sons of Lord Wimborne and Aunt Cornelia, Lady Wimborne, who was sister of Lord Randolph and greatly loved admirer of Winston. Both cousins became MPs.

Haldane, Captain Aylmer, DSO (1862–1950) Friend and fellow officer of Winston. Commanded fatal train party in South Africa, and like Winston was made prisoner and escaped. Became a knighted general.

Haldane, R. B. H. (1856–1928) Army reformer after South African War. Secretary of State for War, 1905–1912. Lord High Chancellor, 1912. Competitive friendship with Winston.

Haig, General Sir Douglas (first Earl Haig of Bemersyde) (1861–1928) Succeeded French as Commander in Chief in France, 1915. Steadfast soldier and steady friend of Winston.

Hamilton, General Sir Ian (1853–1947) Served in India and South Africa with Winston, commanding mounted infrantry in capture of Pretoria. Commanded Army at Gallipoli, 1915.

Hopkins, Harry (1890–1946) Benefactor, reformer, statesman. Special adviser and assistant to Franklin D. Roosevelt. Noted for his nobility of mind and good sense. Became close friend of Winston.

Hozier, Nellie Sister of Clementine. *See* Romilly.

Ismay, General Sir Hastings "Pug" DSO (1887–1965) Chief of Staff to Winston, 1940–1945, and a vital link in the chain of command.

Jerome, Leonard (1817–1891) Father of Jennie Churchill, Lady Randolph, and husband of Clara (1825–1895). Newspaper proprietor and financier.

Jeune, Lady (1845–1931) Married, 1881, Sir Francis Jeune, later first Baron St. Helier. Famous hostess, friend, and supporter of Winston.

Law, Andrew Bonar (1858–1923) Conservative MP and leader of his party, 1911. Chancellor of the Exchequer, 1916–1918. Prime Minister, 1922–1923.

Lawrence, T. E. "Lawrence of Arabia" (1885–1930) Soldier (leader of the Arab Revolt), writer, archaeologist, airman, motorcyclist. Admirer and friend of Winston.

Lindemann, Frederick (first Viscount Cherwell) (1894–1952) "the Prof" Scientist and personal assistant to Winston. Loved by all the family.

Lloyd George, David (first Earl Lloyd George of Dwyfor) (1863–1945) Liberal MP and statesman and occasional friend and ally of Winston. Chancellor of the Exchequer, 1908–1915. Prime Minister, 1916–1922.

Lytton, Victor (second Earl of) (1876–1947) Civil Lord of the Admiralty, 1916, 1919–1920. Married Pamela Plowden, Winston's first love, 1902. Lifelong friend and associate of Winston.

MacDonald, James Ramsay (1866–1937) Labour statesman. MP, 1906. Lost seat because of his pacifism in the Great War. But returned to Parliament and Prime Minister in first Labour administration, 1924. Led national coalition, 1931–1935 though expelled by his party. Despised by Winston.

Macmillan, Harold (1894–1987) Soldier in Great War. Conservative MP Minister Resident in North Africa, 1942–1945. Succeeded Eden as Prime Minister, 1957–1963. Unadmired by Winston.

Marlborough, Charles Richard (ninth Duke of) (1871–1934) "Sunny." Lifelong friend of Winston. Succeeded to title, 1892. Married Consuelo Vanderbilt, divorced, 1920, she later married Jacques Balsan.

Marlborough, George Charles (eighth Duke of) (1844–1892) "Bertha," Married, 1869, Lady Albertha, divorced, 1883.

Marlborough, John Winston (seventh Duke of) (1822–1883) Married, 1843, Lady Frances Vane, "Fanny" (1822–1899).

Marsh, Sir Edward (1872–1953) First Class Clerk in Colonial Office, 1905. Private secretary to Winston, 1905–1915, 1917–1922, 1924–1929. Debonair aesthete and patron of the arts. Beloved by Winston and Clementine.

Martin, Sir John (1904–1991) Civil servant. Private secretary to Winston, 1940–1945, principal private secretary, 1941.

McKenna, Reginald (1863–1943) Liberal statesman. As First Lord of the Admiralty, 1908–1911, obliged to swap jobs with Winston at the Home Office, to his chagrin. Mutual distrust thereafter.

Montagu, Edwin (1879–1924) Conservative MP. Secretary of State for India, 1917–1922. Close friend of Winston and Clementine. Married, 1915, Venetia Stanley.

Montagu, Judy Daughter of above.

Moran, Lord see Wilson

Mountbatten, Captain Lord Louis, DSO, later Admiral of the Fleet (first Earl Mountbatten of Burma) (1900–1979) Son of Admiral Prince Louis of Battenberg. Socialist admirer of Winston while considering him to be a megalomaniac. Deft manipulator and opportunist. Appointed last Viceroy of India to secure its independence.

Moyne, Walter Lord, DSO (1880–1944) Statesman, soldier, millionaire (Guinness beer). Friend of Winston and Clementine. Murdered while Depty Minister of State, Cairo.

Plowden, Pamela see Lytton.

Romilly, Colonel Bertram, DSO (1878–1940) Heroic soldier badly wounded in Great War and nursed by Nellie Hozier, who married him, 1915. Two sons, Giles and Esmond.

Rosebery, Archibald Philip (fifth Earl of) (1847–1929) Prominent Liberal politician. Succeeded Gladstone as Prime Minister, 1894. His horses thrice won the Derby. Close friend and associate of Lord Randolph and of Winston in his early political days.

St Helier, Lady see Jeune.

Salisbury, Robert Arthur (third Marquis of) (1830–1903) Conservative MP, 1853. Foreign Secretary, 1878. Prime Minister, 1885, when Lord Randolph resigned as Chancellor of the Exchequer. Assisted Winston.

Seal, Sir Eric (1898–1972) Civil servant. Principal private secretary to Winston as First Lord of the Admiralty and Prime Minister, 1939–1941.

Sinclair, Sir Archibald, DSO (first Viscount Thurso) (1890–1970) Soldier, statesman, lifelong friend of Winston and Clementine. Secretary of State for Air, 1940–1945.

Smith, F. E. (first Earl of Birkenhead) (1872–1930) Advocate, Ulster supporter, wit, reckless politician, and heroic drinker. Lord Chancellor, 1919. Secretary of State for India (1924–1928). Winston's closest friend.

Smuts, Jan Christian, Field Marshal (1870–1950) South African soldier and politician. Prime Minister of South Africa, 1919. Much respected and admired by Winston.

Stanley, Venetia (1887–1948) Clementine's cousin and close friend. Confidante of Asquith as Prime Minister until her marriage to Edwin Montagu.

Trenchard, Hugh, Lord, Marshal of the RAF (1873–1965) "Father of the RAF." His brilliance at once recognized by Winston when he was placed in charge of the RAF in 1920.

Vanderbilt, Consuelo see Marlborough, ninth Duke of.

Welldon, Right Reverened James (1854–1937) Winston's firm, brilliant, and percipient headmaster at Harrow. Later Dean of Manchester, 1906–1918, and Durham, 1918–1933.

Westminster, Hugh Richard Arthur DSO (Duke of) (1879–1953) "Bendor" Immensely wealthy close friend of Winston. Fought in South Africa and Great War.

Wilson, Sir Charles, MD (Lord Moran) (1882–1977) Winston's personal physician from 1940. An articulate, sympathetic, intelligent doctor, but with dubious ethical standards.

Winant, John Gilbert (1889–1947) "Gil" American Ambassador to Britain, 1941–1946. Greatly admired and loved by Winston.

THE MARLBOROUGHS
Abridged Table

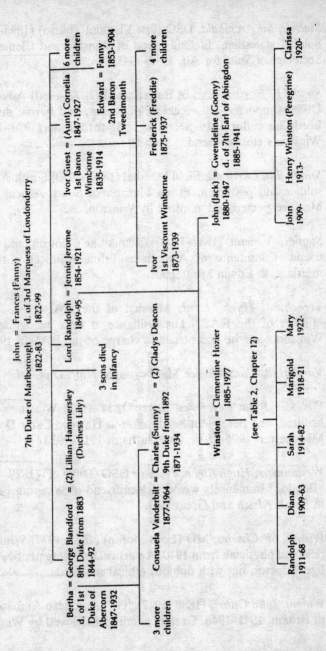

CLEMENTINE HOZIER
Abridged Table

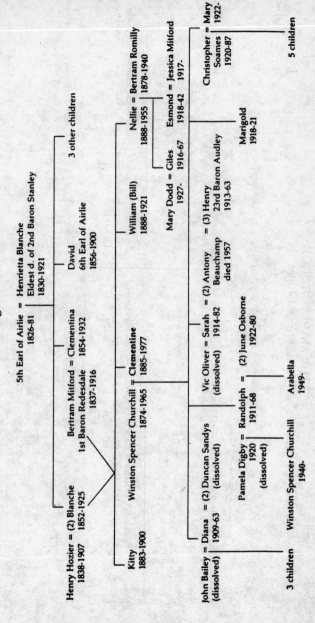

1

The Dinner Party

On a damp March evening in London, in 1908, Clementine Hozier returns home, tired and hungry after a hard day's work. She has been giving French lessons at two shillings and sixpence an hour. Clementine lives with her mother at a small terraced house, 51 Abingdon Villas, off Kensington High Street, and money is always desperately short. Because she and her mother are descended from one of the oldest and most distinguished Scottish families, the Ogilvys of Airlie, there is never a shortage of invitations to balls and dinners. But social life is expensive to maintain: gowns, white kid gloves, shoes, hairdressing, cab fares if you have no carriage, and so on. The beautiful, distinguished twenty-three-years-old Clementine is much in demand, but cannot often go out.

Her mother greets her at the door. 'There is a message from Aunt Mary, dear. Just arrived. Can you come to dinner, please. One of her guests has fallen out, and that leaves her with thirteen.'

'Mama, I'm so tired. I really don't want to go. I've no gown ready and no clean gloves.'

Inside the little parlour – so different from the great hall at Cortachy Castle, the ancestral home – Blanche Hozier takes a firm stand. Aunt Mary, Lady St Helier, an aunt to Blanche by marriage, is a veritable empress of London social life who knows, and organizes, everyone. She has been singularly helpful to Clementine after her 'coming out'. 'You really cannot let her down,' Blanche Hozier says firmly. 'Now just go upstairs and change.'

On that same evening, a similar little struggle is taking place just two and a half miles to the east, at 12 Bolton Street, off Piccadilly. There, a rising young politician, accustomed to getting his way, is taking a deep hot bath after a long day in the House of Commons. His thoughts are broken by a voice, speaking through the steam: 'You are dining out and will be late,' his private secretary, Eddie Marsh, reminds him uncompromisingly.

'Where am I going?'

'To Lady St Helier's.'

'I am not going,' declares Winston Churchill. His old nanny, Mrs Everest, would recognize the petulant note with a slight trace of defiance in it. 'It will be a great bore.'

'But you can't do that.' Eddie is outraged. 'Especially not to her. You've only got to remember how kind she was, making Sir Evelyn Wood get you to the Omdurman campaign.'

Reluctantly, Winston gets out of his bath. He is putting on weight and keeping his tailor busy. It does not bother him in the least. He dresses, and shortly before he is ready, Eddie goes downstairs to hail a cab.

Clementine is at the mansion in Portland Place on time, but for an anxious period Lady St Helier fears that the unwelcome thirteen-to-dinner will be her fate in spite of her efforts. She can keep her guests waiting no longer. The guest of honour is Sir Frederick Lugard, Governor of Hong Kong, but more renowned for his soldiering and for his explorations and administrative achievements in East and West Africa. With him is his powerful and uncompromising wife, Flora, Lady Lugard, one-time colonial editor of *The Times*, who disapproves root and branch of everything that Winston Churchill represents.

Halfway through dinner Winston turns up, full of glib excuses, and sits down at the only empty chair, between Clementine and Lady Lugard. Winston's youngest daughter, Mary, will later write: 'Since Winston was, at the time, Undersecretary for the Colonies, he might well have been expected to devote a good deal of his attention to the distinguished and knowledgeable Lady Lugard; however, he turned almost at once to the ravishing young woman on his left, and monopolized her for the rest of the dinner.'

They have met before, but it is unlikely that either of them refers to that unpromising occasion, which may well have been expunged from Winston's memory. Clementine was introduced to Winston by Winston's mother, Jennie, at a ball some four years earlier as the daughter of an old friend of hers; moreover, Jennie's brother-in-law, Sir Jack Leslie, is godfather to Clementine. Abstracted and tongue-tied as Winston often is on introduction to a young woman – no small talk, no practice in light flattery – he failed to ask her to dance, and she was whisked away by another. Because almost everything she had heard about Winston was unfavourable she was offended but not greatly disappointed.

Now here he is, next to her, and there is no escape. In a very short time she is enchanted by his attention, admiring of the agility of his mind, laughing at his jokes and anecdotes, warmed by his personality. She has met many up-and-coming young men, but none who sparkles more dazzlingly, none who leads her so confidently into new worlds of unfamiliar dimensions.

The effect Clementine has upon Winston is startling. Customarily, he is a lingerer at the table when the women withdraw, with a great cigar burning as strongly as the political conversation. Tonight he is first away to the drawing room, heading unerringly toward Clementine. The effect upon Lady Lugard, who has been almost totally ignored by Winston on her right, can only be imagined; but she will later write (as she had written in *The Times*) of 'wild Winston . . . an ignorant boy, so obviously ignorant in regard to colonial affairs and at the same time so full of personal activity that the damage he may do appears to be colossal'.

Winston and Clementine talk together through the rest of the evening, occasionally breaking into laughter, ignoring the other guests in their total absorption in each other. Later, neither of them will ever remember a single word they uttered. When they at last gather to collect their coats, Clementine has to endure teasing from some of the other women – but not from Lady Lugard.

Clementine's upbringing was as unstable as her family

background was distinguished. Born in 1852, her mother, Lady Blanche Ogilvy, was the first child of the fifth Earl of Airlie and Henrietta Blanche, the eldest daughter of the second Baron Stanley, a good mix of the best Scottish blood. Blanche had grown up a fetching, flighty girl who indulged in passing whims and fancies, flirting outrageously whenever the opportunity arose, laughing a great deal, and learning little. One of her granddaughters has written: 'Her angelic countenance belied a very humanly passionate nature, and, as she grew older, she was to cause her parents grave anxiety by her wayward and capricious spirit.'

Blanche loved dearly her younger sisters Griselda and Maude; she was also fond of her brother, David, younger by four years, who was to inherit the earldom, though he disapproved of her flighty carryings-on. But she was closest of all to her younger sister Clementine, who married a man sixteen years older than herself, Bertram Mitford.

Like her younger sister, Blanche tended to admire men a good deal older than herself, just as she greatly admired her brother-in-law Bertram. She was 26 years old, known in the family as Aunt Natty, her beauty matured, when she met an army colonel, Henry Montague Hozier. He was a remarkable man, fourteen years older than Blanche, of dashing appearance, with many battles behind him in China and Abyssinia. He had become military correspondent to *The Times*, and covered the Franco–Prussian War for that newspaper. He was a highly successful pioneer of radiotelegraphy, had become secretary of the corporation of Lloyd's, the world-famous insurance underwriters, and was responsible for setting up Lloyd's world-spanning wireless-telegraphy link.

Colonel Hozier had not made a great fortune, but he had made something of a name for himself when he first met Lady Blanche Ogilvy. He was not, however, of very good character. His business ethics were suspect, though they never got him into serious trouble; and when he decided he would marry Blanche he failed to tell her that he had been the guilty party in a divorce and had been a co-respondent in another divorce.

4

The Ogilvy family had no reason to doubt the honour of this suitor. He came from a perfectly respectable Glaswegian family (his father was the first Baron Newlands). The Ogilvys were also anxious to get naughty Blanche 'settled'. The marriage went ahead, and very swiftly fell into ruins. The colonel had decided views about a wife's place in the home; Blanche wanted fun and excitement, flattery, and men about her. And she wanted children, which her husband refused to give her.

They had a house in Grosvenor Street, Mayfair, but fortunately Colonel Hozier was away a great deal, and Blanche found further freedom and independence in their small house in Scotland, which allowed her to keep in touch with her family, and especially her sister Clementine and Bertram.

It is impossible now to be accurate about the sequence of events, the consideration, the conversation, perhaps even the laughter, that culminated in the momentous domestic decision that Bertram should sire Blanche's children as well as his wife's. However wide the search, no better father could have been found. Bertram was good-looking, strong, kind, and (as was to be proven) obliging. He was also fecund.* He and his wife had already produced six children when Blanche's first child, Kitty, was conceived, and more were to follow.

Aunt Natty's second child was born on 1 April 1885 (April Fool's Day, and after a very brief labour in London), another daughter. Blanche named her Clementine after her sister. Three years later, like a final generous offering by her brother-in-law, Blanche gave birth to twins, a boy and a girl, to be named Helen and William – Nellie and Bill.

After this tidy if unorthodox start, the Hozier children led, for a while, a relatively settled nursery life, seeing little of their mother (but that was not unusual) and even less of

---

*His second son, David, the second Baron Redesdale, also fathered seven children, including the Mitford girls – Nancy, Diana, Jessica, and others.

their 'father'. Two years after the birth of the twins, Colonel Hozier decided he had had enough. He, quite reasonably, accused his wife of adultery, a fact that was whispered fairly loudly in the family, and told her he was going to separate from her. When the father of the children and Blanche's brother, David, attempted to organize some sort of maintenance for her – she had scarcely a penny of her own – Colonel Hozier rounded on them and threatened to expose his wife as an adulteress. Why should he pay an adulteress, and pay for children that were not his own?

Eventually, an agreement between the estranged pair was patched together. Hozier, the colonel who had never wanted children, now demanded the custody of the two eldest girls, Kitty and Clementine, while the twins were left in the care of Blanche, who was to receive a modest allowance. The innocent peace of the nursery was over. The colonel sent the two girls in his charge to a sort of female Dotheboy's Hall in Edinburgh. When they complained about the conditions, he promised to take them away, but never did. Blanche, discovering their whereabouts, tried to steal them away, failed, and settled into some rooms overlooking the school. From the window, she could at least give cheer to Clementine and Kitty when they passed on strictly disciplined walks.

This experience, and others equally bizarre, gave rise to an exceptional solidarity and affection between the sisters. They were very different girls in personality: Kitty, preferred and spoilt by her mother, was spontaneous, violent, and fearless; Clementine was shy and buttoned up, already with inflexible principles and short on joy and laughter. Kitty's beauty was that of a young Spanish aristocrat, while Clementine's touched on northern stateliness and finely sculpted features. All that the girls had in common was a sharp-pointed nose.

With stalwart support from her brother-in-law Bertram and her brother, David, Blanche at length regained possession of her elder children when her husband was away, and they were never again to leave her care. But that did not mean a settled life for the four children. According to the degree of their poverty, they travelled from one rented property to another. Only their education remained consistent, or as steady as could be contrived. Governesses came and went, some discharged for inadequacy, others discharging themselves for lack of pay or ability to cope with the tempestuous eldest girls. Long summer holidays were spent up in Scotland with old Lady Airlie, the one woman who could discipline them, even Kitty.

Blanche went away for long periods. She was a compulsive gambler and could persuade men friends to take her to the casinos of northern France without difficulty. 'She would skip about all over the place,' recalls one of the family today, 'and you only had to look at her to see the roving eye.'

'Even in old age Aunt Natty was distinctly "fast",' the family historians have recounted. Her nieces, the Mitford girls, relished her company and reputation, Diana loving her for being 'the first unprincipled grown-up who came our way'.

Sometimes she visited her favourite French town, Dieppe, with her children. It had a good casino, good shops at which to spend her winnings (when there were any), a large British colony, and (for one who appreciated the arts) many artists, writers, and musicians.

There was an additional and less frivolous reason for Blanche to be in Dieppe in the winter of 1899 with Kitty and Clementine. Word had reached her that her husband had recently determined to recover the two eldest girls – if necessary, by force – as an act of revenge against his wife. So she sensibly decided to hide them, and herself, away in a little rented house on the French side of the English Channel.

On the evening of 16 December, while the family, with their friend the painter Walter Sickert, were chatting by the light of the fire, Clementine, aged 14, suddenly saw a face peering through the window of the sitting room. There was little light from their log fire, but she was quite certain she was being examined closely by the man outside. Blanche Hozier saw the figure, too, and recognized him as her husband. She at once seized her two children and dragged them to the floor out of sight.

7

The front doorbell rang, and rang again. Kitty started to answer it but was pulled to the floor again by her mother. There was silence for a while, then came the sound of something being pushed through the letterbox. This was followed by the brief reappearance of the face at the window.

By way of explanation, Blanche said calmly to the painter, 'That was my husband. I expect he brought a letter. Kitty, go and see.'

There were two letters, one inviting Kitty to dine at her 'father's' hotel, the other inviting Clementine to lunch with him the day after. The reaction of the mother and two daughters reflected their characters. Blanche Hozier treated the matter with seeming calmness, making no objection to the children being entertained by her husband, but providing them with an escort in the form of Justine, their reliable French maid. Kitty was highly excited at the prospect, and wondered what she would wear, while Clementine dreaded the whole idea.

Over her dinner with the colonel the next day, Kitty was offered a pony and a dog if she would come to stay with him. Then it was time for Clementine's ordeal. She was almost too shy to talk, but her 'father' continued to ask her questions about their life, and then told her, 'I suppose your mother has told you that in future you will be living with me . . .' The girl was horrified at this news, which at last loosened her tongue. She told him that indeed she had not heard, and that she thought her mother would not let her and Kitty go.

At the appointed hour of two p.m., Justine arrived to take Clementine away. The colonel appeared angry at this interruption, and he pushed Justine from the room, at the same time thrusting a gold coin into her hand. Now terrified, and trapped, Clementine still kept her wits about her, and when the colonel turned to select a cigar, she ran for the door and rushed outside, where Justine was awaiting her. The two hurried down the road, closely pursued by the colonel, whose curses could be clearly heard until he at last gave up the chase.

8

A few weeks later, another dreadful event in Clementine's childhood occurred, and it was much worse than the attempted kidnap. Her sister Kitty contracted typhoid fever and died just before her seventeenth birthday. Clementine did not enjoy the same depth of love from her mother as Kitty had done, but now they were united in mutual grief. Blanche gave up the Dieppe house and returned to England, where she acquired the rental of a little house on the high street of Berkhamsted. The twins joined them here, and Clementine and her younger sister went to the local grammar school.

Clementine, growing more beautiful and statuesque with every passing year towards womanhood, was happy in Berkhamsted and became an accomplished scholar. For a time, she wanted to pursue a university career, but she was also easily beguiled by the delights of social life when she was allowed to have her first taste of them. This was made possible by Lady St Helier, to whom Blanche turned when she saw the first signs of her daughter's social ambitions. This kind and powerful woman took Clementine to dinner parties and balls, buying her first ball dress, which was quite beyond Blanche's means, and generally setting her on her way in the social season.

At the age of 18, Clementine met at one of her patroness's parties a brilliant barrister-banker, the son of the third Viscount Peel, Lord Sydney Peel. He was fifteen years older than Clementine, charming, courtly, a brilliant academic (a fellow of Trinity College, Oxford), a veteran of the Boer War, in which he was decorated. He proceeded to court Clementine ardently and gracefully, taking her to the theatre, sending her a bunch of white violets every day, and, when she spent a winter in Paris with her mother, coming over every weekend to spend a few hours with her. They were secretly engaged, not once but twice; and perhaps this hints at Clementine's hesitancy and lack of confidence. But her mother approved of the match, and Aunt Mary pressed her strongly to accept.

Clementine's instinct continued to hold her back, and when another suitor appeared, Lionel Earle, a man nearly

9

twice her age, she became engaged to him, more as a means of extricating herself from an increasingly difficult situation than out of love. This, too, was broken off. There was a good deal of family outrage this time, with wedding presents having to be wrapped up and sent back, but Blanche stood by her daughter through the storm. They had grown closer to one another, especially since the death in 1907 of Henry Hozier, who had always been an embarrassing impediment between them.

By 1908, when Clementine was 23, her beauty was fully matured. 'Queen she should have been,' Cynthia Asquith, the prime minister's daughter-in-law, once described her. 'Her superbly sculptured features would have looked splendid on a coin.' Her eyes were hazel-green, her hair ash blond, and she held herself and walked with a grace that 'turned all eyes'. She was immediately identifiable in any gathering and was often, and simply, referred to as 'the beautiful Miss Hozier'.

Beautiful indeed! But older women, as shrewd as Cynthia Asquith, also recognized a coldness, a lack of spontaneity, a reluctance to drop the drawbridge and admit even her friends, let alone her acquaintances, to her private feelings. In the four years of courtship, Sydney Peel had become aware of the difficulties in penetrating to her heart, and heaven knows he had tried.

And so, at the time of the fateful dinner party, Clementine's heart was unattached, and the hostess and some of Blanche's friends were becoming secretly concerned about this wonderfully attractive young woman who seemed all too ready to rebuff any advances and evade any risk of having to make a decision. Not at all like her mother!

The guests at Lady St Helier's house that March evening had caught a glimpse of a newly aroused Clementine Hozier, a quite different being from the diffident, quiet, and self-apologetic young woman they had previously known. What, they asked themselves, was the special quality in that rising politician – not noted for courting pretty girls – to have brought about this metamorphosis?

10

2

The Marlboroughs

'On the 30th November, at Blenheim Palace, the Lady Randolph Churchill, prematurely, of a son.' The year was 1874, and the adverb 'prematurely' in *The Times*'s announcement had been thought a desirable precaution because the wedding, seven and a half months earlier, had caused a great stir in society, and neither the Marlboroughs nor the bride's family wished there to be any misunderstanding.

'My mother,' Winston wrote, 'always seemed to me a fairy princess: a radiant being possessed of limitless riches and power . . . She shone for me like the Evening Star.' Her grandson described her as a woman of exceptional beauty in an age of famous beauties; and every reference to this remarkable woman takes note of her grace, beauty, intelligence, and unquenchable liveliness. Edgar D'Abernon, first Viscount and a notable diplomat, first set his eyes on Jennie outside the Viceregal Lodge in Dublin soon after she was married. To him she appeared 'a dark, lithe figure, standing somewhat apart and appearing to be of another texture to those around her, radiant, translucent, intense':

A diamond star in her hair, her favourite ornament
– its lustre dimmed by the flashing glory of her eyes.
More of the panther than of the woman in her look,
but with a cultivated intelligence unknown to the
jungle. Her courage not less great than that of her
husband – fit mother for descendants of the great
Duke. With all these attributes of brilliancy, such
kindness and high spirits were universally popular.
Her desire to please, her delight in life, and the
genuine wish that all should share her joyous faith
in it, made her the centre of a devoted circle.

11

And these words were from a characteristically cautious diplomat.

Jennie's family stemmed from early eighteenth-century Huguenot stock, persecuted and driven out of their homeland. Her father, Leonard Jerome, was a fifth-generation American and the fifth of eight boys whose 'animal vitality seems to have slightly distressed their diligent God-fearing parents', Leonard being 'the most restless and rebellious'. The Jerome farmhouse near Syracuse, New York, was substantial, as fitted the Jeromes' relative affluence. Here, when he was not at school or working on the farm, Leonard hunted deer, fished, and learned to respect the rattlesnake and bear.

Leonard Jerome's early achievements were modest; one of his brothers had already made a small fortune before he had graduated from Princeton. Leonard studied law and practised for a while in booming western New York State; he tried his hand in various businesses, including the purchase of a newspaper jointly with one of his brothers. He prospered, and he met and married Clara Hall, who was 'possessed of a curious dark brooding beauty', stemming from the strong element of Iroquois Indian blood in her veins. She was brought back by Leonard to a substantial house next to his brother's in Rochester.

The newspaper prospered, and at 32 Leonard left for New York City where he and several of his brothers hurled themselves with relish into the fast world of Wall Street. They were all young, ambitious, energetic, and hell-bent on becoming millionaires. They did so quite quickly. Jennie, the second of four daughters born to Clara and Leonard – one had died at the age of 7 – was born in 1854. She was brought up first in New York, then in France, to which Clara took her brood to escape from her husband's increasing and flagrant infidelities. In Paris, while her mother slipped comfortably and swiftly into the social circle of the imperial court, Jennie and her younger sisters, speaking fluent French, completed their education and soon embraced the brilliant social life themselves, encouraged by the strongly pro-American Emperor Napoleon III and his beautiful Empress Eugénie.

It was less than a century since the French Revolution, but there was not much sign of *égalité* in the Paris of the 1860s, and the court was only slightly less lavish and extravagant than before the Revolution. Life in New York had reflected to the point of vulgarity the wealth of Leonard Jerome, but as Clara once said of Napoleon III, 'I have found the Court I want.' Early in 1868, Jerome suffered a severe financial setback, to the tune of one million dollars. This by no means bankrupted him, but he decided to lease his house and see how his family were getting on in Paris. He found Clara fatter and the girls taller and very *soignée*. Jennie's 'flamboyant beauty was already beginning to show', but she told him, 'I'm *never* going to marry. I am going to be a musician.' Although she was musically gifted, there seemed little likelihood of this.

Leonard Jerome found all three girls a handful. 'Can't you control them? Why are they so wild?' he complained to Clara.

'Well, dear,' Clara replied spiritedly. 'They are *your* daughters.'

Not long after the arrival of their father, the girls became aware that their life at the court and in high society in Paris was threatened by France's conflict with Prussia. This political conflict soon turned to violence, war, and a Prussian invasion, and in August 1870 the family fled on the very last train out of Paris, with only a few clothes and precious possessions tied up in sheets. From Deauville they sailed for England, 'which I now saw for the first time,' Jennie, now 16, recalled. 'A winter spent in the gloom and fogs of London did not tend to dispel the melancholy which we felt. Our friends scattered, fighting, or killed at the front; debarred as we were from our bright little house and our household goods, it was indeed a sad time.'

Clara and the girls were back in Paris in 1871, however, and their father back in New York, where he lived alone. He had lost his touch in the world of financial speculation

13

and suffered a series of blows that led to his claiming he was ruined. But it was only relative ruin: he continued to live comfortably and in any case had already settled a large fortune on Clara. It was his pride that had seriously suffered. And then came the news from Paris in a letter from Clara: Jennie, his precious, exquisite, beloved twenty-year-old Jennie, was engaged to be married. Moreover, Clara described the betrothal as rash, hasty, and impulsive. 'You must return by the next boat,' she added. The news could hardly be worse. Who *was* this young man, Randolph, who planned to marry his daughter? He was a scion of the Spencer-Churchill family, his father being the Duke of Marlborough. That sounded impressive, of course. But Leonard also learned that the Duke opposed the marriage, and that was tantamount to a gross snub. Leonard was furious and at once cabled that he would not give *his* consent either.

Winston was to spend a number of years writing a eulogistic biography in four volumes of his great ancestor John Churchill, first Duke of Marlborough and Britain's most renowned general. As a young boy, refighting with his armies of toy soldiers the Duke's battles at Blenheim, Ramillies, Oudenarde, and Malplaquet, Winston was sowing the seeds of his pride and his determination to emulate this first duke in his lineage.

John Churchill's triumphant life – including his victories that shaped the future of Europe – has been written about by many more than the second Winston Churchill and Thomas Lediard, his first biographer in 1736. When this first Duke of Marlborough died in 1722, heavy with honours and wealth, he had achieved all for his country and for the cause of stability and freedom that could reasonably be expected of any man. And so vast was the palace of Blenheim that the nation had dedicated to him, that it had never been sufficiently completed for him to reside in it. No one was more aware than the Duke himself that this mountain of stone would be the greatest of all memorials to him.

John Churchill, first Duke of Marlborough, had two sons, both of whom predeceased him. The title acquired the additional name Spencer, and in so doing lost touch with its inspiring past, while the vast fortunes withered through incompetent management. As with a sick, aging man, what was needed was a transfusion of new blood, preferably from the north or from Ireland. This was provided when the seventh duke, John Winston Spencer-Churchill, married Lady Frances ('Fanny') Anne Emily Vane, daughter of the third Marquis of Londonderry, in 1843. This remarkable woman possessed the right blend, even if at first it seemed a trifle overstrong. She did better than the first duke's wife: Frances produced two sons who survived beyond infancy: George, who took the title Blandford, and Randolph. Though both inherited a measure of instability, Randolph showed signs of potential greatness.

Randolph Spencer-Churchill (it took his elder son to diminish the 'Spencer' almost to the point of non-usage) was a strange, fascinating, and unsettling man, with an appearance dominated by protruding eyes. There was a touch of the rake about him, but his arrogance and apparent lack of consideration for others were leavened by real kindness towards and concern for the unfortunate. His health was uncertain and his disposition highly nervous; no doubt the two were linked. His intellect was both spear and sword, with the keenest cutting edge; his ambition was boundless; his scruples and self-control were minimal; and his charm, when summoned, was exceptional.

He had many devoted friends, all of whom would have agreed that, at the age of 24, he was in need of a stabilizing influence. This could be provided only by a satisfactory wife, a woman who would certainly need to be not only beautiful, but also intelligent and dashing, yet with the strength and steadying influence Randolph would always need. Consciously or unconsciously, Randolph recognized these qualities at his first meeting with the woman he would one day marry, Jennie Jerome.

Cowes Week, the regatta that closes the London social

season and precedes the mass slaughter of birds on the grouse moors, was notorious as the most notable venue for the young to meet and fall in love, or consolidate the earlier amorous overtures of the summer season. In the summer of 1873, Leonard Jerome had written from New York in the knowledge that his wife and two elder daughters had left Paris and would be at Cowes: 'I have no doubt you will see many nice people and will have Cowes all to yourselves as far as Americans are concerned . . .'

The Jerome girls and their mother did indeed meet 'many nice people', and looked forward to meeting more at a reception and dance on board a Royal Navy frigate. The hosts and hostesses were the Prince and Princess of Wales, heirs to the British throne, and their Russian equivalents, the Grand Duke Cesarewitch and Grand Duchess Cesarevna, on the evening of 12 August. It was just the sort of occasion the girls and their mother relished.

Lord Randolph Churchill had a similar invitation. When his eyes fell on Jennie he arranged, within minutes, for an introduction, and a moment later she was in his arms for the quadrille. He was a hopeless dancer, and detested it. They sat out the next dance, and 'though her eager feet hated to miss one moment of a waltz, some vibrant quality in this young man with the prominent eyes and changeable expressions held her interest'.

Jennie asked her mother to invite Randolph to dinner, and he came and they talked and talked. But it was not until the third occasion after their first meeting, when Clara had been prevailed upon to provide yet another dinner party and invite, with some misgivings, the same young lord, that Randolph made known his feelings. So did Jennie. Randolph proposed and was accepted. It was the perfect setting: a garden flooded with moonlight, with the light of the stars above and the light of the boats on the ocean. They were intoxicated by their mutual love, both of them for the first time.

The Duke of Marlborough, on hearing his son Randolph's

excited announcement that he intended to marry this American girl, first made enquiries about her family. Jerome? Who were these Jeromes? Leonard Jerome, the girl's father, was a sporting 'and I should think vulgar kind of man', he learned. Jerome and his two brothers were stockbrokers, and 'one of them bears a *bad* character'. Worse was to come. 'Everything that you say about the mother and daughters,' the Duke told Randolph, 'is perfectly compatible with all that I am apprehensive of about the father . . .'

There was another, unstated, snag of great concern to the Duke: a political one. The parliamentary seat of Woodstock, in which the vast estates of Blenheim lay, was held by an unpopular conservative who would certainly be beaten by the radical candidate at the next election. This was an intolerable prospect. George, Marquis of Blandford, his elder son, would inherit the title and so be disbarred from Parliament. So the Duke had long ago set his heart on Randolph's standing at the next election. He was popular and would win the seat, barring any serious impediment, such as being married to some flashy American woman.

Meanwhile, Jennie had won round her father (she always did), and Leonard suddenly was in favour of 'the greatest match'. 'Between you and I and the post – and your mother etc. *I am delighted* more than I can tell. It is magnificent.' But such joyous sentiments did not break the impasse. This came about only gradually, the Duke suggesting to Randolph a one-year interval before he reached a final decision. Then politics, which had at first proved such a serious impediment, now – 'thank goodness' – resolved everything. There was a general election on 3 February 1874; Randolph was elected with a comfortable majority. Still nursing many reservations (as did his son, about being a Member of Parliament), the Duke gave his consent.

April in Paris. And what a beautiful April it was! The two utterly disparate families assembled to inspect one another, arrange settlements, and attend the wedding – Leonard Jerome from New York, then the Duke and Duchess from Blenheim, their elder son and three daughters and other relations, and Clara and her other two daughters. Everyone was very polite and determined that this was to be a happy occasion after the stormy start to the relationship. Clara even let it be known that she thought the Duke 'a perfect dear'. There was a slight, somewhat squalid tussle about settlements in which the Duke, through his solicitors, revealed himself to be quite as tough as the New York financier.

The Duke and Duchess had to return home before the wedding at the British Embassy on 15 April, but everyone understood and their absence in no way diminished the colour and happiness of the occasion. After the wedding breakfast, Jennie and her father left for the embassy in an open carriage with four grey horses and postilions, and with half of Paris (or so it seemed) cheering them along the boulevards in the sun. Dr Edward Forbes conducted the marriage ceremony, with Francis Knollys, the Prince of Wales's representative, as best man.

The French honeymoon was 'deliriously happy but all too brief'. On the last day of April the couple reached the Channel and crossed the next day in brilliant spring sunshine. Then the train to London, thence to Oxford, and at last to Woodstock and Jennie's spectacular if temporary new house. Jennie had seen pictures of Blenheim and its wonderful gardens and rolling parkland. Randolph had described it many times. Now, here at last, was the reality.

A large party of the Duke's tenants and Randolph's constituents had met them at the station and amidst cheers had taken the horses out of the carriage and had themselves dragged the carriage through the town and out to the palace.

The place could not have looked more glorious [Jennie wrote of this memorable moment], *and as we passed through the entrance archway, and the lovely scenery burst upon me, Randolph said with pardonable pride, 'This is the finest view in England.' Looking at the lake, the bridge, the miles of magnificent park studded with old oaks, I found*

18

*no adequate words to express my admiration, and
when we reached the huge and stately palace, where
I was to find hospitality for so many years, I confess
I felt awed.*

But Jennie was not one for revealing that she was impressed,
by anyone or anything. She knew that from the moment
she stepped from the coach she would be under the closest
observation, but it did not in the least bother her. On the
contrary, she determined to show that she was used to grand
living – moreover, grand living against a background of artis-
tic appreciation and accomplishment, the refined court life of
France.

> *The Duke and Duchess were waiting on the wide steps
> to greet her with kindness, slightly tinged by conde-
> scension* [wrote Jennie's great-niece]. *She watched
> them closely to see what an American daughter-in-law
> could be like. In this house criticism would always be
> easy to arouse. Jennie soon enjoyed the small malice
> of showing herself better educated than their own
> daughters . . . In vain had Leonard tried to teach
> this ebullient daughter not to show off.*

Unaware that most of the old families of Britain regarded
royal families (even the British one) with distant disdain
when they considered them at all, Jennie prattled on about
the French court; then, unasked, she settled herself at the
piano and played and played, exquisitely.

She did, however, manage to restrain herself from commenting on the dingy style of the table – 'frumpy old table
mats, water decanters with ordinary thick tumblers, the kind
we use in bedrooms', as she told her mother. She also wrote
of the complete absence of style and the adherence to rigid
routine and ceremony day after day in this cold, massive
mausoleum. Very dull, very dispiriting.

No one can say who was the more relieved, the Duchess
or Jennie, when the duty visit was over and the newly-weds

could return to London and settle themselves into the Charles Street house they had been given, and Jennie could throw herself into the hurly-burly of the season. As for Randolph, he made a highly successful maiden speech in the House of Commons and accompanied his beautiful, much-admired wife to balls and dances with the Prince of Wales, Princess Louise, the Duke of Atholl, the Buccleuchs . . .

For many weeks, for too many weeks after she knew she was pregnant, some thought, Jennie continued to accept every invitation and danced through the night 'with all the vigour and unjaded appetite of youth', she once wrote. She continued to ride, and she always rode fearlessly. Randolph made no attempt to restrain his bride. On the contrary, he loved to see her whirling round and round dancing the mazurka, dark eyes shining and laughing with the joy of it, at four in the morning when most other couples were wearily sitting it out.

By October, the big London houses had been closed down, and the country houses opened up for the winter season. This did not mean any respite from dancing and night-long parties, and riding in Rotten Row gave way to hunting and balls. Pregnant seven and a half months, Jennie restrained herself to the extent of riding at a slow pace rather than following the hounds across the Oxfordshire countryside, leaping the hedges and gates, and suffering the inevitable falls. But she could not be restrained from following the guns, and that could be a strenuous business, too.

On Tuesday 24 November, Jennie insisted on walking with the shooters over rough ground. Unbalanced by her weight, she took a bad fall. It was nothing, she said, and carried on, covered in mud. She did not appear to have suffered any damage, and on the Saturday she took a rough drive in a pony carriage, which even Randolph thought 'rather imprudent'. That same evening, he danced with her at a party at Blenheim Palace – until Jennie whispered in his ear words he had never expected her to utter: 'I am feeling unwell. I think I will lie down.'

Blenheim Palace was not designed for childbirth. The

route to Jennie's distant rooms lay through the largest library in England and the longest domestic corridor anywhere, a quarter mile of it. She never made it. She got as far as a ladies' attiring room, 'strewn with velvet capes and feather boas', and collapsed.

Stretched out on a makeshift bed, she continued to suffer pains off and on through that Saturday night and all day Sunday, during which she was comforted for most of the time by Frances, Duchess of Marlborough; Clementine, Marchioness of Camden; and Bertha, Marchioness of Blandford, the wife of Randolph's elder brother. All Saturday night the rain beat at the windows, and the last leaves were torn from the Blenheim Park oak trees by the wind. The forty-three-year-old local doctor, Frederick Taylor, struggled through the storm from Woodstock to supervise the ministrations. The birth, when it came, was extremely difficult and painful.

A baby boy was born at 1.30 a.m. on Monday 30 November 1874 – 'wonderfully pretty', according to the proud father, with dark eyes and hair and the little button nose characteristic of the Churchills. There was no cradle or even baby linen for him, and as an emergency measure these were obtained from the more farsighted pregnant wife of the local Woodstock solicitor. A nurse and a wet nurse were quickly summoned through the good offices of Dr Taylor. The obstetrician from London, who had been telegraphed but had not been able to get a train on Sunday evening, owing to the heavy fog that had followed the storm, arrived at breakfast time, and by then the boy was washed and dressed and looking perky and eager to face the challenges of infancy.

Telegrams were also despatched to Leonard Jerome in New York and to Jennie's mother in Paris. Letters followed, and the Duchess was able to write three days later to Clara Jerome:

I am happy to send you a most favourable report of dear Jennie and her little Baby. She is progressing steadily towards Convalescence. She has no Fever,

*the Milk is subsiding satisfactorily. Her appetite is
fairly good & her strength keeps up well. The little
Boy is a very healthy pretty little Child & I think will
be a large Child in time.*

The Prince of Wales, who was so positively to shape the lives
of father Randolph and his baby son, despatched twenty
brace of pheasant from Sandringham to the maternity wing
at St Bartholomew's Hospital, of which he was president, as
if it were a tribute to motherhood, though he knew nothing
of the birth.

For the first time that anyone could remember, and certainly for the first time in Randolph's experience, Jennie
was placid and contented in her bed, complaining not at
all, sleeping well without medication, and patiently awaiting
permission to get up. Eight days after the delivery, she was
allowed onto a sofa, and she was on her feet, looking more
radiant than ever, for her baby's baptism. This took place
at the Blenheim Chapel and was performed by the palace
chaplain, Henry Yule, on 27 December. The baby was
named Winston Leonard Spencer-Churchill, with Leonard
an acknowledgement of the American connection.

On the following day, father, mother and child took the
carriage to Woodstock station, where they had enjoyed
that tumultuous reception scarcely eight months earlier.
That evening they were settled in Charles Street. Well off,
exceedingly well connected, handsome and privileged, with
a comfortable home in Mayfair, the mother blissfully happy
and content with her first child, and the adoring husband at
the very outset of his political career: what more could this
young family expect?

3

Loving Brothers

Alas, it was not long before a damaging scandal clouded the idyllic life of Randolph and Jennie, a scandal that was to have momentous repercussions for both Winston and his father. The most powerful social figure in the lives of this newly married couple was Edward Prince of Wales, the eldest son of Queen Victoria and heir to the throne. The Prince of Wales was a gregarious, hedonistic, much admired (and socially much feared) prince, who had been for long excluded from any responsibility of importance by his disapproving mother. This had led him into a self-indulgent life, which featured numerous beautiful women, gambling, and horse-racing.

On 11 October 1875, shortly before Winston's first birthday, the Prince of Wales left England for India, ostensibly on a tour of imperial solidarity, but also taking in a great deal of pig-sticking and big-game hunting, balls, levees, and the other forms of fun so heartily enjoyed by His Royal Highness.

The prince took with him a number of his cronies, not all of them noted for the purity of their morals, including Prince Louis of Battenberg, who would later share the favours of the celebrated actress Lillie Langtry with the prince; Lieutenant Lord Charles Beresford; Lord Carrington; Colonel Owen Williams; and Williams's brother-in-law, the Earl of Aylesford.

Aylesford, aged 26, was nicknamed 'Sporting Joe' for his raffish and sometimes violent style of living. He had married a gentle, pretty woman named Edith, who bore him two children and bore her husband's manners patiently. The Countess, living alone in the great Aylesford seat, Packington Hall, had attracted the attention of Randolph's elder brother,

George Blandford, heir to the dukedom, in her husband's absence. In fact, he left Blenheim and his own family and for a while established himself, and his horses, in an inn near Packington Hall, for reasons that at once became the subject of feverish local gossip.

Blandford might as well have moved in altogether for all the concealment he attempted. He came over to the countess's house in the evening and stayed until the morning. He had the same ardent nature, the same uncompromising determination and highly developed sexual appetite, as his younger brother, and by February 1876 he had persuaded Edith to leave her home and children and, in the absence of his wife, to come and live with him. Probably not all that much persuasion was needed, for 'You do not know,' – as Edith wrote to her mother-in-law after this dramatic step was taken – 'you never can know, how hard I have tried to win [my husband's] love, and without success, and I cannot live uncared for.'

For a short time it seemed as if the situation might be contained and the news confined to the two families. But George Blandford was hell-bent on two divorces and never mind the scandal. His brother, Randolph, did his best to dissuade him from this extreme step, but otherwise backed his cause to the hilt, to an extent that even Blandford found worrying. The Prince of Wales, in India with Aylesford, on hearing the news backed his companion and let it be widely known how strongly he felt about Blandford's caddish behaviour. Aylesford was released from the India party and hurried home to face the scandal.

But, asked Randolph in his efforts to support his brother, was the Prince's own record in his relationship with Edith Aylesford entirely blameless? Letters lent to him by the Countess indicated that it was not, and Randolph let this news be widely known, though the letters were in truth no more than flirtatious in their content. With unbridled arrogance, he now called on another wife who had been left behind on the India trip, the Princess of Wales no less. Would Her Royal Highness please ask the Prince to persuade Lord

24

Aylesford to drop any divorce proceedings? Certain revelations might be embarrassing if read out in court. 'There are these letters, Your Royal Highness . . . you do understand, Ma'am, that if made public, the Prince will never sit on the throne.'

This threat of blackmail did *not* amuse Queen Victoria when her daughter-in-law at once took a carriage to Buckingham Palace to inform her. 'What a disgraceful business!' said the Queen. Everybody was soon involved: the Prime Minister, Benjamin Disraeli, and the Cabinet, and the Lord Chancellor. The situation became more deeply embroiled when it was learned that the Prince of Wales, who had regarded himself as a close friend of Randolph and often in the past had dined at his house with his enchanting Jennie, now proposed to challenge him to a duel. Furthermore, when the Prince finally returned from India, he announced that not only would he not be dining in Charles Street in future, but that anyone who received Randolph and Jennie would be excluded socially as far as he was concerned.

This amounted to ostracism by the Court and society of the proud Marlboroughs, something that neither the Duke nor his younger son, to say nothing of the convivial Jennie, was prepared to face. However, the wily Prime Minister found a way out, though the Duke was reluctant to follow it, mainly because of the expense it would involve. The viceroyalty in Dublin could be made available, and the new viceroy would require a secretary, prestigious posts for father and son. So in January 1877 Blenheim Palace was suddenly emptied of its august residents, their relations and retinue of servants, their horses and carriages, and a fair proportion of their furniture, and one infant boy, Winston, whose father by his reckless impetuosity had caused this considerable upheaval.

The most important person in the special saloon carriage attached to the Irish Mail train out of Paddington Station on this January morning, in the eyes of two-year-old Winston, was his nursemaid, Mrs Everest, or 'Woom'. Winston loved and admired his mother and father without

25

restraint or condition. He might complain later of their neglect of him, sometimes but not always with reason. They might break promises and order things for their own, rather than his, convenience. But they remained his beloved parents.

Mrs Everest had become the steady rock in Winston's childhood, always present, always to be relied upon. ('Mrs Everest it was who looked after me and tended all my wants,' wrote Winston. 'It was to her I poured out my many troubles, both now and in my schooldays.') She was a stout, round-faced woman emanating kindness and goodwill, good sense and firmness – the perfect nursemaid. The few surviving letters she wrote while in service with the Churchills reveal a wide range of expression and an economy in the use of punctuation. 'Mr Winston,' she wrote of him to Jennie, 'walked from Cheveley up the house yesterday & said he left all his bad throat in the train he feels nothing of it . . .' She was born at Chatham in Kent in 1833 and always talked lovingly of what she thought of as the most beautiful county, 'the garden of England' with its succulent soft fruits and orchards. (This early indoctrination influenced Winston, many years later, to make Kent his home. When she died Winston wrote to Jennie, 'I shall never know such a friend again.')

By the time Winston was two, Mrs Everest's charge had long since made up for any deficiency in size and development caused by his premature birth, but it was still too early to distinguish any signs of special strength in his face. Even the experienced Everest (as she was invariably referred to by all except Winston and the domestic staff, to whom she was Mrs Everest) had not yet discerned any special behavioural characteristics. There was perhaps an infant petulance and impatience that might – any nursemaid would surmise – become troublesome. A well-developed head of dark russet hair formed into a fringe above a pair of wide-set blue eyes, a modest up-tilted nose, and a positive, uncompromising mouth, full and a touch sensuous like his mother's; and he had a tough little chin, marked by the same single line that also divided his upper lip. He was going to be good-looking, of that you could be certain.

Well removed from the mutter and gossip and baleful cloud of the Prince of Wales's set in London, Randolph and Jennie, their boy and their entourage of servants settled into a new life in the Little Lodge, their ample house in the heart of Dublin, near the Duke's residence, the Viceregal Lodge. Far from being thought of as social outcasts seeking escape from the London Court, the Churchills became at once the very hub of social life in Ireland, which suited Jennie admirably. There were balls and receptions, dances and dinners, levees and drawing rooms, a miniature mirror of London but by no means rated as inferior. As for the hunting, in Ireland it was in a class of its own, and Winston's picture of his mother, when images began to fix on the sensitive plate of his memory, was 'in a riding habit, fitting like a skin and often beautifully spotted with mud. She and my father hunted continually on their large horses; and sometimes there were great scares because one or the other did not come back for many hours after they were expected.'

But almost all the lasting memories of these early formative years relate to violence and soldiering. When Mrs Everest took him for a walk in Phoenix Park, it was not like feeding the ducks in Hyde Park. More often than not, there would be riflemen at practice, the explosions blood-stirring and not in the least alarming to Winston or his nursemaid. What did alarm Mrs Everest was the prospect of meeting the real enemy in Phoenix Park, those terrible Fenians who murdered people and blew up buildings. Winston was a casualty of one of these scares when Mrs Everest took fright at the approach of a body of men she thought were Fenians. The fear was transmitted to Winston's donkey, who threw him, leading to concussion.

In a house in Phoenix Park there lived the Irish Under-secretary, Thomas Burke. Burke gave Winston a drum to beat, a very suitable present. But later Winston learned from 'Woom' that this kind man had been murdered by Fenians with another man called Cavendish in this same park, confirming Mrs Everest's fears that it was a most unsafe place.

Then there was what Winston called 'my first coherent memory', the unveiling of the statue to Field Marshal Gough, that 'illustrious Irishman whose achievements in the Peninsular War, in China and in India have added lustre to the military glory of his country', the 'man with a lust for danger'.

These blowings-up and killings, Winston learned, had been going on for a long time. Oliver Cromwell had lived a long time ago, but on one visit to a friend of his father's, Winston was shown a large tower that had been blown up by Oliver Cromwell. Fires and explosions were still going on. Much excitement was built up, for example, by the imminence of a visit to the pantomime. Many children were to go in a party, and the rendezvous was the Viceregal Lodge, whence they drove to the castle where it was to be performed.

Winston remembered clearly his first experience of the aftermath of disaster, the flurry and dismay in the air that met them on arrival. 'I am sorry, children,' they were told. 'There has been an accident and there won't be a pantomime after all.' The theatre had been burnt down, consuming the manager. Only his keys survived. The ghoulish delight on hearing this tale was powerful compensation for missing the pantomime, and next day they were all taken to see the ruins. Winston 'wanted very much to see the keys, but this request does not seem to have been well received'.

Besides lighting the taper of Winston's militarism, which was to grow into a mighty blaze, the three years of early childhood in Dublin had a powerful side effect on his father. Until the break in his social life in England in 1876, Randolph had shown little interest in politics and rarely gone to the House of Commons. Nothing much was expected of him by anyone, including himself. The frivolities of social life with Jennie at his side had almost totally consumed him, and she had no ambitions for him to 'make his mark'.

Two factors brought about a remarkable change in this self-ish, self-indulgent, pleasure-seeking, and previously unimportant man: first, the banishment from his life in London and Oxfordshire and the indignity for a proud Marlborough of becoming *persona non grata*; and second, the distress and starvation he saw all around him in Ireland. Suddenly Lord Randolph Churchill was seized with a mission.

The first sign, unrecognized at the time, of the new Randolph was seen late in the first year of exile. He had already come home several times to attend the Commons, but on this occasion, armed with knowledge and confident of the rightness of the cause he was to espouse, he created a sensation by attacking his own party's policy on Ireland. As a close witness to the poverty and suffering of the Irish people and the failure of the British government to do anything about the maladministration of the country, he said in the course of a speech in Woodstock, 'There are great and crying Irish questions which the Government have not attended to, do not seem inclined to attend to and perhaps do not intend to attend to.' Neither Disraeli (now Lord Beaconsfield) nor the Duke was much pleased by this.

However, in the broad spectrum of the Conservative Party's policies (such as they were) this speech of Randolph's was merely an irritating, quickly forgotten sting. And no breath of blame was attached to Randolph when at the general election in April 1880 the Conservative Party was swept from power. With their huge majority it looked as if the Liberals under Gladstone were now set for a decade or two of supremacy. But this did not take into account – could hardly be expected to take into account – the rocket-like political ascendancy of Randolph Churchill.

The advent of a Liberal government marked the end of the Duke of Marlborough's viceroyalty of Ireland, much to his relief. It also meant the end of Randolph's office as his father's secretary. So, little more than three years after their departure on the Irish Mail from London, they were back on board the steamer to take them home again to Blenheim and London.

The Spencer-Churchills had left as a family of three; they returned as a family of four, for Winston now had a younger brother, hardly large enough to interest him, but visibly a member of the human race, and visibly a male. Jennie assured Winston that this baby would soon grow up into a boy he could play with, but at five years, the future seemed to Winston unreliable, like the pantomime, and anyway not easy to visualize.

Jack's birth, on 4 February 1880, was as difficult as Winston's (there is good reason to suspect that there had been miscarriages in between the two boys). At first, Jack was not expected to live, having been born with one eye damaged and a twisted artery near the heart, which might have burst at any time. In appearance, Jack – or Jackie sometimes – was similar to Winston, but with brown rather than russet-red hair, and with the same characteristic of one line dividing the forehead, the upper lip and the chin.

Ever vulnerable to family canards, Randolph, it was said, was not Jack's father. Jennie, it was gossiped, had had an affair with John Strange Jocelyn, fifth Earl of Roden, who had entered Jennie's bedroom after climbing a drainpipe. But Roden family records show that he was in England for the whole of 1879 and arrived in Ireland only on inheriting the earldom the month Jack was born, when he agreed to stand as godfather. (Rumours of promiscuity swirled around Jennie throughout her long, glittering social career. With her exceptional vivacity, she did attract many male friends and admirers, including the Prince of Wales, but according to close members of the family, Jennie did not find the sexual act particularly pleasurable, and most probably never went to bed with any of the 'lovers' gossip enjoyed ascribing to her.)

Apart from their similarity in appearance, by the time Jack was a year old it was already clear that he was a very different sort of boy from Winston. Mrs Everest never discriminated between them, loving both with all her heart, but she noticed

30

all the contrasts in style and manner of the boys. Winston was wayward, reckless, impatient with authority, mischievous and pugnacious; Jack, on the other hand, was placid, conformist and anxious to please, as much an introvert as his brother was an extrovert. Both boys had an appetite for knowledge, but Winston's was insatiable. While Winston resented the discipline of learning, Jack accepted and appreciated his teachers' guidance. When the two boys, aged 7 and 13, were staying with their grandmother Duchess, she wrote to Jennie to report that Winston 'is a clever Boy & really not naughty but wants a firm hand', whereas 'Jack requires *no* keeping in order'. And at the end of the stay, with Winston going back to school, the Duchess confides, 'Entre nous I do not feel very sorry for [Winston. He] certainly is a handful. Not that he does anything seriously naughty except to use bad language which is bad for Jack [who] is a good little boy & not a bit of trouble.'

What surprised and touched Mrs Everest about the boys (and she was often touched but rarely surprised) was Winston's rapid development of affection for his brother. A gap of more than five years is often too wide to bridge, but a protective love for Jack provided the foundation for the closest male friendship in Winston's life. He never patronized Jack, and Jack's reciprocal love never touched sycophancy. They were completely compatible. Even before Jack was on his feet, they played together for hours, quite tirelessly. When they were separated, first by school and then by their professions, they wrote frequently, and in letters from Winston to their mother he often asked after his brother, especially when Jack was unwell.

From school, aged 11, Winston wrote asking his mother to give Jack his best love and tell him he would soon be home, when they would have some fine battles with their toy soldiers. And later, when there was a prospect of a visit by Jennie or Mrs Everest, he nearly always asked them to bring Jack too.

Even before Winston returned from Dublin to England with

his family, his education had begun, and very unwelcome it was, too. Winston never really came to terms with formal learning, and recalled with horror the day 'I was first menaced with Education'. Lessons 'took one away from all the interesting things one wanted to do in the nursery or in the garden. They made increasing inroads upon one's leisure. One could hardly get time to do any of the things one wanted to do.' In fact, lessons were an all-round nuisance, and remained so until they were over and done with and he could face the real world outside the classroom.

Like it or not, a governess had come briefly to the Little Lodge, Dublin, and something even more threatening raised its hideous head when they returned to London: boarding school.

Randolph took a house in St James's Place off St James's Street, a handsome Georgian house with direct access to Green Park, one hundred or so yards distant, and more important politically, next door to Sir Stafford Northcote, Randolph's nominal leader in the House of Commons. Northcote took soundings, through Lord Beaconsfield, on Randolph's standing at Court. He was, it seemed, 'all right so far as the Queen was concerned', less so with the Prince of Wales, a man slow to forgive at any time. The grievance, it was suggested, might be forgotten in inverse ratio with Randolph's success in politics: 'The Prince is always taken by success,' Northcote wrote. Randolph's freshly fuelled fire of ambition was to see to that, but at a price for Winston – and himself.

In early 1880, Winston's lack of knowledge of his father's professional life was but a molehill to the mountain of unconcern in Randolph for his son. If Winston had been sent away to boarding school while his father had still been leading the aimless social life of three years earlier, he still would have heard from him seldom and seen him rarely. But some sort of contact would have been maintained. Instead, from all outward evidence, his father might not have existed, although Winston frequently wrote to him, and the love and admiration he felt for Randolph increased rather than diminished.

The school was St George's, Ascot, a new, very expensive, very fashionable establishment that maintained connections with Eton and was run by a headmaster with the Dickensian name of the Reverend H. W. Sneyd-Kynnersley. Winston was sent to St George's at the beginning of November 1882, shortly before his eighth birthday; his arrival in midterm, after all the other new boys had settled in, accentuated his misery and loneliness. Soon after, he wrote to his mother: 'I am very happy at school.' But a half century later he wrote, 'How I hated this school, and what a life of anxiety I lived there . . . I counted the days and the hours to the end of every term, when I should return home from this hateful servitude.'

Little evidence of the trouble he had at St George's is evident in his letters. These are as brief as he dared write them, uninformative and cryptic, ill-spelt, and often with complete words missing. There are reminders of how many days there are before the end of term, but as most boys prefer home to school, these need not be interpreted as reflecting any misery or homesickness. There are, however, early signs of two concerns that were to become preoccupations: shortage of money and his mother's apparent lack of interest in him, almost as if when he was out of her sight he was out of her mind.

'I must ask you to send me a little money . . .'

'It is very unkind of you not to write to me before this, I have had only one letter from you this term . . .'

'I want you to come down and see me, let Everest come and Jack . . .'

These pleadings from school became more ardent as he grew older, was able to express himself more articulately, and (as he saw it) suffered increasing neglect and penury.

Winston's more serious troubles at St George's – the beatings and humiliations – were reflected only in his school reports. But his parents now belatedly began to entertain doubts about the school. Mrs Everest had seen the scars of beatings on Winston's buttocks after every term. On 22 July 1884, when Winston was still only 9 years old, the evidence of his harsh treatment was so appalling that she reported it to Jennie, who took immediate steps to take him away.

Winston did not record his relief at the news, only (in *My Early Life*) that he suffered from a low state of health, which was true enough, but his condition certainly included a low state of spirits. He was not at this age a strong boy and was liable to fall foul of every passing infection.

But for Winston, the summer months of 1884 – a beautiful summer, too, with day after day of unbroken sunshine – marked the end of misery, the hell of Ascot replaced by the heaven of Blenheim, playing in the park, by the lake, up the trees, with the added spice of a brother who had suddenly become a companion and playmate, who was keen to battle it out with the toy soldiers in elaborate campaigns. 'Fate, Time, Occasion, Chance, and Change' were all suddenly flowing favourably, and the cup of joy was filled to overflowing when he heard that he would never return to the clutches of the Reverend Sneyd-Kynnersley.

Winston was also conscious of a transformation in the political fortunes of his father. Everybody seemed to be talking about this handsome, well-turned-out young man with the ample drooping moustache, the swagger in his step, and arrogance and ambition in his great eyes. Everyone recognized him on the street, and he was the centre of the political news and comment in the newspapers and journals. Early in the year Randolph had made a slashing and memorable attack on the Prime Minister, Gladstone. The speech was a wonderful example of the previously concealed wit and powers of oratory of the Member for Woodstock. He followed this up with an announcement that he proposed to stand as Tory candidate in the heartland of the Liberal Party, the central division of Birmingham. Almost overnight Winston's father had become an *enfant terrible*, a thorn in the flesh not only of the Liberals but also of the more supine and traditionalist Tories.

Winston revelled in his father's new-found popularity and notoriety. Excitedly, he wrote to his mother from school (16 March 1884) that they were betting two to one that his father would get in for Birmingham. From New York, Jennie's father wrote to her of Randolph's sudden rise to political fame: 'I confess I am amazed, so young! so reckless inexperienced and impulsive!' Later in the year, after Randolph was told by Lord Salisbury that he would be the Secretary of State for India if the Tories won the next election, Randolph decided to visit the sub-continent to make himself known there and improve his knowledge of the country.

The temporary loss of his father coincided for Winston with a new phase in his life, too. After making many enquiries about a suitable school following the disaster of St George's, Ascot, Jennie heard of a little place in Brighton run by two unmarried sisters, Charlotte and Kate Thomson, at 29–30 Brunswick Road, Hove. What she wanted for Winston was firmness and kindness, and above all a healthy environment. Not only was Brighton famous for its invigorating air, but the family doctor, Robson Roose, one of the most celebrated physicians of the time, lived there and would normally be available if required.

Winston immediately settled down at this comfortable establishment where learning was fun, and he responded to the kindness of the two women and their staff by behaving a great deal better than before. He enjoyed the swimming and riding and even the less exciting walks along the seafront. With his tenth birthday, he had acquired a stamp album and brought it home with the first of his colourful foreign stamps to show Jack, along with much else that he could share with his brother.

The family had now moved from St James's to a tall, handsome, white stucco, end-of-terrace house at Marble Arch, 2 Connaught Place. The high sash windows, with balconies, and the smaller windows of the other three floors, overlooked Hyde Park to the south, while to the north, beyond the iron gates and fence, there was a view up the Edgware Road. This was to be Winston's home for the next eight years.

We can imagine, then, the train from Brighton arriving at Victoria Station, decorated for Christmas, on the warm afternoon of 19 December 1884, the sun shining all the way

35

through Sussex and Surrey. One carriage is reserved for the Miss Thomsons' pupils, all in their best uniform, most of whom have not drawn breath since their embarkation at Hove Station ninety minutes earlier. Outside in the forecourt the family carriages are drawn up, the coachmen keeping a keen eye on the crowd emerging from the station in order to identify their charges.

Jack is with the coachman, King, and it is he who identifies Winston first. He shouts and waves his scarf. King restrains him from jumping down for fear he will be lost in the crowd; Winston, waving his cap, breaks through. 'Hullo, Jackie . . . Hullo, King – look, there's my trunk, the porter with the white beard has it!'

King descends from his seat, helps the porter up with the school trunk marked 'W. S-C', and tips him sixpence. There are Christmas decorations in the station shops, and some of the cabbies have decorated their horses with holly and bunting.

Jack says, 'Only six days to Christmas, Winny. Six days. Lady de Clifford came to tea yesterday and when she was leaving she whispered to me, "I have bought some soldiers for you for Christmas. They're called *The Nile Expedition*."'

'By jove, you are lucky,' answers Winston. 'But she shouldn't have told you all the same.'

Jack responds, 'She said you had so many that I ought to have some too.'

'You can be the Mad Mahdi,' says Winston, 'and I'll be General Gordon. He's bound to beat those savages, you see.'*

The street gaslights are being lit by the lamplighters up Park Lane; and in the big houses belonging to the very rich

---

*General C. G. ('Chinese') Gordon, a great public hero, had reached Khartoum in the course of an expedition to relieve garrisons within rebel-controlled territory. But his force was besieged by the Mahdi. Winston's campaign in miniature was not reflected in the tragic events that followed.

– first the Duchess of Gloucester, then Viscount Crowhurst, the Marquis of Londonderry, Sir Thomas Colebrooke Bt, Lady Elizabeth Hope Vere (at number 18), and others – the maids are drawing the curtains, glancing out at the heavy traffic as they do so.

Jack, nearly 5, is already a great chatterer and is spurred on by the excitement of his brother's return and the latest news he has to impart.

'They're going to build a huge great tunnel outside our house, Winny.'

'Oh, don't be silly,' Winston replies scathingly. 'What would they do that for?'

'It's going to go all the way to the City – all the way along Oxford Street, Mama told me. She's furious. She says it'll make a terrible mess.'*

Winston pursues the subject no further. They are now almost at Marble Arch – and there, on the corner, is home! Mama will be more accurate with the news. Tunnel indeed!

'And Woom told me they're going to cut right through America, too. It's going to be a canal, like the Suez Canal, she says.'

The carriage turns left round Marble Arch, which stands in the dusk like a giant tombstone. The horse-buses and cabs and scattered coaches are making for the shops in Oxford Street, open late for the Christmas trade, and decorated with tinsel and streamers and holly. King expertly drives the two handsome greys round the corner of Bayswater Road and Edgware Road and through the gates, acknowledging the gatekeeper with his whip, into Connaught Place. The porch of number 2 is lit by a large single gaslight, and the coach has hardly come to a standstill before Robertson, the butler, has opened the front door, welcoming the two boys with a smile. Beside him, tail floating from side to side, is an overweight dog.

---

*The Central tube line.

Winston jumps down from the carriage, leaping up the two steps, greets Robertson briefly, and flings himself onto the dog, who responds with much licking. 'Oh Chloe, have you missed me? Oh Chloe, you've got so fat. No one's taking you for walks, are they?'

'Oh yes, they are,' says Jack. 'Woom and I take him into the park every day.'

Jennie appears from the drawing room at the sound of her boys' voices and stands on the landing at the top of the stairs. She is dressed in a long dark blue velvet dress embellished with a single diamond pendant, and behind is her sister Leonie, chubbier and less beautiful than Jennie, and her husband Jack Leslie, who have come to stay for the Christmas period to keep Jennie company.

Winston races up the three flights. Jennie bends down to embrace him, asking how he is and 'Was the train ride jolly?' Jack is trying, but unsuccessfully, to get confirmation from his mother about the tunnel. Leonie is asking about school, and did Winston see the sea earlier in the day? Winston, at mention of the sea, tells his mother, with just a faint note of self-satisfaction, that he has written a letter to his father, who *is en route* to India.

But all this takes only a brief time, and Jennie is heard to say firmly, 'Your tea's ready upstairs, boys. And Everest is anxious to greet you.' Then she turns back to the long drawing room, from which other voices can be heard. Winston and Jack race up the wide staircase, while the knife-boy, Edgar, and the even younger Pip carry the trunk awkwardly up the servants' steeper and narrower winding staircase at the back of the house.

'Woom! Woom! – hullo Woom!'

'The Most Extraordinary Young Man I Have Ever Met'

Winston's time at the Miss Thomsons' school in Brighton remained happy. By contrast with the hell of St George's, 'I was allowed [he wrote] to learn things that interested me: French, History, lots of Poetry by heart, and above all Riding and Swimming.' There was riding three times a week and swimming in the sixty-by-twenty-foot municipal baths whenever the weather allowed it: 'I dive . . . and keeping body perfectly straight until I reach the other side keeping under the water the whole time.'

Winston's letters home reveal his constantly developing powers of pleading with his mother. Jennie was often forgetful and even neglectful of her sons at school. Her life was a constant round of pleasure-seeking and social and sporting occasions, whether or not her husband was at home. She failed to visit them after indicating that she would, and she forgot to send Winston things he needed, and often had to be reminded. Jack, when he eventually went away to school at Elstree, just north of London, does not appear to have resented the omissions and neglect generally. But Winston, intemperate, impatient, proud and egotistical, could not bear to have his wishes frustrated and was up to all the tricks of importunity, begging and bullying by turn. With his father he was much more discreet, time and again saying that he quite understood his not writing when he was so busy, let alone visiting him, but could he please send a few autographs as his friends would appreciate them?

Winston was struck down by pneumonia at school on 12 March 1886, and was soon in a very dangerous condition. Dr Robson Roose hastened to his bedside and gave up all thoughts of his other patients, in London and Brighton, in favour of the Duke of Marlborough's nephew. Randolph was summoned by telegram, and Jennie booked in at the nearby Bedford Hotel. For several days Winston was at death's door, and no sooner had Dr Roose succeeded in getting down his temperature from over 104°F than another climax sent it soaring again. Jennie sat for long hours at his bedside, and even for Randolph things political went 'rather kriss-kross'. Not until 17 March did Winston's temperature stay down long enough for there to be a note of optimism in the doctor's report, though even then Mrs Everest, who also had hurried down from London, was not allowed to see him in case the excitement might be too much for the boy. In Parliament, friends and foes alike of Randolph – Lord Salisbury himself, Sir Michael Hicks Beach, and many more – expressed their sympathy and their relief when Winston's health improved. For a day or two it seemed as if half the socially and politically prominent people in Britain were concerned about the health of the future heir-apparent to the Dukedom of Marlborough.

Brighton's reputation for a healthy climate was not much dented by Winston's attack of pneumonia, and on the whole he was mercifully free of childhood ailments while with the Miss Thomsons. But for convalescence, and convenience in the summer holidays, Mrs Everest often took Winston, and later, Jack, to stay with her married sister, Mary Balaam, at Ventnor on the Isle of Wight. Mary's husband, John, was a senior warder at Parkhurst Prison, and they lived with their son Charlie, a year older than Winston, at 2 Verona Cottages. This was a little two-up-two-down stone dwelling, which could have fitted into one of Blenheim's smaller bedrooms.

The Balaams filled an important role in Winston's early childhood. Here at Ventnor, Mary and Mrs Everest provided a humble, sensible, domestic milieu by contrast with the grand comings and goings of Blenheim and Connaught Place where any attention Winston received was of a fleeting nature. Only teachers and the servant class, in Winston's experience, were capable of steady, unfailing interest in him, something he always expected and rarely received.

At Ventnor John Balaam, who had been in the prison service for thirty years, would take Winston out on the Downs for long walks when the warder would tell him of riots and mutinies, and the injuries he suffered as a result. Understanding Winston's enthusiasm for battles, the two of them followed the details of the Zulu War of 1879. 'There were pictures in the papers of these Zulus,' wrote Winston. 'They were black and naked, with spears called "assegais" which they threw very cleverly. They killed a great many of our soldiers, but judging from the pictures, not nearly so many as our soldiers killed of them.'

Conveniently for John Balaam, some act of violence or some catastrophe outside the prison seemed to occur whenever young Winston was staying with them, giving them plenty to talk about. There were engravings in the magazines to study in detail of the Tay Bridge collapse when a whole train and its passengers were hurled into the river. And the *Eurydice* disaster occurred only a mile or so from Verona Cottages. It was on a brisk, gusty, but mainly sunny Sunday afternoon in late March when John Balaam and Winston, only 3 years old, were walking on the Downs admiring a frigate, with all sails set, heading for the Solent – a stirring sight at any time. According to Mr Balaam, who seems to have been something of a romantic, she was a troopship returning from some distant war.

Suddenly a black cloud blew up from the north-west, obscuring the sun and then filling the whole sky. The first heavy flakes of snow whipped into their faces, and the calm day was turned into turmoil by a great wind. The warder picked up Winston and ran for home. A few days later as they walked together on the cliffs where that fine sailing ship had been, three masts now stuck out from the water, all that could be seen of the brave swamped frigate. There was a naval tug alongside lowering divers. She was not a troopship but, even more tragically, a boys' training ship returning from a voyage to the West Indies. More than one hundred boys

41

had been drowned, along with the regular crew. Even now as they watched, a boatload of corpses was being towed towards the shore, to Winston's ghoulish satisfaction, and Mr Balaam took off his hat in respect before turning away and taking Winston home.

At Ventnor, too, there was nearly always a playmate closer to Winston's age than Jack. Charlie made a great companion, a year older than Winston. Later, when the Balaam boy had decided on a career, Winston was able to help him with family references for the bank where he wanted to work.

It was while Winston was at Brighton in the care of the Thomson sisters that his father passed through the final triumph and tragedy of his brief political career. By the summer of 1886 Randolph had gained for himself such a powerful reputation within the Conservative Party that he was appointed both Leader of the House and Chancellor of the Exchequer. However, he by no means enjoyed the full confidence of Lord Salisbury, who distrusted him and recognized his unsteadiness. As Leader, Randolph was brilliant and conscientious. 'Lord Randolph has shown much skill and judgement in his leadership . . .,' commented the Queen at the end of the first session.

In the House, with an audience before him, Randolph showed no sign of failing powers. But friends and colleagues were noting that his good sense was weakening, and this, with his naturally mercurial and impetuous nature, led him into serious indiscretions. He made policy statements of the most profound kind without reference to the Prime Minister or his fellow ministers. Early in October 1886, at a time when Winston was taken up with swimming and games, *Julius Caesar*, and (significantly in view of his father's activities) *Paradise Lost*, Randolph was delivering what his grandson Randolph, Winston's son, later described as 'a fateful speech', which 'created a sensation'. Almost everything that he advocated on foreign and home affairs ran counter to government policy. Then he immediately went secretly abroad until the dust settled. Speculation among his family and friends, as well as his enemies, about his health was increasing.

Randolph was an inveterate gambler who once told an aspiring young politician, 'Politics are more of a gamble than other careers; but look what big prizes there are.' But his behaviour during the final weeks of 1886 suggests that the odds for his political survival, let alone his becoming Prime Minister, had lengthened to a hundred to one. In mid-December Randolph was embroiled in a struggle with the heads of the two services, Lord George Hamilton who was First Lord of the Admiralty and W. H. Smith at the War Office. Randolph thought their funding demands were too high and that more money should be spent on raising agricultural wages and other worthier welfare causes. Neither of these ministers would agree to lower their estimates.

Consulting nobody, not the Queen (with whom he was staying) nor even Jennie or his closest friends, Randolph wrote a long letter on Windsor Castle-headed paper to Lord Salisbury saying that because no compromise could be reached 'I cannot be responsible for the finances' any longer and offering his resignation. After a prolonged and agonizing silence from the Prime Minister, Randolph's letter was published in *The Times* and his resignation accepted. When asked why he had not refused to accept Randolph's resignation, Salisbury commented, 'Have you ever heard of a man having a carbuncle on his neck wanting it to return?'

In view of Randolph's power and popularity, his resignation was immensely damaging to Salisbury; but it was fatally damaging to Randolph. In spite of all the Churchill-Marlborough families' belief that Randolph's time would come again, he was in effect at Christmas 1886 cast into the wilderness, where his health rapidly deteriorated. In all the family, no one's faith in Randolph was stronger than that of Winston, the adoring, admiring son who so longed for an intimate relationship with him and was never granted it.

It is difficult to overestimate the influence on Winston of his father's political downfall, just as it is fruitless to speculate on the shape of Winston's career if his father had become

Prime Minister, a position he was almost certain to have achieved but for the ravages of some undiagnosed disease and their effect on his judgement.

Five months after his father's resignation, Winston at his Brighton school took his first political step by applying to join the Primrose League, an organization for spreading Conservative principles, co-founded by his father four years earlier. What is more, he wished to be a member of the Brighton branch *and* the local one in London. 'Would you send me a nice badge as well as a paper of Diploma?' he beseeched his mother. Even at twelve, Winston never did things by halves, and he loved to have something to show to the world.

The year 1887 was a critical one for Winston for another reason. Shortly after becoming a double member of the Primrose League, he learned that his parents had decided on his public school, and that it was to be Harrow, and not Eton, the family school for generations, or even that brainy establishment Winchester, where his cousin Sunny Charles, future ninth Duke of Marlborough, had been for three years. There were two chief reasons for this decision: first, there was the importance of a healthy situation, Harrow being on a hill, Eton among the mists and damp of the Thames valley, which were regarded as unsuitable for a boy who had already nearly died of pneumonia; and second, the husband of Randolph's sister, Fanny Marjoribanks, had just entered his son Edward for Harrow and spoken highly of the new young headmaster.

After the terrors of Sneyd-Kynnersley and the motherly kindness of the Thomson sisters, Winston was now to face a teacher of an altogether different calibre in the Reverend James Welldon, the headmaster of Harrow School from 1885 to 1898. Welldon, an old Etonian and brilliant classics scholar, had a fine intellect and a deep understanding of boys. His sermons were works of art; a number of those he delivered at Harrow were published in book form. He was only 31 when he was appointed, and 34 when Winston came under his care. A fine, muscular, bull-like figure, Welldon never married and was cared for domestically at Harrow by his unmarried sisters.

So, on 17 April 1888, Winston was taken to this new school, with many exhortations from his father and mother in his ear (and the extensive new school uniform in his trunk). There he found himself in one of the small houses and in bottom place in the lowest form, where he 'continued in this unpretentious situation for nearly a year'.

It was soon publicly known that Lord Randolph Churchill's elder son was at Harrow, and these were times when a son of a notable politician attracted public attention. At school parade every morning, crowds would gather to look out for Winston, and he would often hear the exclamation, 'Why, he's last of all!' There is no evidence that he was shamed or embarrassed by this; it is much more likely that he viewed it as proof – alas false – of his father's continuing fame.

Before Winston began at Harrow, the decision had already been made that he would pursue an army career, with Sandhurst Military College as the next step. This was decided during one of Randolph's extremely rare visits to the children's quarters at 2 Connaught Place. As usual, Jack and Winston were engaged in a mighty battle, with some fifteen hundred troops, including cavalry and artillery. According to Winston, his father had studied the field of battle for a long time and was certainly impressed, for he then asked his son if he would like to go into the Army. 'I thought it would be splendid to command an Army, so I said "Yes" at once: and immediately I was taken at my word.'

So, within a few days of the beginning of Winston's first term at Harrow, he had joined the school's military wing, the Corps, and from that time he became more and more concerned with military training: 'The toy soldiers turned the current of my life.' On 12 May, he fought his first 'battle', on an open stretch of ground at Rickmansworth against Haileybury school. It was not much of a beginning. He had no military uniform yet and was assigned the humble role of

45

blank-cartridge carrier. What's more, Harrow was beaten. But two days later, he wrote an account of this battle for his mother, complete with diagram. 'It was most exciting.'

Jennie was treated to a number of these reports throughout his time at Harrow, but read them only perfunctorily.

Within a few weeks of entering Harrow, Winston was also writing to Jennie, 'I hope that you are enjoying *yourself* at *Ascot* [races] as much as I am enjoying *myself* at *Harrow*.' In these early days after Brighton, everything was new and exciting and *big*, especially the swimming pool, which was 'more like the bend of a river than a bath'. The Corps, too, was a wonderful novelty. Jennie or Jack and Mrs Everest came down most weekends, and there is no doubt that Winston was enjoying himself. He was making new friends or picking up old friendships again. Besides Dudley, son of Lord Tweedmouth, Winston's uncle, there were two boys from Brighton, Luke White and Harry Stirling, whose mother was a friend of Jennie's. (Harry later fought with the Coldstream Guards in the Boer War, while another friend, Jack Milbanke, was to win the Victoria Cross in that same war for rescuing a trooper under heavy enemy fire.) There was a great camaraderie amongst the boys destined for the Army. They might be above toy soldiers now, but there was much army and fighting talk, and planning of tactics for the next 'battle'.

An incident at the swimming pool, where the boys spent so much of their spare time, basking between dips, 'eating enormous buns, on the hot asphalt margin', hints at the reason for Winston's popularity amongst his contemporaries. He is still in his early days at the school, but Winston has already discovered the delight of taking boys by surprise and pushing them into the water. He sees a vulnerable figure, naked but for a towel, standing and ruminating at the water's edge. It is too good an opportunity to miss, and Winston creeps up quietly, seizes the towel, and in the same movement pushes hard into the boy's back. There is a great splash, followed by an emerging victim already swimming strongly towards

46

him, his purposeful activity contrasting chillingly with the awesome silence and frozen posture of all the other young boys about the pool.

Winston races off, realizing that this is not someone of his age, but three years older, a fact confirmed by the speed with which he is caught and thrown into the deepest end of the pool. When Winston in turn emerges and climbs out, he is surrounded by his contemporaries, all twittering like starlings. 'You're in for it now!' 'D'you know what you've done?' 'That was Amery – sixth former, head of his house, gym champion . . .'

Realizing at once that there is only one course he can now take, Winston advances humbly on 'the potentate in lively trepidation'. 'I am very sorry,' he says in his slightly lisping voice. 'I mistook you for a Fourth Form boy. You're so small.'

This does not go down at all well, and in a sudden recovery worthy of his father in hot political debate, Winston adds, 'My father who is a great man is also small.' This was not actually true. But Leo Amery, glancing at this boy with the blue defiant eyes, red hair, freckled face, at once laughs. 'You're a cheeky little nipper,' he exclaims and turns away towards higher things and more elevated companionship.

From the first to the last of Winston's terms at Harrow it was quite impossible to ignore his presence, and on the whole he attracted both affection and admiration from his contemporaries. One of the head boys in his time, James Tomlin, who became a notable churchman at Canterbury, recalled:

> The one vivid memory that I have of him, corroborated independently by two of my Harrow friends, is of this small red-haired snub-nosed jolly-faced youngster darting up during a house debate, against all the rules, before he had been a year in the house, to refute one of his seniors and carrying all before him with a magnificent speech.

Winston's first term at Harrow revealed a boy of complete independence and non-conformity, slovenly and careless, not just difficult but impossible to arouse unless he had already cultivated an interest in a subject. Every effort by his Latin and Greek teachers, even the headmaster, failed to ignite the slightest spark of interest in these subjects. The mathematics teachers had an equally difficult time with him. How on earth was he to survive three or four years of this fruitless, tiresome regimen, he asked himself. His teachers had the same doubts. Before the end of Winston's first term, his housemaster, sharing the opinion of another master, reported to Jennie that he may not have been '*wilfully* troublesome; but his forgetfulness, carelessness, unpunctuality, and irregularity in every way, have really been so serious, that I write to ask you, when he is at home to speak very gravely to him on the subject.'

However, given a subject he enjoyed, like history or English, his powers appeared limitless. It was no trouble at all to memorize twelve hundred lines of Macaulay, to write essays of charm and erudition ('the ordinary British sentence . . . is a noble thing') showing an astonishing range of vocabulary and construction – or at the other end of the spectrum, score twenty-two out of twenty-five with the rifle. By contrast with 'the perverted pedantry' of Latin and Greek, the savour of Shakespeare was so appealing that he learned entire plays by heart, from time to time correcting publicly the misquotations of his masters.* This was not done out of either discourtesy or a need to boast. It was done spontaneously, out of an innate desire for truth and accuracy. Whatever dreadful trials his masters suffered at

---

*As Prime Minister during the Second World War, Winston, invited by Laurence Olivier and Vivien Leigh to see their production of *Richard III*, showed that he knew this play by heart, and put off the cast, by muttering all the speeches. He knew as well all of *Henry IV* and *Henry V*.

this precocious boy's hands, they had to admit that he spoke from the heart, without guile or subterfuge. A true son of his mother, he was proud, fearless and indifferent to any impression he might make. Most Harrow boys would rather be beaten than be seen with their old nannies. But when Mrs Everest arrived, plump and wearing an old-fashioned bonnet, Winston lovingly embraced her regardless of the number of watching boys. And he would be contemptuous of any teasing later.

It was not Winston's fearlessness that led him to speak out on every occasion, regardless of tact and suitability. It was not even his lack of self-discipline. It was his unselfconsciousness and spontaneity, in addition to his urge to enunciate the truth as he saw it. He was also, it has to be added, already in love with his own voice and his powers of exposition, and the attention they brought him.

Even Welldon, for whom he entertained great affection and respect, was an occasional victim of Winston's tongue. 'Churchill,' the headmaster addressed Winston severely one day over some dispute, 'I have very grave reason to be displeased with you.' Winston came back at once with, 'And I, sir, have very grave reason to be displeased with you.'

One of his contemporaries has written of Winston at this time: 'No doubt he was handicapped by his own idiosyncrasies, for he resolutely refused to absorb anything that did not interest him, and was even selective in his choice of masters from whom he was willing to learn. He consistently broke almost every rule made by masters or boys, was quite incorrigible, and had an unlimited vocabulary of "back-chat", which he produced with dauntless courage on every occasion of remonstrance.' Beaten by a senior boy, Winston arose and spoke (one is sure with a steady voice): 'I shall be a greater man than you.' He was given two more slashes for that bit of cheek.

The only people to whom he humbled himself were the two most important women in his life, Jennie and Mrs Everest. He could not bear to displease his old nanny, and accusations of extravagance and improvidence from her went deeper than those from his mother, whom he once described as his 'banker'. He was not above asking Mrs Everest for funds when his finances were desperate, and once or twice she had to plead poverty. Jennie heard about these gifts and was very angry. In one letter to his mother during his first term at Harrow, he wrote, 'Please don't scold Everest for giving me 5/-', and in response to some strong criticism of his performance, 'Don't be cross with me any more. I will try and work, but you were so cross to me you made me feel quite dull. I have kept my room pretty tidy, since you came . . . I will try to work harder . . . I am not lazy and untidy but careless and forgetful.'

But to no one else did Winston show remorse. An apology to a man was not something he was prepared to consider, for it might weaken his pride and status. But at this time criticism from women for whom he felt affection caused him genuine pain, and he felt great regret at any distress he might, however unintentionally, have caused them.

As an adult, Winston affected to have disliked his time at Harrow, and it was not until he became old and the most famous man in Britain that he harked back sentimentally to his Harrow days, even returning to the school to sing the old Harrow songs with the boys. If he was quite often unhappy there, it was not so much caused by any dislike of the institution as a combination of impatience and boredom with the attempts to mould him into a stereotype of the Victorian public schoolboy and drum into him knowledge in which he had no interest. When he was interested, his capacity for learning was infinite. When uninterested, he gave an impression of laziness and stupidity.

But Winston's first and irremediable reason for 'disliking' Harrow was no fault of the school's. He just wanted it over and done with – finished and behind him so that he could begin to make his first mark upon the world before the long march to the top. For that, as sure as could be, was his intention, and an indifferent performance was not even given the benefit of consideration. But how was he to realize his mountainous ambition by joining the Army, which was a career for the less gifted, having only limited status?

He had it all worked out. His untidiness, his feckless-ness, extravagance, bumptiousness, obstinacy and lack of self-discipline all served to conceal the master plan that he had developed covertly since his days at Brighton. He was, no less, to use the Army as a stepping-stone, to use it for the experience it would give him, together with the opportunity to make his mark. First he must make this mark, then he must exploit it politically, get into Parliament, and rise to become a great statesman.

His ambitiousness and competitiveness were recognized in the family. 'I am very ambitious to beat the others,' Winston wrote from Brighton, in connection with a play competition. 'I shall have a hard job to beat the others . . . but I think I can make a pretty good attempt.'

'I take the greatest interest in your welfare & progress,' replied his Grandmother Duchess. 'Am pleased to see you are beginning to be ambitious! You have a great example of industry of your dear Father & thoroughness in work.'

Yes, 'dear Father' indeed! The performance of dear fathers has been a spur to young men since the beginning of recorded time. And if the father has been a victim of ill luck or unjust treatment, the spur is then supercharged. As the years at Harrow went by and there was still no sign of Randolph's return to power, his son's determination to succeed in his place, and right a great wrong, became even more powerful.

No one, not even Mrs Everest, appears to have been privy to the depths of Winston's ambitiousness, except for one man. Sir Felix Semon was the most distinguished laryngolo-gist of his time, highly intelligent, physician extraordinary to the Court and to royal families abroad, and loaded with honours and decorations. When Winston was sixteen he con-sulted him about his lisp, which was a mild one but always giving him trouble.

Semon examined him after Winston had asked if he could correct the impediment. The physician was puzzled.

51

'Why are you so concerned?' he asked. 'It won't interfere with you in the Army.'

'Well, sir, I certainly intend to go to Sandhurst, that is true,' Winston replied. 'And afterwards I shall join a regiment of Hussars in India. But it is not my intention to become a professional soldier. First I want some experience. And then one day I shall become a statesman like my father. But when that day comes and I have to make an important speech, I don't want to be haunted by the idea that I must avoid every word beginning with "S".'

There was a pause; then Semon told Winston that there was no organic defect. 'But with practice and perseverance you will be able to cure yourself of this slight disability.' Winston was clearly disappointed. He had thought the impediment could be dealt with swiftly with some minor operation. Four guineas seemed a lot of money for this bit of vague advice.

What he could not know was that Felix Semon had been a great deal more impressed with Winston's demeanour than his defect, and when he saw his wife in the evening he told her, 'Augusta, I have just seen the most extraordinary young man I have ever met.'

5

'To Pursue My Father's Aims . . .'

There was little evidence of future greatness to be seen in Winston's last terms at Harrow, least of all in his examination results. For some time now he had been in the headmaster's big house. Welldon, in his anxiety to avoid the ignominy of failing to get such a prominent pupil even into the Army, began to pay him special attention. 'Mr Welldon has been taking such a lot of trouble in arranging private lessons for me . . .,' Winston wrote to Jennie. 'He really takes more trouble of me than any other ten boys.'

But all this extra trouble did not produce the required results. Winston tried to persuade his father that the reason for his dismal record was that he was now in the Army Class, a requirement at Harrow for any boy set on Sandhurst. Winston hated the Army Class and claimed that nearly all the boys heading for Sandhurst hated it, too. It occupied two hours of every working day, which usually resulted in low marks in other subjects. 'The Army Class,' he told Randolph, 'takes me away from all the interesting work of my form & altogether spoils my term.'

The preferable alternative, in Winston's eyes, was to go directly into the Army through the Militia. His great friend Jack Milbanke had gone into the Army by that route; why should not he? But no, it was to be Sandhurst, his father insisted. But how would he ever make it to that exalted establishment?

'Your report which I enclose is as you will see a *very* bad one. You work in such a fitful inharmonious way that you are bound to come out last,' Jennie complained. 'Look at your place in the form!'

Winston generally replied to parental criticism humbly and with apologies, and reassurances and rosy hopes –

'I am bound to get a good report next time . . .' He rarely did, and the petty misdemeanours multiplied. He got a good 'swishing' from Welldon when he and other boys were reported for breaking windows in an abandoned factory, and a thorough ticking-off from Mrs Everest for his habitual, and ever-increasing, extravagance. He persuaded his father to give him a new bicycle and within the month had fallen off and concussed himself badly enough to be bed-bound: he was accident-prone as well as undisciplined. Nothing seemed to go right for him. 'All my contemporaries and even younger boys seemed in every way better adapted to the condition of our little world,' Winston confessed. 'It is not pleasant to feel oneself so completely outclassed and left behind at the very beginning of the race.'

Even the rare pleasure of a visit from his father was tarnished by his own inadequacies. Randolph took him and Jack Milbanke out to lunch at the King's Head Hotel. Milbanke and Randolph talked as if they were equals, 'with the easy assurance of one man of the world to another . . . But alas I was only a backward schoolboy and my incursions into the conversation were nearly always awkward or foolish.'

Winston's one consolation in his last terms at Harrow was his newly discovered skill at a sport at which he never expected to shine: fencing. He found he had a natural aptitude for fencing, being nimble on his feet, deft with his arm, and fast in his reactions. No one could touch him. 'I have won the Fencing,' he told his mother at the end of March 1892. 'A very fine cup. I was far and away first. Absolutely untouched in the finals.'

There was also some comfort for Winston in the pets he kept. During all his earlier days at boarding school he had missed Chloe and the other dogs and his pony at home. Mrs Everest often referred to the dogs in her letters, and to 'three little pups up in the nursery', one of which – Turvy – was adopted by Winston. He was not allowed to live with Winston at Harrow, but his pony Gem was stabled at the school and was ridden whenever he had time.

In September 1891, when Winston was 16, he determined

to have the company of a dog, too. 'I have never had a decent dog of my own,' he pleaded with his mother, '& Papa told me he used to have a bulldog at Eton so why not I at Harrow.' And naturally, it had to be a bulldog – a bulldog of excellent pedigree, costing £10. 'I can get whelps from her worth 30/- each.' Mrs Everest intervened at this point, with sensible, down-to-earth advice. Winston had proposed selling his bicycle to help fund the cost of the bulldog. She thought this quite improper. 'His Lordship gave you the bicycle & he would not like you to part with it', and the bicycle would afford him more pleasure than a 'dangerous dog'. However, the deal was done, Randolph appears not to have minded, and to Winston's delight, his father greatly admired the bulldog.

In spite of his long, restless journeys abroad in search of his health, Randolph's relations with Jennie remained stable and affectionate. On all family matters, especially concerning the boys, they consulted one another frequently, Jennie having to take all the initiatives when her husband was away. From being the darling of the press, Randolph became a pariah with the Conservative newspapers after his resignation. Gossip about his marriage, previously suppressed, began to be freely bandied about. The London representative of the *New York Sun*, at less risk than English reporters, actually asked Jennie in a letter if her marriage was 'on the rocks'. Jennie gave the letter to Randolph to deal with. He did so by informing the journalist in uncompromising terms that if he repeated or printed such scurrilous nonsense, there would be immediate libel proceedings.

Such proceedings would almost certainly have been successful. The whole of society knew that the pair were utterly loyal to one another in spirit, and equally that the marriage was now in name only. Jennie made no attempt to conceal her affection for other men, nor to flaunt it, nor to claim or deny that they were innocent relations – which they certainly were. Such behaviour was beneath her contempt.

Jennie's steadiest admirer was Count Charles Kinsky, a

dashing Austrian diplomat and man-about-Europe, a prominent rider to hounds who had won the Grand National steeplechase in 1883 at the age of 33. Kinsky judged that one way to Jennie's heart was through her elder son, and he made much of Winston, who returned his affection. From his privileged philatelic base in Europe's embassies, Charles Kinsky was a great supplier of foreign stamps for Winston's collection.

At the celebrations for Kaiser Wilhelm's visit to London in 1891, Kinsky took Winston to all the sights and displays: 'The fireworks were wonderful . . . Then there was the Battle of the Nile. The ships actually moved and the cannonading was terrific . . .' Winston was beside himself with delight. Charles Kinsky became Winston's hero and surrogate father. Until this Austrian married in 1895 he was often to be seen in attendance on Jennie at Connaught Place and Banstead Manor, the country home near Newmarket rented by the Churchills for Randolph's racing activities.

For a while, racing and breeding and, unfortunately, gambling provided Winston's father with some sort of consolation for his failing political activities and failing health – the two, alas, going hand in hand. Randolph was suffering from an acute toxic confusional illness. He was a passionate man who had always experienced hypertension and had had no wish to enter Parliament.

'He was not trained for Parliamentary work, much less Ministerial work,' one of his grandsons has written. 'So he had to learn: history, the intricacies of finance, administration, and the ways of bureaucracy. He suffered in consequence from overwork, and he also had worries about money.'

For Randolph, the stress of the Aylesford affair, the virtual banishment from his own country, was followed by the sudden and powerful missionary zeal that overcame him as he became aware at first hand of the fearful maladministration of Ireland and the suffering of the people. From an uncaring backbench MP who enjoyed the good things in life without any conscience, he became seized with a mighty ambition for power in order to right the great wrongs of this unhappy country.

All this was too much for his nervous system, and Dr Roose, as was common at the time, prescribed belladonna as an anodyne and laudanum as a tranquillizer. Randolph found the effects highly beneficial and, typically for a man of his temperament, took the drugs in increasing doses, as the family records reveal. The debilitating effect over a period of time, exacerbated by a steady consumption of alcohol, led to the political excesses and follies that increasingly marked his downfall.

Sudden fears, bewilderment and impulsive behaviour, along with a tendency to aggression alternating with complete withdrawal from life – these were the standard consequences, and they were all suffered by Randolph.

His family and friends were appalled by the onset of Randolph's disease and its remorseless advance, but his political enemies, who were numerous, used it to denigrate him. The completely unsubstantiated story was spread that he had contracted syphilis from a serving girl at Blenheim while Jennie was pregnant, and as a result had been obliged to abstain from further intercourse with his wife. Moreover, this conveniently dovetailed with the rumour that he was not the father of Jack – 'so different in every way from Winston', as people were constantly asserting.

This cruel canard in fact had only a limited effect on Randolph's political career, for by 1892 he was dying politically and physically. There was little that Dr Roose could do. Randolph's hearing had become so poor that he did not realize how slurred and hesitant his speech had become. His sense of balance was going, and his palpitations were all too evident to his family and friends, but not to himself. Yet on 17 February 1893, he let it be known that he was to make a major speech on one of his favourite subjects, Irish home rule. The performance was so pitiable – he stumbled over his words and ran out of breath, seemingly only half conscious of his whereabouts – that members left the chamber in embarrassment.

*

57

Winston's practice of ignoring all that failed to interest him may have diminished during these last terms but had not disappeared. The result was that, in spite of all his special coaching, he failed by a wide margin to pass the 'Further' entry examination. He learned of this disappointment in August 1892 while staying at Banstead and enjoying a lazy and blissful time with Jack and friends and with his pony and dog and hens (a new enterprise), a veritable menagerie of pets.

Welldon, after all the trouble he had taken, was not pleased when he heard, and he wrote to Winston that he 'must come back to school resolved to work not by fits & starts but with regular persistent industry'. Randolph was equally displeased and threatened him with a career in business if he failed again, citing several City magnates, including Nathan Rothschild, Horace Farquharson, and his old friend Ernest Cassel, as possible sponsors.

Winston's last term at Harrow was unlike all those before it. He had finally disciplined himself to work hard and steadily, fearful of a second failure and the loss of public esteem and self-esteem this would cause. He was further kept out of mischief by the presence of Jack, who enjoyed the customary privilege of sharing a room with his elder brother in Welldon's house. Winston gave his beloved brother all the guidance in the ways of the school that he needed.

Winston reported on Jack's health and general well-being. 'Jack has been getting on very well & has come out top in Essay.' And he sent his mother details of the decoration and furnishing of their joint room. Winston also asked anxiously when Jennie was coming to see them. But neither boy was to see his mother for some time, for Jennie was seriously – even dangerously – ill.

The news reached Winston and Jack through a letter from Randolph, who had returned to London from Scotland as a result of an urgent telegram from Dr Roose. Jennie was suffering from acute peritonitis, and the new operation for the removal of the appendix was considered too dangerous:

this was still ten years before King Edward VII's life was to be saved by this surgery.

It was not a good time for Winston to be troubled by worry about his mother. Just over four weeks before his first papers, he wrote to Randolph:

> *Dear Papa,*
> *I received your letter this morning. I am dreadfully sorry to hear Mamma was so bad. I do hope she will soon be better and that you will let me know every day how she is.*
> *Is it any good writing to her?*

Fortunately her condition had slightly improved when he sat his first papers on 29 November 1892, the day before his eighteenth birthday.

But Winston remained confident that all would be well in his exams, and more important, Welldon was optimistic. 'His work this term has been excellent,' the headmaster reported to Randolph. 'He understands now the need of taking trouble, and the way to take it, and, whatever happens to him, I shall consider that in the last twelve months he has learnt a lesson of lifelong value . . . I should say he has a very fair chance of passing now . . .'

Randolph waited as anxiously as Winston for the results. But the father had other anxieties. In fact they had multiplied with Jennie's serious illness. His debts had at last caught up with him. His brother, Blandford, had died at the age of 48, Randolph's nephew Sunny succeeding to the Marlborough title, and Randolph had been reduced to selling 2 Connaught Place and ceasing to rent Banstead Manor, a place of joy and relaxation for all the family. And his own health was still fast deteriorating.

Poor Randolph, whose 'transitory life' was 'in trouble, sorrow, need, sickness', suffered a further blow while in Dublin for Christmas. 'Come at once. Winny severely injured – Jennie', ran the telegram. So this was the biblical 'other adversity'.

59

'Walden, pack my bags at once – we are leaving for Bournemouth.'

This is what had happened. Jennie and the two boys were staying at Canford, Branksome Dene, outside Bournemouth, the home of Randolph's sister Cornelia. She was married to the industrial tycoon Ivor Guest, first Baron Wimborne, and much loved in the family and within a wide circle of friends. The boys were playing in the garden with one of the sons of the household, Freddie. As usual with these teenage boys, the game was a boisterous one – on this occasion a game of tag, with Winston as the quarry.

The chase had already lasted twenty minutes, but Winston was as determined as ever to claim victory by reaching the house without being intercepted. He was short of breath and anxious to make a final escape, when he remembered a possible shortcut across a flimsy rustic bridge that spanned one hundred and fifty feet across a deep cleft in the sandy pine forest.

Winston was halfway across, victory within his grasp, when to his dismay he saw Jack barring his way; then, on turning, he spotted Freddie approaching the other end. He was the victim of a trap, and capture now seemed certain.

'But in a flash,' Winston recalled, 'there came across me a great project.' The tops of the pine trees reached the level of the footbridge and were not, he calculated, too far distant. If he leapt into space he could seize the nearest stem and let himself down rapidly to the ground, some thirty feet below.

Many years later, Winston's son believed that he was influenced in his daring decision by the example of Horatius:

> Without two more
> . . . who will stand on either hand,
> and keep the bridge with me
> what else was there but to plunge?

It was no River Tiber below, however. It was hard ground. Winston's courage was sublime, his calculations absolutely

60

wrong. Some of the branches broke his fall but not by much. The boys heard the thud of the impact and saw him spread-eagled at the base of the tree, unconscious.

Jack raced back to the house. Jennie saw him coming and ran to the door to meet him. 'Winny jumped over the bridge,' he panted, 'and he won't speak to us.'

Jennie ran inside again, holding her dress for greater speed. In a moment she had summoned aid and seized a bottle of brandy. Winston was picked up fifteen minutes later and tenderly carried back to the house, covered by a rug, still quite inert, as he was to be for three days. Telegrams flew, to London, to Blenheim, to Randolph in Dublin.

Winston had ruptured a kidney. More seriously, he had damaged his spine, so that forever after he suffered a slight stoop, by contrast with Jack's erect stance. 'It was more than three months before I crawled from my bed,' he recounted in *My Early Life*. This was typical hyperbole. He was out and about again within a few weeks. But then, as one of his nephews has remarked, those memoirs contain a good deal of fiction.

Ever anxious to communicate, Winston in less than a week was writing letters describing the drama of the occasion and his brush with death to friends and relations, and on 4 February he was taken to 'Dr Brighton' to recuperate, staying with his aunt, Duchess Lily, Blandford's recently widowed wife. Within one month of the accident, Jennie was despatching cross letters telling him that he will have to 'settle to yr work soon otherwise you will have a scramble for it', while Dr Roose advised against 'hard study . . . and vigorous exercise'. The need to settle to his work arose from the dismal news that he had failed his Sandhurst examination again. Now there was nothing for it but a 'crammer', just as soon as Dr Roose pronounced him fit for the strain.

At 5 Lexham Gardens in west London there was an 'educational establishment' presided over by a retired army captain, Walter James. After thirty years of cramming boys who for one reason or another had failed their army examinations once, twice, or sometimes three times, there was absolutely nothing Captain James and his staff did not know about the intricacies and patterns of thought of the civil service examiners. This did the trick, at last.

On 3 August 1893, Winston learned that he had passed, not triumphantly but sufficiently, his marks still reflecting his high talent in a subject like English history, which he enjoyed, and dismal inadequacy in Latin, in which he scored just 362 out of 2,000 marks. He was on his way to Dover with Jack and Jack's holiday tutor for an unexpected treat, a walking tour in Switzerland, when he read his name in the newspaper as a successful candidate. He at once sent telegrams with the news to his father, to Welldon, and to Duchess Lily, who had given him such a good time at Brighton. She wrote back, 'I was so pleased to get your wire today and to know that you had "got in"!!!'

Winston's marks were enough to get him into the cavalry, but inadequate for the infantry, which demanded higher standards. This did not imply a greater stupidity among cavalry officers, but the cavalry demanded greater expenditure, at least £200 extra a year, on a servant and the upkeep of a horse, while an infantry officer was required to pay for only a servant. Winston did not mind in the least and looked forward eagerly to the dashing life of a young cavalry officer with, as well, hunters and later a string of polo ponies.

So it was in high spirits that Winston entered on this holiday, walking great distances with Jack and climbing all the best mountains. He was eager to 'do' the Matterhorn, but this required expensive guides and was, according to Jack's tutor, too dangerous. It might have been safer than boating on Lake Lausanne. Once again showing his proneness to accidents, on a calm day in August he 'saw death as near as I believe I have ever seen it', even nearer than when, only a few months earlier, he had hurled himself into space and failed to seize that pine tree.

Winston had hired a boat, with a protective awning against the sun, and with Jack as a companion, he rowed out into the middle of the lake, where they stripped and took a dip, swimming no more than a hundred yards from the boat. But even this proved to be too far, for a breeze got up and with the awning acting as a sail, blew the boat out of reach.

Winston began to pursue it, thankful that he was a strong swimmer; but every time he almost had his hand on the stern, the breeze gusted and took it away. It was a nightmare situation, for the shores of the lake were far distant. 'I now swam for life,' he recounted, and at last, when close to exhaustion, he seized the gunwale and dragged himself on board, and then seized the oars to return to Jack.

The happiness of this holiday was marred not by this episode, which was only terrifying, but by a long letter from his father. Read with the advantage of hindsight, it is easy to account for its tone and message by the condition of Randolph's health. But at the time, it was a savage blow for Winston. Far from congratulating him on passing into Sandhurst, he upbraided him for his poor marks, which would lead his father into the extra expense of supporting a cavalry cadet. Moreover, Randolph had used all his influence to ensure that Winston would get into the 60th Rifles, 'one of the finest regiments in the Army'. The letter was alternately sarcastic in tone and haranguing, sparing him nothing, referring to his 'idle useless unprofitable life' probably leading to 'a shabby unhappy & futile existence' as an adult.

Winston later confessed that he 'was pained and startled by this communication' from the man he had always so loved and admired, and he returned sad and chastened at the end of August for his entry into Sandhurst on 1 September 1893.

The Royal Military College, Sandhurst, is set in agreeable Surrey woodland close to the village of Camberley. On the long drive up to the main buildings, Winston caught glimpses of lakes, one for swimming and the other for boating, cricket and football grounds, a golf course, tennis courts, and (more meaningfully) large asphalted parade grounds. Beyond immediate sight were stables, riding schools, shooting ranges, racquet courts and a huge gymnasium. The main building, which he first saw through the late summer birch leaves, was long, low, and spotless white, the home for 360 cadets.

These cadets, of whom Winston was now one, were, he learned, divided into three stages of training. Each company of sixty was led by a captain, who appointed three grades of under-officers from the most promising cadets; each company had its own quarters, including recreational facilities, and competition was encouraged.

It was said that the regime combined the evils of the life of the private soldier with those of the private schoolboy. But the discipline was many times stricter than at any school, and from the 6 a.m. start to the formal evening dinner the cadets had scarcely a moment to themselves.

Half the time, the working-blue-clad cadets were in the classrooms studying tactics and military history, topography, and military law; the remainder of the day was spent shooting, drilling, riding (a great deal of this), and practising blowing up bridges or constructing fortifications.

It was intensely demanding, and Winston at first complained of great weariness. The routine was not made easier by his passing through a period of poor health, with several boils that had to be lanced and painful teeth that had to be extracted. Mrs Everest was reduced to a fine state of concern for 'my darling Winny', her letters giving firm instructions about self-treatment, Eno's Fruit Salts being her favourite potion.

Stress and worry were contributing factors to this poor health and weariness. There were several reasons for this. Family finances had declined dramatically. It was not enough that Randolph and his family had been obliged to give up both the town and country houses, and squash in with his mother at 50 Grosvenor Square. Their overheads, it had been decided, must be cut to the bone – even the staff, even Mrs Everest herself.

Shortly before his arrival at Sandhurst, Winston learned that Fanny, the Dowager Duchess, who controlled all the servants at Grosvenor Square and was herself feeling the need for economy, had insisted that Mrs Everest must be sacked, on the grounds that with Jack at Harrow and Winston in the Army, she was no longer needed. Randolph and Jennie acquiesced, and Jennie told Winston.

This news troubled him greatly, and at last on 29 October 1893, he wrote a long, impassioned letter to his mother.

> . . . *if I allowed Everest to be cut adrift without protest in the manner which is proposed I should be extremely ungrateful . . . She is an old woman – who has been your devoted servant for nearly 20 years . . . Look too at the manner in which it would be done. She is sent away – nominally for a holiday as there is no room at Grosvenor Square for her. Then her board wages are refused her – quite an unusual thing. Finally she is to be given her* congé *by letter – without having properly made up her mind where to go and what to do.*

Winston goes on to suggest 'a *good* place' must be secured for her first and that she should be given a pension for life. 'Dearest Mamma – I know you are angry with me for writing – I am very sorry but I cannot bear to think of Everest not coming back much less being got rid of in such a manner.'

This letter appears to have softened, a little, the hard Marlborough hearts at 50 Grosvenor Square. The deed was done, but more mercifully. A suitable situation was found for Mrs Everest at the other end of the country – Barrow-in-Furness – where she appeared to be happy though sorely missing her boys, and she was given a modest bonus and a pension of £2.10s a month. She never knew how passionately 'darling Winny' had interceded on her behalf.

Pressing money worries for Winston himself – much more serious ones than he had suffered at Harrow – were a contributory reason for his ill health. Because of these money difficulties, Winston became seriously embarrassed with late subscriptions and other obligations, got into debt, and sold some of his possessions.

In answer to Winston's appeal for a sovereign to tide him over, Jennie replied sharply, '. . . you are spending too much money – & you *know it*. You owe me £2 & you want more besides. You really must not go on like this – think of all yr bills besides!' Winston claimed to have cut his mess bills by fifty per cent, but still had to resort to the pawnbroker. 'If therefore as the 30th Nov. [his birthday] approaches or Christmas draws near you feel as if you would like to commemorate both or either of these auspicious birthdays – a chequelet should above all things fill my heart with joy and gratitude.'

It is impossible to grade levels of anxiety and stress, but there can be no doubt that Randolph's poor health remained an abiding worry. Winston also began to understand the reason for the irrationally angry letters from his father, who a few years earlier would have been proud of his successful entry into Sandhurst and would, for instance, have treated more tolerantly the damage Winston had caused, through the rigours of Sandhurst training, to a good watch Randolph had given him.

Winston's resilience, resolution, high spirits and relentless ambition overrode these handicaps. In spite of the stresses and anxieties, he was doing what he wanted to do: learning the skills and arts of soldiering, becoming an exceptional rider (missing the college championship by a whisker), becoming a first-class shot, and making more friends than he made in all his years at Harrow.

He also began to 'make his number' with great politicians of the time, thanks to his father, who introduced him to Gladstone and to future and past Liberal prime ministers such as Lord Rosebery and Herbert Asquith, and many others, and to notable military figures who were to play their part in Winston's future, such as Lord Roberts and Colonel John Brabazon.

His name and his attractive appearance and manner ensured that he was never at a loss for entertainment during leave from Sandhurst:

> *I have had a very pleasant week in London* [he writes to his mother 22 July 1894]. *People have been very kind and I have had lots of invitations to lunch and to dances. I went to Stafford House on Tuesday*

66

– Lady Leconfield's ball Wednesday, Devonshire House Thursday, Grosvenor House Friday . . .

In this same letter Winston told of a visit, 'quite alone' with a girl called Molly Hacket, to Harrow to see Jack. Winston had met Miss Hacket at Blenheim back in December 1893, described her to Jennie as beautiful, and was clearly attracted to her. Molly was the daughter of George and Adela Hacket of Moor Hall, Warwickshire, and just ten weeks younger than Winston, for whom she quickly acquired an affection, in no time at all begging for his photograph. She got 'lovely sweets' at first, and in weeks her letters were signed 'Best love' instead of 'Yours very sincerely', and showed clear signs of flirtation.

It appears that Winston's response to all this was muted, although he clearly enjoyed being with her and admired her appearance. But Molly was bent on marriage and twelve months later was engaged to someone else.

In keeping with the times, Winston also conceived a fascination for the young musical comedy actress Miss Mabel Love, who sent him her photograph and met him after her show at the Lyric Theatre. Even if he had neither the time nor the money to become a 'stage-door Johnnie', he clearly enjoyed the brief affair with this star of the West End and was the object of some envy from old friends, such as George Wilson (from Harrow), who wrote, 'How did you manage to meet Mabel Love, I rather envy you as pretty females are few and far between down here . . .'

A few months later, by contrast with earlier records, Winston passed out of Sandhurst with honours, twentieth of his batch of 130. This proved, at least to himself, that he was bright enough 'when things mattered'.

> *I passed out of Sandhurst into the world* [he wrote of this time]. *It opened like Aladdin's cave. From the beginning of 1895 down to the present time of writing* [1930] *I have never had time to turn round.*

Lord Randolph Churchill's final decline spanned Winston's

period at Sandhurst. His father steadily lost lucidity and coherence, and his appearance became grotesque and embarrassing. His mother, the old Duchess Fanny, who had so recently lost her older son George (Blandford), realized how disturbed his mind had become when she received a letter from her son berating Winston for only just scraping into Sandhurst, including this statement about Winston's education: 'The whole result of this has been either at Harrow or at Eton to prove his total worthlessness . . .' This confusion between his own schooldays at Eton and Winston's at Harrow reflected the mental condition to which he had become reduced.

There were one or two attempts at a political comeback but they ended in disaster and were the more poignant because intermittently there were glimpses of the old orator and political tactician. In the summer of 1894 he conceived the idea of going round the world with Jennie as an escape and a search for a cure. The doctors agreed, though with reservations, and the couple set off with their servants on 27 June 1894.

In their absence, Winston approached Dr Roose and extracted from him the first clear, frank summary of the state of his father's health. The doctor had belatedly diagnosed Randolph's illness as *delirium tremens* from drug overdose, and Winston was appalled at the seriousness of his father's condition: 'I had never realized how ill Papa had been and had never until now believed that there was anything serious in the matter,' he wrote in confidence to his mother. On 24 November he was called to Roose's surgery and told that his father's condition had now deteriorated so swiftly that he was breaking short his tour and returning home immediately. He arrived in the last days of the old year and was taken to 50 Grosvenor Square, the Marlboroughs' London home.

Lord Randolph Churchill was dying. All efforts at concealment ceased. Daily bulletins were published in the press. Letters of commiseration arrived in hundreds from friends and political foes alike and from the general public, who had in the past watched in wonder as if he were a climber poised for the triumphant last steps to the summit. Instead, he had stumbled and fallen to this sorry end.

Winston was summoned and installed himself in a nearby house. He found that his father was almost incapable of speech. The two sons sat at his bedside with their mother. During Randolph's moments of lucidity, Winston learned that his father approved of his progress and was reconciled to his becoming a cavalry officer. His last coherent words to him were, 'Have you got your horses?'

In the early morning darkness of 24 January 1895, Winston was awakened by a servant. 'I have been told to ask you to go to your father, sir.'

Winston dressed and hurried out into the square where the gas lamps still burned and the sound of wheels and horses' hoofs was muffled by the lying snow. There were lights burning at number 50 and the door was at once opened for him. His father had been in a deep coma for some time and Dr Roose indicated that he might go within minutes. He did so, peacefully and painlessly, at 6.15 a.m.

Winston was just 20 years old. The Army had recently matured and hardened him and taught him both steady judgement and control of impulse. The flames of ambition were still there, as bright and hot as ever, but now better ordered, for Sandhurst had taught him that the 'fire that's closest kept burns most of all'.

The intelligence had always been there, with flashes of genius that shrewd observers had already recognized. It had not matured swiftly, but perhaps was all the better for that. Of the audacity, both physical and cerebral, there was never any doubt. He was on nodding terms with the greatest in the land, and his name alone offered an enormous advantage. Familiarly, he lacked money, for his pay was just £120 a year, and his mother had only the allowance that trickled through from her late father's estate. But that was a small handicap compared with the crusader's spirit, summed up by the words he wrote of himself at this time, when he became his own master: 'There remained for me only to pursue my father's aims and vindicate his memory.'

6

Under Fire at Twenty-one

Two soldiers figured importantly in Winston's military career. They were named, euphoniously, Bindon Blood and John Brabazon. Colonel Brabazon, as he was when Winston first met him, was a penurious Irish landlord, with an inherited passion for horses and the Army. He was a fine-looking man, with a tremendous moustache, piercing grey eyes, and grey curly hair parted in the middle. He affected the style of the dandy, processed through the season, through the Court and through clubland with stately grace, and was never heard to pronounce an 'r' in his life. 'Where is the London twain?' he once asked the Aldershot stationmaster. And when told it had left: 'Gone! Bwing another.'

Brabazon knew everyone, was an intimate of the Prince of Wales, and possessed charm and conversational powers that attracted the most beautiful women of his time, though he abstained from marriage. His courage and military record, when there was little enough campaigning to be had, were impeccable. His broad chest was ablaze with medals and clasps. He was also well read, which was about as rare in the Army as was his appointment, through the intervention of the Prince of Wales, as Colonel of the 4th Hussars over the heads of long-serving officers of that regiment.

Bindon Blood, another Irishman of extended lineage, whose ancestor Colonel Thomas Blood came near to stealing the Crown Jewels from the Tower of London in 1671, was quite as handsome as Brabazon, though with fine blue eyes and a moustache that exceeded even Brabazon's in luxuriance. From 1877 to the conclusion of the Boer War in 1901, Blood contrived to take part in almost every campaign, covering himself in as many honours, medals and clasps as Brabazon. Born in 1842, he lived to see his

70

protégé, Winston, as Prime Minister after the fall of France in 1940.

With the death of his father, Winston could press without restraint for an appointment with a fine cavalry regiment; and there was none finer than Colonel Brabazon's 4th Hussars. Before he died, Randolph had made contingency plans should Winston have to enter a cavalry regiment, and had spoken with Brabazon, who was an old friend.

Shortly after Randolph's death, Jennie carried out the first of countless steps to advance her son's career. She wrote to Colonel Brabazon to ask his assistance, if he approved and there was a vacancy, in ensuring that Winston was appointed to his regiment. Brabazon replied instructing Jennie exactly how to work this, through the military secretary, the aged Sir Reginald Gipps, and the almost equally aged Duke of Cambridge, a grandson of George III and Commander in Chief of the Army for no fewer than thirty-nine years.

The machinery creaked into action, rather more rapidly than usual, thanks to the Marlborough name, and within a month of Randolph's death, Winston was installed at Aldershot as a lieutenant in the renowned 4th Hussars. Training was a great deal tougher than he had anticipated. 'A terrible tyrant', the regimental riding master, nicknamed 'Jocko', supervised the riding school. For weeks on end, between nights of pain from bruises and cuts, Winston and his contemporaries, both officers and troopers, learned to mount and dismount bareback at the trot and to jump a high bar with hands clasped behind the back and without saddle or stirrups. Falls were inevitable, a particularly savage one putting Winston to bed for two or three days, while others made walking impossible for even longer.

Gradually Winston's muscles and sinews adjusted to the shock treatment of the riding school and, later in the summer, to manoeuvres, which entailed eight hours in the saddle and then two hours 'stables', followed by polo. This was supplemented by occasional steeplechasing, which he had to admit to Jack was dangerous.

All this activity kept his mind from the death of his father, which had deeply affected him. But the sudden death of the woman who had been closer to him than any other in his life brought renewed sadness and depression. Mrs Everest's passing followed closely on that of Jennie's mother, Clara, and was therefore the third in a year of bereavement.

When Winston heard that Mrs Everest was seriously ill, he hastened to her bedside with a doctor, ordered a nurse, and sat with her until she fell into unconsciousness on the evening of 2 July 1895. The old lady, who had dedicated her life to children and given hardly a thought to herself, died in the early hours of the next morning. 'I shall never know such a friend again,' Winston wrote to Jennie. 'I feel very low – and find that I never realized how much poor old Woom was to me.'

Before returning to Aldershot, Winston diverted to Harrow, not wishing Jack to learn the news from a telegram. 'He was awfully shocked but tried not to show it.' Winston also made arrangements for the funeral, which he attended with Jack a few days later. Jack and he paid for a headstone, and Winston ensured that fresh flowers were to be placed on the grave on every anniversary of her death.

If Mrs Everest, and her death, pointed sadly to the past and 'with regret to the old days at Connaught Place when fortune still smiled', two first meetings at this time could later be seen to be carrying potent seeds of the future. One of these was with the recently married Duke and Duchess of York, at dinner. The Duke had had to give up a prosperous naval career when he became heir apparent to the throne. 'I was very glad to be asked,' noted Winston, ever eager to meet those of high rank and importance.

The second meeting, a little later, and one which pointed to the almost immediate future, was with Bindon Blood. General Blood was a lifelong friend of Lord William Beresford, who had married the twice-bereaved Dowager Duchess 'Lily' (Lillian Hammersley). 'Bill' Beresford had won the Victoria Cross in the Zulu War, was a great sportsman as well as a soldier, and had been military secretary to two successive

72

viceroys of India. Winston loved him, and the two men remained close friends until Bill died in 1900.

The Beresfords had a beautiful house near Dorking called Deepdene, and here Winston first met the accomplished and impressive General Blood. He recognized immediately that this was a man who had a greater knowledge of Indian military affairs than anyone alive, and the 4th Hussars were shortly to be stationed there. Not only had the general just returned from successfully storming the Malakand Pass, on the north-west frontier of India, but in any future trouble, there or elsewhere, he was the officer most likely to be in command. 'He thus held the key to future delights,' Winston wrote shamelessly. Before they parted, the young Lieutenant had extracted a promise from the elderly General that in the event of another Indian campaign, he would be allowed to come with him.

When it was not campaigning, these were leisurely years for the British army. The pace of events was sedate, the time for recreation and relaxation ample. Officers who could afford it took five months leave each year, ten consecutive weeks if they so wished. For those in a cavalry regiment, fox-hunting was encouraged, and many hunted three or four times a week. After completing training at Aldershot, the regiment was due to move to Hounslow barracks, much nearer London, until it moved to India in 1896.

At the end of August, Winston felt stale and dissatisfied with life. Soldiering was all very well, and he liked the discipline and the responsibility. But it was not, as he told his mother, his 'métier'. Politics still called, more clamorously than ever, but the old problem remained. To be sure of success in a political career, he must establish his name in his own right, make his mark and show his enterprise. He still held to the belief that the Army offered him the most rapid and effective method of doing this.

Wars and punitive expeditions were rare events this year, and as Winston noted sorrowfully, 'Nowadays every budding war is spoiled and nipped by some wily diplomatist.' But no

73

– there *was* a campaign going on, in a corner of the Spanish empire rather than the British empire. Well, that was better than nothing. Winston made enquiries.

The colony of Cuba had for long been a thorn in the flesh of Spain's empire. The Cubans, who were fighting for their independence, were a very tiresome and insurrectionary people in the eyes of the authorities in Madrid. Winston took a neutral political view of these Caribbean affairs, but he did want to get to the seat of a war, to hear the whine of bullets, prove his courage, and tell the world about events through the newspapers. In Cuba, he could perhaps make his first small mark as a war correspondent, combining for the first time soldiering with writing.

One of Winston's friends at Aldershot was Reggie Barnes, a few years older than himself, with a lively sense of enterprise, who, like Winston, could not afford a season's fox-hunting at home and preferred the idea of bigger game abroad. Colonel Brabazon approved the idea, and so did Jennie, less enthusiastically. Winston and Reggie would have to go by way of New York and men *hated* that city, she said unaccountably, adding, more truly, that it was terribly expensive.

However, Winston was already at work preparing for this two-subaltern expedition, trading relentlessly on his father's associations. The most important of these was the present British ambassador in Madrid, Sir Henry Drummond Wolff, who thought it an excellent idea and spoke to Spain's Minister for Foreign Affairs, who arranged for the backing of the Minister of War, who in turn provided letters for the Spanish commander in Cuba. In London the Director of Military Intelligence provided maps and made certain specific requests for information. The *Daily Graphic* agreed to publish, for a modest fee, Winston's despatches from the front.

The two young men were at sea by 2 November, and in New York by the tenth. On this his first of many visits, his mother's land and the people impressed him at once. 'What an extraordinary people the Americans are! Their hospitality is a revelation to me and they make you feel at home and at ease in a way that I have never before experienced,' he wrote

74

to Jennie. And to his brother, 'This is a very great country my dear Jack.' And a few days later, summing up his conclusions to his brother, he wrote of the nation's vulgarity:

> I think mind you that vulgarity is a sign of strength. A great, crude, strong young people are the Americans – like a boisterous healthy boy among enervated but well bred ladies and gentlemen . . . Picture to yourself the American people as a great lusty youth – who treads on all your sensibilities . . . but who moves about his affairs with a good hearted freshness . . . Of course there are here charming people who are just as refined and cultured as the best in any country in the world . . .

Winston and Reggie's host in New York City was a forty-one-year-old prominent lawyer and politician, Bourke Cockran. He impressed Winston by his breadth of view, his intelligence and his conversation and kindness. He was an extremely wealthy man whose apartment at 763 Fifth Avenue provided lavish accommodation. The hospitality was limitless, and instead of staying for a day or two, the young men extended their visit to a week before embarking on a train (private stateroom by courtesy of their host) for Key West, where they embarked for Havana.

In the Cuban capital, the authorities treated them as if they were a deputation of military support by Britain, which later caused some embarrassment to the War Office. Every facility was offered to them, with free passes to any destination, transport, escort – and warnings that the insurgents might strike anywhere at any time, particularly at railway stations, which were heavily armoured and guarded. The Commander in Chief in Havana telegraphed the general in the field at headquarters, and Reggie and Winston set off in good heart, keen to witness a battle.

After a long and tiresome train journey in great heat, they caught up with a mobile column of Spanish troops under the

75

command of a General Valdez, a fearless and extrovert soldier who exhibited himself to the enemy in white uniform and sparkling decorations, on a grey horse. How honoured he was to have these two distinguished soldiers and representatives of a great and friendly power! How much (he exclaimed through the interpreter) he looked forward to having them at his side! And how delighted he would be if they would join him for dinner that night!

In a few hours they were off, thankful to leave behind the disease-ridden town where they had camped, off on a march through the insurgent districts, visiting garrison posts and clearing out the enemy when opportunity allowed.

'Behold next morning,' wrote Winston, 'a distinct sensation in the life of a young officer! It is still dark, but the sky is paling . . . We are on our horses, in uniform; our revolvers are loaded. In the dusk and half-light, long files of armed and laden men are shuffling towards the enemy . . .'

The enemy made no appearance that day or the next – days during which the column marched some eighteen miles between dawn and dusk, excluding a long siesta. And then on the fourth day, there was heard the sound of firing from the rear of the column. Soon the vanguard was being attacked too; and on this morning, the dawn of his twenty-first birthday, 'I heard shots fired in anger, and heard bullets strike the flesh or whistle through the air.'

Later, the officers were attacked while bathing in a river and were forced to retire in a state of semi-exposure; their encampment was attacked at night, and finally General Valdez cleverly manoeuvred his column so that the Spaniards could close with the enemy force ensconced in open ground and drive them into a hectic retreat.

Winston and Reggie arrived back thankfully to the flea-bitten Gran Hotel Inglaterra on 5 December, 'after a very exciting fortnight and very glad we were to return to civilization and to return safely,' he wrote to his mother. 'Our luck has been almost uncanny. Every train, every steamboat has fitted exactly. We missed two trains that were both smashed up by the rebels by about half an hour. We went into a town

76

in which every sort of dreadful disease was spreading and finally if without any particular reason I had not changed my position about one yard to the right I should infallibly have been shot.'

Back in New York, the two subalterns enjoyed further hospitality, but received a (mainly light-hearted) wigging from the press, which, like British newspapers, was totally opposed to the Spanish cause. But Winston had his medal from the Spanish army – his first of many – and the *Daily Graphic* published all five of his long despatches, signed 'W.S.C.' The editor wrote to him: 'Your letters and sketches have been extremely interesting, and were just the kind of thing we wanted.' Better still, he enclosed a cheque for twenty-five guineas, Winston's first earnings from his pen and a source of great satisfaction.

Even before Winston had joined the 4th Hussars, he had been thinking about supplementing his inadequate pay and allowance from his mother of £500 a year with his writing. His letters when he was not yet 12 years old already show his facility, his feel for words, and his range of expression. His contributions to the Harrow school magazine, written under a pseudonym, were markedly superior to the usual run of articles, and his account of life at Sandhurst for the *Pall Mall Magazine*, in which the standard of writing was very high, was something of a model of its kind, graphic, concise and with touches of humour to encourage the reader:

> . . . The canteen – an institution conducted on lines which would satisfy the most intemperate Temperance lecturer – is crowded with cadets busily engaged in purchasing bread, cakes, fruit, dough-nuts, cigarettes, and milk. The last is sold in paper bags, which hold the milk indifferently well, but make excellent missiles . . .

There is no doubt that Winston enjoyed the art of writing, and had done so as early as his days at Brighton, where he managed to acquire a typewriter. Now these despatches published in the

Daily Graphic, followed when he reached home with an article in the *Saturday Review*, encouraged him to develop his talent, combining pleasure with publicity and remuneration.

His money worries continued insolubly, and like the inadequate outsiders he sometimes backed in the steeplechases, he limped from one high fence to the next, and the course never seemed to end. All too often the letters he exchanged with his mother were marked with arguments and acrimonious comments concerned with money. The trouble was that they were both extravagant and irresponsible about money. All her life Jennie had given no thought to the morrow and considered her own extravagance to be incurable. When she recognized the same weakness in her son she sometimes became almost distraught with guilt that quickly turned to anger. After Randolph's death she began to work her way at an accelerating pace through her American capital, while Winston more and more often got himself into debt as he found himself unable to pay even his mess bills. However, by sometimes frantic manipulation, he managed to run a string of polo ponies and, apparently forgetting the recent row with Jennie about his debts, wrote blithely to her (6 July 1895), 'I have bought a nice charger for £80 which will have to be paid for within a month or so.'

Since Randolph's death it had been unsuitable for Jennie to remain at 50 Grosvenor Square, and she had been moving from place to place, at home and abroad, staying with friends or at hotels. Winston and Jack, and Mrs Everest before she died, longed for her to settle in a home, for their own sakes as well as for Jennie's. On Winston's return from Cuba, Jennie had at last settled into a house at 35a Great Cumberland Place, a stone's throw from 2 Connaught Place. Winston brought with him 'excellent coffee, cigars and guava jelly to stock the cellars'.

In this pleasant house during the weeks after his return, Winston plotted new campaigns that might earn him attention and honours and prevent the need to follow his regiment to India. On 29 May 1896, he took advantage of dining with Lord Wolseley, the new Army Commander in Chief – 'and in fact all the powers that be' – to talk about troubled South Africa with Joseph Chamberlain. A few weeks later he was plotting, and manipulating 'all the powers that be', to join the 9th Lancers, who were likely to go out there and likely to see some fighting. 'My dear Mamma you cannot think how I would like to sail in a few days to scenes of adventure and excitement – to places where I could gain experience and derive advantage – rather than to the tedious land of India.'

Winston also still hankered after Egypt and the Sudan, and as the time neared for the 4th Hussars to leave England for their nine-year-long stint in India, he used all the influence he could muster to get out to Egypt as a galloper – or military aide – to Kitchener, the commander there. But all Winston's efforts were fruitless.

> *When I speculate upon what might be and consider that I am letting the golden opportunity go by I feel that I am guilty of an indolent folly that I shall regret all my life* [he wrote to Jennie on 4 August]. *A few months in South Africa would earn me the S.A. medal and in all probability the* [British South Africa] *company's Star. Thence hot foot to Egypt – to return with two more decorations in a year or so – and beat my sword into an iron despatch box.*

Soldiering, fighting, acclaim, medals, Parliament, and (not long delayed) the ministerial despatch box: that was the programme of his ambitions. And he was being frustrated. Mercilessly upbraiding his mother for not using her influence more ruthlessly, he told her from his barracks, 'You can't realize how furiously intolerable this life is to me when so much is going on a month away from here.'

The late summer days ticked by. Containing his anger and regret and persuading himself that the fates anyway could not be denied – and, with his luck in life so far, might have riches in store for him after all – Winston gathered together his possessions. With his fellow officers, he boarded the SS *Britannia* at Southampton and sailed for India on 11 September 1896.

7

War Without Quarter

Winston Churchill at 21 years was a fine-looking young man, muscular, of medium height (5 feet 6$\frac{1}{2}$ inches), with a full head of russet-tinged hair and a face marked by positive features, especially his mouth. The determined, 'bulldog' mouth and the frank, blue, wide-set eyes first attracted attention. His skin was fair and susceptible to extremes of temperature. On the passage to India he described himself to his mother as 'being very fat', but this was only relative. Corpulence was still distant in time, and the hard riding in the Hussars had kept down his weight, otherwise inclined to rise, such was his appreciation of good food and drink.

His health had not been robust during his growing years. Boils and his teeth had given him much trouble and led him to fuss about himself. He had suffered most of the standard ailments, but was a stalwart recoverer from disease as well as accidents. He always hotly denied that he was accident-prone, taking it as a slight. But it was nevertheless true that he had more than his fair share of falls and cuts and bruises.

Having been a slow developer, Winston's character had by no means become fully formed at this age. He had left behind his school laziness, though he already dearly loved a daytime doze, but not his unpunctuality. Once, he had arrived at Deepdene late and in disgrace. Duchess Lily and Bill Beresford were having a large weekend party, which included the Prince of Wales. It was considered a great honour for Winston that he had been invited at all. To the surprise of his fellow passengers in the train, he had to resort to changing into evening dress before them. When he at last arrived, eighteen minutes late, the august, fretting host, hostess and guests had not gone in because they numbered thirteen, and that was unacceptable to the heir to the throne.

The Prince rebuked him severely: he liked his food and did not care for unpunctuality, especially from a young subaltern who ought to know better.

'I do think unpunctuality is a vile habit,' Winston once confessed, 'and all my life I have tried to break myself of it.' He never succeeded.

His masters at Harrow, often exasperated beyond measure by his forgetfulness, carelessness, and unpunctuality, had always declared that he was not *wilfully* troublesome. Jennie described him at 16 as 'at the ugly stage, slouchy and tiresome'. But that had disappeared with his adolescence, and any lingering slouchiness had long since been harshly corrected by the 4th Hussars.

He was now exceedingly good company, a good raconteur who appreciated irony and the more active side of regimental life. He was popular with his regimental friends, was intensely competitive, and took part gladly in all the rowdier aspects of mess behaviour. By contrast, he could shut himself off from his surroundings and read for hours on end.

At Brighton, aged 12, he had asked for *Jess* and *She* by H. Rider Haggard, Rudyard Kipling's *The Light that Failed* (a harrowing book), and Robert Louis Stevenson's *Treasure Island*, which he read many times. His cousin later described how Winston's 'adventurous spirit fastened on *King Solomon's Mines*. He read it twelve times and once drove its author "haggard" in the course of a cross-examination. "What did you mean . . .?" he insisted on one disputed point, and the author confessed he did not know himself.'

At Harrow his reading taste turned to military works, but it remained catholic. We hear of a mysterious, anonymous novel called *Euthanasia*, and a triple-decker novel by Frank Frankfort Moore called *I Forbid the Banns*. From his father's bookseller, Bain's in the Haymarket, which became his own, he ordered William Lecky's *European Morals*, Thomas Hardy's *Jude the Obscure*, H. G. Wells's *The Invisible Man* (a great favourite), Thomas Macaulay's *Essays* and *History of England*, Henry Hallam's *Constitutional History of England*, Adam Smith's *Wealth of Nations*, and Plato's *Republic*. He prepared for himself a timetable for reading these heavier, longer works in his determination to improve his mind and provide the weight and background for his future political career.

The banjo briefly figured among his musical instruments when he was only eight; he enjoyed singing and joined the choir at Harrow, until his father told him that it was a waste of time. 'So I left the singing class and commenced drawing.' He wrote to his mother from Harrow, 'I am getting on in drawing and I like it very much. I am going to begin shading in Sepia tomorrow. I have been drawing little Landscapes and Bridges and those sort of things.' A correspondent who had received an illustrated letter from Winston congratulated him: 'There is no reason whatever why you should not make some use of your sketching, certain it is, it will certainly be a source of amusement to you.'

As for games and hobbies, Winston at this age became impatient with card games, whist in particular, but *en route* to India he developed a great enthusiasm for chess. Besides stamps, he collected butterflies, which always fascinated him. And when he arrived in India, he took to growing roses, an enthusiasm that lasted for all his life.

Winston was, at 21, a moderate drinker, but like most of his fellow officers, smoked heavily. While at Sandhurst, he thanked his father for sending two boxes of his best cigarettes. 'I keep them for after lessons,' he wrote, 'and smoke commoner ones in the daytime.' At this time he was also experimenting with cigar smoking, but Randolph did not approve. 'I don't think I shall often smoke more than one or two a day – and very rarely that,' Winston reassured him.

Winston's love of pets had, we have seen, formed early in life, and he was rarely without one or two dogs, even in the most remote places. In spite of the pain his horses caused him through excessive riding and falls, he remained deeply attached to them. In India, he had a beautiful chestnut Arab, Firefly. 'He is a great pet & prefers above all things bread & butter or a biscuit,' he told his mother. Among riders of great experience and skill, Winston stood out as exceptional; he was already becoming a first-rate polo player, an enormous asset in a cavalry regiment stationed in India.

The arrival at Bombay was one of the great moments in Winston's early life. The voyage out had lasted twenty-three days, calling at Gibraltar and Port Said, passing through the Suez Canal by moonlight and searchlight, and enduring the extreme heat of the Red Sea, before slipping across the cooler Arabian Sea from Aden. As soon as the *Britannia* neared Bombay and the great hot landmass of India, the temperature rose again. For the one hundred officers, it had been a passage of comfort and pleasure; for the eleven hundred men below decks of the trooper, close to hell.

Winston had occupied himself writing letters, reading and playing chess and piquet. Hugo Baring, Reggie Barnes and Ronald Kincaid-Smith had become his closest friends and most frequent games protagonists. He reported the food as excellent, the progress peaceful, the heat not overbearing.

At the beginning of October 1896, nearing Bombay, the temperature is in the high eighties. By noon it is possible to make out the smudge of shoreline ahead, misty and quivering in the heat. Winston is looking at it through his telescope, which has been in frequent use over the past weeks.

We can imagine him saying to Hugo as he hands him the telescope, 'It'll be good to get ashore.'

'Yes, five o'clock, isn't it, we're due to disembark?'

'The men will be thankful, too.'

By four o'clock that afternoon, Bombay harbour embraces their ship, with the teeming city on the peninsula to the west and a palm-fringed shoreline to the east, rising to tumbling high hills inland. The smell of humanity and eastern food lies heavy on the air. The sun is low in the west, silhouetting Malabar Hill, the minarets of palaces and temples, and the commercial buildings and warehouses of the great city.

Between the hove-to *Britannia* and the docks, many hundreds of small boats rise and fall on the swell like scavenging seabirds, awaiting the moment of disembarkation when they can offer their services.

83

Hugo Baring is at the rail beside Winston, both officers wearing informal uniform and topees. For the first time since Port Said, the entire complement of the trooper, as well as the crew, are on deck, observing and commenting on the magnificent panorama to the west and the contrasting view to the east with its promise of unknown awesome square miles of jungle, mountain ranges, great rivers and mysterious cities.

'The men are not going ashore until the evening – around eight o'clock,' Hugo remarks.

'Because of the heat, I expect.'

'Yes, but we can choose our own time.'

Already several fellow officers are calling out to the nearest boats, which race towards a gangway being lowered from the *Britannia* amidships. In a moment the competitive bargaining is bedlam. Ronald Kincaid-Smith, Hugo Baring and Winston make their way down to the main deck. The guards at the head of the gangway salute as they descend the steps.

'That nigger over there is trying to charge three rupees,' a heavily sweating officer is calling out. 'Don't go near him. One rupee's quite enough.'

Kincaid-Smith, the senior officer in their little party, takes command, holding out a rupee coin and promising another when they are ashore. Cash in advance works wonders, and the three of them are soon crouching in the little skiff. It takes some fifteen uncomfortable minutes, across the undulant swell, to reach the quays of the Sassoon dock.

'We came alongside of a great stone wall,' recounted Winston, 'with dripping steps and iron rings for handholds. The boat rose and fell four or five feet with the surges. I put out my hand and grasped at a ring . . .'

It is a straightforward enough action, and a necessary one if he is going to get his feet upon the shore. But this first step upon Asian soil has dire consequences. The skiff falls away before he reckons it will. He feels a sharp pain in his shoulder as he swings to try to place his feet on the stone. The sudden strain tears the capsule holding the shoulder joint together, without actually dislocating the shoulder joint.

Winston is in considerable pain, holding his right shoulder

with his left hand, as he mounts the steps, cursing and turning to call down to the others to take care. He has no idea yet that he has suffered long-term damage that will handicap him severely, prohibit games like tennis, and cause him to play polo with his arm strapped to his side. It is a melancholy beginning to his army career in India. Accident-prone indeed.

For the present, in the hurly-burly of arrival, and then the disembarkation of more than one thousand men and some five hundred tons of luggage, Winston does not expect, or receive, much sympathy, and all the next day, from 4 a.m. to dusk, he is on his feet supervising the unloading and packing on to the train of all their arms and equipment, from lances and Martini-Henry rifles to tents and saddles – 'a tremendous business,' he writes to his mother.

Bangalore – far inland, midway between the Arabian Sea and the Bay of Bengal, in southern India – was the 4th Hussars' eventual destination. It was reached by stages along the railway route south from Bombay, with the first rest camp at Poona. Winston was enchanted by it all, except the Anglo-Indian ladies – 'nasty vulgar creatures' – and found that mess life lacked very few of the comforts of home, with punkah-wallahs to stir the air and iced drinks to further offset the heat. His personal staff included a butler, dressing boy and head groom. 'All you had to do,' Winston noted with satisfaction, 'was to hand over all your uniform and clothes to the dressing boy, your ponies to the syce (or groom), and your money to the butler, and you need never trouble any more.'

He slipped into the new way of life rapidly and easily, writing home after a few days that he felt as if he had been in what Colonel Brabazon called 'that famous appanage of the Bwitish Cwown' for years. Once again, as his father's son, he was treated with deference everywhere and invited to dinner at the best tables.

But the futility of regimental life at Bangalore soon began to bear down. Only two months after his arrival he heard that at home there was to be a by-election in East Bradford, a seat that he was confident he could win for the Conservatives. What a calamity! If only he had been in England instead of 'being an insignificant subaltern' isolated somewhere in the middle of India. 'Life out here is stupid dull & uninteresting,' he complained to his mother.

In the essence of what he wrote home at the time, and remembered later, one can feel the frustration, grating like file against file through his expressions of exasperation. He had asked Jennie to send him the weekly edition of *The Times*, and this kept him *au courant* with political developments at home, but the length and frequency of his letters to his mother on contemporary political themes reflect the dearth of serious conversation in the regiment.

His old American friend, Bourke Cockran, also exchanged long letters with Winston, and that was a further solace. To him Winston described Bangalore as having a beautiful climate and being for many reasons 'an agreeable place to live in'. But to his mother, for whom he is prone to paint the gloomiest picture in his search for sympathy, it 'resembles a 3rd rate watering place, out of season & without the sea, with lots of routine work and a hot and trying sun – without society or good sport – half my friends on leave and the other half ill.'

Winston's impatience to be gone – either on leave in England to strengthen his important connections, or to some frontier campaign for a medal, or better still to Egypt – was like a running sore. In December he applied to the Adjutant General in Simla for 'special service' in Egypt, and at about the same time Jennie, in answer to her appeals on his behalf to the Commander in Chief, Sir Herbert Kitchener, learned that Winston's name had been put down on the list of officers to accompany him.

This news certainly cheered him up, and in any case he was far too ebullient to allow himself to be cast down for long over this delay in his progress. Polo, in spite of the injury to his arm, filled much of his spare time. He read a great deal, enjoyed tending the roses around the bungalow he shared with Reggie Barnes, added to his butterfly collection from the marvellous variety available in Bangalore, and danced and flirted with the few pretty and fewer pretty and intelligent girls. Standing out among these was Pamela Plowden, with whom he fell instantly and deeply in love. With appealing spontaneity he wrote of her to Jennie the day after he first met her. She was, he told her, the most beautiful girl he had ever seen. And he already planned to take her to Hyderabad and show her the city – on an elephant, for the sensible reason that the natives spat at you if you were walking.

Pamela Plowden soon became a serious influence in Winston's life. He adored her and listened to her advice and respected her judgement in a way he never had with any other young woman. Their correspondence on his side is moving and respectful towards her; hers, alas, appears not to have survived. She was an interesting woman of whom we learn little at this time.

During this first period in India, Winston travelled far and wide. Like everyone serving in the subcontinent, he had to be prepared to travel three or four days in a train for a few days' stay. It took over four days to reach Calcutta, but that did not deter Hugo and Winston from attending the famous Calcutta races for a week, both of them driven by the social side of the event as much as by the racing itself, as in England. The races were held at the very end of the year, over the Christmas period, and Winston was determined to meet as many influential people as he could pack into the time. His letters to his mother, written in the jolting train *en route* back to Bangalore, assiduously and shamelessly list them. Everyone (except the appalling Elgins, Viceroy and Vicereine) was a possible recruit to the army of supporters he was gathering for the major advance up the ladder of success that was never far from his mind.

Winston was by no means isolated by his distance from London from the cares of now being head of the family. The least disagreeable of these responsibilities was Jack – his progress

87

at Harrow, his general welfare and above all, his career. He consulted Jennie frequently about this, and she in her turn put forward proposals – the Army, like Winston, but she could not afford a smart cavalry regiment; in business in the City; the bar; or perhaps first a university education? In a letter (14 January 1897) to Jennie, Winston recommended most the Army – 'I think him absolutely cut out as a soldier.' Jack concurred. But Jennie persisted that she could not afford to put him in the Army. It almost broke Jack's heart, but ever pliant, he said he would do as she wished – and he did indeed go into the City, with high hopes at least of doing something to recover the family's fortunes, although he loathed every minute of his work there.

The truth was that Jennie's finances had reached their nadir – which had the inevitable consequence that her attacks on Winston's improvidence reached a new strength. Moreover, she had been swindled out of a large lump of capital by a crooked financier. By 1897, she had spent about one-third of the capital she had inherited from her father and was living in considerable elegance at Great Cumberland Place on £2,700 a year, out of which (she claimed) £800 went on Winston and Jack and over £400 for house, rent, and stables, leaving her with £1,500 for everything else – food, servants, entertaining and so on. But while Jennie was reading these severe lessons to Winston about the need for economy, she did not consider economizing herself. She ordered the most luxurious food for her dinner parties, never gave a thought to her dress and millinery expenditure, and stayed in Monte Carlo and in Paris at the Hotel du Thin, in the greatest luxury.

The crisis continued throughout 1897, and in January 1898 she took out a vast loan of £17,000 to clear her debts and Winston's, too, though they were minuscule compared with her own. The conditions of this loan did not appeal in the least to Winston, who stood eventually to lose £700 a year from his share of the family estate. It was all extremely distasteful, and mother and son were close to falling out seriously over the crisis.

*

Against Jennie's wishes, and the advice of the Prince of Wales, Winston determined to return on leave in May 1897. The Diamond Jubilee celebrations promised to be spectacular, but Winston was less interested in the occasion than in meeting, or refreshing his acquaintance, with the chief political figures of the time.

Back home in Great Cumberland Place, where he was warmly greeted by his loving mother in spite of her misgivings about his absence from his regiment, Winston conducted his campaign. First, he would give a political speech, to be prominently reported. His father's friend, Captain FitzRoy Stewart, secretary of the Conservative Central Office, must fix that.

Second, he had to ensure that he attended the very best celebrations connected with the Diamond Jubilee and the regular summer season.

Third, he must let it be known to the right people that he was interested in a seat in Parliament.

None of this was difficult to arrange, but time was short. He made a study of party meetings involving rallies, fêtes, and bazaars, surveying 'this prospect with the eye of an urchin looking through a pastrycook's window'. Finally, he chose Bath, where the Primrose League was holding a Jubilee meeting at Claverton Manor.* The organizers were delighted to have the great Randolph Churchill's son as first speaker. Winston's début on the platform was on 26 July 1897, and he was able to utter the cliché for the first and last time, and amid laughter, 'Unaccustomed as I am . . .'

It was a brilliant speech, which he had spent a lot of time preparing. He spoke about the six thousand workmen killed and the quarter million injured every year without any compensation under law, and how the Tories were correcting that injustice; against home rule for Ireland proposed by those 'discredited faddists', the Liberals; and the Tory mission

---

*Now the American Museum.

'of bearing peace, civilization and good government to the uttermost ends of the earth'.

This speech – and the cheers that greeted it – were more widely reported than Winston could reasonably have expected. The national as well as the provincial newspapers and the weekly journals carried columns on it, and the general view was that it was 'an auspicious début on the platform' by the young officer and son of the founder of the Primrose League, 'which delighted his audience by the force and mental agility he displayed'. There was much speculation on how and when Lieutenant Winston Churchill would seek a seat in Parliament.

Then there were race meetings to attend, where he met again old friends and influential figures in politics, and visits to the Turf Club, where he had been recently elected a member. He was certain to meet more men of power at Deepdene. Was it not here that he had first been introduced to Sir Bindon Blood? By a stroke of fate, which from time to time singled out Winston, for better or for worse, he here began his long journey to his first campaign as a fighting soldier *and* war reporter.

In fact, it was at Goodwood races, whence the house party had gone for the day, that Winston received the news that, on the very day he had made his maiden political speech, Pathan tribesmen on the Indian frontier had risen in revolt against British rule. 'I was on the lawns of Goodwood in lovely weather and winning my money' when he read in the newspaper that a field force of three brigades had been formed to suppress this uprising. It was to be led, almost inevitably, by Sir Bindon Blood.

Winston left with his winnings, explaining breathlessly to Beresford and his aunt, Duchess Lily, that Sir Bindon had promised to take him on his next campaign. He raced to the nearest telegraph office. Telegrams flew, with apologies to some, including Jack whom he had hoped to see again in Paris, and above all to the general – 'Sir, I am available and ready . . . Your generous offer . . .' So precipitate was his departure that he left behind some of his luggage, including his polo stick, and – how could he? – his new little dog, Peas. (All had to be despatched by the unfortunate Jennie.)

The fastest route to India was by P&O express train, which did not even stop at Paris, via Turin to Brindisi, and then the fast mail boat to Egypt – and India. Twelve days in all. It was all fixed within hours. His august host dined him at the Marlborough Club and took him with a farewell party to Victoria Station. The train was due to leave. 'Where is our friend going?' demanded the inebriated friends. 'He goes to the East tonight – to the seat of war,' Bill Beresford announced grandiloquently. Winston loved that – not 'going out to India' but 'to the East . . .' 'To the front?' asked the members of the Marlborough Club. 'I hope so, sir. I hope so.' And then he was off.

The second voyage to India was one of misery and anxiety, lacking even the comfort of his fellow officers. There was no message from General Blood at Brindisi, nor again at Port Said. In the Red Sea there was a stupefying damp heat of over 100°F, and at Bombay still no message. Winston was cast down with disappointment. Then the long rattling train journey to Bangalore. Surely there would be something at the regiment? But no. Had the report in the newspapers been a fabrication? Evidently not, for all southern India was drained of troops to meet the trouble on the north-west frontier, which was growing daily more critical. Fretting far from the scene of action, Winston started writing a novel, a political romance he called it. If the reality of war evaded him, at least he could turn to his other great enthusiasm.

At last, at the end of August, there arrived a letter from Sir Bindon Blood. It could not have been more friendly and encouraging. He had had to make up his personal staff before leaving and had no billet for him. But come as a war correspondent by all means, and once installed in that capacity, perhaps he could 'do a little jobbery on your account'.

Thanks to Reggie Barnes, the regiment's temporary adjutant, Winston got leave and was off again before the end of the month, travelling over two thousand miles to the scene of action. From Umballa in the North-West Provinces, he wrote to Jack a summary of the situation, the frontier being 'a scene of great trouble and excitement'. All the remains of the old Islamic conquest, the fierce warlike tribes of the frontier regions, were in revolt against British rule, he told Jack. Great danger of a massive invasion threatened. To meet this, 40,000 extra troops so far had been brought in, in addition to the regular defence complement of 10,000, to push back the tribesmen and then to exact vengeance by destroying villages.

On the sixth morning of this seemingly interminable railway journey (with a break at Rawalpindi), Winston arrived at the railhead at Nowshera. This left a further forty miles to be negotiated, through burning heat, in a pony cart, to the summit of the Malakand Pass, which General Blood had forced three years earlier.

The General returned triumphantly from a punitive expedition a few days after Winston's arrival. 'Sir Bindon Blood was a striking figure in these savage mountains . . . with his standard-bearer and cavalcade,' Winston recalled. General Blood was in his element, planning a march into enemy-held territory lasting probably one week, when they were certain to see action. They would pass through hard campaigning country, in great heat, with few facilities and much danger from these Pathan tribes and others who knew every rock and every bend in the rivers.

Winston told the General that he had been accredited to the Indian newspaper the *Pioneer*, which he had arranged in case his mother failed to persuade any London editor to take him on. But she had not failed him. She had spoken to Randolph's old friend, Sir Edward Lawson, proprietor of the *Daily Telegraph*, who had warmly welcomed the idea. 'Tell him to post picturesque forcible letters,' he telegraphed Jennie, who passed the news on through the new telegraph office at Nawagi.

To Reggie Barnes, back in the tranquillity of Bangalore, Winston wrote a long letter of as high quality as anything he wrote for his newspapers, telling of night firing into the

camp, which the British troops (11th Bengal Lancers) hated,
of the encampment of some two thousand tribesmen only
seven miles away, of scouting trips on horseback, and above
all of the strangeness of this war, in which 'half the show is
run by bluff'. He told of riding through a village full of hostile
armed men with a fellow officer and just two mounted native
orderlies. The enemy glared threateningly, and Winston's
companion trotted the last few yards separating them and
ordered them all to stand and salute them. 'They refused at
first and really things looked very black,' Winston continued,
'but somehow they do recognize superiority of race – and at
last they all got up. It was like lion taming . . .'

When Winston was not out scouting and gathering material, he was writing long letters home and the first of his
Daily Telegraph despatches. The midday temperature was
well above 100°F, and here there were few comforts, certainly no ice.

Then on 15 September, messing as always with the General, Winston learned that on the following day they were
off on their long-expected punitive expedition, sweeping the
tribesmen before them, burning every village, and killing
all who resisted. The Sikhs, who were part of the force,
were sometimes found burning their wounded prisoners,
too. 'There is no doubt we are a very cruel people,' Winston
confessed to Barnes.

The first day's fighting in what became known as the
Malakand Campaign presented Winston with all – and
perhaps a little more – of what he had been seeking, and
enough material to fill an issue of both the *Pioneer* and the
Daily Telegraph. It was also marked by disaster.

Sir Bindon Blood had determined to destroy some fortified villages at the end of the Mohmand Valley that were
held by a great number of tribesmen. He advanced early
in the day, with Winston at his side, his force consisting of
a squadron of the 11th Bengal Lancers and four companies
of the 35th Sikhs.

At the head of the valley, the tribesmen could be seen in

vast numbers, half-concealed by boulders along the terraces of the valley side. Here Winston left the General and joined with the cavalry for an advance up the slope, firing their Lee-Metford magazine carbines as they ascended – all but Winston, who feared for his shoulder and used his pistol.

After half an hour of this skirmishing, and with the enemy retreating up the hillside, the cavalry gave way to the Sikhs, who continued the attack on foot, with Winston riding among them on his pony. The return fire was very hot, and he dismounted, continuing to advance with the Indian troops until they reached the first of the villages – a village really only in name for it consisted of loopholed hovels, which were at once set alight. No enemy was in sight. It was as if the Afridi tribesmen had had enough. The retreat was ordered, and the place was a mass of roaring flames when the Sikhs pulled out to return to the valley floor.

Winston had now remounted and remained among the last to leave. In a moment the action was transformed by the sudden reappearance of the tribesmen, shouting and screaming hideously, and in great numbers pursuing the withdrawing Sikhs and their officers down the hillside. The execution was terrible, both among the British officers and the Indian troops.

At one moment Winston turned in his saddle and saw an officer falling. The Afridis fell on him like hyenas on a dying buffalo, hacking at his body with their swords. At thirty yards range, Winston emptied the chamber of his revolver at them. For a moment they desisted, then continued their ugly butchery. A sepoy lay wounded close by. Winston again dismounted, handing over his pony, and with another subaltern, dragged him screaming over the rocks: anything to get him away through the whistling fire and flying rocks. Later he complained to his mother that, on the one hand, his uniform was stained by the man's blood, and on the other that no-one appeared to notice this act of gallantry – 'given an audience there is no act too daring or too noble. Without the gallery things are different.'

Now, in spite of his weak shoulder, when others had taken

over the wounded man, Winston seized an abandoned Martini rifle and, firing as steadily as he could, considering his breathlessness, succeeded in hitting (he thought) four men. Gradually, the officers rallied their men and, reinforced by a company of the Buffs, began volley firing at the hundreds of tribesmen who were still pouring in a bloodthirsty frenzy down the hillside. Dozens of them fell, and the rest turned and fled.

As at half-time in a desperate game of football, the men rested and ate their lunch as best they could. It had been a bad morning, and this engagement was only one of many in the surrounding countryside, not all of them successful. But that was not the end of it for the Sikhs and the Lancers. The order was given to advance again, up that steep, blood-soaked slope, to recover the village and at the same time their prestige, as well as what was left of the bodies of those who had fallen.

This time the advance was better organized. The tribesmen appeared to have had enough for the day and there was little opposition. Both the Sikhs and the British soldiers had had enough fighting for one day, too, having lost 150 of the 1,300 men who had started out.

Back at the encampment, after suffering an immense thunderstorm that broke over the weary ranks, Winston took stock of his personal situation and of the day's fighting – the bloodiest since the Afghan War – for his report to the *Daily Telegraph*. His sense of pride and fulfilment after being shot at from 7.30 a.m. to 8 p.m. was almost overwhelmingly exhilarating. 'I rode on my grey pony all along the skirmish line where everyone else was lying down in cover,' he told his mother exultantly. He was playing for high stakes, he conceded, but his life had been a pleasant one, and after all it was quality rather than quantity that a man should strive for. 'Still I should like to come back and wear my medals at some big dinner . . .'

Winston need not have worried that his courage was without a witness. Sir Bindon Blood himself wrote of that day's action:

He joined me as an extra ADC – and a right good one he was. . . . He saw more fighting than I expected, and very hard fighting too! He was personally engaged in some very serious work in retirement, and did excellent work with a party of Sikhs . . . using a rifle which he borrowed from a seriously wounded man.

Much more fighting lay ahead in this campaign. The General succeeded in extending Winston's leave, and he saw service with the Buffs and the Mohmand Field Force, again being under intense fire – on one occasion continuously for five hours. Time and again he witnessed death and gallantry, and on one sadly memorable occasion, he saw British infantry run, leaving their officer on the ground.

Towards the end of his service at the front, he wrote to his mother about the nature of the campaign:

> *The danger & difficulty of attacking these active, fierce hill men is extreme. They can get up the hills twice as fast as we can – and shoot wonderfully well with Martini Henry rifles. It is a war without quarter. They kill and mutilate everyone they catch and we do not hesitate to finish their wounded off. I have seen several things wh. have not been very pretty . . .*

And now, from faraway Bangalore, Winston's colonel was judging that his restless subaltern had had enough leave and enough fighting for the time being. He sent a telegram ordering his return. Reluctantly, Winston packed his kit, said goodbye to the officers at whose side he had fought, and after a month's campaigning that had included more action than he could have dreamed possible, embarked on the long, hot train journey back to his regiment.

8

'The Shoddiness of War . . .'

The year of the Good Queen's Diamond Jubilee, 1897, was also for Winston Churchill the year when his command and courage in war settled any doubts in his mind of future greatness. Just as he had read from Dr Johnson that 'every man thinks meanly of himself for not having been a soldier,' he knew now the reverse of this adage, from the immensity of self-confidence stemming from proof of his courage. The experience of the year 1897 told him what he had always suspected: that there was no limit to what he could do with his life.

The wearing of his medals 'at some big dinner', as he had told his mother, would certainly give him immense satisfaction. Vainglorious perhaps, but he thought of them rather as a student views good marks that will take him to the next stage towards his graduation. With a prophet's eye and strengthened as always by the spirit and memory of his father, Winston in 1897 saw his career stretching ahead through the new century, rising higher and higher. So clearly did he observe his star, he was already telling people that one day he would be Prime Minister. And from this time, too, on every occasion when he heard the whine of bullets about his head and then ignored them and escaped them, his conviction hardened.

A dreaded bar to Winston's political future was removed with the birth of a son to Consuelo and Sunny Marlborough in September 1897. Now there was virtually no risk of his succession to the dukedom, which would have prohibited his sitting in the House of Commons.

At the very end of this year Sir Bindon Blood's 'Despatches' were published. They singled out Winston for his courage and

97

resolution at a critical moment. Everyone of importance at home would read that. His cup was full.

In a revealing letter to his mother from Bangalore after his return, he wrote of the irrelevance of bullets. 'Besides I am so conceited I do not believe the Gods would create so potent a being as myself for so prosaic an ending.' Fame, he added, sneered at, melodramatized, and degraded as it may be, was still the finest thing on earth.

> Nelson's life should be a lesson to the youth of England. I shall devote my life to the preservation of this great Empire and to trying to maintain the progress of the English people. Nor shall anyone be able to say that vulgar consideration of personal safety ever influenced me.

Could any mother have been given a clearer, more robust and more moving account of the career intentions of her son?

It was becoming increasingly clear to her that Winston, who had sometimes stretched her patience and tolerance almost past bearing, could well become a man of greatness. She was shrewd enough herself to recognize the signs, in his letters and in their meetings when he was last home on leave.

Suddenly, after Malakand, frivolities like polo lost their appeal. The Hyderabad Tournament, previously anticipated with such fervour, became a 'nuisance'. And later, polo 'fills a vy different position in my mind to what it did last year'.

For the present, a novel to be called *Savrola* he had begun was put away, for Winston had conceived an exciting literary project to follow up the new reputation he had achieved as a soldier. He was going to write a book about the Malakand expedition. He could already visualize it, substantial in format, finely bound, his name prominent on the cover, in the windows of London booksellers. 'The publication of the book will be certainly the most noteworthy act of my life,' he wrote to Jennie, adding the important provision, 'Up to date (of course).'

In the first ten weeks after Winston's return to his regiment he immersed himself in the writing of this account, to be called *The Story of the Malakand Field Force: An Episode of Frontier War*. Every day he worked for not fewer than five hours, partly under the press of competition from another officer, who had a similar ambition, and also to retain the topicality of the subject. His discovery of powers of application he did not know he possessed was almost as important for his self-esteem and self-confidence as his personal part in the campaign of which he was writing.

With great urgency, he sent off the manuscript to his mother on the last day of 1897, with maps and a photograph of his hero, Sir Bindon Blood, to follow.

While this book was being set up in type, Winston was already embarking on another campaign in India, while at the same time using all his powers of persuasion with Jennie, and with men of influence in the Army, to get an appointment to Egypt. Egypt: that was his next goal, and then the inevitable campaign to regain the Sudan and avenge General Gordon. What a campaign that would be – 'then I think I shall turn from war to peace & politics!' 'Oh, how I wish I could work you up over Egypt!' he wrote to Jennie while she was already engaged on the time-consuming and complicated task of getting Winston's book published and, almost desperately, trying to sort out the family's financial affairs with a seemingly hopeless accountant. 'I know you could do it with all your influence – and all the people you know. It is a pushing age and we must shove with the rest.'

Meanwhile, Winston himself was like a fisherman with half a dozen lines to attend to, casting one and reeling in a small or bigger fish at others, never idle. Besides these rods, he still had to concern himself with selling his polo ponies, with Jack's future in consultation with Jennie, and with complaining about the meanness of the *Daily Telegraph* in paying him only £5 a despatch, when each was a coup for the newspaper, placed on the front page.

The Malakand book was received with almost universal praise, ranging from fine notices to a letter (one of many) from the Prince of Wales, who congratulated him on the book's success. He found it 'generally excellent' and told Winston that 'everybody is reading it, and I only hear it spoken of with praise.'

Frustrated by his failure to bring pressure to bear on the authorities over his Egypt–Sudan ambitions from India, Winston got leave to return home. He hoped to be able to manipulate the controls with a firmer and more direct hand in London, and perhaps discover why Kitchener was apparently so hostile to the idea of allowing him to join his expedition. He arrived in London in early July 1898. Jennie, with the stimulus of Winston at her side, redoubled her efforts, even writing to Kitchener himself as an acquaintance. The great man replied with the utmost courtesy that he was besieged by young officers wishing to join him, and he simply had no room. Sir Evelyn Wood, the Adjutant General of the forces, was brought in, without, at first, useful result.

A new twist to the campaign now took place. Winston had already received letters of praise for his Malakand book from some of the highest in the land, including George Curzon, future Viceroy of India, and from that great soldier Lord Roberts, national hero of the Afghan wars. Now, soon after his return to London, there arrived at 35a Great Cumberland Place a letter from the private secretary to the Churchills' old family friend and foe Lord Salisbury. He was in his third term of office as Prime Minister and Foreign Secretary, a figure of almost unimaginable respect and *gravitas* in the nation. Not only did the great man praise Winston for his book, but he added that he would very much like to talk to him about it.

We see, then, Winston Churchill, dressed in a light grey morning coat, bow tie (as always throughout his life), and top hat, hailing a horse cab in Great Cumberland Place. It is a beautiful Friday afternoon, 8 July, the crowds are out in Hyde Park, and there is much traffic down Park Lane and Constitution Hill, past Buckingham Palace – no royal standard flying: the Queen is at Osborne – towards Whitehall and the Foreign Office.

At the appointed hour of four o'clock he gives his name and is taken to Lord Salisbury's room. The great man walks from his desk to the door to meet him. He has changed little since Winston last met him, figure of medium height, stout but no more so than was customary, almost bald but with a rich white full curly beard. His eyes are kind and wise.

'How very good to see you again, Winston. You have indeed had some adventures since we last met.' He conducts him to a small sofa in the centre of the spacious room looking out over Horseguards Parade and the Admiralty. There the twenty-three-year-old subaltern and sixty-eight-year-old statesman sit side by side.

'I have been keenly interested in your book,' Salisbury begins encouragingly. 'I have read it with the greatest pleasure and, if I may say so, with admiration not only for its matter but for its style. The debates in both Houses of Parliament about the Indian frontier policy have been acrimonious, much misunderstanding has confused them.'

Salisbury continues: 'I myself have been able to form a truer picture of the kind of fighting that has been going on in these frontier valleys from your writings than from any other documents which it has been my duty to read.'

What music is this for Winston's ears! Lord Salisbury now begins to ask specific questions that show how attentively he has read *Malakand*, and Winston replies easily and crisply, his slight lisp contrasting with the older man's deeper voice. The two men get along splendidly. At one point Winston glances at the great clock on the wall. It shows twenty minutes past the hour, and, anxious not to overstay his welcome, he moves as if to leave. But Salisbury is clearly intent on continuing the conversation, and it is half past four when he stands up and walks with Winston towards the door.

'I hope you will allow me to say how much you remind me of your father, with whom such important days of my political life were lived,' says the Prime Minister, adding: 'If there is anything at any time that I can do which would be of assistance to you, pray do not fail to let me know.'

The two men walk together through the double doors, held

open for them. They shake hands, Winston with a little bow. 'Thank you, sir. I am most grateful to you.'

Outside, in Whitehall, the sun appears to be even brighter. The whole world has suddenly changed for the better. Of course, Winston tells himself, I do not want to put the old lord to trouble on my account. On the other hand (as he was to write), 'It seemed to me that the merest indication on his part would suffice to secure me what at that time I desired most of all in the world . . .'

Several days passed. Winston continued his campaign of attrition, his mother at his side. But this did not deter him in the slightest degree from meeting the most important appointment of his infant political career. This was a speech at Bradford, where his father had been so politically active and where there was a possibility of adoption as a member. He had a packed, enthusiastic audience, and he and they loved every minute of it. 'Go on for another hour!' came the cry. And 'Come back, lad.' More important, the speech was hailed by the press.

Winston returned to London, found no progress in his more immediate ambition, and realized that he had only days left if he was not going to be too late for the expedition. He *must* take advantage of the Prime Minister's offer. A mere conversation with Salisbury's private secretary led to Salisbury's summoning Lord Cromer (virtual dictator of Egypt, who happened to be in London) and asking him to prevail upon Kitchener to call for Winston. Even this failed to move the General, who was deeply suspicious of Winston – a scribbler for the newspapers, who used his name to gain any number of privileges to which he was not entitled and who in any case was only 'using' the Army to forward his political career. That was how Kitchener regarded him. Winston, now in despair, tried one more move.

The future Lady St Helier – Aunt Mary to Blanche Hozier – was also a friend of the Marlboroughs and knew Jenny and Lord Randolph. Winston also knew her well and admired her greatly – not least for the immense range of her connections. Among them was the Adjutant General of the Army, Sir Evelyn Wood, who was known to have mixed feelings about Kitchener and the way he surrounded himself with toadies and acolytes. Would she, he asked her, ask Sir Evelyn whether he knew that Kitchener had even ignored a request from the Prime Minister to grant him an appointment with the Army in Egypt?

The future Lady St Helier did just that. Two days later a reply was received from Egypt, addressed personally to Winston: 'You have been attached as a supernumerary Lieutenant to the 21st Lancers for the Sudan campaign. You are to report at once . . .'

For young Winston preparations for war extended beyond the routine check on his weapons and uniform – and above all the medals and clasps. War had to be paid for, and that evening he arranged to meet his old friend Oliver Borthwick, son of the proprietor of the *Morning Post*. Winston's earlier efforts for Fleet Street had been so well received that he now had no trouble fixing up a deal for sending a series of letters to the newspaper at £15 column.

The following morning there was another rushed departure – but not before he made a call at his gunsmith's. With his vulnerable right shoulder, he knew that he would be at a grave disadvantage with a lance. He looked through a number of pistols and chose a beautiful Mauser, with a capacity of ten cartridges in a clip. Thus equipped, with plenty of ammunition, and lacking only leave from his regiment, he took the train to Dover, the Channel packet, and the fast train to Marseilles – 'to the East, to the seat of war' again.

The river war of 1898 can be called the last medieval crusade and the first exercise of twentieth-century combined operations, which culminated in the D-Day landing of 1944. Moslem divisions marched forward fearlessly under colourful banners to fight hand to hand with sabre and sword, and cavalry charged to break their ranks, whilst Maxim guns with

103

a rate of fire of 1,000 rounds a minute, howitzers, and naval artillery of the most modern design filled the air with their lethal projectiles.

Khartoum and the greater part of the Sudan had been in the hands of the Dervishes since the city had been besieged and captured and General Gordon killed on 26 January 1885. In Britain, the political need to regain this vast lost territory and avenge the death of 'Chinese' Gordon had never relaxed over more than thirteen years. The immense, powerful, and expensive military expedition led by Kitchener (the 'Sirdar'*) represented Lord Salisbury's, and the nation's, determination to settle the matter once and for all. The expeditionary force for the culminating assault was made up of 8,200 British and 17,600 Egyptian soldiers, 2,500 horses, 3,500 camels, and 1,100 donkeys and mules. Forty-four pieces of artillery were backed up by thirty-six naval guns mounted on river gunboats, and there were no fewer than forty-four Maxim guns in all.

To transport this great force, with all its supplies of food, fodder, tents and ammunition, was a logistical nightmare, involving movement by train, boat and hard marching. Winston, who had arrived in the nick of time in Cairo, described the 1,400 journey as swift, smooth, and punctual. The train took them to Assiout, and stern-wheel steamers to Aswan; thence (leading their horses), they went round the cataract at Philae. More steamers took the army from Shellal to Wadi Halfa, where a newly constructed railway of 400 miles took them safely to their base camp at the point where the waters of the Atbara flow into the Nile. Ahead, 200 miles distant, lay another river meeting, between White Nile and Blue Nile, at Khartoum itself. From now on it was all marching, with hopes high for a great battle and the destruction of Arab power in the Sudan.

*Kitchener's title as Commander in Chief in Egypt.

104

At one point on this long journey, Winston doubted that he would even be present at the forthcoming battle, and that instead his body would be left, bones picked white by vultures, in the desert. It happened like this: he was deputed to supervise the transfer of some stores. The task took longer than he reckoned, and it was dusk when he set off on his pony to catch up his column at its first camp.

With the Nile at his side, it seemed a simple enough navigational task. The stars were clear in the night sky. But suddenly dark clouds obscured this stellar compass, and after some hours Winston realized that he was hopelessly lost. It was futile to continue, exhausting his pony upon whom his life depended; so he lay down, as thirsty and hot and anxious as his pony, whose reins he tied round his waist. There was no sleep for horse or rider that night, but before dawn the clouds cleared, the stars reappeared, and with their guidance, Winston steered back towards what he hoped was the Nile.

Dawn broke, magnificently, revealing desert bushes that progressively became higher until the first palm trees appeared. The pony scented water, increasing its pace regardless of the thick thorns; then, 'immense and mysterious in the growing light, gleamed the Nile'.

Like thirst-stricken millions before him, Winston waded in drinking the waters, while his pony thrust its nose deep, 'and gulped and gulped in pleasure and relief'. Still ravenously hungry, Winston later chanced on a family in a mud hut who found food for him and his horse – and then, at length, he succeeded in catching up his comrades. It had been an alarming and chastening experience.

In 1885, the Dervishes' leader, the adored and feared Mahdi, had died – his great sacred tomb dominated the ruins of Khartoum – and the Khalifa now commanded the seasoned, disciplined, and well-equipped force of some sixty thousand men, including cavalry and a modest force of artillery. But would this formidable army challenge the British-Egyptian force or fade into the immensity of the desert to bide its time? This was a speculation that had preoccupied the entire army

105

since its departure up the Nile. By the end of August, the Anglo-Egyptian army was almost within sight of Khartoum.

With his uncanny knack of contriving to place himself at the heart of events, Winston is one of the first with the news that there are Dervishes between Kitchener's force and their destination. He is dressed for war, light jacket buttoned to the neck, subaltern's patches and pip on his shoulders, campaign ribbons above his breast pocket, Sam Browne belt, Mauser pistol in its holster, and riding breeches, and carrying that universal protection against tropical sun, the pith helmet.

He is only 23 years of age and certainly looks no older, although there is already a hint of receding hair. His square face, with wide-set blue eyes, is formed into an expression of serious self-conviction and ruthlessness: any hint of the sentiment and tenderness we know he possesses is quite expunged. He wishes to look the warrior before battle, and succeeds.

We can see him, then, on the morning of 1 September, part of an advance patrol provided by the 21st Lancers, trotting out on his horse with his troopers through the rough bush towards a broad swell of sand that might provide them with early sight of the enemy, if enemy there is. They are only eighteen miles from Khartoum: if the Khalifa and his army have not fled and are intent on intercepting Kitchener's army, they must surely catch sight of the enemy's advance patrols today.

It is strange how, in circumstances like these, atavistic instincts seem to take over, and it is possible to *sense* the proximity of an enemy. Now, at 10.30 on this hot, sultry morning, the dusty air carrying the sweet scent of the thorn bushes, these excited instincts are supported by rumours of sightings from trooper to trooper. From the top of the swell of sand, Winston and his small party rein in their mounts. Ahead of them, only a short distance away, the squadron outriders, like a long line of pointing dogs, are stationary in their saddles.

Soon, a subaltern rides up, smiling broadly at Winston.

106

'Enemy in sight!' he says proudly, as if responsible for their presence.

'Where?'

'There,' he says, pointing at the quivering horizon. 'Can't you see? Look at that long brown smear. That's them. They haven't bolted.'

Even with his field glasses, Winston cannot distinguish native figures in the brown smear. But confirmation arrives with the undeniable authority of the regimental sergeant-major, back from the farthest outpost line. Moments later, an order arrives for a subaltern to advance to the outpost line and report to the Colonel.

Winston trots forward and in a minute is beside Colonel Martin. 'Good morning,' Winston is greeted. 'The enemy has just begun to advance. They are coming on pretty fast.' The Colonel points to the long brown line, now with immense clouds of dust marking the movement. 'I want you to see the situation for yourself, and then go back as quickly as you can without knocking up your horse, and report personally to the Sirdar. You will find him marching with the infantry.'

So Winston, who has never set eyes on Kitchener, is not only to see this lofty figure, but to report the sighting, position, and advance of the enemy! Conscious of the importance and urgency of his task and the need to save the strength of his horse for the imminent battle, Winston canters and trots away on his message delivery. From the spur of a hill, he is enthralled by the sight of the entire British-Egyptian army advancing in battle array, followed by the rows of artillery and with long strings of supply camels taking up the rear. On the river are countless supply sailing ships towed by stern-wheel steamers, which stain the sky dark with their funnel smoke, while in their midst, like diamond jewels in a crown, advance the large white naval gunboats. What strength, what power!

Now on a level with the advancing armies, Winston experienced some difficulty in identifying the Commander in Chief and his party – a 'cavalcade' as he later called it. But there

107

it was, in the centre of the thousands of marching infantry, identifiable by a banner as bright red as that of any of the Dervish flags, and behind it the Union Jack and the Egyptian flag.

There was no difficulty in recognizing the Sirdar, 'Godlike erect, with native honour clad'. He rode alone before his two standard bearers and his headquarters staff, all riding into battle as if posing for the official war artist – a sight as impressive and romantic as any Winston would ever see in his lifelong association with war.

Winston wheeled round his horse and approached Kitchener from behind, slowing when he was just behind him. He saluted and the General turned and acknowledged his arrival, while Winston noted 'the heavy moustaches, the queer rolling look of the eyes, the sunburnt and almost purple cheeks and jowl' and knew that he was in the presence of a considerable figure, no matter that he had done all that he could to prohibit Winston from serving with him.

'Sir, I have come from the 21st Lancers with a report,' Winston began, and recounted in detail the situation beyond the horizon, and the enemy's movements and rapid advance when he had last seen the Dervishes. There was silence between the two men when Winston had completed his concise and exact report, and the only distinct sound was the crunch of their horses' hooves in the sand, above the drone and rumble of the army marching in unison on all sides.

Kitchener spoke in a deep, precise voice.

'You say the Dervish army is advancing. How long do you think I have got?'

Winston did not hesitate for a moment with his answer. 'You have got at least an hour – probably an hour and a half, sir, even if they come on at their present rate.'

Kitchener tossed his head, in a way that left Winston in doubt as to whether he concurred or was sceptical of the estimate. But this was followed by a reassuring, if slight, bow. Winston saluted and reined in his horse, leaving the General and his headquarters party to slip past him. Other senior and junior staff officers followed in their train, and one of these called out cheerfully to Winston, 'Come along with us and have some lunch.'

The scene was suddenly being transformed, like a stage between acts, the masses of infantry ceasing to march and instead forming themselves into a huge arc with their backs towards the Nile. Others busied themselves cutting down thorn bushes and creating with wonderful speed a long continuous fence – or *zeriba* – as a defence line.

Closer, and more comforting, was the equally rapid creation of a picnic – more a *fête champêtre* – for the officers. Biscuit boxes appeared from nowhere, stacked by orderlies into tables that were in turn covered by white oilcloths and then large dishes of bully beef and every sort of pickle, to be washed down by a generous number of bottles of cold wine. If this was an army that marched on its stomach, then how could it fail to win the imminent battle? And it was Winston's message that had made it all possible!

'I attacked the bully beef and cool drink with concentrated attention,' he later recalled. 'Everyone was in the highest spirits and the best of tempers. It was like a race luncheon before the Derby.'

But there was to be no 'Derby' – no battle – that day. When Winston rode back to the outpost line and his squadron, he saw that the Dervishes had unaccountably halted in their rapid march, and the only gunfire that broke the silence of the desert was a tremendous *feu de joie*, the smoke rising from thousands of wildly wielded rifles, before the great mass of dark men lay down as if to rest for the night.

Winston's squadron was ordered back, a section of the high *zeriba* being removed to allow their entry. Dinner was already being prepared, and the men took away the officers' horses to a place reserved for them under the steep bank of the river. In company with a fellow officer, Winston took a dusk stroll along the Nile, exchanging greetings with some of the officers aboard the gunboats, which were anchored for the night close to shore. How smart these naval officers looked in their white uniforms, by contrast with the dusty Lancers! But it was the cavalrymen who had set eyes upon the enemy, and Winston and his companion were besieged by serious questions as well as mocking comments offering accommodation if the Dervishes drove them into the river. The young lieutenant commanding one of the gunboats, who gave his name as David Beatty, called across the short strip of water, 'How are you off for drinks?' He was holding up a bottle of champagne. 'We've got everything in the world on board here. Can you catch?'

The bottle came sailing through the twilight and splashed into the water. Winston waded in up to his knees and retrieved it gladly from the mud. Waving good night to the senior service, the two subalterns made their way back to their temporary mess in triumph.

The dawn of 2 September 1898 remained sharply in Winston's memory for all his life. In its vivid glory it matched the scene that greeted him as he led a forward patrol out from the *zeriba* and up the same ridge from which he had witnessed the Dervishes' advance on the previous day.

At first there was nothing to see except distant dark patches against a dark background of desert. But like the first glow of a fire, the light seemed to sweep across the limitless waste before them, creating a shimmer that fast intensified and sparkled, while the dark patches began to move restlessly and form into mighty shapes. The sight of 60,000 desert warriors in a mass some five miles long, awakening and checking their glinting weapons in the half-light, was beyond imagination; but this was the reality. The Khalifa's army was assuming disciplined formations, and as the first touch of sunlight skimmed the desert, the Dervishes were seen to be already advancing, and advancing swiftly.

Winston unbuttoned his breast pocket, extracted his field service book, and wrote in it: 'The Dervish army is still in position a mile and a half south-west of Jebel Surgham' – the prominent hill on the observers' right. He marked it for top priority and ordered a corporal to gallop to the Commander in Chief. By the time he was off, in a cloud of dust, the enemy had formed into ordered ranks, as neat as any display on those long benches in the nursery at 2 Connaught Place. The flags and banners, their colours vivid in the early sun, were as glorious as any Winston had devised for those same childhood armies.

The great mass of the Khalifa's force appeared to be heading for the north side of the peak of Surgham, although a division, estimated by Winston as six thousand men, was already clambering up the flank of the hill. The corporal returned from the Sirdar with a message, 'Remain as long as possible, and report how the masses are moving.'

The nearest part of the great mass of the enemy was less than a quarter mile distant, and some of the outriders half this distance. Winston ordered fire to be opened on these scouts, and the return fire sent up the first spurts of dust about them.

Winston's duty being to remain alive in order to continue his reports, he ordered his party back to a higher ridge, which gave them an unprecedented panoramic view of both armies. Kitchener's armies were still behind the *zeriba*, poised to open fire, the infantry formed up two deep. Behind was the artillery, guns trained, awaiting the order. On the river, the gunboats had advanced upstream, and as Winston watched, he saw the first flashes of their guns, followed seconds later by the sound of the detonations. They were firing at the river forts with a new form of explosive – lyddite – and at the Mahdi's sacred tomb, its ninety-foot-high white dome shining like a giant jewel in the sun. Already damaged the previous day, it rapidly disappeared under a giant cloud of dust and falling rubble, for the Dervishes the ultimate desecration and provocation.

It might have been the signal for the defiant roar that at once broke out among the Dervishes, growing in volume so that it filled the hot dawn air and reached the farthest ranks of the British-Egyptian army, while the Dervishes' proud emirs paced before their men beneath their vivid banners. One great division passed by Winston and his party at no more than two hundred yards, but ignoring them as they breasted the southernmost shoulder of

111

Surgham in long lines, ignorant, or fearless, of their imminent fate.

As they came into full silhouette view of the Anglo-Egyptian gunners, two or three batteries and all the gunboats opened an intense shrapnel fire at 2,500 yards range. The effect was instant and devastating. Surgham might have been a giant anthill trodden upon by giant boots, leaving their mark and a mass of crushed, wriggling victims. 'I saw the full blast of Death strike this human wall,' Winston later recalled. 'Down went their standards by dozens and their men by hundreds. Wide gaps and shapeless heaps appeared in their array.'

But there were survivors, and these marched relentlessly on, diverting only to avoid heaps of their dead comrades. Those with rifles fired them wildly. It was as impressive as it was awful.

At that moment a trooper raced up to Winston's party and delivered a message from the squadron's major. Return at once. The infantry are about to open fire.

Winston led his men at a steady trot back to the *zeriba*, which they entered as the most tremendous fusillade was opened on the wretched Dervish survivors from two and a half divisions of highly trained infantry and all the batteries of artillery.

As the first wave faltered, the Khalifa sent in more and more reinforcements, hoping to overcome the defenders by sheer numbers. Instead, they merely added to the carnage, until an estimated twenty thousand corpses lay on the sandy approaches to the *zeriba*. Some of the Dervishes with rifles lay among the dead and opened up an intermittent fire on the thorn hedge, causing some casualties, but soon these withdrew or were ordered back or were killed. The Khalifa was by no means defeated, still possessing twice the numerical strength of Kitchener's army, which had now determined to cut out of this fortress and march into Omdurman and Khartoum before the enemy could fall back on their city.

Winston, at the 21st Lancers' base by the river, was becoming impatient. He felt in need of action, both for the glory and excitement and for the demands of journalism. How could he describe for the *Morning Post*'s readers the ebb and flow of this great conflict in the desert between Moslem and Christian from below this steep river bank of the Nile?

But the cavalry's time was near. Orders arrived for the 21st to leave the protection of the *zeriba*, reconnoitre the road to the city, and head off any Dervish attempt to cut them off and enter the city first. Horses were mounted and weapons checked, Winston leaving behind the standard lance and relying on his Mauser, sword and carbine. The four troops of the four squadrons of the regiment – sixteen in all – with Winston leading the twenty-five Lancers of the second-to-last troop, hastened south out of the *zeriba*. Once clear, the trumpet sounded 'trot'. Not a man, and certainly not Winston, doubted that there would be a charge before the day was over.

It came sooner than they expected, though. Almost at once the Lancers became the target of scattered groups of Dervishes, who fired into the mass of men and horses, causing a few casualties. The density of the enemy increased, until finally the Colonel ordered, 'Right wheel into line,' the preliminary to a charge, and the Lancers now broke into a gallop.

Before him Winston could see a long line of crouching blue figures firing at them, and beyond – boundless desert. From his troop's position in the charge they would just catch the enemy's left. He brought his Mauser to full cock and increased the speed of the gallop, heading between two figures immediately ahead. They both fired as he neared them. Both missed him, but were almost certainly responsible for the death of the trooper immediately behind him. At that same moment, he saw that it was by no means boundless desert beyond. There was in fact a deep ditch, from which there sprang an ambush of hundreds of Dervishes, armed with rifle, sword or lance, a solid phalanx of the enemy.

Winston had been trained in the Hussars to believe that infantrymen – and especially native infantrymen – would

113

break before a charge. He and the rest of the Lancers did not know that these Dervishes not only were utterly fearless but had had many years of experience of cavalry charges in their long wars with the Abyssinians and others. Now, to Winston's left, where the enemy was most dense, he was aware that the Lancers had been brought to a standstill by weight of numbers, and were fighting for their lives from the saddle or on the ground; and the noise of hand-to-hand combat was unlike anything he had heard – atrocious, brutal, and animal-like.

Winston's troop, less the casualties already suffered, succeeded in forcing their way through and up the bank on the other side.

The danger was by no means over, however. A tremendous hand-to-hand struggle was taking place to his left, and screaming Dervishes were scattered everywhere about the desert, waving their arms and spears, some in groups, others singly. One of them threw himself to the ground before Winston's pony as if in obeisance, but actually with raised gleaming sword for the hamstringing cut. Winston leaned from the saddle and put two shots into him at three yards range. At once another figure appeared from nowhere, sword raised. At the last moment, Winston fired at him, the muzzle of the Mauser actually grazing its second victim. On the left a third enemy as suddenly appeared, a horseman this time, a medieval horseman, it seemed, in helmet and chain mail, and brightly coloured tunic. Winston fired again and the horseman swerved away.

He was suddenly alone, and no further assailant appeared. Where was his troop? Had they all been killed? He put his pony into a gallop and found the survivors already faced about for the regulation second charge. As he reined in amongst them, a single unseen Dervish sprang up from the ground, attempting to attack all about him. The troopers stabbed at him with their lances as if he were some snake, wounding him repeatedly, but the zealot came on, heading now for their leader. At a yard range Winston fired his Mauser and the man fell dead.

And now for the second charge. All Winston's troop – less six missing – were prepared for it. He turned to one of his sergeants and asked him, 'Well, did you enjoy that?'

'Well,' replied this old veteran of so many scraps, 'I don't exactly say I enjoyed it, sir; but I think I'll get more used to it next time.'

The men who heard this comment burst out laughing, and the tension was eased, even though the scene was not altogether humorous. The survivors from the Lancers who had been in the heart of the fighting were struggling from the field of battle – horses on three legs, pouring blood, 'men staggering on foot, men bleeding from terrible wounds, fish-hook spears stuck right through them, arms and faces cut to pieces, bowels protruding, men gasping, crying, collapsing, expiring. Our first task was to succour these,' Winston wrote later.

There was, after all, to be no second charge, no further loss of good men and good horses – they had already lost a third of their horses and seventy officers and men killed and wounded. The Colonel ordered carbines to be drawn, and the squadrons moved off to the sound of trumpets, dismounted within three hundred yards of the remaining enemy in the ditch; and cleared them out with rapid fire, gaining final possession of the field. The way to Khartoum was open for Kitchener, who took possession of the ruined city and of Omdurman, while the Khalifa, his surviving warriors and their families, disappeared into the wastes of the desert.

Winston managed to send off a telegram to Jennie the following day to tell her he was safe, and a day later wrote to her at length, telling her that he believed he was about the only officer in the Lancers untouched by enemy action, neither his uniform, saddlery, nor horse. 'I shot five men for certain and two doubtful. The pistol was the best thing in the world.' And the charge 'passed like a dream . . . Nothing touched me. I destroyed those who molested me and so passed out without any disturbance to body or mind.'

But in the end he was not entirely undisturbed. He had lost two good friends, and when he lay down that night he admitted he was worried: 'I speculated on the shoddiness of war. You cannot gild it. The raw comes through . . .'

Worse, far worse, than the shoddiness of war was, he believed, the vulgarity and lack of compassion of the Sirdar in victory. Nothing was done for the thousands of Dervish wounded, left to bake and die slowly in the desert. Winston himself rode over the battlefield with a fellow officer, Lord Tullibardine, giving a sip of water here and there to the dreadfully mutilated natives. They had no chance of survival, and his description of the sight of piles of the dead and wounded struck down by shrapnel bursts and Maxim fire – acres of dead and dying – makes dreadful reading.

Besides the earlier bombardment of the Mahdi's tomb, Kitchener ordered the remains within to be removed and cast without ceremony into the Nile – all the bones save the skull, which he ordered to be brought to him.

There was not often laughter at Kitchener's headquarters, but there was 'some rare ribaldry among Kitchener and his staff as they – and Kitchener himself – played with the skull and discussed what to do with it. Kitchener was reported to have unwisely suggested various uses for it, as his inkwell or drinking cup, or that it should be sent to the Royal College of Surgeons in London. There was even talk of its being used as a football.'

This episode, reported both in the *Morning Post* and in Winston's subsequent book, *The River War*, appeared to confirm what he had earlier written of Kitchener to his mother – 'He may be a general but never a gentleman.'

But it also confirmed in Kitchener's mind the unsuitability of having journalists doubling as officers under his command. The split between the two men was to have the direst consequences.

Cavalry are notoriously expensive to maintain in the field, and after the battle there was no place for the 21st Lancers in Kitchener's army. In a letter from Wadi Halfa, Winston wrote thankfully to his mother that he would be home very shortly.

9

The Prisoner of War

Among the growing number of prominent people who were becoming aware of Winston's exceptional qualities and potential was the Prince of Wales. By 1898, Albert Edward – 'Bertie' – had been heir to the throne since 1841 and, excluded from all important matters of state by his ill-advised mother, left to create a role of his own. Blessed with a sweet-natured but sometimes exasperating wife, the Prince had indulged himself in a wide range of pleasures, but had also shown in practical terms his patriotism and dutifulness to the monarchy, the nation and the empire. Above all, he was interested in people, in those who would be the established leaders of the future when – surely it must come one day? – he became King Edward VII.

Latterly the Prince had once more been a close supporter and friend to Randolph Churchill and been grieved by his downfall and tragic decline in health. Jennie had captivated him from their first meeting with her beauty, charm and vivacity. As soon as Winston gave some evidence that he might be a chip off the old block, the Prince began to take an interest in his career, which was sustained until his death, as Edward VII, in May 1910.

Like all those in touch with the centre of events, the Prince had learned of General Kitchener's reluctance to have Winston on his expedition and his disapproval of Winston's using the Army for self-advertising newspaper reporting. He also knew how Winston had circumvented the General's wishes and fought at Omdurman, reporting the campaign in the *Morning Post* and publicly expressing disgust at the action of Kitchener in defiling the Mahdi's tomb and encouraging the killing of prisoners.

The Prince had already told Winston that he thought he

should stick to the Army for a while longer before venturing into politics. When Winston returned from Egypt, the Prince clearly considered that the young subaltern was in need of a further word of fatherly advice and warning. A few days later Winston received a letter from the Prince, then in Scotland, telling him somewhat sternly that he agreed with Kitchener 'that an officer serving in a campaign should not write letters for the newspapers or express strong opinions of how the operations are carried out'. The Prince also gently warned Winston that if he intended to write a book about the expedition he should 'write it as a history & not with military criticism which so young an officer as yourself, however clever you may be, should avoid as a matter of discipline'. Finally, and as a gesture of friendship, the Prince of Wales hoped that Winston would come and see him to tell him about the campaign and about his plans. Winston dined at Marlborough House on 22 October, after having dined two nights earlier with the international banker Ernest Cassel and fifteen other men, 'none of whom were wholly undistinguished for conversational powers'.

Having delivered his homily by letters, it is certain that the Prince was charming, encouraging, and enquiring about Winston's future; it is equally certain that both to the Prince and to Cassel and his friends Winston made clear his intention of leaving the Army and taking up a political career – in support of which he had several immediate speaking engagements: at Dover, Rotherhithe and Southsea. All three were highly successful, and Winston was tremendously encouraged by their wide and favourable reporting, especially in the newspapers edited by Cassel's dinner guests.

Winston knew that he would have to return to India briefly before resigning his commission, in order to tidy up his affairs and, if possible, take part in his last army polo tournament. This he planned to do at the end of November, and in the meantime he had plenty to do at home, cultivating politicians, writing his new book, to be called *The River War*, and paying attention to Miss Pamela Plowden.

Winston's courtship of Pamela Plowden was as intermittent as his appearances in London, but the letters between them were as steady as his love for this beautiful and talented young woman. In one letter before he returns to India, he writes of the constancy of his love. '[It] is deep and strong. Nothing will ever change it.'

Miss Plowden was intrigued by Winston and pleased at his attention. She followed his progress, in print and in the Army, with deep attention. She admired his courage but was concerned at what she saw as his impetuousness and his disregard for popularity. 'I will admit,' he wrote to her, 'that you are quite right and that I make unnecessary enemies. The question is – Is it worth it? I confess I think so in many cases. It's an extravagance that is all . . .'

A young woman does not much care for her suitor to be spoken about roughly in public, and there is no doubt that Winston was regarded by many people as bumptious, conceited, 'pushy' and – said some – unscrupulous in his methods of furthering his ends.

In Pall Mall clubs, especially the service clubs, questions were being asked about his irregular behaviour in not only taking extended leave seemingly whenever and wherever he wished, but then using it to write for the newspapers and, moreover, writing critically of the service and officers in the service whose uniform he wore.

'What is the position of Lieut. Spencer Churchill in Her Majesty's Army?' demanded an anonymous officer in the columns of the *Army & Navy Gazette*. 'According to the Army List he is a junior subaltern in the 4th Hussars. According to announcements in the press he is anything but that, for we find it openly stated that this young officer . . . is acting as a special correspondent here, there and everywhere.'

The attack was long and powerful, and widely read. Miss Plowden would certainly have heard of it if she had not read it, and it was by no means the only public criticism of her friend.

On a seemingly more trivial level, while Winston was a Marlborough to the core, he had no title. His connections were unimpeachable, but his fortune was non-existent. The only roof over his head was his mother's, even if he could make himself comfortable at Blenheim Palace whenever he wished.

Intriguing, yes. Wonderful company, charming, courageous, ambitious (goodness, yes!), good-looking – all these qualities, but, Pamela believed, incapable of affection. Winston stoutly denied this. Their relationship continued, not always easily, broken by Winston's arrivals and departures. He knew it must be precarious, with so many rich and titled suitors waiting in the wings – with their easy life-style, comforts and great estates. Then, how long would she have to wait for Winston to be able to marry . . .?

On the evening of 2 December 1898, Winston bade goodbye to his brother and mother at 35a Great Cumberland Place and went off reluctantly to India. He did not in the least relish the journey, and always abominated rough sea crossings. 'I hate the sea and have a constitutional aversion to travel.'

Back at Bangalore, he was welcomed as a regimental hero, and he wore his new Sudan medal with appropriate pride. But there was to be no serious soldiering. Things were relatively quiet in the great subcontinent, even at the north-west frontier. Polo and his new book were to be his chief preoccupations for the next three months before he was due to return to England, a civilian again, seeking a seat in Parliament.

Back home again, Winston was gazetted out of the Army on 3 May 1899, and was approached about standing for a seat in Parliament on the same day. This was on the morning after dining with two future prime ministers, Sir Arthur Balfour and Herbert Asquith, and others of mighty political influence. Deputations from other constituency associations were also hovering, like moths about a candle. But the most likely and promising constituency was one of the two vacant seats at Oldham, in Lancashire.

By the end of the third week in June, when Winston returned from a highly successful visit to the town, the candidature was his. With a prominent trade union official as running mate in this prosperous working-class cotton town, he threw himself into the campaign with great vigour. He called himself a Tory democrat, harking back to the days and the political philosophy of his father. 'I regard the improvement of the condition of the British people as the main end of modern government.'

But the two Tories were up against powerful Liberal competition, one of them being a scion of a mill-owning family, the other a future cabinet minister, Walter Runciman. It was a great fight, this first parliamentary election for Winston, and he enjoyed it almost as if he were on the north-west frontier amidst the whine of bullets. Sunny Marlborough gave him a hand, but Jennie – who might have been more valuable to him – was not able to come.

To the end of the fight and the polling, Winston would make no prediction of the outcome, and when the result was declared late on the evening of 6 July, it was easy to see why. Both the Liberals had attracted more voters, but the difference was measured in a few hundred.

'I returned to London,' Winston wrote later, 'with those feelings of deflation which a bottle of champagne or even soda-water represents when it has been half emptied and left uncorked for the night.' No one from the Conservative Party came to see him at Great Cumberland Place.

Throughout the campaign Winston had remained in touch with Pamela Plowden, telling her about his meetings and speeches and wearing her charm for luck. He would have loved her to be at his side, but knew that it would not be appropriate. Now that it was all over, she consoled him in his disappointment. He was certain that she loved him and would remain constant. When she left the country early in September, he told his mother how lonely he was without her.

> The more I know of her [he wrote], the more she
> astonishes me. No-one would understand her as I do.
> Yet I am always seeing new sides to her character.
> Some are good & some weak – yet I like them all –

121

*indeed this is becoming quite an old story and I fear
I shall provoke a smile.*

The other great antidote to the sadness over Oldham was the
progress and imminent publication of *The River War*. This
appeared in two handsome volumes in early November. It
was subtitled *An Account of the Reconquest of the Soudan*
and traced the origins of the campaign back to the early
days of the century. The dedication, by permission, to Lord
Salisbury, lent this new book a special cachet, and the account
marked a great improvement in clarity, style and construction over *Malakand. The River War* revealed that Winston,
at 24, was already a fine historian, although 1,000 pages on
a campaign that might soon be looked upon as a minor one
was certainly excessive.

Winston arranged for copies to be sent to the dedicatee, to
his most important political friends, and to friendly soldiers
like Sir Evelyn Wood and Lord Wolseley – though not to
Kitchener, who was treated unsympathetically. Publication
was fixed for 7 November. But by that date Winston was
thousands of miles away and at the outset of another chapter
in the adventure of war.

On Friday 2 June 1899, Winston had breakfast with Cecil
Rhodes at the Burlington Hotel in London to discuss the
growing crisis in South Africa. Rhodes had been Prime
Minister of the Cape Colony at the time of the infamous
Jameson raid, when a small force of determined Britons
set out in support of an insurrection in Johannesburg by
excessively taxed non-Boers against the Boer government
of the Transvaal.

The quarrel between white Boer and white Briton was
deep-seated, with origins going back to the late eighteenth
century. The Dutch had established a staging post at the Cape
in 1652, which had served the Dutch East India Company's
ships, bound for the East, for many generations. The native
population was negligible, and as the post enlarged into a
colony the native bushmen made their way into the interior,

while the black Hottentots were absorbed, intermarried, and became known as Cape coloureds. A great influx of persecuted Huguenots from France enlarged the white population, and the Cape became an important pastoral colony.

This Dutch possession was ceded to Britain under the Treaty of Amiens in 1814, and reforms granting equality to all, regardless of colour, were instituted. This equality was contrary to the beliefs and religion of the Boers, who in any case spoke their own Afrikaans language. As a result, between 1834 and 1838 some ten thousand men, women, and children packed their wagons and moved north in what became known as The Great Trek.

These Boer refugees established their own republics in the rich farming land north of the Vaal River and to the east, conquering native tribes and putting down their roots in this new territory. But they did not enjoy peace for long. The discovery of diamonds, and then gold, led to the arrival of thousands, mainly British, seeking their fortune. These 'uitlanders', as they were called, were heavily taxed and denied the vote. At length, they appealed for help against this injustice from the British government.

Negotiations between Britain and the Boer President, Paul Kruger, for political recognition of the uitlanders broke down on 31 May 1899, a few days before Winston's meeting with Cecil Rhodes, and the crisis was the chief topic of conversation between the two men over breakfast. Rhodes was certain that war was now imminent, and by the end of their talk Winston agreed.

Even through the Oldham by-election and its aftermath, Winston followed events in South Africa, his keen nose scenting imminent battle. At Blenheim during the weeks of high summer, with the failure of Oldham behind him, Winston was engaged in the completion of the book on the Sudan campaign. So he was still describing the conclusion of one war while his ear was cocked for the renewed sound of faraway drums.

By September, with the breakdown of further talks between the Boers and Britain, the talk of war had extended from Whitehall and the armed forces to the streets and pubs of the nation. Britain had not fought a war against a white enemy for almost half a century, and this was no native uprising, the foe not Dervishes or Afridis or mutinous Indians. These people were of mainly Dutch stock who shared a faraway land, diligent farmers and Christians. But they employed black slaves and treated the British within their midst little better. Moreover, they were heavily armed with the most modern weapons, eagerly supplied by the Dutch and Germans, who were entirely sympathetic to their cause.

On 18 September, while in London, Winston was telegraphed by the *Daily Mail* to ask if he would go to South Africa as that newspaper's war correspondent. Rapidly, in turn, Winston telegraphed his friend Oliver Borthwick of the *Morning Post*, telling him of this offer and making a proposal that he should act instead for Borthwick's newspaper. Winston's suggested terms were £1,000, plus his expenses and the copyright of anything he wrote, for four months, and £200 per month thereafter. No foreign correspondent had ever been paid a comparable fee, but the management of the *Morning Post* were prepared to accept, and they telegraphed Winston to that effect without delay. The days of £5 a column were evidently long past!

Winston completed his preparations rapidly, inviting his 'man', Thomas Walden, to accompany him, and took the precaution of applying for a commission in the Royal Bucks Hussars so that he would enjoy the privileges of an officer. He also carried with him letters of introduction to rich and successful people in the Cape from the Colonial Secretary, Joseph Chamberlain, and from Alfred Beit, who had made a mountainous fortune in South African gold and diamonds.

The Boers issued an ultimatum on 9 October demanding the withdrawal of all British troops from the frontier regions within two days. The first shots were exchanged on 12 October, and Winston sailed two days later. There were many on board, including General Sir Redvers Buller, who was to take command of all army forces and believed nothing of importance would happen until he arrived in South Africa.

Others believed optimistically that it would be all over before they docked.

There was plenty of time to study the new Commander in Chief on the voyage to the Cape in the *Dunottar Castle*, a vessel that reflected some of the characteristics of its most important passenger: slow, ponderous, steady, unexciting. Of Buller, Winston was to write:

> He looked stolid. He said little and what he said was obscure. He was not the kind of man who could explain things, and he never tried to do so. He usually grunted, or nodded, or shook his head, in serious discussions; and shop of all kinds was sedulously excluded from his ordinary conversation.

On the long, calm, sun-drenched voyage, nothing was permitted to disturb the daily routine, and it seems that no thought was given to accelerating by one knot the speed of the vessel with its vital contingent of troops. By the time the *Dunottar Castle* slipped into Table Bay in darkness, they had all been without any hard news since leaving Madeira, except a brief message from a homeward-bound ship. Now what they learned was extremely disturbing.

The Boers had invaded Natal and attacked the British forces at Dundee, inflicting severe casualties. The British had counterattacked, they learned, driving the invaders from Talana Hill, but losing their general in doing so. The Boer commanders were showing great skill and determination. 'We have greatly underestimated the military strength and spirit of the Boers,' Winston wrote home to his mother, and '. . . a fierce and bloody struggle is before us in which at least ten or twelve thousand lives will be sacrificed and from which the Boers are absolutely certain that they will emerge victorious.'

These ominous words were written on a train travelling east from Cape Town, for Winston and two other correspondents were attempting to reach Durban before the

Dunottar Castle and General Buller, something not difficult to achieve. The three men completed their journey from East London to Durban in an extremely uncomfortable coasting vessel, and at once headed for the eye of the war, the town of Ladysmith.

Ladysmith was – and remains today – a small town on high, undulating ground north of the Tugela River and some hundred and twenty five miles north of Durban. Here General Sir George White, with 12,000 troops, was attempting to hold off a strong force of invading Boer troops. Instead of yielding ground, as the Government intended, until General Buller could bring up reinforcements, White did the worst possible thing and sent out an offensive party to meet the enemy. It was easily surrounded, and 1,200 men were made prisoner. Then he drew in his forces and allowed himself to be besieged in Ladysmith.

All this Winston learned during the few hours he remained in Durban before taking the train north, 'to the seat of war'. He was also told that an old friend from days in India, Ian Hamilton, now a general, had joined General White. As Winston was to discover, the whole world seemed to be foregathering in Natal. Flat on his back in a hospital in Durban, he found another old friend, Reggie Barnes, now suffering from a bullet wound in his thigh. 'The Boer is a deuced clever fighter,' he told Winston. 'Very skilful with horse and rifle.' Barnes was determined to get fit to rejoin the fighting before it was all over.

Accompanied by Walden and J. B. Atkins of the *Manchester Guardian*, Winston took the train to Pietermaritzburg and there commissioned another train to take them as far as the Boers would permit. In surrounding and besieging Ladysmith, the Boer troops had cut the railway line at Colenso, where an iron bridge carried it over the Tugela River. Having penetrated almost as far as this, their train was forced to retire to the little village of Estcourt.

Here, surrounded by the dreary, hostile veldt and with only a few Dublin Fusiliers and Durban Light Infantry to defend the township, Winston came across still other familiar faces, notably Aylmer Haldane and Leo Amery, from Harrow days, who was acting as war correspondent for *The Times*. With Atkins, the three set up some tents in the railway yard to await events. Like most journalists, they had provided themselves with the comforts of life, including a first-rate cook, provisions and good wine. By day they awaited news; in the evening they entertained the local officers.

There was mounted reconnaissance from Estcourt daily, for there were enough Boers in the vicinity to wipe out the defenders very swiftly if they so wished. On the fifth evening, the commander of the troops, Colonel Charles Long, gave instructions to Haldane to take an armoured train that had been prepared for the fighting to reconnoitre the enemy. It was a very bad idea, a man on horseback being far less vulnerable than a train, which was no faster.

Haldane was to arm his train with an ancient nine-pounder naval gun, manned by sailors, and take with him two companies of soldiers as well as some civilian platelayers in case they had trouble with the line. Haldane thought Winston would like to join him, though, he recognized full well the dangers of the enterprise. Winston agreed, though with serious misgivings. The train, consisting of a gun truck, three armoured trucks, a breakdown gang truck, and tender and locomotive in the centre, steamed out of Estcourt before dawn on 15 November.

Desperately vulnerable, with smoke and sparks pouring from the smoke-stack, the train trundled across the veldt for fourteen miles, stopping from time to time to report its position by telegraph. At Chieveley station they learned that the place had been briefly occupied by Boers during the night. It was now just after seven in the morning. There was still little daylight. Haldane reported his position and was ordered to fall back on the little township of Frere and warned that a party of fifty Boers had been reported in the vicinity.

Before the train, now in reverse order, with the locomotive behind three wagons and its tender, could gather momentum, Winston made out, through the driving rain, a number of figures moving on a hill beside the line between them and their destination. They appeared, on closer inspection, to be wheeling out guns, and when they were very close,

> instantly bright flashes of light opened and shut ten or twelve times. A huge white ball of smoke sprang into being and tore out into a cone, only as it seemed a few feet above my head. It was shrapnel! – the first I had ever seen in war, and very nearly the last! The steel sides of the train tanged with a patter of bullets.

The driver accelerated the train, and with the advantage of a down gradient and the protection of a cutting, saved them from further damage. They were going at a great pace when they emerged from cover, and Winston was now worried about the state of the line ahead. He might well be! Almost at once there was a stunning shock, which threw down everyone and brought the train to a grinding halt.

The leading carriages had been derailed and were on their side, blocking the track, and on the slopes of the hill above many figures were seen running and then falling amongst the rocks and shrubs. The cracking sound of rifle fire and the sucking sound of passing bullets and the rattle of others striking the armour plate of the wagons filled the air.

Winston is in the rearmost truck, with Haldane and the naval crew for the gun, which dominates the centre of the truck. When he pulls himself to his feet after the crash, he raises his field glasses to try to make out what has happened. The leading wagon, with the breakdown gang, has turned over on to its back and, from the cries he can hear, has severely injured some of the men. The next two wagons are both derailed and blocking the line, one of them on its side.

'I'll go forward and see if I can get those trucks off the line,' Winston says, ducking down behind the armour plate.

Haldane says he will try to keep the enemy's fire down with the naval gun and rifle fire from the Dublin Fusiliers in the two forward coaches. With the volume of Boer fire undiminished, Winston leaps down beside the line. He runs fast under cover of the two intact trucks, urging the men to keep up a steady fire on the enemy. Just as he is passing the locomotive, there is another great crash and flash of light overhead – another shrapnel burst – causing the driver and fireman to leap out of the cab. Winston sees that there is blood streaming down the driver's face. He is holding a rag to it and cursing loudly.

'I'm a bloody civilian,' he complains. 'What do they think I'm paid for? Killed by a bloody bombshell – not bloody me, thanks – I'm off!'

Winston restrains the man and persuades him to let him examine his wound. It is only a flesh wound on the scalp. 'It's all right – more blood than anything else,' he reassures him. 'And believe me, no man is hit twice on the same day. And anyway, if you stick to your duty after being wounded, you're bound to get a medal – you might never have another chance.'

The driver and the fireman reluctantly return to their cab to await orders, and Winston runs on, ordering the men in the derailed trucks to give assistance to the injured breakdown gang. A quick glance at the derailment and he returns to the armoured gun wagon, which is keeping up steady fire on the Boer positions.

'The line is blocked,' Winston shouts at Haldane through a loophole in the armour. 'But I think I can clear it with the engine.'

'Right – we'll try to keep the enemy engaged.'

Winston returns to the locomotive, stripping himself of his Mauser and binoculars before getting down to work. For more than an hour, in pouring rain and under continuous rifle and shell fire, using the combined force of the engine and the muscle power of the unwounded men, they struggle to clear the line. With one final butt that threatens to throw the engine and tender off the line, they manage to squeeze it past, only for the debris and damaged wagon to fall back and block the line again, separating the locomotive from the intact wagon.

The driver and the fireman are doing wonders. Winston

129

climbs on the footplate beside them. Like all of them, he is soaking wet, both from the rain and his own perspiration.

'We'll have to content ourselves with the wounded – the rest will have to retreat on foot,' he tells the driver, and then turns to a major who has been leading the men in their work and supervising the care of the wounded. 'Will you get the wounded on to the tender, sir? It's all we can do.'

It is a wretched task. Some of the men are badly shot about, and they have to be packed like sardines. At last there is no more room. 'Ease forward now,' Winston orders. A bullet ricochets from the steel side of the tender. It is amazing that he has not been hit during the seventy-five minutes when he has been completely exposed. 'I'll come with you as far as the bridge.'

The driver eases forward the regulator, and the engine gathers speed slowly, into a cutting which gives some cover, and onward towards the steel bridge over the Blue Krantz River. 'Stop here to let me off,' Winston tells the driver. 'I must go back to the Captain.' He climbs over the wounded men stacked on the footplate, wishing them well.

He hurries into the cutting, expecting to meet the vanguard of the retiring troops. Instead, out of the rain there appear two figures – only two, and unfamiliar in silhouette: flapping cloaks, slouch hats, and – final confirmation of the worst – with levelled rifles, at a range of one hundred yards.

Winston turns and begins to run between the lines, dodging from side to side, the sucking sound of near misses close to his head. He has to get out of this damnable cutting, this trap. He leaps to the steep side, glancing back to see one of the Boers now kneeling for steadier aim, pulls himself up the bank, hurls himself under a wire fence, drops into a slight depression that affords some temporary cover, lies there panting, considering what to do next. The deep gorge of the river is only a few hundred yards distant. That would afford him all the cover he needs. He rises to his feet to make a dash for it . . .

A cry comes from the other side of the cutting. A horse-man is drawing up sharply. He is waving a rifle and clearly

130

ordering his surrender in a guttural tongue. Winston reaches for the comfort of his Mauser, determined to shoot it out. It is not there; of course, it is with the engine driver! Only further flight can save him from capture. He glances again towards the river gorge, yet knowing that the worst shot could not fail to hit him – and these Boers, he has heard, shoot like the devil.

'So I held up my hands and surrendered myself a prisoner of war,' Winston later wrote. General Louis Botha himself, leader of the commandos, claimed later that he personally had made the capture, and Winston eagerly seized on this and believed it all his life. But both men were boasting. It was Field Cornet Oosthuizen, under Botha's command, who effected this prize capture.

10

Fighting Enemies, Making Enemies

Winston loved to make much of his regret that he ever returned from the engine and tender to rejoin Haldane and the soldiers and their officers. 'I cursed, not only my luck, but my own decision.' We can pass this by, with an indulgent smile. Winston was, as always, hell-bent on getting the best of all worlds. He had shown his courage, succeeding under the ferocious fire of the Boers in extricating the locomotive *and* the wounded. Then, once satisfied that all had witnessed this triumph against hopeless odds, returned loyally to his comrades. It certainly would *not* have done to have been the only unwounded man to have escaped on the train!

Winston had determined that, once back with Haldane and his now surrounded officers and men, he would fight successfully with them, beating off the Boers and retiring on foot, or he would be captured along with the rest. If captured, he either would contrive to be repatriated as a non-combatant or, better still, would escape and return in a blaze of glory.

In the event, Haldane and the other officers were forced to surrender before any fighting took place, as a result of the showing of the white flag by a pair of troopers, which prohibited the rest from opening fire. Several hundred mounted Boers were soon on the spot, calling on them to lay down their arms, holding umbrellas against the rain with one hand and waving their rifles threateningly with the other.

When Winston was ordered to join the other prisoners, he says, he sat drenched and miserable on the ground among them, 'meditating blankly upon the sour rewards of virtue'. Another account takes a different view. Aylmer Haldane wrote of the misery of everyone except Winston. As they marched off in the pouring rain, Winston appeared quite cheered by the thought that although he had temporarily lost his post as war correspondent, the events of the past two hours had helped 'considerably in opening the door for him to enter the House of Commons'. After all, those who had escaped on the engine and tender would take back with them the story of his gallantry and of how, but for Winston Churchill, they too would be in the hands of the enemy. They 'would not fail,' claimed Winston, 'to make the most of what they had seen when they got back to Estcourt'.

Everyone was soaked through when they at length arrived at a small railway station. Here the prisoners were locked up in a baggage room, while Churchill, singled out for special security, was locked alone in the ticket office. For three days and nights, partly in heavily guarded trains and partly marching, the prisoners made their way towards Pretoria. Skirting Ladysmith, they heard the crack and echoing explosions of the besieging guns. Would it ever stop raining? It seemed not. Never for a moment on this miserable journey did they have a chance to dry their clothes.

They arrived in the capital on 18 November. The men were marched off to their cage at the racetrack, while the officers were taken to a secure school, heavily guarded, where they met the British officers who had been captured in earlier engagements.

In England, Jennie was staying at Escrick Park, in Yorkshire, her host and hostess being Lord and Lady Wenlock, with their pretty little daughters, Ursula and Margaret. As the party was about to dine on 16 November, a telegram addressed to Jennie was brought in. 'Unpleasant news capture hundred men from armoured train Ladysmith.' It was signed by Moreton Frewen, who presumably would not have sent it unless it involved Winston. And after dinner there came further news from the *Morning Post*. 'I regret to inform you that Mr Winston Churchill has been captured by the Boers: He fought gallantly after an armoured train in which he was travelling had been trapped.'

Jennie's belief in the survival capacity of her elder son was, it seemed, confirmed once more. When her friends

133

congratulated her she responded with a confidential smile that served to indicate that *she* had never had any doubts. 'Winston is indestructible': she never spoke these words, but by her demeanour and expression they were implicit.

If no-one appeared able to match Winston's talents for escaping bullets, it was also true that no-one, in or out of uniform, possessed his capacity for attracting publicity, favourable or unfavourable. Within two days of the train action, the *Natal Witness* was reporting on Winston's bravery, as described by one of those wounded who escaped in the locomotive, Captain James Wylie. These accounts were taken up by some of the London newspapers, and there was even talk of Winston's being awarded the Victoria Cross.

The war correspondents for the *Daily Mail, Manchester Guardian* and *Daily Telegraph* and Leo Amery of *The Times* all let it be known that Winston had behaved with outstanding gallantry. But by this time he had many enemies at home besides Kitchener in South Africa. Envious voices, political voices, pacifist voices, were soon heard, eager to discredit Randolph Churchill's bumptious son, who equally sought favouritism and spurious glory.

These accounts of Winston's gallantry in the British South African press also appeared to give the lie to Winston's claim to his captors that he had acted in a strictly civilian capacity during the engagement. He hotly claimed that he had been unarmed, which was true latterly, and that he took no part in the fighting, only arranging for the wounded to be taken away.

A few days after Winston's capture, the Boer General Petrus Joubert wrote to Francis Reitz, Secretary of State of the Transvaal:

> *I understand that the son of Lord Churchill maintains that he is only a newspaper reporter and therefore wants the privilege of being released. From [enemy] newspapers it appears entirely otherwise and it is for this reason that I urge you that he must be guarded and watched as dangerous to our war. . . .*

Jennie knew nothing of all this, only that Winston was a prisoner of war, unwounded, that he expected soon to be released, and, through Pamela Plowden, that he was writing confidently and affectionately to her. But Jennie was not idle either. Prominent people in England and New England had conceived the idea of sending an Anglo-American hospital ship out to Cape Town. Forty thousand pounds had been raised, and as an American-born celebrity of great influence, Jennie was asked to sail out and manage it.

In the Pretoria school where Winston and his friends were incarcerated, the lessons were on one subject only: the art of escape. Talk was of little else. Every possibility was explored. The most daring plan considered was to capture all the guards and their weapons, release the troops at the racetrack, and create an insurrection in the centre of Pretoria, even taking over the city.

More realistically, Winston and Haldane and an Afrikaans-speaking sergeant, Brockie, who had convinced his captors that he was an officer, found that there was a possible escape route through a latrine window to an unilluminated piece of ground, over a wall, and into a garden. The area was covered by an armed guard, but on occasion he moved to exchange words with a companion. Once outside, they would head for the Portuguese colony of East Africa, some three hundred miles distant, walking by night and hiding by day. That was the plan.

An attempt scheduled for 11 December was aborted: the guard remained as immobile as a statue. The next evening Winston took advantage of a moment when the guard was lighting his pipe to drop down, only a yard or two from him, and leap up and over the fence. Haldane was less lucky. He was spotted by the sentry when he was about to drop down beside Winston, who was waiting for him. There was a sharp challenge. Aylmer Haldane had no alternative but to return in humiliation.

Winston waited anxiously for his fellow conspirators to

make a further attempt, aware that he had little chance without the support of the Afrikaans-speaking Sergeant Brockie. Finally, without compass or map, and only some chocolate in his pocket, Winston made off. He rated his chances at about nil, 'but I felt that I would have a run for my money and see how far I could get'.

There had been a plan devised by the three conspirators, to attempt to take the train from Pretoria to Delagoa Bay in neutral East Africa, but it was rejected as impractical. Winston now judged it to be his only possible route. Disregarding any consideration of concealment, he walked down the middle of the brightly lit road into the centre of Pretoria, humming a tune to indicate the insouciance he did not feel, and found the railway station and then the line likely to lead east towards his destination.

This line he followed for some distance on foot, avoiding guarded bridges, until he reached the first station. Assuming that the next train would stop here, he positioned himself some two hundred yards beyond it, hoping to intercept it before it regained much speed.

'Suddenly I heard the whistle and the approaching rattle,' Winston recalled. 'Then the great yellow headlights of the engine flashed into view. The train waited five minutes at the station, and started again with much noise and steaming. I crouched by the track . . .'

Two hundred yards was too far, Winston soon discovered. The train was going too fast for comfort as it thundered up beside him. He grasped for, and missed, a grip, risking dislocation of his vulnerable shoulder. He grasped again – and finally seized a handhold and was swung off his feet; he felt his way to the couplings to the next truck and climbed up. The cargo was empty coal sacks. It could be worse. They might be filthy, but they made warm, comfortable bedclothes, he discovered, as he burrowed into them.

Winston awoke long before dawn. He had no idea how far he had travelled or where he was. But instinct told him to quit the train before daylight. He did so, bruising and shaking himself as he fell into a ditch. At dawn he found he was in a rich farming valley, with kaffirs working under the supervision of mounted Boer farmers. Lying in long grass, he holed up here all day, counting the trains in anticipation of another free ride when darkness fell.

But the trains to freedom seemed to die with the day. For several hours Winston awaited his chance. The moon-flooded veldt remained silent, and for the first time he felt an outcast in this world – as indeed he was.

There were few occasions in his life when Winston was at a loss to know how best to act. He reported later that he set off towards some distant fires from a kaffir kraal before retracing his steps on realizing the futility of seeking help there, then changed his mind and set out again. An hour or two later, the lights had become formed into the glare of furnaces, which outlined in the darkness the wheel of a mine lift.

There seemed nothing to lose now in appealing for help. He had escaped on an empty stomach, and the chocolate he had eaten had served only to give him a raging thirst. Separated from the other dwellings, he saw a single-storey house. No light shone from it, until Winston knocked loudly at the front door. A head appeared from a window. A voice called out, '*Wer ist da?*' It was not especially friendly.

Winston replied that he had had an accident and needed help. A brief pause. The head disappeared. The front door opened, revealing a young man holding a lantern. Behind him was a tall older man with a pale face and a moustache, and a revolver. This time the older man spoke in English. 'What do you want?'

Without thought or preparation, Winston found his imaginative processes hard at work devising some cock-and-bull story about being a burgher, one among a number of a train on the way to join their commando, skylarking – which led to his falling out . . .

The man lit another lamp, placed it on a table before him, beside the revolver, and bade him come in. He wanted to know more about this accident. Winston accepted that the time had come for the truth, with a prayer that the reception would not be too hostile.

'I am Winston Churchill,' he told the man with the lamp and the revolver. 'War correspondent of the *Morning Post*. I escaped from Pretoria. I am making my way to the frontier. I have plenty of money. Will you help me?'

Without a word, the tall man, whose name was John Howard, walked towards the door and bolted it. Not promising, thought Winston, not at all promising. Then Howard approached him, hand extended. 'Thank God you have come here!' he exclaimed. 'It is the only house for twenty miles where you would not have been handed over. But we are all British here, and we'll see you through.'

A number of mines in the Transvaal were managed by Britons, and for practical reasons these men had been encouraged to give their parole and remain in spite of the war.

'You must be famished,' said John Howard.

Winston agreed and busied himself with the whisky and soda and cold leg of mutton offered to him by his generous host.

Winston's escape adventure was by no means over. But with John Howard and four more British subjects on Howard's staff eager to do anything to see Winston through to freedom, the chief danger and anxiety were now over. For two days and nights, Winston was secreted in abandoned stables deep in the recesses of the mine, where he was well supplied with whisky and food. The Boer hue and cry was intense, for it was suspected that he would head for the railway line to Delagoa Bay. A price was put on his head – 'dead or alive' – and his description and photograph were published widely.

But all the while his new allies were formulating plans for the last leg of his journey. Then on 19 December at 11 p.m. Winston was taken from the mine and hidden in a tiny cell in the centre of a wagonload of wool bales that were due for export by a local English storekeeper.

The long freight train jerked into motion on time, and Winston settled back in reasonable comfort – certainly in

138

greater comfort than on the first leg of his journey. He had bottles of cold tea, two roast chickens, sliced meat, bread, a melon, and, for emergencies, a loaded revolver. Daylight was breaking as the train gathered speed.

At Kaap Muiden station on the Transvaal side of the frontier, there were many Boer soldiers hanging about the platforms, and the train was thoroughly searched, but Winston remained undetected. He had memorized the names of all the stations, and when at length he squinted out from his hiding place and saw the name Ressano Garcia, he knew he was safe and in Portuguese territory. He at once burst out from his wool cell, shouting with relief and in celebration of his freedom. No one appeared to take any notice, even when he fired shots into the air with his revolver.

At the British consulate in Laurenço Marques, the welcome union flag fluttering outside, Winston was given all that he needed – 'a hot bath, clean clothes, an excellent dinner, means of telegraphing . . .' The newspapers were full of black news about the progress of the war, defeat following defeat at the hands of the audacious and well-equipped Boers. The next day every English South African newspaper would carry happier news. Dominating the headlines was the story of Winston's escape from his prison camp. Not one of the newspapers, then or later, made any reference to the information from behind the enemy lines that his release as a non-combatant was probably imminent anyway. For publicity purposes, he had got away in the nick of time, and Churchill luck had followed him thereafter.

Oliver Borthwick at the *Morning Post* office was the first to inform Jennie that Winston had escaped, adding sardonically that 'knowing his practical turn of mind I have no doubt that he knows what he is about and will turn up with an extra chapter of his book finished in a few days' time at some English encampment. So do not be uneasy,' he added. Jennie was not in the least uneasy, but very happy for his sake that he was free from his captors.

After the first news from Reuters of Winston's freedom,

which made all the lead headlines, the newspapers remained silent for the days when he was crossing the veldt on foot or by train, or holing up under the care of John Howard. Then on 22 December Joseph Chamberlain's office was telegraphed from Cape Town that Winston had arrived at Delagoa Bay the previous day. Within minutes the news was transmitted to Jennie and passed on to Jack and all the Marlboroughs, and to Pamela Plowden. (Pamela's telegraphed response to Jennie was brief and to the point: 'Thank God – Pamela.')

Fearful that Boer sympathizers in the Portuguese colony might attempt to recapture Winston and smuggle him out of the country, a party of armed Britons in Laurenço Marques escorted him noisily to the quayside and to a steamer that was sailing for Durban that night. In less than forty-eight hours, Winston was stepping ashore on to British soil. He expected to be warmly welcomed, but could hardly have anticipated the reception he received on 23 December. Several bands were playing on the dockside. Flags and bunting fluttered in the breeze. Dense crowds cheered and sang. Local dignitaries, civil and military, jostled to shake his hand before the crowds surged forward to hoist him high on shoulders.

Winston remained aloft, smiling and waving, until deposited on the town hall steps. 'I was received as if I had won a great victory,' he wrote. A speech was demanded, and ready as always with a few well-chosen words, Winston made one. Renewed cheering!

He wished to leave at once for the front and still managed to catch a train for Pietermaritzburg that evening. Early the following morning, Christmas Eve, he was on his way again, heading for Buller's headquarters at Chieveley. Here he was confident of a warm reception from the one general who seemed to understand and like him.

'Winston Churchill turned up here yesterday escaped from Pretoria,' Buller wrote to a friend. 'He really is a fine fellow and I must say I admire him greatly. I wish he was leading

140

irregular troops instead of writing for a rotten paper. We are very short of good men . . .'

Winston echoed this last cry in a despatch to the *Morning Post* when he appealed for more irregular corps. 'Are the gentlemen of England all fox-hunting?' he demanded provocatively. 'Why not an English Light Horse? For the sake of our manhood, our devoted colonists, and our dead soldiers, we must persevere with the war.'

This reflection on 'the gentlemen of England' was not well received by everyone back home; no more was the news of his escape, in spite of the local accolades. There was real vitriol in the attack of the *Phoenix*, published when he was still in prison camp: '. . . hoping that Mr Churchill will not be shot. At the same time the Boer General cannot be blamed should he order his execution.' The *Daily Nation* and *Blackwoods Magazine* both accused him of doing the dishonourable thing and breaking his parole.

The accounts of Winston's courage at the attack on the train had backfired, so that the influential *Westminster Gazette* (among others) confessed that 'we hardly understand the application which Mr Churchill is reported to have made to General Joubert asking to be released on the ground that he was a newspaper correspondent and had taken "no part in the fighting".'

Winston defended himself against these 'ungenerous' attacks by claiming that he was not responsible for the stories brought back by the wounded and the railwaymen. Indeed not, but he had earnestly hoped that his bravery in the face of enemy fire would be observed and reported, and for this reason there was something in the *Westminster Gazette*'s claim that 'he cannot have the best of both worlds'.

But the additional accusation that he had broken a parole that had never been given offended Winston deeply, if only because it could be damaging to his political aspirations. He therefore later instituted proceedings against *Blackwoods:* the case was not defended and he was given a full apology. A sadder business altogether was Aylmer Haldane's public claim that he had been left in the lurch by Winston, who, having made use of Haldane's plan, then compromised the chances for his fellow conspirators to escape. In fact, Haldane later made an even more daring escape than had Winston, by tunnelling out of the school, but without the publicity, and the two men never recovered what had been a warm and mutually admiring relationship.

General Redvers Buller, recipient of the Victoria Cross, corpulent, elderly, slow on his feet and in the working of his mind, heavy with honours and drifting white beard, was totally unfitted, at the age of sixty, to command an army corps against the mobile and well-equipped Boers besieging Lady-smith. All his military life he had been a 'number two', mostly to the brilliant Field Marshal Garnet Wolseley. 'I have never credited myself with much ability on the inventive side,' he once confessed; although, given orders, he had once been quite efficient at carrying them out. But he paid concerned attention to his men, who loved him, and he had managed to attract a similar affection from the public.

Winston found Buller in poor spirits. He had been rebuffed at Colenso, with severe casualties, and was almost reconciled to the idea that General White in Ladysmith had better sur-render before his army (and the inhabitants) were starved out. By contrast, Winston, with his aura of gallantry and with the episode of the train and his dramatic escape from the Boers to his name, represented the shining star of success in Buller's brief campaign.

'What is it you would like?' the General asked Winston after greeting him. (Buller had a lisp, like Winston, but caused by a horse in India having once kicked out all his front teeth.)

'I would like to see more fighting, sir. But I must also continue to send back despatches to my newspaper.' With the outcry at home after Winston had both fought and reported critically the battle of Omdurman, the Army Council had ruled that this dual activity must cease. Buller ignored this objection, and later Winston was able to tell Jennie glee-fully, 'Sir Redvers Buller has given me a lieutenancy in the

SA [South African] Light Horse, without requiring me to abandon my status of correspondent so that evidently I am in very high favour.'

Winston at once pressed home his advantage. He had learned that Jack had temporarily quit his job in the City and sailed for Cape Town.

'Would it be possible, sir,' Winston asked Buller, 'for you to arrange for a lieutenancy in the same regiment for my brother who is on his way out here as a volunteer?'

This, too, was dealt with at once through the good offices of Julian Byng, the regiment's colonel.

So the toy soldiers of Connaught Place were to become reality, with the two brothers in command of their own men. But, thank goodness, in this real war they were on the same side; for over the following days in January 1900, the most bloody and futile fighting of the war so far occurred on the approaches to Ladysmith before it was relieved.

The 1,400-foot hill, Spion Kop, was gained and lost amidst the most dreadful hand-to-hand fighting and uniquely inept leadership. For the first time, the troops of both sides found their courage tested too far, and there were shameful surrenders among the British troops and refusals to fight among the burghers.

'The scenes on Spion Kop were among the strangest and most terrible I have ever witnessed,' Winston wrote home to Pamela. He added:

I had five very dangerous days – continually under shell & rifle fire and once the feather in my hat was cut through by a bullet. But – in the end I came serenely through . . . now we have the bloodiest fight of the war immediately before us – a supreme effort to break through the Boer lines. We are but grains of sand in the waves of the sea. What can we do but what we think is for the widest form of best?

Pamela, who had sent him a hamper of food from London for her brother-in-law, Major Edgar Lafone, trapped in

Ladysmith, wanted him to come home, but Winston would have none of that. 'I should forfeit my self-respect forever if I tried to shield myself like that behind an easily obtained reputation for courage . . . My place is here: here I stay – perhaps forever.'*

In these last days before Ladysmith was relieved, Winston experienced at their fullest the joys of his dual career as soldier and reporter. Those who served with him, including his brother, saw him trotting about the field of battle on his little pony as if inviolable by bullets and shelfire, pausing to take notes one minute, the next rallying the men in the face of enemy attack. They were over the Tugela River now, up the hillsides, over the Boer trenches, and on the road to Ladysmith.

Jack's introduction to the field of battle was a severe one, too. A Boer detachment suddenly opened 'a very hot fire'. Everyone in Winston's company lay down to seek cover – everyone except Winston. But it was Jack who was hit by a bullet, Winston who was unharmed. The wound was not a serious one, but required hospitalization. By chance, Jack became one of his mother's first patients on board her ship, and for a few days the family of three were reunited 8,000 miles from home.

After further heavy fighting, on 28 February Major Hubert Gough of the 16th Lancers succeeded in breaking through and riding into Ladysmith at the head of his squadron. The reception by the garrison and the women and children was tearful and rapturous. They had been trapped, short of everything, for 118 days, shelled by day and night. 'The

---

*The hint at his possible death in battle keeps reappearing in his letters written during his Indian and African campaigns. This practice must be excused as youthful melodramatics, for the tendency quite disappears in maturity when he is under fire on the Western Front in 1915 and 1916.

144

contrast between the robust troopers of a dozen battles and the pale, emaciated defenders of Ladysmith was great,' wrote one eyewitness. Churchill was only a few minutes behind, riding hard with the Earl of Dundonald, who had got wind that the way was open.

> *Never shall I forget that ride* [wrote Winston in his despatch for the *Morning Post*]. *The evening was deliciously cool. My horse was strong and fresh . . . Ladysmith was within our reach at last . . . The excitement of the moment was increased by the exhilaration of our gallop. Onward wildly, recklessly, up and down hill, over the boulders, through the scrub . . . We turned the shoulder of a hill, and there before us lay the tin houses and dark trees we had come so far to see and save.*

After making himself known to General Sir George White, Winston was invited to dine with him that first evening, also sitting next to his old friend General Ian Hamilton, and beyond him sat General Sir Archibald Hunter. Dundonald and Gough were there, too, leading Winston to exclaim that never before had he sat in such brave company 'nor stood so close to a great event'.

On the following days, while the celebrations continued and the shellfire damage to the town was repaired, Winston dealt with a number of personal matters and telegraphed a long report to the *Morning Post*. Pamela's brother-in-law, Major Lafone, he discovered was in hospital and too ill to appreciate the food hamper. So Winston ate it himself. He also drank a bottle of priceless 1825 brandy Jennie sent him from her hospital ship, and asked her for one or two more bottles, preferring it, he wrote, to the 1865 brandy he had brought out himself. He also appreciated the reviews of his novel, *Savrola*, which had at last been published both in New York and London. They were by no means wholly flattering. Some reviewers compared the novel unfavourably with his more recent military accounts, but excused it as a piece of juvenilia, better on action than on people. But the book attracted a lot of attention and sold well.

Winston was much more concerned by the hostile response to his campaign against treating the defeated enemy harshly. The war was by no means over with the relief of Ladysmith, but with every yard of advance into liberated country in Natal, more rebellious Boers once again came under British jurisdiction. 'I urge generous counsels upon the people of Natal,' he appealed.

For the citizens of Ladysmith who had been bombarded for nearly four months and suffered near starvation as well as danger, it did seem a trifle early to be talking of forgiveness. The spirit of Winston's campaign was just and farsighted, but for the present he took a hammering locally and from the Conservative press in Britain, even from his own newspapers, the *Natal Witness* and the *Morning Post*.

By contrast, editors in Britain and the United States were now clamouring for his services as the hero of Ladysmith. His agent in London had extravagant offers for magazine articles and even an extended lecture tour. This was sweet music to Winston's ears, but he did not waste time listening beyond the first bars of the overture. 'Make sure that I get not less than £2,000 as an advance on royalties for my new book,' he commanded Jennie, now back thankfully in London. She had no difficulty in doing so, although she herself was deeply preoccupied with courtship. George Cornwallis-West, widely regarded as the handsomest man in England, had fallen in love with her and proposed marriage. The trouble was that he was almost exactly the same age as Winston and therefore twenty years younger than Jennie. The Cornwallis-West family strongly disapproved of the match; Winston, when consulted by Jennie, considered that she should put her own happiness before everything.

The strength of the presence of Winston in Ladysmith can be judged by several recorded incidents in the liberated town. For example, one day soon after the relief, Sir George White was standing talking to a number of officers. 'A young officer came up to the group: with a good deal of sang-froid and not much ceremony,' reported this eyewitness, 'he made his way through the group, and in a very audible voice at once engaged [White] in a short conversation, then went off. An older officer said to Sir George, "Who on earth is that?" He answered, "That's Randolph Churchill's son Winston: I don't like the fellow, but he'll be Prime Minister of England one day."'

Then there was Percy Scott. Winston had met, and admired, this naval captain who had ingeniously contrived to remove four of the heavy guns from his cruiser off Durban, fitted them on makeshift carriages and transported them up for the defence of Ladysmith. After Scott had left, he expressed his regret in a letter to Winston that he had not shaken hands with him before his departure. 'I am very proud to have met you,' wrote the Captain, 'because without any luck you have made a wonderful career.' He added, 'I feel certain that I shall someday shake hands with you as Prime Minister of England, you possess two qualifications, genius and plod.'

This naval captain's admiration for Winston was not shared by the hierarchy at the new headquarters of the new Commander in Chief, Field Marshal Lord Roberts, who had replaced Buller. Roberts had read Winston's despatches in the *Morning Post* and had taken strong exception to his criticism of an army chaplain's sermon to some five thousand troops during a lull in the heavy fighting about Spion Kop. What an opportunity for an uplifting sermon! Winston had exclaimed. Instead of which 'a chaplain with a raucous voice discoursed on the details of "The siege and surrender of Jericho".' In addition, Roberts's chief of staff was none other than Kitchener, still hot with resentment at Winston's criticism of his conduct at Omdurman.

It was hardly surprising, therefore, that when it became clear that a new offensive against the Boers was imminent and Winston applied to be attached as a bona fide war correspondent, he received no reply. It soon became clear that he was facing the same all-too-familiar trouble with Kitchener. Eventually, two of Winston's supporters at General Headquarters, Generals Nicholson and Hamilton, prevailed upon Roberts to allow him to come. The Field Marshal reluctantly agreed, and like some grumpy schoolboy had the most terse possible letter sent to Winston, making clear that it was only 'for your father's sake'.

The pathetic childishness of Field Marshal Lord Roberts and the venom of Kitchener were further revealed in two incidents. Winston and an officer companion were ambushed by a group of Boers and subjected to intense fire at short range. Winston's companion mounted his horse and escaped, but Winston's horse panicked and bolted before Winston could swing into the saddle. On foot, and dodging amongst the bullets, Winston faced recapture or death. Then a scout suddenly appeared and, at terrible risk, helped Winston up behind him and rode off through the bullets, one of which struck the horse.

Winston described this incident vividly in the *Morning Post*, suggesting that the scout deserved the Victoria Cross. But nothing – not even a minor medal – was forthcoming. Winston and everyone else knew that if anyone but he had been saved, the man would have been properly rewarded.*

Shortly after this escape, Winston, with his cousin Sunny Marlborough, was attached to Ian Hamilton's column. These two men, both descendants of the great John Churchill, were the first into Pretoria, after covering 400 miles in forty-five days, and were also the first to liberate the prisoners of war, many of whom Winston had left behind less than six months earlier. But even then more fighting lay ahead, and in the last action in which Winston took part, he acted with stunning bravery and resourcefulness.

---

*When, seven years later, Winston was in a position to authorize a decoration, the scout was awarded the Distinguished Conduct Medal.

Many years later, as a venerable retired and knighted general, Ian Hamilton wrote:

> My column . . . lay opposite and below a grassy mound, bare of rocks or trees . . . The crestline was held by the Boer left. The key to the battlefield lay on the summit but nobody knew it until Winston . . . somehow managed to give me the slip and climb this mountain, most of it being dead ground to the Boers lining the crestline as they had to keep their heads down owing to our heavy gunfire. He climbed this mountain as our scouts were trained to climb on the Indian frontier and ensconced himself in a niche not much more than a pistol shot directly below the Boer commandos – no mean feat of arms in broad daylight and one showing a fine trust in the accuracy of our guns. Had even half a dozen of the burghers run twenty yards over the brow they could have knocked him off his perch with a volley of stones. Thus it was that from his lofty perch Winston had the nerve to signal me, if I remember right, with his handkerchief on a stick, that if I could only manage to gallop up at the head of my mounted Infantry we ought to be able to rush this summit . . .
>
> The capture of Diamond Hill meant the winning of the battle . . . also it meant that it was the turning point of the war.

In the judgement of Winston's commanding general, this was 'an exhibition of conspicuous gallantry' (the phrase often used in recommendations for the Victoria Cross). But Roberts and Kitchener refused any kind of recognition, which made Hamilton 'furious with impotent rage'.

After the victory of Diamond Hill, the Boer War was to decline into guerrilla activity and sporadic brushes with the enemy – a sad and not always glorious business that led to many deaths and much suffering. For Winston, there

149

were more pressing demands on his time and attention at home – to set out towards what his devoted friend and ally, Ian Hamilton, called his 'high perch on the political Diamond Hill'.

Winston, reunited with Thomas Walden, embarked in the same ship, the *Dunottar Castle*, that he had sailed out in to the war only nine months earlier.* Those thirty-six weeks had transformed his public reputation, matured his judgement, and smoothed some of the sharp edges in his personality as they had developed his character. More than ever he was convinced that he was a phenomenon and that there was nothing on earth beyond his powers to achieve. He landed at Southampton on 20 July 1900, having occupied himself on the voyage in completing yet another book, *Ian Hamilton's March*.

---

*Walden, Winston's personal servant, joined the Imperial Light Horse in Winston's absence, after recovering Winston's Mauser and binoculars from the locomotive.

11

Winston 'Crosses the Floor'

Winston came home to a hero's welcome. His arrival date was in all the newspapers, so many letters of congratulation and invitations were waiting for him at Jennie's house. But Jennie herself was, for once, not at the port to welcome him home. Her marriage to George Cornwallis-West was imminent, and Winston had arrived only just in time for it. At 45, Jennie was as lovely as ever, and they made a striking couple standing in the sun outside St Paul's Church in Knightsbridge, all the Churchill family providing a show of solidarity, but the Cornwallis-Wests conspicuous by their absence. (Nor did the Prince of Wales approve: he wished his name to be excluded from the wedding-present list.)

This marriage led to a certain loss of intimacy in Winston's relations with his mother, who had always been first in his thoughts, always his first confidante. She was, he believed, the one person who comprehensively understood him, his processes of thought and his ambitions. Any severance as a result of this unpredicted marriage was beyond considera-tion, and Winston made clear to his young contemporary stepfather that he had nothing but friendly feelings for him. For his part, Cornwallis-West overwhelmed Winston with gratitude for his generous attitude – so unlike that of his own family.

A second new set of circumstances that Winston had to face was a good deal more welcome and exciting. Just as he had been forewarned of Jennie's imminent wedding while still in South Africa, so his political contacts in England had let him know that a general election was not far off. No other constituency than Oldham was in his mind, and within five days of his return he had been chosen to fight this seat, which last time he had missed by such a narrow margin. And what a welcome he had there, as both a war hero and a Conservative candidate! No fewer than ten thousand people, he claimed, turned out to greet him. Bands played, flags were flown, and he was cheered wherever he went.

These were hectic days for Winston, complicated by the fact – which he had not expected – that his mother was to let 35a Cumberland Place, depriving him of his only roof. Sunny came to his rescue and gave him the lease of a flat at 105 Mount Street. It was for only two years, but it would see him through until he could find, and afford, a place of his own.

Then, as always, money: he could no longer accept an allowance from Jennie, whose debts were paid off by her new husband but who had very little left after that. Winston had accumulated some £4,000 of capital, mainly from his books and articles, although Ernest Cassel had made him £500 profit in the decisive way that money magicians had. He hoped to make quite a bit more from his books and had planned a lecture tour in England, Canada and the United States after the election. Sunny, with further generosity, was contributing towards his election expenses; and, on condition that he lived frugally (never an easy task for him), Winston thought he could get through 'the lean years' ahead.

But everything depended on his winning his seat at Oldham, and he prepared for the imminent campaign with all the guile and dedication he could summon, encouraged by the knowledge that he was nationally famous enough to be reported wherever he spoke. Within less than two weeks of his return he had persuaded George Wyndham, Undersecretary of State for War and an old disciple of his father's, to take him round the House of Commons. At the traditional tea on the terrace, many MPs came up to wish him well and to congratulate him on his heroism, his escape and his despatches in the *Morning Post*, which had made a strong impression. Among them was Joseph Chamberlain, the Secretary of State for Colonies, who was to be a powerful supporter. Two more of his closest friends and advisers were John Morley and Lord Rosebery. Rosebery, another close friend of Randolph's, had been briefly Liberal Prime Minister in 1894. He fired up Winston, who was often asked to stay at Rosebery's country place near Epsom and felt at his best in the older man's company. John Morley held a special charm for Winston. He delighted in Morley's conversational powers and always enjoyed his company even though he was a Liberal, and one of those who deplored the Boer War.

But Winston's most valuable supporter at the general election, which was now fixed for 1 October, was Chamberlain. He was regarded by those who supported the Boer War (and they were the majority) as the one politician responsible for turning early setbacks into the more recent military successes. When he came to Oldham to speak for Winston, both men received a tremendous welcome from their followers, and an equally vocal hostile reception. Both men being fighters, they relished this discord, and everyone agreed that it was a great evening.

During the last days of September the campaign was intense. At that time elections were spread over several weeks. The first results could influence later voting – it was even possible for a defeated candidate to stand for another seat – and Oldham was one of the first. Then, not only was the Boer War issue a subject of fierce debate and even violence, but there was also the cotton issue. Oldham lived by cotton, which was being challenged by cheap American imports. It was not easy going for Winston. Hero he certainly was, but there was a deep radical strain in this Lancashire industrial town, and it was hard to break voting tradition.

Winston begged Balfour to come and speak, but he was too busy with his own constituency. He twice begged his mother to come, citing the committee's belief in the importance of the feminine presence and the fact that his fellow Conservative candidate's wife was being helpful. But Jennie was having a lovely time in Scotland and failed her son.

The last few days before polling were noisy, acrimonious and taxing: three or four speeches a day on makeshift platforms against the noise of heckling, shaking hands, knocking on doors, keeping his wits and his sense of humour about him. Winston had little confidence that he would succeed this time. If he had relied on *The Times* the morning after polling, he would have had to reconcile himself to defeat: 'Mr Winston Churchill, who evidently possesses many of his father's gifts, and will, no doubt, make some day a figure in Parliament, was defeated . . .' By two votes apparently. This was hastily corrected, and the next morning *The Times* made amends with an adulatory leading article. The other newspapers took full advantage of this howler. 'Mr Winston Churchill, who is well accustomed to the fortunes of war,' commented the *Illustrated London News*, 'could have borne defeat with a very good grace.'

He no doubt would have done, but he had polled 222 votes more than the Liberal Walter Runciman, though sixteen fewer than Runciman's fellow Liberal, splitting this double constituency between the two parties and giving the Conservatives an encouraging early gain. Congratulations poured in from all points of the compass, from South Africa, from his leader Lord Salisbury, from Lord Curzon at Viceregal Lodge in India, Lord Rosebery, Joseph Chamberlain and countless others in the Army and in politics, and from citizens whom Winston had never met.

Winston scarcely had time to answer all these goodwill messages, for he had now to put his weight to the Conservative wheel in other constituencies.

> *I have suddenly become one of the two or three most popular speakers in this election* [he wrote to his old American friend Bourke Cockran], *and am now engaged on a fighting tour, of the kind you know – great audiences (five or six thousand people) twice & even three times a day, bands, crowds and enthusiasm of all kinds.*

Although earlier in the year Winston and Pamela Plowden had exchanged the most loving and thoughtful letters, it seems that this delightful and intelligent young woman had found since his return cause for doubts about Winston's suitability as a husband for herself. She knew that he was not likely to be well off, and she had a taste for comfort. She saw little prospect of comfort, its accompanying serenity, or the social season's joys as the wife of a penurious politician with boundless ambition. Perhaps, too, his abrasiveness, which she had criticized in the past, was an increasing worry to her. Winston's sensitive antennae rapidly recorded Pamela's lessening enthusiasm for their relationship, and noted too her wish to get married. He certainly was not ready for marriage now or for some time, so – as with all things – he made a rational if agonizing decision to suggest an end to their intimacy.

The parting was 'sweet sorrow'. Pamela married a less turbulent but highly talented politician, Lord Lytton, and became a countess and the mother of two sons and two daughters, and did not want for what Winston called 'her sweet and abundant milk of life'. But their friendship remained warm until her death. Writing to her of friendship five years after her marriage, Winston said, 'Alas with my busy selfish life – I fear . . . I fail too often in the little offices which keep friendship sweet and warm. But you always understand me and pardon, because you know me and care about me . . .'

Winston shrewdly and sensibly cashed in on his military and political successes for his English lecture tour, committing himself to no fewer than twenty-nine appearances up and down the land, talking under the title 'The War as I Saw It'. The houses were packed, the lectures enormously successful, gathering notices in the national as well as the local newspapers. To his delight, in one month he netted £3,782 15s 5d.

By contrast, the North American tour, which spanned the turn of the century, was unrewarding considering the effort that went into it, partly because he was in the hands of a grasping 'vulgar Yankee impresario'. In addition, both the Irish and the Dutch immigrants in several cities organized hostile campaigns. But from Toronto on the first day of the new century, Winston was able to write to Jennie that he had earned £10,000 without any capital behind him in less than two years – and not one person in a million could have done that, he boasted.

Three weeks later, he read of the death of Queen Victoria, 'a great and solemn event'. On the day of the old Queen's funeral, Winston sailed from New York to face this new century and his new life as a politician.

At the beginning of 1901 the British nation was still pre-occupied with the Boer War. Expectations that it would soon be over had been dashed. Defeat of the Boers on the field of battle by overwhelmingly more powerful forces and British control of the vital railways had merely driven the determined enemy underground. Small, highly mobile Boer forces on their swift, sturdy ponies were difficult to pin down and destroy. The recapture of Pretoria, which had led to the so-called 'Khaki' general election – and to Winston's election to Parliament – had not led, as expected, to the surrender of the Boer forces.

The first session of the new Parliament, opened by Edward VII, reflected the concern of the people about the conduct of the war, the efficiency and size of the Army and its leadership. No subject could be more suitable for the new member for Oldham, who had witnessed the fighting at first hand, knew as well as anyone the problems of the soldiers, from private to general, and was an intimate acquaintance of Sir Alfred Milner, the High Commissioner for South Africa. Moreover, every member knew that he was an up-to-the-minute authority on South African affairs and that his brother Jack was still fighting there.

Everyone who knew Winston predicted that he would soon take advantage of his reputation. He was already being alluded to as 'a young man in a hurry'. But few members expected him to make his maiden speech as early as the fourth day of this session. As soon as word got around that he would be called on the evening of 18 February, the House began to fill with members from both sides, and in the ladies' gallery could be seen his mother and four of his aunts, like exalted first-nighters bent on seeing their idol on stage.

Of all these strangers and members, perhaps only Jennie knew how weak Winston was at spontaneous debate and at modifying his speech to meet new circumstances. He had spent unnumbered hours on the preparation of this speech, writing it out in several drafts, and then – because it was against the etiquette of the House to read a long speech – learned it by heart. The sheets of paper would be in his hand, and he could pretend to refer to them as notes and, according to parliamentary custom, flourish them to emphasize a point. But he would be talking entirely from memory.

Winston was to follow that fiery Welsh radical David Lloyd George, who was due to move an amendment, and Winston prepared the opening of his speech accordingly. Unfortunately, Lloyd George decided not to move the amendment and opened his speech by announcing this, throwing Winston into a near panic. Mercifully, he was sitting next to a member, Thomas Bowles, of great experience who had sensed Winston's unease and diagnosed its cause. 'Why not open with something like this?' he whispered. '"Instead of making his violent speech without moving his moderate amendment he had better have moved his moderate amendment without making his violent speech."'

Winston had not welcomed anything so much since the sight of water after that night in the desert. When Lloyd George at length sat down, Winston was thankfully able to include this apt observation in his opening comment, and thus got off to a good start. From then on everything went his way. The essence of what he had to say in reference to the Boer War also applied throughout his political life, and almost half a century later was expressed as the 'Moral of the Work' in the six volumes of his history of the Second World War: 'In war: resolution. In defeat: defiance. In victory: magnanimity. In peace: goodwill.' The war, he maintained, must be pursued vigorously while keeping alive the hope that the Boer leaders would accept the generous terms of surrender offered to them, though they might 'stand or fall by their

157

old cry, "death or independence".' Anticipating the cheers of Irish members on hearing this cry in the House, Winston had prepared a crushing rejoinder:

> I do not see anything to rejoice at in that prospect . . . [the Irish members] would be well advised cordially to co-operate with His Majesty's Government in bringing the war to a speedy conclusion, because they must know that no Irish question or agitation can possibly take any hold on the imagination of the people of Great Britain so long as all our thoughts are with the soldiers who are fighting in South Africa.

This brought forth loud cheers from the government benches. And Winston ended on just the right note: 'I cannot sit down without saying how grateful I am for the kindness and patience with which the House has heard me, and which have been extended to me, I well know, not on my own account, but because of a certain splendid memory which many honourable members still preserve.'

Members on both sides of the House were quick to offer Winston their congratulations, many of them referring to 'his illustrious father'. Joseph Chamberlain commented, 'Friends and intimates of his father will have welcomed [the speech] with utmost satisfaction in the hope that we may see the father repeated in the son.'

Winston got a good press, too, the next day, and better still, an extensive coverage. Even *The Times*, as reserved about Winston as about his father, described the speech as 'highly successful'. From India he later received a letter of congratulation from George Curzon, not on this maiden speech but for having won and retained the ear of the House. He added, sagaciously and perhaps warningly, 'There is no more difficult position than being on the benches behind a government. It is so hard to strike the mean between independence and loyalty.'

The Viceroy of India feared that Winston, whose admiration and love for the memory of his father was so deep, might emulate him too closely, to the point when he, too, would be politically cornered and cast into the wilderness. Over the coming months, many of Winston's friends and many who had never met him were anxious that they were seeing the first signs of this suicidal policy. Was it not an omen, many people argued, that within days of his marvellous maiden speech he was attacking the Secretary of State for War on his extravagant and inappropriate proposals for 'reforming' and enlarging the Army? It might have been his father speaking.

Winston's self-confidence and belief in his cause were not in the least dented by attacks inside and outside the Commons. But after only a few months, he was finding himself more and more out of sympathy with the Conservative cause and the leaders of the party. The gap between him and the Conservative Party was visibly widening as he became increasingly in sympathy with the less radical Liberals. On holiday in Scotland that summer he was rarely seen with Conservatives, while he stayed five days with his Liberal uncle, Lord Tweedmouth. 'I have seen a lot of the Liberal Imperialists lately,' he told his old friend and confidant the Liberal Lord Rosebery. 'Haldane* and Edward Grey . . . and Asquith very kindly took the chair for me at [a lecture].'

Already in his first year as a member of parliament Winston found himself associating with other dissidents in the Conservative Party who came to be known as the Hooligans, by reason of their outrageous behaviour, or as Hughligans, after one of their number. They were all extremely high-born and intelligent: Arthur Stanley and Lord Percy, sons of the Earl of Derby; Lord Hugh Cecil, a son of the Prime Minister, Lord Salisbury; Ian Malcolm, who had recently married the illegitimate daughter of Lillie

---

*Richard Burdon Haldane, Liberal MP, and no relation to Winston's Army friend Aylmer Haldane.

Langtry by Prince Louis of Battenberg; and Winston. They made a formidable and entertaining fivesome and gave the political commentators a lot of fun.

This number could hardly form a centrist party, but their more serious aim was to bend the Conservative Party towards greater liberalism – a hopeless cause at that time. But in Parliament they fought for greater efficiency in expenditure on the Army in order to divert funds to welfare services for the poor. Winston had been deeply moved and influenced by Seebohm Rowntree's book *Poverty: A Study of Town Life*. Rowntree, a Quaker, was a philanthropist and member of the 'chocolate family' based in York. In spite of the enlightened conduct of this business, there was dreadful poverty in that city and many others in the land. This book, Winston told an audience, 'had fairly made my hair stand on end'.

Like Rowntree, Winston was concerned that in a nation that was rich in resources, cultivated, successful in the sciences and arts, and the creator of the greatest empire the world had known, so many of its people lived in poverty and close to starvation. The easing of the suffering of the poor and dispossessed had now become the substance of his political policy and was to remain so until the creation of the welfare society, for which he was more responsible than any other statesman, with the possible exception of David Lloyd George, the brilliant Welshman with whom Winston was to be so strongly associated. At the same time, he did not consider it in the least contradictory that, like his mother, he continued to live as if there were no tomorrow. Through thin times and flush times, Winston never gave what he considered vulgar thought to the cost of his food and drink, or anything else for that matter. At the same time he gave the most earnest consideration to the value of his services in writing and lecturing. He already loved gadgetry and 'the latest thing'. He was one of the earliest purchasers of a motor car, in July 1901, and from that time his taste for the best in cars equalled his taste for the best in champagne – tastes that later settled on the products of Rolls-Royce and Pol Roger. His cousin, Sunny Marlborough, felt obliged to point out that

Winston's four hunters were costing him some £400 a year and as he hunted for only twenty days a year, this worked out at £20 a day. 'Needlessly extravagant,' he pointed out censoriously. Winston's capital, like Jennie's before him, was being steadily reduced and required supporting from time to time with lectures, for which he was paid astonishingly high fees.

Winston's other great causes were army reform and tariffs. As a manufacturing nation Britain had for some time been seriously handicapped by the introduction of tariffs among its worldwide customers. As these began to bite, the nation resorted to exporting more machinery, coal, iron, and other metals, which enabled previous consumers of her manu-factured exports to be self-supporting or even to become exporters themselves. For example, British shipbuilders were heavily engaged in building the Japanese Navy and at the same time teaching this newly industrialized people how to build battleships of their own – which they did extremely successfully by about 1904.

Protectionism was in the air. Winston believed passionately in interdependency against independency. It made for peace, he argued, and was an important reason for European peace over the past twenty-five years. He believed that the path of protection was a slippery one, which would be countered by more tariffs abroad and would inevitably, among other disasters, lead to the destruction of Britain's dominance in banking, brokering and warehousing. A home market monopoly led to higher prices and lower quality and, as in the United States, to the development of great trusts. Tariffs were bad for the people, Winston contended, bad for the economy, bad for the empire, and bad for the nation.

The cause of free trade became Winston's first preoccu-pation during the summer of 1903, and he was the chief power behind the creation of a Conservative splinter group that later came to be called the Free Food League. This grew to include sixty Conservatives in the House, a far greater number than the rival Tariff Reform League.

Under the flaccid leadership of A. J. Balfour, the Conservatives were tearing themselves apart, and no-one was more responsible for this than Winston. Many of the loyal old guard were distraught at this state of affairs, and the Liberals were overjoyed. But Sunny Marlborough, a staunch loyalist, regretted that he and his cousin were at the parting of the political ways:

> I am also grieved to feel that you are going to take such an aggressive part in opposition to the Fiscal proposals of AJB [Balfour] and JC [Joseph Chamberlain]. It will mean your ultimate severance from the Tory party and your identification with Rosebery and his followers. I deplore the hasty position you have taken up.

In the midst of all this controversy inside the family and inside the Conservative Party, an old veteran and supporter of Winston, Lord Salisbury, fell fatally ill. It was almost like the death knell for the party he had served and led for so long when he died on 22 August.

Winston was by no means totally taken up with creating discord in and out of Parliament during 1902 and 1903. Throughout his political life he almost always had some item of injustice upon which he sharpened his teeth. Aside from his enduring fight against poverty, two smaller and more specific occasions came to his notice.

At Winston's old college, Sandhurst, there had occurred a series of mysterious fires. Accusations of incendiarism were made against three cadets, but no evidence of guilt was discovered. When the fires continued, an order was issued by the War Office and read out to an assembly. Unless the guilty were found within forty-eight hours, all cadets of C Company (where the fires had broken out) would be rusticated and all their servants (mostly old soldiers) discharged unless they could prove they were elsewhere when the fires broke out.

Among them were the three cadets who had already been found not guilty.

Winston took up this cause in a long letter to *The Times*, pointing out not only the injustice of this decision but also the suffering and financial difficulties it would cause. He argued that the War Office and the commandant were themselves guilty of violating three principles of equity: suspicion is no evidence, accused must be allowed to defend themselves, and they are innocent until proved guilty.

The matter became a great *cause célèbre*. The correspondence in *The Times* became acrimonious. The Hooligans persuaded some peers to raise the matter in the House of Lords. At length the Army Commander in Chief himself, and hero of the Boer War, Lord Roberts, intervened and promised that each case would be considered independently, the result of which was that all but two cadets and all the servants were reinstated and the commandant replaced.

Some weeks earlier, Winston and the Hooligans also combined in an attack on the military authorities in South Africa. A newspaper editor who had served a sentence in prison for a published libel on Kitchener had expressed a wish to come to Britain on personal grounds. The military authorities had refused him permission because there were quite enough people already in Britain 'who disseminated anti-British propaganda'.

Winston was no doubt quietly approving of anyone who libelled Lord Kitchener, but more seriously, this high-handed action against a citizen who had served his term was a gross abuse of power. The matter was raised in the House, but the motion condemning the action was lost by a substantial margin, in spite of many Conservatives voting with the Liberals.

Winston's early years as an MP were not entirely occupied with fighting his larger and smaller causes, with establishing even more firmly his reputation and name (albeit not always favourably, but he did not care about that), and with enhancing his relations with the great in the land. As

163

a personable young bachelor and a member of an exalted family, and with a dazzling reputation as soldier, writer and politician, he was never short of invitations to stay in the great houses of the land. His hosts ranged from Edward VII at Balmoral and the Duke of Sutherland at Dunrobin, to more modest estates in the home counties. His range of friends was enormous. As a fine shot, he shot everything in season – partridge, woodcock, pheasant, stag. He continued to hunt in spite of Sunny's warning of extravagance.

Sir Ernest and Lady Edwina Cassel invited Winston on a trip up the Nile – in, of course, immense luxury. The august guests included the Duke and Duchess of Connaught, the King's younger brother and sister-in-law, the King's mistress, Mrs Keppel ('very good company'), and more personally, Winston's Aunt Leonie and two of his father's closest friends, Sir Michael Hicks-Beach, recently Chancellor of the Exchequer, and Sir John Gorst, who had been Financial Secretary to the Treasury. They whiled away the warm winter days, chatting, playing, eating and drinking, and visiting temples and sights along the Nile valley. Winston took up bridge, enjoyed it, and was very bad at it. He overbid disastrously, as he later did at backgammon.

By the spring of 1904 the gap between Winston and his party had grown so wide that it appeared unbridgeable. The Conservative committee at Oldham had been restless about their member for some time. In January, a resolution was passed that in effect cut Winston off from all support at the next general election. Friends and allies began looking about for likely alternative seats. Opportunities seemed to be available at Sunderland, Birmingham and Manchester. Winston bided his time. There was still work to do at the House. Meanwhile, nothing reveals his determination to cross the floor and take the Liberal whip more concisely than these few words (from many) in a letter to his old ally Lord Hugh Cecil: 'I am an English Liberal. I hate the Tory party, their men, their words & their methods. I feel no sort of sympathy with them.'

As always, he was thinking through the mind of his

father. What would *he* have done under these circumstances? Randolph had been uncompromising in his principles and beliefs, decisive in his actions. Would he have 'crossed the floor'? Winston believed that he would have, just as he had resigned as Chancellor of the Exchequer – no matter that he had been a whisker away from the premiership. And it was these same Conservatives, these Tories, these Unionists, who had ganged up and destroyed his father. Yes, Randolph would have left them.

Then why, it may be asked, had Winston stood as a Conservative little more than three years earlier? The answer was that it was then inconceivable that he could have stood as a Liberal: his family, his Marlborough upbringing, his father's political beliefs – everything he felt by instinct rebelled against any association with the Liberal Party. Now, however, circumstances, and the Conservative Party, had greatly changed. In April 1904 Winston's future was as exciting for him as it was dangerous. His mind was clamorous with plots and causes, he was embracing more closely Liberal ideas, and he was meeting prominent active Liberals privately. A luncheon with Lloyd George was an eye-opener, and he had a long and impassioned talk with him. A few months ago he had referred to the Welsh firebrand as 'a vulgar, chattering little cad', but now he described their conversation as 'very interesting and not altogether unsatisfactory'.

Soon after this, a dreadful thing happened. On the afternoon of 22 April, Winston was delivering a long speech, which he had as usual learned by heart. It was hardly an inspiring subject, the Trades Unions and Trades Disputes Bill, but he had a nearly full House, with all members attentive to his plea on behalf of the unions. 'The influence of labour on the course of legislation in Parliament is negligible,' he declared emphatically, 'compared with the influence in this House of company directors, the learned professions, the service members, the railway, landed and liquor interests . . .'

Suddenly Winston faltered, looked about him in dismay as if he had been struck an unseen blow, sat down, and covered

165

his face with his hands, uttering these words: 'I thank hon. Members for having listened to me.'

Hansard reported formally, 'The hon. Member here faltered in the conclusion of his speech, and, amid sympathetic cheers, resumed his seat after thanking the House for having listened to him.' (In fact, there were jeers from some of his enemies, too.)

Winston was appalled by the experience and left the House. His prodigious memory, of which he was so proud, had suddenly and for no apparent reason failed him, leaving him floundering. The implications were too awful to contemplate. There were many older members present who could recall those last pathetic and embarrassing speeches by his father, and it appeared as if they might have witnessed a recrudescence in the son of the father's brain failure.

This was what was most worrying Winston as he took a cab back to Mount Street, contemplating the subject of inherited genes and the end of his political life. The following morning his brother-in-law, Sir Shane Leslie, Sir Alfred Harmsworth, the newspaper proprietor, and his brother Jack all visited Winston to offer condolences and practical help.

Another friend, Jack Seely, provided the greatest reassurance. Seely had fought with Winston in South Africa and been awarded the DSO, then returned to contest and win the Conservative seat for the Isle of Wight, although he had recently crossed the floor to the Liberals. Seely sought the advice of a doctor friend who specialized in brain damage. It was, this physician suggested, a form of sudden brain anaemia, a syncope of the memory cells, brought on almost certainly by overstrain. It was most unlikely to recur, he advised, but a rest was desirable.

Strengthened by this news and a very brief rest, Winston chose the afternoon of 31 May 1904 to switch his allegiance. He walked into the chamber and up to the bar, looked with deliberation to right and left, bowed to the speaker, turned decisively to his right, and sat down next to David Lloyd George, in the same seat his father had occupied when in opposition. The uncertainty was over. He was a Liberal.

There were those who said it was about time, too. Others grieved or were angered. There were many who accused him of being a turncoat, even of treachery. Few thought it a wise step for such a young politician to take.

For Winston, heart-searchings and doubts were out of sight, were not even beyond the horizon. He had done what he had to do, and his heart and mind were on the future. To the new Lord Salisbury he later wrote:

> *I readily admit that my conduct is open to criticism*
> *– not – thank heaven – on the score of its sincerity,*
> *but from the point of view of taste. I had to choose*
> *between fighting & standing aside. No doubt the latter*
> *was more decorous. But I wanted to fight – I felt I*
> *could fight with my whole heart and soul . . .*

12

Back to Africa

At a time when anti-Semitism was widespread in Britain, Winston proved publicly that he was not only untainted, but, like his father, was as comfortable with Jews as with anyone else. Prejudice of this kind was utterly alien to him. On the day he crossed the floor of the House, the *Manchester Guardian* published a long letter from him attacking the Aliens Bill, which had come up for its first reading in Parliament.

Anti-Semitism in Russia – as in Germany later, in the 1930s – had driven out of that country many thousands of Jews, most of them poor and many of them illiterate. One of the most popular new homes they sought was Britain, with its long tradition of hospitality to the downtrodden and dispossessed. This led to national anxiety, easily whipped into flames by the forces of prejudice. The result was the Aliens Bill of 1904, which conferred on the Home Office unprecedented new powers to keep out of the country 'undesirable' aliens. The Jewish community in Britain was outraged. Lord (Nathan) Rothschild claimed that the bill would provide 'a loathsome system of police interference and espionage, of passports and arbitrary power'.

Winston attacked the bill for the new powers it proposed to confer on the police and customs officers. The undesirables would always get through by cunning or cash, he claimed. 'The simple immigrant, the political refugee, the helpless and the poor,' he wrote, '– these are the folk who will be caught up in the trammels of the bill and may be harassed and hustled at the pleasure of petty officials without the smallest right of appeal.' The bill would please those with racial prejudices against the Jews and 'those who like patriotism at other people's expense'.

Winston's case was unanswerable. 'We can only wonder

that an English gentleman should make such proposals to the House of Commons in the twentieth century.'

Although published in the *Manchester Guardian*, the letter was addressed to a prominent Jew in Manchester, Nathan Laski, who was chairman of the Jewish Board of Guardians. There was a special reason for this. For months Winston had known that, hardly surprisingly, he had lost the confidence of his old supporters in Oldham, and his new allegiance to the Liberal Party sealed the coffin. Meanwhile, discreet enquiries about his political future emanated from Manchester North-West, a constituency with a strong Jewish community, including Chaim Weizmann, the future President of Israel. The Aliens Bill, which had taken nine years to prepare, was dead within two months, a credit mark to Winston leading to an invitation to stand for Manchester North-West at the next election. Nor could this election be long delayed. 'Victory is assured,' wrote Nathan Laski triumphantly.

All this Winston was able to relate to his oldest and certainly most powerful Jewish friend, Ernest Cassel, in August. Cassel was a great lover of mountains and had built himself an extraordinary villa in Switzerland, 7,000 feet up and poised on a spur between two valleys. It was accessible only on foot or by donkey. At the end of the long climb to the villa you were confronted with a four-floor house, equipped with every luxury and with breathtaking views in every direction.

In this mountain air, Winston felt in better health than at any time he could remember. In the mornings he read and wrote, in the afternoons he walked and climbed, and in the evenings he played bridge and talked. The company was good, including Edward and Alex Colebrooke (the latter shortly to become Lord-in-Waiting to the King), and the conversation well-informed. Cassel was a mine of inside knowledge about international finance and the people who managed it, and the present and future politics of Britain were discussed exhaustively and with a great deal of worldliness and laughter. Winston, glowing with his success over the Aliens Bill and plotting his future with his customary zeal and optimism, was in a seventh heaven.

169

One of the most important of the many subjects of conversation that summer in Switzerland was the decline of the Conservative Party under the supine leadership of Arthur Balfour. Policy was moribund, the front benches without a sparkle. The administration was clearly in a state of terminal illness, but it took a long time to die, and its dying gasp reflected its enfeebled condition. Balfour resigned on 4 December 1905, and the King sent for the Liberal leader, Sir Henry Campbell-Bannerman.

Although an elderly and somewhat colourless man, Campbell-Bannerman enjoyed the confidence of the new bright young stars of the Liberal Party, who were to change the face of the nation over the next ten years – men like John Morley, Walter Runciman (who had earlier lost to Winston at Oldham), Reginald McKenna, Herbert Gladstone (youngest son of former Prime Minister William Gladstone), Lloyd George, Herbert Asquith and, of course, Winston.

Winston had been unwell over his thirty-first birthday and was still recovering when Campbell-Bannerman began to form his administration. Winston was offered the appointment of Financial Secretary to the Treasury, a very considerable promotion in his political career at his age. Young he might be, but he was shrewd enough to recognize that he would here be in the shadow of Asquith, slated for the Treasury as Chancellor of the Exchequer. By contrast, the Colonial Office, he learned, was going to the Earl of Elgin, who would be in the Upper House and, when he was not there, was likely to be looking after his Scottish estates. After some difficulty Winston got his way and became Colonial Under-Secretary, and at midday on 10 December he met his superior by appointment at his house in Eaton Terrace to discuss plans. 'We have rather a tough job before us,' Lord Elgin had written, '– but with your assistance I hope & believe the Colonial Office will make a good show.' The word 'assistance' was a misnomer; Winston was determined to run the Colonial Office with as little interference as he could contrive.

But he would certainly require assistance himself in fulfilling his duties, and he now qualified for a private secretary. He was aware of the importance of his choice. Even before his own appointment, Winston had kept his eyes open for a suitable candidate, and he had been introduced to – among others – a young man of immense erudition, charm and good looks, Edward Marsh. Marsh came from a scholarly background, his father being Master of Downing College, Cambridge. Marsh himself had a sparkling record, having acquired a first-class degree with distinction in classics at Trinity College, Cambridge. There was no great wealth in the family, and in 1896 he became a second-class clerk in the Colonial Office. By 1905 he had already been an assistant private secretary to two ministers, both of whom were able to recommend him.

Marsh's biographer described him as 'an aesthete of acute perception and an ornament of society with an inexhaustible fund of small talk'.

Marsh's shrewdness and keen observation are revealed by his summing-up of Jennie:

> She was an incredible and most delightful compound of flagrant worldliness and eternal childhood, in thrall to fashion and luxury (life didn't begin for her on a basis of less than forty pairs of shoes) yet never sacrificing one human quality of warm-heartedness, humour, loyalty, sincerity, or steadfast and pugnacious courage.

Of Marsh himself it has been written (by Christopher Hassall):

> Edward Marsh was a scholar. He was also, and for many years, a great deal more, making active appearances where men of academic temperament do not normally feel at home – such as dancing his way through every ball of the London season, travelling

171

on foot to the source of the Nile, playing mah-jong
with the King of Portugal . . .

It might be thought doubtful (and was thought so by Marsh
himself) that Winston Churchill and Edward Marsh could
have anything in common. Winston thought they might get
on well, and was confirmed in his belief by none other
than Pamela Plowden – now Lady Lytton. Pamela helped
to complete the match and dispel Marsh's doubts. 'The first
time you meet Winston,' she told him, 'you see all his faults,
and the rest of your life you spend in discovering his virtues.'
Marsh went on to dine alone with Winston that evening,
and afterwards concluded, 'He was the man for me, though
I could still hardly see myself as the man for him.'

Shrewd observers disagreed. Lady Constance Lytton wrote
in answer to the news of his appointment, 'How movingly
exciting about your new job. I have a theory about secretaries
that they should be the opposite poles in type from the
secretaryee . . . I think you and Winston Churchill will add
another proof of it to my list.' And so it proved to be. 'Eddie'
Marsh became Winston's shadow and mentor and devoted
friend for life, the relationship never fading, even when, with
Winston out of office, Marsh had perforce to be seconded to
another minister.

Almost at once, Marsh was thrown willy-nilly into Winston's hectic election campaign in Manchester, where they
took rooms in the Midland Hotel. The constituency included
the financial and commercial centres of the city, a prosperous
residential area, and a very much less prosperous urban area
of slums. The campaign required a great deal of walking, and
Winston chose the slum area on their first evening. At one
point he paused, looking about him in horror. 'Fancy living
in one of these streets,' he exclaimed to Marsh, 'never seeing anything beautiful, never eating anything savoury, never
saying anything *clever*.'

Winston had a formidable fight on his hands, in spite of
Laski's optimism. The seat had been held for more than
twenty years by a local Conservative businessman and had

on several occasions not even been fought by the Liberals, so hopeless was their cause thought to be. Winston's chance improved when the sitting member decided at the last minute not to run again, but he gave his powerful support, and presence, in favour of the new Conservative candidate. Also in Winston's favour was his rigid stand against tariffs and for free trade, music to the ears of the business community. The Jewish vote, too, was an important asset.

It was all over by 13 January, Manchester like Oldham being one of the first constituencies to poll. The result was a spectacular victory: Winston had turned the vote right round. With eighty-nine per cent of the electorate voting, he gained a lead over the Conservative candidate of more than twelve hundred votes. Moreover, the landslide towards the Liberals was reflected throughout Manchester and the whole country. Winston, and Eddie Marsh in his new elevation, were witnessing the first British political revolution of the twentieth century.

Winston's conquest of Manchester North-West coincided with the publication of his most important book so far in his writing career, his thousand-page biography of his father. He had embarked on this monumental task soon after he was first elected to Parliament, and had contrived to research the work and write the two substantial volumes in the course of a full parliamentary and social life – a *tour de force* even by his standards.

The work involved travelling to the country estates of aged retired politicians and working through trunks of ancient papers and much else besides his father's own formidable archives. The entire manuscript was completed by September 1905, when Winston made careful enquiries about a literary agent. He finally settled on Frank Harris. Harris knew the literary world inside out and had edited several newspapers and magazines, and he agreed to negotiate on Winston's behalf on a ten per cent commission basis over and above £4,000. Seven major publishers were approached, the best offer coming from Macmillan, and a startlingly generous offer it turned out to be, with an advance of £8,000 and a fifty-fifty division of profits between author and publisher after Macmillan had made a profit of £4,000.

Harris later became a discredited and notorious figure for his own *My Life and Loves*, but he was certainly an effective literary agent – the guarantee being little short of £300,000 in 1990 money.

One of the book's first admirers was Eddie Marsh, who was given an early copy. *Lord Randolph Churchill* became, and remained, his favourite Winston book. Most reviewers shared Marsh's judgement: the book's press was extensive and rewardingly favourable. Amongst the important newspapers, only the *Daily Telegraph* attacked the book, and at the same time made a scandalous attack on the subject, describing Randolph as a dishonourable man who treated his friends atrociously and was 'careless with the truth'.

Sunny Marlborough was especially outraged by this attack, which was clearly motivated by political considerations, and he demanded (and received) a public apology from the editor, at the head of the leader column.

Aside from his natural ability and intelligence, Winston was ideally equipped to deal with the problems of his position at the Colonial Office. He had travelled widely – far more widely than his immediate superior – and above all he understood and had witnessed at first hand the problem of South Africa. If India was the jewel in the imperial crown, South Africa was the gold in which it was set. The mineral discoveries in the Transvaal were immensely valuable, and the farming was as good as anywhere in the world. But the years of fighting had blighted the land and disrupted the lives of the people. For a small war it was perhaps the most expensive in history.

The policy of the new Liberal administration was to recover the land and unify the people. 'We hope to build upon the reconciliation and not upon the rivalry of races,' was Winston's definition of British aims. The previous Conservative government had hoped to reconcile the defeated

Boer leaders to a strictly limited form of self-government in the Transvaal, for the present. Apart from a few cautious Liberals, the new government proposed a scheme for greater autonomy for the Boers.

In order to meet the new British government's colonial administrators, the Boer authorities had sent to London Jan Christian Smuts. Smuts was a highly educated (Christ's College, Cambridge), articulate and intelligent South African, and a close associate of General Botha's. Smuts requested an early meeting with Winston, and the two men talked together for the first time on 19 January. Mutual respect quickly developed as Smuts made the case (he was a barrister-at-law) for immediate self-government for the Transvaal and the Orange Free State.

One of the most important issues was that of the financial future in the Transvaal. There were strong British fears that a self-governing Boer community would fail to attract the money desperately needed to rebuild confidence in the future of the Transvaal and (less so) the Orange Free State. The Liberal government sought to attract British migrants in order to redress the imbalance in population, but the memories of the war were too fresh in people's minds for South Africa to be an attractive proposition for emigration.

Thanks to the steadiness and wisdom of Botha, Smuts and other Boer leaders, the outcome was eminently satisfactory even if – from the British point of view – the virtual independence of Boer South Africa was a reversion to the situation before the war. The new Transvaal constitution was promulgated in December 1906, and in the following February, only just a year after the British general election, the Boer Het Volk party emerged the narrow winner. Stability was maintained, the mining industry went from strength to strength, and three years later the unification of South Africa took place.

Winston emerged as the darling of the Liberal Party for his successful negotiations, and became the hated enemy of the Conservatives for 'giving away' so much.

*

Just as Winston could encompass the writing of a long definitive biography while conducting his own political life, the burden of the Colonial Office was not so heavy that he was unable to keep alive his military interests. Europe was a dangerous continent in 1906. Russia had recently suffered, and put down, a revolution and had lost a major war against Japan in the Far East. Rumania and Greece were at each other's throats. In the previous year, Germany and France had almost come to blows during the Morocco crisis. Above all, Germany, possessor of a massive army, was swiftly building a navy, which already threatened to challenge Britain at sea. Winston, along with other farsighted people, was coming to the view that a major European war could break out within the next decade. It was not yet time to clean his Mauser, but in order to be prepared he decided to examine as closely as permitted the armies of Germany and France.

This was not difficult to arrange, thanks to his name, his achievements and his office. In August 1906 he was told by the German Embassy in London that he would be welcome to observe the late-summer manoeuvres of the German army in Silesia, staying as a personal guest of the Kaiser, Wilhelm II, King Edward VII's nephew. He was instructed to wear military rather than diplomatic uniform, including levee dress for the formal occasions. He always enjoyed dressing up as a soldier, though some of his items were missing and he had to borrow from Sunny his plume and leopard skin of the Oxford Hussars.

Winston was immensely impressed by the size and the 'massive simplicity & force about German military arrangements', he told Lord Elgin. 'I am very thankful there is a sea between that army and England.' But what if the control of that sea were lost?

During the following summer (1907), Winston followed the French army manoeuvres by invitation, and the two knowledgeable reports he prepared for the War Office were much admired. These army exercises also marked the beginning of one of Winston's closest friendships. Frederick

Edward Smith (or 'F. E', as he was always known famili-arly) had been a great admirer of Randolph's and was a Conservative protectionist who strongly disapproved of Winston's crossing the floor to the Liberals. He was a successful barrister and scholar, a man with a wide-ranging mind, and an irrepressible conversationalist. Winston never allowed political differences to interfere with personal friend-ships; his political estrangement with Sunny did not conflict in the least with his affection for his cousin. The two young men – F. E. the older by two years – hit it off perfectly, and others in their company wondered at the brilliance of the talk in its range and variety. Just as Eddie Marsh had come into Winston's life as a wise and gentle aide and guide in 1906, so F. E. flew into Winston's cosmos like a shooting star in 1907. 'Our friendship was perfect,' wrote Winston. 'It was one of my most precious possessions.'

After witnessing the French manoeuvres together, the two men drove in a powerful borrowed car through France, 7,000 feet over the St Bernard Pass, and down into Italy, where Winston met Sunny Marlborough at Venice. F. E., who had business to attend to, had already driven home, leaving the two cousins to continue a more leisurely journey via Vienna to Malta.

At this Mediterranean island colony the expedition took on a different colour. While comfort, pleasure and the satisfac-tion of good viands were always an important consideration for Winston, they were never allowed to interfere with his duties. Lord Elgin had agreed that a thorough survey of Britain's East African colonies would be valuable, and Winston arranged for it to be conducted in appropriate style. Between early October 1907 and mid-January 1908, the national newspapers and journals followed the progress of this expedition, which also took in Cyprus *en route* to the Suez Canal.

For company, Winston had (at first) Sunny, Eddie Marsh and the husband of Winston's Aunt Sarah, Colonel Gordon Wilson, and Winston also took with him his devoted servant, George Scrivings. Everywhere they went they were treated

177

with immense respect and consideration. The Admiralty provided the party with the 5,600-ton cruiser *Venus*, and Winston was given the ship's admiral's quarters, complete with stern walk. 'The Captain is unceasing in his efforts to promote our comfort, & all the officers are most civil & attentive,' he told Jennie. But Winston never really enjoyed the sea, even under the most advantageous circumstances, and he also complained to his mother about the roughness as well as the sultry heat of the Red Sea.

Neither the heat nor the bad weather for one moment reduced the pace of Winston's work during this voyage. Eddie Marsh was kept busy all day – on one day for eleven hours – taking dictation and transcribing it. Just as pen and sword had accompanied Winston on his military expeditions, so pen and portfolio were the insignia of these travels. Whitehall was bombarded with papers reporting and recommending over a wide range of subjects, most of them far from his brief and dealing with diplomacy and financial matters. Civil servants were outraged at this irregular behaviour, especially as this novice in his department wrote as if he were Prime Minister, and an imperious one at that. 'He is most tiresome to deal with,' commented the Permanent Under-secretary at the Colonial Office, Sir Francis Hopwood, to Lord Elgin, '& will I fear give trouble.' Indeed he did, and for all his life.

Meanwhile, as with all his expeditions, military or civil, the world had to be told about it, and money earned. A magazine had agreed to pay him £750 for five articles, and from·these (as usual) a book rapidly developed. It was called prosaically *My African Journey*, and it remained in print for almost all Winston's life.

Winston was received like some native god at Mombasa – and at all his points of call subsequently – before proceeding up-country in his private train. As the two best, and most enthusiastic, shots in the party, Winston and Colonel Wilson occupied themselves for most of the journey towards Nairobi in a seat rigged over the locomotive's front buffers, rifles at the ready. At a sign, the driver would stop the train, while the two men took pot shots at zebras and wildebeest, gazelles and great birds.

At Simba, the train was shunted into a siding while they set off on foot into the bush. This turned out to be more challenging, and they had some anxious moments with charging rhinoceroses. 'I fired at the big one with a heavy 450 rifle & hit her plum in the chest,' he wrote to Jennie. 'She swerved round & came straight for us at that curious brisk trot which is nearly as fast as a horse's gallop, & full of surprising activity . . . The vitality of these brutes is so tremendous that they will come on like some large engine in spite of five or six heavy bullets thumping in to them. You cannot resist a feeling that they are invulnerable & will trample you under foot however well you shoot . . .'

They travelled vast areas of this beautiful countryside, on foot, by car and by train, then staying with the Governor of British East Africa in Nairobi. On by railway again to Lake Victoria, which they crossed in a steamer to Entebbe and Uganda, to Kampala and Jinja and the immense Ripon Falls, thence by train and steamer to Khartoum, a reconstructed and peaceful city now. 'That was where Lyttleton advanced – there, just east of the flanks of Mount Surgham. And there, over to the left, that's where the 21st Lancers made their charge . . .'

Even now, nearly a decade after that bloody battle, death still seemed to haunt these sandhills and desert. The heat and some infected food proved too much for George Scrivings's constitution, and after a short illness he died on Christmas Eve. Winston was heartbroken. Scrivings had been a loyal servant for years, while his wife had acted as cook-housekeeper to his bachelor household. A funeral service was hurriedly laid on, and he was buried with full military honours (he was an ex-soldier) that evening. 'The Dublin Fusiliers sent their band,' Winston told Jack, 'and a company of men, and we all walked in procession to the cemetery as mourners, while the sun sank over the desert, and the band played that beautiful funeral march . . .'

Winston reached Paris on 13 January, where he met and

179

stayed with Sir Ernest Cassel for a few days, arriving in London on 17 January. After his long absence, he faced a year of immense change in his circumstances and fortunes, which made 1908 the most important year in his life. Political developments were dramatic enough, but they can be consigned to the bottom drawer, at least for a while, by contrast with the transformation in his personal life.

With the advantage of hindsight, one of the letters awaiting him in London was a pointer to the one event that no-one at that time could forecast. The letter was from his old love and eternal friend Pamela Lytton. She was winter-sporting (or rather, her husband was skating) and had taken time off to write Winston a welcome-home letter. In it she wrote of Scrivings's death, of which she had heard 'in a round about way'. 'How he loved you (& no-one can do without love) . . .'

13

A Walk in the Rose Garden

For several years now, Winston had become increasingly aware that there was a hollowness in his life that ached to be filled. But the problem of filling it was not easy to solve, for he was also increasingly preoccupied with his ambitions and causes, and the tempo of his life gave him only the briefest moments for personal reflection. He was like a passenger in an express train racing through, say, the Po Valley, with scarcely time to glance out through the window to admire the scenery.

It was not that he lacked appreciation of the attractions of women. He was always half or wholly in love, but as with Pamela Plowden, who would certainly have accepted him if they had not both known that circumstances made him unready for marriage, there was always – it seemed – some impediment. He had fallen in love with and proposed to a Miss Muriel Wilson, but this beautiful young woman did not, it seems, match up to his intellectual expectations. In the course of a perhaps overlong motor tour through Italy in 1906 with her and others, he told his mother that 'nothing could exceed the tranquil *banalité* of my relations with [Muriel Wilson] but I am very glad I came.'

A year later, at the time of Louis Botha's visit to England, there were rumours (unsubstantiated) of another engagement. Botha had brought with him his attractive and cultivated daughter, Helen, and word of this 'engagement' had reached Muriel Wilson in the south of France. She was one of the first to congratulate him.

The actress Ethel Barrymore was another lady friend. They were extremely fond of one another, and their friendship endured – as the others did. But she later conceded that she would have found the world of politics beyond her capacity.

181

This time, things were different. Did Winston open his heart to Eddie Marsh when he got home to Bolton Street that night of the dinner party when he had sat down next to Clementine Hozier and engaged her attention? Did his secretary tease him by saying, 'Think what might have been your loss if I had not got you out of your bath?' We don't know. We do know that Winston had already decided to pursue this courting of Clementine with his usual resolution and speed, and that he was not going to be deviated in his aim to make Clementine his wife.

Another event at this time had led Winston to recognize the deprived and unsatisfactory nature of his domestic life. While he was on his African tour he received a long letter from Jack. The brothers were as close as ever, in spite of their divergent careers, and shared the house in Bolton Street. After leaving the Army, Jack had reluctantly continued his City professional life with Cassel, advancing steadily but not at a pace that allowed him to marry and set up his own establishment. For many years Winston and Jack had both known and been fond of Lady Gwendeline Bertie, a daughter of the Earl of Abingdon. It had been a rather sisterly relationship for both young men, but in the summer of 1907, for Gwendeline – or 'Goonie', as she was known to them – it developed rapidly into something more.

In his letter, Jack told his elder brother, 'A very wonderful thing has happened. Goonie loves me. . . . I have loved her for a long time – but have always attempted to put thoughts of that kind out of my mind – because I felt I had nothing to give her – and also chiefly because I never for one moment imagined that she would ever care for me.'

Winston wrote to his 'dear Goonie' to congratulate her, and she wrote back passionately but tragically, for the current financial crisis in the City made Jack's future even more uncertain. Goonie's mother took the strong line of prohibiting her daughter from even meeting Jack for the time being, let alone marrying him. Months of misery between the two lovers were endured before Jack managed to obtain a guarantee of income that led the couple, strongly encouraged by Winston, to decide to marry on 7 August 1908. It was a civil wedding, 'for all the world as if it was an elopement – with irate parents panting on the path', Winston told Clementine. This was not quite true: the father and mother were present, but very reluctant supporters of the marriage. That made no difference to the couple, who were both radiantly happy – 'the triumphant Jack bore her off amid showers of rice & pursuing cheers – let us pray – to happiness & honour all her life.' The prayer was answered.

By this time in the summer of 1908, the briefer courtship of Winston and Clementine had advanced mightily, and letters of growing affection were being exchanged. Both were committed to other responsibilities at widely separated parts of the country, but at last in early August it seemed possible that they could meet.

Clementine was at Cowes for the yachting, and now, at Winston's urgent behest, agreed to come to stay at Blenheim and then go on to Salisbury Hall, Jennie and George's place. She was anxious about these visits on two counts: first, the usual concern of any girl meeting the family of which she might one day be a part, and second, and more prosaically, the fact that she had only one laundered and starched dress to wear – and, of course, no personal maid.

Remembering how his father had courted his mother at Cowes, and after their marriage had brought her to Blenheim, Winston wrote to Clementine, 'I want so much to show you that beautiful place & in its gardens we shall find lots of places to talk in, & lots of things to talk about.'

And so we can see this beautiful twenty-three-year-old girl, with her modest luggage, bidding farewell to her host and hostess, the Godfrey Barings, at Nubia House overlooking the Solent, and being taken to the ferry by the coachman. It is Monday 10 August. It is raining, but soon the sun comes out, and it becomes a warm and beautiful day for the journey and for the events that must imminently unfold.

The train from Southampton takes her through the rolling

Hampshire and Berkshire countryside. Clementine spends part of the journey writing to her mother: '. . . I feel dreadfully tired & rather shy . . . I feel like in a dream & can do nothing more intelligent than count the telegraph poles . . .' She sees also the harvest in full swing in the fields, some fields being cut by lines of men with scythes, the larger ones by horse-drawn reapers. A halt and then on to Oxford, arriving at 5.20 p.m. The train comes to a hissing halt – and there, with a porter at his side, is the waiting figure of Winston, feet slightly splayed, wearing an unbuttoned tweed suit and bow tie, with no hat. There is just a fleeting moment for her to cast a loving glance at him through the carriage window; then he recognizes her and bounds forward . . . 'My dear, how wonderful . . .!'

Winston had driven his own car to the station – the two were inseparable – and after the porter had put the trunk and hat-box in the back, passed Clementine a pair of passenger's goggles and donned his own cap and goggles. Chattering all the while about Sunny and their fellow guests – 'just Sunny and the F. E. Smiths and my Mama and my secretary, Eddie Marsh' – Winston climbed into the driving seat. After one reassuring smile at her, he drove stylishly out of the station forecourt, into Oxford, through the city's quiet streets – it was summer vacation – and out on to the dusty Woodstock Road.

Winston drove fast along the straight road, and conversation was impossible until they slowed down for the narrow high street of Woodstock. Once he had quoted his father in his biography: It was 20 August 1873. 'I met, soon after my arrival at Cowes, Miss Jeannette Jerome . . . I passed most of my time with her and before leaving asked her if she loved me well enough to marry me; and she told me she did.'

During the dinner at Lady St Helier's that had brought them together, Winston asked Clementine if she had read his biography of Lord Randolph, and when she replied that she had not he promised to send her a copy. He forgot to do so. But now he remembered that passage and quoted it to

184

her as they drove along the winding drive that revealed new wonders at every turn.

Sunny was there to greet her at the great entrance, and Jennie, and then Freddie and Margaret Smith . . . Such a welcome! 'Ethel will take you to your room, dear, and we'll have some tea waiting for you . . .'

Later, Clementine had a long hot bath and time to contemplate in solitude the wonders of this great palace, with the sun low over the rolling parkland and the famed oaks, time, too, to contemplate Winston's cousin, the Duke, whose wife Consuelo had left him two years ago. Was it her imagination, or did he appear lonely and rather sad? And the Smiths, who had been so particularly kind at tea. And the good-looking and amusing Edward Marsh . . .

Before eight o'clock, Clementine descended the great staircase for dinner, her fears and doubts renewed in spite of the evident warmth of her welcome. Whenever it was possible, 'I stood for fear of getting my dress crumpled.' (She need not have worried. The ever-percipient Jennie had arranged for a maid to take away her worn dresses and wash, press, and starch them.)

After dinner, and before the party broke up for bed, Winston invited Clementine to walk in the rose garden after breakfast, and she accepted. Was this the time he had chosen to propose to her? Why else could she be here? Men did not customarily write letters in the intimate terms he had used unless their intentions were serious. And he had told her they were serious. As long before as April, he had written of a party, 'How I should have liked you to have been there.' He wrote of life's incompleteness, without naming her, but adding, 'I am a solitary creature in the midst of crowds . . .'

Punctual as always, Clementine came down to breakfast on the morning of Tuesday 11 August. There was no sign of Winston, and she ate at first alone and then with Sunny, and later with the others. Sunny, the assiduous host, who was privy to Winston's intentions to propose to Clementine today, sent an urgent message for him to get up and come down quickly. Meanwhile, how best to fill in her time?

185

Clementine was disappointed and decidedly put out. For a moment, it crossed her mind to leave at once for London. Then Sunny said, 'Dear Miss Hozier, would you honour me by accompanying me on a drive round the park? There is much to see.'

It was almost lunchtime when they returned. The weather looked less settled and there were showers around. But Winston was down at last, seemingly unconscious of any gaffe or omission, and at once gave all his loving attention to Clementine. It was raining after they had finished lunch, and it was not until late in the afternoon that the sun came out. Winston now invited Clementine for the much-delayed visit to the roses. Those who saw them walk off across the lawn noted not only their equal height but also the sense of intimacy between them. Surely the guests' suspicions of the reason for this outing were as strong as Sunny's certain knowledge.

The sky was exceedingly dark and threatening, in no way reflecting the state of mind of the couple. They were still far from the roses when they saw that the lake before them was pockmarked with the rain that was sweeping towards them. The nearest shelter was a little Greek temple looking out over the lake. They ran towards it and sheltered inside before they got too wet, and Winston wasted no more time in declaring his love and proposing to Clementine. 'Yes, Winston, I will . . .' Later, she said, 'But we must keep this a secret between us until I can tell my mother.' Winston agreed, and the rain declining, they left behind the Greek temple and headed back towards the house.

As swiftly as the rain had come, so the sun followed it. The vigilant Duke emerged from the door, anxious to be the first to hear the news. And so he was. Forgetting his promise, Winston broke away, raced up the slope like a schoolboy, and flung his arms round Sunny's neck. 'She has accepted – Clementine will marry me . . .!' He was almost incoherent with excitement as he repeated the news to the others. No-one was more pleased than Jennie. Her son had for long needed a wife, and who better

186

than this ravishing and intelligent girl? Now, it seemed, both sons would be married in one year – almost within weeks of one another, for when everyone asked when the wedding was to be, Winston had replied, 'Oh soon – yes, soon!'

It was arranged that Clementine should travel up to London the next morning, 12 August, in order to ask her mother's consent. For once, Winston was awake early and eager for the glorious day to begin.

> *My dearest* [he wrote from his bedroom],
>   *How are you?*
>   *I send you my best love to salute you: & I am getting up at once in order if you like to walk to the rose garden after breakfast & pick a bunch before you start . . .*
>
>

Always
W

Winston then wrote a letter to Blanche Hozier telling her of their mutual love, of his own 'great & sacred responsibility', and of his determination to make Clementine happy. It was not in fact delivered for, on reaching Oxford station with Clementine later in the morning, he impetuously boarded the train with her.

> *When we got to Paddington* [Clementine wrote to her sister] *I went off alone . . . & told him to follow in half an hour – I wanted to see the Min* [her mother] *alone first & also I was not sure if she would be dressed! . . . Well, W arrived presently & I left them alone & everything was all right . . . My dear, I have the most lovely ring – a fat ruby with two diamonds . . . Min, Winston & I returned to Blenheim in the afternoon – We were all dog-tired but no matter – Min was most delightful at dinner & looked lovely in her white lace arrangement . . .*

The letters and telegrams poured forth from Blenheim, and later Bolton Street, with the news of the engagement. To his first love, Pamela, Winston wrote, 'I am going to marry Clementine & I say to you as you said to me when you married Victor – you must always be our best friend.' His other loves were high on the priority list, Muriel Wilson writing, 'Bless you dear Winston & I can't tell you how really delighted I was to get your wire.'

To Jack and Goonie, Winston wrote:

> It is done & done forever.
> I am to marry Clementine almost at once.
> I hope we shall be happy like you are, and always all four of us bound together by the most perfect faith & comradeship.

The King, who was taking the waters at Marienbad, was among the first to be told, and Winston sent on his 'best wishes for your happiness' to Clementine, adding, 'There are no words to convey to you the feelings of love & joy by wh my being is possessed. May God who has given to me so much more than I ever knew how to ask keep you safe & sound.'

The official announcement of the engagement was made on 15 August from Salisbury Hall, where Jack and Goonie, still on their honeymoon, Jennie and George Cornwallis-West, and Winston and Clementine, all foregathered. The news came as a surprise to many people who had no knowledge of the swift courtship and had in any case expected a great match for Winston, for, well connected as she was, Clementine was not widely known to the public and was virtually penniless.

The wedding was fixed for 12 September 1908, at St Margaret's, Westminster, in Parliament Square. It was convenient to have it while the House was in recess, but it did mean that many of his political intimates would be away and unable to attend. Lord Hugh Cecil agreed to be best man, however, and many figures from Winston's earlier years were to be present, and both families in abundance. Dr Welldon agreed to give the address, and Sir Ian Hamilton and Sir Bindon Blood represented Winston's military past. Then his recent friends F.E. and Margaret Smith could come, as well as the political colleague he had once despised but was now close to, David Lloyd George.

As do many engaged girls before a wedding, Clementine found the strain of waiting on the one hand and the rush to have her trousseau ready in time on the other hand, as well as the stress of responsibility and the raising of doubts – about her love and his love – a great trial. At one point she confided her anxiety to her young brother and asked him if she should break off the engagement. He was only 20 years old, but he was 'the man of the family', and he rose to the occasion. He correctly declared that she had already inconvenienced many friends by breaking off her last official engagement and must on no account humiliate this 'public personage'. It was only a brief lapse of self-confidence, and she was soon all right again.

> Great numbers of well-dressed people lined all the roadways leading to St Margaret's. The police were present in considerable force, mounted and on foot, and their services were quite necessary to marshal the crowds. . . . Within the church political opponents joined with friends and colleagues in expressing their goodwill. The church was decorated with masses of white chrysanthemums, lilies and feathery spiraea . . . towering palms and heaped up banks of ferns . . . while sunshine through the stained glass windows streamed full upon the flowers.

Lady Blanche Hozier (*The Times* noted) was in purple silk, Lady St Helier in black with a black and silver bonnet, Jennie in dark mushroom with a large hat trimmed with dahlias. The bride was 'a slim, dignified figure in white ivory satin with a flowing veil of soft white tulle escorted by Mr W. Hozier, RN, her brother'.

After the service, which ended with 'Now Thank We All Our God', the bride and groom, best man and close family and friends retired to the vestry to sign the register. It was indeed a solemn and glorious occasion, but politics could not be entirely excluded, and this was what Winston and Lloyd George discussed while waiting to sign the register. It was something that Clementine would have to get used to.

Lady St Helier – 'Great-Aunt' Mary – who more than anyone else had brought the couple together, had offered to give the reception at her house in Portland Place, where only six months earlier Winston and Clementine had first sat and talked side by side. It was a great popular occasion, with East End 'pearlies' dancing in the street outside. (They especially loved the groom because he had defended their right to trade as costermongers in the streets of London.) Among the multitude of presents on display were a gold-topped malacca cane from the King and a scallop-edged silver tray from the Prime Minister and all members of the government, who had signed their names on the back.

Then at 3 p.m. Clementine withdrew to change out of her wedding dress into a 'smart grey cloth costume finished with a deep black satin sash, a large black satin hat adorned with one long sweeping ostrich feather'. The couple departed in a carriage for Paddington Station, cheered by a huge crowd and scattered with rice. Sunny had offered them Blenheim Palace for the first part of their honeymoon. It was just short of thirty-four years since Winston had been baptized there. A special train took the couple from Oxford to Woodstock, where they were met by cheering crowds and the ringing of bells, just as Randolph and Jennie had been greeted.

And now, as Winston wrote in the last line of his early memoirs, 'I married and lived happily ever after.' It would be satisfactory to record that this much-quoted claim was entirely true, but like much in that book, it was an exaggeration.

The Emerging Statesman

As Prime Minister, Sir Henry Campbell-Bannerman had presided over the great Liberal upsurge marking the first decade of the new century. He was a shrewd and much-liked man who had succeeded in holding together a team of brilliant but unruly ministers, and there was real sadness when it became clear that his health was failing early in 1908. There was no doubt who his successor would be.

Herbert Henry Asquith was a man of immense intelligence, wit, sagacity, wiliness, and ruthlessness, whose powers of administration and organization marked him out for success as soon as he turned from the bar to politics at the age of 34. He rose rapidly and became Home Secretary in 1892, and with the return of the Liberal Party served under Campbell-Bannerman as Chancellor of the Exchequer. His first wife died in 1891, and three years later he married the remarkable Margot Tennant.

Margot was the sixth daughter of a baronet, and at the time of her meeting with Asquith was one of a set that combined hard hunting with social intellectualism, one of 'The Souls', which comprised young men and women of generally high rank and exceptional brains. Arthur Balfour and George Curzon were typical of the male membership, Lady Brownlow and the Duchess of Sutherland amongst the women. Margot herself wrote immodestly in her *More Memories* that 'The Souls was a foolish name given by fashionable society to myself and my friends . . . There has been no group in society of equal distinction, loyalty, and influence. None of us claimed any kind of superiority or practised any sort of exclusion.'

Margot liked to be at the centre of the stage, preferably in a shocking role. At all times she said what she thought with total spontaneity and enjoyed any effect she caused. In a literary tussle with Lady Londonderry, who had many acolytes around her at the time, about the merits and demerits of a new volume of essays, Margot was accused of not even having read the book. 'I thought it unnecessarily rude and more than foolish,' Margot recalled. 'I looked at her calmly and said: "I am afraid, Lady Londonderry, you have not read the preface. The book is dedicated to me."'

When Randolph Churchill resigned as Chancellor of the Exchequer, destroying his career, Margot told him that he had resigned 'more out of temper than conviction'. Not in the least put out, Randolph invited her to dinner and seated her next to the Prince of Wales.

Campbell-Bannerman had died on 22 April. The King was staying in his favourite hotel in Biarritz and decided to break custom (but not his holiday) by asking Asquith to come to him and kiss hands in France. The sovereign and his first minister had already discussed suitable appointments in London, and Asquith had indicated that Winston could have the Admiralty, the Local Government Board or the Colonial Office.

Winston would dearly have liked the first of these, but it would have meant superseding his uncle, Lord Tweedmouth, who was not well but would be deeply hurt at his nephew's ousting him. Finally, Winston was offered and accepted the appointment of President of the Board of Trade.

The title bore little relationship to the functions of this office, which, anyway, was in a run-down state and in urgent need of reform. One of the first commitments of this new administration was to the welfare of the working people. This was close to Winston's heart, and the appointment allowed him to put into effect his newly acquired theories on how best to relieve the sufferings of the unemployed, the poor and the elderly. Only the end of *laissez-faire* and the introduction of state intervention could bring this about, notably through agencies to channel men into jobs, ensure a basic minimum wage and provide for working men and their families in times of ill health or hardship. During his two years at the Board of Trade, labour exchanges began to appear throughout the land, legislation was passed that controlled the practice of sweated labour, and the foundations were laid for unemployment insurance, with contributions from employees and employers.

These reforms had become doubly necessary as a result of the slump of 1907 and 1908, which led to a sharp rise in unemployment, much suffering and the dangerous labour unrest that Winston was shortly going to have to face.

He was now in the Cabinet, and by a law of 1705 he had to resign his parliamentary seat and seek re-election as a result of this promotion. In the milder political climate of recent years it had become customary for the opposition to abstain from putting up a candidate, which precluded the need for a by-election. But by 1908 the Tory Party was having no truck with that, especially when the candidate was the hated turncoat Winston Churchill.

So in the middle of the turmoil of job-changing – and at the outset of his courting of Clementine Hozier – Winston had to return to the hustings at Manchester. As last time, his opponent was William ('Jix') Joynson-Hicks, an able and determined Conservative, bent on revenge. It was a brisk, relentless campaign in which Winston was defending a small majority after the enactment of some legislation that was deeply offensive to the wealthier people of the constituency. Moreover, many ill-informed voters were persuaded by Joynson-Hicks that the Government had thrown away the fruits of the Boer War, in which so many British lives had been lost. When the votes were counted, it was seen that the 6.4 per cent swing from the Liberals had given the Conservatives the margin they needed. Winston conceded defeat. The *Manchester Guardian* made the bold prediction, 'You have not done with Mr Churchill yet.'

Winston took the defeat philosophically, ascribing it, at least in part, to a hostile Conservative press. One local newspaper went so far as to repeat the accusation that he had broken his parole while a prisoner of the Boers. He again sued for libel and forced the paper to apologize and withdraw the accusation.

The Liberal Party soon found a safe seat for Winston, at Dundee in Scotland, where the sitting member had been elevated to the peerage. Like Oldham, Dundee was primarily a working-class, medium-size, industrial town with a strong radical tradition. With a Labour candidate to contend with, besides the local Tory (and a temperance man, too), Winston pushed his radical views with great emphasis. He attacked the House of Lords, the powers of which the Liberals were determined to restrict, with special ferocity, and announced to his listeners that an old-age pension scheme was to be introduced.

In his onslaughts against the Labour Party as well as the Conservatives he ran rings round his opponents. With the exception perhaps of Lloyd George, there was no greater orator in the land, and he had his audiences spellbound. On 9 May Winston was returned with a majority not far short of double the votes of both his opponents.

The marriage of Winston and Clementine was to suffer many disappointments and anxieties. But the honeymoon had the glow of pure gold. After a few days at Blenheim, they travelled to Lake Lugano in northern Italy and thence to Venice. 'We have only loitered & loved,' he wrote to Jennie, 'a good and serious occupation for which the histories furnish respectable precedents.' But even the lure of beautiful Clementine could not entirely distract him from all his work. The *Strand Magazine* articles on his East Africa trip were being assembled into a book, and he very badly needed the advance of £500 his new agent, Alexander Watt, had negotiated. He promised Watt that he would provide an extra 10,000 words, to bring the book up to a respectable size, by the end of September.

When they returned to London, the writing finished, the honeymoon over, they settled temporarily at 12 Bolton Street. But in four months the lease was due to expire, so they went house-hunting, and found just what they wanted in Eccleston Square – a proper family house, accessible to Belgravia in one direction and the Houses of Parliament on the other side of Pimlico. New aspects of Clementine's character now revealed themselves to Winston, her economy and good, yet practical, taste.*

Quite unlike Winston's mother, Clementine had been brought up to practise domestic economy, like most Scottish girls. For her, a booklet wedding present, *House Books on 12s a Week*, was valued as highly as a canteen of silver; certainly it was as much used. When it came to furnishing and carpeting the new house, she ingeniously contrived to use the carpets from Bolton Street, having them cut and stitched so that nearly all the rooms, except the dining room and the stairs and the servants' quarters were covered – 'and cheap linoleum for about £2' would do for the servants.

Winston warmly approved while at the same time being slightly puzzled about this zeal for economy, which had rarely penetrated his personal life. But it did now. She tried to make him cut down on his cigar smoking and his expenditure on clothes. He might be the worst-dressed man in Asquith's ministry, but not in his underclothes. Asquith's daughter Violet learned of this through Clementine's whispered outrage.

> She told me that Winston was most extravagant about his underclothes. These were made of very finely woven silk (pale pink) and came from the Army and Navy Stores and cost the eyes out of the head. This year according to her calculations he had spent something like eighty pounds on them. When I taxed him with this curious form of self-indulgence he replied, 'It is essential to my well-being. I have a very delicate and sensitive cuticle which demands

---

*She let rip only in her bedroom, which she had decorated in the fashionable *art nouveau* style.

the finest covering. Look at the texture of my cuticle
– feel it [uncovering his forearm by rolling up his
sleeve for Violet]. I have a cuticle without a blemish
– except on one small portion of my anatomy where I
sacrificed a piece of skin to accommodate a wounded
brother officer . . .

Clementine was also at first greatly shocked at Winston's
gambling, less on ethical grounds than because he was
not very successful at it, and they could not afford the
losses. She also showed the censorious side of her nature
in disapproving of Jennie's gambling, too, especially because
from time to time Winston had to help her out of her
debts, George Cornwallis-West being quite incapable of
earning a livelihood. Clementine tried her utmost to conceal her doubts about Jennie because she knew how much
Winston loved his mother and how close they had always
been.

By contrast, Goonie was a blessing, and a confidante in
mother-in-law crises. From the first time they met, the
wives of Jack and Winston struck a mutually affectionate note. It was a pleasure for the brothers, too, to see
their wives so happy together. They were quite different
in temperament and outlook, and a splendid example of
Winston's belief that harmony was often found between the
unlike.

To Winston's carefully concealed distress, Clementine's
affection did not extend to his cousins, Ivor and Freddie
Guest, and their father Lord Wimborne. She secretly dreaded
visits to Canford Manor, although she shared Winston's affection for his aunt, Cornelia (Spencer-Churchill), the boys'
mother. Ivor and Freddie she found brash and conceited,
and did not care for their manners. At bridge one evening,
Clementine's youngest daughter relates, Ivor Guest lost his
temper and threw his cards into Clementine's face. She
immediately stood up and left the room. The following
morning she insisted on leaving, and Winston was obliged
to accompany her.

By the standards of Winston's social world and background, Clementine could be judged suspicious of intellectualism, as over-critical and puritan in her outlook, especially in her early years of marriage, and Winston was doubly grateful when his friends and relations appreciated the warmth of her heart and the depth of her appreciation of the kindness in others. Through Winston, she was often with some of the cleverest people of her generation, who found her shyness and reserve difficult to penetrate, though for Winston's sake they concealed their opinion of her. Besides being clever, they were also sharp and cynical in their observations. Asquith once told his confidante, Venetia Stanley, that, while he was 'quite fond' of Clementine, she 'is *au fond* a thundering bore!' On another occasion, when offered the present of a beautiful dress by Mrs Keppel, the King's mistress, she refused it. Asquith commented: 'Clemmie is very "particular", isn't she?'

Considering her position in society (to say nothing of her beauty), it may seem odd that she was quite often lonely. But what with her husband often being absent, always being busy, and habitually excoriating the rich and the titled and allying himself with the natural enemies of his class while frequently staying at Blenheim with his ducal cousin – with all this and her shyness, she did sometimes have cause to feel isolated and lonely.

But at all times and on all occasions, she was supported by Winston's undivided love and, within a few weeks of their wedding, by the knowledge that she was expecting their first child – and then by the reality of this baby.

A few extracts from Winston's speeches and letters while at the Board of Trade serve to highlight his beliefs and his determination to remedy the injustices of the time. For example, on education: 'Is it not a terrible thing that the whole of our educational system upon which so many millions are lavished, stops short at the age of 14, and that boys and girls, just at the age when they ought to receive training and discipline . . . are allowed to slip away from all

197

guidance and control?' He proposed, as a cure, 'an altogether unprecedented expansion in technical colleges and combination schools to train our youth in the skill of the hand, as well as in the arts and letters . . .'

With the rate of unemployment almost doubling between 1907 and 1908, he mocked those who sought a solution by creating tariff barriers, which were no more than an 'impudent irrelevance'. State intervention could be part of the cure, and in the short term, advancing the construction of warships would alleviate unemployment on the Tyne and the Clyde. To the First Lord of the Admiralty, Reginald McKenna, he wrote in September 1908:

> *I never contemplated the laying down of Dread-noughts* [large battleships] – *even as a basis for discussion – but I know you have about twenty smaller ships which have to be constructed every year, and I should have thought that nothing would be more easy than to have placed seven or eight of these during the period* [i.e., the winter] *when work is so much needed.*

McKenna agreed.

At this time, Winston took a benign view of trades unions, and he felt keenly for those workers, mostly migrants, who became victims of 'sweated labour' without any protection against unscrupulous employers.

> His feebleness and ignorance generally renders the worker easy prey to the tyranny of masters and middle-men – only a step higher up the ladder than the worker – and held in the same relentless grip of forces – where those conditions prevail, you have not a condition of progress, but a condition of progressive degeneration . . .

This was part of a long speech to introduce his bill, the Trade Boards Act, in 1909, which was to fix minimum rates for time-work in the 'sweated labour' industries, with penalties for offenders.

On introducing workers' insurance and labour exchanges, Winston spoke to the Cabinet of the responsibility of employers for their employees, who in turn must contribute to the cost of their welfare from their wages for the times when they were incapable of work. Later, he was to say, 'Insurance brought the miracle of averages to the rescue of the masses.' As for the labour exchanges, they would, he contended, provide information on the need for tradesmen at particular locations, to tell 'workmen where not to go and where to go'.

The exchanges and unemployment insurance were complementary, he declared. 'They were man and wife, mutually supported and sustained by each other.'

The more successful that Winston and Lloyd George, as Chancellor of the Exchequer, were in converting Britain into a welfare state, the more unpopular they became with the landed gentry and the wealthy. The bitterness was very deep, and feeling ran high. There is no doubt that Winston especially was a prime target. After all, he had nearly become a duke himself, and his aristocratic connections were impeccable. Yet he was frequently attacking the House of Lords, calling it 'a miserable minority of titled persons who represent nobody, who are responsible to nobody and who only scurry up to London to vote in their party interests, their class interests and in their own interests'.

Both Winston and Lloyd George were particularly vitriolic in their attacks against dukes, and this could only lead to family friction and a conflict of interests. Lloyd George's opinion of dukes rang up and down the country after a speech on 30 July 1909: 'A fully equipped duke costs as much to keep up as two Dreadnoughts, and dukes are just as great a terror and they last longer.' Sunny Marlborough was manfully restrained, and there were no cross words between the two cousins at Blenheim. But his tolerance was stretched too far on one occasion when Clementine was staying there with her sister Nellie, and Winston was absent. Lloyd George had just made an important speech on the proposed reforms of land ownership, which made unhappy listening to all landowners. Clementine and Nellie, both of radical persuasion, read reports of the speech in the newspapers the following morning, praising it warmly, loudly enough for Sunny to hear.

Later in the day, while they were all at lunch, a telegram arrived from Lloyd George for Clementine that needed an urgent reply. She slipped away to one of the writing tables in the room. Sunny found this more than he could bear and called out, 'Please, Clemmie, would you mind not writing to that horrible little man on Blenheim writing paper.'

Furious at this rebuke, Clementine left the room, had her bags packed, and ordered transport to the railway station. Sunny intercepted her in the hall, apologized abjectly, and begged her not to leave. But Clementine was not that easily mollified and insisted on departing for London.

Winston tended to belittle incidents like this, but to Clementine's chagrin, with the political scene becoming more and more violent, class against class, this couple were difficult to accommodate amongst their Conservative friends and relations. After all, Asquith's ministry was bent on bringing about the greatest political upheaval of modern times in its determination to bring some measure of justice to the disadvantaged. The construction of the foundations of a complete welfare state, of schools and colleges, labour exchanges and hospitals, all had to be paid for, and in great part out of the pockets of the rich taxpayer.

Winston's cousin Ivor Guest, for one, was going to be heavily hit by the new proposals, in 1909, on death duties. The immensely wealthy Lord Wimborne had transferred his estates to his son in 1907, with the knowledge that he had only to survive one year for the transfer to be free of death duties. Now Lloyd George proposed to increase the period to five years, and retrospectively at that. In a long letter to Winston his cousin claimed that he would be paying thirty per cent on a capital of £1,250,000 or £375,000 – or about £14 million in

1990 money. When Ivor followed this up with a visit, Winston wrote to Clementine, 'Ivor Guest has just been to me in a great state . . .' But then, who could blame him?

The heat of the national conflict was certainly intensified by the violent language used on both sides. Winston was as guilty as anyone in his party of embittering the opposition. From King George V down, there were countless people in the land, friends as well as enemies, who wished Winston would display more restraint in his speeches, especially around election time. Amongst the middle- and working-class people he had countless admirers who recalled the hero of the Boer War, the cavalry charge at Omdurman, and now his evident deep concern for easing the lot of the poor. George V himself, fresh on the throne after the death of his father, sent a message through Margot Asquith 'that if you wd just keep up that moderation of language wh had struck so many in this election you wd not be at all unappreciated'. And as for clever Margot herself, what better advice could she offer Winston than this:

> *The fact is dear Winston (I am the most genuine woman in the world & I know from our talk you will xcuse my frankness) you have a unique opportunity . . . of improving yr position in the eyes of the best element both in politics & society. Believe me cheap scores, hen-roost phrases & all oratorical want of dignity is out of date. You have only to say to yrself 'Margot Asquith is a little boring & over-earnest but she is right. Loyalty, reserve & character pays more than all the squibs & crackers. I have got a beautiful young wife, an affectionate heart & love of amusement. I will make the Court, the Colonies, the West and the East end of London change their whole views of me . . . I shall thrive on being liked instead of loving abusive notice & rotten notoriety.'*

During these early years of marriage, amidst the smoke of social and political battle between the entrenched and the 'revolutionaries' of the Liberal Party, Winston took advantage of opportunities to travel outside the corridors of Whitehall.

In the autumn of 1909 he succeeded in combining his twin but seemingly disparate interests, in army and social matters, by visiting both labour bureaus and military manoeuvres (at the invitation of the Kaiser) in Germany. The trip was conducted almost entirely by motor car, with Eddie Marsh and F. E., who provided the car. 'There is such a sense of independence about motoring,' he wrote to Clementine, 'that I should never think of going by train, if the choice offered.' He was in Strassburg for their first wedding anniversary and wrote to 'My darling Clemmie':

> *A year to-day my lovely white pussy-cat* came to me, & I hope & pray she may find on this September morning no cause – however vague or secret – for regrets. The bells of this old city are ringing now & they recall to my mind the chimes which saluted our wedding & the crowds of cheering people. A year has gone . . . My precious & beloved Clemmie my earnest desire is to enter still more completely into your dear heart & nature & to curl myself up in your darling arms . . .*

Winston found the manoeuvres awe inspiring and was as impressed as ever by the German military machine. But the prospect of this power of destruction being released was

---

*Their letters are spattered with soubriquets and decorated with drawings of the creatures so identified. Clementine was always 'Cat', 'Pussy-Cat' or 'Kat'; their first child was identified as 'Puppy-Kitten', or 'PK'; Winston himself began as 'Pug' or 'Amber Pug', but developed, seemingly painlessly, into 'Pig'. The third person was frequently used in this context.

utterly repugnant, refuting all accusations that he loved war. He put it to Clementine like this: 'Much as war attracts me & fascinates my mind with its tremendous situations – I feel more deeply every year – & can measure the feeling here in the midst of arms – what vile & wicked folly & barbarism it all is.'

Twelve months later, Winston's visit to Greece and Turkey could not, he regretted, be conducted by motor car. Seasickness was compensated for, to some extent, by a call at Monte Carlo, where he contrived to make a profit of £160 on the tables. On his return he and Clementine went off together to stay with the Lloyd Georges at their place in northern Wales near Criccieth. The two men were the corps commanders in Asquith's army of reform and now got on extremely well together. There was at this time no dispute about policy, but plenty to plot and debate, between motor rides through the beautiful mountainous countryside, and golf and bridge in the evenings. Clementine, ever on the alert to protect Winston and cautious and uncertain of herself with all his political colleagues, did not wholly trust Lloyd George, while greatly admiring him. Winston once told Clementine that Lloyd George, over a dinner together, had been 'full of your praises – said you were my "salvation" and that your beauty was the least thing about you'.

In fact, Clementine was going through a period – mercifully brief – of suspicion that her husband was having an affair with one, if not several, of his old flames. It is true that he had once proposed to, and been turned down by, Muriel Wilson and that his manner with her, and with Pamela Lytton, to whom he had been so close for so long, continued to be mildly flirtatious. Nor did he modify his behaviour when Clementine was present: that was not in his character. He also flirted in a fatherly way with the Prime Minister's twenty-two-year-old daughter, Violet. But for all his married life, he remained innocent of adultery. 'He was not made that way,' a member of his family remarked. 'And anyway he was too busy chasing his ambitions.'

But Clementine was clearly nursing a grievance when she

told him of her suspicions little more than a year after their marriage. It prompted him to write:

> *Dearest it worries me vy much that you should seem to nurse such absolutely wild suspicions wh are so dishonouring to all the love & loyalty I bear you. . . . They are unworthy of you & me. And they fill my mind with feelings of embarrassment to wh I have been a stranger since I was a schoolboy . . . they depress me & vex me – & without reason.*
>
> *We do not live in a world of small intrigue, but of serious & important affairs. I could not conceive myself forming any other attachment than that to which I have fastened the happiness of my life . . . it offends my best nature that you should – against your true instinct – indulge small emotions & wounding doubts. You ought to trust me for I do not love & will never love any woman in the world but you . . .*

The two greatest domestic issues that threatened Asquith's ministry and even the stability of the nation were the Liberal struggle to get through Parliament a budget that would pay for the new welfare measures, and the restlessness of the wage-earners against working conditions, unemployment, and reductions in pay. The two were not unrelated, and both were set against the background of a world slump.

Lloyd George needed no less than £21 million extra to finance the Government's social plans, a sharp increase in naval expenditure, and sundry other needs, including – because of the tremendous increase in motor traffic – new roads. Tobacco and alcohol were easy targets, partly because brewers were thought of as *nouveaux riches* and were not respected members of society. But an increase in death duties and the introduction of land value duties and a supertax on annual incomes above £3,000 hit hard at the affluent.

A tremendous wailing arose from the shires; ancient back-woodsmen peers and barons who had not been to London, let alone to the House of Lords, for years, were persuaded to clamber into unaccustomed trains and enter the battle. Constitutionally, the Lords could refuse to pass into law any except fiscal bills. But now, after the Commons had passed the budget by a majority of 379 votes to 149, the Lords rejected it by 350 to 75. Asquith forthwith moved a resolution that the action of the Lords was a usurpation of the rights of the Commons and was therefore unconstitutional. This meant that there would be an immediate general election, the theme of which was inevitably the privileged and rich trying to evade taxation called for by the people: 'the People versus the Peers'.

This election cost the Conservatives about one hundred seats, and although the Liberal majority over the Conservatives remained narrow, they had the support of the Labour Party and others. In simple terms (and the constitutional situation was now becoming both critical and complex), the alternative to a veto bill to trim further the power of the House of Lords was the creation by the King, under pressure from Asquith, of several hundred peers all disposed towards the Liberal cause and capable of fighting off all efforts by the Conservative peers to halt the bill.

Under this pressure and the threat of a bill to replace the pressed House of Lords with a second chamber constituted on a non-hereditary basis, their lordships yielded and passed the budget without a division. Neither a mass-production line of peers nor a veto bill was eventually called for. After further bitter fighting and another general election, the teeth of the House of Lords were drawn, so that they could only delay and not throw out any bill from the Commons.

By this time (July 1911), Winston had long since moved to the Home Office, where he was fighting another battle – a battle that demanded of him all his discretion, determination and courage.

Winston's appointment dated from the general election of January 1910 and represented the reward not only for his contribution in bringing about another Liberal victory, but also for his work at the Board of Trade. He was clearly due for further promotion, and the position of Home Secretary provided it. Here he would be responsible for the police and prisons, for magistrates, courts, and legislation on criminal justice, for the fire service and control of immigration, and – especially during his term of office – for the maintenance of law and order.

Winston could expect trouble from the suffragettes, campaigning for votes for women, and he had plenty of it. But the number of strikes, and their size and violence, was unexpected. There had been few labour problems recently, but by the spring of 1910 he was forced to deal with them in abundance.

The first was in May at Newport in Monmouthshire, where non-strikers over a dispute were beaten up by a handful of strikers. The temperature rose rapidly, the local police and supporting police from outside could not keep control, and the mayor appealed to the Home Office for troops. These were not finally required, for after some ominous looting and violence, the strike petered out.

The next serious strike took place among miners in the Welsh Rhondda valley, a much larger and more widespread affair involving some thirty thousand men. Frustrated in their attacks on the collieries, some of the more violent men took to looting, especially in a village called Tonypandy. Here there were three days of violence, completely out of the control of the police, even when reinforcements were brought in from Swansea and Bristol.

Troops were called for again, and Winston authorized the despatch of 200 mounted Hussars and two companies of infantry. But he fully understood the seriousness of facing strikers with bayonets and cavalry instead of police truncheons, and held back the military while making a last appeal to the strikers. The appeal was ignored and the troops were sent, but by the time they arrived the rioting was over from sheer exhaustion, and most of the smashed shops were empty.

A storm of criticism, like strikers' brickbats, fell about the Home Secretary. There were three sources of protest: from those, like *The Times*, who thought Winston had been dilatory – 'Mr Churchill hardly seems to understand that an acute crisis has arisen, which needs decisive handling'; from others who thought he had been too lenient; and from some who declared it to be harsh and provocative to use bayonets and mounted soldiers against unarmed working men. The myth of Winston's violence born of this affair was perpetrated by Winston's critics, and for the rest of his life he was liable to have 'the Tonypandy scandal' hurled in his face by those who chose to see him as a bloodthirsty militarist.

There was more trouble, among the dockers this time, in June 1911, followed by a near-total railway strike. The dock strikes spread with alarming speed, inflamed by the refusal to raise intolerably low wages and the unprecedented heat of the summer, which made even rational discussion difficult. Winston had no alternative to sending in the troops, who camped in London parks and in full public view in provincial cities. The looting and rioting were particularly savage in Liverpool and Llanelli, where troops opened fire, killing a number of rioters.

Winston anticipated a 'grave upheaval':

> Serious crises have been in recent years, and very often lately, surmounted only by a narrow margin of safety, and now specially a new force has arisen in trades unionism, whereby the power of the old leaders has proved quite ineffective, and the sympathetic strike on a wide scale is prominent. Shipping, coal, railways, dockers etc etc are all uniting and breaking out at once . . .

Predictably, Winston's handling of the strike-ridden months during his term of office as Home Secretary was approved of by his own party, while the Conservatives protested that he had not been harsh enough and the Labour Party found him much too harsh. Moreover, for his part in another, merely local scene of violence, he was criticized for being too intrepid.

207

In December 1910 a gang of burglars was seen to be tunnelling into a jeweller's shop in the East End of London. Half a dozen police were alerted, and they closed in on the gang, who opened fire, killing three policemen and wounding two with their Mauser pistols. The burglars then escaped to a house in Sidney Street, where they locked themselves in, clearly intent on killing anyone who came near. The police appealed for troops to be called to the scene, their own revolvers being inadequate for what had turned into a military-style siege.

When all else failed, the crooks resorted to setting their house-fort on fire. Meanwhile, Winston could not resist the lure of whistling bullets and the excitement of danger. He and Eddie Marsh (armed with an umbrella) arrived with a police escort. By now reporters and photographers were present in abundance, but it was Winston and Eddie who claimed the best, and most dangerous, observers' position.

Winston did not remain a spectator for long. He soon assumed the position of commander in chief, and when the fire engines arrived he forbade them from doing their duty, judging it more sensible to let the murderers burn to death, which they did, than to risk a single fireman's life.

Eddie Marsh, unaccustomed to live bullets, later wrote, 'You can't imagine the extraordinary sensation it was to see a fusillade going on in a dim little London street – and still more to see the fire brigade standing by encouraging the burning house to burn.' Afterwards Eddie became the centre of conversation at every dinner table he attended. He was equally amused by being one of the subjects of a motion picture of the incident shown in the local theatres. It was headed 'Mr Churchill directing the operations', and was received with boos and catcalls from the Conservative cockney crowd.

While not actually booing him or calling out, 'Shoot him!', Winston's critics did feel, with some reason, that he had had no business there, subverting the police and fire officers. In the Commons, Arthur Balfour commented, 'He was, I understand, in military phrase, in what is known as the zone of fire – he and a photographer were both risking valuable lives. I understand what the photographer was doing, but what was the right honourable gentleman doing?'

Winston had always reckoned that, as an ex-prisoner himself, he enjoyed a special sympathy with criminals serving long sentences, particularly now that prisoners were better educated than in the past and so suffered more than their predecessors from want of stimulation.

On 20 July 1910, he told the House:

> We have to consider now that it is forty years since the Education Act of 1870 was passed, and that we have got a class of men in our prisons who need brain food of the most ordinary character. There have from time to time been occasional lectures given in the prisons, and a few months ago the Somerset Light Infantry had their band in Dartmoor Prison and it played to the convicts. It was an amazing thing the effect which was produced on all these poor people . . . I have been able to arrange with the Treasury for a small sum of money – only a hundred pounds a year – which will enable four lectures to be given a year in every convict prison.

Besides easing the lot of prisoners, amongst other prison reforms, he was determined to reduce the total number of prisoners. In 1910 there were 184,000 men and women serving prison sentences out of a total population of 42,000,000.* Many of these were serving terms for failure of payment of a fine, and no fewer than one-third were in for drunkenness. 'In the case of drunkenness,' Winston reasonably observed in the House, 'the enforcement of a fine is a far better

---

*Today's figures, which are considered grossly excessive, are 46,000 out of 56,000,000.

209

punishment than a committal to prison; for his release is very often celebrated by a prisoner but a fine effectively enforced means a period of temperance.'

As to wretches who were unable to pay a fine 'in default of having the money with them in their pockets', it was an unnecessary and injurious operation to pack them off to prison. 'The State loses its fine, the man goes to prison, perhaps for the first time. A shocking event.' Fingerprints are taken, and he is photographed and whisked off in a black maria just as if he had committed a capital offence! Why not give the fellow time to pay?

There were many doubts about this change of policy, especially as the deterrent effect would be reduced. But Winston pressed ahead, with the result that the numbers imprisoned for non-payment of fines fell in ten years from around 95,000 to 5,000. Another long-term reform effected during Winston's busy twenty months at the Home Office was an extension of the Children Act of 1908, intended to keep young people out of prison. During the debate on this new measure, Winston pointed to the rowdyism and vandalism of high-spirited undergraduates at the great universities, which led to promptly paid fines, and the humiliation and bad effects (and expense to the state) of a prison or Borstal sentence for working-class youngsters for the same offences. As a result of this measure the prison population under 21 years of age fell from around 12,000 in 1910 to about 4,000 ten years later.

Winston also reduced the prison population by introducing 'suspended sentences' for minor offences and the extension of probation for young people. More indirectly, criminality was reduced by his recommendations for aftercare for released prisoners.

One class of prisoner whose numbers he had no means of reducing was the extreme wing of the suffragette movement. By the time he was appointed to the Home Office, Winston had received much attention from these highly militant women intent on extending the vote to their sex by violent means and he had first-hand experience of their wish to go to prison to draw attention to themselves. The leaders of this long-drawn-out campaign were Emmeline Pankhurst and her daughters, Christabel and Sylvia. One of these daughters and a friend had been so troublesome at a meeting at which Winston was speaking that the police dragged them outside. The next morning they were fined. They refused to pay and were sentenced to a week in prison. Winston's offer to pay their fines was refused.

Winston's own views on extending the vote to women were quite clear. 'I am anxious to see women relieved in principle from a disability which is injurious to them whilst it is based on grounds of sex,' he once wrote to Henry Brailsford, the radical university lecturer and honorary secretary of the Conciliation Committee for Women's Suffrage. But as Home Secretary, responsible for law and order in the land, and as a private citizen, he was strongly opposed to the violence of the Pankhursts' campaign.

Clementine, too, supported the suffragist cause until the violent element got out of hand – and until she had had personal experience of its ruthlessness. Arriving at Bristol railway station with Winston in November 1909, they were greeted by the local Liberal hierarchy. But amongst them there lurked a suffragette with a horsewhip, which she attempted to use against Winston. In defending himself, he seized her wrist, and there was an unpleasant and dangerous scene as the woman countered by forcing him back to the edge of the platform. The train had just begun to gain momentum, and the strength of the woman's attack, supported by its surprise, seemed likely to push Winston on to the line. Clementine, separated from the struggling figures by a pile of luggage, clambered over it, seized her husband's coat-tails, and dragged him back just in time.

This sort of behaviour – the smashing of politicians' windows (a concrete slab landed within a few feet of Margot Asquith at dinner), the disruption of public assemblies – lost the suffragettes much sympathy, especially amongst women. After a particularly violent demonstration in Parliament Square, when the police lost their composure and counter-attacked vigorously, Winston became the target for even greater malevolence.

If women were most strongly opposed to the militant suffragettes, Mrs Pankhurst included in her ranks a number of men who were prepared to go to extremes. Brailsford could be intemperate, but a well-connected young man, Hugh Franklin, was plain violent. On 26 November 1910, at a meeting in Bradford, he heckled Winston throughout his speech and later attacked him physically on the return train to London. As he struck out with a whip, he shouted, 'Take that, you dirty cur!' He was sent to prison for six weeks, but that did not bother him in the least.

The suffragettes remained a thorn in the flesh of the Liberal Party until the Great War. 'We are getting into vy gt peril over Female Suffrage,' Winston wrote in December 1911. One trouble was that only sixty per cent (the property owners) of the male adult population had the vote anyway, and to impose on the electorate 8,000,000 women voters against the wishes of the people would have had a violent and disastrous effect. 'How can the PM [Asquith] honourably use the Parlt Act to force it upon the King, when he himself declared it to be a disastrous mistake?' Winston asked in the same letter to the Chief Government Whip, Lord Elibank.

In another anxious letter to Sir Edward Grey, the Foreign Secretary who was in favour of female suffrage, Winston wrote:

> It is because I am so deeply disturbed at the prospect I see ahead that I write to urge that an effort should be made to see whether we cannot come together on a referendum – men or women or both – I do not care. Your own honesty and candour will I am sure lead you to admit that the opinion of the country has never been tested on the subject.

The period in Britain's history between the death of the old Queen in 1901 and the outbreak of the Great War in the late summer of 1914 is popularly viewed as the golden sunset of a glorious imperial age of peace and splendour, when the arts and the art of living achieved a new height – an age of reform and contentment and patrician pleasures: balls in winter, parties on the lawn in summer, Diaghilev and the Russian Ballet . . . And at another social level, cotton workers in the north and cheerful cockneys in the south, off on cheap day returns to the seaside.

The truth was quite different. It is true that great social changes and improvements were set in train; there were great improvements in education and great achievements in all the arts, in medicine, and in the sciences. As Winston was one of the earliest to demonstrate, the motor car offered to the better-off marvellous mobility and freedom from the restrictions of the railway. Better education created the demand for better mass-circulation newspapers. All this is true, and this decade and a half revealed a wonderful new vitality lacking in the last fifteen years of Queen Victoria's reign. Clothes became less formal and stereotyped, and the previous hard dogma of the Church softened.

But this same period, which saw Winston rise from the back benches of the Commons to become one of the most prominent statesmen in the land, also witnessed much restlessness and violence that threatened the nation's stable structure. The country was not far distant from revolution in 1911 and 1912, and it is not wild speculation to imagine the reality of a working-class uprising if the Great War had not intervened. Who could have imagined in 1895 the extremes to which educated women were prepared to go – arson, violence, hunger-striking leading to force-feeding in prison, even fatal martyrdom?

Politics, which had been a mainly gentlemanly business before the Liberal renaissance, first intruded into social life and then was tarnished by violence at meetings and verbal abuse at a new low level in the Commons. There was also an alarming threat to peace in Europe, and as this grew Winston's political activities turned from social issues and stability at home to the defence of the nation and the empire.

15

'Your Father Has Just Offered Me the Admiralty'

On 31 May 1909, Goonie Churchill had her first child, John George. Her experiences were greatly comforting to Clementine, who was nervously expecting her own first child in two months' time. Goonie had gone out to dinner the previous evening, walked home and gone to bed as usual, to be awoken by 'a new sensation' at 2 a.m. Three hours later, after almost no pain, the baby was delivered.

Clementine did not have such an easy time with her baby, but a fine girl was born at home in Eccleston Square on 11 July 1909. Winston was thrilled and insisted on bathing baby Diana (as 'PK', or 'Puppy-Kitten', was christened) from a very early age. Clementine did not breast-feed the baby and felt run-down after the birth and in need of a rest. She found it at a house called Carpenters, which was on the estate of Crabbet Park at Southwater, near Brighton, the property of Wilfrid Scawen Blunt.

Blunt was a charming, immensely rich and talented man of 69, a considerable poet who had travelled widely in Arab countries and India and published many books, with titles like *Seven Golden Odes of Pagan Arabia* and *Satan Absolved*. Blunt was a close friend of Blanche Hozier's and had known Clementine since she was a child. He was very glad to offer her the hospitality of the house, then and many times in the future.

While Clementine was recuperating in the Sussex air, with her mother and her sister Nellie, Louis Blériot flew across the English Channel from Calais to Dover, an epochal feat at that time. Blunt noted in his diary (29 July) how pleased Victor Lytton's father would have been. 'He always maintained

214

forty years ago that the true solution to the flying problem lay in a machine which should be heavier, not lighter than air.'

The event was also seriously noted by Winston, and it was to influence his ministerial policy in scarcely more than two years' time. He could spare the time to visit Clementine only once or twice during her stay, but from London (where he was in nominal charge of the baby) he sent frequent reports on PK's progress. 'The nurse is rather inclined to glower at me as if I was a tiresome interloper,' he complained. 'I missed seeing her take her bath this morning. But tomorrow I intend to officiate!'

Winston was further delighted when Clementine gave birth again on 28 May 1911. Clementine had long since decided it was a boy ('Chumbolly') this time, and so it was. He had to be, and was, christened Randolph. This time, Clementine nursed the baby herself and wrote from London to Winston at Blenheim:

> *I am very happy here, contemplating the beautiful Chumbolly who grows more darling & handsome every hour, & puts on weight with every meal; so that soon he will be a little round ball of fat. Just now I was kissing him, when catching sight of my nose he suddenly fastened upon it & began to suck . . .*

Clementine felt the full strength of mother-love for her children while they were still babies, and had yet to learn of her change of attitude when they became children.

To the sorrow of Winston and Clementine, the next baby miscarried, and after that she enjoyed a rest from child-bearing for a while, no doubt on doctor's orders. Winston's attachment to family life and his unselfconscious and public affection for his children at a time when the nursery quarters and the drawing room were still well separated, surprised many people, especially those who saw him as a political ogre. Considering his own deprivation of parental affection as a small child, this behaviour becomes less surprising in a man who was naturally affectionate and had a warm heart.

*

Winston's involvement with the Royal Navy was one of the most important factors in his political life. We go back to 1907 in order to trace its origins. In his days at the Colonial Office, and three years before George V succeeded to the throne, King Edward VII wrote a letter from the royal yacht off Toulon in which he stated, 'I am watching your political career with great interest. My one wish is that the great qualities you possess may be turned to good account & that your services to the State may be appreciated.'

A week or two later, Winston received an invitation to stay with the King where he was spinning out the end of the winter at Biarritz. Winston arrived on 19 April 1907, and was not surprised to find himself in interesting company. This included the King's and his own friend Ernest Cassel, together with Cassel's rather mousey daughter, Maud, and her extremely lively daughter, Edwina Ashley.

But the figure who stood out in the King's party at the Hotel du Palais was an admiral of whom Winston had heard much but had never met. John Arbuthnot Fisher was First Sea Lord, at present carrying through radical reform of the service he loved but knew to be locked in outmoded practices, manned by too many sinecurists and traditionalists who objected to change as strongly as any deeply entrenched senior civil servant. Thanks to 'Jacky' Fisher and a few other 'brains' in the service, some of the worst practices (like throwing overboard shells for gunnery on manoeuvres because firing stained the brass) had already been dealt with, and Fisher had startled the world the previous year by building in twelve months a revolutionary battleship, HMS *Dreadnought*, which was bigger, faster and more heavily gunned than any other in the world.

Fisher had a modest background, loathed toadies and had advanced up the navy's promotion ladder without social influence or wealth [wrote his authorized biographer]. Fisher's life cause was the Royal Navy, which he regarded almost as a branch of his beloved

Church of England. As a great reformer, parables and Biblical quotations and aphorisms rattled like shrapnel amidst the thunder of his naval guns, firing at failure and defects in the service or despatching spine-chilling threats at the future enemy. 'The Germans will smell hell when they find us at Cuxhaven!' he once predicted. And of dilatoriness in building submarines, 'Give peace in our time, O Lord!' for this is the old, old story! 'We strain at the gnat of Perfection, and swallow the camel of unreadiness.'

Fisher's vision was far beyond the range of a twelve-inch naval shell. He not only backed the submarine but prophesied the giant battleship-sized submarines of the 1970s and 1980s. He advocated converting the Navy from coal (home produced) power to oil power, which had to be brought in by sea: 'We will build a pipeline under the English Channel.' This scheme, rejected during Fisher's time, later became the 'invention', known as 'Pluto', of Lord Mountbatten's staff for the D-Day invasion in 1944. Fisher was also the first to back the creation of a fleet air arm soon after Blériot's Channel flight.

   Prophet, eccentric, conspirator, originator, a charmer and inspirer, but an unforgiving enemy, Fisher attracted admirers as he repelled those who distrusted him and his devious practices. Thanks to his work before and during his term of office as First Sea Lord, the Royal Navy was twice as efficient as the moribund, top-heavy service upon which the nation had depended for its security in Victorian times. His energy appeared limitless. At an age when many people dream of retirement, he would be up at 5 a.m. and would say his prayers in Westminster Abbey on the way to the Admiralty, which he would reach before the cleaning ladies. He loved the company of young women, could dance them to a standstill and was never short of a mistress. His affair with the Duchess of Hamilton was as long-lived as King Edward VII's with Mrs Keppel.

   Although Fisher hated war as strongly as Winston, he was

217

not perhaps the ideal delegate for the 1907 Hague Peace Conference intended to humanize modern warfare. 'You might as well talk of humanizing hell!' he exclaimed at one point. 'War is the essence of violence. Moderation in war is imbecility.' In total, no two men in Britain had more enemies than Fisher and Winston. But they were almost handcrafted for one another, and the relationship that developed was warm and portentous.

Fisher was the first to arrive at Biarritz and had already seen the King. When Fisher and Winston met, they were surprised that they had never done so before.

> We talked all day long and far into the nights [Winston later recounted]. He told me wonderful stories of the Navy and of his plans – all about *Dreadnoughts*, all about submarines, all about the new education scheme for every branch of the Navy, all about big guns, and splendid Admirals and foolish miserable ones, and Nelson and the Bible . . .

Within a few hours, Fisher had become Winston's naval 'teacher'. The King watched them together with amusement. 'I call them the chatterers,' he noted in his diary. Later in the same year, Winston turned up without an appointment at the Admiralty.

> I was whirled off [to the Ritz] [Fisher wrote]. I had two hours with him . . . He is an enthusiastic friend certainly! . . . He said his penchant for me was that I painted with a big brush! and was violent! I reminded him that even 'The kingdom of Heaven suffereth violence, and the violent take it by force.'

On Asquith's accession to the premiership in 1908, Fisher told him that he would like to have Winston at the Admiralty as First Lord. But he went to the Board of Trade and ever after regretted that he had not pushed for the Admiralty, where, he was confident, he would have worked splendidly in harness with Fisher. Instead, their new friendship was dented when Winston, like Lloyd George, fought against a further increase in funds for the Navy in 1908–1909, preferring the defence money to be diverted to the social services. In the end, Fisher got his extra dreadnoughts anyway, and for once forgiving in victory, Fisher suggested facetiously that two of the battleships should be named HMS *Winston* and HMS *Churchill,* the other two HMS *Lloyd* and HMS *George.*

Friendship was re-established late in 1911, when, ironically, Fisher was no longer at the Admiralty, having resigned in a characteristically heated conflict with his sharpest enemies. On Fisher's resignation as First Sea Lord, he was replaced by Sir Arthur ('Tug') Wilson, an unmarried admiral as hard and unyielding as the oak of one of Nelson's three-deckers. Loved and feared by the lower deck, he would have been more at home in the Napoleonic navy than in this era of almost bewildering scientific and technical advances. His civil chief was Reginald McKenna, a fine administrator who played the part of the arrogant and unbending patrician too keenly for the comfort of some of his contemporaries. Wilson and McKenna were eleven years older than Winston, but the three men shared the same rung of the political promotion ladder.

This, then, was the pair at the Admiralty in control of the nation's affairs in the spring of 1911 when a serious international crisis occurred. At this time, Britain's ally, France, was still busily colonizing North Africa. An expeditionary force had been sent to Fez as a preliminary move towards the annexation of all Morocco. But this process was militarily, and politically, threatened by the arrival at the port of Agadir of a German gunboat. The Germans said this was 'to protect our interests'. The French thought otherwise: they judged that the Germans were making a preliminary move towards cutting off a large slice of the cake for themselves. The British, already in a state of deep anxiety about the ever-growing strength of the German fleet, suspected that it was a first move by the Kaiser towards acquiring a naval base in North Africa – which could threaten Britain's Atlantic and Mediterranean trade in time of war.

In Britain the alarm spread quickly, fanned by the press. Winston became involved in the crisis when he learned at a party in the garden of 10 Downing Street that the police, who were under the jurisdiction of the Home Office, were responsible for guarding the nation's naval cordite reserves. This was news, and shocking news, to the Home Secretary. Just 'a few constables,' remarked Sir Edward Henry to Winston over his cup, 'that's all we have.' As Henry was Chief Commissioner of Police, Winston had to take this astonishing statement seriously.

On returning to the Home Office, he learned that McKenna and Admiral Wilson were both absent in the midst of this crisis, Wilson shooting grouse in Scotland. 'But you must at once send a contingent of Royal Marines to guard this treasure,' Winston told the officer in charge of things at the Admiralty. The officer refused: not his responsibility. So Winston raised the telephone to the War Office.

The Secretary of State for War was Winston's old friend Richard Burdon Haldane. The Boer War had exposed the many shortcomings of the Army, and Haldane had been given the task of restoring its efficiency and morale. His reforms had transformed the service. Besides serving in Asquith's ministry, he was a contemporary and close friend of the Prime Minister, and while he did not share Asquith's burning ambition and admitted that he, Haldane, had 'no attractive presence' and 'a bad voice', he was quite as clever as Asquith, even if he was big and unhandsome.

Haldane responded at once to Winston's appeal, and within a few hours the two depots housing 'the teeth of the Navy' were secure from sabotage. But that was only the first chapter in the story that was to transform the senior service and the career of Winston Churchill.

The Times meanwhile investigated the state of the Fleet if Germany had decided to go to war over the Agadir business, which many people feared. This newspaper discovered that the divisions of the Home Fleet were either in southern Ireland, had only nucleus crews on board, or had sent their crews off on four days' leave.

> What a chance for our friends across the water! [exclaimed Haldane]. Supposing the [German] High Seas Fleet . . . had gone straight for Portland, preceded by a division of destroyers, and after a surprise night torpedo attack had brought the main fleet into action at dawn against our ships without steam, without coal, and without crews!

Winston, backing him up, confessed to Lloyd George, 'I cannot help feeling uncomfortable about the Admiralty. They are so cocksure, *insouciant* and apathetic.' The post mortem on this crisis revealed that the Admiralty possessed no written war plans or a war staff and that while the Army had contingency plans fully worked out to send six divisions to France to support the French left flank in the event of war, and the Navy knew this, the Navy had no plans to convey them across the Channel and, further, had no intention of doing so. The Navy had long since made up its mind that the Army's role was to defend the homeland, not to allow itself to be wastefully swallowed up in some Continental war.

Asquith could hardly credit all this, and Haldane threatened to resign unless the Navy began to put its house in order. No one could deny that Fisher had worked mightily for the Navy and had carried out wonderful reforms, had built revolutionary new ships, had improved the quality of the personnel, and had concentrated the Fleet in home waters where the real danger lay, instead of continuing to allow it to be scattered about the world, 'showing the flag' from Tierra del Fuego to the Yangtse River. But now the Admiralty was feeling the absence of his reforming zeal. Something had to be done, Asquith decided.

Towards the end of September 1911, with the Agadir crisis

close to solution but the nation still in a half-belligerent, half-fearful state, Winston was invited to stay at Balmoral. He did not enjoy the same easy relationship with George V as he had with his father. He found him, by contrast with Edward VII, stiff, stuffy and humourless, and his wife, Queen Mary, an equally strong contrast with the outgoing, friendly Queen Alexandra, whose tinkling laughter so readily cheered up the solemnity of the royal residences.

Nor did Winston find the rest of the company at this hideous Highland mock-castle either stimulating or much fun. 'Unexciting' was the word he used to Clementine to describe his fellow guests. There were a number of Connaughts, the Duke being the immensely dull third son of Queen Victoria; Sir Francis Hopwood, with whom Winston had already crossed swords; and Dr Francis Laking, the royal physician, who took advantage of the occasion to remind Winston that he had helped to bring Clementine into the world.

'It would be jolly' if she were there, he had told Clementine. But it was not customary for ministers' wives to be invited too, and she remained not far away at Airlie Castle with her family. For Winston, the high point of his visit was the arrival of his new red Napier car. He was inordinately proud of this fast machine, which (to Clementine's dismay) had cost over £600. Soon after its arrival, he left Balmoral and drove off, as usual inaccurately and too fast, along the undulating roads and through the beautiful scenery of this part of Scotland, relishing the Napier's power and handling. Clementine, remembering his unpunctuality, had warned him that luncheon at Airlie, where her grandmother ruled with demonic rigidity, was 'at 1:30 *to the second by Greenwich time*'. Here he thankfully greeted his family, spent the night, and then on the morning of 27 September motored off in the Napier again to stay with the Asquiths.

Ever since Winston had confided to her that McKenna was going to be moved from the Admiralty, Clementine had known that this appointment was Winston's heart's desire and that he hoped this visit to the Prime Minister would settle the matter. She had been invited too, but at the last minute decided that she might inhibit the proceedings and remained at Airlie Castle.

Winston prefers to drive alone rather than with his wife, who tends to fret if the speedometer approaches thirty mph. In the beautiful autumn sunshine he makes short work of the journey, and we can imagine him at the wheel as Archerfield, his destination, comes into sight. It is a beautiful, enormous Adam house, lent by Asquith's brother-in-law, Frank Tennant, on the breathtakingly beautiful coast of East Lothian. Winston drives more slowly down the long, winding, tree-flanked drive, still in full leaf, which leads to the house. Beyond are the gardens leading to the private golf course, which for the Prime Minister is one of the great charms of the place. (In fact, as Winston knows, so keen is Asquith to make the fullest use of his holiday home, that he takes a sleeper train from London on Friday evening, returning on the night train on Sunday.) And beyond again is the limitless twinkling blue of the Forth estuary.

The first to greet him, almost before the car comes to a halt, is Asquith's daughter Violet, a tall, elegant, willowy figure with a welcoming smile on her face. She knows why he is here and has already spoken to her father in his favour.

'Dear Winston, how lovely to see you!' Violet would have welcomed him. 'You must come at once for tea – outside on this beautiful day.'

On the terrace at the back of the house, overlooking the water, Margot and her husband are already drinking tea. Margot hastens to kiss Winston, and Asquith rises to greet him warmly. 'Ah, good. Time for a round before dinner.'

Winston is notoriously uneven with his clubs, sometimes driving far and with considerable accuracy, while at other times, when distracted by a thought or something a fellow player says, the skill with his hands and arms dissolves. On this visit, Violet recalls later that at the ninth hole in one round, he asked her the name of a shrub whose orange berries intrigued him. She told him it was called buckthorn, 'the olive of the north'.

*He rose like a trout to the fly of any phrase and his
attention was immediately arrested and deflected from
the game* [Violet wrote]. *'The olive of the north –
that's good. The buckthorn of the south – that's
not so good' – and during the remaining holes he
rang the changes on every possible combination and
permutation of this meagre theme, which took his
mind and eye completely off the ball. My father was
intensely amused, and gratified. He crowed in triumph
at luncheon. 'Winston was four up at the turn but once
he heard about the "olive of the north" he never hit
another ball and lost the game.'*

On the second day, Winston is told that Haldane is coming
over from his house at Cloan. This is bad news. Haldane must
know that the Prime Minister will make up his mind about
the Admiralty in the next day or two, and Haldane, having
cleaned up the Army, is bent on doing the same job for the
Navy. And he is a very close family friend of the Asquiths'.
Later, Haldane wrote:

*I drove over to Archerfield as soon as I had got to
Cloan. As I entered the approach I saw Winston
Churchill standing at the door. I divined that he had
heard of possible changes and had come down at once
to see the Prime Minister.*

*It was as I thought. Churchill was importunate
about going himself to the Admiralty from the Home
Office. He had told Asquith that the First Lord must
be in the Commons. As I was by now in the Lords
this looked like a difficulty . . . Obviously Churchill
had been pressing Asquith hard . . .*

Winston, as temporary host, greets his rival warmly, ensuring
that Haldane's car is taken to the motor house. Haldane
has driven himself, enjoying handling a motor as much as
Winston.

'Are you pleased with your Mercedes, Dick?' Winston

might have asked him as a lead to talking about his own car.

'Yes, very. Fast and reliable, and I've had very few punctures considering what a heavy car it is.'

'And you don't find the left drive a nuisance?'

'No, not really. And I saved £300 buying it at Stuttgart when I was in Germany watching the manoeuvres.'

Their hostess is approaching down the hall; Winston only just has time to boast about his Napier, and Haldane has none to show his interest.

The weather is still warm and clear enough to have tea on the terrace. Violet is picking some late roses and waves to the new arrival, while the three men set about their favourite occupation, talking politics. Margot pours the tea, no doubt thinking with amusement that it would scarcely be possible to find three men of such different appearance – Winston still so youthful and puckish in spite of his receding hair and bald patch and slight paunch; Haldane almost monstrously fat, in a heavy black suit, his puckered face constantly changing in expression, clever wide-set eyes darting from one to the other of his companions as he talks about the Army in a rather high-pitched voice; and her husband, looking so handsome and young – he was 57 two weeks ago – his face scarcely lined, and with a full head of hair even if it has been grey for some years.

It would be difficult to find a greater concentration of brains amongst three men, Margot also muses; but then, she is scarcely ever with men who are not exceptionally clever, thank goodness.

After spending the afternoon discussing the naval crisis, without reference to the imminent vacancy at the Admiralty, Haldane rises from the table in his immense bulk (he has eaten even more cake than Winston). 'I must be gone, Prime Minister, but I'll be back tomorrow as you suggested.'

Margot and Asquith accompany him back to his car, while Winston remains at the table with Violet. They can hear through the house with its open doors the sound of Haldane's Mercedes starting and then the crunch of its tyres on the gravel. For once, conversation is constrained between them. Winston longs to confide in Violet his doubts and puzzlement about the avoidance of the subject of the succession at the Admiralty – no getting down to brass tacks until the next day. And Violet longs to hear what has just transpired between the three men; perhaps she will learn later from her step-mother, who is told all. They talk instead about roses – the picked roses lying on the table, hybrid tea roses, floribundas, the climbers (glancing at the second, muted flowering of the Gloire de Dijon) above them on the house, and the roses Winston once grew in India when he was a subaltern.

Then Asquith reappears, demanding instantly a round of golf: 'Come along you two, another threesome.'

At dinner that evening, as usual the wine flows as freely as the conversation and is of the same high quality. Although himself very fond of drink, Winston no doubt reflects, not for the first time, how really heavy drinkers press their friends to excess as a comfort and an antidote to their own guilt. But the trouble with the Prime Minister is that, increasingly, others have to cover up for his inebriation in the House of Commons. 'On Thursday night the PM was vy bad: & I squirmed with embarrassment,' Winston had divulged to Clementine earlier in the year. 'He could hardly speak: & many people noticed his condition. . . . It is an awful pity, & only the freemansonry of the House of Commons prevents a scandal.' That night, Winston recalls, he and some friends had only just managed to get him away before he would have had to speak on a subject so complex that he would have been completely lost.

On this night at Archerfield, after Margot and Violet have left the table, the brandy goes to and fro across the table, with Winston taking half as much as his host and adding water each time. The talk is all of the German threat, and Asquith's contributions steadily become more hesitant and slurred. As his head falls and his breathing becomes stertorous and steady, Winston slips away. The butler is well practised in dealing with this situation, Winston has observed

226

in the past: an 'accidental' knocking against his chair, some loud removal of plates by the parlourmaid. . . .

Having learned of the expected time of Haldane's arrival the next day, Winston happens to find himself close to the front door as the Mercedes races down the drive. And he finds it agreeable to recognize rather less warmth in the minister's greeting. 'Well, Winston, still here, I see.'

'It's such a jolly place that I couldn't resist the PM's extended invitation,' he might have retorted.

Today it is so warm, with scarcely a breath of wind, that Margot orders a cold lunch on the terrace, with plenty of pickle for Winston and a large cold ham to satisfy her other guest. Asquith is late joining them, and when he does appear is in a rage. 'Those wretched Italians – it's just as we expected. They've declared war on Turkey this morning, and Sir Rennell Rodd* has just telegraphed that their navy's on its way to Tripoli.'

Margot asks, 'What does this mean, Henry?'

'It means that those abominable curs, those ice-cream vendors, are taking over Cyrenaica and Tripolitania. And Turkey will fight them.'

Luncheon proceeds in a subdued mood for a while, until the hock cheers everyone up (Violet drinks lemonade) and Winston asks what Asquith intends to do with the Mediterranean Fleet – putting in before he has time to answer: 'I would immediately put it on a war footing and send it on manoeuvres off the North African coast.'

'Well, Prime Minister,' Haldane interjects, 'I am sure you would not allow such a provocative proceeding.'

At the end of the meal, Asquith asks his wife to order coffee for two in his study and then leads his two guests inside. As he opens the door to his study, he says – with a twinkle in his blue eyes – 'I'm leaving you two alone for a

*The British Ambassador in Rome.

227

while so that you can settle between you who's going to the Admiralty.'

The two men laugh uneasily at Asquith's order, but settle down with their coffee and brandy. The proceedings will be conducted with friendliness and dignity, as the Prime Minister knows.

Winston plays his top card first. 'I really think it is out of the question, Dick, that the Admiralty's affairs can be conducted at this critical time from the Upper House.'

Haldane takes a time lighting his cigar. Winston's is already well alight.

'It is perfectly possible and in many ways has advantages,' he replies at length. 'If we can have the Prime Minister in the Upper House, as we frequently have – why not the head of a department? And remember, Winston, the public know me as someone who has cleared up the Army's augean stables, and would trust me to do the same for the Navy. And you – you're seen as an Army man – and a very gallant one; and you once told me you *hated* the sea!'

They both laugh at this. The smoke of cigars fills the room.

'I truly believe, Dick,' Winston replies, 'that the Navy will be more suspicious of you than of me.'

'Why do you say that, pray?'

'Because the admirals will be suspicious of your broom that has cleaned up the Army, and they will be offended at not having their own broom. Or, to switch metaphors, it'll be for them like washing in someone else's bath water.'

Haldane then makes an interesting suggestion, and as an advocate for many years, his timing is perfect. 'I believe that I can do all that is necessary at the Admiralty within twelve months. Then, my dear Winston, if you could act as caretaker, so to speak, at the War Office for that time, you would then switch to your heart's desire at the Admiralty.'

'And you?' Winston is clearly puzzled, at least until he hears Haldane reveal that the Prime Minister has already offered him the Lord Chancellorship, and he would take up the offer in one year's time rather than now.

Winston is grinning like a mischievous but highly clever boy and shakes his head. 'I never have heard you at the bar, Dick, but I am sure you are a brilliant advocate. But you can't trick me with your cunning compromise.'

'May I put this to the PM all the same?' Haldane eases himself slowly from his armchair.

'How can I refuse you this privilege?'

Later in the afternoon, Winston is walking between the flowerbeds as Asquith accompanies Haldane back into the house for the War Minister's departure. 'With all due respect to your admirable Papa, Violet,' Winston exclaims, 'but they do look rather like a pair of music hall comics at the end of their act.'

Violet laughs. 'Was it a good act, do you think? Is the crowd cheering?'

'It is *not*,' Winston replies on a serious note. 'It is left thoroughly uneasy.' It is the first reference, albeit oblique, to the subject uppermost in both their minds.

Later in the afternoon, Asquith invites Winston – but significantly, not his daughter – for a round of golf. It is a keenly fought game, conducted in near, and unaccustomed, silence. They really start to talk in earnestness only on the way back from the eighteenth hole.

'I wonder,' Asquith begins, with a note in his voice of confidentiality with which Winston is familiar. 'I wonder, Winston, if you would like to go to the Admiralty?'

'Indeed I would,' Winston replies without any hesitation, his heart lifting as high as the wheeling seagulls above them.

Violet is just finishing tea in the drawing room with her stepmother when the two men arrive back. Looking up, she sees in Winston's face 'a radiance like the sun'.

> 'Will you come out for a walk with me – at once?' he asked [Violet recalled]. 'You don't want tea?' 'No, I don't want tea.' We were hardly out of the house when he said to me with grave but shining eyes: 'I don't want tea – I don't want anything – anything

in the world. Your father has just offered me the Admiralty.'

In late September, night comes early in Scotland. As the two friends walk down towards the sea the flashing from a lighthouse begins, and at the same time, like a theatrical celebration of Winston's new command, two great battleships come into view, slipping out to sea from their base at Rosyth up the Forth. War threatens and Winston is in command of the greatest fleet in the world.

16

Shaking Up the Admiralty

After Violet and Margot Asquith, the first women to hear Winston's highly confidential news that he was going to the Admiralty were his wife and mother. Clementine, who guarded secrets with total security, was told everything in detail soon after he arrived at Airlie Castle from Archerfield on 29 September. As he had exclaimed to Violet the previous evening, 'Look at the people I have had to deal with so far – judges and convicts! This is a big thing – the biggest thing that has come my way – the chance I should have chosen before all others.' Then, as if anyone who knew him could doubt it: 'I shall pour into it everything I've got.' Clementine was ecstatically happy for him, and in her practical, down-to-earth way, was soon enquiring about the size of Admiralty House (which came with the appointment), the number of servants they would need to run it, and other housewifely details.

To Jennie he was more circumspect, confining himself at first to the news that something really big had come his way. 'You thrill me with curiosity. Is it a change of office?' she asked. 'I hope a good one . . . I am longing to see something of you and hear all your news.'

When at last the announcement was made of the changes in Asquith's cabinet, Winston was inundated with congratulations from his friends and family, with Sunny Marlborough and the F. E. Smiths being especially excited and pleased for him. Eddie Marsh was delighted for Winston's sake, though it meant an even more ruthless working routine for him – 'We have made a new commandment,' he wrote. '"The seventh day is the Sabbath of the First Lord, on it thou shalt do all manner of work."'

The part of the press that by now automatically condemned

231

everything Winston said and did was predictably hostile to the appointment. *The Spectator* advised its readers that 'he has not the loyalty, the dignity, the steadfastness, and the good sense which make an efficient head of a great office. He must always be living in the limelight, and there is no fault more damning in an administrator.'

The *Standard* sounded a cautionary note:

> Mr Gladstone once defined Lord Randolph Churchill as 'a young man in a hurry'. Lord Randolph's son is also a young man in a very great hurry to do striking things, and to give the world the fullest opportunity for appreciating his remarkable talents. Absorbed in these preoccupations he cannot slacken the pace to consider other people's susceptibilities.

The romance and challenge of Winston's new appointment suited his temperament perfectly. 'These were great days,' he recalled. 'From dawn to midnight, day after day, one's whole mind was absorbed by the fascination and novelty of the problems which came crowding forward. And all the time there was a sense of power to act, to form, to organize: all the ablest officers in the Navy standing ready, loyal and eager, with argument, guidance, information . . .'

The visual grandeur of the Fleet, on manoeuvres or even at anchor, now moved him as deeply as that of the Army on exercises with its great sweeping movements of cavalry and the infantry in all its colourful glory.

> *I recall vividly my first voyage from Portsmouth to Portland, where the Fleet lay. A grey afternoon was drawing to a close. As I saw the Fleet for the first time drawing out of the haze a friend reminded me of 'that far-off line of storm-beaten ships on which the eyes of the Grand Army had never looked', but which had in their day 'stood between Napoleon and*

232

the dominion of the world'. In Portland Harbour the
yacht lay surrounded by the great ships; the whole
harbour was alive with the goings and comings of
launches and small craft of every kind, and as night
fell ten thousand lights from sea and shores sprang
into being and every masthead twinkled as the ships
and squadrons conversed with one another . . .*

Winston soon revealed his merits and faults to the Admiralty
staff at the levels that associated directly with him. They
found his drive and energy, his power to work and his
powers of expression, his talent for rapid analysis and com-
prehension, all on a different level to those of anybody they
had previously worked with. On the other hand, his aggres-
siveness and truculence, his denial of any other judgement
than his own when once he had made it, were hard to bear.
Because they seldom or never saw him socially, they had no
conception of his charm and social conversational powers.

McKenna before him had been a real Admiralty man,
backing his admirals in all contention, defending them
against outside pressure. For example, if they did not want
a naval war staff he was certainly not going to impose one
on them. Aloof and patrician he may have been, but he was
one of them all the same. Winston clearly was not. He had
come to stir up trouble, *that* soon became clear. He wanted
to change things, 'make a splash', dig into everything.

The function of the political head of the Royal Navy had
no clear terms of reference, and the depth of enquiry by First
Lords into the multitude of functions of the service varied,
but customarily did not go very deep. Admirals could be
trusted, McKenna would have said. The First Lord's chief

---

*From Admiral Alfred Thayer Mahan's *The Influence of Sea Power
upon the French Revolution and Empire, 1793–1812*, published
in 1892.

responsibility was to represent the service in Parliament and ensure its efficient running. McKenna and his two predecessors had stirred up little or no mud at the Admiralty, which made the arrival of Winston even more of an unwelcome shock. Suddenly in their midst was a young man who went to sea with the Fleet, who examined dockyards and depots, ratings' rations, and standards of gunnery at first hand (operating the controls himself), and who questioned personnel at all levels, asking ordinary seamen what they thought of their officers and asking junior officers what they thought of their superiors.

The ever-alert German Naval Attaché reported back to base from London: 'The sea-officers of the British Navy are often enraged against Mr Churchill . . . for the youthful, civilian Churchill, on his frequent visits to the Fleet and dockyards, puts on the air of a military superior. Through his curt behaviour he offends the older officers . . . And thus, according to many, through his lack of tact he injures discipline by his ambition for popularity with the lower ranks . . .'

He had not been in office for twelve months before he was giving wireless instructions to the commanders in chief at sea from Whitehall, and 'on the return of the ships to harbour he lectured to the flag officers on how the manoeuvres should have been conducted, and this even before the Umpire had completed his report!'

Wherever he went through the Fleet, Winston left a trail of hurt feelings and resentment at his abrupt manner and his arrogance. If he had been a civilian politely anxious to learn, it would not have mattered much; it is always pleasing and flattering to pass on specialized knowledge. But here was an ex-Hussar subaltern with a reputation as a show-off who was antagonizing his most senior officers and was always throwing his weight about on the decks of His Majesty's men of war. It was not a formula for popularity, but that was not a consideration in Winston's mind. He wished to learn and then reform, regardless of anyone's feelings, and with the speed of one of Fisher's new battle-cruisers.

It has also to be said that Winston impressed a number of

the less hidebound junior officers, partly because his suspicions about the usefulness of officers rose in ratio with their age. Admiral Sir William James recalls that, when he was Gunnery Lieutenant of the Home Fleet flagship in 1912, he and his fellow junior officers learned with interest that Winston was coming to sea with them to watch night-firing practice:

> *His curiosity about the service for which he was responsible* [the Admiral wrote] *seemed to the older officers almost indecent. They had no intention of putting themselves out when he came on board.*
>
> *After the night firing was completed, I invited our visitor to the wardroom. It was now past midnight and we found only a sprinkling of officers who had been concerned with the night firing. We sat down by the fire and Churchill began to pepper me with questions about our system of control and what steps we were taking to improve the performance of the guns and searchlights. The wardroom gradually filled, and soon a large circle of officers was listening intently to the discussion, into which Churchill soon drew many of those who had hitherto avoided him.*

'Jacky' Fisher was the man who was to figure, through good days and bad days, in Winston's first years with the Navy. The strength of his influence on the course of the First Lord and the Navy during this period cannot be exaggerated. Between their first meeting at Biarritz with King Edward and the mutual distancing of the two men when Winston opposed the high naval estimates of 1908–1909, the politician and the sailor were writing to one another about the Navy: for Winston it was like a correspondence course in the structure and future of the service. Since then Fisher had retired, as usual amidst the rumble of thunder, to live in Switzerland, and the two men had been out of touch with one another. Now, within a day of his installation at the Admiralty, Winston wrote, 'I want to see you vy much.

When am I to have that pleasure? You have but to indicate your convenience & I will await you at the Admiralty.'

Fisher's reply from Lucerne was prompt and encouraging:

> *You have 'the desire of your heart' I think getting to the Admiralty, and I now feel free to be with you again which of course is a pleasure as I don't forget past days which proved we had views in common and mutual regard!* You were very good to me! *and I used to enjoy my many lunches and dinners with you at Bolton Street! Well, dear old Cassel sent me a note that you had been enquiring about me so I sent him a telegram to say I would meet you . . .*

Winston would have dearly liked to have Fisher as First Sea Lord, but he recognized the political difficulties after Jacky's acrimonious departure. It was not the time to reopen old wounds, and Winston had to be content with as close communication and consultation as could be arranged. He did not lack Fisher's advice, first on appointments. Fisher had approved of and promoted young officers with brains and enterprise, searching always for those who shared his enthusiasm for work and had radical new ideas.

Among these were men like Sir John Jellicoe and Prince Louis of Battenberg, both of whom had worked closely with Fisher on the conception of the *Dreadnought* battleship. Fisher saw Jellicoe as the future Nelson when war came, and he admired the King's German-born cousin. 'Battenberg,' Fisher told Winston, 'is *ideal* for First Sea Lord – he has to perfection the German faculty of organizing a great Naval Staff and in debates at the Committee of Imperial Defence [CID] you will find him incomparable.'

Winston did not follow all the recommendations at once, but every name Fisher recommended was noted with five stars in his mental assessment. For instance he replaced Admiral Arthur ('Tug') Wilson as First Sea Lord with Admiral Sir Francis Bridgeman, who looked a more malleable officer and was in favour of the creation of a naval staff, and he made Battenberg Second Sea Lord. Captain Mark Kerr, an able enough officer, was passed over for the youngest and most brilliant admiral in the Navy, David Beatty, who had first drawn attention to himself in a most appropriate manner by throwing Winston a bottle of champagne from his Nile gunboat. Beatty was appointed Winston's naval secretary.

At first, Winston's appointment to the Admiralty made little difference to Clementine's daily routine. In spite of the nursemaid, she had much of the final responsibility for the two infant children. She had persuaded Winston that they could not yet afford to live in the Admiralty, so they remained in Eccleston Square. On most nights they either gave dinner parties or were out with friends and professional associates, especially the Asquiths, the F. E. Smiths, Jack and Goonie, and Ernest Cassel in his enormous mansion, Brook House, on Park Lane. In winter, they sometimes spent weekends in London, especially that first winter of 1911–12, to accommodate Winston's seven-day working week. But at other seasons they usually stayed in the country, often at Salisbury Hall with Jennie and George and at Blenheim with Sunny.

Horse-racing did not in the least attract Clementine, disapproving as she did of gambling and 'the racing crowd', but she took up hunting to fill in the time when Winston was away from London, which was much more frequent than when he had been at the Home Office. At first, Sunny Marlborough gave her guidance and looked after her:

> *I have just come back from a long day's hunting* [she wrote to Winston]. *It was the greatest fun – Sunny took charge of me and gave me a lead over the stone walls. We found at once, and had a lovely run over the vale. Sunny was most kind . . . We went over some quite big places. I took all the fences after Sunny . . .*

It was at the end of the next month after this letter, and after much more hunting, that Clementine had her miscarriage. It seems probable that it was brought on by this unaccustomed hard exercise – just as Winston's own premature birth had been induced by Jennie's hunting. Clementine seemed at first to get over this quite well, while experiencing the awful anticlimax of failure. 'It is so strange to have all the same sensations that one has after a real Baby, but with no result,' she wrote to Winston.

But later, and for some months, she rarely felt completely well, and in the midst of his tours of inspection and visits to the Fleet, Winston suffered much worry about her. 'I am most grieved to find that the rosy views of [your doctor's] earlier telegrams have not been confirmed,' he writes to her, '& that you have had a return of the pain & only a fair night . . .'

Besides Admiralty House ('we really cannot afford it'), one of the benefits of being First Lord was the use of a luxuriously appointed Admiralty yacht. The *Enchantress* was like a slightly scaled-down version of the royal yacht *Victoria & Albert*, a graceful, single-funnel steam yacht of 3,500 tons. Winston had on board an office and all the necessary equipment and personnel to run the Admiralty from it while steaming with the fleet or visiting naval bases at home and abroad. Clementine loved it, not only for its comfort and the attention she received from the yacht's company, but also because she could entertain as lavishly as Winston could wish at no expense to themselves.

In April 1912 Winston decided to visit bases in the Mediterranean, call on Admiral Fisher and at the same time entertain the Prime Minister and his family and tour several historic cities, something Asquith and Eddie Marsh would especially enjoy. But above all, this early summer cruise of the *Enchantress* would offer health-enhancing convalescence for Clementine. Among those invited were the Asquiths and his daughter Violet; Winston's and Clementine's mothers; Clementine's sister Nellie (loved by all wherever she went); Edwin Montagu and his future wife, Venetia Stanley; the Liberal Chief Whip in the Commons, Master of Elibank; Prince Louis of Battenberg; Eddie Marsh and his new colleague in Winston's office, a reluctant David Beatty; James Masterton-Smith, Winston's permanent secretary; and Asquith's private secretaries, Sir Maurice Bonham Carter and Sir Roderick Meikeljohn.

After a great send-off at Victoria Station on 22 May, this exalted and amusing party headed for Paris in a special pullman carriage, according to Violet 'full of Cabinet boxes, newspapers, letters, flowers'. In Paris there was an 'ambrosial banquet' at Voisins after hot baths at the Ritz, and then re-embarkation on board the same de luxe French train that had swept them from Calais earlier. The *Enchantress* was awaiting them at Genoa and took the party, in all the promised luxury, to Elba in order that Winston could visit Napoleon's house, which turned out disappointingly to be an insignificant villa. Thence to Naples, where they all disembarked for a wonderful day at Pompeii, again according to Violet's diary, 'wandering down the long lovely silent streets among the little courts and houses of the dead where grass and flowers grow'.

Jacky Fisher had been persuaded to travel from his hotel at Lucerne to talk about the Navy to Asquith and Winston. Those of the *Enchantress*'s passengers who had not before met Jacky Fisher were keenly looking forward to the appearance of this volatile and notorious admiral. Violet Asquith's diary entry on the day he came aboard, 24 May, reads:

Back to the yacht for luncheon – and *there was Lord Fisher*! in the flesh . . . I examined him minutely and tried to diagnose his mood and his potential placability. His eyes, as always, were like smouldering charcoals – lighting up at his own jokes. He was very friendly to Father and Prince Louis but glowered a bit, I thought, at Winston. To me he retailed a stock of anecdotes, puns, chestnuts and riddles which might have come out of crackers . . . As the day wore on I noticed signs of mellowing in Lord F. which I feel will turn to melting before long. I whispered at tea to Winston: 'He's melting.' His mind was far away. He gazed at me blankly and said in a hard, loud voice: 'What's melting?' Distracted, I replied: 'The butter,' which brought me an 'old-fashioned look' from our hostess, who eyed the bread and butter anxiously.

Later, Violet observed that 'Lord F. and W. were locked together in naval conclave . . . I'm sure they can't resist each other for long at close range.' And the next day's entry opens, 'Danced on deck with Lord Fisher for a very long time before breakfast.'

Fisher clearly made a 'hit' with the Prime Minister's daughter. Her stepmother, Margot, was less susceptible to his charms, and Clementine, while applying all the circumspection she could muster, was from the outset suspicious of the Admiral. She fully understood Winston's need of him, but was relieved that his disruptive capacity precluded his return to office as First Sea Lord and Winston's partner.

Admiral Beatty, a professional if ever there was one, was observing everything with a keen sailor's eye. 'That old rascal Fisher arrived on board directly we got here,' he wrote to his wife, Ethel, the Marshall Field heiress, 'looking very well and young, never stopped talking and has been closeted with Winston ever since. Wasn't that something to come to Naples for?'

Fisher himself wrote to a friend:

> I was nearly kidnapped and carried off in the Admiralty Yacht! They were very sweet about it! My old cabin as First Sea Lord all arranged for me! I had a good time and came out on top! The Prime Minister is 'dead on' for my coming back, and he has put things so forcibly to me that, with great reluctance to re-enter the battle field, I probably shall do so!

What was really being settled on board the *Enchantress* was not the prospect of Jacky Fisher coming back as First Sea

240

Lord (as his friend might have interpreted from his letter), but, of all prosaic but momentous considerations, the future fuel for the Royal Navy. The inefficiency and inconvenience of coal-fired boilers had been underlined by the progress of oil-firing and turbine power. If the future Navy was to be dependent on oil, it would be imported oil, largely from the Middle East, with all the wartime hazards this would involve. But Britain *was* coal. Scratch down a few feet, and there it was. (The fact that a long miners' strike had recently come near to crippling the nation was considered irrelevant.) Now Churchill, with Asquith's support, was to set up a 'commission on oil'. And he wanted Fisher to be chairman. The preliminary talks on board the *Enchantress* were later followed by a letter Winston wrote to Fisher after his return home. It began:

> We are too good friends (I hope) and the matters with which we are concerned are too serious (I'm sure) for anything but plain language. This liquid fuel problem has got to be solved, and the natural, inherent, unavoidable difficulties are such that they require the drive and enthusiasm of a big man. I want you for this . . .

Meanwhile, serious business in the *Enchantress* alternated with rapturous occasions at blissful places:

> We are lying at anchor in the great harbour [Syracuse] where the Athenians fought 2,000 years ago [Violet wrote in her diary on 28 May]. I have just been bathing in it before breakfast with Winston and Clemmie. . . . W. is never so happy as in the water.
>
> [Then, on the same day but twelve hours later] We went up to the Greek theatre towards sunset and lay there among wild thyme and humming bees and watched the sea changing from blue to flame and then to cool jade green as the sun dropped into it and the stars came out.

241

As this beautiful yacht – stocked with the finest provisions and wines, provided with every comfort, and manned by a picked crew – cruised from island to island and port to port, each passenger followed his or her inclination. Asquith and Eddie Marsh loved Greek ruins, while Winston saw them in terms of military significance. Some went on adventurous picnics, others preferred to swim or paint. In the evenings there were tables of bridge that reflected in their play the personalities of the contestants. 'Little boat-loads of Syracusan musicians came and sang to us round the yacht in the dark as we played Auction [bridge] after dinner,' wrote Violet.

One of the most eager players was Asquith. He was also the worst, the construction and rules of the game being unsuited to his particular form of genius. 'Winston was even more dangerous,' according to Violet, 'for he played a romantic game untrammelled by conventions, codes or rules. When playing in partnership they made a happy, carefree and catastrophic combination.' And when Winston's private secretaries were paired with their master it was sheer hell, for both took the game seriously and could not afford the losses.

For David Beatty, the *Enchantress* outing was becoming too much to bear. All he wanted was to get back to his work:

> Oh dear! I am so tired and bored with the whole thing. Even the weather isn't kind: cloudy and cold with heavy rainstorms . . . And the party on board bores me to tears. Winston talks about nothing but the sea and the Navy and the wonderful things he is going to do. Mrs Winston is a perfect fool, I never met a truer or better specimen of the amiable fool. Old Asquith is a regular common old tourist; spends his time immersed in a Baedecker Guide and reading extracts to an admiring audience. On shore it makes me ashamed to have to introduce him as the Prime Minister of Great Britain. Prince Louis is of course charming, but not terribly exciting.

Malta, seat of British naval might in the Mediterranean, provided the first almost-royal welcome for the yacht and her passengers. Steaming slowly into Grand Harbour early in the day, they were greeted by the fleet with gun salutes, bugle calls and the hoisting of flags on the great men of war, while admirals and flag lieutenants, grand soldiers like Kitchener and Ian Hamilton, came on board with all the formality the Royal Navy could muster. Then came functions and banquets and dances and receptions, culminating in going to sea in a battleship to watch gunnery practice against a towed target. All the spectators were issued with earplugs against the thunder of the guns – 'little glass stoppers with *anchors* – so like the Navy!' Unfortunately, to the Admiral's embarrassment and Winston's outrage, not a single hit was scored.

The reception by the French authorities at Bizerta was almost as grand and in some respects ludicrous, with Winston contributing his own act of shouting loudly in his execrable accent and old vocabulary questions of a highly confidential nature, such as '*Où sont vos soumarins?*'

Clementine suffered another relapse at this time, and she was thankful when the *Enchantress* at last set course for home, via Gibraltar. Further weeks of anxiety were to follow before her gynaecological problems were solved and she returned to her customary cheerfulness and good health. But for more than another year she ensured that she did not conceive another child. She had been thoroughly frightened by the extent of her illness and the failure of a number of the finest medical brains to cure her.

By contrast with the sumptuous voyages Winston and Clementine made in the *Enchantress*, there were other occasions when they had to face political hostility that was extremely uncomfortable and even dangerous. Irish politics and the issue of home rule for the Irish brooded over Britain like a menacing storm cloud throughout this period, splitting the nation and Parliament. Winston had not concerned himself closely with the problem of Ireland and the project of 'Irish autonomy in Irish matters' until Asquith succeeded

Campbell-Bannerman, who had been an enthusiastic advocate of home rule. But as soon as Winston recognized the importance of the impending conflict he made himself a (if not the) leading advocate.

Although he had more than enough to do as First Lord of the Admiralty with a gigantic reform programme, laying down new oil-fired turbine battleships (the biggest, fastest, and most heavily gunned in the world), creating a naval air service, building enough submarines to satisfy Jacky Fisher (except that he was never satisfied), and much else – Winston was never content with only the job in hand. Foreign affairs, the state of the *entente cordiale*, the progress of the Home Office reforms he had left uncompleted – these and many other issues came within his purview by his judgement, if by no-one else's.

Early in 1912, shortly before Clementine's miscarriage, Winston decided to take the Irish problem to its roots in Belfast, against the warnings of many of his friends and advisers. The volatility of the situation was worse than it had been for a long time, the Catholics in the city as determined that home rule should embrace all Ulster as the 'Orange' Protestants were that they would not submit to Catholic rule from Dublin.

Clementine decided to accompany Winston. She thought her presence might cool passions. Winston and her friends did not agree. But it was difficult to deter Clementine when she had chosen what she reckoned to be the correct course. A hall was booked for Winston's address, and the Ulstermen countered by occupying it with a sit-in. A football ground was reserved instead.

Trouble was never far away even before they arrived on the night ferry, though it was of a nature unrelated to Irish affairs. With advance notice of Winston being on board, the suffragette movement filled the ferry with activists, who shouted all night long, 'Votes for women! Votes for women!' which precluded any idea of sleep.

The depth of the Protestant hostility was evident as the ferry tied up, the whole docks area being plastered with anti-home rule posters, and a jeering crowd threatened them all the way to their hotel. All day long it was almost like Paris during the French Revolution, with the hotel as the Bastille. Clementine noted Winston's calm and how 'the opposition and threats seemed to "ginger him up"'. She determined to match his courage.

> As they started on their long drive to the Celtic Football Ground, [a local newspaper reported] the crowd surged round the car and, despite the strong escort of police, very nearly overturned it. As the cars in the cortège slowly made their way through the milling mass, men thrust their heads through the windows, uttering menaces.

But as soon as they reached the Falls, the dividing line between Protestant and Catholic Belfast, there was a dramatic change in the manner of the crowd, with cheering replacing booing, smiles and cries of welcome instead of threats and curses. In spite of the pouring rain, there were thousands of eager listeners at the football ground, filling every pause in Winston's speech with cheers.

Asquith's Liberal ministry pressed ahead with a home rule bill, against the strong opposition of the Unionist Irish members and the solid phalanx of the Conservative Party, in spite of numerous concessions by the government. Two years later, with the bill about to become law, Sir Edward Carson and his Ulstermen were preparing themselves for armed conflict. On 14 March 1914, Winston, encouraged and briefed by Lloyd George and Asquith, made a strong speech upholding the will of the British people, excoriating the Conservatives, and defying armed opposition within the United Kingdom. He concluded:

> We are not going to have the realm of Great Britain sink to the condition of the Republic of Mexico . . . If all the loose, wanton and reckless chatter we have been forced to listen to these months is in the end to

disclose a sinister revolutionary purpose, then I can only say to you 'Let us go forward and put these grave matters to the Proof'.

Civil war appeared so imminent that Winston ordered a battle squadron to move close to Belfast, ostensibly on manoeuvres. Troops moved to guard military depots in Ulster, railway lines and bridges, and special dispensations were made for army officers and men who had roots or close associations with the province. As a counter-move, Carson's Ulster Volunteers carried out gun-running on a huge scale – he claimed some 35,000 rifles and 3,000,000 rounds of ammunition. The mass resignation of Brigadier Hubert Gough, commanding the 3rd Cavalry Brigade, and fifty-seven of his officers in sympathy with Carson's Unionists – referred to euphemistically as the 'Curragh Mutiny' – heightened the crisis. Civil war on a large and tragic scale was avoided only by the outbreak of war in Europe.

Winston's powerful and even provocative role in the Irish crisis of 1912–14 made him many more enemies in the land. Those who tried to get him to temper the violence of his attacks – notably Margot Asquith and Clementine – had little success. It still seemed to many who were close to him that in his determination to pursue his causes without compromise he actually relished making new enemies. Even the sovereign was not immune.

As the Irish crisis was rapidly building up, Winston followed custom by proposing names for new warships shortly to be launched. It was important that these names, above all others, should be right – euphonious, rousing, yet solemn – for between them these ships would be the crowning glory of the Battle Fleet, as fast as most battle-cruisers yet almost indestructible by gunfire.* One of the names Winston put

---

*None was so destroyed in two world wars.

246

forward was that of Oliver Cromwell, who had, after all, cut off his sovereign's head and been responsible, more than anyone else, for the deaths and miseries of the native Irish.

George V, through his secretary, Lord Stamfordham, unhesitatingly turned down this name. A year later, the name Oliver Cromwell appeared again, among others, on Winston's list. Again the King turned it down. Refusing to accept defeat, Winston strongly argued the case. Oliver Cromwell was one of the founders of the Royal Navy, he argued. 'I am quite sure that nothing in history will justify the view that the adoption of such a name would constitute any reflection . . . upon His Majesty's Royal House . . . The bitterness of the rebellions and tyrannies of the past has long ceased to stir men's minds.'

That scarcely seemed to be the case in Ireland, as the King sharply reminded his First Lord; moreover, only seventeen years ago when it had been proposed to erect a statue to Cromwell in London, the idea had been thrown out by Parliament by a majority of no fewer than 137 votes; which did not appear to lend weight to Winston's claim that he was 'satisfied that the name would be extremely well received'.

This, one would suppose, finally settled the matter. But Winston did not care for his wishes to be frustrated, even by his King, and was about to prolong the argument when Prince Louis of Battenberg, whose ears were always close to palace affairs, interceded. He reminded Winston that in his experience with three sovereigns, no First Lord had questioned a decision about names. 'I am inclined to think the Service as a whole would go against you in this choice.'

To Prince Louis's amazement – and the amazement of many others privy to it – another ship-name argument broke out later concerning another of these super-Dreadnoughts. Winston wanted Pitt, after the two great statesmen of that name. Not dignified, claimed the King. The last two naval vessels with that name were coal hulks. Anyway, there was 'always the danger of the men giving the Ship nicknames of ill-conditioned words rhyming with it'. The King could be

247

described as an authority on service foul language, having served in the Navy for fifteen years, which had left him with a fine turn of obscene vocabulary.

Again, Winston had to bow to superior rank, but he did not enjoy doing so, and like the bad-tempered schoolboy he could still be, sought petty revenge. He 'happened' to chance on some figures in the naval estimates relating to the cost of running and maintaining the royal yacht, *Victoria & Albert*. 'I have been looking into the expenditure of the last five years,' he informed Lord Stamfordham soon after this last dispute. 'I am sure the King would be surprised to see the enormous charges wh are made for quite small things . . . After I am more fully informed, His Majesty wd probably wish me to lay the result of the investigation before him?'

His Majesty could hardly say no, as Winston had calculated. A point up! But in fact, there also occurred a decline in George V's regard for his First Lord, whom he did not much trust anyway, not since he had shown such outrageous disloyalty to the Conservative Party almost ten years earlier.

After the doctors had finally cured Clementine's gynaecological troubles in the late summer of 1912 she and Goonie and their children left for a long convalescence by the seaside in Kent. The house was suitably named Rest Harrow and had been lent to her by Waldorf and Nancy Astor.*

Winston was so busy that he could make only brief and intermittent visits to his beloved 'Kat' and scarcely had time to write, though he sent telegrams daily. Meantime, Clementine kept Winston informed of domestic details:

> *I have had a delicious blowy afternoon on the Beach with the Babies. You would have laughed if you had seen Randolph eating his pap for supper. If ever the*

---

*Like Jennie, Nancy Astor was American-born. She was to become the first woman MP.

*spoon contained too much milk & not enough solid
he roared with rage & insisted on solid food being
scooped up.* [Alas, there was no Mrs Everest!] *Diana
says her prayers so sweetly & with great dignity. God
keep Papa & Mama & Little Randolph & make
Diana a good little girl for Jesus Christ's sake, Amen.
Randolph goes to sleep holding his Nurse's hand &
gurgling and cooing like a Ring Dove. Tomorrow
comes George. Thursday Goonie & Saturday Oh Joy
my Pig. Come early not late dear one.*

Eight days later, Winston was able to give Clementine the
good news that he could come down again.

*I have made no plans for Sunday next except to
come down quietly and see you. We ought to find
a really good sandy beach where I can cut the sand
into a nicely bevelled fortress – or best of all with a
little stream running down – You might explore and
report . . .*

In spite of Winston's earlier dislike of the sea – and one
or two of those voyages to the East had been extremely
uncomfortable – the voyages in the *Enchantress* and his new
responsibility for the Royal Navy had quite converted him.
'Winston has taken to the sea like a duck to water,' as a friend
put it somewhat inexactly. But as always, he was also looking
ahead and upwards.

A month after Winston had been appointed to the Admiralty, Asquith ordered the standing subcommittee of the CID
(Committee of Imperial Defence) to consider the future of
aviation for the Army and the Navy. He appointed Haldane
as chairman. The Agadir crisis earlier in the year and the
ever-growing threat of German naval rearmament were two
of the reasons for this urgent step, when the French army was
taking aviation seriously and Germany had advanced far with
passenger-carrying zeppelins. The findings of this committee
were strongly supported by Winston from the start, and he

took a personal hand in the formation of the Royal Naval Air Service (RNAS).

Headquarters of the RNAS were set up at Eastchurch on the shores of the Thames estuary, and here, under Winston's watchful eye, the first pilots were trained in 1912. Once momentum had been gained, progress was swift, with Winston, strongly egged on by Fisher, following every detail. It was the reconnaissance benefits of the aeroplane that most appealed to the Navy, and therefore plane-to-ship communication was essential. By June, Commander Charles Samson, to become one of the great pioneer naval pilots, installed a primitive wireless set in a Short seaplane, took off and found he was able to transmit messages up to a range of ten miles.

The following year, 1913, saw the RNAS mature into a small but accepted part of the Fleet, manned mainly by enthusiastic and bold young officers, as unafraid of being considered eccentric as of the act of flying, which was in itself a hazardous undertaking. In a minute of 26 October 1913, Winston called for 'three new types of machine: first an oversea fighting seaplane, to operate from a ship as base; next, a scouting seaplane, to work with the fleet at sea; and last, a home-service fighting aeroplane, to repel enemy aircraft when they attack the vulnerable points of our island, and to carry out patrol duties along the coast'.

With his customary far-sightedness, and with the steady encouragement of Fisher, Winston was already envisaging roles for the aeroplane and seaplane far beyond those of reconnaissance: the possibility of these aircraft carrying machine-guns (long before the Army gave thought to the future fighter), bombs, mines, and torpedoes were all being considered from 1912. But not only the equipment and the multiple roles seized his imagination. Just as he went to sea and submerged (not liking it much) in submarines, and was prepared to face a force gale in a small destroyer and to watch night-firing practice with the Fleet, so now he determined to fly.

'He was fascinated by the idea of flying,' remembered one

of the dashing young pilots of the time, 'but he admits that side by side with desire was also a dread of going into the air for the first time.' However, sensing 'the vulgarity of fear', to which he sometimes referred in connection with close fighting on the ground, he ordered the pilot of a naval hydroplane to take him up over Cromarty Firth on 6 October 1913.

Winston found his first flight a wholly agreeable experience, and a week or two later was telling Clementine about another 'very jolly day in the air':

> *First we all went over to Eastchurch where we found dozens of aeroplanes, & everyone flew . . . I let the military & naval officers fly across the river with me to our other air stations in the Isle of Grain – a delightful trip on wh I was conducted by the redoubtable Samson. Here we found another large flock of seaplanes in the highest state of activity. Just as we arrived & landed, the Astra-Torres airship, wh I had sent for from Farnborough, arrived, and the Generals & I went for a beautiful cruise at about one thousand feet all round Chatham & the Medway. . . .*
>
> *It has been as good as one of those old days in the S. African war, & I have lived entirely in the moment, with no care for all those tiresome party politics & searching newspapers, & awkward by-elections, & sulky orangemen [Ulster Irish] & obnoxious Cecils & little smugs like Runciman . . .*
>
> *How are the chickens? The world will be a vy interesting place for them when they are grown up . . .*

Winston decided to celebrate his thirty-ninth birthday, five weeks later, by taking a flying lesson. His instructor was a Royal Marines captain, Gilbert Wildman-Lushington, who reported excitedly to his fiancée that evening.

> I started Winston off on his instruction about 12:15 & he got so bitten with it, I could hardly get him out of the machine, in fact except for about ¾ hour for

lunch we were in the machine till about 3:30. He . . . is
coming down again for further instruction & practice
. . . I've never had such a day in my life . . .

But poor Wildman-Lushington had used up all but a few
days in his life. On 2 December while coming in to land at
Eastchurch, he sideslipped into the ground and was killed.

Winston was shocked and grieved by this accident, which
again underlined the hazards of this pioneer flying. He at
once sat down and wrote a letter of commiseration to the
pilot's fiancée, Miss Airlie Hynes: 'To be killed instantly
without pain or fear in the necessary service of the country
when one is quite happy and life is full of success & hope,
cannot be reckoned the worst of fortune. But to some who
are left behind the loss is terrible.'

Clementine correctly reckoned that Winston could so
easily have been the passenger-pupil in the aeroplane. She
feared dreadfully for the life of her husband, who was in any
case five years beyond the maximum age considered suitable
for pilots. But Winston continued his instruction, when time
allowed, without pause. Clementine was not the only one
fearful for his life. None of his new instructors fancied the
responsibility for his safety. 'As an instructor,' one of them
wrote, 'one was *over*-careful with WSC. We were all scared
stiff of having a smashed First Lord on our hands . . . WSC
was always bucketed about from one instructor to another.'
And certainly no-one wanted the responsibility for letting
him solo. 'If anything happened to WSC the career of the
man . . . would be finished.' Besides, he was without question the worst pupil any of them had tackled, suffering the
same lack of timing and co-ordination that made him such a
terrible driver.

Sometimes he would go up as many as ten times in a day.
'He couldn't bear to make mistakes. He always wanted to
correct them at once.'

Winston's family was becoming increasingly alarmed by
his insistence on continuing to fly. 'I do not suppose that I
shall get the chance of writing you many more letters if you

252

continue your journeys in the Air,' wrote Sunny. 'Really I consider that you owe it to your wife family and friends to desist from a practice or pastime – whichever you call it – which is fraught with so much danger to life. It is really wrong of you . . .'

And F. E. asked him brusquely, 'Why do you do such a thing as fly repeatedly? Surely it is unfair to your family your career & your friends.'

At last, to the relief of all his family and friends, and his admirers everywhere, an event occurred that finished for the time being Winston's flying career. He had invited over from France the great French aviation pioneer Gustav Hamel, and Winston was there expecting to greet him after his Channel crossing. He never arrived, and no trace of him was ever found. On 6 June 1914, Winston wrote to Clementine, who was expecting their third child: 'I will not fly any more until at any rate you have recovered from your kitten . . . This is a wrench, because I was on the verge of taking my pilot's certificate . . .'

He did not go into the air again until his duties obliged him to do so, years later, when planes were much safer.

17

Troubles with Admirals

To the increasing dismay of his friends and especially of Clementine, who worried about the number of enemies Winston made, the new First Lord quarrelled with his admirals with scarcely a pause. The mere sight of a thick gold ring on a sleeve caused Winston's suspicions to be aroused, while a youthful lieutenant with the gleam of courage and ambition in his eye was met with nothing but approval.

Take the unfortunate Admiral Poore. Richard Poore, aged 60, was the hero of many campaigns on land and sea in the last century, and now held the prestigious command of the Nore, an anchorage off Sheerness which embraced the RNAS headquarters at Eastchurch, including the Navy's first carrier, HMS *Hermes*, under Captain Gerald Vivian. Vivian had made a decision over the use of some nearby land that was the responsibility of the RNAS. When Winston arrived in the *Enchantress* to check on progress, he asked one of Vivian's subordinate officers if he thought that his captain's plan was the best available.

'No, sir,' said the lieutenant, after being pressed. And he described his own plan, which Winston thought was much better. Winston then informed Captain Vivian that his lieutenant's plan was much superior to his own and should be implemented. The row when he left can be imagined. But the lieutenant had been instructed by Winston to inform him directly if his own plan were not carried through, and he told his superior of this.

Captain Vivian complained to Admiral Poore, who complained to Prince Louis of Battenberg, now First Sea Lord. Churchill, through his network of informers, learned of this, and gave orders that any communication addressed to the Admiralty referring to the matter was to be passed to him.

This was not done. A letter arrived direct from Poore on this subject, addressed to Admiral Jellicoe, Second Sea Lord. 'In this letter Sir Richard Poore proposed to report what had happened, and to state in strong terms his view that such action was bound to undermine discipline.' Jellicoe judged the tone to be too strong and returned it with a note of mild rebuke, suggesting more temperate tones.

But he was too late. By now, Winston had given personal instructions to the Admiralty post room to open any communication from Admiral Poore's command. As a result he saw both Poore's and Jellicoe's letters. Winston 'went dancing mad', it was said, and declared that he would order Admiral Poore to haul down his flag.

Winston found himself in very deep water now. He had exceeded his powers on many occasions, but to dismiss a senior admiral without reference to the Board of Admiralty was outrageous, said the Board in the strongest language. As in the charge at Omdurman, Winston was committed and could not hold back now. Indeed, drawing his Mauser, he started to fire. If any member of the Board criticized him on any matter whatsoever he would be obliged to resign.

Prince Louis of Battenberg, the affable semi-royal negotiator, intervened. He kept the scandal from George V, begged Admiral Poore not to demand a court martial as he threatened, and begged him to apologize. Poore indignantly refused, but finally gave in when Prince Louis hinted unflatteringly that Winston was not responsible for his own actions. Sir Francis Hopwood, Winston's old antagonist, now Additional Civil Lord at the Admiralty, wrote that Poore had been told that 'Churchill was so much off his head over the whole business that Poore need take no notice of it.'

That was the end of that crisis, 'but we shall have it again in some form', concluded Hopwood.

Prince Louis had been promoted to First Sea Lord under circumstances that were as embarrassing for him as they reflected poorly on Winston's methods and tact. After Admiral Sir Arthur ('Tug') Wilson had been dismissed as First Sea Lord, Admiral Bridgeman soon proved himself unable to satisfy Winston's great demands. For one thing, his health was not very good, and unwell people irritated Winston inordinately. Bridgeman had supported him over the creation of a naval war staff, for that was why he had been appointed in the first place, but otherwise he proved negative and Winston decided he ought to go. He had conceived a high opinion of Prince Louis for his organizational powers, tact and discretion, and he ignored warnings from Lloyd George that, as a German by birth, his position might be untenable in time of war with Germany.

Bridgeman was popular among his fellow flag officers, and Winston, warned by Clementine, realized that he might have to be more diplomatic in getting rid of him than in the case of the unmarried, unpolitical Tug Wilson. When Bridgeman suffered another bout of illness in November 1912, Winston seized the opportunity. First, knowing the King's admiration and affection for the Admiral, he took advantage of an audience with George V to inform him that Bridgeman's continuing ill health was proving a severe handicap. This prepared the ground for what was to follow.

Next, Winston wrote a letter to Bridgeman to say how sorry he was that he had still not recovered from his chill, which prevented his returning to London, and that he had been meaning 'for some time to write to you about your health'. He had observed 'how heavily the strain of your great office has told upon you' and regretted that the strain was unlikely to diminish and that, in the event of war, it might prove too much. 'If therefore you should feel disposed at this juncture to retire,' Winston continued, 'I could not, whatever my personal regrets, oppose your wish, and I believe that such a step would be a relief to you.'

Bridgeman's reply from his country house suggested that he might well consider retiring, and he thanked Winston for his 'kindly-meant' letter. Winston then wrote to the King suggesting that the First Sea Lord's retirement was a *fait accompli*, adding that it would be appropriate, perhaps, for him to be promoted Admiral of the Fleet.

Alas, the situation was suddenly transformed when Winston's political enemies, who were as common as partridge in the shires, got wind of 'the demand' for the First Sea Lord's resignation and converted the Admiral's acquiescence to indignant refusal. The Conservative press and party rose up in defence of this abused admiral who had served his country so nobly – and all that.

To Bridgeman, Winston regretted any misunderstanding. 'There is absolutely no truth in the idea that any difference in policy or procedure or any divergence or incident between us influenced me at all. Honestly, I only thought about your health . . . and what would happen if war began and you broke down.' But it was too late. Bridgeman, whose character was no stronger than his health, had now been convinced by Conservative Party friends that he had been shabbily treated, and these same friends, egged on by the Conservative newspapers, forced a debate in the House of Commons on 20 December.

After facing a barrage of attacks, Winston went over to the offensive:

> When Sir Francis Bridgeman came to the Admiralty [he claimed], I knew nothing of the state of his health. I found him, where he shone, in command of a great Fleet and I naturally assumed he was in full strength and vigour. It was with much regret that I quite early discovered that his health was impaired . . . In early November the First Sea Lord was on a week's leave and was immediately laid up with illness. It was three weeks before he was permitted by his doctor to return to London.

Winston, moreover, had corroborative evidence of Bridgeman's poor state of health, and Bridgeman's *own awareness of it*:

> On 25 November [Bridgeman] wrote to a colleague on the Board saying that he had been very much

depressed about his health [continued Winston], that he had had two attacks of bronchitis within a few months, and this, coming on top of appendicitis, seemed to have weakened his constitution. He sometimes, he said, felt inclined to give up his post.

Not content with one broadside, Winston now delivered the *coup de grâce*, quoting what Bridgeman had written to the greatly admired Admiral Beatty: 'He said he was so very ill the night before that he had actually taken up his pen to write his resignation, but feeling better the next day he had not done so.'

That settled the matter. Nevertheless, the Bridgeman affair did Winston's reputation no good at all. 'The whole matter is damnable, undignified and extremely bad for the service,' commented a future First Sea Lord, Rear-Admiral Wester Wemyss.

Winston's difficulties with admirals continued almost to the outbreak of war in Europe – in fact, to within a few days of the first fighting. Admiral Sir George Callaghan, aged 62, commanded the First Fleet. He was loved and admired by all, and there was no question of ill health in his case, for he was as tough and robust as any 30-year-old.

But Fisher had drummed into Winston, time and time again, that Jellicoe must lead the Fleet in war, and Winston believed that Fisher was right. On 31 July 1914, when war became almost inevitable, Jellicoe was told that when it was declared he would take over command from Callaghan. Jellicoe, a sensitive and kind man, and also a close personal friend of the Callaghans', was horrified. Also, Jellicoe was junior to many flag officers, which would make the discharge of his duties even more difficult and uncomfortable just when he would require all his skills and powers at their highest pitch. Over the next few days, Jellicoe repeatedly signalled Winston, begging him to rescind the order. Beatty supported him, and so did Prince Louis, but Winston was unyielding.

On the morning of 4 August, with war only hours away,

Jellicoe boarded Callaghan's flagship and took over command. 'I hope never to live again through such a time,' he wrote later. 'My position was horrible. I did my best but could not stop what I feel is a grave error . . . the tragedy of the news to the C-in-C [Commander in Chief – i.e. Callaghan] was past belief, and it was almost worse for me.'

On this same day, Clementine, who had suffered much anguish over Winston's admiral troubles, wrote to him about 'the deep wound in an old man's heart'.

> Please *see him yourself & take him by the hand and (additional) offer him a seat on the Board, or if this is impossible give him* some *advisory position at the Admiralty . . . His lips will then be sealed and his wife's too. Don't think this is a trivial matter. At this moment you want everyone's heart & soul. If you give him a position of honour and confidence, the whole service will feel that he has been as well treated as possible under the circumstances, & that he has not been humiliated.*

Recalling the terrible row over the Bridgeman affair, Clementine emphasized that Winston would not want 'Lady Callaghan & Lady Bridgeman to form a league of retired Officers' Cats, to abuse you. Poor Lady Callaghan's grief will be intense but if you are good to him now it will be softened.' Winston as usual took Clementine's advice, which was always very freely available, and Callaghan was later appointed Commander in Chief at the Nore.

Clementine lost an important round in her non-stop battle with Winston for economy when they moved from Eccleston Square into the Admiralty in early April 1913. Winston had been longing to move into the spacious official premises since his appointment. There he would be able to entertain in the style expected of the First Lord, and he would be conveniently 'living on the job'. Clementine finally yielded regretfully, knowing how much it would please her husband, who reassured her that he would in future commit himself to all sorts of economies. 'Remember I am going to turn over a new leaf! That I promise,' he wrote to her. But he did not.

Winston was conveniently absent on board the *Enchantress* for the move, while Clementine struggled with the Office of Works, who provided all the standard-issue furniture. 'I am afraid altho' we are allowed to "choose" our bedroom furniture it will be difficult to get anything attractive as the "choosing" is to be done out of a grim catalogue,' Clementine wrote stoically. 'I really think they ought to have a woman at the head of the Office of Works – someone like your Mama.' And later: 'House moving is going on & there is no resting place for the soles of my feet. I am now sitting in a desolated library (ink-pots & pens gone) . . .'

'I am afraid it all means vy hard work for you,' Winston sympathized.

When life became impossible at Eccleston Square, Clementine moved for a weekend to the Asquiths' home at The Wharf, Sutton Courtenay, near Oxford, a red-brick residence on the river, of modest size for the number of residents and guests usually to be found there. Asquith and his daughter Violet picked her up, without the children, who were at Salisbury Hall, and drove her away. 'I felt it was the end of a chapter of my life,' she wrote to Winston. 'Leaving a house where one has lived nearly four years is as much of an event in a "Kat's" life, as changing from Home Office to Admiralty for a statesman!'

Mercifully, the weather was fine and they seem to have spent most of the time on the golf course. Besides Clementine, 'the congested Wharf' (as Asquith described it) found room somehow for the Prime Minister's friend Robert Ross, of Oscar Wilde notoriety, and Edwin Montagu. Montagu, Asquith wrote to Venetia Stanley, 'was in an introspective and sombre mood: declared that he had never known what it was to be free from physical & mental pain: and complained that he amused nobody & that nobody amused him'.

A letter from Winston arrived for Clementine at The Wharf. 'It will be nice coming back to the Admiralty,' he wrote, adding a warning note about the *Enchantress*, which the Prime Minister's wife enjoyed almost too much. 'Do not commit yourself & the yacht unnecessarily to Margot, if you can help it. But I know how discreet you are.'*

Clementine's youngest child has given us a clear and touching picture of her mother at home at the Admiralty at this time, coping with a husband who was gregarious and liked the luxuries of life – and especially food. 'I am easily satisfied,' he would joke, 'with the very best.' Fortunately, she did not have to make provision for many large dinner parties, nor did they often attend them. Besides their families, they saw most of their political friends, like Edward Grey, the F. E. Smiths, Ernest Cassel, Venetia Stanley, Edwin Montagu and most frequently, perhaps, the Asquiths. Herbert and Margot were often at the Admiralty, or the Churchills were at 10 Downing Street during the week or The Wharf at weekends, playing much golf and bridge.

Clementine was always early awake, unlike Winston, who usually worked far into the night, and she would write letters in bed, or read, until breakfast, and then the cook would come up to take her orders for the day. Winston would sometimes come in at this time, in dressing gown and carrying the newspapers, free with suggestions on what they should eat that evening: 'Let's have Irish stew – with lots of onions!'

There would probably be one or both of their children on or around the bed, and Winston would pick them up and kiss them and joke with them, with Clementine watching lovingly but sometimes anxiously when the play became what she thought was boisterous. Her disposition was inclined to be

---

*Clementine's discretion could be relied upon, but the Asquiths spent three weeks on board the *Enchantress* in the Mediterranean and Adriatic from 8 May just the same.

nervous even at this age, and this increased over the years, although she was personally as courageous as Winston, both morally and physically.

Clementine had never reconciled herself to living in a circle of political friends whom she regarded as cleverer than herself, more worldly and amusing, and never overcame her sense of inferiority. But, censoriously, she thought that all this cleverness only partly concealed a brittle cynicism and inadequacy in moral values. In this she was certainly right, but her efforts to conceal her disapproval were not always successful. Those who got to know her, which was sometimes difficult, were fond of Clementine, and not always just for the sake of Winston; but a tendency to priggishness (by contrast with her sister and Goonie) let her in for some private criticism. Clementine's virtues, like her stunning beauty, were there for all to see, though her regard for her own looks was carelessly unselfconscious compared with the way she presented her views and attitudes.

Winston saw none of all this, and would not have done even if his friends had been less careful to conceal their opinions. Clementine remained for him what she had always been – a woman without faults, her nature as perfect as her body. He might flirt outrageously with clever and attractive young women like Venetia Stanley and Violet Asquith, sometimes to Clementine's discomfiture, but he remained loyal to her in every meaning of the word.

The nagging about his extravagance, the barbs she released so freely and often publicly about his friends and associates, the uncomfortable economies she imposed on their household and, less successfully, on him, he endured then in a surprising and touchingly naive way as all part of the marriage process. Time was to change this, and rows in later years were to assume heroic proportions. For the present, however, he was dutiful and almost abjectly submissive, to Clementine's immense satisfaction, and he was (as he ended his letters) her 'ever loving and devoted husband'.

From the day Winston took over the Admiralty, he was

faced with a very difficult political dilemma. At the Board of Trade and the Home Office he had been able to pursue, in continuation of his father's beliefs, a policy of economy in expenditure on the armed forces to the benefit of the welfare of the poor and unemployed and to improve medical and educational services. This policy reflected basic tenets of the Liberal Party, but as always it was essential to maintain the security of the nation for political reasons and out of a sense of responsibility. It was just bad luck that the great revival of Liberalism coincided with the most dangerous military challenge Britain had had to face since Napoleonic times, and Winston was in charge of the first line of defence.

The building of HMS *Dreadnought* in 1906 had intensified the battleship race instigated by Germany in the late 1890s. This ship was so superior to all its contemporaries that it overnight made every other battleship virtually obsolete; thus, the numerical advantage Britain held over Germany became virtually irrelevant. This was one of the sticks used to beat Fisher, but he could correctly answer back that all the great naval powers had plans for an all-big-gun battleship, and Britain had stolen a march on them (and especially on Germany) by completing one in twelve months instead of the more usual three years.

Germany began building her own Dreadnought-class battleships and by 1914 had sixteen to the Royal Navy's twenty, far too narrow a margin for Britain's safety. And even this advantage had been achieved only as a result of the most strenuous efforts by British shipyards and Winston's endeavours to squeeze the money out of the Treasury. From being a critic of heavy rearmament Winston overnight had to become an advocate of increased warship building and thereby made enemies of his earlier friends and allies in the war for Liberal economy.

After he had been in office for scarcely one year, Winston got wind that Germany's ally Austria was planning to build a Dreadnought fleet, too. Austria's navy had previously been weak enough that the French could have coped with it in the event of war, allowing Britain to reduce her Mediterranean

Fleet to a skeleton force and build up further her naval power at home. Lloyd George especially had been nagging Winston about naval expenditure, and Winston replied by citing this new threat, with documentary evidence:

18 November 1912

My dear David,
Look at this. Do you realise what it means if it is true?
It is no use being vexed with me and reproaching me. I can no more control these facts than you can.
Should the Austrians build three extra Dread-noughts beyond anything yet foreseen or provided against, we shall have to take further measures. What measures I cannot now say: but an equal provision in some form or another will be necessary . . .

Winston's position was further worsened by the Canadians' reneging (as the result of a change of Prime Minister) on an agreement to pay for three Dreadnoughts and by the failure of negotiations conducted, in turn, by Cassel, Haldane and Winston himself, to persuade Germany to let up on her Dreadnought building. Conversations with the Kaiser proved equally futile. The Germans argued that it was all very well for Britain to propose what Winston called 'a naval holiday' when she had such an advantage in numbers.

The naval estimates of 1914–15, which Winston had to begin to prepare in late 1913, represented the climax of the political dispute, which split the whole country, over naval expenditure. More ships meant more men to train to man them, more fuel to power them and more storage space for the fuel, and more or bigger docks and more expenditure to maintain them, while the development of aviation and sub-marines entailed the creation of entirely new and expensive services. Moreover, the search for greater deadliness was the most expensive item of all. A battleship at the turn of the century had cost less than £1 million; now the figure was nearing £3 million.

When it became known in the Cabinet that the new estimates would be well over £50 million for the first time, there was great outrage amongst Winston's critics. Five members of the Cabinet, including Walter Runciman and McKenna, who were known to be unfriendly to Winston, wrote a letter to Asquith to make clear their alarm:

> . . . the total is unprecedented; the increase is unexampled at a time of international calm; and the impression powerfully created that we are leading the way in yet more rapid outlay.
>
> These proposals expose us to Parliamentary attack far more serious than the sporadic efforts of a few Liberal 'economists'. The Labour party will surely be driven to go to any lengths in dissociating itself from such increases; defection by a substantial group on our own benches is likely . . .

Margot Asquith, extremely improperly, wrote on 10 Downing Street headed paper to the Chancellor of the Exchequer, Lloyd George: 'Don't let Winston have too much money – it will hurt the party in every way – Labour & even Liberals. If one can't be a little economical when all foreign countries are peaceful I don't know *when* we can.'

The Prime Minister himself was attempting at this time, and until the estimates were passed, to keep the quarrellers within his party separated, so his wife's intervention (if he knew of it) was not helpful. As for Winston himself, he was beset on all sides, and there was talk of his resignation *and* of his taking the entire Board of Admiralty with him, which might prove a fatal blow to Asquith's administration.

Reporting the situation to the King, Sir Francis Hopwood (another of Winston's non-friends) wrote:

> Our affairs are very critical . . . The fact is the Cabinet is sick of Churchill's perpetually undermining & exploiting its policy and is picking a quarrel with him. As a colleague he is a great trial to them.

But their battleground is very ill-chosen as in consequence of their indolence he has probably got chapter
& verse for every item of the Naval Programme.
[He had!]

Some members of Winston's family, including Sunny, Aunt
Cornelia (Lady Wimborne), and Clementine herself, were
worried about his future, whether or not his policy was the
right one. Aunt Cornelia wrote:

> *I am going to write very frankly, and I know you
> won't take it amiss, because I love you and care
> so much for your career. I have an instinct you are
> going wrong. Even the ablest of men may wreck their
> political life, witness your dear Father, by an error of
> judgement and I who saw him eating out his heart in
> years of disappointment feel I can't keep silence. You
> are breaking with the traditions of Liberalism in your
> Naval expenditure; you are in danger of becoming
> purely a 'Navy man' . . .*

Asquith continued to work tirelessly for a compromise
between his warring factions in order to present a united
front when Winston presented his estimates. Winston, it
might seem to his Prime Minister, was feeling the strain
more than Asquith himself. 'I dined at the Churchills last
night,' Asquith wrote to Venetia Stanley. 'Winston slept
placidly in his armchair while I played bridge with Clemmie,
Goonie & the Lord Chief Justice* being our antagonists.
However, he did sometimes nod off after dinner, waking up
later to become a rejuvenated creature just when everyone
was ready for bed.'

But success for Asquith was close. By dint of a mixture of

---

*The Lord Chief Justice was Rufus Isaacs, created later Lord
Reading, Viceroy of India.

knocking heads together and forcing compromises out of the 'economists' as well as the 'navalists', agreement was reached on 11 February. 'Dearest Mama,' Winston wrote to Jennie on 10 February, 'I think the naval estimates are now past the danger point & if so the situation will be satisfactory. But it has been a long and wearing business wh has caused me at times vy gt perplexity.'

With this crisis behind him, all that was left for Winston to do was to present the estimates to a highly critical House of Commons on 17 March 1914: present them to the Conservatives as if they could not be any greater and to his own party and Labour members as if they could not possibly be any smaller. It was the sort of juggling challenge that he faced with relish.

We can see him, then, rising from his usual seat on the front bench, a sheaf of notes in his right hand, nodding towards the Speaker and then casting his eye over the packed benches on both sides, assessing their mood before opening his speech. Any member who remembers him a decade ago when he first entered the House will note his slightly more ordered appearance, thanks to his marriage, but his inevitable bow tie is already askew. He has put on a good deal of weight in the time, too, jowl well rounded, waistcoat buttons at full stretch, and hair receding towards the bald patch on his crown. He leans forward as he speaks, the tilt of his head expressive and his gestures the more effective for being few. His voice is clear, the lisp much less pronounced than it once was.

'These are the largest estimates for naval expenses ever presented to this House,' he begins equivocally, 'but I hope the House will not think it necessary on that account that I should introduce them in the longest speech ever delivered.' In the event, the speech lasts for two and a half hours, a personal record if not a House record.

> The burden of responsibility laid upon the British navy is heavy, and its weight increases year by year [he continued later]. All the world is building ships of the greatest power, training officers and men,

creating arsenals, and laying broad and deep the foundations of future permanent naval development and expansion. Besides the Great Powers, there are many smaller States who are buying or building great ships of war . . . None of these Powers need, like us, navies to defend their actual independence or safety. They build them so to play a part in the world's affairs. It is sport to them. It is life and death to us . . .

The speech was a *tour de force*, the greatest as well as the longest in his Parliamentary career. Even Lloyd George applauded it, and there were many on the opposition benches who reluctantly and privately gave it a high rating. The press divided according to party, as usual, but those of Liberal persuasion gave it a very high rating. The *Daily Telegraph* described it as 'the longest, and perhaps also the most weighty and eloquent, speech to which the House has listened from a First Lord of the Admiralty during the present generation'. The Liberal papers also gave Winston full credit, although the more radical were critical of the very high figures proposed, while the *Daily News* sounded a new and interesting note in describing 'the folly of speculating heavily in Dreadnoughts at a time when the best opinion is coming round to the view that the Dreadnought cannot live with the submarine'.

The Times, on the other hand, was worried about the lack of emphasis on building Dreadnoughts and, with the cancellation of the Canadian contribution, was particularly concerned about the loss of strength in the Mediterranean. 'What does Mr Churchill propose to do?'

Some years before Winston was appointed to the Admiralty, a number of the most senior and influential admirals – among them Prince Louis of Battenberg and Jellicoe – had been pressing for a full-scale test of the mobilization of the Navy's Royal Fleet Reserve – the 'Third Fleet'. These reservists numbered some twenty thousand, and while the men had been called up before, usually in small numbers to specific ships, there had never before been a mass mobilization.

In his search for economy, Winston had been reluctant to authorize this expensive proposal. But after the summer manoeuvres in 1913, the Board suggested that the cost could be more than offset by scrapping the 1914 manoeuvres while the conclusions drawn from the 1912 and 1913 manoeuvres were studied in detail. Winston welcomed the proposal in anticipation of a tough struggle ahead over the estimates.

Both Prince Louis and Jellicoe were now long accustomed to Winston's methods of implementing proposals. He was, after all, a politician, with different priorities and standards from those of a naval officer. The first step was to get down something in writing, for the record, which made clear the attribution to himself. There was no surprise, therefore, when these two admirals received a memorandum on 22 October 1913, that contained their proposals as if they originated from Winston himself:

> . . . I am drawn to the conclusion that it would be better to have no Grand Manoeuvres in 1914–15 but to substitute instead a mobilization of the Third Fleet. The whole of the Royal Fleet Reserve, and the whole of the Reserve Officers could be mobilized and trained together for a week or ten days . . .

Later, Winston wrote in his memoirs, 'Prince Louis agreed. The necessary measures were taken and the project was mentioned in Parliament on the 18th March, 1914.' But Winston's memory failed him on this point. In fact, he incorporated his announcement in his estimates speech of 17 March, where it must attract the maximum attention from a packed House, rather than as a mention in the debate on the estimates the following day, when fewer members would be present and the announcement probably ignored by the press:

> We have decided to substitute this year for the grand manoeuvres [he stated] a general mobilisation of the

Third Fleet. We are calling up the whole of the Naval Reserve for a period of eleven days. . . . This test is one of the most important that could possibly be made, and it is really surprising to me that it has never been undertaken before. The cost including the bounty [bonus] of £1 will be about £50,000. Having no grand manoeuvres yields a saving of £230,000, so there is a net saving of £180,000.

This mobilization began on 15 July, and Prince Louis accompanied Winston to the naval base at Chatham to watch the reservists arrive, draw their kits, and proceed to their ships. All the Third Fleet men of war then headed for Spithead and the rendezvous with the First (regular) Fleet.

Here [wrote Winston], *on the 17th and 18th July was held the grand review of the Navy. It constituted incomparably the greatest assemblage of naval power ever witnessed in the history of the world. The King himself was present and inspected ships of every class. On the morning of the 19th the whole Fleet put to sea for exercises of various kinds. It took more than six hours for his armada, every ship decked with flags and crowded with bluejackets and marines to pass, with bands playing and at 15 knots, before the Royal Yacht, while overhead the naval seaplanes and aeroplanes circled continuously . . .*

At the time Winston was presenting the naval estimates to Parliament, Clementine knew that she was pregnant again and that, after her miscarriage last time, her activities during the summer would have to be limited: no tennis, no riding, and, later, no swimming. Apart from a slight illness in early May 1914, which kept her separated from her children, her health remained good. Later in the month, she and her mother and Nellie left with the children and the nursemaid for Dieppe, a town she always loved and where her mother largely resided. She was happy there, with her family about her, the only darkness – like an ever-threatening thundercloud – concern about money.

In spite of all the economies she practised, the cost of running Admiralty House and the failure of Winston to tame his extravagance led to steady spending above their income. Even if Clementine had been able to throw off her worries by the French seaside, she would have been reminded of them by Winston's letters. He was trying to establish a substantial loan through a life insurance policy, but as he told her in a letter, 'My business proposals do not go smoothly – for the reason that the insurance companies try to charge excessive premiums on my life – political strain, short-lived parentage & of course flying.'

Early in June, Winston visited the French naval school at Cherbourg, and afterwards travelled overland to Dieppe to spend a few hours with his family before being picked up by the *Enchantress* to continue an inspection of naval stations. 'The Babies were sad when they found the *Enchantress* had sailed away in the night,' wrote Clementine.

Winston was as busy as ever, naval preoccupations being matched by the seemingly intractable problem of Ireland, which completely divided the nation. It also distracted the people from the steadily deteriorating international situation after the assassination in Serbia of Archduke Franz Ferdinand of Austria and his wife on 28 June.

Meanwhile, Winston determined that there should be some sort of a family holiday in which he could participate if only intermittently. For several years he and his brother Jack had rented adjacent cottages at Overstrand on the Norfolk coast, where Diana and Randolph and Jack and Goonie's sons, Johnny, aged 5, and Peregrine, eighteen months, could play on the beach. Pear Tree Cottage and Beehive Cottage should have been named in the plural for both were conversions, by Edwin Lutyens, of terraces of fishermen's cottages, each with six bedrooms and a billiards room as well as the usual accommodation downstairs. A winding path led down the low sloping cliff to the seashore where fishermen's boats

271

were still drawn up onto the sand for lack of a harbour. 'The sands are firm and good,' records the local guide book – alone a good enough reason for Winston to choose this village.

On 12 July a larger and more impressive vessel than one of these boats hove to offshore: the *Enchantress* again, with Winston on board. He came ashore to see his family for a few hours, as he had at Dieppe a few weeks earlier.

> *It was quite forlorn leaving you last night* [he wrote to Clementine later]. *I don't know why a departure to the sea seems so much more significant, than going off by train. We watched your figures slowly climbing up the zigzag & slowly fading in the dusk: and I felt as if I were going to the other end of the world . . .*

He was going only some seventy-five miles away to London, but the world was, within a week or two, to become a very different place, never to be the same again. Austria was hell-bent on revenge against Serbia, where the archduke and his wife had been assassinated. The latest ultimatum delivered to this small state, which Winston described as 'the most insolent document of its kind ever devised', made war, which would besides draw in Russia and Germany, and France and Belgium, and Britain and her empire, almost inevitable.

On Friday afternoon, 24 July, ministers were due to leave London for their country places. Winston was still determined to get away at least for a night or two with his family. There was a Cabinet meeting at 2.30 p.m., and he strode the short distance from the Admiralty to 10 Downing Street, where Asquith presided and as Prime Minister began to deal with the first item on the agenda – the implementation of home rule for Ireland.

Suddenly the proceedings were interrupted by a secretary who entered the cabinet room and silenced the subject under discussion for years: a further and more savage ultimatum had been sent to Serbia, virtually precluding any possibility of avoiding war. Suddenly Ireland was pushed aside, being replaced by national survival against the awesome war machine of the Central Powers, Germany and Austria-Hungary. After a while, Asquith adjourned the meeting until the next morning – a Saturday, which alone underlined the urgency. Winston hurried back to the Admiralty to check with Prince Louis on the state of the Fleet. The First and Second Fleets were at Portland, but the reservists manning the Second Fleet would shortly be discharged and the rest given 'manoeuvres leave', while the Third Fleet ships, manned entirely by reservists, were already on their way to their home ports where the crews were to be paid off on Monday. Winston had a preliminary discussion with Prince Louis, his First Sea Lord, about the possible need to halt the dispersal of these reservists.

That Friday evening Winston was driven to Brook House in Park Lane to dine with his old friend Cassel. He was not surprised to find there already Herr Albert Ballin, the German shipping magnate, almost as rich as Cassel and quite as ardent in his efforts over the past year to ensure peace between Germany and Britain. Ballin was also a close friend of Kaiser Wilhelm II and Alfred von Tirpitz, Germany's Jacky Fisher and the creator (with the support of the Kaiser) of Germany's High Seas Fleet.

The mood was bleak and pessimistic. The conversation kept pace with the placing and removal of dishes and covered every aspect of the international crisis. At one point, Ballin recalled a conversation he had had with Bismarck. 'I remember him telling me the year before he died that one day the great European War would come out of some damned stupid thing in the Balkans . . .'

Ballin continued, addressing Winston now: 'If Russia advances against Austria because Austria attacks Serbia, we shall have to march too. And if we march France must march. And then what would England do?'

'Well, Herr Ballin,' Winston replied, 'it would be a mistake for Germany to presume that Britain would necessarily do nothing.'

On Saturday morning, Winston attended the Cabinet and

then walked back across Horse Guards Parade to the Admiralty. There Prince Louis awaited him – a grave, tall figure in morning coat, still crashingly handsome at sixty years, with a fine full greying beard, which had once tickled the cheeks of Lillie Langtry and other courtesans of her day.

Although almost more patriotic than any Briton, Prince Louis was suffering much anguish. For what he had for so long feared seemed now to be almost inevitable: war with the land of his birth. His accent, after all, was still strongly guttural; he had many relations in Germany; one of his brothers-in-law, Prince Henry, was an admiral in the German navy; and all his property was in Germany. Prince Louis was inclined to be censorious at the best of times, and today he could hardly contain his indignation at the disappearance to the country of most of the Cabinet, including his own senior, who was about to leave him in sole charge of the Navy while he went off to the seaside. 'Ministers with their weekend holidays are notorious,' he later told his younger son, Dickie.

> I have given instructions to the GPO to keep the telephone switchboard open twenty-four hours a day [Winston told his First Sea Lord before leaving]. Therefore you may ring me at any time, and I shall telephone you every few hours in case you have any news. The most critical decision that we are likely to have to make concerns the Third Fleet. Once discharged, most of the men, and their officers, will go directly off on their holidays and be difficult or impossible to trace. But I need not tell you that the decision will be highly sensitive politically as well as practically.

Imagine for a moment Winston descending from his Admiralty car at Liverpool Street Station just before 1 p.m. on this Saturday afternoon. There are few people on the platform, and once on the train, carrying his small Gladstone bag and stick – he always travels as light as possible – he makes his way straight to the dining car.

The train stops at Chelmsford, Ipswich and Norwich, where Winston has to change into a local train for Cromer, arriving at Overstrand at 3.30 p.m. There brother Jack greets him and walks with him to his big open car outside the station. We can be sure they talk of nothing but the crisis. Jack has grown up taller by some five inches than his older brother and appears even taller for he holds himself well.

'How were things when you left, Winny?'

'Critical, dangerous and threatening.'

'All three?'

'I dined with Ernest and Herr Ballin last night. Both were well informed on the feeling in Germany. Both thought war was almost inevitable. Now I intend to bury my head in the sands of Overstrand for a day or two. How is Goonie? How are your chicks?'

It has not rained for some days and the road along the coast between the sand dunes is dusty. Fishing boats, we can imagine, bob offshore, and distantly through the haze a cruiser with four tall funnels makes its way north towards the Humber, trailing a long stream of black smoke.

'Everyone's down on the beach,' Jack says as he draws up off the road behind Pear Tree Cottage. 'Shall we go down to join them?'

'At once – now. Time is more precious here even than in London.'

The two fathers, stripped now of their jackets and waist-coats, hurry down the two-hundred-yard-long sunken lane called The Land. From the shallow cliff top at the end they pause and look down at their families on the sandy beach below. Rugs are spread, there are two wicker baskets for pic-nic teas. Diana and Randolph appear to be deeply absorbed in the construction of a castle, with Randolph in noisy charge in spite of his younger age; while Johnny and Peregrine are displaying more activity in the shallows of the sea, splashing one another. Their mothers, both in deck chairs, turn at the sound of their husbands' call. Goonie leaps up at once, calling, 'Winnie darling!' while Clementine, heavy with child, confines herself to a cry of welcome and a wave of both arms. Already the children are running towards them . . .

Winston waves back, but remarks to Jack in a sombre tone, 'Perhaps we are observing the last glimpse of happy, carefree peace either of us will see – for some years: yes, for *some years*.'

That evening before dinner, Winston got through on the telephone first to Cromer. For this, he had to walk to the house of a neighbour, Sir Edgar Speyer, who had one of the few telephones in Overstrand. The operator then connected him directly to the Admiralty. It was not a good line and he had difficulty in hearing what Prince Louis had to say, but it seemed that Serbia had accepted the outrageous Austrian ultimatum. Winston had wanted to avoid crisis talk as far as possible in the few hours of family life that he had stolen, but it could not be avoided altogether, and there was general relief at the dinner table.

'I went to bed with a feeling things might blow over,' Winston recalled. 'We had had . . . so many scares before. Time after time the clouds had loomed up vague, menacing, constantly changing; time after time they had dispersed . . . Reassured by these reflections I slept peacefully, and no summons disturbed the silence of the night.'

At nine o'clock on the following, Sunday, morning, Winston telephoned Prince Louis again – and again the line was a bad one, with much static and crackle. What little Prince Louis had heard – and it was only Foreign Office rumour – was not good. Austria, egged on by Germany, was still not satisfied. 'I will telephone you at midday,' Winston told him.

'I went down to the beach and played with the children,' Winston wrote of that morning. 'We dammed the little rivulets which trickled down to the sea as the tide went out. It was a very beautiful day. The North Sea shone and sparkled to a far horizon. What was there beyond that line where sea and sky melted into one another?'

First Lord and First Sea Lord spoke again, though scarcely audibly, at midday. But all the news Prince Louis had to offer was bad. Austria was clearly bent on invasion. Her troops were on the frontier. One order only was necessary. As Ballin had said, if they marched, Russia would support her ally Serbia, just as Germany would support her ally Austria and invade Russia . . .

Prince Louis seemed to be asking about the reservists of the Third Fleet. Should they be released? And what about 'manoeuvre leave' for the First Fleet? Prince Louis claimed later that he was unclear about his instructions; the only thing he *was* clear about was that the decision must be his, as the man on the spot, and that the First Lord would return to London that evening.

But by the time Winston was due to arrive, at around 9 p.m., it would be too late. If leave was to be halted, if the reservists were to remain with their ships, the order must be given at once. A momentous political decision was therefore in the hands of a naval officer. Was this deliberate? Prince Louis always believed it was.

After little more than twenty-four hours with his family, Winston regretfully kissed the children and Clemmie good-bye, and Jack took him to the station. The sky had clouded over, and the storm and rain that had affected the rest of the country earlier was clearly about to sweep over East Anglia.

At Liverpool Street Station, a car raced Winston to the Admiralty. Special editions of the Sunday newspapers were on the streets and Winston bought a number of them. They told only of increasing tension and the likelihood of a great European war. Prince Louis, who – except for a brief sleep – had been on duty continuously since Winston had left the previous day, greeted him solemnly. 'Yes, I made the decision some time ago,' the First Sea Lord told him. 'I wrote it out myself. "Stand the Fleet fast." It was just in time.'

Winston congratulated him, at the same time commiser-ating with him. It could not have been easy taking this first hostile step against the land of his birth. Then Winston had himself driven to his old home, 33 Eccleston Square, where the Foreign Secretary still lived. The only other person there besides Sir Edward Grey was his private secretary and the senior clerk at the Foreign Office, Sir William Tyrrell.

'How are things, Edward?' Winston asked.

'We view the situation very gravely,' the Foreign Secretary told him, and Winston knew that things could scarcely be worse, for Grey was a man not given to hyperbole.

'We are holding the Fleet together, otherwise the reservists would have dispersed by now, and many more gone on leave. Shall I make a public announcement or will that only exacerbate things?'

Both Tyrrell and Grey agreed that the Admiralty should proclaim it at once. 'It might have the effect of sobering the Central Powers and steadying Europe.'

Back at the Admiralty, Winston called for the secretary, Sir Graham Greene, and between them they drafted an announcement, which appeared in all the newspapers the next morning.

Asquith had been playing golf while Winston was speeding back to London on Sunday afternoon. But he returned to London on the Monday morning for the first of many urgent Cabinet meetings. Venetia Stanley learned all about what was going on, as usual, in a letter Asquith wrote to her in the afternoon. 'We seem to be on the *very brink*,' he told her, 'but near or far, you are my beloved & fill my thoughts and heart. *All love*,' he concluded.

After a second Cabinet meeting that Monday evening, in which 'at least three-quarters of its members were determined not to be drawn into a European quarrel,' Winston wrote a more measured letter than Asquith's to Clementine at Overstrand. 'Europe is trembling on the verge of a general war,' he wrote.

Everything tends towards catastrophe & collapse. I am interested, geared up & happy. Is it not horrible to be built like that? The preparations have a hideous

278

fascination for me. I pray to God to forgive me for such fearful moods of levity. Yet I wd do my best for peace, & nothing wd induce me wrongfully to strike the blow. I cannot feel we in this island are in any serious degree responsible for the wave of madness wh has swept the mind of Christendom . . . We all drift on in a kind of dull cataleptic trance . . .

Winston and Prince Louis had earlier in the day despatched a preliminary 'very secret warning' to all British naval commanders in chief throughout the world. 'Be prepared,' it ran in part, 'to shadow possible hostile men-of-war and consider dispositions of HM ships under your command from this point of view . . . No unnecessary person is to be informed.'

On the following day, 28 July, with still no light in the darkness, Winston called in his Chief of Naval Staff, Admiral Doveton Sturdee, and Prince Louis for an early conference. The momentous decision was taken to despatch the First Fleet (now to be called the Grand Fleet) to its war stations in the north.

To-morrow, Wednesday, the First Fleet is to leave Portland for Scapa Flow [ran the Admiralty's signal of 28 July, 5 p.m.]. Destination is to be kept secret . . . Course from Portland is to be shaped to southward, then a middle Channel course to the Straits of Dover. The Squadrons are to pass through the Straits without lights during the night and to pass outside the shoals on the way north . . .

Winston, now quite as romantically in love with the Navy as he ever had been with the Army, allowed his imagination to play on this great transfer of power he and his staff at the Admiralty had set in motion:

We may now picture this great Fleet, with its flotillas and cruisers, steaming slowly out of Portland

279

Harbour, squadron by squadron, scores of gigantic castles of steel wending their way across the misty, shining sea, like giants bowed in anxious thought. We may picture them again as darkness fell, eighteen miles of warships running at high speed and in absolute blackness through the narrow Straits, bearing with them into the broad waters of the North the safeguard of considerable affairs.

At Pear Tree Cottage, Clementine felt isolated from the momentous events taking place in the capitals of Europe and fretted about the baby who had begun to move in anticipation of imminent birth. At the heart of the crisis in London, Winston kept her as closely in touch as he could within the limits of security. On 28 July he made a perhaps unconscious reference of comfort to her in her anxiety about the unborn child. 'The two black swans on St James's Park lake have a darling cygnet – grey, fluffy, precious and unique. I watched them this evening for some time as a relief from all the plans and schemes.'

Just one week after Winston had hastened back to London to face the crisis, he sat down at one o'clock in the morning, after a day of Cabinet meetings and critical work at the Admiralty, and wrote:

> Cat – dear,
> It is all up. Germany has quenched the last hopes of peace by declaring war on Russia.

On the last day of July, Winston could report that the Navy was ready for any eventuality, with the battleships at Scapa Flow, the great anchorage in the Orkney Islands north of Scotland, and at Cromarty further south; while at Rosyth, under the command of the admired and dashing Admiral Beatty, lay the battle-cruisers, the swift scouting wing of the Grand Fleet.

To George V, whose first thought was always for the Navy, Winston wrote, 'The general position and strength of the British Fleet Squadrons & Flotillas is regarded as satisfactory by the Board of Admiralty.' And to his wife, still at Pear Tree Cottage and very fretful, he wrote, 'There is still hope although the clouds are blacker & blacker . . . everybody is preparing swiftly for war and at any moment the blow may fall.'

It fell at 11 p.m. (midnight, German time) on 4 August after Germany had declared war on Russia and the day before the German armies crossed into France and Belgium. As the excited, innocent crowds cheered in the streets of London and in Trafalgar Square within earshot of the Admiralty, Winston authorized the despatch of this signal to all naval vessels and establishments: 'Commence hostilities against Germany.'

18

Sea of Troubles

By an ironical and fateful chance, Kitchener had been appointed head of the Army after Britain declared war on Germany. Suddenly and unexpectedly, therefore, the thirty-nine-year-old ex-Hussar and head of the Navy found himself working in harness with the sixty-four-year-old soldier who had done his best to frustrate Winston's career and made himself a target for Winston's contempt. Kitchener had remained hostile to Winston over the intervening years, just as Winston continued to despise Kitchener. 'Churchill hates Kitchener,' Wilfrid Blunt wrote in his diary [3 April 1910], 'who, he told us, once prevented his entering the Egyptian Service, and was always rude to him, he does not know with what reason.' But the heat of war (for the time being, anyway) burned away the mutual hostility of these two men who now had to work together.

One of the first tasks of the Royal Navy in the event of a Continental war was to transport an expeditionary force to France. Within five days of the outbreak of war, the first units of this force embarked on transports for the short crossing to France. The Admiralty warned Jellicoe, commanding the Grand Fleet, that the enemy knew of this movement of more than a hundred thousand men across the Channel, with all their horses and equipment, and that 'the Germans have the strongest incentives to action . . . They may well argue that a raid or raids now upon the East Coast would interrupt, confuse and probably delay the departure of the Army.'

Delay had to be avoided at all costs, for the French and Belgian armies were already hard pressed. Winston sought every means of speeding up the transportation:

My dear Kitchener,
   *I find on enquiry from our Transport Department
that if the ships go only by night, the passage may
take nearly twice as long. In these circumstances,
after consultation with the First Sea Lord, I think
the risk from submarines must be faced. Otherwise it
will throw out all your railways arrangements as well
as those for embarkation and transport, and cause a
delay which I expect you would regard as fatal . . .*

The transporting of the Army to France 'was a period of great
anxiety to us,' Winston wrote. 'All the most fateful possibilities
were open. We were bound to expect a military descent upon
our coasts . . . or a naval raid into the Channel to cut down
the transports . . . The great naval battle might begin at any
moment . . . It was a period of extreme psychological tension.'
   In fact the operation was completed between 9 August and
22 August without loss of or injury to a single man.

Although Clementine took no part in this opening drama
and was not even at Winston's side, she too was suffering
'extreme psychological tension'. It had been agreed between
the two families that Clementine and Goonie and their children and nursemaids should complete their late summer
holiday, while Winston remained in London and Jack joined
his regiment and went off to the war. Clementine felt starved
of news at this most critical time. She was accustomed to
being privy to all the most important and confidential Cabinet
and international intelligence.
   On the first day of the expeditionary force's move to
France, she wrote to Winston:

*I am longing to get your letter with the secret news. It
shall be destroyed at once. I hope that in it, you tell
me about the expeditionary force. Do I guess right
that some have gone already? Be a good one and
write & feed me with tit-bits. I am being so wise &*

> good & sitting on the Beach & playing with my kittens,
> & doing my little housekeeping, but how I long to dash
> up & be near you and the pulse of things.

When Clementine failed to get any hard news out of her husband, she wrote to him again, this time with a trace of impatience: 'I was disappointed because I hoped you were going to tell me about the Expeditionary Force. Do send me news of it. When it is going, where it will land . . .'

It is easy to understand Clementine's anxiety, but her advanced state of pregnancy was leading her to be more than usually emotional and thoughtless. She took no account of the vast pressures under which Winston was working, and failed to understand his position and the need for secrecy now that war had been declared and was not just a threat. The following day, she received only a terse note from him:

> My dear one,
>   This is only a line from a vy tired Winston. The Expedy Force about wh you are so inquisitive is on its road & will be all on the spot in time. I wish I cd whisk down to you & dig a little on the beach. My work here is vy heavy & so interesting that I cannot leave it.
>   Now I am really going to knock off.
>   Ever your loving
>   W

Ignoring the implied rebuke, Clementine replied with a long formula of health instructions about not smoking too much, avoiding indigestion, taking an early morning ride, and going to bed well *before* midnight ('You *must* have eight hours sleep every night to be your best self'). Clementine's intentions were irreproachable, but this was perhaps an inappropriate time to be laying down a good health formula.

Winston was not the only member of her family to cause Clementine agitation. She and Nellie had decided that their mother should no longer remain at her home in Dieppe, which could easily be threatened by the advancing German

284

armies. So Nellie went over to bring her back to Pear Tree Cottage, Clementine's understanding being that the two of them would help look after her. Lady Blanche Hozier was a good deal less spirited than she had once been, and her health was not robust.

When she arrived at Overstrand she was exhausted by the journey, and instead of being accompanied by Nellie she only brought a letter from her. It seemed that Clementine's sister had suddenly decided that she must involve herself in war work and had gone to the Astors' great house, Cliveden, which was to be converted into a convalescent home. This was happening all over the country among the rich as a gesture of patriotism and solidarity.

Clementine was not pleased at having sole responsibility for their frail mother thrust upon her when she was so heavily pregnant and virtually without servants. It also precluded any possibility of taking a day or two off, as she had planned, to go up to London and stay with Winston. But now she heard that Nellie had gone off to Belgium to join a nursing unit.

This was too much. Clementine sat down and wrote an immensely long letter to Winston – page after page – in condemnation of her beloved sister and her selfishness.

> *It is all cheap emotion. Nellie is not trained* [she wrote]. *She will be one more useless mouth to feed in that poor little country which in a few days will be the scene of horrible grim happenings. Nellie's obvious and natural duty is to look after Mother. . . . I feel quite ill this morning, as I have had a very bad night & this on top of it has really upset me . . .*

Winston, between running the Navy at war, attending Cabinet meetings and keeping *au courant* with fellow ministers and their activities and with events in France and Belgium, and Russia and Serbia, and a great deal more, fulfilled his family duties as well as he could. Secret from Clementine, he rather admired the spirited Nellie for hurling herself into the war. He was also amused that when the enemy overran her medical unit, she was, as he had been fifteen years earlier, locked up in a railway station waiting room. He was also delighted that she had spent some of the time scrawling on the wall:

> Our good King George is both
> Greater and wiser,
> Than all other monarchs
> Including 'der Kaiser'.

In spite of this indiscretion, the unit, and Nellie, were allowed to continue treating British casualties and eventually allowed to go home.

Winston was less preoccupied with the goings-on of Clementine's sister than with his wife's safety, and it is difficult to understand why he did not insist on her ending her holiday and returning to London. Most of the other holidaymakers along the Norfolk coast, which was the nearest part of the country to Germany, had gone home early, and Winston knew that his big Napier car, which could contain them all at a pinch, needed repair.

> *It makes me a little anxious that you should be on the coast. It is a 100 to one against a raid – but still there is the chance, and Cromer has a good landing place near. I wish you would get the motor repaired and keep it so that you can whisk away at the first sign of trouble.*

But while deeply concerned and irrational about many of the domestic events of this critical time, Clementine was transformed to her old self when it came to personal danger, even with the children beside her. When her mother suggested that the Germans, with their knowledge of Clementine's whereabouts, might send an aeroplane to kidnap her and hold her to ransom 'for several of our handsomest ships', Clementine instructed Winston 'not to sacrifice the smallest or cheapest submarine or even the oldest ship', for she would prefer him to be a 'Spartan' for allowing her to die bravely and unransomed.

All this nonsense came to an end when Clementine and her 'kittens' returned to London for the birth of her baby. But war events conspired to make this the worst possible time to do so. In France and Belgium the fighting was fierce and critical, with Germany well on the way to knocking out France completely according to the 'Schlieffen plan'.* Brussels had rapidly been invaded, and only the great port of Antwerp held up the German advance on to the vital French Channel ports. The Germans were besieging this city with 60,000 troops, and during the first days of October the Belgian government and king declared that they would have to evacuate. If this should happen, the last Belgian defences were certain to fall.

Winston had already made a number of visits to France, unable to resist the lure of battle. He was a friend and admirer of General Sir John French, the British Commander in Chief, and also had the excuse of visiting the naval flyers and a Royal Marines contingent. On 2 October Asquith decided to accept Winston's offer to go to Antwerp to promise the wavering Belgians reinforcements and diversions, and to put some steel into their resistance. It was the kind of urgent, dramatic and dangerous mission that set his Marlborough blood flowing faster.

Writing to Venetia Stanley (who, unlike Clementine, was still privy to everything that went on at the seat of power), Asquith explained:

> The intrepid Winston set off at midnight . . . He will
> go straightaway & beard the King and his ministers

---

*Field Marshal Graf von Schlieffen (1833–1913) created a scheme to achieve victory over France and Russia by knocking out France swiftly in six weeks by a great wheeling movement through Belgium, and then transferring the victorious armies to the east to crush Russia.

and try to infuse into their backbone the necessary quantity of starch. . . . I don't know how fluent he is in French, but if he was able to do himself justice in a foreign tongue, the Belges will have listened to a discourse the like of which they have never heard before. I cannot but think that he will stiffen them up to the sticking point.

Asquith was right. Winston persuaded the Belgian government to postpone their departure and then went off in a motor car to inspect the defences for himself. It was a chilly day and he wore a long black overcoat with broad astrakhan collar and his usual black top hat, and swung his silver-topped walking stick. In his customary manner, he completely ignored the enemy fire from howitzers, rifles and machine guns and astonished the Belgian troops by taking complete charge of the situation, criticizing the siting of guns and trenches and emphasizing his points by waving his stick or thumping the ground with it. He then climbed back into his car, waiting impatiently to be driven to the next section of the front line.

Later, when the reinforcing Royal Marines arrived and were settled in, Winston came along to inspect them, dressed suitably for this more maritime occasion: 'enveloped in a cloak, and on his head wore a yachtsman's cap,' observed an accompanying journalist. 'He was tranquilly smoking a large cigar and looking at the progress of the battle under a rain of shrapnel, which I can only call fearful.'

Carried away by all this military endeavour and by memories of handling great armies in the playroom of 2 Connaught Place, Winston signalled Asquith with the proposal that he should forthwith resign his office as First Lord and take command of all the forces defending Antwerp. 'I feel it my duty to offer my services, because I am sure this arrangement will afford the best prospects of victorious result . . .'

Asquith, describing this offer as 'a real bit of tragi-comedy', sent 'a *most decided* negative' in reply. He went on to confide in Venetia Stanley the Cabinet's response when told of this exchange of telegrams. 'I regret to say that it was received with a Homeric laugh. W. is an ex-Lieutenant of Hussars, and would if his proposal had been accepted, have been in command of two distinguished Major Generals, not to mention Brigadiers, Colonels &c . . .' Winston was summoned home, and with his departure the Belgians relapsed into defeatism, surrendering the city on 10 October.

When the news of this one-man reinforcing expedition by the First Lord got out, it was criticized by his regular press enemies (such as Howell Arthur Gwynne, editor of the *Morning Post*) as irresponsible and vainglorious, and by his friends as foolishly courageous. Asquith was undisguisedly relieved. Lacking confidence in the Admiralty Board, he had virtually been running the Admiralty in Winston's absence in addition to all his other responsibilities.

As if to confirm that his offer did not stem from a fit of madness, Winston on return again begged to be relieved of the Admiralty in order to take up some big military command. 'Having, as he says, "tasted blood" these last few days, he is beginning like a tiger to raven for more,' Asquith wrote. Later, Winston reflected, 'It was a sporting offer, and I was very lucky not to be taken at my word.'

Edward Grey, on the other hand, was high in his praise of Winston's expedition to Antwerp. While at a Cabinet meeting, he wrote to Clementine, 'I feel a glow imparted by the thought that I am sitting next to a Hero. I can't tell you how much I admire his courage & gallant spirit & genius for war.' Clementine's own feelings about the Antwerp business were not nearly so clear-cut. She had at first 'been startled by the suddenness of Winston's departure', anxious and distressed during the last days of her pregnancy while he was under fire in the field, and finally had given birth at the Admiralty while he was still absent. Later, when she learned of his offer to resign his post and become a soldier again, she thought it absurd, ill-advised and selfish.

Even in later years, Clementine remained concerned with her own feelings about this lapse in judgement, this dereliction of family responsibility. She disregarded the immense

289

courage it involved and the important military benefits: the postponement of Antwerp's surrender gave Belgium's allies the time needed to reinforce, and retain throughout the war, the vital Channel ports.

After an audience with the King at Buckingham Palace, Winston hastened down the Mall to the Admiralty where he had a joyful reunion with his wife and admired the day-old girl baby – who already revealed a tuft of red hair like his own.

After recovering from her labour and the birth of her child, Clementine recuperated at the country residence of their friend Sir Philip Sassoon in Kent. Again, Goonie came with her, and Jennie visited them. Now, with the addition of baby Sarah, Jennie had five grandchildren. Jennie's George was fighting at the front, had in fact been at the siege of Antwerp, and remained a source of concern even though their marriage had broken up and they had been divorced the year before. Jack was in the trenches, too, and Goonie 'was in a great state of anxiety' about him, Clementine told Winston. But Winston was able to telephone a few days later to reassure his sister-in-law that her husband had been posted to the safety of General Sir John French's staff.

In the early days of the war, the Navy was enjoying greater good fortune than the Army, and the first victory at sea happily coincided with the only visit to London from Overstrand made by Clementine and her children. Two of the Navy's fire-eaters, Commodores Reginald Tyrwhitt and Roger Keyes, impatiently waiting for the enemy to come out and face battle, devised a provocative movement off the German island of Heligoland with their light forces and submarines.

The German navy ran a daily protective patrol of destroyers against British minelaying off the German coast. The plan was to lure these destroyers, and other men of war that might come out to support them, into the vicinity of the submarines and light cruisers, and then, additionally, fall upon them with battle-cruisers coming down secretly from the north. The operation at first went awry when the Germans turned the tables on these two aggressive commanders by sending in powerful reinforcements more swiftly than expected. But the battle-cruisers arrived on the scene in the nick of time. With their heavy guns they sank three German cruisers and a destroyer without any British losses and returned to base before the Germans could send in their battle fleet.

It was hailed as a greater victory than, in material terms, it really was. 'We had a great reception,' Tyrwhitt recorded. 'Every ship and everybody cheered like mad. Winston met us at Sheerness and came up to Chatham with us and fairly slobbered over me. Offered me any ship I liked and all the rest of it . . . Everybody quite mad with delight at the success of our first naval venture.' Clementine wrote to Keyes of his 'splendid victory' and invited him to lunch at the Admiralty.

More important than the considerable weakening of the enemy light forces by this victory was the caution and defeatism instilled into the German naval command. The Kaiser was greatly displeased, and all ranks in the German navy, which already suffered from a sense of inferiority, succumbed to depressed spirits.

From the day war broke out, Winston had been imbued with the certainty that luck would be on his side, as it always had been in military operations. He had mastered his job as First Lord and was confident in his commanders and the Board of Admiralty and in the ability of the Grand Fleet to meet any German threat at sea. In spite of his brief longing to be a general, he relished his work, gloried in its power and responsibility, and looked forward eagerly to the expected clash of the two fleets, the modern Battle of Trafalgar that must end in the defeat of the German High Seas Fleet.

In fact, his cup of luck at the Admiralty was almost empty already. As some farsighted theoreticians, including Fisher, had predicted, the new weapons of naval warfare, the underwater mine and the torpedo, were already having a decisive influence. Submarine (U-boat) periscopes, real or imaginary, were so frequently sighted by ships of Jellicoe's Grand Fleet, that 'periscopeitis disease' set in among lookouts. A solitary roaming seal was enough to send the whole Fleet into a dither. There were scares even in the anchorage of Scapa Flow, leading to the ships putting to sea and, at one time, retreating to the west coast of Scotland and Ireland.

The fear of the submarine's torpedo was intensified many times over when the Germans scored their first successes. The first victim was the flotilla leader HMS *Pathfinder*. Then, on 22 September, a triple tragedy shocked the Navy and the nation. Since the beginning of the war a constant patrol had operated close to the German and Dutch coasts to give early warning of any attempted German attack on the Channel transports or incursions by mine-layers. The ships employed on this work were old armoured cruisers that, unlike the men who manned them, were expendable. The 'live bait squadron' was their unofficial black definition. Three of these big ships were patrolling, without destroyer escort, at low speed on a steady course early in the morning, when one of them was struck by a torpedo. No one saw its trail, and at first no-one knew whether it had been a mine or a torpedo.

As the ship began rapidly to settle, the Captain ordered the other two armoured cruisers to close and take off the survivors. Their boats were in the water on their rescue work when one and then the other armoured cruiser were also struck and in their turn began to sink. Fewer than one thousand of the 2,200 officers and men were eventually picked up by other ships.

Blame was attached to the Captain, to the destroyer commander for not being there, and to the two responsible admirals commanding the squadron, who were also not present. Why were the ships zigzagging and travelling no faster than ten knots? Why was not a proper lookout being kept? Why did not the other two ships at once scatter instead of presenting themselves as sitting ducks? None of these questions was properly answered. Roger Keyes, among others, had warned of the suicidal nature of this patrol. Winston himself had issued a memorandum five days earlier recommending that the patrol be withdrawn. So he was in the clear, but he was also in charge.

If anyone was to blame it was the Chief of Naval Staff, Admiral Doveton Sturdee, but Winston wanted no scapegoats at the Admiralty. It might have been better if he had, for the press threw the blame at him. Fortunately, the next, and much worse, disaster was kept from the public altogether. Almost simultaneous with the Grand Fleet's retreat from the North Sea to the Atlantic, a high-priority and secret manoeuvre, a German minelayer succeeded in evading all patrols to lay a large number of mines off the coast of northern Ireland.

One of these mines was struck by the Dreadnought *Audacious* on the morning of 27 October. She heeled over, taking in a great deal of water. While she was under tow by the transatlantic liner *Olympic*, which luckily failed to strike any other mine, a number of American passengers had time to aim their cameras at the dramatic sight, and some of the photographs appeared in American newspapers the following week. The almost-new battleship later that day blew up and sank, and this loss brought to near parity the number of Dreadnoughts in the German and British fleets. It was well that the Germans did not know that the ship had sunk or that, thanks to the absence from its northern bases of the Grand Fleet, they could, for the present, range the North Sea without fear of being intercepted.

Later on that same morning of 27 October, Winston called at 10 Downing Street in 'a rather sombre mood' with the news of the *Audacious* sinking. What was more ominous than the loss of this great modern Dreadnought, which had cost all of £2.5 million, was that it had sunk as the result of a single exploding mine, in spite of its elaborate underwater protection and compartmentation. It was one thing for an old armoured cruiser to succumb to a single torpedo, but not a modern 25,000-ton battleship! What would be the result if a few U-boats got in among the Grand Fleet at sea?

'[Winston] has suffered to-day a terrible calamity on the

sea,' Asquith informed his adored Venetia, 'which I *dare* not describe, lest by chance my letter should go wrong.' However, he could not bear to keep secrets from her, and the next day he described the catastrophe in detail, naming the ship.

Winston's run of ill luck was not yet by any means over. In the same letter, 28 October 1914, Asquith also referred to the depredations of the German cruiser *Emden* in the Far East, which in three months sank or captured seventeen British merchantmen. 'She is certainly an undefeated sportswoman!' declared Asquith, as if describing a steeplechase. 'Seven ships are hunting her, but she seems to have a charmed life & an unfailing reserve of resource.'

The *Emden* was only one vessel of the powerful German East Asia Squadron under the command of the experienced and fearless Vice-Admiral Count Maximilian von Spee. He flew his flag in the *Scharnhorst*, one of his two eight-year-old armoured cruisers. His squadron disappeared into the vast wastes of the Pacific on the outbreak of war, appearing only briefly at lonely Pacific islands in order to load coal from their colliers or take in fresh provisions and water.

Their threatening presence and the failure to hunt them down over many weeks held up troop convoys and meat and grain supplies for Britain from Australia and New Zealand. This distant danger was not understood by the general public – at least not until another British catastrophe occurred a few days after the *Audacious* had gone down in home waters.

With the intention of doubling Cape Horn and falling upon the rich British shipping traffic out of the River Plate, Spee anchored off the remote Easter Island. Here a British rancher, who knew nothing of the European war, was gratified to sell at an inflated price virtually all his cattle, and British archaeologists on the island studying the unique giant statues were puzzled that the ships' nameplates had been obscured. Spee steamed south for Tierra del Fuego and eventually the South Atlantic.

The first clue to reach the Admiralty of the intentions of Spee was contained in an intercepted radio signal stating that his squadron was moving east across the Pacific, mentioning Easter Island as a destination. Of all the naval forces searching for the Germans in the Pacific, it now appeared that the most likely to intercept them was a squadron commanded by Rear-Admiral Sir Christopher Cradock, which used the Falkland Islands as its main base. Cradock was a popular and fine leader of men who had let it be known that, when his time came, he wished to die either in action or on the hunting field – where he spent much of his life ashore. His force consisted of two ancient armoured cruisers, far inferior to the Germans' and one modern light cruiser, the *Glasgow*.

Winston had already shown that he was not content simply to observe his tactical experts in the Admiralty – notably Prince Louis and Sturdee. It was he who drafted telegrams and arranged dispositions of the Navy's ships, whether in the Mediterranean, the North Sea, the Atlantic or the Pacific. These two senior admirals might make a few suggestions themselves, but their role was mainly to nod concurrence: in fact Prince Louis was nicknamed 'I concur' Battenberg. So it is Winston's hand behind the wording of the telegrams relating to the hunt for Spee and the action that followed.

The German force, now reinforced with three modern, fast light cruisers, approached the Chilean coast. Recognizing Cradock's great inferiority in firepower, Winston promised him a powerful and much more modern armoured cruiser and a pre-Dreadnought battleship. 'When you have a superior force,' ran the Admiralty telegram of 14 September, 'you should at once search Magellan Straits with squadron, keeping in readiness to return and cover the River Plate, or according to information, search as far as Valparaiso northwards, destroy the German cruisers, and break up the German trade.'

A month later, Cradock was informed that the armoured cruiser was being diverted elsewhere, and the battleship turned out to be the *Canopus*, built at the time of Omdurman, no better armoured than von Spee's cruisers and with a maximum speed of 15 knots. Moreover her heavy 12-inch guns were so old that they could range no further than the German 8.2-inch guns; and her crew were all inexperienced reservists who had never once fired their old guns.

Cradock calculated that this battleship would be more of a liability than a reinforcement, and having been spurred on more than once by Winston's telegrams, he passed through the Magellan Straits and into the Pacific. He had his urgent orders. The fact that he had been let down and been confused by ill-worded telegrams counted not at all. The going might be rough, the hedges high, and his mount inadequate, but he was not to be diverted from his quarry.

The two squadrons made contact at dusk, in rough seas, off the Chilean town of Coronel on 1 November. With his superior speed, Spee manoeuvred so that as the sun sank beneath the horizon, the British ships were silhouetted against the scarlet glow of the evening sky, while his own squadron was obscured. The German ships had won the top gunnery award of the German navy two years in succession. With dreadful inevitability the *Scharnhorst* and her sister ship, *Gneisenau*, tore apart and sank the British armoured cruisers. There were no survivors.

Once again, the finger of accusation pointed to Winston.

> The principal reaction was that there had been bungling at Whitehall [one naval historian has written]. The Admiralty arrangements were at fault and Cradock was placed in a dangerous position when he was allowed to look for a powerful squadron with an inferior force. The headlines of the half-penny press were about the 'fearful odds'.

Beatty commented, 'If ever there was an occasion which displayed bad judgement on the part of the Admiralty, you have it there . . . I fear [Winston] will try and throw blame on to poor Kit Cradock.' This is exactly what he did do.

The one man who at this time could not share the blame

was Prince Louis of Battenberg. He, poor fellow, had already been sacked. There were two main reasons for this. First, as Lloyd George and others had predicted, his German name and birth soon became unacceptable after war was declared. All over the country crowds went on the rampage, smashing up shops with German names, threatening the lives of citizens who had long since been absorbed as émigrés, even stoning German breeds of dogs.

Asquith had calculated that Prince Louis might get away with it if the Royal Navy early on fought and won a great victory at sea. This had not happened, which accounts for the second reason. The Navy had not fought another Trafalgar because the Germans would not come out. There was nothing anyone could do about that. Instead, misfortune had piled upon misfortune, and even before the loss of the three armoured cruisers at the hands of one German submarine commander, a whispering campaign had begun.

Two unsavoury figures stand out at this time as the conspirers in Prince Louis's downfall. One was Horatio Bottomley, the editor of *John Bull* magazine, which pandered to the lowest instincts of its readers – self-righteousness, xenophobia and cruelty. 'Blood is said to be thicker than water,' ran one editorial, 'and we doubt whether all the water in the North Sea could obliterate the blood-ties between the Battenbergs and the Hohenzollerns when it comes to a question of a life and death struggle between Germany and ourselves.'

The second was the retired admiral and MP, Lord Charles Beresford. In Parliament, Winston had once said of him, 'Before he gets up he does not know what he is going to say, when he speaks he does not know what he is saying, and when he sits down he does not know what he has said.' Beresford reciprocated Winston's feelings, but his hatred of Winston was tepid compared with his loathing for Prince Louis – the 'Germhun' – who, he believed, had denied him his chance of becoming First Sea Lord.

Matters reached a head on 28 August when Beresford was heard in the hall of the Carlton Club to be making accusations about German spies, a popular topic at the time. Prince Louis's name was mentioned, and Beresford said he was under close suspicion and ought to resign forthwith. Word of this reached Winston, who wrote the next day to Beresford accusing him of uttering calumnies 'in clubs and other semi-public places'.

> *In time of war the spreading of reports likely to cause mistrust or despondency is certainly a military offence. Your name is still borne on the retired list of the Navy. It is not possible that this matter should be passed over. The interests of the country do not permit the spreading of such wicked allegations by an officer of your rank.*

Winston then threatened Beresford with 'serious action' unless he received an 'absolute retraction'. But Prince Louis's position was already untenable. Because of his vulnerability, he could do nothing right. Everything that went wrong, even negatively the failure of the German fleet to come out and do battle, was blamed either directly on him or, perversely, on his failure to guide and control Winston. Beatty believed that he was sacked 'because he did not keep a proper check on Winston and ran the show himself, instead of allowing him (W) to do it'.

Prince Louis's inevitable resignation was brought about by the clamour against him, which soon undermined his confidence and was reflected in his performance. He became listless and defeatist. Winston understood the reason, but he also knew that he had to go.

On the day of the *Audacious* catastrophe, Winston told him that he would have to resign. It was a 'delicate and painful interview', according to Asquith. 'Louis behaved with great dignity & public spirit.' A formal exchange of letters took place, expressing regrets and thanks on both sides, and then this most excellent and efficient officer, now broken in spirit, disappeared into obscurity.

Again on this same eventful day, 28 October, Winston let it be known that there was only one admiral to take Prince Louis's place: Jacky Fisher. Six years after Winston had turned down the Admiralty when Fisher was First Sea Lord, he now proposed to bring him out of retirement to work in harness with him. Asquith had some misgivings about how well this pair of strong and self-assertive men would get on. The King was frankly outraged at the idea, and his private secretary talked of the monarch's 'violent aversion'. During the long and bloody contest between Beresford and Fisher, which had resulted in the resignation of both admirals, George V had firmly backed Beresford and accused Fisher (more or less openly) of splitting the Navy down the middle.

George V put forward the names of a number of 'palace' admirals. Winston said he would have none of them. Asquith told the King's secretary 'that nothing wd. induce me to part with W, whom I eulogised to the skies, and that in consequence the person chosen must be congenial to him.' The word that Fisher was coming back raced round the senior echelons of the Navy, causing a good deal of outrage among his old enemies, and concern among his admirers. 'I am afraid he is *too old* [seventy-four years] and of course the Service don't trust him,' wrote Beatty to his wife. '. . . I cannot see Winston and Jacky Fisher working very long together in harmony.'

But even the most outraged believed Fisher would at least be able to contain the wilder excesses of the First Lord. They were not, fortunately, in a position to know of Winston's real reason for bringing Fisher back to the Admiralty. 'I took him because I knew he was *old* and *weak*, and that I should be able to keep things in my own hands.'

When Winston divulged the news about Prince Louis to Clementine, she was unsurprised that he had been forced to resign. Ever mindful of the power of admirals' wives, she commiserated with Princess Louis of Battenberg, a forthright granddaughter of Queen Victoria. 'What a pain & wrench it is you can imagine . . .,' the Princess wrote to her lady-in-waiting. 'We are not going to mope or hang our heads; all of these whom we like & respect know that the "man-in-the-street & Clubs" is quite in the wrong.'

Clementine was also surprised and deeply anxious about Winston's choice of Fisher as his First Sea Lord and quite agreed with King George. She had never trusted Fisher and considered him malevolent and megalomaniacal. This seemed to be confirmed when Winston was in Paris at a meeting. He had asked her to 'look after the old boy for me'. So she invited Fisher alone to lunch one day. After he had left, as she supposed, she was surprised to find her guest lurking in the passage off the sitting room. 'She asked him what he wanted,' Winston's youngest daughter noted, whereupon, in a brusque and somewhat incoherent manner, he told her that, while she no doubt was under the impression that Winston was conferring with Sir John French, he was in fact frolicking with a mistress in Paris.' She shut him up and told him to get out.

After Winston's surprise appointment of Fisher, Clementine tried to suppress her doubts about his choice and breathed not a word of her suspicions. And of course, she had plenty else to occupy her mind. Besides nursing her baby and supervising the older children, she had the domestic running of the Admiralty to cope with, and the economies that this entailed made it more taxing than if she and Winston had enjoyed a private income. There also was a lot of entertaining to do, and both her mother and mother-in-law took up a lot of attention.

Above all, Clementine, ever responsible, ever concerned, had to share the duties, frustrations and anxieties of her husband. These were, as Winston described them, stirring days, and except for Asquith as Prime Minister with overall command, Winston's duty of running the Navy was the most critical and weighty. Every day, and often at night too, great decisions had to be made that affected the security of the nation and the lives of thousands of men. Moreover, he took nobody on trust and if he delegated anything, he followed the matter up later, sometimes more than once; and as at Antwerp and in his visits to General French in France, he

Lord Randolph Churchill, 1876

Lady Randolph (Jennie) Churchill, 1876

LEFT: Mrs. Everest, Winston's nurse

BELOW: Jennie with Jack and Winston at time of Randolph's death, 1894

FAMOUS ESCAPES

Winston Churchill's Escape from Pretoria.

Winston as overnight celebrity in 1899

Winston with his fiancée, Clementine Hozier, in 1908 (Hulton-Deutsch)

Winston and Clementine playing with Randolph, 1912 (Peregrine Churchill)

Winston with his secretary, Edward Marsh

Winston and Clementine at the Royal Naval Review, 1919 (Hulton-Deutsch)

Campaigning in Epping, 1924 (Peregrine Churchill)

Budget Day, 1929 (Clementine, Sarah, and Randolph on Winston's left) (Hulton-Deutsch)

LEFT: Winston is met by Clementine on his return from America after the crash of '29 (Hulton-Deutsch)

BELOW: With Diana at her wedding in 1932 (Hulton-Deutsch)

extended his interests into every cog and shaft of the war machine – usually finding them in need of oil and repair.

There are surviving records covering most of the days Winston was at the Admiralty that show the limitless range of his interest in the war, far beyond what could reasonably be expected of a First Lord. For example, on 5 September 1914, Winston proclaimed:

> There is no doubt that a large number of American citizens of quality and character are anxious to fight on our side. The value and advantage of such aid cannot be overrated . . . It ought to be possible to organize in Canada an American volunteer force . . . Nothing will bring American sympathy along with us so much as American blood shed in the field . . .

A few days later (10 September) he is writing to David Lloyd George at the Treasury about the allowance for war widows: 'The 5/- pension is a scandal. No soldier's wife shd be dependent on charity.'

And two days after that he is complaining to his old friend and colleague Austen Chamberlain about his policy over Ireland, which he thought unnecessarily provocative and amounting 'to a grave weakening in the forces that can now be gathered together for the prosecution of the war'.

Unsurprisingly, Kitchener is one of Winston's most frequent targets, though a veneer of courtesy and consideration is unbroken (for now) between the two men. On the inadequate output of guns:

> I am sure, myself, that more could be done by the firms than is being done at present. For instance, after you told me of the pressure you had put upon them and that their complete limits had been reached, our people went round and obtained undertakings from the trade to produce 700 rifles a week more additional to all that had been ordered by you.

This is not a formula for happy relations!

More than anyone else, Clementine recognized the dangers behind what many of his colleagues considered to be 'dabbling and interference' outside his department. She also discerned the potentially explosive situation in the hierarchy of the war machine. Within the Admiralty there was now an unsteady and inflammatory First Sea Lord of nearly seventy-four years, with whom Winston had disagreed only a few years earlier. Winston had also brought back Tug Wilson in an advisory capacity, after earlier sacking him as First Sea Lord, and he was only one year younger than Fisher. Uncomplaining as Tug was, with duty first under all circumstances, there could not have been much love there.

Outside the Admiralty, Winston had many enemies other than Kitchener; but this field marshal alone was like some skipper of a munitions ship who is a careless chain-smoker. Then there were newspaper proprietors and editors only just hidden behind trees flanking the road; and finally there was King George himself, strictly limited in executive power, but an immense influence behind the scenes and deeply suspicious of Winston.

Clementine knew all this, loved her husband dearly and proprietorially, and worried for his well-being and safety while knowing that 'safety' was not a word that figured in his vocabulary. Clementine was truly a worrier anyway, and now, with war raging and with three young children, she became more edgy than ever.

Did she have the confidence to believe that Winston would not only survive, but triumph, and triumph not only over the enemy at home, but also over the enemy abroad? She was not by temperament an optimist and could be a depressive. But she also had mountainous faith in her husband, which she confided in him whenever the need seemed to arise.

The question remains unanswerable. But we do know with reasonable certainty that she did not consider, among the possible shorelines upon which his ship of state might founder, the far distant Gallipoli Peninsula, in Turkey.

Turkey was not even at war with Britain when Winston first

considered and then rejected the idea of any serious danger from this quarter.

> *There is no need for British or Russian anxiety abt a war with Turkey* [Winston wrote to the Foreign Secretary, his friend Grey, on 6 September 1914] . . . *The price to be paid in taking Gallipoli wd no doubt be heavy . . . A good army of 50,000 men & sea-power – that is the end of the Turkish menace.*

19

'In Rather a Funk . . .'

The atmosphere at the Admiralty was quite transformed by the arrival of Jacky Fisher, who commanded the energy of a thirty-year-old, the volatility of a volcano, and a freshness of ideas quite equal to Winston's. Where for many weeks in the First Sea Lord's office gloom, despondency and inaction had ruled, now (as in his earlier reign) there arrived long before dawn the stumpy yet autocratic, fast-moving figure of Britain's most famous admiral. At once memoranda and telegrams were studied, prepared and despatched, his pen racing across the page in his bold writing, full of quotations, exclamation marks and double underlinings. 'In these morning hours,' Winston was to write, 'he gave his greatest effort, transacting an immense amount of business, writing innumerable letters and forming his resolutions for the day.' By the time Captain T. E. Crease, his naval assistant, had arrived he had done half a day's work. In another hour or two, he could expect to be called to Winston's office.

So late into the night did Winston work, and so early to bed and early to rise was his partner, that between them they were 'very nearly a perpetual clock', as Fisher called it. Or, as defined by Winston, 'We thus constituted an almost unsleeping watch throughout the day and night . . .' Winston also wrote:

> We made the agreement between ourselves that neither of us should take any important action without consulting the other, unless previous accord had been reached . . . We had thus formed, for the first time, an overwhelmingly strong control and central authority over the whole course of the naval war . . .

In addition to his normal duties, Fisher was putting in hand an enormous new programme of construction, with most of the ships being designed for his pet project. This was a typically radical, even sensational, plan that he had first mooted after his visit to Russia with Edward VII, his great admirer and supporter, as long before as 1908. Like Tug Wilson and nearly all naval officers of his generation, Fisher was appalled at the idea of Britain despatching an army to fight a Continental war, and now considered that he had been proved right by the virtual extinction of the British expeditionary force that the Navy had taken to France in August.

Fisher's concept was simple. The Navy would land a great Russian army on Germany's Baltic coast, less than ninety miles from Berlin. The 'Baltic Project', he called it. Backed by Winston and Lloyd George, Fisher put in hand 'a great Armada of 612 vessels, to be rapidly built . . . to carry out the great project'. The armada was to consist of monitors, fast, light battle-cruisers with a shallow draught, minesweepers and minelayers, hundreds of landing craft, and auxiliary ships. By the end of 1914, the construction of most of these vessels was under way.

As discussions went ahead in the Cabinet and with the Russians on the Baltic Project, the new positive attitude at the Admiralty was reflected in two victories at sea, which recovered for the Navy much of the loss of face and reputation it had suffered after the first weeks of the war. The defeat at Coronel neatly coincided with Fisher's return to power, and with Winston now temporarily reduced to the role of consultant in matters of ship dispositions, Fisher took decisive and rapid corrective steps. Two battle-cruisers, the *Invincible* and the *Inflexible*, were detached from Beatty's scouting force, and a third was despatched to the West Indies, to Beatty's and Jellicoe's dismay.

Two of the battle-cruisers headed for the Falkland Islands in anticipation of Spee making for the Atlantic, and the third, *Princess Royal*, was intended to intercept the Germans if they broke through into the Caribbean by way of the recently opened Panama Canal. This was done with great secrecy and at considerable risk, for in their absence the German fleet would have a superiority in battle-cruisers in the North Sea. But the risky move was typical of Fisher, who believed strongly that boldness was rewarded with luck. The two big battle-cruisers arrived at Port Stanley, in the Falkland Islands, and in less than twenty-four hours, smoke on the southern horizon told of the arrival of the Germans. What timing! What incredible good fortune!

In the pursuit and gun duel that followed, both of Spee's big ships were sunk, just before the weather closed in. Two of his light cruisers went to the bottom too, the third being caught and destroyed later. The Navy, and the nation, were jubilant.

> *It has done us all a tremendous amount of good getting the news* [Beatty wrote to his wife], *and I hope will put a stop to a lot of the unpleasant remarks one can detect in a certain portion of the Press that the British Navy has been an expensive luxury and is not doing its job . . . Now the victory belongs to old Fisher, & nobody else, who sent them out directly he arrived at the Admiralty, and all credit is due to him.*

Winston concurred generously, but with a reservation:

> *10 December 1914*   *Admiralty*
>
> *My dear – This was your show & your luck.*
>
>   *I shd have sent one Greyhound* [battle-cruiser] *& Defence* [armoured cruiser]. *This wd have done the trick.*
>
>   *But it was a sizzling coup. Your flair was quite true. Let us have some more victories together . . .*
>
>   *Yours ever*
>   *W*

Winston had learned a great deal about the Navy since his appointment to the Admiralty more than three years earlier, but the astute Fisher, already a captain in the Royal Navy when Winston was born, had spent his whole long life in the service, much of it studying tactics and dispositions. He knew that the *Defence*, an armoured cruiser – a predecessor to the battle-cruiser and three knots slower – *might not* have been enough to ensure the destruction of Spee's squadron. The other old armoured cruisers accompanying the *Invincible* and *Inflexible* had had the greatest difficulty in keeping up, which allowed one of the enemy to escape into suddenly deteriorating weather. Another of Spee's big ships might well have escaped, too, if the British had had only one ship both faster and more heavily gunned than the *Gneisenau* and the *Scharnhorst*.

Fisher's (and Winston's) luck held a month later in another savage action, this time in the North Sea rather than the sub-Antarctic. In spite of the Kaiser's caution in the use of the German fleet, occasional raids by fast forces were allowed, to provoke the British by bombarding coastal towns in tip-and-run raids and in the hope of cutting off and destroying inferior forces. The bombardments, causing the death of civilians, created much anger, and Fisher and Winston were furious, too, when one day, due to a misunderstanding of signals, German battle-cruisers got away unscathed.

But all went well on 24 January 1915. British intelligence had been reading German naval signals from the beginning of the war, and on the morning of the twenty-third Winston was interrupted by a visit from Admiral Sir Henry Oliver, the Chief of Staff and Wilson – Fisher being unwell. 'First Lord,' said Wilson, 'those fellows are coming out again.' The 'fellows' were Admiral Franz von Hipper's battle-cruisers – four in all.

Plans were speedily completed for Beatty's battle-cruisers to take the Germans by surprise at first light the following morning. The interception was brilliant, surprise was complete, and in a running battle Beatty (though his ship was badly hit) cut off and destroyed one of the enemy heavy ships. It was, admittedly, Hipper's weakest, but its sinking was well photographed and appeared triumphantly in the

307

British newspapers; and the German Commander in Chief was sacked for incompetency.

The Battle of the Dogger Bank, as it was named after its locale, further cheered everyone up, and the Navy's (and Winston's) reputation was now quite re-established. Beatty was furious that he had not sunk more of the enemy ships, but all the same the performance of the commanders was certainly in sharp contrast with an earlier action in the Mediterranean.

At the outbreak of the war, and long before Fisher was called back to the Admiralty, the only German squadron other than Spee's operating in foreign waters was Admiral Wilhelm Souchon's in the Mediterranean. He had only two ships under his command but they were modern and exceptionally good, better than any that Spee had in the Pacific. One was the battle cruiser *Goeben*, his flagship, and accompanying her the light cruiser *Breslau*.

Facing this German force was France's Mediterranean Fleet – mainly old ships whose first concern was to keep open trade and troop movements with France's North African colonies – and the British Mediterranean Fleet. This had once been the jewel in the crown of the Royal Navy, but with the growing threat from Germany, Fisher had, during his first long term as First Sea Lord, concentrated the Navy's main strength in home waters. To ensure maritime control of the Mediterranean, Winston had retained a force of three battle-cruisers, four older armoured cruisers under Admiral Sir Ernest Troubridge, several light cruisers and a sufficiency of destroyers and submarines. Overall command was in the hands of Admiral Sir Archibald ('Arky-Barky') Milne, to the vocal fury of Fisher, who was not yet back in office.

Winston had received some explosive words from Fisher about this appointment, and to a friend Fisher wrote of this and another appointment: 'Winston, alas! (as I have had to tell him) feared for his wife the social ostracism of the Court and succumbed to the appointments of two Court favourites

. . . a wicked wrong in both cases! Winston has sacrificed the country to the Court.'

It is true that Winston at this time was attempting to build bridges with his sovereign after the row over ships' names and judged that it was not worth another row over the appointment of Milne, an equerry to the King, who so badly wanted the Mediterranean command.

Milne was shadowing the *Goeben* and *Breslau* during the last hours of peace, but by a supreme effort from his engine-room staff, Souchon managed to outdistance the British battle-cruisers and, like Spee in the Pacific, disappeared without trace for a while. And again as during the preliminaries to Coronel, the war staff and Winston, at the Admiralty, fired off confusing signals to the Commander in Chief while Milne made the mistake of assuming the German ships would head for the Atlantic.

Admiral Souchon did nothing of the kind. After bombarding French ports in North Africa, he followed secret orders from Germany and headed for Turkey, which was not yet at war but was more friendly to the German than the Allied cause. Milne succeeded in picking up Souchon's trail, and it seemed certain that Admiral Troubridge would be able to intercept the German ships early on the morning of 7 August.

While speeding through the night with the four armoured cruisers to the likely point of interception, Troubridge's flag captain succeeded in persuading him that they stood no chance against the faster, more heavily gunned German battle-cruiser. To his eternal shame and the shame of the Royal Navy, Troubridge deliberately avoided battle, although it was four ships against one and his total broadside was heavier than Souchon's.

The German ships therefore escaped and arrived off Cape Helles in Turkish waters on 10 August. The man in the British street thought that this was the second-best thing to sinking the German ships, which had shown that they were not prepared to stand up and fight. Asquith tended to agree with this fallacy. With sublime arrogance and poverty of imagination, he wrote:

We had a Cabinet this morning as usual. The only interesting thing is the arrival of the *Goeben* in the Dardanelles & her sale to Turkey! . . . As we shall insist that the *Goeben* shall be manned by a Turkish instead of a German crew, it doesn't much matter: as the Turkish sailors cannot navigate her – except on to rocks or mines . . .

Winston invited Fisher to lunch at the Admiralty the following day. The conversation is not recorded, but its tone may be judged by Fisher's reply to Eddie Marsh's letter of invitation: 'I am APPALLED at the *Goeben* incident! I looked up the "Naval Gazetteer" of the Old [Napoleonic] War yesterday for precedents! I see the wording of the telegram to Milne should be "Haul down your Flag and Come on Shore" . . .'

The German present to Turkey of these men of war was a master diplomatic coup at a critical time in Anglo-Turkish relations. Just before the outbreak of war British shipyards had completed an order for two Dreadnought battleships for the Turkish navy, one of them a giant armed with more heavy guns than any other in the world. These were intended to give Turkey total naval superiority over her arch-enemy, Greece, and they had been paid for largely by national patriotic subscription. The Turkish crews were already in Britain and plans were complete in Constantinople for joyous celebrations on their arrival in the Bosporus.

As war with Germany became more and more likely during the last days of July, Winston fretted about these brand new, powerful battleships. What if they were intercepted by the German navy and forcibly taken over? Or more likely, what if they became the subject of a diplomatic agreement between the two countries? They would, in either case, become an important and possibly decisive addition to the German High Seas Fleet at the very outbreak of war. Winston decided to act ruthlessly and quite illegally by ordering troops on board to prohibit the Turkish crews from boarding, and he confirmed British possession by hoisting the white ensign on both battleships.

The Turkish authorities were appalled and protested strongly, pointing out that they had paid for them and they were, therefore, Turkish property. It was pure piracy! Docks to accommodate them in Turkey had been completed by British firms, and British prestige in Turkey was expected to soar with the Dreadnoughts' arrival from British yards. The news of this last-minute 'theft' was spreading throughout the Ottoman Empire as the *Goeben* and *Breslau*, evading the might of the Royal Navy, arrived triumphantly off the Turkish coast. Shortly after, they hoisted the Turkish flag, with much fraternization between the Turkish and German crews, who continued to man them, against Asquith's wishes and expectations.

The outcome of all this was inevitable. The last suspicions, the last distrust of Germany by some of the younger members of the Turkish government disappeared; relations became closer, and German military aid and 'advisers' arrived in Constantinople. By 22 September, Winston is writing to Grey: 'We are suffering very seriously from Turkish hostility. Our whole Mediterranean Fleet is tied to the Dardanelles . . . the German grip on Turkey tightens and all preparations for war go steadily forward.'

Until now, Turkey had adhered to the international treaty allowing free maritime passage through the Dardanelles, the narrow funnel between the Black Sea and the Mediterranean. The Russians relied on this for military aid from the West and for the export of Russian grain to pay for it. But on 29 September a German officer ordered the completion of a minefield across the Dardanelles, which would seal it off. A month later Winston learned that the *Goeben* and *Breslau* had steamed into the Black Sea from Constantinople. Flying the Turkish flag, but still with German crews, they bombarded Russian ports. Britain and France slid into war with Turkey a few days later. Steps were taken to defend Egypt against a Turkish land attack. The new Commander in Chief of the British Mediterranean Fleet, Admiral Sir Sackville Carden, instituted a full blockade off the entrance to the Dardanelles, and from long range bombarded some of the forts that Turkey, with the active help of Germany, had recently established.

So, while fighting for their lives in France and Belgium, the Allies had made for themselves a new enemy in the Near East as a result of the flaccid performance of Milne (Fisher: 'He ought to be shot'), the cowardice of Troubridge, and the precipitate action of Winston in seizing the two new Turkish battleships. Lloyd George never had any doubt that it was the last of these that had drawn Turkey into the war, and told Winston so. He was not pleased.

The entry of Turkey into the war, the severing of Russia's only year-round artery (the Arctic route was frozen all winter), and the threat to Egypt and the Persian oilfields, to the Suez Canal, and even to India posed a fearful dilemma to the Allies. Among the many peacetime contingency plans conceived by the Admiralty was for a combined services assault on Gallipoli, and this plan concluded that 'it would involve a great risk, and should not be undertaken if other means of bringing pressure to bear on Turkey were available.'

Moreover, the record of bombardment of forts from the sea was a poor one. 'Any sailor who attacked a fort was a fool,' Nelson had once remarked. It was one thing to hit a six-hundred-foot-long battleship, quite another to destroy a camouflaged or hidden gun and its few square yards of mounting. As recently as 1882 the entire Mediterranean Fleet had bombarded the forts at Alexandria, and Fisher, who had commanded the most powerful battleship there, could testify that it had taken ten hours at point blank range to silence the crudely sited Egyptian guns. The German guns mounted on the Gallipoli Peninsula were immeasurably more powerful.

However, something had to be done, if only to ease the pressure on Russia. On 25 November at a War Council meeting, Winston proposed a joint Army-Navy attack on the peninsula. Kitchener was outraged: 'Certainly not – we can't spare the men from the Western Front.' So that was that. Five weeks passed, during which the Western Front settled into deadlock, and still no great victory at sea occurred. Then at the beginning of January 1915, a further appeal arrived from Russia, where there was no deadlock on the fighting fronts and Turkish troops were menacing the Caucasus.

This time the Russians were assured that something would be done. All manner of plans were devised and came up for consideration at War Council meetings. At the tail end of one of them was that the Navy should force the Dardanelles with some of the many old British and French pre-Dreadnought battleships.

Winston pounced on this, recognizing it as a godsent opportunity for the Navy to *do* something – make a real 'splash', a real contribution to the war effort. He at once drafted a signal to Admiral Carden. Could it be done? 'The importance of the results would justify severe loss . . .'

Carden responded cautiously, but on the whole encouragingly. He proposed bombarding the entrance and inner forts in turn and then the defences in the 'narrows', after which he would clear the minefields and steam into the Sea of Marmara. The operation would call for a large number of ships.

Winston was buoyant with enthusiasm when he presented this plan to the War Council on 13 January. Such was his power of persuasion that he carried all before him. Even Kitchener approved: it would not require a single one of his troops.

Asquith spent a part of this long meeting writing to Venetia. He told her who was there and the seating. 'You won't often see a stranger collection of men at one table.' He did not at this stage give her the details of Winston's proposals, but later, as if this young woman of less than half his age possessed the military wisdom of Solomon, wrote, 'I wanted so much at the earliest opportunity, and while the impressions were still fresh, to talk to you, & get your opinions about to-day's War Council.' He then 'at once postponed my interview with the King' in order to have this talk.

Winston claimed his plan 'made a deep impression', and this view was substantiated by one of those present, Lord Hankey, who told how 'the idea caught on at once. The whole atmosphere changed. Fatigue was forgotten. The War Council turned eagerly from the dreary vista of a "slogging match" on the Western Front to brighter prospects, as they seemed, in the Mediterranean.'

Of all those present only the two old admirals, Wilson and Fisher, remained silent. Fisher saw his Baltic Project fading into the distance, the armada of vessels designed for it being diverted to Winston's new hare-brained scheme. Nevertheless, he considered it diplomatic to humour Winston by giving it his qualified support for the time being. He did this by making the startling proposal that the new super-Dreadnought, the *Queen Elizabeth*, should do her initial gunnery practice with live ammunition against the Turkish forts instead of harmlessly into the sea. Her fifteen-inch guns, the most powerful in the world, must surely shatter the forts with a few salvoes.

Winston was delighted at this proposal, especially coming from his First Sea Lord and thus signifying his approval of the whole operation. The War Council now concluded that 'the Admiralty should prepare for a naval expedition in February to bombard and take the Gallipoli Peninsula, with Constantinople as its objective.' Nothing was said about what the Fleet was supposed to do when it reached this great city.

With the green light flashing, Winston and his staff went into urgent action, despatching old battleships, persuading, without difficulty, the French to send a squadron, and collecting a force of minesweepers from the nation's fishing fleets, together with the fishermen, who were given temporary naval status.

As always, Winston confided these secret plans in Clementine, who shared his first enthusiasm and excitement. But as the days passed she became aware, through her husband's daily recounting of every detail of progress, of the equivocations of Jacky Fisher, 'from violent opposition to wild enthusiasm, and back again to grumbling disapproval'.

Jacky Fisher never hesitated in slamming Winston to his commanders behind his back:

> The way the War is conducted both ashore and afloat is chaotic! [he wrote to Jellicoe]. It's amusing how Winston makes out that in all types you are ever so much stronger than when you assumed command of the Fleet. I simply keep reiterating, 'He has only 29 battleships available at present.' He can't get round that fact! So off he goes on another attack on your arrangements . . .

Then, after outlining Winston's Dardanelles plan and the number of ships it will require – '*all urgently required at the decisive theatre at home!*' – Fisher tells the Commander in Chief that there is only one thing for it, 'that is to resign! But you say "*no*", which simply means I am a consenting party to what I absolutely disapprove. *I don't agree with one single step taken . . .*' Did Fisher disagree even with his own crucial step of sending out the *Queen Elizabeth*, with all the risks of her destruction by mines or German U-boats which were expected shortly?

Clementine's suspicions about the old Admiral's loyalty were clearly correct, but her husband pooh-poohed her fears. He knew of her antipathy to Fisher and passed it off as one of her feminine prejudices. But another feminine instinct was also alerted at this time, that of Asquith's daughter Violet. 'I said both to my father and Winston,' she later recounted, 'that though I did not doubt Lord Fisher's genius I thought him dangerous because I believed him to be mad.'

Whether or not Fisher was mad, there can be no doubt that the head of a great fighting service in the middle of a great war who can change his mind about a great new proposed offensive four times in one day, as Fisher did, should at once have been dismissed. In fact, this would not have been necessary. All Asquith had to do was to accept his resignation, and there were plenty of opportunities: eight between January and May. But resignation by the most admired and popular admiral in the land would prove highly damaging to Asquith and his administration. 'He is always threatening to resign,' Asquith confided in his diary. And, 'A personal matter which rather worries me is the growing friction between Winston and Fisher.' Indeed there was. Every day, so it seemed, Winston was reducing the power and responsibility of the Board and taking it back into his own hands. Even Fisher was now reduced to little more than an initial-signer on Winston's orders direct to commanders at sea. Winston was doing *everything*. 'He always wins the argument,' the once all-powerful Admiral declared plaintively.

On the morning of 28 January, Asquith decided to knock heads together. Winston had put forward another and additional offensive plan in the form of a naval bombardment of the enemy port of Zeebrugge, Belgium, much used by U-boats. In a private meeting before the War Council meeting, Asquith persuaded Winston to give up the Zeebrugge operation, which had anyway been put forward only as a debating sacrifice. Fisher must, for his part, cease opposing the Dardanelles.

With this settled, all three went off to the meeting. When the subject of the Dardanelles was reached on the agenda, Fisher astonished everyone by silently stalking off towards the door, as if wiping his hands of the whole business. Kitchener, like any good soldier, was the first to react. He raised his great frame and strode to the door in pursuit. He caught up with the errant Admiral, took him to the window, and tried to persuade him to return. 'It is your duty to return. If you have changed your mind about this proposed operation you must explain why. I appeal to your patriotism and sense of duty.'

This fortunately or unfortunately did the trick, for the time being anyway. The Field Marshal and Admiral returned to their seats. Although everyone else was embarrassed they pretended the incident had never occurred, and it was deleted from the minutes while the meeting was resumed. During the lunch break Winston tackled the old man, and by persuasive argument, made Fisher give him his support.

316

As Fisher recounted later, 'When I finally decided to go in, I went in the whole hog, totus porcus.'

'This I took as the point of final decision,' Winston wrote. 'After it, I never looked back. We had left the region of discussion and consultation, of balancings and misgivings. The matter had passed into the domain of action.' But he was as aware as Fisher, and all other members of the War Council, that there was a heavy risk element in attempting to break through the Dardanelles without a major military landing. Then, quite by chance, a few days later, it was agreed by the War Council to send a complete division of troops, the 29th, to Greece if she would agree to join the war on the Allied side. The Greeks promptly refused the offer, and Winston argued that if Kitchener could spare them from the Western Front as a bribe for the Greeks, he could certainly spare them for action against the Turks. 'We shd. never forgive ourselves if the naval operations succeeded and the fruits were lost through the army being absent.' If nothing else, Winston's claim underlined his anxiety about a Navy-only assault.

Kitchener, never strong in debate and almost as vacillating as Fisher, fell for this argument and agreed. Winston was overjoyed. With a well-equipped division of regular troops, the operation could not fail.

Winston had already decided, following an earlier failure to procure troops from Kitchener, to send a couple of naval brigades, which had earlier seen service at the siege of Antwerp. Violet Asquith first heard of this while dining at the Admiralty with Winston and Clementine. Winston, referring to criticism of his, and their, performance at Antwerp, then exclaimed, 'This will make them sit up – the swine who snarled at the Naval Division!'

He was, according to Violet, 'dressed in dark green plush' and suffering from influenza, but this did not in the least diminish his spirit, which was burning with enthusiasm for the Dardanelles operation.

He discussed every aspect of the strategy, naval and military, with tremendous zest [Violet reported], and

317

then breaking off he said to me with sudden gravity, 'I think a curse should rest on me because I am so happy. I know this war is smashing and shattering the lives of thousands every moment – and yet – I cannot help it – I enjoy every second I live.'

This news of the future of the naval brigades was especially interesting to Violet, for her brother Arthur ('Oc') and dear friend, the poet Rupert Brooke, were both serving in the Hood Battalion of the brigades. When Rupert Brooke heard the news, he was even more lyrical about the prospect of imminent action than Winston.

Oh Violet – it's too wonderful for belief. I had not imagined Fate could be so benign. I almost suspect her [he exclaimed] . . . Oh God! I've never been quite so happy in my life I think. Not quite so pervasively happy; like a stream flowing entirely to one end. I suddenly realize that the ambition of my life has been – since I was two – to go on a military expedition to Constantinople.

The entire Board of Admiralty, headed by Winston and Fisher, went down to Dorset on 25 February to inspect the naval brigades before their departure and watch the King taking the formal march past. Winston was in a uniform he had designed himself and quite unlike any other. 'Inventing uniforms is one of Winston's chief pleasures and temptations,' Clementine divulged to Asquith, who commented waspishly about this one: 'It will cause universal derision among our soldiers!'

Clementine and Violet had decided to take part in the proceedings, and the two women, on horseback, cantered down the lines of men, pausing from time to time to talk to them. Soon, the King arrived, also on horseback. Violet wrote, 'Then there was the formal march past. I felt a great thrill when the Hood Battalion went by and when Colonel

Quilter roared "Eyes Rrright" and all their faces turned . . .
Winston glowing with pride in his troops.'

Later the hierarchy had lunch, and as Winston was present,
'every form of luxury' was served, including marrons glacés,
foie gras, and champagne. A few days after this, Violet saw
her brother and Rupert off on their troopship from Bristol.

> Rupert walked with me along the narrow crowded
> decks, down the plank stairs [Violet recalled]. I said
> goodbye to him. I saw in his eyes that he felt sure
> we should never see each other again. Oc took me
> over the gangway and we talked for a few moments
> feverishly – 'I shall come back,' he said. 'I may be
> wounded but I shall come back.'*

For a while it seemed that, after all, the naval brigades might
be the only troops available to support the bombarding ships
at the Dardanelles, for Kitchener, playing the part of 'second madman' in the War Council, had changed his mind
about the 29th Division. They would, after all, probably
be wanted in France. In any case, there were the naval
brigades and an Australian–New Zealand force (Anzacs)
in Egypt. 'What did Mr Churchill propose these large forces
should do, when they reached the Dardanelles?' Because of
the mesmerizing effect Kitchener had on Asquith and on
all his colleagues except Winston, no-one else protested.
A week later Kitchener temporized to the extent of saying he would make no final decision until he saw how the
Russians fared in a ferocious battle taking place on the
Eastern Front. Fruitlessly did Winston argue with his old
antagonist that the way to relieve pressure on the Russians
was to go for Constantinople, via the Dardanelles: that was

---

*Rupert Brooke died even before he reached the Dardanelles. Oc
survived, though wounded four times and losing a leg; he was
awarded the DSO and two bars.

the whole *raison d'être* of the operation, as Kitchener had earlier agreed.

Never had anyone seen Kitchener so obdurate, and at least in part this was caused by recent 'fearful rows' he had had with Winston on quite other topics, like Winston communicating directly with Sir John French at the fighting front about the conduct and progress of the war on land. Another typical dispute was over Kitchener's point-blank refusal to accept thousands of desperately needed rifles from Brazil – 'I do beg you not to let this opportunity slip. Soon the chance may be gone for ever,' Winston pleaded with the Secretary of State for War, disregarding Kitchener's known dislike for outside interference.*

Kitchener relented in the end about the 29th Division, but as a result of his pique and hesitancy there resulted a delay of some four weeks in the despatch of this vital division. The first bombardment had by then taken place. The outer forts had fallen before the rain of high explosive, including the *Queen Elizabeth*'s fifteen-inch shells, and Admiral Carden had declared he needed only fourteen more days to complete the destruction of the German-Turkish defences.

The pattern of events now assumed the shape of some Greek tragedy. Carden's fourteen days increasingly revealed both the difficulties and miscalculations of the Navy. General Sir Ian Hamilton, Winston's old campaigning friend in India and South Africa, had assumed command of the land forces off the Dardanelles when they arrived, and at once telegraphed Kitchener about the Navy.

The Admiralty have been very over-sanguine as to what they cd do by ships alone [Asquith wrote after

---

*On 14 May Winston despatched an urgent memorandum to the commander of the Royal Naval Division: 'Every care shd be taken to recover the rifles of dead & wounded men. We are literally at the end of our store . . .'

hearing of this from Kitchener]. Every night the Turks under German direction repair their fortifications; both coasts bristle with howitzers & field guns (outside the forts) in concealed emplacements; and the channel is sown with complicated & constantly renewed minefields.

The ease with which the outer forts were crushed turned out to be highly deceptive. The Fleet was now faced with forts, mobile howitzers, minefield batteries and minefields.

The minefields blocked the passage of the Straits and kept the Fleet beyond their limits [Winston explained later]. The minefield batteries prevented the sweeping of the minefields. The forts protected the minefield batteries by keeping battleships at a distance with their long guns. The mobile howitzers kept the battleships on the move and increased the difficulty of overcoming the forts. So long as all four factors stood together, the defences constituted a formidable obstruction.

Winston might have added, but did not, that the general standard of navy shooting was weak and that when the fall of shot was 'spotted' either from the air or from ships closer inshore, the gunlayers rarely adjusted their aim, which was not at all good anyway.

Winston's brother, Jack, had been sent out to this new theatre of war to serve on Ian Hamilton's staff, and he too wrote of the difficulties and failures of the Navy: 'All the stories of forts being silenced are greatly exaggerated . . . the enemy have mobile guns, and we were shelled yesterday at the very entrance to the Straits. Our minesweepers are not strong enough and are too few.'

This was written on the day following the disastrous 18 March, one of the black days of the Dardanelles operations. Admiral Carden, ill and already worn out by worry, had been superseded by Admiral Sir John De Robeck, a much more positive figure, who planned a supreme effort to finish off the inner forts once and for all. The operation opened with his four most powerful ships, including the *Queen Elizabeth*, penetrating the straits and bombarding the narrows forts, while two more battleships behind them engaged the intermediate-defence batteries.

These ships were followed by six more battleships and then another half dozen, all pounding away and using up immense quantities of ammunition, while higher into the sky than the seaplanes could fly, there arose a gigantic cloud of smoke and dust. It scarcely seemed possible that any gun, let alone any gunner, could survive this rain of destruction. It was intended that the minesweepers should now go in and clear the way for the advance into the Sea of Marmara. But these little ex-fishing boats, bucking a 4-knot current, were met with such a murderous Turkish fire that they simply turned about and retired. And who could blame the men? They had not been trained to face enemy guns, nor had they expected anything like this.

At the same time, the mines they had been expected to clear began to take effect. The French battleship *Bouvet* was first to go, in a massive explosion that killed almost all her 650-man crew. The battle-cruiser *Inflexible*, one of Beatty's precious 'Greyhounds', was next to strike a mine, and she limped off with a severe list, followed minutes later by another British battleship. Yet another, going to the aid of her consort, struck a mine – and both foundered later.

At this point De Robeck called off the attack, fearing that there would be no ships left if he persisted. It was perhaps as well that he did not know the truth of the damage he had inflicted on the Turkish guns: only two fourteen-inch guns and two or three smaller guns put out of action, and not a single gun guarding the minefield had been touched. But what the Commander in Chief did know at the end of this tragic day was that he could never get through with his ships while the minefields remained, and they would remain until the Army landed and cleared the guns protecting them.

Back in London, Winston did not agree with all this and

considered De Robeck was not showing sufficient thrust. The Admiral 'feared losses may be heavy' if he attempted another attack. 'I think it will be necessary to take and occupy the Gallipoli Peninsula by land forces before the Navy can break through,' he reiterated.

Winston's theme remained that losses were to be expected. 'As for the old battleships, they were doomed in any case to the scrap-heap. Every ship lost was being replaced . . .' And Asquith thought that De Robeck 'seems to be in rather a funk'. Still the Admiral refused to be moved. 'For the Fleet to attack the Narrows now would jeopardize the success of a better and bigger scheme and would, therefore, be a mistake,' he telegraphed on 26 March.

No-one else at the Admiralty or in the War Council was prepared to override the man on the spot, and it was generally (but not formally) agreed that the big new offensive must not take place until Hamilton's armies had arrived, prepared landings, and carried them out. And aside from the Anzacs and the naval brigades and some French troops, the main body, the 29th Division, was still on the high seas and would not be ready for weeks. Meanwhile, the enemy quickly recovered from the big bombardment, and worked day and night shifts to perfect and reinforce the peninsula's defences. But worse still, as Winston lamented:

> Henceforth the defences of the Dardanelles were to be reinforced by an insurmountable mental barrier. A wall of crystal, utterly immovable, began to tower up in the Narrows, and against this wall of inhibition no weapon could be employed. The 'No' principle had become established in men's minds, and nothing could ever eradicate it.

20

The Treacherous Shores of Gallipoli

Although written many years later, Winston's judgement of the dominant negative in all aspects of the Dardanelles operations is borne out by contemporary records. At the top, Asquith became increasingly doubtful about the wisdom of 'Winston's sideshow'. Kitchener remained as ambivalent about it as Fisher, and both became increasingly pessimistic. Admirals Jellicoe and Beatty and the entire Board of Admiralty loathed it.

Only the soldiers on the spot, and especially the Anzacs, were bullish and longed for the landings and for action. But they had to contend with some fearful blunders before they could do so, in spite of all the reform the Army had enjoyed since the Boer War. The store ships were packed incorrectly for unloading onto the beaches and had to be sent to Egypt to be repacked, leading to further delay. Security virtually did not exist, the Egyptian newspapers announcing all the troop movements in detail as if reporting passenger-liner movements in peacetime. There was no attempt to make a surprise assault. The Turkish gunners, with German officers, were solidly dug in, the machine-gun posts were perfectly sited to make any landing a murderous business, and the barbed-wire entanglements were laid like massed spiders' webs down to the shore's edge and even into the sea.

The mass landings took place on 25 April. Thousands were killed and wounded. From above, the pilots of spotting seaplanes could see the stains of blood spread ever wider from the shore and from wrecked craft that never reached it. The courage of the men was sublime, but they could hardly prevail against such defences.

For home consumption, a series of bland or optimistic reports of progress were despatched by the information staff.

'The operations are being continued and pressed forward under highly satisfactory conditions,' reported *The Times* on 6 May. In fact, only a toehold was gained here and there, and by 9 May the Army was deadlocked, held up by barbed wire and machine guns as solidly as on the Western Front. And, also as in France, the only solution seemed to be to send more men 'to bite barbed wire'. But Winston had another idea. He knew, as they all knew, that to abandon the operation now would not only be a body blow to Russia, but would also discredit the Allied cause in the Balkans, throughout the Moslem world, and in India. They *had* to keep it going. His idea was to renew the bombardment and make another attempt at a naval breakthrough to the Black Sea, cutting off the Turkish and German forces on the peninsula.

This proposition was listened to by the War Council. Incredibly, considering the dreadful losses on 18 March, only Fisher opposed it – and opposed it hotly, on the grounds that it must lead not only to further sinkings, but to another drain on naval strength in home waters. Then, on the night of 11–12 May, a German-manned Turkish torpedo boat crept out of the Dardanelles and put a torpedo into the battleship *Goliath*, which sank at once, with the loss of 570 lives. It might as easily have been the *Queen Elizabeth*.

This was too much for Fisher. He at once demanded the return to home waters of this valuable super-Dreadnought. Kitchener was outraged. To the hard-pressed Army, this battleship was not only the Army's headquarters but the symbol of the Navy's strength and support. Winston pointed to the great superiority already enjoyed by Jellicoe in home waters, but Fisher wrote to Asquith (13 May): ' . . . I desire to convey to you that I honestly feel I cannot remain where I am any longer, as there is an inevitable and never-ceasing *drain daily (almost hourly)* of our resources in the decisive theatre of the war [i.e., the North Sea].' Moreover, at this time intelligence was building up at the Admiralty that the German fleet was planning at last to break out.

Fisher got his way after this threat of resignation, Kitchener and De Robeck were placated by the promise of two old battleships and two new monitors and a small fleet of other ships to take the *Queen Elizabeth*'s place. Winston carefully defined the actual numbers and types of ships at a War Council meeting on 14 May.

Clementine was made aware of every step, every new crisis, every new dashed hope, of the Dardanelles operations, from their conception. Like Asquith's Venetia Stanley, she was Winston's confidante for all that went on in the War Council, at the Admiralty, and off those distant hostile shores where once Greek had fought Trojan, and Christian crusaders had clashed with Moslem hordes.

'Is Fisher behind you?' was Clementine's frequent question. 'Yes,' Winston would always reassure her. 'He is sorry to see his Baltic Project postponed, but he recognizes the need to support Russia and is anxious to see his Navy successful and acclaimed. Besides,' he would observe more pragmatically, 'if he vehemently opposed the campaign and it was successful – and successful it will be, my dear – then he would not only lose face but his cherished and carefully cultivated reputation for "full speed" and "damn the torpedoes"* would be left in tatters.'

Clementine retained complete confidence in every aspect of the plan and every man involved, except Fisher. She accompanied Winston to Charing Cross Station to wish godspeed and success to Major General Sir Ian Hamilton and Major Jack Churchill. She commiserated with Admiral Carden in his losses and his sickness, and she shared her husband's confidence in Admiral De Robeck. But every time she learned of another Fisher threat to resign, and the almost immediate retraction, of the Admiral's clashes with Kitchener, of his opposition to withdrawing more ships from home waters one day and his enthusiastic suggestion to

---

*'Damn the torpedoes! Captain Drayton, go ahead! Jouett, full speed!' – David G. Farragut, 5 August 1864.

326

despatch the Navy's newest and most powerful battleship the next day, her suspicions grew.

Winston and Clementine's preoccupation with the Dardanelles campaign was almost complete. Sometimes at dinner and bridge with the F. E. Smiths, the Asquiths and Violet, Venetia Stanley, Balfour, Edwin Montagu, and other of their friends, the conversation would deviate from this one burning issue, only to return minutes later. Winston's daughter Mary has told of how, 'During these anxious, fateful months of the spring of 1915 even the nursery world at Admiralty House, cocooned and sheltered in its upstairs existence, was aware of some threatening cloud which seemed to brood over their parents' life.' Mary has written, too, of her eldest sister Diana 'sensing the atmosphere of anxiety' and ending her prayers at night 'with an earnest plea: "God bless the Dardanelles."'

Jacky Fisher awoke at his usual early hour on the morning of 15 May 1915. The previous day had been full of controversy, disturbing and at times tempestuous. He had no doubt that today would be as bad or worse. But this seventy-four-year-old sailor had always enjoyed a good fight, and he was feeling fit and ready. 'I attribute my present vitality,' he once wrote, 'to the imbibing of my mother's milk beyond the legal period of nine months.' And only the other day he had written, 'I feel like twenty.'

It was his custom to conduct at least two hours of business before breakfast, and while dressing he speculated on what he might find on his desk after the War Council row the day before. There would certainly be papers from Winston, written late at night or in the small hours.

Like nearly all naval officers, Fisher dressed smartly, even out of uniform. He wore this morning a black double-breasted four-button suit, white shirt with wing collar and black bow tie. Lastly, he put on his black shoes, which he always polished himself in the evening.

It was only a short distance from his quarters on the north side of the Admiralty Arch. As usual, there were few people about at this hour, although the sun had risen an hour earlier and was already flooding the courtyard. Fisher mounted the two flights of stairs to the first floor. The First Sea Lord's office was immediately ahead, the petty officer on guard clicking heels to attention and saluting him. His private secretary and stenographer was standing by his desk. 'Good morning, sir.'

Fisher hung his hat and coat on the stand behind the door and sat down at his desk. It was as clean and tidy as a quarterdeck before inspection, the silver inkstand gleaming, so often polished that the inscription was beginning to fade: 'To Captain John Arbuthnot Fisher CB, RN from the Officers and Men of HMS Inflexible, Christmas Day 1882.' Round, steel-rimmed spectacles on the end of his nose, the old man began flicking through the pile of papers that had been placed in front of him. At some he merely grunted and put them aside; others he ticked or scribbled on with a vivid comment, inevitably with an exclamation mark, and to others again he dictated a brief reply.

Then he came across a memorandum of four typed pages, with the Admiralty heading and each page marked at the end with Winston's familiar initials. Fisher read them through in complete silence, replaced them on the unread papers, and stared ahead at the massive painting of the Battle of Trafalgar on the far wall. He spoke to his private secretary: 'Please present my compliments and apologies to Captain Crease and ask him to attend my office as soon as is convenient.'

When the secretary had left the room, Fisher took a sheet of memorandum paper and began writing in his large flowing hand:

15 May 1915

First Lord
After further anxious reflection I have come to the regretted conclusion I am unable to remain any longer as your Colleague. It is undesirable in the public interests to go into details . . . but I find it increasingly difficult to adjust myself to the increasing

daily requirements of the Dardanelles to meet yr views
– As you truly said yesterday I am in the position of
continually veto-ing yr proposals.

This is not fair to you besides being extremely dis-
tasteful to me.

I am off to Scotland at once so as to avoid all
questionings.

Yrs truly
Fisher

He folded the paper once, placed it in an envelope which
he addressed to 'The First Lord', sealed it, and placed
upon it one of the 'URGENT' stickers he had personally
introduced almost at the outset of his reforming crusade so
many years ago.

'Ah, Captain Crease, I am so sorry to get you up so early,'
we can hear him saying. He indicated a chair to his loyal naval
assistant. 'I am sorry to say that the good news I brought you
last night was premature.'

'How do you mean, sir?' Tom Crease was forty years old,
a tactful, dedicated, and also amusing officer. He recalled
their conversation at seven o'clock the previous evening,
soon after Winston had left. Fisher had told Crease that
he need not pack up yet as the meeting with Churchill had
been satisfactory, and Fisher's resignation – which he had
threatened so often – was at least postponed. The row over
how many ships and naval guns should be sent out to the
Dardanelles had been settled by compromise, and Fisher had
given Crease the figures involved verbally. In a jocular vein,
Fisher had concluded, 'But I suppose he'll be at me again.'

'I mean, Crease,' Fisher said now, the lines on his forehead
deep with anger, 'that the First Lord has gone back on our
agreement last night. Just look at these figures.'

Captain Crease studied the four-page memorandum in
silence. 'The figures are certainly in excess of those you
quoted me last night, sir.'

'Indeed they are. *Nine* heavy monitors, four instead of two
"Edgars" [cruisers] and *five* fifteen-inch monitors.' Fisher

329

pointed to item 6, the last. 'And note, will you, that this has been added even after the typist has completed his work.'

Item 6 was in Winston's own small rounded hand. '. . . in view of the request of [De Robeck], I consider that two more E boats [the latest submarine] shd be sent to Dardanelles.' This reference to draining off submarines to the operations that Fisher so detested, when submarines were so desperately needed at home, outraged him more than anything else: 'You see now, my dear Crease, that there is no limit to the First Lord's appetite, and the longer the Dardanelles adventure is allowed to endure, the greater the demands will become. I have therefore already written to the First Lord tendering my resignation. It is regrettable, but while my responsibilities and views are being constantly overridden by the First Lord, I have no alternative.'

Fisher then told his naval assistant that after calling on Lloyd George to explain the situation he would be leaving for Scotland to stay with friends – 'out of the way of pressmen and other questioners. My decision is final.'

By some chance, as if the burden of the message might be too great for Winston, Fisher's letter of resignation was delayed and reached Winston's office when he had already left for a meeting with Grey at the Foreign Office. On his way back across Horse Guards Parade shortly after 10 a.m., he was met by his secretary, Masterton-Smith, with what Winston described as 'an anxious face'. 'Fisher has resigned, and I think he means it this time,' Masterton-Smith said, handing him a letter.

Winston read it there and then and handed it back to his secretary. 'Well, it's not the first time, as you know. I don't think we need to take this too seriously.'

But he was soon forced to do so, and for the first time feared for his own future. In this partnership he had always known that if one went down, the other would go down with him. They were like two men operating the pump of a leaking ship that could be kept afloat only by their joint efforts. It was little more than six months since Fisher's

330

return to the Admiralty had been hailed by the country as a popular triumph. Fisher was the national hero who would put the Navy to rights and counter the baleful influence of the politicians – Winston Churchill in particular. Remember the Falklands victory – nay, annihilation?

If Jacky Fisher now found it impossible to reform and work at the Admiralty, the finger of blame pointed at one man only. Winston realized all this, and when he reached the Admiralty and found the blinds down in Fisher's office and no sign of him anywhere, he knew that things were serious. No one knew where he had gone – only that he had said he was taking the train to Scotland at once.

Without going to his own office, Winston hastened back across Horse Guards Parade to Downing Street. The sun was now high in the sky, and Big Ben was booming 11 a.m. The policeman on duty at 10 Downing Street saluted him, and the butler let him in without delay. Winston handed to Asquith Fisher's letter of resignation. 'We must not let this happen, I'm sure you'll agree.'

After reading the letter, Asquith sat down at his desk and scribbled a short note:

> *10 Downing Street*
> *Whitehall SW*
>
> *Lord Fisher*
> *In the King's name, I order you at once to return to your post.*
> *H. H. Asquith*
> *15 May 1915*

Maurice Bonham Carter,* one of Asquith's private secretaries, was given this to deliver personally to the Admiral and ask him to come to see the Prime Minister. This was not easily accomplished, as no-one knew where Fisher was. Eventually

---

*Soon to marry Asquith's daughter Violet.

an Admiralty messenger volunteered the information that he had been seen walking towards the Charing Cross Hotel from Parliament Square. (He had been praying in Westminster Abbey.) The hotel manager had been told not to divulge Fisher's presence, but was obliged to relent when the Prime Minister's name was mentioned, and the young man found Fisher reading the newspapers. Bonham Carter delivered the note and the message, and with the utmost reluctance Fisher agreed to come to Downing Street later.

It was early afternoon when Fisher left the hotel to walk back down Whitehall. It was a Saturday, and London had assumed its usual weekend calm in spite of the war and the political storm that was about to burst upon the nation. This calm extended even to Downing Street, where at number 10, Fisher learned that the Prime Minister was not in. He was attending the wedding of his one-time parliamentary private secretary Geoffrey Howard MP, to the Honourable Christina Methuen, the only daughter of Field Marshal Lord Methuen, at Henry VII's Chapel, Westminster Abbey. This was quite fortuitous, as Lloyd George soon arrived on some business and by chance met Fisher in the lobby. It was their first meeting of the day, as Lloyd George had not been at his office when Fisher had called earlier.

> A combative grimness had taken the place of his usually genial greeting; the lower lip of his set mouth was thrust forward [Lloyd George recalled].
>
> 'I have resigned!' was his greeting, and on my enquiring the reason he replied, 'I can stand it no longer.' He then informed me that he was on his way to see the Prime Minister, having made up his mind to take no further part in the Dardanelles 'foolishness', and was off to Scotland that night.

Lloyd George tried to persuade him to postpone his departure until Monday so that at least he could present his case before the War Council. 'I'm not waiting another hour,' Fisher persisted obstinately.

'But as far as the Council is concerned, you have never expressed any dissent from the policy and plans,' argued Lloyd George. 'I haven't heard one word of protest from you.'

Fisher replied, 'Mr Churchill is – or was – my chief. And by the traditions of the service I'm not allowed to differ from him in public.' He continued, 'At the very beginning I made my views clear privately to the Prime Minister, in the presence of Mr Churchill, and it was up to Mr Asquith whether my objections were made known or kept confidential.'

It was difficult to answer this, and the need to do so was avoided by the arrival, in his wedding tails, of Asquith. 'There was no reception,' he declared indignantly. 'They decided it was not appropriate at this time. Whatever is the world coming to?' He was clearly cross at his deprivation of champagne. The Prime Minister then grumpily greeted his ministers and invited Fisher into his office. It was 4 p.m. and a few minutes later Asquith realized that this time Fisher was deadly serious. He was going to resign, which meant that not only Winston would face the wrath of the nation: his own position was at grave risk, and the Government seemed likely to fall. Their only chance of survival lay with Fisher. *Everything* must be done to persuade him to change his mind, and the only person he still might listen to was Winston.

Later that afternoon, for the second time in the day, Winston called at 10 Downing Street. The problem was clear-cut. Naval reinforcements of all kinds were desperately needed at the Dardanelles for Ian Hamilton and De Robeck, and also to placate Kitchener for the loss of the *Queen Elizabeth*. But Fisher, too, must be appeased in order to bribe him back, so a cut from the proposed figures would have to be offered. Exactly what these figures were to be was not recorded at the time or divulged later by either Winston or Asquith. Neither is it recorded who suggested, as an added bribe, that Fisher should be offered a position in the War Council.

Because Fisher flatly refused to see him, Winston wrote a letter, using all his very considerable persuasive powers. 'The only thing to think of now,' it began, 'is what is best for the country and for the brave men who are fighting. Anything which does injury to those interests will be vy harshly judged by history on whose stage we now are . . .' He appealed to Fisher's loyalty and courage, and he reminded him that he, Winston, had taken his political life in his hands with the King and Prime Minister in insisting on having him as partner and that Fisher's resignation would invest with an air of disaster this 'mighty enterprise' of the Dardanelles in the eyes of the world. And 'our rupture will be profoundly injurious to every public interest'.

The 'rupture' was bound to come anyway. It was not only Admiral Beatty who knew that Winston and Fisher could never work together for long: they were like two positives in an electrical circuit or like the age-old conflict between soldier and sailor.

'His heart is ashore, not afloat!' wrote Fisher to McKenna (16 May), adding, *The joy of his life is to be 50 yards from a German trench!'*

And yet the mutual love and admiration was deep, and perhaps that is the reason why the partnership had survived for so long. The eight resignations and the eight withdrawals were not entirely frivolous or proof of poor judgement or old age; the resignation withdrawals, sometimes within minutes of being tendered, were motivated by the knowledge that only from within the Admiralty could Fisher still hope to influence events, tame the wildness (as he saw it) of his master, and confirm his loyalty to Jellicoe, who frequently begged him to remain in power.

The spark was Winston's slipping in of additional reinforcements to those agreed after the War Council meeting and their personal meeting at 6.30 p.m. on 14 May. Not for the first or last time, Winston had pushed his luck too far. The Admiral's fury and despair were fuelled by his certain conviction that Winston thought he could hoodwink him. He had tried it before and would no doubt do it again – if given the chance.

Later, Winston naughtily tried to hoodwink the readers of his memoirs in his determined attempt to clear his name. Writing to explain, but not to justify, Fisher's resignation, he asked his readers to imagine how 'the old

Admiral, waking in the early morning, saw himself confronted again with the minutes proposing the reinforcements for the Dardanelles . . .'

But the word 'again' is deceptive. As Captain Crease confirmed, 'Late at night you altered the minute and added to it . . .' It was in fact the first time Fisher (or, later, Captain Crease) had seen the minute in its new form suggesting additional reinforcements, including those suggestions added in Winston's own hand.

On Sunday morning, 16 May, Fisher replied to Winston's appeal to withdraw his resignation. It was not true, he told him, that Winston had been unaware of his hostility towards the Dardanelles operations:

> How could it be otherwise when previously as First Sea Lord I had been responsible for the Defence Committee Memorandum stating the forcing of the Dardanelles to be impossible! You must remember my extreme reluctance in the Prime Minister's room in January to accept his decision in regard to the Dardanelles . . .
>
> Ever since (as, I fear, to your great annoyance!) I have been, as you truly said the other day, in the unpleasant position of being antagonistic to your proposals, until the series of fresh naval arrangements for the Dardanelles you sent me yesterday morning convinced me that the time had arrived for me to take a final decision, there being much more in those proposals than had occurred to me the previous evening. . . .
>
> YOU ARE BENT ON FORCING THE DARDANELLES AND NOTHING WILL TURN YOU FROM IT – NOTHING. I Know you so well! . . . You will remain. I SHALL GO. It is better so. Your splendid stand on my behalf with the King and the Prime Minister I can NEVER forget, when you took your political life in your hands and I really worked very hard for you in return – my utmost . . .

Fisher did not take his train to Scotland at once. More drama was to be found in the postscript to his story even than in the last chapters. He returned to his office, where he wrote the letter above, removed his personal possessions and settled down to watch events, but not to participate in them yet, in his official quarters on the other side of Admiralty Arch.

Meanwhile, in the newspapers and in letters and telegrams from his friends and admirers, the appeals to him to stay poured in. 'LORD FISHER MUST NOT GO' headlined the *Globe*, asking 'Lord Fisher or Mr Churchill? Expert or amateur?' *The Times*, which had savaged Winston since the failure of the landings, proposed that not only should Fisher not be allowed to go, but he should be promoted First Lord in Winston's place. The *Daily Telegraph* agreed.

Jellicoe, speaking for the Grand Fleet, said he would rather lose some ships than see Fisher leave the Admiralty.

And Beatty wrote, 'If it is of any value to you to know it, the Fleet is numbed with the thought of the possibility. Please God it is NOT possible for we absolutely refuse to believe it . . .'

Lord Esher, an old and powerful friend, hinted that Fisher should be given the revived title of Lord High Admiral. Fisher's beloved friend Queen Alexandra, with whom he had danced so many waltzes on so many quarterdecks (in spite of her lameness), wrote peremptorily: '*Stick* to your *Post* like *Nelson*! The Nation and we all have such full confidence in you and I and they will not suffer you to go. You are the Nation's hope and we trust you!'

It would have been better if Fisher had done as he had promised and left for Scotland at once. The vain old man had always been susceptible to flattery, and all this was going to his head. Now he suddenly saw a chink of light in the darkness. Asquith at this time had more to cope with than the Dardanelles. On the very day of Fisher's resignation, *The Times* had exposed a shell-shortage scandal, which at once grew to gross proportions. As Winston was being publicly castigated for the Dardanelles, the War Council (not Kitchener – he was inviolable) and Asquith in particular were being blamed for the shell scandal, which was costing thousands of lives:

> The want of an unlimited supply of high explosive was a fatal bar to our success [complained *The Times*] . . . British soldiers died in vain on Sunday because shells were needed. The Government, who have so seriously failed to organize adequately our national resources, must bear their share of the grave responsibility.

At the same time a great offensive in France, in which the Germans used poison gas for the first time, had ground to a halt. Impasse again, with thousands more dead with nothing to show for it. Herbert Asquith, so unflappable, so bland and arrogantly confident, had his back to the wall, which Fisher threatened to demolish behind him. If this administration should fall, Winston was certain to fall with it. And, Fisher reasoned, what opportunities might not then come his way? This question became even more interesting after a talk with Grey at the Foreign Office and after receiving a letter from Asquith begging him to do nothing and say nothing. Fisher took this advice. It was the one sensible thing he did in this crisis.

As much for Clementine as for Winston, every day of the awful week beginning on 16 May seemed like a lifetime. For Clementine, personal involvement began on that Sunday. In the morning, Winston answered Fisher's violent but affectionate letter by refusing to see him or to ask for the withdrawal of his resignation. Winston used every argument he had used before, with some new ones, including the risk that the Italian government, poised on a knife-edge of indecision, would fail to come in as an ally. The reply to this came within the hour – Admiralty messengers were having a busy weekend, too – and said little. Then there was a cheerful letter from General French at his headquarters: 'We have had a really good fight today,' and French invited

337

Winston to come on another visit 'when you can'. Evidently no hint of the raging crisis had crossed the Channel yet.

In the middle of that Sunday afternoon, Winston returned from his office to Admiralty House. Clementine was with the children, but for once he took little notice of them, which led Clementine to realize that the crisis had by no means blown over.

'James* has been speaking to the PM,' Winston told her, 'but I really need to talk to him face to face. He is down at The Wharf with Margot and Violet, and Maurice will be joining them. He suggested that we dine there tonight.'

Clementine was surprised at this short notice and said so. 'You would like me to come? It's as urgent as that?'

Winston confirmed that it was and asked how soon she could be ready. Half an hour later, the parents kissed goodbye to the children, who were left in the charge of their nanny, Higgs. 'You must be good – especially you, Randolph,' said Winston. 'We'll be back late but we'll be here when you wake up in the morning.'

There was no question of using an Admiralty car. Anyway, Winston loved driving. It was a fine, calm late afternoon, with the sunset hours away at almost 8 p.m., and there would no doubt still be light in the sky when they returned. Clementine and Winston were well wrapped up and wearing goggles, although for most of the way they would be on metalled roads with little dust. Nor was there much traffic on the Oxford road, which they followed through Denham, Beaconsfield and High Wycombe, up over the Chilterns where the beeches in new leaf were at their best.

At the start of the journey, we can be sure that Clementine asked for a detailed account of what had been happening during the earlier part of the day. He would then have told her in detail of his many meetings and interviews, and given her his views and asked for hers. As they passed through the

---

*James Masterton-Smith.

villages and small towns of Buckinghamshire, people sitting outside pubs and their cottages in the evening sun might have turned their heads and followed, with expressions that were mainly unfriendly, the red Napier with 'Mi'lord and his Lady' speeding by. Why wasn't that man in khaki? No one would have recognized, beneath his cap and scarf and goggles, the First Lord of the Admiralty (one of the most famous men conducting the war) and his beautiful wife.

Before they reached Sutton Courtney, south of Oxford, Winston told Clementine the good news. Among his closest associates in the Admiralty, now that Fisher had gone, old 'Tug' Wilson had not only agreed to stay but had told him – after an hour's consideration – that, yes, he would be prepared to take over from Fisher.

'Oh, that's capital!' exclaimed Clementine. 'And what about the others? Will they stay? Will they serve under the old man?'

'Yes, they are all behind us. So the talk of a split due to my dictatorial methods is as malicious as I knew it to be.'

When they arrived in the village, Clementine was in good spirits from the news and refreshed by the country air. She went into the house before Winston, who was putting up the car's hood with the help of a gardener, in anticipation of the night journey back to London.

Margot offered Clementine tea, and they sat and gossiped by the drawing-room window overlooking the lawn and the river. 'I thought you were going to overlap with Reggie,'* Margot remarked in her forthright way. 'That wouldn't have done, would it, my dear Clemmie? Fortunately he went off in his motor just before you arrived. This place is like Waterloo Station today.'

We can imagine them chatting and watching Winston crossing the lawn and heading for the river, clearly in a

---

*Reginald McKenna, Winston's resentful predecessor at the Admiralty.

pensive mood. 'I hope Henry is not too long with B,'* Margot remarked, 'Dear B. spent the morning with the King, dressed quite informally for the weekend. Low blue turned-down collar and golfing clothes, would you believe it? He said the King wanted to know all the goings-on at the War Office with this shell scandal talk. He doesn't like to hear anything against Kitchener – in fact he told B. he wished he would be made C in C over French and conduct the war in France personally . . .'

While Margot prattled on, her stepdaughter Violet was boating back from a little trip up the river with a friend. She caught sight of Winston standing on the river bank, looking (she wrote later) 'like Napoleon at St Helena'. She stepped out of the boat and greeted him, taking his arm for a walk up and down the lawn.

Of the political situation, she asked him, 'Didn't you realize you were on the edge of a volcano?'

'No,' Winston told her. 'Jacky and I have always got on so well. We never differed on any principle. And I certainly supposed that he was completely loyal.'

'Can't you make him change his mind, Winston?'

He laughed with a trace of bitterness. 'God knows, I've tried. But he seems as impervious as the Rock of Gibraltar. See this' – and he pulled a letter from his pocket – 'it is the answer to my second long appeal to him.'

Violet read the letter in silence:

Dear Winston, –
As usual your letter is most persuasive, but I really have considered everything and I have definitely told the Prime Minister that I leave to-morrow (Monday).
Please don't wish to see me. I could say nothing as I am determined not to. I know I am doing right.

Yours,
Fisher

---

*Maurice Bonham Carter.

She folded the letter and handed it back. 'Yes, I see what you mean. What a strange man he is! For some years I have thought him mad. He was half mad when he came on board the *Enchantress* that time at Naples. Do you remember? It seems another world ago.'

The sun was low in the sky and they went in to change for dinner. Later, Violet recalled that stroll in the garden in her diary:

> Poor darling W. – there is a naive and utterly disarming trustfulness about him. He is quite impervious to the climatic conditions of other people. He makes his own climate and lives in it and those who love him share it. In an odd way there was something like love between him and Fisher – a kind of magnetic attraction which often went into reverse. Theirs was a curiously emotional relationship – but as in many such they could neither live with, nor without, each other.

When Clementine came down to dinner from the bedroom assigned to them for the evening, she noticed that Winston and Asquith were missing. Edgar Vincent, Maurice Bonham Carter, little Prince Paul of Serbia, Violet, Margot, and one or two others were all there, but the Prime Minister and First Lord were noticeably absent. Asquith and Winston soon joined them, both looking quite relaxed. Violet had earlier noted that 'Clemmie was naturally very upset and as ever very brave.' But it was quite a cheerful dinner, she also recalled.

Later, on the road back to London, Winston would have told Clementine in detail of what had transpired in those few minutes in Asquith's study. 'I showed him Jacky's final letter of resignation, and then I said that my office was at his disposal if he thought it necessary to make a change. "No, I have thought of that," he said. "I do not wish it, but can you get a Board?"'

341

'And so you said, yes, you could. Thank goodness for dear "Tug" Wilson! And what a contrast with Fisher!'

They were climbing in second gear up the steep, zigzagging road on the north-west slopes of the Chilterns. What little light was left in the sky at 10 p.m. was shut off by the close-set, towering beech trees, and the twin beams of the acetylene lights picked out in yellow the road, the steep bank on the right, and the steep drop to the left.

'I told him that Wilson would take over from Fisher, and the rest of the Board had stood fast.'

'Surely you must be safe, then?' Clementine asked anxiously.

'For the present. Yes, for the present, but perhaps not for long. Maurice took me aside after dinner and indicated that because of the shell scandal on top of Fisher's resignation, the opposition might have to be consulted about the next step.'

'You mean he thought a coalition –?'

'It could be, and you know what they [the Conservatives] think of me.'

Big Ben was sounding midnight when Winston drove the Napier into Admiralty Yard. Clementine could reasonably claim on his behalf that it had been a busy and dutiful day. She could not know that Sunday had been a placid ocean compared with the stormy seas of Monday.

There is no gauge to register the depth of bitterness and anger. In any case, of the three men most damaged by the crisis of mid-May 1915, Asquith's sufferings were of a different nature from those of his First Lord and First Sea Lord. Just as this final crisis for his government was blowing up, with the nation reeling from the torpedoing of the liner *Lusitania* (1,198 passengers drowned, including many children and 128 Americans), the failure of the new offensive in France, the grinding to a halt in Gallipoli, and the Zeppelin air raids, Asquith suffered a personal blow. Venetia Stanley suddenly, without any warning, told him of her engagement to his friend and colleague Edwin Montagu. It was almost more than he could bear. 'I don't believe there are two living people who, each in their separate ways, are more devoted to me than she and Montagu,' Asquith wrote to Venetia's sister in despair. 'And it is the irony of fortune that they two shd. combine a death-blow to me.'

If not quite a death-blow, the sudden loss of this intimacy certainly affected Asquith's judgement and led him to a more precipitate formation of a coalition government than might otherwise have been the case. There was no wilier or more experienced politician, and had his resolve not faltered so rapidly, he might well have saved his government. Italy was on the very brink of joining the Allies, and did so on 23 May. The anger of the British people against the Germans had never been so intense, and conditions of near riot prevailed. Asquith could easily have traded on this instead of silently deploring it. He could have fended off the attacks and demands of Andrew Bonar Law, the Conservative leader, just as he could have disregarded the advice of Lloyd George, who was bent on a coalition for his own political advantage. But as Asquith admitted in a *cri de coeur* to Venetia, her sudden absence as a loving confidante was 'the most bitter memory of my life,' causing politics and the survival of his administration to fade into relative insignificance.

It is highly probable, though not certain, that Winston could have survived the resignation of Fisher if it had not been for the defection of Venetia Stanley, that clever spoilt darling of the Prime Minister, who confessed that her behaviour had been 'treacherous', that every day before her confession had ended in tears. 'How awful you must have thought me,' she confessed to Asquith. Asquith had no minister he admired more than Winston, but he had to be sacrificed as a condition, imposed by the Conservatives, of Asquith's remaining Prime Minister.

Winston knew nothing of the emotional turmoil of his chief, or even of Asquith's decision to form a coalition government, when he began his last battle for political survival. On Monday 17 May, two days after Fisher's resignation and the day when, unknown to Winston, Fisher began to have second thoughts, Winston spent most of the morning preparing a statement for Parliament explaining the new arrangements he was making at the Admiralty. Before calling on Asquith with his text for approval, he dropped into the House and visited Lloyd George in his office. Winston's old confederate told him at once that the political crisis and Fisher's resignation could be corrected only by the formation of a coalition government and that he would resign unless this happened at once.

Winston agreed. 'I have always favoured a coalition, as you must know, but I hope any new arrangement can be deferred until the new Admiralty Board is appointed and settled in.'

'No, I disagree,' Lloyd George replied abruptly. 'The action must be immediate.'

Winston was taken aback by the Chancellor of the Exchequer's verbal violence. He could not know that his old friend had been making calculations and that they were not favourable towards himself. Lloyd George believed that salvation for the Liberal Party, and his own political future, lay in coming to terms swiftly with the opposition, with Asquith still as Prime Minister. He knew, too, that Winston was totally unacceptable to the Conservatives.

Winston left in an uneasy frame of mind. What on earth was going on? He repaired to 10 Downing Street again. Asquith received him 'with great consideration', but it was the smile of the executioner. When Winston showed him the statement he was to make to the Commons that afternoon, and the formation of the new Board of Admiralty, Asquith shook his head sadly.

'No, this will not do,' he said. 'I have decided to form a national government by a coalition, and a very much larger reconstruction will be required. The whole nation is filled with gratitude for what you have done,' he continued ominously. 'I do not have to tell you of my admiration.'

So it had come to that. Dismissal. The suddenness of the blow was stunning. But as he stood there in this familiar room, studying Asquith's clever face and stumpy figure in black morning coat, Winston had already decided that he was going to fight; though this was not the time to open fire. He must work out his campaign in detail. Instead, he said: 'If there is to be a change, Prime Minister, may I suggest that Mr Balfour should take my place. He has been a party to all our secrets. His appointment would be far the best that could be made.'

Asquith thanked him and Winston recognized that he had already decided in favour of Arthur Balfour. 'Now, about you. Will you take office in this new government?' Then, recalling Winston's earlier desire to revert to being a soldier, added, 'Or would you prefer a command in France?'

Before Winston could reply to this offer, who should be shown into the room but David Lloyd George. Had he come to be in at the kill? Oh, no, it seemed as if he had followed Winston in order to give them both advice. After a brief greeting, Lloyd George said, 'Why do you not send him to the Colonial Office? There is great work to be done there.'

A whole era in politics had passed since Winston had been promoted from Undersecretary at the Colonial Office. From running the war at sea, back to running the colonies in time of war? The suggestion was ludicrous and insulting. Winston kept his voice steady: 'I think not, Prime Minister.'

This little fragment of tragicomedy was broken by *enter a messenger*. He was, in fact, one of Asquith's secretaries. 'Mr Masterton-Smith has been on the telephone, Mr Churchill. Very important news . . . You must come back to the Admiralty at once.'

Leaving the executioner and witness, Winston hastened from the room. 'It took only five minutes to get to the Admiralty,' Winston later recalled. 'There I learned that the whole German Fleet was coming out . . .' With the Chief of Staff and the Second Sea Lord at his side, Winston took over complete command, signals pouring from the War Room at the Admiralty like confetti. With every decision – 'Send five submarines to Harwich . . . Send the Tribal destroyers to join . . .' – and every minute that passed, Winston was conscious of the exciting prospect: a great victory in the North Sea must preserve his position, especially as Fisher had refused to return to his post – even at this critical moment. It was an act of defiance from which Fisher would never recover; it lost him the support of the entire Board of Admiralty.*

After he was satisfied that all steps had be n taken to bring about a meeting between the two fleets that might end the war altogether and would certainly hasten it, Winston found time to deal again with his own crisis. This personal battle was at a more advanced stage than the threatened clash in the North Sea.

> *So far as I am concerned* [he wrote to Asquith] *if you find it necessary to make a change here, I should be glad – assuming it was thought fitting – to be offered a position in the new Government. But I will not take any office except a military department, and if that is not convenient I hope I may be found employment in the field . . . I should be sorry to leave the Admiralty, where I have borne the brunt, but should always rely on you to vindicate my work here.*

Now Winston at last felt that he must go to bed, reflecting on the day: 'In the morning I had prepared for a Parliamentary ordeal of the most searching character; in the afternoon for a political crisis fatal to myself; in the evening for the supreme battle at sea. For one day it was enough.'

But even as Winston fell into exhausted sleep, the German commander in chief was about to reverse the course of his fleet. So there could now be no reversal of Winston's fate in a great naval battle.

---

*Later, when he was told of Winston's departure, he laid down conditions for his return, conditions that would have made him virtually 'admiralissimo', accountable to no-one! By then no-one bothered to answer. Violet was surely right: he *was* mad.

'I Thought He Would Die of Grief'

The rage of Winston's numerous enemies, now that they thought he was on the run, was unbridled, the language – verbal and written – beyond reasonable grounds. Geoffrey Robinson, editor of *The Times*, flushed with the sensation he had caused by exposing 'the shell scandal', was among the more moderate critics in the leader he wrote for his newspaper that morning. It was one of those 'we-can-no-longer-keep-silence' pieces, and concluded:

> When a civilian minister in charge of a fighting ser-
> vice persistently seeks to grasp power which should
> not pass into his unguided hands, and attempts to
> use that power in perilous ways, it is time for his
> colleagues in the Cabinet to take some action. Such
> is the stage which they appear to have reached.

The *National Review* wrote of his 'arrogance' and 'disastrous blunders'. 'The departure of Mr Churchill from the Admiralty was never anything but a question of time; and the period of time depends upon how much people would stand.'

Winston had not time at present for reading these attacks or the more violent ones in the less 'respectable' papers. He needed no written evidence that he was in the eye of the storm. In the struggle for survival, he wrote to Asquith: 'Above all things I shd like to stay here – & complete my work . . . Everything has been provided for and the naval situation is in every respect assured. After four years admin-istration & nine months war I am entitled to say this . . .'

He went on to suggest that Balfour should go to the War Office, in place of Kitchener, and then all 'wd work with perfect smoothness'. But forgetting the scorn he had poured on Lloyd George's insulting suggestion that he should go to the Colonial Office, he now wrote, 'If an office like the Colonies wh was suggested were open to me I shd not be right to refuse it . . .'

For a while there seemed to be no friend or even a boat in sight to save him from the sinking ship.

Apart from Clementine and his close friends, the only people who offered Winston support were (to his surprise) Tug Wilson and his old friend J. L. Garvin, editor of the *Observer*. Wilson wrote to say that not only would he serve under him, but he would not serve under anyone else. For a while, this generous offer gave Winston a flicker of hope, but it was soon dashed: things had already gone too far.

Garvin's letter, too, gave Winston a great lift:

18 May 1915
Private

My dear Churchill,
A thankless hour but behind you is the one initial act historic and imperishable, and your career is only beginning. Good will come out of it all. A first class man is never fully known (says the sage) until he shows the rapidity with which be recovers from a blow. Your fighting heart will be quits with fortune in twenty-four hours or less! and here, on this difficult, political battleground at home is the 'front' for you, & where the country needs you.*

Yours ever sincerely,
J. L. Garvin

The following Sunday, the *Observer* was the only serious newspaper to back Winston to the hilt and pour praise upon his record.

*He refers to 'standing the Fleet fast' in late July 1914.

ABOVE: Randolph at his marriage to Pamela Digby in 1939 (Hulton-Deutsch)

RIGHT: The famous poster of 1940

"LET US GO FORWARD TOGETHER"

ABOVE: Viewing London's bomb damage from the Thames in 1940 (Hulton-Deutsch)

BELOW: Winston presents a letter from King George VI to Franklin Roosevelt in 1941

With General Dwight D. ("Ike") Eisenhower before D-Day in 1944 (G. Treuhaft)

Winston on his way to the House of Commons on VE Day, 1945 (Syndication International)

Chartwell (Peregrine Churchill)

Winston painting in the south of France (Peregrine Churchill)

In retirement

ABOVE: Clementine and Randolph, 1962 (Hulton-Deutsch)

ABOVE: Sarah and Clementine after Winston's funeral (Hulton-Deutsch)

LEFT: Sarah after viewing her father's body lying-in-state, 1965 (Hulton-Deutsch)

The last ride: Winston's coffin leaving St. Paul's Cathedral after the funeral service

Whatever satisfaction Garvin's letter gave Winston, it was overwhelmed by the multitude of intrigues that were building up about him. Even the King, who distrusted him and had never forgiven him for bringing back Fisher, was up to dirty work. To his wife, Queen Mary, George V wrote approving of a coalition government: 'Only by that means can we get rid of Churchill from Admiralty. He is intriguing also with French against K [Kitchener], he is the real danger.' This charge was completely untrue.

Winston at one stage was reduced to sending documentary evidence of his innocence to Bonar Law, the Conservative leader who was insisting on a coalition that would exclude him. These Admiralty papers purported to refute 'the charge that I am to blame by my interference with the naval experts' for the disasters of Coronel and the sinking of the three armoured cruisers by a single German U-boat.

Winston next drafted a statement, intended for the press, defending his policy over the Dardanelles, and took it to Lloyd George and Grey. They both thought this a disastrous idea as it would imply that things were so bad out there that excuses were needed. Among the many other people of power on whom he called was Max Aitken (later Lord Beaverbrook), who recorded that Winston 'was clinging to the desire of retaining the Admiralty as if the salvation of England depended upon it'.

Those close to him, and above all Clementine herself, watched with agonized sympathy Winston's ordeal and desperate last-ditch fight for survival. 'My heart was wrung for him,' exclaimed Violet Asquith, who told of meeting him by chance in the House. She had caught him in a black moment.

> He took me into his room and sat down on a chair
> – silent, despairing – as I have never seen him. He
> seemed to have no rebellion or even anger left. He
> did not even abuse Fisher, but simply said, 'I'm
> finished.' I poured out contradictions, protestations

– but he waved them aside. 'No – I'm done. What I want above all things is to take some active part in beating the Germans. But I can't – it's been taken from me. I'd go out to the Front at once – but these soldiers are so stuffy – they wouldn't like my being given anything of a command. No, I'm finished.'

Violet was reduced to tears by this outburst and her failure to convince him of his true greatness. 'My faith in him and in his fortunes was absolute.' Her mind went back to that afternoon at Archerfield House when Winston had been like an excited schoolboy at achieving his ambition to run the Navy. And now? Was it any use interceding with her father? She consulted Maurice Bonham Carter, who declared at once that it would not be. 'He has done his damnedest but the Tories won't have Winston at any price,' he told her. 'It is after all their hatred of Winston and their blind belief in Fisher which has brought about this crisis.'

Violet kept asking the question to which there was no answer: 'What balm was there for Winston's wound – the sharpest and the deepest wound he suffered in his whole career?'

We get another glimpse of both Clementine and Winston from the diary of Lady Cynthia Asquith for 27 May:

I lunched at the Admiralty with the 'setting sun' minister. Saw Clemmie alone first for a little. She looks very sad, poor thing. Winston came in rather late from the first Coalition Cabinet. He looks unhappy, but is very dignified and un-bitter. I have never liked him so much. Clemmie said she had always known it would happen from the day Fisher was appointed, and Winston said that, if he could do things over again, he would do just the same with regard to appointing Fisher as he says he has done really great organizing work. I think his [Winston's] nature – though he may be unscrupulous and inclined to trample on susceptibilities of sailors . . . from eagerness – is absolutely devoid of vindictiveness, unlike the half-caste* Fisher who really runs amok from malevolent spleen . . .

During lunch, it seems, Winston cheered up and showed his resilience by boasting of the Cabinet meeting he had attended. 'There I was after ten years in the Cabinet, and five years in the most important office, still by ten years the youngest member!' He also described himself as experiencing the 'austerity of changing fortune'.

Edwin Montagu, not perhaps the most sensitive of beings, called on Clementine at Admiralty House, too. 'She was so sweet,' he told Venetia Stanley, 'but so miserable and crying all the time.' He felt later that he had not adequately consoled her, and wrote her a letter which was at once a moving tribute and an expression of trust in Winston's future:

> *Winston is far too great to be more than pulled up for a period. His courage is enormous, his genius understood even by his enemies and I am as confident that he will rise again as I am that the sun will rise tomorrow . . . Be as miserable as you must about the present; have no misgivings as to the future; I have none, Winston I am sure has none and I know that in your heart and amid your gloom you have undaunted confidence in the man you love.*

But within this misery, Clementine nursed an increasing contempt for Asquith, the man who had brought about the downfall of her husband, and swore that one day she would dance on his grave. On 20 May she unwisely but typically wrote a long letter to Asquith, praising Winston and pouring scorn on all those who had conspired to see him gone. She suggested that it was the press that had made up Asquith's

---

*Fisher was born in Ceylon, and because of his swarthy appearance, his enemies suggested his mother or father was Sinhalese.

mind. 'If you throw Winston overboard you will be committing an act of weakness . . . he has the supreme quality which
I venture to say very few of your present or future Cabinet
possess – the power, the imagination, the deadliness to fight
Germany.'

Asquith did not condescend even to reply. But the contents
of the letter had wide distribution, as it was read out aloud to
guests at table to amuse them. 'She wrote me the letter of a
maniac,' he complained to Venetia Stanley.

When she was an old lady, Clementine told Winston's
biographer, 'When he left the Admiralty he thought he
was finished . . . I thought he would never get over the
Dardanelles: I thought he would die of grief.'

The Conservatives would not countenance Winston even at
the Colonial Office. The price for their co-operation was
Winston's political extinction. All they would allow him was
chancellorship of the Duchy of Lancaster, a token courtesy
title with absolutely no power, although Asquith did at least
insist that he should sit in on War Council and Cabinet meetings for the time being.

On 27 May less than one week after he had controlled
the pursuit of the entire German High Seas Fleet, Winston
went to Buckingham Palace to receive the seal of the Duchy
of Lancaster. The day before, his last at the Admiralty, he
learned that the threatened U-boats had indeed arrived at
the Dardanelles and had already sunk a battleship. Delay
and procrastination – the two greatest robbers of victory in
war – had decided the outcome of the most enterprising and
exciting operation of the Great War, on any front and at any
time. It was an irony of the first order that the one man most
responsible for the fatal delay in the despatching of the 29th
Division and the landings on Gallipoli, Field Marshal Lord
Kitchener, arrived without appointment at the Admiralty on
the last day of Winston's rule there, to commiserate, in his
own austere fashion.

'What are you going to do?' he asked.

'I have no idea, nothing has been settled.'

The soldier then spoke kindly of their work together and prepared to leave. 'Well,' he said, 'there is one thing at any rate they cannot take from you. The Fleet was ready.'

Kitchener never knew that Asquith had wished to get rid of him, too, but had been too fearful of public opinion to order the execution. Instead, this strange man, who was as inscrutable as he was incapable of understanding Winston, was drowned while in the care of the Navy, little more than a year later. The cruiser in which he was sailing struck a German mine, as had so many more of the Navy's ships at the Dardanelles, thanks to his delaying military support.

Sunny Marlborough was among those relatively few who wrote to sympathize with Winston in the wilderness. 'I gather that you have been flung a bone on which there is little meat,' he wrote. 'The fare is poor but I suppose you will think it wisest to live on emergency rations pro tem.'

For Clementine, Winston's cousin spoke with more truth than his metaphor might have suggested. Their income was suddenly reduced from £4,500 to £2,000 a year, and prices were rising as the economic effects of the war began to bite. Grey's lease on 33 Eccleston Square had not yet expired, and they had to find somewhere to live. The 'austerity of changing fortune' discouraged Clementine and Winston from buying another house, and he wired to Jack, who was still with Hamilton off the Dardanelles, asking if they might move into his house in the Cromwell Road. Asquith had suggested that they should remain at Admiralty House for the time being, but Clementine was not taking any favours from *him*, and anyway wished to throw off the dust of that dwelling, and the Navy.

So, after a short emotional convalescence in Ivor Guest's house in Arlington Street, they moved in with Goonie and her children, to the delight of both Clementine and their children. But the almost intolerable strain of the past weeks led Winston and Clementine to seek some refuge from the hurly-burly of wartime London and its associations with the shame and indignity of loss of office. They found what they wanted in a farmhouse in a remote wooded valley in Surrey not far from Godalming. Like Pear Tree Cottage, Hoe Farm had been converted by Edwin Lutyens. It was quite big enough for both families, and the two 'flotillas' of children (as Winston called them) – Diana (6 years), Randolph (4), Sarah (9 months), and Jack and Goonie's Johnny (6) and Peregrine (2) – had the run of the big garden and wooden summerhouse. 'It really is a delightful valley and the garden gleams with summer jewellery,' Winston told his brother.

Eddie Marsh, who had been at Winston's side throughout the recent ordeal and shared his sufferings, now shared his appreciation of Hoe Farm. It was, he wrote to Violet Asquith, 'the most exquisitely lovely place, and the real English country in all its glories and to me cruel beauty of the first day of perfect early summer.' But Winston was not constituted to be satisfied for long with bucolic pleasures and the sounds of birds. The deprivation of office, the release from responsibility for great decisions, the loss of all the trimmings of power, left him empty and bitter.

'I am miserably sorry for Winston,' Marsh continued in his letter to Violet. 'You can imagine what a horrible wound and mutilation it is for him to be torn away from his work there – it's like Beethoven deaf.'

Only weeks earlier, Winston had begun each day in bed, surrounded by papers and red boxes crying out for urgent attention. Replies and demands for action would be dictated, telephone calls to fellow ministers and to the giants of Fleet Street and the City would be made, memoranda would be initialled with scribbled comments. Now, suddenly, no-one consulted him, sought his advice or suggested meetings. All he received was the occasional letter from some friend or acquaintance appealing for a magistrate appointment, almost the only responsibility his new position granted him.

Watching him pacing about the garden, sunk in a gloom only momentarily lifted by a romp with the children, Clementine and Goonie felt grieved and frustrated that nothing seemed to lift his spirits. Temporary alleviation was at last provided by a distraction that grew to be a great relaxation

354

and hobby in later life. Goonie was an amateur artist who loved painting. The scenes about the garden, fields and woods of Hoe Farm particularly appealed to her. Winston's attention was attracted to her with her easel, and after watching her abstractedly one day, he was suddenly drawn to, and then fascinated by, the art of painting.

The two women did all they could to nurture this interest, hoping that he might find some release from his misery. Paints and palettes and easels were purchased in Godalming, and encouragement and praise for Winston's early efforts were lavished upon him. Sir John Lavery and his wife, neighbours in London and both distinguished painters, were invited down to Hoe Farm to offer instruction.

The therapy worked like a dream. In transforming the image before him on to canvas or paper, Winston found he could totally absorb himself, without a sliver of intervening thought for the troubles of his life. The only association between previous experience and this new world of painting was the determination to excel. Every painting had to be better than the last, and Sir John Lavery was for a time like the Fisher of 1911 and 1912 – guide, teacher and 'sure and steady counsellor', as Winston had once described the Admiral.

Although without any executive powers, Winston had been co-opted on to the Dardanelles Committee, on which he could bring a limited degree of influence and at least could follow the progress – and lack of progress – of the operations. But after a while, hamstrung and frustrated, he wearied of argument and pined for action. At least on a battlefield, he could influence events personally. Anxious not to arouse Clementine's fears unnecessarily in case he failed to get an appointment, he confided in Goonie, who could pass on his wishes for action to Jack.

As soon as he heard, Jack reacted unfavourably. 'I hope you will not attempt such a thing,' he wrote to Winston on 3 July. 'You would sacrifice such a lot and gain so little . . . you would be twice as useful at home as here.' But then he went on to suggest an alternative, that Winston come out to the Dardanelles for three weeks and compile a report for the Cabinet.

This idea appealed strongly to Winston. At least he would as a result speak with personal and fresh knowledge in the committee. To his delight, Asquith agreed that this was a valuable suggestion, although he would have to make it clear to Admiral De Robeck and General Ian Hamilton that his mission did not indicate any lack of approval of and confidence in their command.

Arrangements were made in total secrecy in case some of Winston's hard political enemies should attempt to frustrate the expedition. Winston himself took all precautions in his preparations and wrote a long and touching letter to Clementine to be opened in the event of his death. 'Do not grieve for me too much. I am a spirit confident of my rights. Death is only an incident, & not the most important wh happens to us in this state of being,' he wrote. Then, thanking her for teaching him 'how noble a woman's heart can be,' he urged her to 'look forward, feel free, rejoice in life, cherish the children, guard my memory. God bless you.'

On 19 July, just two months after his resignation and after a last weekend at Hoe Farm, Winston attended his last Cabinet meeting for the time being. At its conclusion, he remained behind with the three men privy to the expedition (excluding the King) – Asquith, Kitchener, and Grey. He was saying goodbye to them when Lord Curzon returned and witnessed the shaking of hands and messages of goodwill. When told of the reason, he expressed surprise but added his own good wishes.

A few minutes later, Curzon passed on the surprising news to his Conservative colleagues, who were outraged and suspected they were witnessing the beginning of the re-habilitation of their enemy. Why else the secrecy? Bonar Law led the attack, informing Asquith that there was widespread objection to the plan and that the coalition itself would be put at risk if Winston were allowed to go.

Winston, who had so nearly got away with it, at once backtracked and that day wrote a letter to Asquith saying in effect that he did not wish to upset the applecart and proposed therefore to cancel the expedition. Winston knew that he was becoming more and more isolated and that even the limited influence he could still wield was being whittled away. Why was it, for instance, that memoranda requesting information were now being ignored?

Winston's fury was compounded by the return to office, without any reference to himself, of Jacky Fisher. Fisher, too, from his Scottish eyrie, had been nagging away for employment and now had succeeded where Winston had failed. On 4 July Balfour asked him to return to London to act as chairman of a new Admiralty committee, the Board of Inventions and Research. The old admiral sank his pride and accepted, hoping for better things later.

Winston, in a burst of fury at the news, wrote to Asquith in complaint. Here was a man who, weeks before, 'had deserted his post in time of war' and ignored the order to return, who had . . . – the crimes were listed, but still Asquith had approved Balfour's appointment of this discredited old man. As for Clementine's comments, they are unrecorded but certainly were violent.

Winston did not send this letter to Asquith but, in slightly modified form, to Masterton-Smith, who passed it on to Balfour. In reply, Balfour quoted back all the qualities in the old admiral that Winston had praised when they were still working together, claiming that he was highly qualified for the task.

The miserable, futile summer months passed by. There was no breakout in the Dardanelles, which continued to exhaust vast quantities of war materials and heart-rending gallons of human blood. As on the Western Front, trenches exchanged hands at the point of the bayonet, and barbed wire and machine-guns remained in command of events. Even the Dardanelles Committee was run down, and it was clearly only a matter of time before the massive forces now employed in attempting to gain the Gallipoli Peninsula were withdrawn.

In Winston's eyes, the villain of the piece was still Kitchener

357

and his moribund, vacillating, and totally ineffective control of events, both in France and in the eastern Mediterranean. Not only Winston but most of the Cabinet knew he had to go. By the third week in October Winston was making it clear that unless Kitchener was removed he would resign from the Cabinet.

But Asquith still believed that his own position would once again be at risk if he sacked the great soldier, just as he had earlier believed that he might fall if he did not sack Winston. Never had the war run so badly for Britain, never had cynically engineered self-survival and self-interest figured so importantly in the activities of the political hierarchy. Men died by the tens of thousands while politicians played personal power games in Whitehall, with Lloyd George ready to struggle for the War Office as soon as Kitchener was gone. He did go – to the Dardanelles in place of Winston – but held on to his post, to Lloyd George's fury.

At last Asquith was shamed into promising to make a public statement on the Dardanelles situation. Winston contributed his own version of events and defended his own actions throughout. When the Prime Minister made his long-awaited speech on the subject to the House on 2 November he neither made use of Winston's material nor countered any of the public and professional criticism of Winston's part in the expedition. The result, as Winston knew it would be, was that Winston was publicly pilloried and became indissolubly associated with what was to become known as the greatest fiasco of the war.

On 11 November 1915, with exactly three more years of war to be endured by the Western world, Winston resigned from the Cabinet. His stiff letter to Asquith, and the Prime Minister's reply regretting his decision, were published two days later. Winston made a personal statement to the House of immense dignity and good sense. 'One line to say I thought your speech *quite* flawless,' wrote Violet Asquith. 'I have seldom been more moved – It was a fine and generous speech . . .'

The letters of commiseration, congratulation and praise for

his record poured in, both for his speech and for the letter he published in *The Times* two days later. Typical of these, and much valued by Winston, was one from a long-time colleague and future First Lord of the Admiralty, Walter Long:

> *Rood Ashton*
> *Trowbridge*

14 November 1915

> *My dear Winston,*
> *You must let me say very briefly how much I regret your resignation. The combination of great ability & fine courage is none too common, & we shall miss you badly. You have borne much misrepresentation with dignity & self-restraint & I am certain you will maintain this attitude to the end. I wish you the best of luck in your new role whatever it may be.*

> *Yours sincerely,*
> *Walter Long*

Lloyd George confined himself to writing of the speech as 'amazingly clever both in substance and tone', but did add, 'You must soon return.'

As a major in the Oxfordshire Hussars, Winston could join his regiment in France whenever he wished. He wasted no time in doing so. The house at 41 Cromwell Road briefly became like a deranged quartermaster's stores, with gear scattered all over the hall and the whole household in a chaos of emotions and impediments. Upstairs, Eddie Marsh was in tears and Jennie in total despair at her second son's going off to the war. The children were all over the place, only the older two understanding what was going on, and not liking it.

Fortunately, the two people most concerned with this brief buckling-of-sword period, Clementine and Winston, had their emotions under tight control, although Winston found it hard to conceal completely his joy and excitement.

There was a last luncheon party on 16 November. It was a great mistake, though it might have been possible to sustain a muted note of final gaiety if Margot Asquith had not been present. Besides this old queen wasp, there were her stepdaughter Violet, Goonie and Clementine, Nellie Hozier, Eddie Marsh and the departing hero himself.

The conversation was dominated by Margot and Winston and was acrimonious throughout, Margot bemoaning the coalition that had been brought about by Winston and 'reminding him that he had always wanted one' (according to Violet's account).

'The mistake was forming a coalition in our hour of weakness,' retorted Winston. 'We should have sought one not in a position of weakness but one of strength.'

It was a curious time for politics rather than the war to dominate the conversation, but the two had never got on well. Margot resented Winston's cleverness and believed he had let down her husband, and Winston was always prejudiced against clever, argumentative women, especially if they were not pretty.

'Somehow that was not a great success,' Margot commented to her stepdaughter as they left. And Violet thought this 'for once a wild under-statement. For most of us it was a kind of wake.'

On the morning of 18 November 1915, Winston kissed Clementine and the children goodbye. He wore his uniform as a major in the Oxfordshire Hussars, and his weapons and a vast amount of luggage almost filled the taxicab at the door. It was eighteen years since he had taken the train from Victoria Station to join Sir Bindon Blood 'at the seat of war'. That had been little more than a distant frontier skirmish. By contrast, this time it was 'the war of all against all',* and the guns would be heard before he had even crossed the water.

As he had written to his brother, 'I propose to do my utmost to win my way in the Army wh is my old profession & where as you know my heart has long been.'

---

*'*Bellum omnium contra omnes*' – Thomas Hobbes, *De Cive*.

22

'I Am Vy Happy Here'

War may be 'the greatest plague that can afflict humanity', but as anyone knows who has experienced it, war also brings the relief of simplicity and the comfort of single purpose. There is a convenience in dispensing with argument and acrimony that can offset the uncertainties of danger. For Winston this improvement in his state of mind was accentuated by his total lack of fear for himself and by the complexities and frustrations he was leaving behind.

The spanning of that narrow strip of water between England and France excited all sorts of emotions in the minds of the millions on their way to this greatest of all wars. For Winston it meant the regaining of 'a peace of mind to wh I had long been a stranger'. It meant distancing himself from 'that odious Asquith & his pack of incompetents & intriguers'. 'I am vy happy here. I did not know what release from care meant. It is a blessed peace,' he wrote in the heat of war and the chill of a muddy dugout.

Winston had planned to travel directly to his regiment in rest billets not far from Boulogne, but even as the troopship nosed against the jetty, a loudspeaker was calling his name. It was the military landing officer, asking him to report. 'There is a car for you, Major Churchill. It will conduct you to the Commander in Chief's Headquarters.'

The big Crossley took him through the crowded streets of the port, where military supplies of all kinds fought for space on the streets with the market stalls and civilian horse traffic, and out onto the open road leading to St Omer, thirty miles to the east. The weather was damp and grey and cold. At the Château de Blondecque, Sir John French greeted him like an old friend.

Winston, with his considerable gear, was installed in a comfortable room for the night, and he descended to take dinner with French and one or two of his closest staff. There was a great deal of general war talk that night, in the course of which French told him that John Redmond, chairman of the Irish Parliamentary Party, had recently been staying with him and had told the General that the Government was 'descending into the abyss' and that Winston was quite right to quit.

At breakfast the next morning, French got down to detail and asked Winston, 'What would you like to do?'

'I'll do whatever I am told, sir.'

French, who knew there was a growing tide of opinion against himself, told Winston somewhat solemnly, 'My power is no longer what it was. I am, as it were, riding at single anchor. But it still counts for something. Will you take a brigade?'

'Thank you, sir. I would be proud to do so. But before I take on such a responsibility I think I ought to learn at first hand the special conditions of trench warfare. It is fifteen years since I saw any action.'

French considered this for a moment and then offered him any division he wished in which to gain experience.

'The Guards is the best school of all, sir. I would like to be attached to the Guards Division.'

The Guards Division was commanded by General Lord Cavan, 49 years old, who had fought in South Africa and had a formidable reputation. Winston, who had met him only briefly in South Africa, was reintroduced to him a day or two later at the Château by the Commander in Chief. After some preliminary remarks, Cavan offered to send Winston 'to one of the best Colonels I have. You will learn more from Geoffrey Feilding than from anyone else. His battalion goes into the line tomorrow.' The general suggested lunch at his headquarters at La Gorgue the following day.

After packing a nucleus kit, Winston was driven to the Guards' headquarters, where Lord Cavan, after a more

362

austere lunch than at General Headquarters, drove him to the battalion where he was to be a major, an observer under instruction. Then Cavan drove off, 'leaving me like a new boy at school in charge of the Headmaster, the monitors and the senior scholars,' as Winston put it.

It was a severely testing time for Winston, who was conscious of being thought over-privileged, and a politician at that, who had had no experience of tough fighting on the Western Front. They had all recently suffered the brutalities and casualties of the Battle of Loos, which had not been the success expected of it.

Feilding, who had been badly wounded a year earlier, remarked as soon as Cavan had departed, 'I think I ought to tell you that we were not at all consulted in the matter of your coming to join us.'

'I had had no idea myself,' Winston replied, 'but I dare say it will be all right. Anyway, sir, I expect we'll have to make the best of it.'

This was followed by a long silence.

The adjutant was not too welcoming, either. Viewing Winston's much-reduced pile of kit, he remarked that it would be necessary to cut it down. 'There are no communication trenches here, Major,' he said. 'We are doing all our reliefs over the top. The men have little more than what they stand up in. We have found a servant for you, and he'll carry a spare pair of socks and your shaving gear. You'll have to leave the rest behind.'

Winston refused to be put out. 'That's quite all right. I'm sure I'll be very comfortable.' As one contribution towards this comfort, he was provided with a pony for the journey to the front line.

Winston had first heard the rumble of guns while crossing the Channel. He had been much more conscious of the sound at French's General Headquarters and even more so at Guards' Headquarters. Now as they jogged east against a freezing drizzle, the guns became a cannonade and 'the red flashes stabbed the sombre landscape on either side of the road.'

Presently the landscape began to change [Winston recalled]. The shell-holes in the neighbouring fields became more numerous and the road broken and littered with débris. The inhabited country was left behind. The scattered houses changed to ruins. The leafless trees were scarred and split and around them grass and weeds grew tall and rank.

Battalion Headquarters was an old farmhouse, little more than rubble, which still offered some shelter, with the added security that German gunners could not believe that any soldier would use it for this purpose. It had been named Ebenezer Farm, evidently by some Hebrew scholar who knew that this translated into 'stone of help'. From here the movement of the Guards into the line was being organized. There was a charcoal fire and strong tea with condensed milk for refreshment, in lieu of French's champagne.

No offensive was being conducted by either side, but there was more or less continuous German firing to keep the Guards' heads down and interfere with the reconstruction and reinforcement of the trenches, which were found to be in a deplorable condition. Intermittently the German artillery would open up, making a great deal of noise and causing some inconvenience, but very few men were killed or wounded. It was just very arduous and uncomfortable. Officers and men slept where and when they could, usually in ankle-deep mud. No-one ever undressed in the line, and they shaved seldom.

Despite the mud that clung to and saturated everything, Winston found living in the front line a purging experience after the politics of Westminster. Colonel Feilding inspected his thousand-yard length of line once a day and once a night, tramping about through the mud across bullet-swept fields and along the labyrinthine trenches, and Winston always accompanied him. The two officers – the ex-politician and the regular soldier – talked incessantly, Feilding instructing: 'Always ask me anything you want to know . . .' And Winston did and learned fast.

The colonel's reserve soon began to break down and the talk became freer. Winston was struck by the severe discipline exercised here in the front line and by the way the officers mucked in with all the physical work – the draining of ditches, the building up of parapets, the laying down of barbed wire. Much of this work had to be done in the open at night, with bullets whistling about among the men, and there was a steady if small trickle of casualties to be carried back to the dressing stations.

Winston's suggestion that he should live with the companies in the line rather than at Battalion Headquarters was well received by the colonel, who never suspected that there was more than one reason for the proposed change: Headquarters was 'dry', while there was always plenty of hard liquor in the forward trenches. 'As I have always believed in the moderate and regular use of alcohol, especially under conditions of winter war,' Winston noted, 'I gladly moved my handful of belongings from Ebenezer Farm to a Company in the line.'

The company he had chosen was commanded by an old friend from the days of peace who had worked on *The Times*, Edward Grigg. One afternoon during a lull in the shelling, Winston was writing letters in a shelter when an orderly arrived, saluted smartly, and presented Winston with a field telegram. It read: 'The Corps Commander wishes to see Major Churchill at four o'clock at Merville. A car will be waiting at the Rouge Crois cross-roads at 3:15.'

Winston had known the Brigadier, Richard Haking, before the war, too, and now reasoned that it must be for some important reason that he was being ordered to withdraw from the front line like this. It was a foul afternoon of freezing drizzle and there was a certain element of risk involved in crossing open country in daylight. He had gone only a short distance when the German artillery opened up again, and as he looked behind him, he saw heavy shells falling, and he covered the wretched muddy ground as fast as he could.

It was a three-mile walk and he was soaking wet and sweating when he reached the rendezvous. There was a certain amount of enemy activity even here, and he had to wait an hour before a staff officer turned up, without a motor car, explaining that there had been a misunderstanding.

'Do you know what the Brigadier wanted me for?' Winston asked.

'He wanted a talk with you – just a general talk. When I told him about the motor car he said it didn't matter. Another time would do – he just wanted a general talk.'

'Perhaps he didn't realize . . .,' Winston fumed, describing his hour-long trek, 'neglecting my duties in the line, wasting your time and mine.' He was furious. It was already almost dark as he set off back, and later he lost his way in the darkness. 'As I walked I cd see our trenches in the distance with great red brilliant shells flaring over them in fours & fives & cd hear the shriek of the projectiles rising like the sound of a storm.' Thus he described the journey to Clementine.

Exhausted, Winston halted at the first company mess, begging for a drink.

'Hello,' he was greeted. 'You're in luck today.'

Winston was not in a condition to agree. 'I haven't seen much of it,' he said. 'I've been made a fool of. These damned Corps Commanders! Indulging their social inclinations at the expense of their subordinates!'

'Well, you're in luck all the same, as you'll see when you get back to your company.'

Fortified by a tumbler of whisky and water, Winston returned to his company where he was greeted with the news that his kit had been moved to another dugout.

'Why?'

'Yours has been blown up, sir.'

It had indeed. A shell had made a direct hit, exploding within a few feet of where he had been sitting, and taking off the head of the mess orderly who had been inside.

'Suddenly,' Winston recalled, 'I felt my irritation against Brigadier Haking pass completely from my mind. All sense of grievance passed in a flash.'

To Clementine, in telling her of this incident, he wrote, 'Now see from this how vain it is to worry about things. It is all chance and our wayward footsteps are best planted without too much calculation. One must yield oneself simply & naturally to the mood of the game and trust in God . . .'

There were many other escapes as close as or closer than this. On another later occasion the headquarters in which he was eating with several others was hit by a shell that burst in the next room, smashing their dishes and furniture, wounding one of the officers, and covering them all in dust and rubble. Winston conformed to his belief that Clementine should be told all and not be sheltered by voluntary censorship. As to official censorship, he had arranged that their letters should pass through Headquarters and direct to one another, rather than through the censor's office.

These were bad times for Clementine. They had been separated before, when Winston was at the Admiralty before the war, sometimes for a week or two at a time, but in their seven years of marriage never for as long as this, with the pain of separation intensified acutely by the knowledge of the risks he was running by insisting on serving in the front-line trenches. Just as he spared her no detail of the dangers, she made no effort to conceal her anxieties: 'I don't like to make any request which might worry or vex you,' she once wrote, 'but it makes me very anxious to feel that you are staying longer in the trenches than your duties require.' And, 'My Darling Love – I live from day to day in suspense and anguish. At night when I lie down I say to myself Thank God he is still alive . . . I have ceased to have ambitions for you – Just come back to me alive that's all.'

They wrote to one another almost every day, her letters full of family matters and gossip, and accounts of her work. Clementine was in charge of a number of YMCA canteens at war factories at Enfield in north-east London. It was extremely tiring work, in addition to supervising the children and running the home with Goonie. Economy was the order of the day. Jennie had come to live with them at 41 Cromwell Road, letting her own house, and although her contribution of £10 a week to the housekeeping was a great help, she was another responsibility. Clementine had given up the car as an economy, but this meant taking the train which was tiring and time consuming.

One more burden was looking after Winston's material needs. Besides waterproof boots, he wanted a warm sleeping bag, socks and a steady flow of food parcels (carefully specified), and bottles of his favourite brandy. One 'urgent requirement' was for small face towels, two pairs of khaki trousers, a pair of boots and trench wading boots, a warm brown leather waistcoat, and 'a periscope (most important)'.

The house at Cromwell Road was a busy establishment with the two brothers away at the war: the five children took up much of the mothers' time, as the nursery was down to one nursemaid. As soon as Jennie arrived, 61 years of age now, a handsome mature woman again without a husband, she settled down to write magazine articles, at which she had had some experience. Goonie concentrated more on running the household with Clementine away a great deal on her war work. Winston allowed Clementine £140 a month. He thought that should be sufficient. 'Keep a good table . . . entertain with discrimination, have a little amusement from time to time.' It was not always easy to do so with such modest funds at her disposal.

These difficult and dangerous times brought out the best in Clementine, who continued to write, lovingly and concernedly, never grumbling at her lot or complaining at the demands made on her time by the more or less continuous flow of delicacies and comforts demanded by Winston: 'go on sending brandy (my own) & tinned things of the ordinary types (but good quality)' sardines, potted meats, chocolate, cigars, large slabs of corned beef, Stilton cheeses, cream, ham, dried fruit. But at least, 'mind you bill me for all these apart from your own housekeeping.'

Clementine wrote to Winston about the most trivial aspects of domestic life, correctly believing that it would help him to continue to identify himself with their household: how Randolph was behaving, what he had said at tea, how

368

Clementine had simplified things domestically by getting up early and coming downstairs for breakfast. 'I find my morning breakfast lonely without you so Sarah fills your place & does her best to look almost exactly like you.'

There were two weddings to report in detail during those first weeks Winston was away at the front, one joyous, the other anxious. Clementine's sister Nellie had fallen in love with a lieutenant colonel in the Scots Guards, Bertram Romilly. He was four years younger than Winston, who had met him during the Boer War, where Romilly had gained a fine record for bravery and won the DSO. Unfortunately he had been badly wounded in the head in France, and when he met Nellie (one of his nurses) he was thought unlikely to recover. Nellie helped him to do so.

Clementine was worried about this match. 'I don't believe she loves him at all,' she wrote to Winston, 'but is simply marrying him out of pity.' What was to be done? Winston agreed that nothing *could* be done – and he adored his little 'Nellinita', who, according to Clementine, 'vacillated between breaking off entirely, postponement, & immediate marriage with every hour of the day, but now she has hardened into a sort of mule-like obstinacy & says with a drawn wretched face that she loves him, is divinely happy . . .'. Goonie, too, agreed that this was no basis for a sound marriage, but it went ahead nonetheless on 4 December 1915.

A few days earlier, on Winston's forty-first birthday, 30 November, his beloved Violet married Maurice Bonham Carter at St Margaret's Westminster, where Clementine and Winston had married seven years earlier at a happier time. In spite of the war, society and politics did what they could to make this a great occasion, and as Clementine told Winston, 'the town is topsy-turvy with excitement.' She also told of their son as one of the pages, looking '*quite* beautiful in a little Russian velvet suit with fur' and later being 'kissed & admired by dozens of lovely women'.

Besides the reception at Downing Street, politics intruded like a great ghost at the feast, in the form of a military apparition – Field Marshal Kitchener, no less. His despatch to the eastern Mediterranean to report on the military prospects there had provided a convenient postponement of his inevitable dismissal as Secretary of State for War, which would be fearfully unpopular with the British people, to whom he remained the god Thor himself. Other excuses had been found to keep him away from home, but here he was, quite unexpectedly: 'the gigantic figure of Lord Kitchener, whom we all believed to be still far away across the seas,' as the bride remarked.

It was even said that, so determined was he not to be relieved of his appointment, he had carried his locked seals of office wherever he travelled. What Asquith was to do with him now, no-one knew.

On the day of Violet Asquith's marriage, Winston's company was drawn out of the front line for an eight-day break.

> We marched in under brilliant moonlight while the
> men sang 'Tipperary' & 'The Farmer's Boy' and the
> guns boomed applause. It is like getting to a jolly
> good tavern after a long day's hunting, wet & cold
> & hungry, but not without having had good sport.

Lord Cavan invited him to dinner, and over the meal the General discussed Winston's future. Winston felt that he had learned all he needed about trench warfare, and clearly his earlier military experience – as recently as Antwerp – fitted him for responsibility above the company level.

Winston reminded Cavan of French's earlier offer of a brigade. 'I agree with him – agree with him entirely. But my advice is that you take a battalion first,' Cavan said. 'It will look better and give you the chance to experience the intervening rank. You would find it interesting.'

'I am sure I should, sir.'

Clementine, quite independently, offered the same advice at this time. Wherever she went, she told him, she found people 'awestruck at your sacrifice'. She longed for him to have his coveted brigade, '& yet not too soon for fear of partly dimming the blaze of glory in which you have left the country'.

This was music to Winston's ears. It is no reflection on his courage and patriotism to record that he had made the decision to go to France as a soldier in order partly to confound his enemies and impress the public that a middle-aged politician was prepared to share the dangers and discomforts of a front-line 'Tommy'. Just as he had used soldiering as a bridge into politics, he believed that he was accelerating his return to high office in politics by playing on his second skill. Now the higher the rank to which he could show himself worthy, the greater the kudos he would acquire in Whitehall and the country at large.

After another brief session in the line with the Guards, Winston returned again to St Omer to coincide with French's return from London. French had had a difficult time with the War Council and he knew now that his days in command were numbered. But there remained time to ensure that his friend got his brigade. That same evening, 10 December, Winston was able to write to Clementine:

> *I am to be given the command of the 56th Brigade in the 19th Division . . . a regular Division in the Second New Army, & the Bde I shall command comprises 4 Lancashire Battalions. The Division has a good reputation, has been out here some time, & is now in the line, next to the Guards.*

A brigadier had a better chance of survival than a colonel; this Clementine knew all too well. But ever protective of his reputation, she was still nervous that such swift promotion would be misunderstood.

'Of course there will be criticism & carping,' Winston accepted, 'but it is no good paying any attention to that. If I had taken a battalion for a few weeks, it must equally have been said "he has used it merely as a stepping stone etc."'

A day or two later, French was again summoned to London. Asquith had decided that his dismissal could be delayed no longer. When the Prime Minister learned that French had promised Winston a brigade, his sensitive antennae anticipated trouble in the House. So, regardless of the Commander in Chief's commitment and any military considerations, such as Winston's excellent military qualifications, he vetoed the order and immediately wrote and told Winston he could not have his coveted brigade. But he might get a battalion.

No-one with any intimate knowledge of the mind and machinations of Herbert Asquith seriously believed his promises. They were fulfilled only if they suited his particular advantage at the time. The fact that he had offered Winston a brigade immediately upon his resignation from the Admiralty, that he had assured Winston he would approve of *any* promotion recommended by the Commander in Chief in France, was of no weight in the Prime Minister's considerations. He suddenly smelt a whiff of danger, danger that Winston might gain a small notch of credit in the House if he were promoted to brigadier-general, or worse still might be such a dramatically successful brigade commander that when he returned to take up his parliamentary duties again (as surely he would), he might actually threaten his premiership; for there were voices – still only faint – in the land calling, 'Churchill for Prime Minister.'

To Clementine, Winston wrote in wrath:

> *I am inclined to think that his conduct reaches the limit of meanness & ungenerousness. Sentiments of friendship expressed in extravagant terms; coupled with a resolve not to incur the slightest criticism or encounter the smallest opposition – even from the most unworthy quarter. Personally I feel that every link is severed . . .*

There was an anti-Churchill Conservative Member of Parliament for Bath, a nonentity called Sir Charles Hunter B. On 16 December he asked the question in outrage whether it was true that Winston Churchill had been promoted to command a brigade. It was with the utmost satisfaction that Asquith's

Parliamentary Undersecretary of State for War was able to utter a stout denial.

The contrast between the machinations of Whitehall and Parliament and the comradeship of the Western Front was never more marked than in the meeting between Winston and the new Commander in Chief, General Sir Douglas Haig. They had known one another slightly when Winston was a fresh young MP and the soldier was a major. Now Haig was a national hero for commanding the successful defence of Ypres early in the war. Winston was one of the first officers Haig asked to see at General Headquarters on the day he took over from French.

'It is very good to see you out here,' the General greeted him. 'I've heard from Lord Cavan of the excellent work you have done in the trenches.'

'Thank you, sir.'

'I know that John [French] was anxious to give you a brigade, and there is nothing that would give me greater pleasure than to give you one when the time comes.' He took Winston by the arm and they paced across the floor of the room. 'My only wish, Churchill, is that able men should come to the front, and you can count on my sympathy in every way. Meanwhile, would you care for a battalion?'

Winston, delighted at the warmth of the General's manner, said that he would like that very much – so long as it was going into the line. 'Perhaps I could have Captain Sinclair or Spiers as my ADC or second-in-command?' he asked, mentioning two of the officers he knew and trusted most. Further encouraged by Haig's friendliness, Winston asked him if he would like to read his memorandum on trench warfare, which he had just prepared, and this he left with the General.

While waiting to hear which battalion he was to have, Winston had time to visit his family over Christmas – just for a few days, but what wonderful days they were! They were also momentous days in Winston's political career, marking a new step that was to have far-reaching consequences. Since

373

Asquith's blocking of the promised promotion, Winston's fury had not abated. Not content with throwing him to the wolves at home, the Prime Minister was now suffocating his second career in soldiering. It was too much. It therefore came as no surprise to Clementine, who realized better than anyone the depth of her husband's bitterness, that a political straw cast in his direction was seized so avidly.

Garvin, the clever editor of the *Observer* and an inveterate conspirator, had kept closely in touch with Jacky Fisher after his resignation. He was one of the Admiral's warmest admirers and was grieved to see him quarrel with Winston, whom he admired equally. Together with many other more responsible critics, Garvin saw Asquith's government lurching about from side to side, sterility at the Admiralty, procrastination at Salonika and the Dardanelles, impasse on the Western Front, and feet-dragging over conscription by Asquith, although it had clearly become urgently necessary.

On one of Winston's precious evenings, Garvin dined with him and suggested reopening 'the old firm', as he referred to him and Fisher back at the Admiralty, under the premiership of Lloyd George. In reporting the evening to Fisher, Garvin wrote of the 'throwing up of hats throughout the country' this would cause. It was the only way to 'save this country and its allies'.

Fisher was encouraged to believe he could return to power by the favourable reception to a speech he had made in the House of Lords in November and by the imminent end of the Dardanelles campaign, proving that his opposition to it had been correct. There was a muttering to be heard that pressed for his return. 'Does anyone pretend that the naval conduct of the war is not gravely imperilled by his absence?' asked the *Nation*, for example.

Winston also met Lloyd George during his brief leave and found him bitterly opposed to Asquith, determined to fight him over conscription – which Asquith feared would lose him votes – and ready to turn him out if the opportunity occurred. With his political blood racing through his veins again, Winston suggested that the time was *now*. What a triumph it would be to return to the Admiralty under Lloyd George's premiership! With all this exciting new political movement, it was hard to have to pack his kit and prepare to return to France. Indeed such was the pace of events over Christmas that he was still plotting after he should have left for his train – and he and Clementine had to run down the platform to catch it.

Three days later, with Winston back at St Omer awaiting his battalion, Clementine dutifully invited Lloyd George to lunch to sound him out further, on her husband's behalf, about progress of the move to overturn Asquith. But it seemed that the Prime Minister might have got wind of the conspiracy, for he had suddenly nipped it in the bud by agreeing without qualification to conscription – though he went back on it later. Lloyd George's fervour had been extinguished as a result, confirming Clementine's distrust of the Welshman. 'I assure you he is the direct descendant of Judas Iscariot,' she commented to Winston. But her husband did not share her views on him, reserving his biggest broadsides for Asquith.

On the first day of 1916, Winston was appointed to command the Sixth Royal Scots Fusiliers, a war-weary infantry battalion of thirty officers and some seven hundred men. He was thankful to get away from General Headquarters, and he was as determined as ever to make his mark again as a soldier. But the gnat that had bitten him over Christmas would not leave him alone. The sting's poison, for which there was no known cure, was still in his bloodstream as he turned east to the sound of the guns and to his Scottish warriors.

Winston's battalion was out of the line when he took over command. It was a very changed body of men from those who had first come to France in 1914. Half the men and almost all the regular officers had become casualties, many of them at Ypres during the first winter and at the Battle of Loos. They had been replaced by earnest officer volunteers in their early twenties and by tough, brave, but mostly inexperienced Scottish soldiers, with a sprinkling of older reservists.

The news that Winston had been appointed to command them struck the battalion like a German howitzer shell. They were devastated, far worse than the Guards had been, though for the same reasons: exalted aristocrat, arrogant and wily politician . . . No-one mentioned his fighting record, going back to the Indian frontier wars, Omdurman and front-line trench fighting with the Guards.

All their worst fears seemed confirmed by the manner of Winston's arrival, on a black charger, with his aide de camp, Sir Archibald Sinclair, on another black horse, followed by two grooms similarly mounted and, taking up the rear, a limber with an enormous pile of kit and a second limber upon which rested a long bath and a boiler for heating the water.

Later, at the end of lunch with his officers, Winston toured the table, staring into the face of each man in turn, and then addressed them all with these words: 'Gentlemen, I am now your commanding officer. Those who support me I will look after. Those who go against me I will break. Good afternoon gentlemen.'

The entire battalion was paraded in the afternoon, and Churchill, again on his charger, inspected them. They were still, quite properly, 'at the slope' when he suddenly called out, 'Royal Scots Fusiliers – fix bayonets!' – an impossibility under the circumstances, though some of the men dropped their rifles in order to withdraw their bayonets. The adjutant then suggested that the commanding officer should order 'Order arms', when the original order could more conveniently be carried out. Winston's final order was even more difficult to follow – 'Sections right!' – a purely cavalry instruction.

Winston had two weeks in which to improve his own performance and the performance of his battalion, introduce a sense of *esprit de corps*, which had been sadly missing since the sufferings of Loos, and instil pride and respect for their commanding officer. After those first disastrous early days, no-one, except Winston himself, thought he could do so.

But the record speaks for itself, just as Second Lieutenant Jock McDavid wrote of the effect he made:

> After a very brief period he had accelerated the morale of officers and men to an almost unbelievable degree. It was sheer personality. . . . He had a unique approach which did wonders to us. He let everyone under his command see that he was responsible, from the very moment he arrived, that they understood not only *what* they were supposed to do, but *why* they had to do it. . . . No detail of their daily life was too small for him to investigate.

He impressed his special methods of command on his officers in other ways, too. His severity on matters of discipline and form was offset by a peculiar reluctance to punish, which his officers and NCOs believed undermined discipline. He was always ready to give the accused the benefit of any doubt, or even to give the soldier a second chance. More appreciated by his officers was Winston's concern with the battalion's physical comfort – or at least with the reduction as far as possible of the discomforts of cold and wet, which were the main features of daily life in winter on the Western Front. For example, he would not tolerate lice, and before the men took up their position in the line, a great war against lice was conducted and won.

Winston also kept a keen eye on the men's food, ensuring that every opportunity was taken to supplement the basic rations from local farms and from quartermaster's stores, which Winston raided without scruple. 'Bully beef and biscuits were only memories,' one officer recalled. And with the officers' mess he shared out the food and drink parcels Clementine conscientiously despatched – sometimes by King's Messenger.

On 16 January Winston organized a sports day, sing-song and banquet – the sports more frivolous than formal. A large barn had been commandeered for the evening events. 'Such singing you never heard,' Winston reported to Clementine.

Prizes were presented, and there was a banquet for the officers and special rations with lots of drink for the men – and three cheers were called for Winston and an extra one for Clementine. 'Quite a cheery day. The men enjoyed themselves immensely. Poor fellows – nothing like this had ever been done for them before. They do not get much to brighten their lives – short though they may be . . .'

Nine days later, the battalion moved forward to take over its section of the front. Winston had twice visited it and found it far better prepared than that occupied by the Guards before they set about improving it. Then the corps commander arrived to inspect them. He was General Sir Charles Fergusson. Winston had last met him before the Battle of Omdurman, along with most of his staff. What a contrast with that campaign! Omdurman – a battle of constant movement – had lasted just one day, and the British army had faced nothing worse than ill-equipped natives; and now, with fighting aeroplanes wheeling overhead and the most modern and frightful weapons of war, including poison gas, at their command, they were locked into stalemate fighting that might last for years, with armies of millions and the whole weight of the Western world thrown into the war.

After the inspection, Fergusson invited Winston back to his quarters for tea. Expressing himself gratified by the improvement in the battalion, the General said, 'I am truly sorry not to have come to see you earlier. And I am also sorry you have been sent to this battalion which was such a very weak and shattered one.'

The General dismounted and led Winston inside. 'We should have found you a much better one for your purpose, to learn about regimental work.'

'Perhaps, sir, I may be more useful here,' Winston replied. 'So long as the difficulties are recognized, I really preferred to have a battalion which wanted helping along.'

They drank tea standing up and had a good, useful professional talk. Fergusson concluded on a congratulatory note. 'Well, there has certainly been a very great improvement and there's no doubt you have done a great deal of good.'

'Thank you, sir.'

'I am completely confident in your command, Colonel Churchill.'

These were good words to hear before going forward, and Winston reported on them to Clementine as proudly as a Boy Scout with good points.

This was a time for family reflection. He wrote his first-ever letter to young Randolph, comparing unfavourably the farmhouse in which he was living with Hoe Farm and telling him that although the Germans were still some way distant, he was now going to go close and to try to kill them 'because they have done wrong and caused all this war and sorrow'.

Winston reflected also on the other Randolph, his father, who had died twenty-one years earlier, to the day, on that cold dawn in Grosvenor Square when he had been only four years older than Winston was now. He wondered what his father would have thought of his own conduct, but remained convinced that he was doing the right thing.

Later on this same day, Winston rode, like King Henry V, at the head of his officers and men towards the battlefield. Their base was close to Ploegsteert – or 'Plug Street', as it was inevitably anglicized – a village just inside Belgium, with a no man's land between the trenches less than two miles wide. The whole area was subjected to periodical shelling, sometimes intense, with periods of relative peace and tranquillity. In this mutilated countryside, thousands of men lived in trenches and billets, dugouts and makeshift shelters. The whole area – and to the north to the Channel and far to the south to the Swiss border – was given up to fighting a land battle. Here in this small sector, men died or were wounded daily, sometimes only one or two, at other times in larger numbers. In countering an enemy attack, hundreds or thousands might die in one day and night, and even more in an offensive of their own. For the present, the horrors of Loos were behind them; before them (though none knew of it) lay the mass slaughter of the Battle of the Somme.

During the one hundred days of Winston's command, 138

379

of his men were killed or wounded – a modest total for the Western Front in early 1916, but almost fifteen per cent all the same. There was no great battle, but there were sudden, terrifying night raids into enemy trenches, snipers were an ever-present danger, bursts of machine-gun fire swept the open fields, and every day and every night the shells added to the pockmarking of the landscape. Plug Street itself was systematically shelled at one stage, until there was scarcely a building left standing.

> *Commanding a Battalion is like being captain of a ship* [Winston wrote home]. *It is a vy searching test and a severe burden. Especially so when all the officers are young & only soldiers of a few months standing: & when a hundred yards away lies the line of the German army with all its devilment & dodges . . .*

Burdensome though it may have been, there was no doubt that Winston extracted every ounce of pleasure and satisfaction from it, while keeping at bay the ever-nagging ache for politics. One of his lieutenants recalled a moment in the forward trenches as the enemy field guns opened fire:

> The Colonel came along to our trench and suggested a view over the parapet. As we stood up on the fire-step we felt the wind and swish of several whizzbangs flying past our heads, which, as it always did, horrified me. Then I heard Winston say in a dreamy, far-away voice: 'Do you like war?' The only thing to do was to pretend not to hear him. At that moment I profoundly hated war. But at that moment and every moment I believe Winston Churchill revelled in it.

A regular lieutenant, Edmund Hakewill Smith, only 19 years old at the time, remembered, with horror, displays of Winston's fearlessness and joy in danger during walks in no man's land:

It was a nerve-wracking experience to go with him. He would call out in his loud, gruff voice – far too loud it seemed to us – 'You go that way, I will go this . . . Come here, I have found a gap in the German wire. Come over here at once!' He was like a baby elephant out in no-man's-land at night. He never fell when a shell went off; he never ducked when a bullet went past with its loud crack. He used to say, after watching me duck: 'It's no damn use ducking; the bullet has gone a long way past you by now.'

As the weeks passed, Winston found himself becoming more and more deeply involved in his battalion and 'the military machine. It almost seems as if my life in the gt world was a dream,' he wrote. But Clementine did her utmost to keep reality to the fore, writing every day and sending newspaper cuttings and messages from their friends and the 'kittens'. For her, Winston might have been campaigning in India, as he used to do before they met, so distant and different was his world.

On one memorable but only half-real afternoon, she experienced the satisfaction of a common link with him, if only by sound. She was staying at Walmer Castle on the Kent coast and playing golf with her host, Asquith, when she heard the sound of the Flanders guns, caught on the wind. Thinking of him out there in his muddy, dangerous tent, she never wished more to beat the Prime Minister – the man who had sent him there – but unfortunately failed to do so.

Winston was entitled to leave around the beginning of March, and during the last days of February his mind turned more seriously and intensely towards his political future. 'While I never doubt the wisdom of my decision to quit office,' he wrote to Clementine on 8 February, 'I writhe daily at the lack of power to make things move.'

A letter from Sunny Marlborough deploring the state of the Admiralty since his departure, a German newspaper cutting expressing thankfulness that he was out of power, and letters suggesting it was time to come home to fight the war in the Commons, combined to add thrust to his resolve. 'Do come soon,' urged F. E. Smith. 'I am sure it is a good thing to turn up at the proper intervals & see people.' Before taking his leave, Winston sent home explicit instructions on the programme Clementine should make for him. Not a moment was to be wasted and 'I will be vy good & keep all my engagements punctually' – an assurance she hoped, but doubted, he would keep.

Winston returned to London on the evening of 2 March. In spite of all the letters and newspapers he had received, it was only upon his arrival that he learned that in five days' time Balfour would be introducing the naval estimates in the Commons, a critical Parliamentary experience for the new First Lord.

Many men who returned from the thunder of war and the special enclosed world of camaraderie and killing found that their judgement was temporarily impaired. It took time to readjust to the realities of ordinary civilian life. The adaptation to the hurly-burly of political infighting and to a condition of balanced judgement was not something that could be accomplished overnight. It was even said by some that the almost continuous noise from explosions and projectiles had a stunning effect on the brain from which it took time to recover: a form of temporary shellshock.

There was no reason why Winston should have been totally immune from the effects of trench warfare, no matter how great was his courage and how strong his constitution. If his mind had been wholly on the political scene – and how could it have been? – he would have noted in advance the date of the naval estimates. And if he had not lost some of his political judgement he would never have decided impetuously, almost without thought, to make a hostile speech in reply to Balfour's. War, and what to Clementine he described as the 'strain and severity' of life in the trenches, had brought him to the brink of his gravest political blunder.

23

Misjudgements and Misalliances

Between dinners arranged with such care by Clementine, luncheons in clubs, meetings in the House – both arranged and casual – Winston attempted to readjust himself from the whizzbangs of trench warfare to the tumult of politics. He spent an entire day preparing the speech that he believed would lead to his return to power. He made no attempt to conceal his intentions. Indeed, on the night of 6 March, before the naval debate the following day, the Asquiths were invited to dinner at 41 Cromwell Road so that a warning could be offered.

It is an odd reflection on contemporary political-social relations that, after all the accusations and acrimony of the past months – after Asquith had obliged Winston to resign, had refused to bring him back into the Government in even a minor capacity, had erected the barrier against his military promotion, and for political expediency and his own ends, had done him untold damage – Winston was still prepared to have him in his house, along with his wife, whom Winston detested.

It was not Clementine's choice that she should have the Asquiths in her house for dinner, and that Jacky Fisher – of all people – had had to be made welcome a day or so earlier. Winston, she believed, was re-entering the political arena too early, and she had told him so. She had also exhorted him to have no more to do with that mad snake Fisher and that unscrupulous and untrustworthy Welshman David Lloyd George.

Meanwhile, responsibilities of hospitality had to be met, and this was a department in which she never failed – even her detractors had to admit that. She always got the best out of her cooks, who admired and liked her.

The unseasonal heavy snow of recent days and nights

added to the unreality of the evening. It was lying thick in the streets, and owing to the lack of manpower, little effort had been made to clear it. There was a pale luminosity in the dusk light as the Prime Minister and his wife stepped from their motor car, to be saluted by the policeman in cape who had been stationed outside for security reasons.

Clementine noticed the paleness of Asquith's complexion as he was shown into the drawing room; as for Margot, her angular features, jutting chin, beak of a nose and ever-wandering patrician grey eyes had been familiar for so long that they made no mark on Clementine's consciousness: only the calf-length evening gown, of purple silk and wool crêpe with a gauged skirt, made any impact.

The butler took round the Pol Roger champagne, and Goonie and then Winston (apologizing for dilatoriness as usual) joined them. Briefly, but feelingly, the talk was all of the freak weather, which had led Clementine to ensure that the fires were well banked up.

Winston had Margot on his right at dinner, Goonie on his left. 'I shall be speaking in the debate tomorrow,' Winston remarked defiantly over the fish. 'It will be strange indeed to orate to members of Parliament instead of the Jocks in the front line in Belgium.'

'You know very well, Winston, that it is unnecessary for me to enquire which you prefer,' said Margot.

Winston ignored the intervention, and with what Margot later described as 'a glare in his eye', continued, 'Yes, I have a good deal of importance to say about the Navy tomorrow.'

'I have no doubt of that, too.'

Winston then turned his attention to his sister-in-law, enquiring about his brother. Goonie told about her latest letter from Jack, describing the remarkably successful evacuation of the Gallipoli Peninsula. This aroused a bitter comment from Winston. 'Dispossessed of the means to correct the folly of evacuation, all that is left is to have my brother observe and report on it.'

Margot attempted to turn the conversation and bring it round to her host, a move always crowned with success. 'But

384

what a fine exit you made, Winston! You gave up money and position, taking your place with your fellows, risking your life for your country . . . That was a noble thing you did.'

Winston was mollified. It was always such a pleasure to see his mood change from baleful to happy: it was like giving a schoolboy a sweet, Margot once observed. But she never could resist putting in the knife.

'Don't go and spoil it all now.'

Later, Clementine, at the far end of the table, was apologizing for the absence of French cheese, and Winston intervened to claim there was no cheese as good as old-fashioned English farmhouse cheese. Then he quoted one of his Jocks claiming that for a used pair of army boots you could get half a dozen Camemberts at Armentières – and a woman in exchange for a new pair.

Before the ladies left the table, Winston turned back to Margot and to politics. 'Do you think, at this time, a proper opposition in the House of Commons would be a good or a bad thing for the country?'

'I don't see any sign of a proper opposition so that's not easy to answer.' Margot quoted the names of some dissident Liberals, and Sir John Simon, who were sternly opposed to conscription. 'I can't see them all co-operating to unseat Henry.' She said nothing more on this subject but later reported to her stepdaughter that she was convinced that Winston was 'dreaming of an amazing Opposition which he was to lead'.

Over brandy and cigars, Asquith and Winston talked briefly of the next day's debate. The prime minister gave Winston no hint about what Balfour was likely to say, and Winston did not enquire. Instead he announced defiantly, 'I shall speak. I have much to say, and it is only fair to tell you so. There is a great deal wrong with the Navy. It is not getting its ships – few of the ships Jacky ordered have even advanced in construction, let alone been completed.'

Asquith asked mildly, 'And what else will you say?'

'I shall say that it is time to bring back Jacky Fisher, to put some life into that moribund body.'

Asquith said nothing for a moment in reply. He was

generally considered to be above surprise, but if not shocked by this suggestion, he was unprepared for it.

At length and after a considerable draught of brandy, the Prime Minister declared, 'I think you are most unwise, Winston. Believe me, it will do nothing but harm. I beg you not to proceed with this intention.'

As he later reported to Margot on the way home, 'But I fear that I failed.'

When the Asquiths got back to Downing Street, Violet (who had been out elsewhere) was there, asking about their evening. Her stepmother and father gave her a summary of the proceedings. Violet was puzzled why Winston had made no attempt to get in touch with her since his return. They were, after all, close friends. Asquith replied, 'That doesn't surprise me in the least in view of his intentions tomorrow.'

It snowed again during the night, and snow lay thick on the streets and pavements of London on the morning of 7 March. Clementine was well aware of the importance of this day to her husband. She had been over the speech with him several times, and as always he listened carefully to her advice. She approved of almost everything he had to say and could imagine the impact it would make on the House. But, like Asquith the night before, she emphasized again that she thought it the greatest folly to suggest that Fisher should be recalled – the loathed and hated Fisher, who had virtually committed treason only ten months ago in quitting his post at a time of great national danger. At a luncheon with Fisher as guest only a day or two earlier, she had been driven to such a state of emotional upset that she had suddenly burst out, 'Keep your hands off my husband. You have all but ruined him once. Leave him alone now!' The Admiral had become an ogre to haunt her.

C. P. Scott, the great editor of the *Manchester Guardian* and an old supporter of both Winston and Jacky, had been at that lunch, too. Now he was the first visitor of the day at number 41. Scott later recalled that Winston evidently felt his was a serious enterprise, that he would have to face the severest criticism, but 'once I am launched on an enterprise I can never hold back, even if – as in this case – it takes more courage than the war in the trenches.'

After Scott left, Winston went through his speech once again, touching up here and there. Then he looked again at the typical-Jacky letter Fisher had sent him that morning. He had long since become used to the extravagances of Fisher's language, but this was remarkable beyond all others:

> *Providence has placed the Plum back in your mouth.*
> Certain Prime Minister!
> *You have no rival as Leader of the Opposition Such a cry for assuming the position!!!! SO PATRIOTIC!!!!*

And the letter concluded:

> You get Prime Minister!
> That will end the War!
> Nought else will!
> *The Country wants a Man!*
> *Every War wants a Man!*
> Don't go back – accept nothing!

The moment Arthur Balfour sat down at 5.10 p.m., after delivering his naval estimates, Winston stood up in a packed House from his seat on the opposition benches. Like his father's feelings about his speech of resignation, Winston regarded this as the most important he had made in his life, and as he proceeded, castigating every branch of the service – except the admirals and the fighting men – he became increasingly conscious that he was succeeding in his purpose. Among his admirers in the Distinguished Strangers' Gallery, the Prime Minister's daughter had to admit to herself 'that all was calculated to shake the confidence of the House in the energy, initiative and determination of the present Board of Admiralty and to arouse fears that Germany was outbuilding us.' As a sign of Winston's effectiveness, Balfour – not a man of quick temper or passion – at one point rose to interrupt

387

with a protest. He was inaudible to the Hansard stenographer, but Winston's counter-retort was angry in the extreme. At last, almost an hour later, he fell silent. The House was stunned by the oratorical skill Winston had commanded, by his timing and choice of expression in this demolition of the Admiralty's record since he had left it and of the man who had superseded him.

But it was not quite over. There was little more to say, but his last words, after a brief pause, were in their own way more devastating than anything that had come before. 'I urge the First Lord of the Admiralty without delay to fortify himself, to vitalise and animate his Board of Admiralty,' he continued, 'by recalling Lord Fisher to the post as First Sea Lord.'

The entire packed House of Commons was, for once, silenced by this appeal. Members asked themselves, had they heard right? Was it possible that the Honourable Member was advocating the return of this ancient admiral whom he had so recently described as impossible to work with, who had brought about the present enforced coalition and caused the crippling of Winston Churchill's political career?

Observing Admiral Fisher leaving the gallery, an expression of satisfaction on his dark face, Violet asked herself, 'Have I gone mad? Has Winston?' She wrote later:

> He had spoken in calm and measured terms, without excitement and with the utmost deliberation . . . What possessed him? I remembered long talks in which he had poured out his heart to me about Fisher, his vacillations, his constant resignations . . . his desertion . . . Could he possibly believe in the course he was advocating? It would be unlike him to swerve from his convictions. Yet if he believed in it he must surely be deranged?

Violet followed Margot to a private room. Already present there were Eddie Marsh, with tears in his eyes, and Violet's husband, Maurice Bonham Carter, who was speechless. Eddie Marsh asked Margot fearfully, 'Do you think he

388

has done for himself?' With unaccustomed generosity, she answered him, 'He's young – and if he goes back [to France] and fights like a hero it will all be forgotten.'

Winston became aware of the disastrous error he had committed all too soon. Amongst the newspapers, only Scott's *Manchester Guardian* took a generous view of his criticism and proposal to correct the poor record and condition of the Navy. The effect of the speech on the *Observer*'s political correspondent was one 'of stupefaction and bewilderment'. The *Spectator*'s editor wrote: 'To watch this fevered, this agonized struggle to regain the political fortune which the arch-gambler threw away by his own acts is to witness one of the great tragedies of life.'

There were many people inside and outside the House who again recalled Lord Randolph's downfall. 'Surely Winston Churchill must be going off his head like his father did?' a notorious Winston-hater, Admiral Sir Stanley Colville, was heard to remark. Another admiral, Sir Hedworth Meux, attacked Winston in the House for his 'vulgar boasting' and compared Balfour favourably with him. 'Thank heaven, at last we have got a ruler who does not grate upon our nerves!'

Predictably, Fisher returned to his office and wrote:

> *My dear Winston,*
> *SPLENDID!!!*
> *You'll have your Reward!*
> . . . *My heart is very full! I feel the good old times are back!*
>
> *Yours*
> *Fisher*

It did little to lift the gloom encompassing Winston, which darkened further as he listened, huddled and silent, to Balfour's speech in reply the following day. Normally a mild, amusing patrician, Balfour had been infuriated by Winston's attack and the language he had used, and now proceeded to demolish all his claims and by invective and sarcasm make him look a fool. Winston had claimed in his

389

speech that he had reached his decision about recalling Fisher after calm meditation at the fighting front.

'I venture to suggest,' Balfour replied, 'that the clearness of thought which we all desiderate is bought at a rather costly figure if it involves a European war in order to obtain it.'

Then, Balfour spoke of Winston's earlier relations with Fisher:

> The fact remains that the right hon Gentleman, who could not get on with Lord Fisher – I will not say that, but with whom Lord Fisher could not get on – says that Lord Fisher, who according to my right hon Friend neither supported him nor guided him, is nevertheless the man who ought to be given as a supporter and a guide to anybody who happens to hold at this moment the responsible position of First Lord of the Admiralty . . .

Balfour's speech was widely praised, but even the newspapers and magazines that were most critical of Winston's demand for Fisher's recall had to concede that all could not be well at the Admiralty. *The Times* declared that Winston's speech 'will certainly command a good deal of attention because it expressed very vividly the vague popular anxiety which has lately been prevalent about our general naval position'. The effect of the speech, the leader continued, 'was a suspicion that there is a lack of driving power about the present Board of Admiralty'. Another Winston enemy, the *National Review*, considered it was 'not an unmixed evil' because it drew attention to certain unsatisfactory aspects in the administration of the Navy.

But after this major gaffe, everyone in politics and many outside were asking what Winston would do now. Would he persist in his attacks on the Government or return to the front? This was a question that both Asquith and his daughter Violet asked him when they met him on succeeding days.

Winston sent Violet a note asking her if they could meet – not at his house in the embarrassing presence of Clementine. Violet had shrewdly guessed that his misjudgement rested on the belief that he would be praised for his magnanimity towards Fisher, the man who had knifed him in the back, for the greatest of all causes, the success of the Navy. But it had not worked that way at all. The suggestion had been treated as mad or ridiculous.

'I suppose you are against me like the rest of them,' Winston began defiantly.

'You know I could never be against you, Winston,' Violet replied. 'But I am strongly against reinvesting Fisher with any sort of authority because he has proved quite unfit for it. And I am amazed that you could bring yourself to do so.' His friend continued strongly: 'You may forgive what he has done to you. But you don't have the right to forgive the ruin he has brought on others and on the Dardanelles campaign.'

Winston allowed the reference to the Dardanelles to pass. It was both too broad and too agonizing a subject for him. Instead, he spoke of the private sources of information at the Admiralty that had made clear that things were going badly there. 'Fisher's fire and drive could pull it out of the rut and reanimate it.' And then, in reference to Balfour: 'Arthur's never been exactly a dynamo at the best of times.'

Later in their talk Violet asked him about his plans. 'Are you going back to the front? My father told me you might stay here. Is that right?'

'Yes, I've come to the conclusion that it's right for me to remain here so that I can use what influence I have at the heart of things.' Then, rather militantly, he said he had many friends and supporters. 'Have you seen the *Manchester Guardian* this morning?' he asked, and she refrained from reminding him that it was his only real supporter.

Shrewd Violet knew that it must only add to his injuries if he followed his belligerent speech by deciding not to go back to the fighting. But she could not bring herself to say so, for many reasons, the most powerful being that he might follow her advice and then be killed.

The meeting with Asquith at 10 Downing Street the next day was a good deal more down to earth. Winston kept referring to his 'ardent supporters', until Asquith was forced to state baldly, 'At the moment you have none who count at all.' And when Winston rather pathetically asked the man he had so denigrated what he should do, Asquith could only tell him to return to the front. 'There were tears in his eyes when he left,' Asquith told Violet later.

Asquith's real feelings were expressed by his wife in a letter to Balfour after his speech in the Commons, and revealed Margot's contempt for Winston:

> I hope & believe Winston will never be forgiven his yesterday's speech. Henry & I were thunderstruck at the meanness & the gigantic folly of it. I've never varied in my opinion of Winston I am glad to say.
>
> He is a hound of the lowest sense of political honour, a fool of the lowest judgement & contemptible.
>
> He cured me of oratory in the House & bored me with oratory in the Home!
>
> . . . if H [Asquith] had not had a deputation he said he wd have given Winston 10 of the nastiest minutes of his life he was so disgusted.

The person most damaged by the Commons conflict and the pillorying of her husband was Clementine. A leave, which for most wives was a joyous occasion, became something of a nightmare, with the dark shadows of Fisher and Lloyd George, Asquith and Balfour, haunting the corridors of Parliament and of her home. It seemed almost as if the world was divided between those advocating Winston's return to parliamentary duties, which she thought premature, and those who were recommending his return to soldiering, which could so easily result in his death.

This was a time of great pain and stress, which only led Clementine to express her views more emphatically, even shrilly. She deserved all credit for doing her duty as she interpreted it, but alas for Winston, she lacked the shades of expression and the subtleties of persuasion that were required to dissuade him from doing things she thought unwise. These included his attempt to gain command of a brigade rather than a battalion and to reinstate Fisher.

Arguments with Clementine always took on a battlefield complexion when they should have followed the line of one of Winston's favourite later aphorisms: 'Jaw, jaw is better than war, war.'

At the end of this eventful and not very happy or successful leave, Winston told Clementine that he was going back to his battalion, because that was his duty, but that he would soon be making arrangements to return to politics for good.

On 12 March, he once again left 41 Cromwell Road, with his usual great pile of kit. This time, Clementine determined to go as far with him as she was allowed. They had put their car on the road again and drove off, waving to Goonie and the children on the doorstep, down the Dover Road. Two hours later, she finally embraced him at the base of the gangway leading to his man of war. Like all wives and mothers of departing soldiers, her heart was full of anxiety for his safety. But for Clementine there were so many other anxieties. He handed her a letter and asked her to send it at once to Asquith. She already knew its contents. It was to ask him to relieve Winston of his military duties because he wished to take a more direct part in politics, to which he believed he could make useful contributions.

Back at Plug Street, Winston at once wrote her a letter that reflected his confused state of mind. He had, he told her, telegraphed the Prime Minister to ignore the letter he had sent him. He needed more time to consider – 'a few more days of reflection' – something she had so strongly been advocating. So perhaps he did listen to her a little?

My dearest soul – you have seen me vy weak & foolish & mentally infirm this week. Dual obligations, both honourable, both weighty, have rent me. . . . I cannot tell you how much I love & honour you and how sweet & steadfast you have been through all my hesitations & perplexity. . . . I was so grieved to think of you

393

*tired & lonely on the pier as my destroyer swept off
into a choppy sea.*

Clementine deserved all her husband's sympathy. Even after
he had slipped away across the Channel, there were still many
tiresome and tiring matters to deal with. She spent that night
at the Lord Warden Hotel, where she dined alone and wrote a
letter to Asquith to accompany Winston's. The next morning
she drove, by previous arrangement, to Sir Edward Carson's
place at Birchington on the way back to London. Carson,
Winston's supporter and leader of a strong dissident group
in the Commons, was ill in bed. But he was able to talk to
her, and as usual his advice on Winston was as sound and
steady as could be expected of the Attorney-General.

Carson, too, held the view that Winston should not return
from the front yet unless there was a powerful reason for
doing so. He believed that, though his attack on the Navy
was justified, he had been foolish over Fisher.

Clementine drove back to London through pouring rain
and suffered a puncture on the road. She was utterly
exhausted when she arrived home. It was then that she
learned of Winston's telegram to Asquith cancelling the
letter she had posted the previous evening. She reflected
on the irony that she should feel relief that her husband had
decided to remain in danger in the fighting line when surely
all other wives would be relieved and thankful for having
their husbands home. Then she glanced at her sleeping children, said her prayers, and went to bed.

The following weeks were the unhappiest of Clementine's
married life. She knew that it was only a matter of time before
he re-entered the political jungle, which might damage his
reputation again. She knew he was plotting with his political
allies, for he frequently sent letters to her through their privileged uncensored mailing channel to forward to them, a task
she did not care for. On the other hand, she feared for his
safety, especially as his letters still told of shellings and narrow misses and casualties in his battalion. She was also feeling
run down physically and finding her work exhausting.

'Sometimes when I have been out all day canteening I dread coming home to find a telegram with terrible news,' she wrote to him.

The excuse that Winston needed for quitting the front came late in April. His Scots regiment had suffered so many casualties that it was decided to amalgamate his battalion with the 7th, whose colonel was senior to him and would take command. General Haig said he was prepared to give him a brigade but, like so many of the top brass in France, hoped that Winston would instead return to politics and do something about the gross political mismanagement of the war. Under these circumstances, even Clementine favoured his return.

Colonel Winston Churchill had made such a success with his battalion of the Royal Scots Fusiliers that there was not an officer or a man who was not grieved to see him go. Some of the Jocks had propped up his photograph in their dugouts. He had completely identified with them, interesting himself in their welfare and their domestic life back at home. Nothing was too much trouble for him, and during his last days he spent endless time ensuring that his officers found themselves suitable appointments following the battalion amalgamation. On 6 May he gave his officers a slap-up lunch, with much champagne flowing, at Armentières. The general commanding the 15th Division inspected the battalion for the last time the following day, and after that Colonel Churchill was driven away with all his impedimenta. He had fought his last battle.

For a while the happy foursome of Goonie and Jack, and Clementine and Winston, with their children, were reunited at 41 Cromwell Road. The two men, at least for the present, were safe from the horrors of the Western Front, and Jack – upon his return – had been given a staff job at the headquarters of the Anzac Corps, the survivors from the Dardanelles.

Winston was now able to learn in detail from his brother about the last days of that failed campaign and the withdrawal and evacuation of the troops, which was the only part conducted satisfactorily. On returning to the back benches in

Parliament, the Dardanelles dominated his mind and activity. He knew that while that cloud hung over him, he remained politically unacceptable. His first fight, then, was to press for a comprehensive and unprejudiced examination of the campaign from first to last. He knew that he was innocent of blame, and with the death of Kitchener, who would have fought against such an investigation and (Winston believed) have been found to be the leading culprit, there was no longer any excuse for Asquith to postpone it. 'You will readily understand my wish that the truth shd be known,' he wrote to Asquith a month after his return. 'Not a day passes without my being the object of unjust reproach . . . Only the facts can tell the tale: and the public ought now to have them.'

The public was to learn the facts – or some of them – but not 'now'. A royal commission was set up, but not until August did it begin work, and it would be well over a year before its findings were published. Moreover, it remained politically unsuitable to ascribe to the dead hero Kitchener the blame he deserved, especially in his critical withholding of the 29th Division. Winston remained confident to the end of his days that the lost four weeks in the despatch of these regular troops was the prime reason for the failure and that an early breakthrough into the Sea of Marmara, followed by an immediate, powerful, and determined landing before the Turco-German forces had established their defences, would have led to a great victory. The capture of Constantinople and the elimination of Turkey from the war would have followed. Communications with Russia would have been re-established, that great nation would not have had to sue for peace, and there would have been no Bolshevik revolution. So Winston believed.

In fact, the blame for the Dardanelles defeat cannot be placed on the shoulders of one man, and certainly not only on Winston's shoulders. It can be put down to inexperience with the nature of the operation, with weapons that had not been seriously tried in war – mines, submarines, spotting and bombing aircraft, modern naval guns and torpedoes. Neither the Army nor the Navy had had experience of combined operations; and there was no prior feasibility investigation. (There was no Plans Division until 1917.)

The failure of the Dardanelles campaign was a major tragedy of the First World War, probably extending it by two years at the cost of millions of lives. But the men did not die in vain. The experience led to the creation of plans and forces in the Second World War that, in Europe and the Pacific, led to numbers of successful landings accomplished with the minimum loss of life.

Winston's return from France, as Clementine had feared, unleashed a fresh torrent of abuse in the press. Two men who hammered away relentlessly were Lord Northcliffe and Howell Arthur Gwynne, editor of the *Morning Post*. A *Daily Mail* leading article, though unsigned, carried the unmistakable mark of Northcliffe.

> The country has seen a Cabinet Minister who had just intelligence enough to know that Antwerp and Constantinople were places of importance and yet was mad enough to embark on adventures in both places with forces and methods that were insanely disproportionate to the enterprises upon which our unfortunate sailors and soldiers were launched in each case. In the Dardanelles affair in particular a megalomaniac politician risked the fate of our Army in France and sacrificed thousands of lives to no purpose.

Winston was anxious that these continued attacks through the second half of 1916, while the commission was sitting and taking evidence, would prejudice its findings. In fact, after prodigious labours in preparing his case, he began to feel that things were beginning to go his way. But his name was by no means cleared when a new political crisis arose in November, and in spite of more amazing gymnastics, reversals and contradictions, Asquith was at last obliged to tender his resignation to the King on 5 December. Lloyd George took his place as coalition Prime Minister, and now at last Winston thought he had a friend and ally in command who would reserve a senior appointment for him. For some twenty-four hours this seemed likely. Then four Conservatives who had agreed to serve in the new Cabinet said they would at once resign if Winston was appointed in any capacity, and Balfour would not go against this pressure.

Winston was appalled and cast down as never before, suffering a prolonged 'black dog', as he called his moods of utter dejection. Only two men possessed the power of patronage to ensure him a seat in the Cabinet: one, Asquith and the second Balfour who had, as Winston saw it, now acted the part of a Judas Iscariot.

Winston believed, in his innocence and arrogance, that he had a great popular following in the country, that his political enemies were conspiring with the press to keep him out of power, and that his rightful place was in 10 Downing Street. Only one person held the position and power to disillusion him. Her sense of duty towards her husband forced Clementine to define for him the reasons why he made enemies and was not trusted. Only Clementine could, and did, repeatedly and uncompromisingly, attempt to explain why in her view his overconfidence, his disdain and scorn for lesser men, his brusqueness and his refusal to compromise with or even listen to other opinions all told against him.

But Winston was not prepared to subordinate himself to anyone. Ironically, the one naval figure to whom he listened was past his best and unsound with age, while the one Army figure he admired in 1914 – French – was found wanting and relieved of his command. Winston could never have formed a government in 1916 even if, in the most unlikely event, George V had sent for him. He was too awkward, too self-assertive and uncomfortable to work with.

There were two black marks against him in the eyes of many people, including many of his colleagues. But the results at Antwerp justified the gamble by keeping the German army from the Channel ports. And the Dardanelles gamble was the one really imaginative enterprise that could have broken the impasse on the Western Front; it did not come off for many reasons, but one of them was Winston's failure to establish proper relations with Kitchener and forget the past between them.

It was less these two episodes that led Lloyd George to continue to keep Winston from office than his general reputation, his regrettable manner and above all his unacceptability to the Conservatives.

1916 had been a dreadful year of war. The Somme offensive, begun soon after Winston returned from the front, into which the soldiers and the public had put so much faith, had cost tens of thousands of lives and had long since petered out with no significant gain. Similarly, the Dardanelles campaign had failed and cost another 205,000 Anzac and British casualties, plus 47,000 French. The sea battle of Jutland, fought through the afternoon and night of 31 May, had proved a severe disappointment, with greater British than German losses, instead of a second Trafalgar. There were few homes in Britain that had not been touched with grief as a result of the war. Certainly, both Clementine's and Winston's families had lost friends and relations – including several old schoolmates of Winston's.

Clementine could, however, look back on the past year with thankfulness that her Winston had been preserved through so many dangers; and as for his political disappointments, well, they would be corrected, and her confidence in his future greatness was unimpaired. And the year ended on as happy a note as the times allowed. Sunny invited the two families to Blenheim for Christmas – Jack and Goonie, with their John and Peregrine, and Winston and Clementine, with Diana, Randolph, and Sarah. For full measure, Sunny invited the F. E. Smiths and their son and two daughters.

'And so, if for Winston and Clementine,' their youngest daughter has written, 'the winds blew chill outside, and the leaden clouds seemed to hold no promise for the future, the interior scene was warm and glowing.'

24

'Your Politicians Are Even Funnier Than Ours'

At the outset of the year 1917, Winston felt more than ever in the wilderness, without office, without responsibility at the fighting front: a simple constituency member of Parliament with a growing family, little money and diminishing responsibilities. Yet his resiliency and spirits were unimpaired, and never for one moment did he accept that greatness did not still lie ahead. His familiarity with the corridors of power, his priceless social and political connections, above all his ambitions, were intact. He would continue to hammer away in the House, and the weight of his opinions was still felt.

The strain of 1916 had taught Winston and Clementine that they both needed a replacement country retreat, which would also be good for the children, the lease on Hoe Farm having expired. In London, the repossession of 33 Eccleston Square, leaving Jack and Goonie and their family in peace, was welcomed all round, without in any way affecting the friendship and loyalty between the families. It was curious to become reacquainted with the ghosts of the past in their little house – where Edward Grey had replaced the *art nouveau* decoration in Clementine's bedroom, of which she had been so proud.

Winston heard of a place in west Kent that might fit their needs, and he and Clementine went down to look at it. It was very attractive and very run down and would need money to be spent on it. Winston instructed Cassel to sell off some of his American securities (and they were few enough) to pay for the freehold and repairs. It was called Lullenden Farm, near East Grinstead, in rolling wooded countryside, far from the next dwelling and offering the peace and quiet they sought. It was built of local grey stone, long and low, with an old oasthouse that Clementine set about having converted into bedrooms and a dining room for the children. The chief attraction of the house was the single long room from end to end, with a single great centre fireplace, and stairs rising to a gallery.

After laying on mains water and completing other simple modernizations, the family would leave London after school on Fridays and with the car packed with provisions, clothes, paint and canvases, arrive for supper. There then followed two days of relaxation, with Winston painting outdoors whenever the weather allowed and also playing games with the children. 'Bear' was the favourite. Bidding his children to hide their eyes, he would make off and climb a tree. The children – usually Jack and Goonie's children too – would challenge trees in turn, beating the trunk and crying, 'Bear! Bear! Bear!' Then suddenly, with bearlike noises, Winston would drop from a branch and give chase and catch the victim.

Clementine loved Lullenden, loving it for the peace it offered, loving the garden and seeing the children relaxed and happy. She was a country girl at heart and would sometimes hire horses and go off for a long hack with Goonie along the Kent and Sussex bridlepaths.

The air raids on London were increasing in frequency and strength at this time. They held no terror for the children, and Randolph in particular loved all the banging and excitement. Night raids meant being woken up and running down to the cellars, where the grown-ups would be in merry, tolerant mood with plates of cold meat and much champagne and brandy. Clementine, however, found the raids no fun at all, and she became increasingly anxious about the children. After a breakfast-time raid on 24 September by sixteen Gothas, with many bombs falling on the Westminster area, she persuaded Goonie that the children should be sent to Lullenden until the danger passed.

A few days later there was a great exodus. The two families settled in quickly. The children later recalled mostly happy

401

memories of Lullenden. Randolph and Johnny went off to the village school, and 'several brutish local girls' were recruited as nursemaids, although they tended to be softer on Peregrine, the placid one among them. The children also remembered the shortage of food, rationing being severe at this time due to the U-boat sinkings of merchantmen. 'There was always great competition to finish off the jampot.' Important visitors would come to Lullenden to confer with Winston, and they sometimes brought presents for the children – including, one magic day, a box of cream-filled chocolates. These were dealt out equitably after lunch, before the afternoon rest, but one day a chocolate was found missing. No-one could be made to own up, so the nursemaid on duty secretly opened one and filled it with mustard. It was Sarah who was later heard screaming with agony.

Another 'important person' brought down a toy caravan, which could accommodate two of them. It lasted no time at all. With Peregrine and Sarah on board, Randolph pushed it at top speed down a steep slope, at the bottom of which it was smashed to pieces. He readily accepted responsibility, and he was prepared to take the blame for anyone's misdemeanour at one penny a time, entering the details in a notebook and pooh-poohing the terrific whacks the tough country nursemaids could deliver.

Diana, it was recalled, tended to be jealous of Randolph's domination, which was complete and overwhelming, while Sarah and Peregrine – devoted friends all their lives – kept themselves to themselves and out of trouble as far as possible.

Later, as the air raids on London began to fizzle out because zeppelin losses became unacceptably heavy and fighters mastered the daylight bombing attacks by Gothas, Lullenden reverted to the weekend role. This entailed a lot of motoring, but Winston never minded that. He always enjoyed driving and always drove fast, and there were numerous frights and near shaves. On one Monday, Winston and Clementine had only got as far as the nearest village of

Dormansland when their car struck another hard and over-turned. They were only bruised and shocked, and luckily the children were not with them.

Later in the year, the lease on 33 Eccleston Square expired, and at a time when Winston was frantically busy again, they had to find somewhere to live in London. Once again Aunt Cornelia came to the family's rescue. She had a London house to spare temporarily, 3 Tenterden Street, off the north-west corner of Hanover Square.

Many months before this further move, the relaxed week-ends and holidays, painting and playing in the country, had been long since over for Winston. The preliminary reports of the Dardanelles Commission made clear that he was innocent of the wilder charges relating to the conduct of the early part of the campaign, and ascribed much of the blame to Kitchener's delaying of the 29th Division. Winston was jubilant, and Lloyd George found it harder than ever to deny him a Cabinet appointment any longer.

On 16 July the Prime Minister invited Winston to 10 Downing Street and asked him which post he would like, Secretary of State for Air or Minister of Munitions. Winston answered at once, 'Munitions, please,' and Lloyd George agreed. It was a post of utmost importance, which Lloyd George himself had held under Asquith.

Predictably, there was an outcry from Winston's traditional enemies, the *Morning Post* as usual being the most virulent in its comments. Significantly, however, to the men who were fighting the war, Winston's return to a place where he could influence events and above all keep them fully supplied with weapons and ammunition was warmly welcomed.

Clementine was delighted at the news, confident that her husband had emerged from the wilderness and reached more fruitful fields. The appointment required a by-election, as always at that time, so Clementine accompanied Winston north to his Scottish constituency.

In his most important speech to the Dundee elector-ate on 20 July, he spoke philosophically about his own ordeal and isolation, and made special reference to the

403

epochal event of 1917, the entry of the USA into the war:

> There is hardly any public servant of position . . .
> who has been exposed to the full brunt and shock
> of this unparalleled convulsion who has escaped in
> the discharge of his duties without being bruised or
> wounded by the violence and fury of events . . . I
> harbour no resentment of any kind against those who
> have endeavoured to prevent me from returning to
> public office . . .
>
> [And of America he said] We have the immeasur-
> able advantage that while there is scarcely any effec-
> tive reinforcement that can come to our enemies,
> the mighty Republic of the United States, with all
> its resources of virtue, of valour, of wisdom, and of
> power, is coming to our aid, and we have only to
> hold on until she can throw her whole weight into the
> struggle to make our victory decisive and complete.

Winston was returned with a large majority, but the attacks
against him personally and against his appointment continued, and even through his thick skin, he felt the pricks.
His old friend Hankey, invited over to Lullenden, was surprised to hear him say that until this new appointment, he had
had no idea that public opinion was so hostile. Winston also
admitted to Hankey, significantly, that he might have been
'a bit above himself' at the Admiralty.

But from family and friends there flowed a river of congratulation. Aunt Cornelia, in sending her wishes, said, 'You
are just the man for the job,' but could not resist a cautionary
note: 'My advice is stick to munitions & don't try & run
the Govt!'

Winston's first-ever comrade in arms all those years ago in
Cuba, Reggie Barnes, now commanding a division in France,
was delighted: 'Pile up the guns & shells & we will make the
Hun sit up & beg . . .'

*

It cannot be said that Winston at Munitions acted upon Aunt Cornelia's advice. His arrival at the department's headquarters, in Northumberland Avenue, was very similar to his first day at the Admiralty back in 1911. His energy, his curiosity, his dedication, his ingenuity and his need to probe into every aspect of the immense world of arms manufacture amazed his staff. As at one time, while still a boy, he had surprised his master with his power to memorize effortlessly an entire Shakespeare play, he now astonished his officers with his ability to assimilate the immensely complicated details of a gun-manufacturing contract and the technique employed in casting and winding – the 'shrinking on' process – rifling machine advances, developments of coned breech screws and all the other processes involved in gun-making, labour relations in the armament factories, the provisions for accelerating the output of fighting aircraft, and thousands more details.

Then, just as he was never very often to be found in his office at the Admiralty in 1912, now five years later he seemed to his senior staff to be constantly travelling – to munitions factories at home and to military headquarters in France. General Haig remained a friend and was, on the whole, glad to see him at Munitions. On Winston's first visit to the General, Haig noted in his diary:

> Winston means to do his utmost to provide the army with all it requires, but at the same time he can hardly stop meddling in the larger questions of strategy and tactics . . . and his agile mind only makes him a danger because he can persuade Lloyd George to adopt and carry out the most idiotic policy.

Well, maybe! But at that time Haig was planning a great new advance across German-occupied Belgium, including the Passchendaele ridge. Winston advised otherwise. He believed (and said so, of course) that a new offensive should wait until 1918, when overwhelming supplies had been built up. We did not want another Somme disaster, did we? And as if to underline this message, he and Eddie Marsh happened to make a tour of the blasted Somme battlefields where over 400,000 men had become casualties.

Almost immediately after Winston's return to London the Battle of Passchendaele was opened by Haig's armies. The same intense machine-gun fire produced the same frightful consequences. Three thousand were killed and 7,000 wounded on one day alone, and some 240,000 men in all were killed or wounded over the next weeks. Never was Winston's instinct, and genius, for war more aptly and disastrously demonstrated – and recognized by so few.

Back in early 1915 Winston had encouraged and contributed to the design and development of a 'land battleship' that would break the deadlock created by the machine-gun, barbed wire, trenches and fortifications. The idea was taken seriously by only a handful of farsighted military thinkers at first. One day, on Vimy Ridge, Winston developed his idea to a French general and his staff. After he left them, they all laughed at this absurd idea. A British officer who was present was told by the general, 'Your politicians are even funnier than ours.'

In stepping out of the confines of his responsibilities as First Lord of the Admiralty, Winston had become the patron of one of the greatest military weapons of this century. But progress on this 'land battleship' had been slow and was slower still with Winston's departure from office. He had always contended that the tank should be built in great numbers before being used. Instead, it had been used almost casually – intermittently and in small numbers and mostly in the wrong place at the wrong time.

Now at last, at Cambrai on 20 November, by using a strong force of tanks in the van and without a warning artillery barrage, a great victory was won at negligible cost. The Germans were routed and demoralized. Winston's instinct had been right again, and he saw to it that tank production was increased many times over, and, belatedly, cavalry regiments were at last turned into tank regiments.

Winston's military percipience was to be demonstrated again, on the strategic scale, too. The Navy had at last broken the back of Germany's U-boat offensive, which earlier in the year had threatened to starve Britain and cancel the benefits of America's entry into the war. Now, on land, Winston was convinced that Field Marshal Lüdendorff would launch a mighty last-fling offensive in the spring of 1918 to win the war before the Americans could become seriously involved.

At the Ministry of Munitions' headquarters in Northumberland Avenue, a new regime of efficiency was introduced. Statistics, from production forecasts to working hours at tank factories, workers' attendance records to aircraft instrument output, were demanded – 'Pray, on one side of paper will suffice . . .' Typical of his attention to the details of efficiency was his instruction, almost on the day he began work, to establish a Quick Luncheon Club, to which the press was invited on 28 August. The waitresses were dressed in the green overalls and green caps of the women munitions workers, and at 1s 3d, 'The best paid officials as well as their subordinates' could afford the lunch, while everyone benefited from the time saved.

Factory management in many sections of industry was still autocratic and insensitive, and in a parliamentary bill that Winston introduced as early as August, there were provisions for liberating manual workers, allowing them to join trades unions, rewarding loyalty and special skills, and giving encouragement to good faith between management and the shop floor.

The Western Front's appetite for men was never satisfied. As many as one thousand a day were drawn from the munitions industry to the battlefield, and the lost output could be made up only by greater efficiency, by the employment of older men, and above all by women – who came close to providing ninety per cent of the labour for shell manufacture.

These women were seldom involved in labour disputes.

407

The most restless workers, at a time of high inflation and desperate need for their services, were the skilled engineers, who saw their wages being overtaken, sometimes by a hundred per cent, by unskilled pieceworkers. Strikes ensued and had to be settled. When engineering workers were granted a twelve and a half per cent wage increase, others demanded the same. In a number of cases Winston intervened personally in major disputes involving disgruntled workers and neanderthal management who refused to recognize the rights of shop stewards. In the case of one vitally important aircraft factory's dispute, involving equally unreasonable behaviour on both sides, Winston told them that with the full authority of the Defence of the Realm Act, he intended to nationalize the plant, putting management and workers out of their jobs. They came to heel.

During most of his time at Munitions, Winston's press enemies, especially Gwynne at the *Morning Post*, continued their attacks upon him, like children who have learned only one tune, so that even the most loyal, or gullible, readers began to have doubts of their truth. Within the first six months of his regime Winston was unquestionably achieving results: the figures were there for all to see. Even a strongly socialist-pacifist MP, William Anderson, was moved to utter a tribute in the House – '. . . in my opinion he has brought courage and a certain quality of imagination to the task of dealing with labour questions.'

Winston found it as valuable – and enjoyable – to visit the Western Front and call on the generals as he had done when at the Admiralty. In March 1918, when the great German offensive he had predicted before Passchendaele was expected, he visited Haig in his headquarters once again. They talked at length about the preparations Haig had made to meet the attack, and later Winston was taken to the headquarters of his old division, the 9th. Here he met again Hugh Tudor, his old friend from subaltern days in India, now the commanding general. He was 'in high expectation' of the German attack.

'When do you think it will come?' Winston asked.

'Perhaps tomorrow morning. Perhaps the day after.'

Winston later wrote of spending the whole of the next day, 20 March, in the trenches:

> A deathly and suspicious silence brooded over the front. For hours not a cannon shot was fired. Yet the sunlit fields were instinct with foreboding . . . We examined every part of the defences . . . Certainly nothing that human thought and effort could accomplish had been neglected. For four miles in depth the front was a labyrinth of wire and scientifically sited machine-gun nests. . . . Rumours and reasonable expectation that the Germans would employ large numbers of tanks had led to the construction of broad minefields studded with buried shells with sensitive fuses amid wire entanglements . . .

Trench raids in the evening confirmed that the battle would open within hours. Shortly after 4 a.m. Winston was awakened by several severe explosions, which later turned out to have been mines exploded in tunnels dug under the British front-line trenches. A minute later, the 'most tremendous cannonade I shall ever hear' broke out. Winston dressed and went outside. Hugh Tudor was already there. 'This is *it*!' he shouted into Winston's ear. 'I have ordered all our batteries to open. You will hear them in a minute.'

But, though much nearer than the exploding German shells, the two hundred or more British guns were inaudible. It was the greatest bombardment in history, and the sight of the explosions, from horizon to horizon, was something Winston (and all who witnessed it) would never forget. On a forty-mile front, the Germans launched an army of three-quarters of a million men against some three hundered thousand British. It was the Germans' 'last throw', and when Winston was at last prevailed upon to retire from the scene, it did not seem possible that there was any power on earth that could halt this huge and terrifying military machine.

*

In eventually holding this German spring offensive, the British and French had no American support. It was not until 12 September that the Americans were able to launch their first offensive. And to the end of the war, the American army was almost entirely dependent on British and French weapons and ammunition. Of the first million American soldiers, Winston wrote, 'But for the fact that we were able to supply them with artillery, machine guns, rifles, trench mortars, &c., and to feed them with munitions of all kind, no use in the present crisis could have been made of [them].' This added another burden to the load carried by the munitions industry and by Winston's department. The consumption of shells alone was prodigious – for some time Britain had been buying up the entire Chilean nitrate output.

Winston was in France on the day of the first American offensive, which also happened to be his and Clementine's tenth wedding anniversary. Failing a celebration he composed for her a tender love letter:

> Ten years ago my dearest one we were sliding down to Blenheim in our special train . . . I reproach myself vy much for not having been more to you. But at any rate in these ten years the sun has never yet gone down on our wrath. Never once have we closed our eyes in slumber with an unappeased difference. My dearest sweet I hope & pray that future years may bring you serene & smiling days . . .

Love was in the air again for Winston's mother, too. She had met a man of forty-one years named Montagu Porch, an archaeologist of private means, who had fought in the Boer War and joined up again in 1914. For the second time, for the sake of her happiness, Winston and Jack were philosophical about the great disparity in age, though Winston was heard to remark that he hoped marriage would not become the vogue among ladies of 64. There was also the considerable consolation that her money problems might now at last be at an end. (They were not.) They married on 1 June in the presence of Winston and Clementine, and the groom wrote Winston a letter telling of his love, assuring him that he could make Jennie happy, and predicting that Winston and he 'shall be good friends'.

Clementine was with child again during the summer of 1918, but continued to work at her canteens, a strenuous business that eventually resulted in the award to her of a CBE. It was also a worrying summer for her. She had become increasingly aware that she did not seem able to feel or show the same affection for her children as other mothers did, and soon she was to give birth to another. Randolph especially failed to attract her love, and she never seemed to understand that his aggressive and obstreperous behaviour was caused in part by his instinctive response to this coolness.

Clementine worried, too, about Winston and the danger in which he seemed impelled to place himself. Was it really necessary, she wondered, for him to be risking himself in the line of German shellfire and flying to and from France so frequently when there was a perfectly good steamer service? He would put down in fields near Lullenden and arrive in his flying gear, which tickled his romantic nature but terrified Clementine. On 13 June, his plane suffered engine trouble and only just made it to the English shore.

A few weeks later he spent a day or two with his family at Lullenden and then drove them all down to the sea at St Margaret's Bay, near Dover. There was nothing he liked more than playing on a good sandy beach with the children, though he was equally happy digging on his own, especially if there was a little stream to dam or divert. Later in the afternoon, a driver whisked him off to Lympne aerodrome where Captain Cyril Patteson, his favourite pilot, awaited him with his De Havilland DH4 aircraft. While Clementine drove back to Lullenden, Winston once again went off in the opposite direction. His little cabin, with sliding windows and a desk at which he could work on his papers, protected him from the elements, which was as well on this trip as they met

411

a tremendous storm that swept their frail little plane across the Channel in (Winston claimed) about eleven minutes. 'It gives me a feeling of tremendous conquest over space,' he told Clementine, who fretted about him and told everyone, including the children, about her fears for his safety. It did not add serenity to the atmosphere of the home.

Winston was in the air again on the afternoon of 8 August. At a War Council meeting that morning it was confirmed that a British offensive would open that day. He knew that tanks in great numbers would take a leading part, and he was determined to watch them in action. So, the moment the meeting closed, he ordered his DH4 and flew off via Lympne to Hesdin aerodrome, and thence by road to a château that was always at his disposal when he was in France. Here he heard that the German front line had collapsed and that prisoners were pouring back in tens of thousands. Until now Winston had not seriously expected a German defeat until the summer of 1919. Haig, however, had been more optimistic, and it looked possible that he was about to be proved right.

The next morning, 9 August, Winston was driven to the headquarters of the British 4th Army at Flixecourt, and took lunch there with the commander, General Sir Henry Rawlinson, and his own brother, Jack. Everywhere, there was a sense of elation and confidence, as if the tide really had turned at last. The German armies, disillusioned and disheartened by the failure of their spring offensive, were now surrendering in great numbers, their steel-like resolve and battle fitness softening as they retreated over ground they had conquered at such a terrible price only weeks earlier.

Winston and Jack took a car towards the front line, noting the tank tracks everywhere and the comparative absence of shell holes, suggesting a more mobile campaign. There was no doubt that the tanks had taken a critical part in the victory. To the two brothers, who had campaigned in so many corners of the globe and now had been involved in this greatest war in history, often in great danger, for just four years and one week, it seemed as if war and destruction had dominated all

412

their lives. Could it now almost be over – the world at peace at long last?

A few days later, Winston and Clementine, separated by 300 miles and the English Channel, were occupying themselves under strangely contrasting circumstances. Clementine was staying with the family of Sir John and Lady Horner at Mells in Somerset. It was 'full of comfort, beautiful things, sweet smelling flowers, peaches ripening on old walls, gentle flittings & hummings & pretty grandchildren', and here she felt the stirrings of her new child, due in three months. Winston, however, in the same summer heat in Paris, was cooped indoors and involved day after day in conferences in which there was too much dispute and acrimony for comfort. The single link between husband and wife remained, inevitably, the war. In the garden at Mells, Clementine and the Horners and Asquiths, bonded by marriage, experienced a heady sense of hope that the war would soon be over while they mourned the dead of their families – 'the sadness and melancholy of it all'.

But in Paris, the generals and statesmen and hard-faced armament manufacturers of four nations prepared for another year of war and argued about mustard-gas output, the need for thousands more tanks and bombing aircraft, and greater output of high-explosive shells.

Just eleven weeks later Winston was presiding over another meeting, this time in London at the headquarters of the Ministry of Munitions. The only items on the agenda were the disposal of the gigantic mountains of munitions stocks and the conversion of munitions factories to peacetime production – a swords-to-ploughshares operation almost as daunting as the construction of the plants originally. The date was 11 November. The Germans had agreed to halt all military activity at eleven o'clock that morning, when the armistice would come into effect.

The meeting closed shortly before 11 a.m., when Clementine arrived. They both went to the window of Winston's office and he opened it in order to hear the strokes of Big Ben from down Whitehall: in this strange, expectant silence, it would be heard from a great distance. Northumberland Avenue below was empty of people and traffic, as if in hushed disbelief that the carnage was over. Then, at the first stroke of the distant bell, a single figure appeared from one of the offices. For a moment the office girl was alone, but before Big Ben had completed its ring, a stream of people, then a river, then a flood of humanity, burst forth from every door, shouting and waving, linking arms, racing towards Trafalgar Square.

More came up Whitehall, from the Strand, mingling with packed buses – with people dancing and waving flags on the open top decks – and taxis. A surge of joyous sound, a limitless pattern of fluttering colour, filled every street. Winston had ordered his car to be ready, and he cautiously escorted the heavily pregnant Clementine along the corridors of the Ministry, still full of running figures, to the main entrance. Here they were greeted with what Winston described as 'a gigantic pandemonium'. As they struggled into the car, twenty more climbed in with them or stood on the running boards. Thus they threaded their way slowly through the triumphant crowds, edging down Whitehall and into Downing Street. At number 10 there were police on duty to clear their path to the front door, and inside they were taken at once to Lloyd George, just back from Italy, to offer their congratulations.

Winston returned for dinner at number 10 on that first evening of peace. Lloyd George wanted to begin by shooting the Kaiser, but Winston said no. According to one guest, the chief topic of conversation was politics and the inevitable general election.

Four days later Clementine gave birth to her baby at 3 Tenterden Street, another little red-headed girl, their own private peace celebration. They named her Marigold.

25

'Tell Winston We Could Never Have Done Anything Without Him'

For Winston and Clementine, the four years following the four years of the Great War were each unusually eventful and marked by tragedy and success, happiness and misery. The Churchills were now 44 and 33 years of age, fit and vigorous and in the prime of their lives, Clementine still statuesquely beautiful, he good-looking, too, almost as bald as he was to be for the rest of his life, but not yet as overweight as he would become, so he was still able to make a good showing on the polo field. Second perhaps only to the Asquiths, they were the best-known couple in the land, and more than ever, wherever he went and whatever he said was reported. Nowhere a loved figure except among his family and friends, admiration also tended to be conditioned, and hostility towards him was still widespread. The findings of the Dardanelles Commission, while largely reinstating his reputation among the better-informed people, by no means restored his standing among the middle classes and Conservatives, who, if anything, were more hostile than ever. His sturdiest supporters came from the working classes, who associated him with gallant deeds in war and social benefits in peace.

The political split in Britain immediately after the armistice was four-way: the Conservatives were dominant in the coalition government; the Liberals were in decline and were split between Lloyd George, who favoured a continuation of the coalition with himself as Prime Minister, and Asquith, who believed he could restore a Liberal administration (with himself at its head); and there was the fast-growing Labour Party.

Of all these factions, Winston favoured the cause of Lloyd

George, a man he mistrusted almost as deeply as did Clementine but also a man he admired politically and enjoyed socially. By no means all his friends and associates thought his choice a wise one. One of these was Max Aitken, Lord Beaverbrook. This Canadian-born, prematurely wizened millionaire had entered Parliament before the war, had become secretary to Bonar Law and successively a baronet and a baron for his parliamentary and war services. Beaverbrook (long since 'Max' to Winston) had seen much of Winston, especially in France, where he had served as a special observer on behalf of the Canadian forces. They spoke the same language and agreed on most things. Their association was to be long and mutually valuable.

'Speaking to you as a friend,' Beaverbrook wrote to Winston after he had made public his political choice, 'I think you are making a mistake.' He considered that Winston was no natural coalitionist and should have followed his instinct. So did Clementine, and she was glad to have the excuse of her new baby, which she was nursing, in declining to come up to Dundee to help in the electioneering, something she always loathed anyway.

In anticipation of a general election very soon after peace was declared, Winston wrote to Sir George Ritchie (local grocer's boy made good and president of the Dundee Liberal Association) nearly a week before the armistice was signed, in order to prepare for the imminent campaign. He was by no means taking the result as a foregone conclusion. Much had happened, not all of it favourable to himself, since he had last asked for the support of the constituents of this Scottish working-class town.

One hostile party Winston had to contend with was the proprietor of the local newspapers. David C. Thomson was the founder of all three Dundee newspapers, and although one of these was nominally Liberal all of them reflected the views of their Conservative proprietor. And Thomson strongly disapproved of Winston. To offset this possibly fatal disadvantage, Winston persuaded his old friend, Lord Rothermere, proprietor of the *Glasgow Herald* (among many newspapers), to publish a special Dundee edition of that newspaper over the election period and make it freely available to the electorate.

Winston also asked for a meeting with Thomson, confident that he could at least reduce the hostility of this hard man. Invited to the newspaper proprietor's office, he got a very rough reception for a while, but by a combination of threat and charm, partly won him round. On the same day, 26 November, he and his supporter Archibald Sinclair, and George Ritchie, were all physically handled by a mob of 'Bolshevik elements' at a public meeting. Winston relished this kind of reception, enjoyed the full day of fighting, and told Clementine that it had all been a great success.

It must have been, for he was returned with a thundering majority. Lloyd George's coalition won a great victory, the Liberals suffered a massive defeat, and Asquith lost his own seat. In Whitehall, even before the results were announced on 28 December, the rumour was doing the rounds that Winston was to be given both the War Office *and* the Air Ministry.

It was also widely, and correctly, believed that he wished to return to the Admiralty, an appointment that would indicate that his resignation in May 1915 was politically motivated and in no way a reflection on the work he had done for the Navy.

Lloyd George was having none of that, though he did promise it to him for twenty-four hours. As rumour had foretold, Winston was given the dual task of looking after the fledgling Royal Air Force and the Army. His recommendations for his friends and relations were more closely listened to. General (Jack) Seely, who had been gassed and invalided from the Army and been Winston's Undersecretary of State at Munitions, followed him in the same role at the Air Ministry; Lord Londonderry, Winston's cousin also, later came to the same ministry as Seely's successor; and F. E. Smith became Attorney General on Winston's recommendation and was created Baron Birkenhead.

Winston's first task with the Army was to organize and

417

supervise the demobilization of millions of men, while retaining an army of occupation. All except a small core of professionals expected immediate repatriation and a return to civilian life, and there was great anxiety that unemployment faced those who were last out. Idleness, fear and delay were fertile breeding grounds for unrest, and there were rebellious scenes in France and on several occasions outright mutiny.

Every effort was made to hasten the demobilization and keep the priority just: those who had joined up early in the war, those who had been wounded and returned, and men over forty were the first to be released under Winston's hastily revised release scheme. More than half a million were released in the first half of January, and almost as many in the next two weeks, creating a great deal of joy and relief – and much strain on Britain's railway system. In the middle of October Winston announced that the rate of discharge had averaged 10,000 a day and that the demobilization scheme had been completed.

Many of Lloyd George's critics claimed that Winston had been given both these service jobs as a preliminary to merging them in due course, a task that Lloyd George judged Winston could accomplish satisfactorily. The RAF, combining the Army's Royal Flying Corps and the Navy's Royal Naval Air Service, had come into being less than a year earlier (1 April 1918), mainly because of their enormous growth: it was by far the biggest air force in the world, with some 12,000 aircraft and 291,000 personnel. With the coming of peace it seemed in Lloyd George's eyes that it would be more convenient and cheaper for the Army to assimilate it.

Winston's predecessor, Sir William Weir, and Hugh Trenchard (ex-Secretary of State for Air and 'the Father of the RAF'), had brought the force into being and were horrified at any suggestion of amalgamation with either of the other two services. To the relief of both men, as soon as he had time, Winston took Weir into his confidence and sought his advice. 'I was glad of the army troubles [the mutinies] as a

418

breathing space,' Weir told Trenchard's biographer, 'just as I was pleased to be dealing with Winston rather than anyone else. Had he been dealing at the Admiralty instead, the RAF's chances [of survival] would, I'm afraid, have been quite negligible.'

Winston liked Weir, a down-to-earth Scotsman of few words and great abilities, first as a manufacturer of aircraft engines and then, towards the end of the war, as Director General of Aircraft Production. Weir was predisposed in Winston's favour for his dynamic performance at Munitions and as parliamentary representative for a good Scottish seat. No-one, except possibly Trenchard himself, knew more about the formation and the personalities of this young flying service. Among all those whom Weir and Winston discussed, it was clear that Weir's admiration for Trenchard was limitless.

Wasting no time, Winston next called Trenchard to the War Office, telling him that he had not yet made up his mind about the independence of the RAF. Nothing could be better calculated to stir up Hugh Trenchard's passions than any uncertainty about the future of his beloved Air Force. Winston let him flow on and then broke in with the startling invitation, 'How would you like to come back as my Chief of Air Staff?'

Trenchard was completely thrown. 'That's impossible,' he retorted. Referring to Lieutenant Colonel Fredrick Sykes, he added, 'You have one already whether you like him or not.'

Sykes was away in Paris as part of Lloyd George's delegation at the peace talks. 'You leave Sykes to me. Civil flying is going to be under the Air Ministry. We'll call Sykes "Controller of Civil Aviation" and console him with a GBE [knighthood].'

Trenchard, a cast-iron professional soldier since the year when Winston entered the Army, had simple principles of promotion and reward for merit, honours certainly being the prerogative of the King. He was shocked at this idea and, when recovered, could only say that he would think the matter over.

'Well, not for long,' said Winston. 'I can assure you that there'll be no opposition within the Cabinet. So why don't you put down on a piece of paper your ideas on the reorganization of an Air Ministry for peacetime. You do that, and I'll do the same. Then we can exchange notes.'

If Hugh Trenchard had wanted this job above anything else in the world – and perhaps he did – he could not have conducted things better. He completed his study that evening in time for the last post. In 800 pithy words he expressed exactly what was wanted. A week passed before he was recalled to the War Office. The airman found the Minister in merry mood. 'I got your notes,' he began.

'I notice I didn't get yours.'

'I haven't had time to write mine. I've been in Paris,' Winston excused himself glibly. 'You'll be pleased to hear, however, that there's little in yours I can quarrel with. Broadly speaking, I like them.'

Trenchard continued to demur about the appointment. He was clearly concerned, like so many others before and after him, that Winston was taking too much upon himself, and there might be upsets later. But he was finally persuaded – and with that reluctant agreement it can truly be said that the RAF was saved.

There had been, as usual, plenty of criticism of Winston's double appointment. 'This is a grotesque arrangement,' complained the *Daily Mail*. *The Times* gravely doubted that 'any single man can cover the huge span of both these departments of the Army and the Air.' The *Morning Post* deeply regretted that Winston had been offered any appointment, never mind two. None of the newspapers had the slightest influence upon Winston or upon his appointment. The most likely source of deterrence was Clementine:

'Darling really don't you think it would be better to give up the Air & continue *concentrating* as you are doing on the War Office?' she wrote to him in France. 'It would be a sign of real strength to do so, & people would admire it very much. It is weak to hang on to two offices . . .'

For the sake of the future strength and well-being of the

nation's defences, it was as well that this was one of the many occasions when he completely disregarded her advice.

Perhaps more usefully, Clementine did all that she could to halt Winston's folly in starting flying lessons again. As he himself observed, 'It was not, and still is not, common for men over forty to become good and trustworthy pilots. Youth with its extraordinary quickness and aptitudes was almost always the first qualification for an attainment of "Flying Sense".' By 1919 he had acquired an impressive total of flying hours, and he could look back on a period of eight years (with one break) when he had been associated in a supervisory capacity with naval and military flying. He even claimed to have invented the terms 'seaplane' and 'flight' (of aeroplanes).

As with driving a car, he was not at all good at flying, but it had a special appeal for Winston because, while a battlefield peppered with bursting shells and whizzing bullets held not the slightest fear for him, he was deeply fearful every time he went up. The overcoming of this fear provided him with a special challenge he could find in no other dangerous activity.

> *The air is an extremely dangerous, jealous and exacting mistress* [he wrote]. *Once under the spell most lovers are faithful to the end, which is not always old age . . . Curiously enough my apprehensions about going into the air were apparently confirmed by a long series of dangerous or fatal accidents in which I narrowly missed being involved.*

He could cite the death of Gilbert Wildman-Lushington when Winston was first learning to fly, the death of three officers in a new experimental seaplane in which Winston had been practising only a few hours earlier, and an occasion when an urgent appointment had prevented him from flying dual in a machine that had always flown perfectly but, during the flight

421

when Winston would have been in it, had plunged into the ground from a new type of spin, killing the pilot.

There were several other occasions when he had felt the close touch of death, and each had stirred his determination to go on, joystick in right hand, throttle in left hand, balance and control nowhere, carrying out the standard evolutions and the coming down in a smooth *vol plané*.

In the summer of 1919, Winston's instructor was the highly experienced Colonel Jack Scott, who had almost written himself off in a crash at the outset of the war. After a hard day's work at the War Office, Winston motored down to Croydon aerodrome for an evening of instruction. He took off in a dual-control machine, well versed in the particular manner in which a pilot gained height at this airfield with its perimeter of tall elm trees, requiring a turn to the right and then to the left. He accomplished the first of these turns safely, but on the second he somehow lost control of the stick and the machine stalled.

Scott took over but they were too low for him to do any more than switch off the ignition. 'I saw the sunlit aerodrome close beneath me,' Winston recalled, 'and the impression flashed through my mind that it was bathed in a baleful yellowish glare.' Then, in another flash, a definite thought formed in his brain, '"This is very likely Death."'

Not many people survived low-level stalls and spins at that time. The machine struck the ground at about fifty miles per hour, burying its nose deep in the grass and hurling both men violently forward. 'Safe! . . . I leapt out of the shattered fuselage and ran to my companion. He was senseless and bleeding . . .'

Colonel Scott was seriously hurt, with two broken legs, but eventually recovered from his injuries. Winston, with lacerations to his face and legs, recovered in time to preside at a dinner in the House of Commons that evening for General John (Black Jack) Pershing, Commander in Chief of American army forces in Europe. The next morning Winston found himself black all over – from his bruises. Clementine had no need for further entreaties. With a deep sense of guilt at the injury he had caused to the gallant Colonel, he vowed never to fly himself again.

Clementine's relief was offset by other worries that struck her in this first year of peace. Since Sarah's birth in 1914, the family had employed a Scottish nanny, Isabelle, a stout and much-loved woman. One March night, when Winston was away in France, this unfortunate woman was struck by the influenza epidemic – or, because of its scale, more properly termed a plague – that was sweeping Europe in the aftermath of the war. It had already killed hundreds of thousands of people on the Continent and had recently crossed the Channel, unreduced in virulence.

Delirium led Isabelle to pluck little Marigold from her cot and take her into her own bed. Mercifully, Clementine was alerted to this, took the baby away, and tried to get a doctor. They were all busy on other cases and Clementine spent the rest of the night trying to soothe the alarmed Marigold and attend to the dying Isabelle. By dawn Isabelle was dead, and soon after, Clementine herself was struck down with a high temperature. Her case was less serious, but she suffered agonies of apprehension about Marigold. Winston was diverted to stay at Blenheim on his return, until the germs were thought to have dispersed.

At this time, with Winston travelling frequently to France in connection with the peace conference, Clementine was once again fretting about their finances. She was always more worried about money when Winston was absent and thus depriving her of the reassurance he always offered her. It also allowed her to imagine him committing all manner of extravagances, especially gambling. Clementine was seriously house-hunting again in London; prices were desperately high after the war, and she suggested to Winston that they might have to sell their beloved Lullenden.

Another looming expense was a motor car. The red Napier had long since gone the way of all cars. Their friend, the Duke of Westminster (Bendor), had lent Winston a closed Silver Ghost Rolls-Royce during the war, which had been an immense pleasure and convenience, but this had to go back, and in thanking him for 'the beautiful motor car you so kindly placed at my disposal', Winston suggested that he drive it up to Scotland when he and Clementine came to stay in early September.

Winston continued to write for magazines and newspapers whenever he was offered a commission, his agent always getting him unmatched rewards, and Winston never allowing pride to stand in the way of a much-needed fee. His pleasure in his painting was widely known, and he had even put on a show under another name in Paris. As a result, *Strand* magazine asked him to write two articles, with reproductions of paintings of his own choice, under the title 'Painting as a Pastime'. His agent arranged a fee of £1,000 and subsequently sold the American magazine rights for another £600, unprecedented figures for *Strand* or any other magazine.

While she knew how badly they needed the money, Clementine, who would have preferred that he never 'dabble in journalism' of any sort, thought this sort of work about painting 'might cause you to be discussed trivially' and strongly opposed his acceptance of the offer. She was worried, too, that professional painters 'would be vexed' and that his advice 'either might be thought naif or conceited'.

Winston argued back equally vehemently that if it was thought quite proper for Balfour to write about his hobby of golf and Bonar Law on chess, why should he not be able to write about painting? 'I think I can make it very light and amusing without in any way offending the professional painters,' he emphasized to her, without referring again to the much-needed remuneration – some £23,000 in 1990 money. Clementine was not convinced, confident as always that she knew best.

The two articles duly appeared and aroused a lot of interest and praise. They were completely modest and down to earth and were concerned more with how to derive pleasure from the pastime than how to paint. They gave him immense satisfaction, as did the agreement for a subsequent book with the publishers, Macmillan. They also wanted to reprint the life of his father in a new edition. He was to provide a long new introduction and publisher and author would share the profits equally, in accordance with the original contract.

Clementine continued to worry about money, as she had done almost from the day of her marriage. Money had become for her a nagging, unceasing irritation, and she wearily reconciled herself to its continuance for all her life. The steady financial drag of keeping two establishments, children, and servants, as well as entertaining guests who took the best for granted (as did her husband, daily), was a wearing business. It was a good deal heavier burden for her to carry than Winston recognized, although he, too, was daily concerned about their financial condition.

Then, in January 1921, an extraordinary thing happened. On the morning of the twenty-sixth a Cambrian Railway express train from Aberystwyth to Shrewsbury, *The Flyer*, collided head-on with a local passenger train from Welshpool at Abermule. 'The impact was terrific. The engine of the express mounted the engine of the local train and crashed down on the roof of the first coach,' as *The Times* described the catastrophe. The driver of the local train was killed instantly. The express train driver chose to leap from his platform at high speed. But before doing so he threw on the brakes, cut off the steam, and grabbed the signalling tablet – which alone proved his right to be on this length of line at this precise time. He survived, as did his fireman, and was exonerated of all blame.

Among the sixteen passengers who died in the collision was Lord Herbert Vane-Tempest. He was a first cousin once removed of Winston's. He was only 58, fit and unmarried; a director of the Cambrian Railway company, he lived nearby where the accident occurred. Under an old will, Winston inherited the entire Irish estate of his unfortunate cousin. It was worth between £50,000 and £60,000 and brought in an income of £4,000 per annum.

This unexpected windfall transformed Winston's financial position. He was suddenly quite comfortably off. This lifting of the burden of (relative) penury was a unique joy and

425

pleasure. He at once handed over the estate's investments to Jack, who was confident of improving them in the City, and bought himself a Rolls-Royce motor car. But he and Clementine also helped out members of the family who were in need, notably Nellie, who largely lived on her husband's disability pension and wanted to open a little shop to help things along. Clementine's mother was also, as always, in need. Both were assured that they were not to worry any more.

They both felt they wanted a holiday, and it was quickly arranged that Clementine should go off to the south of France – to her favourite hotel, the Bristol, at Beaulieu – and Winston would soon take her away in a comfortable ship to the Middle East, which she had never visited. She wrote to him:

> *I am living in blissful contemplation of our smooth and care-free future; (I mean from a money point of view) & I am laying up stores of health by staying a lot in bed. The last two days I have been thinking of the great pleasure and excitement of going with you to Egypt & Palestine. I am thrilled by the idea & so longing to see you.*

Winston, busy in London and preparing for the voyage (which would be mainly on government business for him), was equally excited at the prospect: 'I shall enjoy so much showing you round some of the places I know so well.' He told her to bring her tennis racquet, promising her the game she loved above all others. As for his own favourite pastime, 'I hope to paint a few pictures in the intervals between settling my business, and naturally I am taking all the right kinds of colours for the yellow desert, purple rocks and crimson sunsets.' As fellow passengers, there would be 'Archie' (Sir Archibald Sinclair, now his private secretary), Colonel Lawrence (of Arabia), and Air Marshal Trenchard, who was coming to study the air control of British-ruled Mesopotamia.

Winston left London on the evening of 1 March, to travel by train to Marseilles, where he would rendezvous with Clementine and board their steamship, the *Sphinx*. He had reported on the state of the children, all excellent in health except Marigold, who had had one or two infections but was better, and left them in the charge of Jennie, who wrote to him from her house in Berkeley Square:

> *Dearest Winston*
> *This is only a line to wish you bon voyage – & a speedy return – Give my love to Clemmie . . . I will look after the children & give you news of them. They are great darlings & do you both great credit!*
>
> *Bless you*
> *Your loving*
> *Mother*

Clementine was enchanted with Cairo and with Jerusalem when they went there later. To ride out to the pyramids on a camel with T. E. Lawrence and that great traveller and Middle East authority Gertrude Bell was a wonderful experience. They lived and travelled in the utmost luxury and met all the politicians as well as the diplomats, archaeologists and Arab and Jewish leaders. There was also, for Clementine, plenty of tennis. Winston painted assiduously whenever he had the chance. On one trip to paint the pyramids he suffered another car accident and also fell off a camel, injuring his hand – but not badly enough to prevent his holding a paintbrush. His accident-proneness did not diminish with the passing years.

Homecomings to young children have ever been poignant and memorable occasions, and Clementine could recall that evening of 9 April in all its detail many years later. Their steamer had taken them to Genoa, which they reached on the third, and thence they had travelled by train all the way to Calais. They were back in London at teatime and went straight to their new house in Sussex Square before collecting the children.

The house was on the east side, facing the gardens, and so catching the afternoon sun. There had been much rebuilding work still to be done when Winston left, but all was in order as instructed, with even the books arranged correctly on the shelves of Winston's study.

They inspected the house thoroughly and with satisfaction, and left their luggage with the servants. Winston telephoned Jennie to greet her and tell her that they were coming round to collect the children. 'Are they well? Have they behaved well?' Randolph, back from Sandroyd prep school, was quite obstreperous, but, Jennie said, she had steeled herself for that, and the girls were too divinely sweet, though little Marigold had a cold . . .

The big Rolls-Royce started at once, and with the top up (it was cold after Egypt) they drove up Bayswater Road, past Winston's childhood home at 2 Connaught Place, down Park Lane – the lights in Cassel's Brook House shining in the dusk – and to 16 Berkeley Square. There the children were, outside the house, hoisting a 'Welcome home' banner as soon as they recognized the car, Marigold well wrapped up and in her nurse's arms. Jennie, who had waited inside, now emerged and came down the steps to greet them . . .

'Mama – Papa!' 'Well, my little Kittens . . .!' 'Randolph, how tall you've grown!' It was two and a half months since Clementine had seen them. At times of great emotion like this she quite cast off the stiffness she felt with her children and of which she was so ashamed.

A cab was summoned for Marigold and her nursemaid and the luggage, while the big children piled into the Rolls-Royce, Randolph demanding that the top should be folded down and becoming at once furious when he failed to get his way. Ten minutes later they were all ranging about their new house, shouting their comments at the tops of their voices, causing the neighbours to wonder what they had done to deserve such a family in their midst . . .

The first government purpose of Winston's trip to Egypt in March had been to preside over a conference for all the senior British officials in the Middle East. He had quit the War Office when Clementine had first left for the south of France, and had begun to immerse himself once again in colonial affairs.

It seemed curious to some of his contemporaries that an office he had seen as beneath him in 1915 he now coveted in 1921. The reason was that he had been seriously frustrated in most of his ambitions as Secretary of State for the Army, though better pleased with his achievements with the RAF. He had failed to create a combined Ministry of Defence; he had failed to persuade Lloyd George and the Foreign Office to take, and persist in, a stronger line on Russia (Winston believed that more serious intervention on the side of the anti-Bolsheviks could have toppled the revolutionary government); he thoroughly disapproved of the Army's commitment to reprisals in the ever-turbulent Irish scene; and above all, he had failed to persuade Lloyd George to come to grips with the confused, unsatisfactory and potentially dangerous situation in the Middle East.

As usual, *The Times* got it all wrong. When it was announced that Winston was to become Secretary of State for the Colonies, *The Times* was both inaccurate and misunderstanding of his motives when it wrote:

> Even Mr Churchill himself would probably say that the experiment [of running two departments] puts too great a strain on the Secretary of State for War. His change to the Colonial Office is a tacit admission that there is little hope of the project for a Ministry of Defence – supreme over Navy, Army and Air Force – being realized.

The dominions were not too pleased about the appointment. His notoriety as the originator of the Dardanelles catastrophe, in which so many New Zealand and Australian troops had perished, still persisted in these dominions; nor was his reputation high in Canada. The Manitoba *Free Press* commented facetiously:

He is going, by a display of his spectacular hustling qualities, so to fascinate the Dominions that they will forget these curious ideas that they have acquired about nationhood and equality, or, if they remain firm in their preference, he graciously meets their views and so lives in history as the emancipator of the Colonies.

In accepting the appointment in principle from Lloyd George on the first day of the new year, Winston persuaded him that he should set up a special Middle East department and gather together as soon as possible a conference in Cairo to settle the outstanding problems. These mostly stemmed from the territories won from Turkey in the war – particularly Iraq, Transjordan and Palestine, all once within the Turkish empire. Many of these territories would become independent eventually, but meanwhile their administration by Britain was complicated and expensive. To simplify and economize was the first concern of the Cairo Conference.

Everything was settled to Winston's satisfaction, and when he returned to London he made a long and detailed statement to Parliament, emphasizing that the nation was pledged equally to restore Arab 'influence and authority' as well as to establish a Jewish national home in Palestine. Expenditure on these territories, £80 million in 1919–20, would be brought down to less than £30 million. The speech was a massive success. 'One of your very best,' commented Lloyd George. 'Hearty congratulations.'

While in France on holiday before her trip to the Middle East, Clementine had written of the Irish troubles, including many murders. As always, she believed that her guidance was desperately needed: 'Do my darling use your influence *now* for some sort of moderation or at any rate justice in Ireland . . . It always makes me unhappy & disappointed when I see you *inclined* to take for granted that the rough, iron-fisted "Hunnish" way will prevail.' Clementine, always the pragmatist but ignorant of the deeply entrenched passions and prejudices of the divided country, really believed 'justice in Ireland' was achievable, and at once.

As Winston had been concerned with Middle East affairs in the first half of 1921, so he devoted the second half of the year to the negotiating of an Irish treaty that would bring peace to that long-suffering land – and not by 'Hunnish' methods, either. By patient, tortuous negotiations, a treaty leading to dominion status for, and eventually the independence of, all southern Ireland was drawn up and approved by the Dail (the lower house of the Irish parliament) in Dublin on 8 January 1922.

One day, Winston believed, Ulster would join with the new free southern Ireland. 'This is our policy,' he stated, but such a union would have to come about with the complete accord of Ulster in her own time. And until that time came, Ulster would be defended as part of the United Kingdom.

Later in January, Winston contrived to bring together at the Colonial Office the two Irish leaders, Sir James Craig for Ulster and Michael Collins for the Irish Provisional Government. He told later of how he left them alone, 'glowering magnificently', and how many hours later, after 'mutton chops, etc, were tactfully introduced about one o'clock', they at last emerged having reached complete agreement on every point.

This agreement may have satisfied the great majority of the people of southern Ireland, but the activities of the Irish Republican Army (IRA), which wished for no compromise, were stepped up and there were countless murders of 'moderates' and of prominent figures in England, in order to demonstrate the IRA's strength and determination. Among those who suffered assassination was Field Marshal Sir Henry Wilson, who was shot outside his front door in London on 21 June.

This outrage led to measures being taken for the protection of cabinet ministers. It was often said that life held few terrors for Winston, and he had already shown on countless occasions his extraordinary public bravery. But he did fear for his life in the air, which had perversely led to his fascination

431

with flying. And just as soon as he became a considerable public figure and circumstances hinted that he might become a target, his fear of assassination manifested itself. He hated deeply the thought of the bomb or the sudden bullet in the back, which would deprive him of any means to fight back.

Certainly the Wilson killing put the fear of God into Winston. He told Clementine that their bed was too obvious a target for a would-be assassin, and he took himself off to the attic, where he rigged a metal shield between himself and the door and slept with a revolver under his pillow. No such protection was offered to Clementine, who might, it could have been argued, be mistaken for him in the darkened bedroom.

A few weeks later Michael Collins himself was the victim of an IRA ambush in County Cork. He was only thirty. His dying message was, 'Tell Winston we could never have done anything without him.'

This accolade, together with the settlements reached in the Middle East, was sufficient to crown with success Winston's brief second period at the Colonial Office.

432

26

Times of Losses

The year 1921, which had turned out to be politically triumphant for Winston, was, by contrast, for Clementine and Winston a year of domestic anguish and pain – a year of sickness and death. Neither his mind nor hers turned naturally towards concepts of Old Testament retribution or payment for fate's gifts. But the fact remained that after the death of his cousin, which had brought such wealth and relief to them, the untimely deaths of friends and family became almost too frequent to be bearable.

It was only a few days after their return from Egypt that Clementine received a dreadful message from Paris. Her brother, Bill, had been found shot dead by his own hand in a hotel bedroom. He was Blanche Hozier's only boy, and as Nellie's twin, especially loved by her. Everyone liked Bill – so unselfconsciously good-looking, cheerful, and lively. He had been a great success in the regular Navy, had served at the Dardanelles, and had survived many dangers. After the armistice, he resigned his commission and went into business.

But Bill, like his mother and twin sister, was a compulsive gambler and several times had had to be bailed out of financial difficulties. Finally, Winston had made him swear never to play cards again. So far as anyone knew, he never did so and was not in any sort of financial plight at the time of his death. Perhaps he found the strain of meeting his pledge too much – and this was what Winston feared, to his great distress.

Clementine and Nellie hastened to Dieppe, where their mother had settled again after the war, and Winston postponed a conference of ministers at the last minute in order to come to the funeral. Clementine had earlier written, 'My poor Mama is so brave and dignified, but I do not think that she will recover from the shock & the grief. She sits in her chair shrunk and small . . .' In his will, Bill had bequeathed to Winston his treasured malacca gold-topped cane, which Winston used every day thereafter for the rest of his life.

The next blow was to Winston's family. At the end of May, only six weeks after Bill Hozier's funeral, Jennie had a painful fall. She was staying with Frances Horner at Mells, her husband being away on business in Nigeria, when she tripped while wearing very high-heeled shoes and fell downstairs. She was badly bruised and hurt her foot and ankle. Lady Horner thought she ought to return to London and see her own doctor.

Jennie had just moved to a house, 8 Westbourne Street, near to Clementine and Winston, and an ambulance met her at Paddington Station and carried her the short distance to her home. Her doctor diagnosed a broken foot and ankle – and worse, that gangrene had already set in. Her foot was removed at once and two weeks later she seemed to be on the mend. Winston telegraphed her husband in Africa that the danger was definitely over. On 24 June she answered Lord Curzon's letter of commiseration: 'I am getting on famously. My poor departed leg served me well for sixty-seven years & led me into some very pleasant walks. I am not to be pitied – now that my grand pain is over.'

Then, without warning, on the morning of 29 June she suffered a sudden, violent haemorrhage. Winston was called, and he ran across Sussex Gardens to her bedside. But she was already dead. Later, on the way out of the house, Winston spotted a letter waiting to be taken up to her room. It was from George Curzon, in reply to hers. He at once sat down and answered it, telling of her painless end after weeks of great discomfort. 'I do not feel a sense of tragedy, but only of loss,' he wrote. '. . . The wine of life was in her veins. Sorrows and storms were conquered by her nature & on the whole it was a life of sunshine.'

Tributes and letters arrived in hundreds at Sussex Square from all over the world. Jennie's death made lead news in *The Times*, the long obituary including this tribute:

A once brilliant and high-stepping figure has passed away. She had all the dash and her full share of the various talents for which American young woman-hood is remarkable. She flung herself ardently into many occupations and amusements: literature, hunt-ing, drama, politics and marriage. . . . Outside the field of strict politics, the dearest wish of this American wife of one Cabinet Minister and mother of another, was to render the United States and Great Britain intelligible to each other. . . . She had been beautiful; she had been brilliant; she filled her life with work and play.

Poor Jennie had been the subject of many jokes among society people for her marriages to men much younger than herself. After George Cornwallis-West ('The Old Wives Tale') left her and before she married again, Sir Henry ('Chips') Channon recalled, there was a brief confronta-tion between Jennie and her ex-husband and Mrs Patrick Campbell, whom Cornwallis-West had recently married: 'I was with Lady Randolph . . . and at the door we met the newly married couple, Mrs Pat and her husband, face to face. There was a tense moment, and we passed on: no word of greeting was exchanged. Soon afterwards Cornwallis-West left her [Mrs Campbell].'

Winston and Jack were among the few who recognized that Jennie hated to be alone and loved to have a man about the house, especially a young and lively man; but in spite of all the jokes, they knew that only her marriage to Randolph had been consummated. Jennie was buried in Bladon church-yard, Blenheim, alongside Randolph on 2 July 1921.

At the time of Jennie's death, elaborate plans for the summer holidays were already complete. All four children were to go to a small private hotel in their favourite seaside resort of Broadstairs in Kent in the care of a French nursery governess, Mademoiselle Rose. Clementine meanwhile was to take part in a tennis tournament at Eaton in Cheshire. In the middle of

August, the children would be taken by train up to Scotland, Clementine joining them *en route*, to the Duke and Duchess of Westminster at their remote estate far in the north of Scotland. Here Winston was to complete the family as soon as he could get away from London.

This timetable had been carefully worked out for the maximum contentment of all. The first break in its neat pattern occurred when Tom Walden, Winston's personal servant for so many years, and before that to his father, was taken ill early in August and had to be taken to St Mary's Hospital in Paddington. Winston visited him several times, but his health did not improve and he died there on 10 August. Winston had been much attached to him and would miss his cheerful presence as well as his intimate knowledge of his daily needs. The event drew his mind back to Khartoum all those years ago and the sudden shock and pain of George Scrivings's death.

News of another illness had already reached Winston by the time he returned from Walden's funeral on 12 August. The children at Broadstairs were very good about writing to Clementine in Cheshire. They told of sunny days and bathing, shrimping and boating. Marigold ('Baba' to the children, 'Duckadilly' to her mother and father) was rather poorly, was better today, then was not so well, ran her big sisters' reports. On 14 August, a message from Mademoiselle Rose brought graver news, and Clementine left her tennis and sped down to Broadstairs. Marigold's condition was clearly serious. The other children were packed off to Scotland in the charge of their nursemaid, Bessie; a specialist was summoned from London; and Winston joined the anxious party. The little girl had a raging temperature and a sore throat. She seemed to rally a little on 22 August, but was still desperately ill. The two parents took it in turns to sit at her bedside. On the same evening, her temperature rose again. Clementine was sitting beside her daughter when Marigold suddenly murmured, 'Sing me "Bubbles",' a song that held a special fascination for her.

Clementine began, 'I'm for ever blowing bubbles . . .'

Marigold put out her hand and whispered, 'Not tonight . . . finish it tomorrow.' The next morning, with Winston and Clementine at her bedside, the little girl passed painlessly away. Many years later Winston confided in his youngest daughter that 'Clementine in her agony gave a succession of wild shrieks, like an animal in mortal pain.'

The pain of the loss was almost beyond bearing. At least they were together and it could be shared – and they were moved and a little consoled by the messages of sympathy that again arrived in a torrent. Venetia Stanley wrote, 'What a cruel year this has been for you and this last blow seems the most cruel and wanton of all. That divine perfect little creature.' Pamela Lytton, Winston's old love from India days, wrote, 'What torture for a parent's heart.'

Perhaps the most moving of all the kind letters came from Aunt Cornelia, who still followed every domestic and political move of her favourite nephew.

> *My dear Winston,*
>   *What can I say to you in the awful crushing sorrow which has come on you & dear Clemmie. My heart just aches for you & I can think of nothing but you two sitting sorrowing in your loss. The only consolation, & it is a great one, you have each other. I can only pray you may be comforted & enabled to say 'Thy will be done.'*
>
>   *Yr fond & loving*
>   *Aunt C*

They buried Marigold at Kensal Green cemetery on 26 August and took the train to Scotland that night to join the children. 'Bendor' and Violet Westminster did what they could to make it a happy time for the children, who were more stunned and confused than grieving for their lost two-and-a-half-year-old baby sister. It was a fine, hot summer, and there were picnics in the matchlessly beautiful hills and valleys, and boating and riding. Then Clementine took the children back to London while Winston went on to stay at

Dunrobin with his old friend Georgie, the Duke of Sutherland, and his wife, Eileen, where he found more consolation in painting the scenery and the sea.

On one of the last days of Randolph's summer holidays, Clementine took all the children to Marigold's grave, and as they knelt round it a white butterfly settled on the flowers. 'The children were very silent all the way home,' she told Winston, and later she gave an account of driving Randolph back to Sandroyd with the two girls and with 'a splendid pic-nic' on the way.

The fates had not yet done with them in 1921. On 22 September, while Winston was still in Scotland, one of their oldest and dearest friends, Sir Ernest Cassel, suddenly died of a heart attack. Clementine, who had been telephoned by the old man's secretary, Miss Stella Underhill, in turn telephoned Winston at Dunrobin. To the dismay of Winston's host and hostess, this was the second time in eleven days that one of their guests had learned of a death to someone close to them. It was here, at about the same time of the day, that young Lord Louis Mountbatten had learned of the sudden death of his father, the one-time Prince Louis of Battenberg, Winston's First Sea Lord in 1914.

The following morning, Winston received a letter from Clementine: 'I have been through so much lately that I thought I had little feeling left, but I wept for our dear old friend; he was a feature in our life and he cared deeply for you . . . He was a true & loyal friend & a good man . . .'

And still the blows had not yet quite ceased, although the last one of the year was not a deadly one – just a nudge, really, to remind them that the fates were always there, ready . . .

Christmas Day was as happy for the children as Clementine and Winston could make it. The next morning, Winston went off to go boar-hunting in the south of France with 'Bendor'. It had been arranged for Clementine to join him after school began. But that same day, one after another, servants and children alike at 2 Sussex Square were struck down with 'flu, all with high temperatures. After all she had been through, Clementine was thoroughly frightened, but had little time to feel any alarm for she was run off her feet attending to the casualties. Nurses were brought in, but still Clementine collapsed, not from 'flu but total exhaustion. By the time she was fit to travel, she was in desperate need of the sun, rest and the comforting presence of Winston. When they parted, Clementine was with child again.

Although still grieving for her lost 'Duckadilly', as she would be for the rest of her life, Clementine enjoyed a happy period in France, and remained happy after Winston came home on 9 January and through the spring and summer in England. As for many women, pregnancy for her was accompanied by good health and less nervous tension. After Winston's return (and to his concern), she played a lot of tennis and with her partner succeeded in winning the Cannes Lawn Tennis Tournament Mixed Doubles Handicap – her best-ever tennis win.

She also emulated Winston by visiting the casino. Unlike others in her family, she never came near to succumbing to the gambling drug, but Winston was amused to hear that she was playing chemin-de-fer and that she had become temporarily so absorbed in it that in a reference to the expected baby, she suggested a bet on the colour of its hair – *'Rouge ou noir.'*

The memories of Broadstairs were too painful to let them consider their old favourite place for the summer holiday break. Instead, Clementine chose the exclusive seaside resort of Frinton, where there was good tennis and plenty of children for hers to play with. She rented a large house, packed up Sussex Square, and made off early in August with all her staff and luggage and bicycles. Winston was abroad, painting in the south of France, but would join them later in the month.

Frinton was a great success. Clementine was too far advanced in her pregnancy to play, but she watched Randolph and Diana partnering one another, lay in the sun, and read. 'I *am* so happy here – It's so comfortable and delicious. I hardly ever go outside the garden but just bask. The children scamper all over the place but I am not (just now) nimble enough to chase after them.'

Winston arrived from France on 24 August and immediately set about constructing Frinton's largest-ever and most elaborate sand castle, which, unlike Canute, defied the tide for several days. Clementine was so enchanted with Frinton that she suggested that they should buy a holiday home in the town; Winston had his eyes on bigger game.

For some time he had been taking an interest in houses for sale in Kent. Under Mrs Everest's influence as a child, he had acquired a special attachment to this county and particularly fancied the deep valleys and hills in the north-west. An agent had sent him details of a large manor called Chartwell, which he had visited and liked. It was near Westerham, tucked in a wooded valley, an Elizabethan house in poor order but with lovely views. There was a well – thus the name – a stream, and a lake in the garden that fell away from the house; a stone wall formed a terrace close to the house. It was on the market at £5,500, and Winston was offered a first option on it. Because of some dry rot revealed by a survey, he got the price down to £5,000.

None of this was known to Clementine, for Winston had decided, as a precaution against her opposition, to present her with a *fait accompli*. Julian Amery learned from Clementine how on a cold March morning, Winston had suggested a picnic with the children down in Kent. Well wrapped up, they drove off from Sussex Square in high spirits. Clementine was four months pregnant and looked forward to seeing the Kent countryside. At length, they drove into a drive, and Winston halted the car by an overgrown lawn close to a large empty house with views across a valley. It seemed a pleasant but curious place to picnic. Table and chairs were set up and halfway through their meal, Winston asked Clementine what she thought of the place. She said she thought it was very nice, but was horrified when he told her it was theirs. How could they possibly afford it? A catalogue of chilling anxieties rose before her.

In fact, the negotiations continued for some time, and it

was not until 15 September that Winston made a formal offer for Chartwell. On that same day, Clementine gave birth to a baby girl, so that it can be said that Chartwell and their last child, Mary, came into the lives of Winston and Clementine on the same day.

Winston had plans substantially to rebuild the manor before moving in, but politics claimed all his attention that autumn. Ever since the 'khaki' election of 1918 the victorious coalition government of Lloyd George had begun to reveal cracks, at first scarcely discernible, but soon widening as political issues became more intense. The Labour Party gained strength, partly as a result of the slump of 1921 and high unemployment – 'the men who won the war now in the dole queue.'

By the Treaty of Sèvres in 1920, Turkey had not only largely lost its old empire, but had had to submit to loss of control of the 'Zone of the Straits', which was neutralized and held by Allied garrisons. No one believed that this could hold for long, but few believed it would be challenged so swiftly by the Turks. This warrior-nation, inspired by a hero of Gallipoli, Mustafa Kemal Atatürk, soon began shamelessly to recover some of its lost territory. Sickened by the prospect of more fighting, France, Italy and Soviet Russia all came to terms with Atatürk. Only Turkey's traditional enemy, Greece, refused to give way; and alone among his ministers, with the notable exceptions of Birkenhead (F. E. Smith) and Winston, Lloyd George backed Greece. Suddenly the Prime Minister saw himself again as a great war hero at the helm of the battleship of state.

The Greeks folded before the fierce advance of the Turkish army (as usual, massacring on the way). At length, the Turkish van reached the boundary of British responsibility at Chanak, a small but vital town on the Asian side of the Dardanelles narrows. Suddenly another Dardanelles campaign threatened. Winston appealed to the dominions for support and got a dusty answer – only loyal New Zealand and Newfoundland offered military assistance.

The British commander was instructed to give the Turks

an ultimatum, ordering their withdrawal. He did not do so. With equal wisdom, the Turkish forces did not attack. Almost no-one in Britain wanted another war with Turkey, but Lloyd George misread the nation's mood and believed that by beating his breast he could get a new mandate for his coalition government in a general election.

As Winston's belligerent demands to support the anti-revolutionary forces in the Russian empire had failed, so his backing for a strong force, preferably international, to oppose Kemal Atatürk was another damp squib. 'Kemal ought to know,' he urged, 'that if he crossed the Straits with 60,000 rifles he would be met by 60,000 – to say nothing of the British Fleet.' It all sounded too much like 1915 over again.

Asquith and Bonar Law, both supporters of the original Dardanelles operation, would have nothing to do with this new sabre rattling. 'We cannot act alone as the policemen of the world,' Bonar Law declared; and Asquith condemned 'the amateurs in Downing Street'. Many Conservatives scented a breakdown in the coalition and the possible reinstatement of an untainted Conservative government.

While the diplomats worked to bring about a compromise (and succeeded at the Mudania Convention), a Conservative meeting voted 187 to 87 to fight an election as an independent party. Lloyd George resigned the same day, and the political troops took up their old battle lines, Winston backing Lloyd George on his coalition ticket.

As 1921 had been a year of political success and personal grief, 1922 was a year of family regeneration and happiness and, finally, political disaster. As he was about to set off to the hustings at Dundee, Winston, who had already seriously damaged himself in a polo accident,* was struck down by

---

*While he was staying at Eaton Hall in April with Bendor Westminster, Winston's polo pony threw him. His bruises kept him in bed for three days and he was ordered to take a complete rest for two weeks.

severe gastro-enteritis. On 17 October, his doctors decided he would have to prepare himself for an operation, and on the following day the surgeons removed his inflamed appendix.

Up at Dundee, everyone rallied round. Clementine threw herself with all the enthusiasm she could muster into the campaign. By 10 November Winston was well enough – though only just – to take the train to Dundee. He had to be carried everywhere, and he made his speeches sitting down. But his first and most important was one and a half hours long, and his oratory at least was unimpaired.

It was a short, rough campaign, and Clementine was fearful that his arrival was too late to restore his reputation among such a volatile electorate. She was right. The result, declared the day after polling, on 15 November, gave the Labour Party one of the seats and an independent the second, both of them with some ten thousand more votes than Winston. He appeared to take defeat well and was encouraged by being followed to the railway station by a group of students who cheered him all the way. Nationally, the Conservatives enjoyed a sweeping victory; the second party was Labour, and the Liberals, split between Asquith and Lloyd George, were a distant third, signalling their demise as a power in the land.

All through Winston's political career, like most people who write for the newspapers, he gave the press too much credit for influencing the voters. Certainly Thomson's local newspapers had been consistently hostile before and during the election run-up. But it was two different sets of circumstances that led to his defeat: the 'warmongering' (as many people saw it) against the Russians and the Turks, and the first-time-ever women voters. Women, as Clementine told him frequently, do not like constant belligerence in their candidates. 'The women put Winston out,' claimed Lord Esher. 'When he loses his temper he looks so damn ugly.'

Winston's friends were stunned by the defeat. What had he done to warrant the desertion of the citizens of Dundee? His old headmaster at Harrow, James Welldon (now Dean of Durham), wrote, 'You will, I think, allow me as an old friend to express my regret, I could almost say my indignation . . . Ingratitude, I am afraid, is apt to be one of the vices of democracy.'

'What bloody shits the Dundeeans must be,' exclaimed T.E. Lawrence.

But Winston tended towards forgiving his errant flock: 'If you saw the kind of lives the Dundee folk have to live, you would admit they have many excuses.'

After more than twenty years, he was without a seat in Parliament – never mind a ministerial appointment. For all his cheerful replies to the letters of outrage and commiseration, he was in a black frame of mind. A friend who dined with him found that he could scarcely bring himself to talk. 'He thought his world had come to an end – at least his political world. I thought his career was over.'

As an antidote to depression, weariness or weak health, there was nowhere to match the south of France, Winston believed. There were always friends to accommodate him, he relished the food and wines, the light suited his painting, and he could work long hours without distraction if he so wished. And then there was always the casino. Winston decided to go away for at least four months, through the worst part of the winter, and among other things, complete his own version of the history of the Great War. For this work he would be paid handsomely, and he hoped further to recover his reputation over his handling of the Admiralty and the Dardanelles campaign.

Winston returned to London in May to test the political waters, play polo and (a rather poor third at this time) see his family. He also sought news of the first volume of *The World Crisis*, which Butterworth had published on 10 April. It had already reprinted twice, he was told, and sales were over ten thousand. Its press had been a mixed one, some reviewers seeing it as a somewhat distorted apologia (as most historians judge it today), others praising it for its frankness.

Letters from friends and political associates were consistently full of praise. Margot Asquith, whose view of Winston was as variable as spring weather, described his book as 'a great masterpiece' and, as always, gave him firm political advice: 'Lie low; do nothing in politics, go on writing all the time & painting; do not join yr former colleagues who are making prodigious asses of themselves . . . Keep friends in every port – lose *no* one. Pirate ships are no use in times of Peace . . .'

There were just audible murmurs through the corridors of Westminster that the Conservative Prime Minister, Stanley Baldwin, looked on Winston favourably and might find him a safe seat and a senior Cabinet post. No-one now believed that his political career was over.

Clementine and Winston, on one another's nerves as never before, saw little of each other during that hot summer of 1923. Clementine took the children away to Cromer, near to Pear Tree Cottage, and with Goonie and her children living with them it was a repeat of that memorable and terrible summer of 1914. Winston occupied himself at Sussex Square correcting the proofs of the second volume of *The World Crisis* and speeding down to Chartwell to supervise the extensive work there. The house had been virtually gutted and its configuration had been so altered that it was almost unrecognizable from its previous appearance. The most significant addition was the large study he was having built for himself.

Clementine was becoming aware that Winston wanted to live there, giving up Sussex Square. She did not think that was a good idea, and there were many clamorous arguments about it. Although a countrywoman at heart, she also loved London and her London friends, and wanted to be near her mother and Goonie. She thought it bad policy for Winston to be so far from his friends and the seat of power. And she was also worried sick about the expense of the conversion of Chartwell, which was rising all the time and had already reached £15,000. As so often in the past, before the Irish inheritance, he had to reassure her: 'I do beg you not to worry about money, or to feel insecure. On the contrary the policy we are pursuing aims above all at *stability* . . .' But to instil a sense of security and stability into Clementine was

445

beyond even Winston's power, and it was very exhausting trying to do so.

Winston had rented a small house nearby while Chartwell was made ready for occupation, and the three older children were invited here later in August to view their future home, only for the weekend. For Winston, entertaining children was mainly a physical activity (no happy families or jigsaw puzzles) involving the construction of something spectacular, though very boisterous outdoor games, in which he invariably took the leading part, could be on the agenda. At Chartwell, where there was already so much building going on, he built an enormous tree house – or 'aerial house', as he called it – in a lime tree, with only nominal assistance from Diana, Randolph and Sarah. Knowing how Clementine would react to this news, he assured her that he would 'take the greatest precautions to guard against them tumbling down'. She was staying with their old friend Oliver Locker-Lamson and his Californian wife, Bianca, at the time. Locker-Lamson was one of the leading early RNAS pilots, had gone into politics, and was soon to become Winston's parliamentary private secretary.

During that summer, contact between Winston and Clementine was infrequent, and before she came down to see the progress on Chartwell and stay at the small rented house, Winston was off again, to go shooting boar with 'Bendor' Westminster at his hunting lodge at Minizan, or yachting in the Mediterranean. 'I write and work in bed all morning as usual,' he wrote to her. 'If the sun shines, I paint.' Gambling at the casino was not often mentioned, unless there were favourable results, but this time he could report winnings of £500 – the annual income of a professional family man. After an extended cruise in Bendor's yacht, with agreeable mixed company and several weeks of concentrated polo – he had brought his own string from Chartwell by train at enormous expense – a threatening political crisis brought him back to London in November.

The issue this time was unemployment, and Baldwin's proposal to introduce protection was countered by the Liberal

446

loyalty to free trade. For the last time, Winston stood as a Liberal. At the conclusion of an extremely acrimonious campaign he was defeated by the Labour candidate. This result reflected the mood of the nation, the Conservatives losing almost one hundred seats and Baldwin leading a minority party against any joint attack by the Liberals and Labour. This attack occurred only a few weeks later, and Ramsay MacDonald, the Labour leader, was called upon to form Britain's first-ever socialist government.

By letting in a socialist administration, the Liberals were finally and irrevocably discredited in Winston's mind. Early in February 1924 he decided to leave the cold country for a month to stay again with Bendor Westminster, where at Minizan he could write articles or paint all day, and start work on volume three of *The World Crisis* in guaranteed peace and quiet. This time he took Clementine with him as far as Paris, where they separated, she heading for Villa Lou Sueil above Eze-sur-Mer, just outside Monte Carlo. This was one of the residences of the Balsans. After her divorce from Sunny Marlborough, Consuelo had married a charming, rich, cultivated Frenchman, Jacques Balsan. Clementine felt totally relaxed and happy with this couple and felt free to unburden herself of her many worries over Winston and the children. 'It is a most peaceful & restful atmosphere.'

On 17 February, Winston received a telegram about a by-election in the Abbey Division of Westminster, a large and prestigious constituency embracing much of the heart of central London and the homes of some one hundred MPs. He went out hunting, the last time for some years, while he considered this news. 'There were no less than eleven pigs *embarras de choix*. I saw seven all together,' he told Clementine, 'including one quite big one, and two others separately galloping through the woods. After a long chase we finally slew a sow. She ran for twenty minutes as fast as the horses could gallop . . .' When he got back on his sweat-soaked horse he had made up his mind to throw in his hat. He sent a telegram to Clementine and prepared to leave the next morning.

Winston arrived back at Sussex Square to find a pile of interesting letters, and poor little Mary, who had just got over measles, down with 'flu and being nursed by Moppett.* Randolph, too, had 'flu. He was at school, but was shortly to come home to recuperate. These domestic upsets in no way disturbed Winston's programme: he merely passed on the news to Clementine. He had decided to stand at the by-election as an independent Conservative. Baldwin and other wise counsels thought this a mistake, while understanding that he did not wish to throw himself into the deep end of the Conservative pool when he had only just dragged himself out of the shallow end of the Liberals'. Regrettably, there had to be an official Conservative candidate, and many establishment people who wanted Winston back regretted that he did not wait for a decent interval. 'Not for the first time in his career [Mr Churchill] has mistimed an important decision and shown himself an essentially disruptive force,' claimed *The Times*.

A new friend and associate of Winston's disagreed strongly with this view and, like many others, got behind him and worked furiously on his behalf until polling day. He was Brendan Bracken, a remarkably shrewd young Irish journalist who was of remarkable appearance, too, with a great mop of bright red hair and thick, steel-rimmed spectacles. He had been recommended to Winston as an agent to sell his newspaper articles abroad, and he did so with great gusto and success. From the first time Clementine met him, however, she took a strong dislike to the man, who became one of the three hated 'Bs', with Birkenhead and Beaverbrook.

Just before polling day, Bracken wrote to his mother, 'We are deep in an awful fight at Westminster and I think we are

---

*Maryott Whyte, 'Moppett' or 'Nana,' was an indigent beloved cousin of Clementine's who, at the age of 27, came to 'help' with Mary and remained as part of the family for many years. She died in 1973.

going to win . . . We are fighting all the three great parties in the State & only Winston could pull it off.' He was very nearly right, too. Just as failure by a handful of votes at Oldham in 1901 was reported, to be corrected to victory almost at once, so Winston was told that he had won by 100 votes. Cheers arose from his supporters, and the news was telegraphed by the agencies all over the world. Alas, when the official figures were announced, it was seen that he had missed by just 43 votes.

This time Winston was not cast down in defeat, for he knew that with such a close result, when so much was loaded against him, it was only a matter of time before he made it back to the House. 'The result is really remarkable,' he wrote to Balfour. 'I am quite satisfied.'

27

Distant Thunder

Ramsay MacDonald's first Labour administration did not last
for long. It depended for its life on the Liberals and on the
extreme left wing of the party, which was full of ideas for
securing closer links with Soviet Russia. For a start, the
Russian Bolshevik government was formally recognized,*
in the expectation of a vast trade deal that would help to
cure British unemployment. Then there was the question of
the formidable pre-revolutionary Russian debts to Britain.
After a lot of haggling, these were settled by a British loan
to Russia. A commercial treaty of a limited nature followed.
But the arrangement was something of a dog's dinner – a
Russian dog's at that – and welcomed by few Britons.

Then there was the incitement to mutiny charge of 5
August against the writer of an article in the communist *Worker's Weekly* calling on the Army not to shoot
strikers if they were ordered to do so. This was suddenly
dropped, amid echoing cries that the socialist politicians
were interfering with the judiciary. On a vote of censure,
MacDonald's government was defeated because the Liberals
were not going to allow themselves to be tainted with the red
brush, and Lloyd George wanted to return to power with a
Liberal-Conservative coalition.

An exceedingly dirty campaign followed. A letter was 'discovered' and published, allegedly from G. Zinoviev, President of the Communist International, instructing Labour
supporters to indulge in a number of seditious activities.
Both the authenticity of this letter and its effect on the

---

*America did not recognize it until 1933.

voting were doubtful. But there was a stench of fear in the air that had an intimidating effect on the middle-class vote. 'No money for murderers,' was Birkenhead's clarion call, referring to the Russian loan. And Baldwin's renouncing of the proposed trade protection measure secured him many wavering Liberal voters.

Winston had been offered the Epping, or West Essex, division, and he fought a short, sharp campaign there for the Conservatives, supported by visits by Birkenhead, Austen Chamberlain and others. He made much of anti-Russian feelings among the electorate, especially in this middle- and lower-middle-class area. 'Why should we be lending money to Russia?' he asked a meeting on 19 October. 'During the war we lent the Russians £600 million when they were fighting bravely on our side, but the Bolshevists, when they made the revolution, deserted the allied cause and repudiated the debt. At the same time they stole £120 million of British property in Russia . . . This was the time when the Soviet Government came, with their hats on their heads, and asked for more.' Winston won at a trot, with 6,000 votes more than the combined opposition.

Baldwin was advised to keep Winston out of any combative appointment, like India ('Look at his violence over Ireland!' was a frequently heard accusation). But the new Prime Minister was recommended by Austen Chamberlain's half-brother, Neville Chamberlain, to give him the Treasury. Baldwin thought about this, then called Winston to his office.

With pipe (Baldwin) and cigar (Winston) well alight and filling the room with smoke, Baldwin asked him, 'Are you willing to help us?'

'Yes, if you really want me.'

'Will you be Chancellor of the Exchequer?'

Winston was astonished, by his own admission, and most uncharacteristically he began to suggest an alternative in Sir Robert Horne, who had previously served in this capacity. Baldwin had to explain at some length why he was not suitable and at last was reduced to asking, 'Perhaps you

451

will now tell me what is your answer to my question. Will you go to the Treasury?'

Now Winston wanted to retort, 'Will the bloody duck swim?' but decided on the more formal response. 'This fulfils my ambition. I still have my father's robes as Chancellor. I shall be proud to serve you in this splendid office.'

It was 5 November, and Westminster and Whitehall and the diners of Belgravia were treated to a fireworks display additional to that of the regular Guy Fawkes night as the word spread of Winston's appointment. Many people, however, refused to believe the rumour that steady Baldwin would make such a dangerous and precipitate decision as to elevate the guilty victim of the Dardanelles, the ex-Liberal star who had turned against the Conservatives in the past and had not yet even formally rejoined the Conservative Party – that Stanley Baldwin could promote Winston Churchill Chancellor of the Exchequer and second-in-line to the Premier seemed inconceivable.

Once again, the letters of congratulation poured in from his family, friends and supporters, while the appointment was, with few exceptions, condemned by the press. One of these exceptions was, surprisingly, *The Times*, which called it 'the most daring appointment . . . but we believe it to be a sound one . . . He has an immense opportunity of showing, what the public have often doubted, that he is capable not merely of brilliant imagination, but of taking the best advice and of forming a sober judgement on it.' Randolph, now at Eton, wrote that he thought it a good thing too.

For Winston, that meeting with Stanley Baldwin at 10 Downing Street was, until 1940, the greatest moment of his political life. The excitement and pleasure and pride were all the greater for the complete unexpectedness of the offer. So much of his political life had been devoted to the vindication of the family name and his father's achievements. This chancellorship had brought the late Lord Randolph so close to supreme power, only to have the premiership snatched from his grasp by Lord Salisbury. Now his son had the task of controlling and reforming the nation's finances, a task he felt utterly confident he could fulfil with glittering success.

That same evening he drove down to Kent to break the news to Clementine. It had been a lovely autumn day, and as dusk fell the bonfires glowed to right and left of the road and the rockets rose high in the sky. Clementine and he had only just moved into the rebuilt house with its completely transformed façade and roof line, and he experienced again the glow of pride he always felt approaching the manor house up the drive, with the laid-out gardens on either side, all his own achievement. And now, on this of all evenings, there was the triumphant news to savour and now to celebrate.

We can imagine Winston entering the house, like any professional man after a hard day's work, calling out, 'Clemmie! Clemmie, I have news – news!'

She rises from her drawing-room chair and joins him in the hall, where the maid is taking his black coat with the heavy astrakhan collar, and his black top hat . . .

They embrace briefly and kiss, and she takes his arm as they walk into the drawing room, where a log fire is blazing in the generous fireplace. 'A good journey, my dear? Tell me the news – what has happened?'

'Baldwin wants me to be Chancellor.'

Clementine is mystified. As he pours himself a whisky and water and her a glass of sherry, she says tentatively, knowing that he had expected an appointment but perhaps not the sinecure of the Duchy of Lancaster again. 'Well, that *is* good news.'

'*Good* news? – good news? Clemmie, it is almost unbelievable news – second to Baldwin's, the highest post in the land. It is splendid! Think – the salary is £5,000 and we shall have a fine London house* so that we can now sell Sussex Gardens and not even have to buy a flat . . .'

---

*11 Downing Street, traditionally the Chancellor's residence, is next door to the Prime Minister's.

The reality is beginning to dawn. Clementine, eyes wide and a great smile on her lips, runs across the room and throws her arms about Winston's neck. 'Oh, my darling Pig – you mean Chancellor of the Exchequer? Baldwin is sending you to the Treasury?'

'That's right, my little Kat. Did you think I was teasing you? Not over anything as important as this. It makes the Admiralty thirteen years ago seem like a puny affair.'

Stanley Baldwin had no reason to regret his dramatic appointment. First, it kept Winston out of mischief else-where, especially in any association with Lloyd George, which he had quite irrationally feared from the moment Winston had won at Epping. And second, he shared *The Times*'s confidence in Winston's ability to run the Treasury successfully. The sheer length of Winston's tenure of office was sufficient proof of that. In almost five years he introduced five budgets, and he could claim to be the first Chancellor to make finance clear to the financially illiterate, and even amusing. The House was always packed for his budgets, and even his worst enemies looked forward to his displays of glittering oratory.

In 1925 it was clearly his duty to return to the gold stand-ard, which was a blow for exporters but essential for the welfare of the nation. He introduced pensions for widows (shades of the pre-war Liberal administration) and reduced income tax, but this proud free trader also introduced import duty on silk and lace. In 1926, Winston introduced a five per cent tax on betting, and could be accused of, so far, favouring the rich, except that he 'raided' the Road (Licence) Fund, previously devoted to upkeep of roads and contributed by the few car owners. He also, the following year (1927), imposed or increased duty on wines, tobacco, imported car tyres, and tableware pottery. The last two budgets showed changes only in detail, except that the bookmakers, having shown a predictable skill in evading the betting tax, were instead now obliged to pay a £10 annual licence fee.

Most of his serious battles during his time at 11 Downing

Street were with the Governor and permanent mandarins of the Bank of England, whom he accused of attempting to run the nation's economy, and with the Navy. In a repeat of his period in office before he went to the Admiralty, he once again took issue with the Navy's expenditure. Under the Washington Treaty of 1922, there was an agreed limit between the great naval powers – Britain, the USA, Japan, Italy and France – on the numbers and size of men of war that could legitimately be built. But the Admiralty, with David Beatty now First Sea Lord, was much concerned about the size of the American navy and, more particularly, of the Japanese navy. The Royal Navy had to fight for every penny, and the Army, too, had to draw in its horns. Winston suggested that his old love, the cavalry, should be reduced to a token force, while there should be more dependence on the invention of which he rightly claimed to be patron – the tank.

By far the most memorable event associated with Winston during the 1920s was the general strike of 1926, in which he played a notable part. This clamorous and potentially disastrous struggle between Baldwin's government and the trades unions left its mark on people's memories of Winston long after his five unsensational budgets. Part of the strike's origins lay in Winston's insistence on returning to the gold standard in the first budget, which had the effect of raising the price of exported coal. The mine owners were already claiming that they were having the greatest difficulty in keeping their heads above water, but their balance statements pointed to a total profit of £58 million over the past four years.

Be that as it may, the mine owners announced in July 1925 that there would have to be a substantial reduction in miners' wages if the mines were not going to fall into bankruptcy. Baldwin's reaction was to appoint Winston as chairman of a special cabinet committee to consider the crisis between the owners and the Miners' Federation, and in particular the practicability and desirability of state control. In the end a subsidy of £10 million was agreed to by the committee and, after consultation, by the two sides.

455

However, by April 1926, with no improvement in the output and sale of coal, the mine owners repeated their earlier threat of wage reductions. When the miners rejected them, they were locked out and coal production ceased. The Trades Union Congress (TUC) then ordered a general strike, to begin at midnight, 3–4 May, in their support. But before this came into effect the typesetters at several newspaper offices refused to handle material hostile to the miners and the TUC, and the battle was on. The Government had about twenty-four hours to prepare the nation for a total absence of railways, buses, newspapers and mail, food, and fuel distribution, and the thousand other facilities that make a complex modern nation operate. All that they had to limit, very slightly, the damage and confusion, were the armed forces, the police and volunteers from the public – who rallied to the cause in hundreds of thousands. Above all, there had to be a source of news and information.

Baldwin declared that there must be a government newspaper and that Winston should be appointed Commander in Chief, a job that would tax even his great powers of speed, decisiveness and organization. Later, when it was all over, Baldwin congratulated himself on his choice, Winston's success, and the way it kept him out of mischief. During this period his natural belligerency could, it was thought, compromise delicate negotiations with men he might regard as traitors hell-bent on communist revolution. (In fact, Winston showed himself to be mild and placatory during the emergency debate in the Commons.)

The *British Gazette*, against the most appalling difficulties, overcome by Winston as they arose, was first published in an edition of 230,000 copies on the morning of 5 May. Winston wrote the leading article, which was decidedly partisan and suggested that the TUC intended to become 'masters of the whole country'. Soon the *Gazette* was selling more than two million copies, and volunteers were driving it all over the country; there was even an air delivery on a modest level. The last edition, on 13 May, headlined its own demise thus: 'Surrender received by Premier in Downing Street'. The

TUC had been forced to capitulate. However, the coal strike continued for many weeks, and great was the suffering of the miners. The importation of foreign coal rose with every day that passed, and many of the mine owners' customers never returned.

Winston could now give his full attention again to the Treasury and to the economic problems that had been exacerbated by the strike.

While managing efficiently the economy of the nation, Winston, even in his fifties, appeared to be still incapable of coping with his family's finances. Age had not tamed his mother's extravagances, and it was evident that the inherited improvidence was as enduring in her son. If Winston had set his heart on something – be it a bottle of hundred-year-old brandy or a long holiday in an extremely expensive French hotel – the cost somehow fled from sight. Clementine had really believed that their money worries were over with the Irish inheritance coming into their hands. There were a few glorious, carefree months, but then Chartwell, with its insatiable appetite for funds and which Clementine so much hated, came into their lives.

In 1924 Winston sold the Irish property, at one stroke writing off the £4,000 per annum it brought in. Not all his capital was at once swallowed up by Chartwell expenditure, but the interest on his capital was greatly reduced. This did not trouble him, as early experience had taught him that he could always considerably augment his income by writing, and this he confirmed once again when he was offered £10,000 by Walter Harrap and £5,000 by Charles Scribner in America for a life of his ancestor, the first Duke of Marlborough.

But in September 1926, in between complex negotiations over a few shillings a week with the striking miners, Winston became aware of serious personal over-expenditure, which Clementine had been aware of for a long time. Winston had reckoned that they could be comfortable on £10,000 per annum, but they were spending much more than that. Regarding himself as a country gentleman with an estate, he had thrown himself into farming at Chartwell. In turn, he had dabbled in beef cattle, sheep, pigs and hens. All proved disastrous. Undeterred, in April he planned to build a dairy for a milking herd. When he proposed this to Clementine, who was away at the time, she wrote a seven-page letter in an attempt to deter him from this new schoolboy's folly, as she saw it.

Now, five months later, he proposed, but did not seriously implement, an economy programme, with Chartwell to be let in the following summer and all the stock except two polo ponies sold. In winter they were to visit Chartwell strictly on a daily basis, with hamper food from 11 Downing Street. The only exception was his study there, so that he could work on his books and articles between the long sessions of estate construction. This construction ranged from a walled kitchen garden (economy again) to a complete cottage for the two older girls, from afforestation to the felling of mature trees for the log fires or to widen the views from the house.

With the same meticulous care he applied to national economies through the Treasury, he laid down a family list that included toothpaste and boot polish, as well as the cost of cigars and wines, laundry allowance, and numbers of guests: 'We must invite visitors very rarely, if at all, other than Jack and Goonie.' But unlike Treasury economies, which were implemented by armies of keen-eyed civil servants, Chartwell economies depended on only the master of the house, widely known for his forgetfulness. Soon names reappeared in the visitors' book, for lunch or dinner or for a night or two. Apart from Jack and Goonie, the most frequent appearances in this leather-bound book were the Birkenheads (the F.E. Smiths), Brendan Bracken and Professor Frederick Lindemann ('the Prof').

Like Winston's, Lindemann's mother was American: she had been taking the cure at Baden-Baden when he was born. His father was Alsatian. Lindemann had worked in the physical laboratory of the Royal Flying Corps (RFC) during the war, learning to fly and studying the dreaded spin by deliberately going into one and contriving to get out of it.

He went to Oxford in 1919, where he became Professor of Experimental Philosophy (physics), retaining the chair until a year before he died, in 1957.

Lindemann became a close friend of Winston's when he was out of Parliament.

> *It was principally to the Prof that my father owed his remarkable insight into the heart of abstruse scientific matters* [wrote Sarah Churchill]. *He was a vegetarian, a bachelor and a teetotaller, all of which things my father deplored . . . He was part of our Chartwell life . . . His exterior was conventionally forbidding: the domed cranium, the close-cropped iron-grey hair which had receded as if the brain had pushed it away, the iron-grey moustache, the sallow complexion, the little sniff which took the place of what normally would have been a laugh; yet still he could exude a warmth that made scientific thinking unfrightening.*

Others who figured at Chartwell were Eddie Marsh, who remained Winston's private secretary, and Bob Boothby, who became his parliamentary private secretary. Then there were the other regulars: Archie Sinclair and his wife, Marigold (after whom Clementine's late daughter had been named); Duff and Diana Cooper; Max Beaverbrook; Violet and Maurice Bonham Carter and their children (Winston was godfather to the eldest); Lloyd George; and another who made a deep impression on the children, T. E. Lawrence, who arrived without notice on his motorbike as an RAF aircraftsman and changed into the robes of a prince of Arabia to dine.

None of these people, or the many other friends and politicians, felt any hint of austerity in the proffered hospitality, and the cost of entertaining was prodigious. But this was exceeded by the weekly wages bill. Besides Bessie and Cousin Moppett, two servants were needed for the pantry and two more for the kitchen, as well as two housemaids and an odd-job man. Then there were two stenographers for Winston (one for very late night work) and another – Margery Street (Streetie) – for Clementine. For outside work, besides the chauffeur, there were a bailiff for the farmwork, a groom, and three full-time gardeners.

This estate and this staff would be modest for a landed gentleman with a substantial income (and no doubt a title to go with it), but for a working politician on a salary and extremely modest private means, it was a formula for disaster, and in the end Winston was prepared to sell to anyone with £25,000: no buyer was forthcoming.

If Chartwell had gone the children would have been almost as disappointed as their father. It had all that was best and most exciting in their lives: games, riding, swimming, tree-climbing, and for some of them and in emulation of Winston, bricklaying and painting. All of them depended for company, fun and reassurance on one another and their cousins. It has been written that Clementine was too busy looking after Winston to have much time for her children. This is true only in a convoluted way. She could have given adequate time to her children if she had not been obsessed with Winston's wrongdoings and malpractices – as she saw them. He was, quite simply, not to be trusted. As it was, her children received a negligible or even negative priority in Clementine's consideration.

It was the minutiae of her husband's political life, his awful cronies – especially Brendan Bracken – and his extravagant life-style, cancelling out all her lovingly conceived economies, that engaged her fretful attention.

Beside all this, her children were secondary targets. But they could not be entirely ignored. She reserved her strongest dislike for her two eldest, Diana and Randolph. Once Diana confided tearfully to her cousin, Anita Leslie, 'I am so unhappy and Mummy is horrid to me because I haven't been a success. I have sandy eyelashes.' Diana longed to leave home and searched hopefully for a husband as soon as she 'came out'. She found one in John Bailey, the son of Winston's friend Sir Abe Bailey, a millionaire South African mine owner. They married on 12 December 1932. In 1935 she

460

got a divorce and married Duncan Sandys, MP, and that was much better, for a while.

During school holidays and at weekends, Jack and Goonie and their children, augmented now by a pretty and exceedingly bright daughter, Clarissa (born in 1920), were nearly always at Chartwell. Jack at this time – when Winston was Chancellor of the Exchequer – was somewhat embarrassed, as a stockbroker, by their relationship around the budget period, when all finances were so sensitive, but their relationship remained as solid as it had always been.

Clementine was remembered by the children, and especially by Randolph and Diana, for obliging them to play tennis, an activity that these two loathed.

> She just loved to organize and had no truck at all with any opposition [Randolph's cousin Anita recalled]. We also hated being forced to act in plays, which Clemmie loved and always assumed everyone else loved, too. When Winston got wind of one of these plays, then he insisted on being stage-manager, ordering everyone around and quarrelling loudly with Clemmie over details.

Of all Winston's and Clementine's children, Randolph from early childhood remained the most dreadful problem. All the qualities of his grandfather and father seemed to have been inherited by him in a topsy-turvy mélange. He was self-indulgent, impetuous, selfish, cruel, emotional and, lacking all mother love, desperately insecure. He also inherited Winston's quick mind and retentive memory, and he wrote well, but almost indecipherably. His charm gained him many friends, but his overbearing, aggressive manner and plain rudeness lost him many more. He was sublimely good-looking as a boy and young man. Of him Anita Leslie wrote:

> No one ever found [him] more abominable than during the first half hour of acquaintance. But those

who did not get angry had to like him even if they were annoyed with themselves at the time. What no-one really appreciated was Randolph's craving for affection.

In Winston's eyes, Randolph could rarely do wrong. But he would rebuke him loudly and vociferously if he was rude to his mother at table. Clementine had the unfortunate habit, which Winston hardened himself to, of talking about people's ailments and organs during meals. Randolph was squeamish about this sort of thing and would tell her to shut up and threaten that he would be sick. Winston would then order the boy to apologize and, when he refused, send him from the room.

While they were still at Lullenden, the American financier and patrician Bernard Baruch was a frequent visitor – as he was for many years after. Winston, for some unknown reason, always called him 'Barney'. This happened to coincide with a popular song called 'Barney With the Goggly Goggly Eyes', a gramophone record of which someone else had brought the children as a present. Randolph conceived a great joke, planting the gramophone close to the door.

When he saw the American financier's limousine drawing up, Randolph put on the record to coincide with his father's appearance. Baruch was entering the room, Winston advancing to greet him, when both men became aware of the playing record. 'Barney . . . goggly eyes . . .' Winston, in a towering rage, seized the record and smashed it on the floor. 'I thought this a frightful thing to do,' Peregrine Churchill remembers.

Later, Randolph's gambling also aroused Winston's fury, which was fuelled by fear that it could ruin him as it had ruined his sister-in-law and brother-in-law, and so many of his own relations. It had, he was obliged to admit, damaged himself a great deal, too. When Randolph wagered £600 on the outcome of the 1931 election, and lost, and then appealed to his father, he received a letter full of invective and disgust. The young man – he was 20 – was living on an allowance after quitting university, but ran a car and kept a chauffeur.

Winston paid up, as he had to on several other occasions when Randolph threatened bankruptcy and shame on the family if he was not bailed out. But pathetically, Winston loved the boy and still strove to believe that he could see in him the qualities and potential of his own father.

Randolph's younger sister Sarah recalled games and pranks at Chartwell when Jack and Goonie's children were staying with them. She would team up with her near-contemporary Peregrine ('Pebin') for energetic games in the woods and recovery in the tree house, while John paired with Randolph.

> While Pebin and I were scampering about in the water garden or the lofty seclusion of our tree-top, the other children led by Johnny Churchill got up to the most extraordinary antics. Johnny was a very fine athlete. He would do the most daring things, running along the edge of the roof, bounding out of windows: this was very difficult for Randolph who did not possess his athletic prowess, but he wouldn't give up and sometimes he had some nasty falls in trying to follow Johnny, and often my heart would be in my mouth.

Peregrine recalls one Christmas at Chartwell when he and Sarah were put in separate rooms for the first time. They were thirteen and were puzzled. When Peregrine asked his mother why, she responded hesitantly, 'Well . . . well, er, you might marry Sarah.' The two children did not actually have that in mind. But, as Peregrine learned later, Clementine, fruit of a cousin-to-cousin relationship herself, would have approved of the match. Peregrine was also Clementine's favourite amongst her and Goonie's children. When she died at the end of 1977, she left him a large sum of money.

Sarah was a very much less flamboyant child than her sisters and Johnny Churchill, and from her own account found the conversation at meals – usually between Winston and

Randolph, and highly competitive – intimidating. She later learned to cope with all this masculine egotism, with the help of a great deal of drink, and became especially close to her father. 'My love for him grew and my hero-worship of him never lessened, but now it was tangible. I wanted to be in the league of people who, if they could not help, at least understood where he was trying to go with an idea.'

The love was reciprocated by Winston, and even (just) survived her running away to America and marrying for a while a popular comedian, Vic Oliver. But drink and an inherited unsteady temperament remained problems for her and for Diana. As for the last, Mary, she could do no wrong with Clementine and Winston: a cheerful, compliant child, she was a delight to have about the house.

In 1929 Baldwin's government failed to achieve a new mandate from the people and fell. In the election Winston was returned at Epping, with a reduced majority. Out of ministerial office, he decided to make a three-month tour of the USA and Canada. He had never been to the West Coast, he planned to revisit the places he first knew in 1900, and he wished to meet the great figures in industry and politics and to promote the last volume of his Great War history, *The Aftermath*. With him he took Randolph, who had just left Eton and was shortly to go up to Oxford; his brother, Jack; and Jack's Johnny. On 3 August the party embarked on the *Empress of Australia* for Quebec. Among the fellow passengers was Leo Amery, whose bottom Winston had once kicked at Harrow and who had subsequently become a friend and political colleague. On the voyage and the subsequent railway journey across Canada, stopping frequently for introductions and speech-making, Randolph was much impressed by the wildness of the land and the beauty of the mountains and lakes. 'Randolph has conducted himself in a most dutiful manner and is an admirable companion. I think he has made a good impression on everybody,' Winston reassured Clementine. The impression he made on many fellow diners (and waiters) was his remarkable capacity for brandy. Later,

Winston wrote of his oratorical skill. 'He speaks so well, so dexterous, cool & finished . . . I love him vy much.'

Later, when they crossed into the USA and drove down to San Francisco, staying at 'dry' hotels, Randolph ensured that there was always liquor available – 'an unfailing Ganymede', as he was to remain for all his life. Farther south, the party stayed with William Randolph Hearst at San Simeon, a figure who greatly intrigued them all: '. . . a grave simple child – with no doubt a nasty temper – playing with the most costly toys,' Winston told Clementine. 'A vast income always overspent: ceaseless building & collecting not vy discriminating works of art: two magnificent establishments, two charming wives [actually one wife and Marion Davies]; complete indifference to public opinion . . .'

They enjoyed the best of everything in Los Angeles and Hollywood, all provided by the banker James R. Page. 'You could not help liking Charlie Chaplin,' Clementine was told. 'The boys were fascinated by him. He is a marvellous comedian – bolshy in politics & delightful in conversation.'

Then they worked their way east, taking in the Grand Canyon; thence to Chicago, where Winston's friend Bernard Baruch met them; and thence to New York, where Winston set himself up with contracts for extremely well-paid articles. On royalties for future and past books alone he had made £6,700 as well as £2,000 for articles. 'I am trying to keep £20,000 fluid for investment & speculation,' he wrote ominously in September 1929. After visiting the Civil War battlefields the party returned to New York at the end of October and witnessed at first hand the Stock Exchange crash. 'Under my window, a gentleman cast himself down fifteen storeys and was dashed to pieces.'

Winston returned to London with his party, in a somewhat chastened financial state of mind. After all his boastings to Clementine, he had to confess when he met her that they had lost no less than £40,000 in the crash. But he also reassured her that he would soon recover the money through his pen and from lectures. To accelerate this recovery, in spite of his interesting but uncomfortable experience in New York, he judged that 'the land of opportunity' would serve him best. With his agent promising him a minimum payment of £10,000 for a lecture tour, Winston embarked on board the German liner *Europa* with Clementine and Diana for New York, arriving on 11 December 1931. The theme of his lectures, as always, had a strong element of Anglo-American fraternity – 'Pathway of the English-speaking people' was typical.

Alas, Winston had delivered only one lecture, at Worcester, Massachusetts, when he met with a serious misfortune on Fifth Avenue, in New York City. This time his accident-proneness had near-fatal consequences. Forgetting about right-hand traffic, he was crossing the avenue on foot to seek out Bernard Baruch's house when he was struck by a car. He was thrown a number of yards and suffered head, chest and thigh injuries. After all the bullets and shell splinters that had somehow missed him in wars and campaigns over the past thirty-five years, and the number of motoring accidents which had left him unhurt, it was ironical that a motor car made him its target on the battlefield of Fifth Avenue.

After more than a week in hospital, Clementine and Diana at his bedside, and the bed itself heavy with cables and letters of concern and commiseration, Winston was allowed to leave, with the prospect of two more weeks confined to the Waldorf-Astoria Hotel. True to the spirit of journalists, and anyway keen to write off the cost of the hospital, Winston wrote a vivid piece for the London *Daily Mail*. 'I certainly suffered every pang, mental and physical, that a street accident or, I suppose, a shell wound can produce,' he wrote. 'None is unendurable.'

Three weeks in the warmth and peace of Nassau helped Winston to recover, and he was able to deliver his next lecture in New York on 28 January 1932. As Clementine predicted, his lectures and accompanying adulation accelerated his recovery. The little party were back in England by 17 March. There on the jetty, surrounded by anxious and thankful friends and family, was a shining new Daimler motor car: a gift from his admirers, who hoped he would not crash it too soon.

*

While on this American lecture tour Winston thought it wise to give himself armed protection against assassination. This was in addition to the private detective, W. H. Thompson, who served him for so many years and was like one of the family. After years of being a potential target for extreme republican elements from Ireland, he now knew that Indian fanatics were the first threat.

By this time, Winston was becoming more and more isolated from Stanley Baldwin's official Conservative policy on the future of India. Since his service in that subcontinent as a young soldier, Winston had become deeply concerned with every aspect of Britain's attitude to India, its people and its politics. He felt a strong sense of paternalism and responsibility towards this enormous part of the empire, which Britain had governed – he believed – justly and to the incalculable benefit of the people. Britain had created for India an army, a civil service, communications (the Indian railway system was one of the greatest and most efficient in the world), and a freedom from strife, as far as this was achievable with Hindus and Moslems for ever at one another's throats.

While the Conservatives believed that India should be gently edged towards dominion status, like Canada, Australia and New Zealand, and eventually to independence, Winston had always held that this policy was premature, that given freedom the minority groups and the 'untouchables', at present enjoying some form of protection by the British, would soon be wiped out. Equally fearful, strife between the two massive religious groups could lead to civil war and the loss of millions of lives.

There was plenty of support in the country and from some one hundred members of Parliament for this policy of caution towards Indian independence. But to Stanley Baldwin and the hard core of the Conservative front bench, Winston's hostility towards official policy on this and other subjects was regarded as typical Churchill unreliability. On 27 January 1931, Winston severed himself from the leadership and the policymaking powers of the party by writing a letter to

Baldwin suggesting that he 'ought no longer to attend the meetings of your "Business Committee"'. Baldwin replied, thankfully, the following day that he was 'convinced that your decision is correct in the circumstances'.

But this severance was much more than a disagreement with Baldwin and the hierarchy. The grey men of the Conservative Central Office, who had detested the rehabilitation of Winston-the-turncoat, seized this opportunity of further discrediting him to ensure he was never offered an important office again after the Conservatives returned to power. It was at this time that the record, the ill health (incurable syphilis), and the drunkenness of his father were recalled. These had been given some sort of highly disreputable credence as long ago as the early 1920s when copies of Frank Harris's banned book *My Life and Loves* found their way into the country. This was specific about Lord Randolph's seductions and consequent syphilis, which supposedly had caused his lingering death. Now, among Winston's implacable enemies, there was much talk of 'like father, like son'. These false whispered accusations were very difficult to rebut, and in unison with character assassination, there now stalked the threat of physical assassination from Indian fanatics.

Winston succeeded in distancing himself even farther from the inner establishment of the Conservative Party over the abdication crisis in late 1936. Almost from the first day of the reign of King Edward VIII on 20 January gossip about his relations with the American divorcée Wallis Simpson, who lived in London with her second husband, began to spread. By early December, it was known that she was applying for a divorce, the inevitable conclusion being that when the divorce was declared absolute, the King would wish to marry her.

Winston was a leading figure, largely behind the scenes, in the constitutional crisis that followed. He had known David, as he was known to the royal family, since he was a young man, even before he became the Prince of Wales. They had shared many experiences and had played many chukkas of polo together over the years. Winston had also observed how the King became a transformed being in the presence of the woman he adored.

While Winston accepted that Mrs Simpson could never become Queen, he deplored what he regarded as the hasty bullying tactics of Stanley Baldwin as Prime Minister, who wanted an instant decision. Winston regarded it as essential for the King to be given time for some formula to be worked out, arguing reasonably that the divorce would not become absolute until April at the earliest. All that the King had to do to avoid the national catastrophe of abdication was to make a declaration that he would not marry 'contrary to the advice of his ministers'.

Winston's few supporters did not include Clementine, who deeply disapproved of Edward VIII's irresponsibility, as she saw it, and there were pealing rows on the subject at home. David, Prince of Wales, was anyway one of the great majority of Winston's men friends for whom she had no time at all and did not hesitate to show it.

The King was grateful for Winston's support and several times asked for his advice. But quite honourably, he found himself unable to accept Winston's formula of playing for time when he knew that his fundamental resolve would be unchanged no matter how many months were allowed to pass. This, in effect, was tantamount to standing down from the throne.

In the House of Commons, where the chamber rang with condemnation of the King and determination to be rid of him, Winston time after time pleaded for delay and patience. Finally he was shouted down from both sides, Winston's last words to Baldwin, amidst the hullaballoo, being, 'You won't be satisfied until you have broken him, will you?'

Baldwin was generally seen as a man gallantly handling a crisis of unprecedented delicacy and difficulty; Winston as a man stabbing him in the back. In this entire unsatisfactory decade, Winston's stock never stood so low as at the end of 1936.

As well, family and financial affairs descended to the

469

depths in the mid-1930s. The two elder daughters married badly, Chartwell remained a terrible burden, Randolph remained a perennial worry, and his own relationship with Clementine was from time to time tempestuous and unhappy. There was never for one moment a threat of the marriage breaking up, and when they were apart their letters were as loving as ever. But the strains were very great, further burdened by Winston's frustration and Clementine's longing to be away from Chartwell or to be there sometimes alone. With all the children 'off their hands', except Mary, who was more like an only child and away at boarding school for much of the time, the bond of child responsibility had much weakened, and having three more-or-less alcoholic children is no great bond in a marriage.

It was also a decade when they had to face the death of some of their closest friends. Edwin Montagu had died early, back in 1924. Sunny Marlborough died on 30 June 1934, much mourned by them both, for he had always been kind and loving towards them, and their friendship had easily survived political differences. His eldest son, Bert, inherited the dukedom, and he and his wife, Mary, continued the same hospitality at Blenheim.

An even greater loss for Winston, but *not* for Clementine, was F. E. Smith – first Earl of Birkenhead – at the early age of 58, on 30 September 1930. He had been the closest of all Winston's friends, personally and politically, and there was added pathos in the fact that he had killed himself with drink. F. E. had all his life been a prodigious drinker, except for one miserable year on the wagon. He once told Bob Boothby, 'Without drink, not only would I have done nothing with my life, I would not have *wanted* to do anything.' His biographer recalls an important case in Leeds when F. E. was still in his thirties:

> While lunching with his clients and their lawyers, at the end of the meal, which had naturally been accompanied by wine, he ordered port. When a glass was brought, F. E. looked at it contemptuously and said

470

that he meant a *bottle*, and proceeded to demolish it;
after which he returned to court and demolished the
opposition.

Clementine told his widow, Margaret, 'Last night Winston
wept for his friend. He said several times, "I feel so lonely."'

Clementine, too, lost several close friends, but perhaps
the most poignant loss for her was the death of Sidney
Peel, who had sought her hand so ardently and for so
long, and in his distress had vowed never to speak to her
again, unlike Winston's pre-marital loves, especially Pamela
Lytton, who remained friends for life. Reading of Peel's
death, Clementine, far from home, told Winston, 'I closed
my eyes; Time stood still, fell away, and I lived again those
four years during which I saw him nearly every day – He was
good to me and made my difficult rather arid life interesting
– But I couldn't care for him & I was not kind or even very
grateful.'

Clementine and Winston's leisure activities kept them apart
for longer and longer periods. Winston liked hunting boar,
playing polo and painting. He had given up polo on his fiftieth
birthday, with much regret, and in the same year Clementine
suddenly started skiing, with Mary, who, at 14, was at the
more suitable age for this sport. This separated the parents
for many weeks in the winter. At about the same time, in the
mid-thirties, Clementine discovered another new pleasure,
cruising.

The richest of all their rich friends, except perhaps Bendor
Westminster, was Lord Moyne, Walter Guinness, of the
brewing family. Moyne was 54 and still extremely active, had
won the DSO in the war, had been an MP, and was a keen
archaeologist and zoologist. He was also extremely amusing
and well informed, a companion for all seasons. In October
1934, Moyne and his wife, Evelyn, invited Winston and
Clementine on a cruise to the Middle East, which included
trips to famous archaeological sites: Winston would have
preferred battlefields. Clementine decided that she loved

471

nothing better than cruising with compatible company in Moyne's luxurious yacht, *Rosaura*. A few weeks after they returned home, the Moynes invited them to go away with them again. Clementine wanted to accept; Winston said no, for he was too busy on his multi-volume *Marlborough*. But seeing how much Clementine wanted to accept, he agreed, rather reluctantly and uncharacteristically, that she should go alone. So on 18 December 1934, the whole family came to see her off on a holiday to the other side of the world that would keep them apart for one of the longest periods in their married life.

At first the party in the *Rosaura* was a small one: Kenelm Lee Guinness, Moyne's cousin, a motor racing 'ace' and founder of the spark-plug firm; his wife; and a young, handsome, and amusing bachelor, Terence Philip. Moyne himself and Vera – the soon-to-be-divorced wife of Sir Delves Broughton – adventurously flew out to Rangoon and joined them there. Madras, Celebes, Borneo, New Guinea, Great Barrier Reef, Sydney and Wellington, New Zealand, were other places they visited, culminating in a voyage round the more succulent Pacific islands.

Nothing like this had ever before happened to Clementine, who might have been missing Winston (she wrote thus in every letter), but was benefiting from a relief from the tension of running him and Chartwell. 'Since Nouméa,' she wrote, 'we have been crossing the trackless ocean calling at various islands. We are quite out of touch, the waters round some of these islands are uncharted . . .'

She was also, for the remainder of the long voyage, out of touch with reality and romantically in love with Terence Philip, although she would never go further than to confess, 'He made me like him.' They fished together, made expeditions to uninhabited little coral islands *à deux*, and talked for long into the tropical night about his world of art and London galleries. Her youngest daughter has written of this time: 'She lived in a dream world of beauty and adventure. She tasted the always heady elixir of admiration, and knew the pleasures of companionship in trivial doings and sayings.'

Clementine was away from home for more than four months. 'It's very nice to be back,' she wrote to a friend, 'but Oh Dear I want to start out again very badly! Mr Pug is very sweet but now he says "NO".' Perhaps it was as well for the security of their marriage that the third cruise in the *Rosaura* was less idyllic than the second. It was 1938, and they left behind a country tense with anxiety about the depredations of the odious Adolf Hitler but divided about how to deal with him. In addition, Moyne had to combine work with pleasure and examine the social conditions in the West Indies, which were depressing to anyone with a conscience.

One night, while they were all listening to a radio broadcast from London in which Winston's much-proclaimed view of the Government's appeasement policy was attacked, Vera Broughton called out, 'Hear, hear!' Clementine might have been able to tolerate this lack of tact, but not their host's failure to rebuke the woman. She at once went ashore and booked herself a passage home, just as, so many years before, she had flounced out of Blenheim. In neither case would she yield to remonstrances or apologies.

Clementine returned to a nation as torn politically as the passengers of the *Rosaura* had reflected in miniature, with Winston's fight for rearmament and the destruction of pacifism at its height.

'The Inevitable Prime Minister'

The ten years between 1929 and 1939, when Winston held no government appointment, when he was subjected to more public disparagement than at any other time in his life, was a period when he contributed as much towards the survival of the nation's democratic freedoms as at any other time in his life. 'The years in the wilderness': he never minded that appellation; he may well have invented it. He was certainly as proud of what he did during the last years of peace as he was of his accomplishments during the years of war that followed. If the people of Britain remained deaf to his cries for building up the country's defences it was because another war, which would be an even more destructive and appalling event than the one from which they had just emerged, might well destroy the world. He said so himself. But because his name was inextricably linked with war, and with unsuccessfully conducted war at that, he was in the public mind a political pariah and bogeyman.

Long after the rise to power of Adolf Hitler, the first preoccupation of Stanley Baldwin was disarmament. The Labour Party offered complete support, and there were very few Conservatives – Winston's old friend Duff Cooper was one – who recognized the danger signals. 'We deny the need for increased air arms,' declared Labour's Clement Attlee. 'We deny the proposition that an increased British Air Force will make for the peace of the world . . . the Government has had its hands forced by the wild men like Mr Churchill.'

Winston had followed the rise to power of Hitler and the Nazi Party with deep anxiety. On 8 September 1933, seven months after Hitler became German Chancellor, Winston received a letter from Duff Cooper that confirmed his worst fears. Cooper had been holidaying in Austria and Germany, and he told Winston that Germany had been 'a remarkable sight. Everywhere and at all times of the day and night there were troops marching, drilling and singing . . . They are preparing for war with more general enthusiasm than a whole nation has ever before put into such preparation.'

Of all branches of British defences, it was the RAF that gave Winston most concern. And it was relatively the weakest. The Royal Navy was, with the American navy, still the most powerful in the world, and far stronger than the German navy. And Winston still believed that it was unnecessary and inappropriate for Britain to support more than a small, highly efficient standing army. But the last years of the Great War had shown the immense importance of superiority in the air, and it was clear that with the advance in the size, range and destructive power of the bomber (the RAF had been developing a powerful force to bomb Berlin in 1918 when the war ended), British cities and industry would be fearfully vulnerable to mass bomber forces.

Because Winston was out of office, he was dependent on semi-clandestine sources of information for his campaign to build up the strength of the RAF. First among these civilians and serving officers who were to be seen slipping in and out of Chartwell and Winston's flat in Morpeth Gardens, was Major Desmond Morton, leader of the Government's Industrial Intelligence Centre. Morton, aged 42, had been aide-de-camp to Field Marshal Haig and was as keen as anyone to avoid a repetition of what he had seen in France. He did not think that stripping the country of its defences was the best way to go about it. Then there were Michael Creswell of the Foreign Office, who was still in his twenties, and Ralph Wigram, also of the Foreign Office, an immensely valuable contributor who was greatly missed when he prematurely died. Squadron Leader Charles Torr Anderson, recipient of the DFC, risked his commission and much else by passing on to Winston a wide range of statistical details about the weaknesses in the service, much of it provided by another serving officer, Group Captain Lachlan Maclean.

As the imminence of war increased, the network widened to include uneasy admirals, Field Marshal Sir Cyril Deverell, and Commander Lord Louis Mountbatten. The First Sea Lord himself, Admiral Sir Ernie Chatfield, persuaded Winston of the earlier folly of placing the Navy's air power in the hands of the RAF, which led to the belated formation of the Fleet Air Arm in 1937.

Winston needed every scrap of authentic information on which he could lay his hands. 'Winston's conjectural scaremongering figures!' was often to be heard in the Commons Smoking Room, but he could prove his accusations to be true, and had to in order to answer questions like this: 'Was there ever such a mad policy put before the House of Commons? Was there ever such a policy enunciated, pregnant with bankruptcy for civilization and indeed with terrible and drastic danger for this country?'

Winston remained extremely reticent about his sources of information, and his critics were furious when he was able to prove the authenticity of his exposures. Even his old friend Maurice Hankey, who was by no means against rearmament, felt it necessary to protest: 'It shocks me not a little,' he wrote, 'that high Officers in disciplined Forces would be in direct communication with a leading Statesman who, though notoriously patriotic beyond criticism, is nevertheless in popular estimation regarded as a critic of the Departments under which these Officers serve.' Winston felt not the least prick of conscience. This was a case, if ever there was one, of the ends justifying the means.

Winston's parliamentary position in 1935 was similar to the one he held after May 1915. He remained in the wilderness because no prime minister dared to appoint him in his administration. Even after the 1935 election, when Baldwin won a landslide victory, Winston, who thought he might be sent back to the Admiralty, was left out. 'This was to me a pang and, in a way, an insult,' he commented. 'There was much mockery in the Press. I do not pretend that, thirsting to get things on the move, I was not distressed.'

Winston returned to his old routine, writing for a living,

painting for relaxation and pleasure, and pushing for all his worth, by any means, for expansion of the RAF. Whatever members of the public as well as the House of Commons might say about his campaign, the RAF naturally loved him. One of the service's biggest problems was how to locate attacking enemy bombers in time to have fighters in the air to meet them. This was just possible by visual and aural means in the Great War. But the Gothas had travelled at around only seventy mph. The speed of the latest German bombers was closer to 240 mph.

In 1934 the Air Ministry set up the Committee for the Scientific Survey of Air Defence, and Winston was invited to one of its meetings on 25 July 1935, to learn that an epochal series of experiments had been completed only the previous day. These indicated that aircraft could now be located in flight by radio-location methods, by night or day, regardless of weather conditions, up to a distance of forty to fifty miles. A few months after the committee's first meeting, radar was invented, multiplying many times over the effectiveness of Britain's air defence. Four years later, when war came, a chain of twenty radar stations (Chain Home, or CH) had been completed along the east and south coasts of England, supplemented by mobile reserve stations and low seeing stations (Chain Home Low, or CHL). Out of power Winston might be, but his bustling influence was behind every stage of this remarkable defence feat in a nation still largely paralysed by pacifism.

When Baldwin resigned and Neville Chamberlain replaced him as Prime Minister, the dead hand of appeasement was colder than ever on the nation's defences. Even after the signing of the Munich Agreement in 1938 and Hitler's subsequent brigandry, Winston was the object of fierce attacks for warmongering and (that old chestnut) disloyalty to the party. As late as March 1939, an attempt – not the first, either – was made in his constituency to squeeze him out, and a rich local landowner was found who would stand against him with the full support of the official association: 'Peace in our time, Oh Lord!'

477

The Conservative MP Sir Henry 'Chips' Channon reflected the majority of his party when he described Chamberlain speaking to the House between the shameful negotiations at Munich: 'I will always remember little Neville today . . . his smile, his amazing spirits and seeming lack of fatigue, as he stood there, alone, fighting the dogs of war single-handed and triumphant . . .' And as Lord Rothermere warned after the completion of the Munich Agreement in October 1938, 'Neville Chamberlain's reputation will not be undermined so long as he is Prime Minister . . . The public is so terrified of being bombed that they will support anyone who keeps them out of the war.'

While Chamberlain basked in the adulation that shone upon him after Munich, Winston had to be content with a few crumbs of comfort and a clear conscience. Of his contribution to the Munich debate in the Commons, Violet Bonham Carter, while congratulating him, asked, 'Will it pierce the shell of those drowsy tortoises dragging us to our doom?' Duff Cooper had resigned as First Lord of the Admiralty over the issue. And month by month, opinion began to turn in favour of Winston and urgent rearmament, in unison with more gross outrages by Hitler – Jewish pogroms; the seizure of Memel, Lithuania; the abrogation of the Anglo-German naval treaty of 1935; and above all the abandonment of the Munich Agreement and the invasion of what was left of Czechoslovakia after Munich.

Even the press was starting to call for Winston's inclusion in the Government now, while some newspapers and weeklies were suggesting that he should take over as Premier. The veteran journalist and one-time editor of *The Times* Wickham Steed wrote percipiently in *Picture Post* (25 February 1939):

Were I asked whether I think Winston would be a good Prime Minister, I should say, 'He might in a supreme crisis be the greatest Prime Minister the country has known since the days of the younger Pitt. But the crisis would have to be so big as to surpass even his powers of dramatizing it.

Chamberlain meanwhile continued to argue that Winston's 'nomination to the Cabinet would be a message of open warfare to Berlin'. But the signing of the Russian-German non-aggression pact, the mounting evidence that Poland would be Hitler's next victim, and the general and speedy acceptance during the spring and summer of 1939 that war could not be avoided all swung public opinion towards the need for Winston's return.

Chamberlain was as blind to American opinion as he was to the reality of Hitler's ambitions. Winston, however, had always been aware that the support of the USA would be critical in any war with the dictatorships of Germany and Italy. He already recognized that relations between the White House and 10 Downing Street would need to be mutually supportive and close when war came in Europe and (as he believed was equally inevitable) in the Pacific. Affairs at home were too critical for Winston to consider a lecture tour, but he did broadcast to the USA. Advocating urgent rearmament, he continued, 'We are left in no doubt where American conviction and sympathies lie, but will you wait until British freedom and independence have succumbed, and then take up the cause, when it is three-quarters ruined, yourselves alone?'

Winston knew that the American Ambassador in London did not share this view. The tycoon Joseph Kennedy was frank in his admiration for Hitler and his achievements, and defeatist about Britain's chance of survival in another German war. On 14 June 1939, Winston dined with Kenneth Clark, the art historian, Julian Huxley and his wife, Walter and Helen Lippmann, and Harold Nicolson. Nicolson later wrote:

Winston is horrified by Lippman saying that the American Ambassador, Joe Kennedy, had informed him that war was inevitable and that we should be licked. Winston is stirred by this defeatism into a magnificent oration. He sits hunched there, waving his whisky-and-soda to mark his periods, stubbing his cigar with the other hand.

'It may be true, it may well be true,' he says, 'that this country will at the outset of this coming and to my mind almost inevitable war be exposed to dire peril and fierce ordeals. . . . Yet these trials and disasters, I ask you to believe me, Mr Lippman, will but serve to steel the resolution of the British people and to enhance our will for victory. No, the Ambassador should not have spoken so, Mr Lippman; he should not have said that dreadful word.'

According to Nicolson, Winston went on to forecast that, in the event of Mr Kennedy's being correct, then 'over there in your distant and immune continent the torch of liberty will burn untarnished and (I trust and hope) undismayed.'

Meanwhile, Adolf Hitler, the man who, Kennedy confidently predicted, would soon overwhelm Britain, used every damning word in his extensive vocabulary to condemn Winston and all his works. Winston had been Germany's *bête noire* since he had taken over the Admiralty in 1911, and Hitler knew that, as regards German interests, he was the most dangerous figure in Britain. Sarcasm was one of Hitler's favourite forms of attack; he believed, rightly, that it was effective with the German people.

In France and Britain [Hitler pronounced after Munich], men who want peace are in the Government. But tomorrow those who want war may be in the Government. Mr Churchill may be Prime Minister tomorrow . . . Mr Churchill may have an electorate of 15,000 or 20,000. I have one of 40,000,000. Once and for all we request to be spared from being spanked like a pupil by a governess.

480

In a speech broadcast to America that Winston made on Sunday 16 October, he replied to this accusation:

> The American people have, it seems to me, formed a true judgement upon the disaster which has befallen Europe. They realize, perhaps more clearly than the French or British publics have yet done, the far-reaching consequences of the abandonment and ruin of the Czechoslovakian Republic.

If only, he lamented, Britain, France and Russia had jointly declared that they would not tolerate the conquest by Germany of a single further square yard of foreign soil, Czechoslovakia could have been saved: 'I hear that they are saying in the United States that because England and France have failed to do their duty, therefore the American people can wash their hands of the whole business.'

For a long period, Winston had contributed regular articles to the London *Evening Standard*, but in 1938 and 1939 he transferred this journalism to a national paper with a far larger readership, the *Daily Telegraph*, whose editor in chief was his old friend William Berry, Lord Camrose. This newspaper charted his views during the last anxious months of peace. In it he advocated a tripartite protective pact between Russia, France and Britain, as in 1914: this was before the German-Russian pact. He also warned his readers of the danger of growing German pressure on Poland. No one who read his column could doubt that Winston believed that war was imminent.

In mid-August, Winston was taken on an extended tour of the French Maginot Line defences, noting ominously how close was the parallel German Siegfried Line. Silence reigned. Only great opposite-facing provocative signs – '*Ein Volk, ein Reich, ein Führer*' on the German side; '*Liberté, Egalité, Fraternité*' inside the French frontier – augured another great conflict, even worse than the last.

Knowing now that this war was only weeks away, Winston

ded to spend a few of the last days of peace in his beloved France with Consuelo and Jacques Balsan. Besides Lou Sueil in the south, they had a château north of Paris, and here Winston read and painted. He was heard to say, 'This is the last picture I will paint in peace for a very long time.' Clementine and Mary joined him. 'There was swimming and tennis and *fraises des bois*,' Mary recalled.

Winston returned to London by air on 23 August, to the news of the German-Soviet pact. The next day Chamberlain recalled Parliament, and an Emergency Powers Bill was passed. Outside, a group of protesters marched up and down with sandwich boards carrying the single word 'CHURCHILL'. Newspapers and posters called out for his return to the Government, as a formal treaty of alliance with Poland, guaranteeing Britain's support in the event of invasion, was hastily drawn up and signed. The Fleet and RAF Fighter Command were put on a war footing, and army reservists were called up. How similar London was to that August of just twenty-five years ago! But this time there was no frenzy, no exultation. War-wise, the people braced themselves for a new ordeal.

With ghastly inevitability, the news filtered through from Warsaw that German tanks had crossed the Polish frontier before dawn on 1 September, that the bombers were already about their work. Winston, at Chartwell, was telephoned by the Polish Ambassador at 8.30 a.m., and he in turn telephoned General Sir Edmund Ironside, the newly appointed Chief of the Imperial General Staff. 'They've started,' he informed the soldier crisply. 'Warsaw and Cracow are being bombed now.'

Winston drove up to London and from Morpeth Mansions telephoned Chamberlain. He was asked to call at 10 Downing Street that afternoon. Was the Prime Minister going to stand firm, or was this going to be another Czechoslovakia? Winston had told his publisher, Sir Newman Flower, the previous day that he believed Chamberlain would this time stand firm. The Prime Minister was looking grave and grey with fatigue and disappointment. He believed that he had done everything possible to avoid this conflict, but, as Winston wrote later, 'he saw no hope of averting war with Germany,' adding that he proposed to form a small war cabinet.

'Will you agree to become a member?' Chamberlain then asked, and Winston said that he would, writing later that 'on this basis we had a long talk on men and measures.'

In the House of Commons that evening, Chamberlain read out a note that had been sent to Germany confirming that, unless German forces withdrew from Poland, 'the United Kingdom will without hesitation fulfil their obligation to Poland.' It seemed at the time that Chamberlain was at last being firm, as Winston had predicted, but the next day, 2 September, Winston's suspicions that even now Chamberlain might temporize were justified. He himself received no call from the Prime Minister and was not present at the afternoon Cabinet meeting. At this, Leslie Hore-Belisha, the War Minister, pressed for decisive action in order to retain the unity of the nation, and Chamberlain agreed to send an ultimatum to Germany immediately, to expire at midnight.

But Winston and the rest of the House received a very different impression of Chamberlain's intentions in the House later. Instead of an ultimatum, Chamberlain talked only of negotiations in the hope that Germany might yet withdraw its troops and tanks and cease bombing to pieces the cities of Poland. The silence that greeted this extraordinary suggestion contrasted starkly with the deafening cheers that had greeted this same Prime Minister after he had handed Czechoslovakia to Hitler on a plate in order to avoid war. Much had happened since October 1938, and there was no doubt that the House was now for war.

That evening a number of Winston's friends gathered in his flat, unified in outrage, and talked through half the night. Some time after midnight, Winston despatched a note to Chamberlain. It was a masterly but veiled rebuke directed at the Prime Minister's indecisiveness and a rather more heavily veiled threat that he was ready to take over the premiership, as some of his associates were pressing him.

At 9 a.m., 3 September, Chamberlain at last sent the ultimatum that would bring Britain into the war within two hours unless Germany withdrew from Poland. No one believed that the Wehrmacht would stop killing the Poles, who were retreating on every front, their cities in ruins. Shortly after the ultimatum expired, Chamberlain spoke to the nation on the radio, announcing that Britain was at war with Germany again – a fact that seemed to be confirmed with great promptitude when the air-raid sirens sounded out over the capital, and the people took to the shelters as the protective balloons rose into the sky. Clementine and Winston were among those who took cover as instructed, Winston clutching a bottle of brandy to his chest.

It was a false alarm, but the sirens acted as a mournful signal that the summer days of peace were over and the nation was embarking on a struggle against a tyrant as cruel and ruthless as any in European history. When the 'all clear' sounded, Winston went to the House, and as he took his seat, he recalled, 'a very strong sense of calm came over me, after the intense passions and excitements of the last few days.' Chamberlain had already sent a message, asking him to call at his room after the House rose.

This Winston did, after delivering a rousing speech, and Chamberlain asked him to join the War Cabinet and take over the Admiralty again. Winston thanked him briefly and withdrew. The day was becoming as tumultuous as 17 May 1915, this time in reverse. He sent a message to the Admiralty announcing his arrival at 6 p.m. But even before he did so, the wireless aerial towering above the building had flashed the message to every ship in the Fleet: 'Winston is back!'

Winston was met at the Admiralty entrance by Captain Guy Grantham, Naval Assistant to the First Sea Lord, who had caused the signal to be sent and now escorted him up the stairs, scarcely able to keep up with him, and led him to his old office.

Twenty-eight years had passed since Winston had entered this office for the first time. One of the things he had done then was to order a large map of the North Sea, held when not in use in a wooden chart case secured at the back of a sofa. Upon it, on every day that he remained in office, the Naval Intelligence Branch recorded the movements and dispositions of the German navy. Winston, delighted to discover that the case was still there, the chart still inside, asked for it to be unrolled and for the previous practice to be reintroduced.

As a sentimental traditionalist, he wanted everything as it had been before, especially an old octagonal table.

> He wanted all his old furniture back and his notorious lampshade [his private secretary remembered]. This was an enormous affair of green silk with butter muslin to diffuse the light, and a long fringe of beads, the whole thing faded and filthy. Eric Seal* had to find and dig out all these objects. After much difficulty, by some miracle he found the lampshade in the vaults of the India Office.

Winston derived comfort from the presence of some familiar faces from the past, too, just as if the earlier war, the years at the Treasury and the years in the wilderness were no more than an extended intermission. The First Sea Lord, Admiral Sir Dudley Pound, for one, had been around in 1914, as a member of Jacky Fisher's staff.

If Winston had reviewed the Fleet, as he had with the King in 1914, only the slab-sized, flat-top carriers would have been new, and their war base was still Scapa Flow, up in the Orkneys. The first threat to the Fleet was the U-boat. And the Navy's most urgent task, as in 1914, was to transport the Army across the Channel to support the French in the same alliance as before.

But in many respects, the Navy of 1939 was very different

---

*Seal (1898–1972) was Principal Private Secretary to the new First Lord, and later to Winston as Prime Minister.

from that of 1914. For one thing, it was less than half the size, and while the battleship was considered the most important class of ship, the Fleet Air Arm, freed from control by the RAF, was growing rapidly – in a few months' time Clementine was to launch one of the new carriers that were already joining the Fleet. As in the RAF, radar was being rapidly introduced, giving the advantage of early warning, and radar would soon be aiming the guns, too.

The Royal Navy remained a force strongly guided by tradition and, alas, by class distinction, but less visibly than twenty-five years earlier. The senior officers, junior officers in the Great War, were a good deal more flexible in their thinking than the hidebound senior officers in 1914, many of whom had been trained under sail and put smartness and seamanship above gunnery and initiative. In the final analysis, the mine and the torpedo had been the arbiters, not the big gun, in the Great War. The enemy mine had defeated the Navy at the Dardanelles, and the threat of the mine and the torpedo had governed tactics in North Sea naval actions. The U-boats' torpedos had come critically near to closing the sea lanes of the Atlantic and starving the Allies of food, armaments and raw materials.

One of Winston's first actions at his desk at the Admiralty was to order a complete set of statistics on the new German U-boat force, while one of the first setbacks he had to face was the sinking of the liner *Athenia*, with Americans among the drowned, by one of these U-boats. The Germans introduced a menacing new magnetic mine, dropped from the air or from fast warships. Just as in 1914 a mine had sunk the Dreadnought *Audacious*, so now in October 1939, a skilful and daring U-boat captain penetrated the defences of Scapa Flow and sank the Dreadnought *Royal Oak*, with the loss of most of its crew.

In 1914 a firm blockade of Germany had been established, cutting off the enemy from all but the Baltic states. At the same time, German raiders in distant seas had caused a great deal of damage before they were destroyed. It was the same in 1939. The most effective and notorious of these was appropriately named *Graf Spee*, after the German admiral of that previous war. She was a small, fast battleship with a range of more than ten thousand miles, modern and heavily armed.

The *Graf Spee* was in the Indian Ocean at the outbreak of war and at once set about sinking British merchantmen, ranging later into the South Atlantic. Like the German admiral after whom his ship was named, the *Graf Spee*'s captain had his eyes on the rich River Plate traffic. But he was spotted by a force of three British cruisers, all greatly inferior in gunpower. Unlike Admiral Troubridge in 1914, when facing the bigger *Goeben*, Commodore Henry Harwood moved aggressively against the *Graf Spee*. Although Harwood's ships were badly damaged, the *Graf Spee* was forced to seek shelter in Montevideo, Uruguay.

'It had been most exciting to follow the drama of this brilliant action from the Admiralty War Room,' Winston wrote later, signifying that he had learned the lesson of direct interference that had cost him his reputation in 1914 and 1915, when signals to the Mediterranean and more distant oceans had confused and demoralized the commanders on the spot.

The *Graf Spee* action aroused much interest in the USA, and *Life* magazine instructed a photographer to fly over the damaged battleship. When the photograph was published, British Admiralty intelligence learned for the first time that the German navy had radar, too. British intelligence also contrived to bluff the Germans that an overwhelmingly powerful force was awaiting the forced emergence, under the Neutrality Act, of the *Graf Spee*. So the German captain steamed out six miles and blew up his ship, and then blew out his own brains in mortification.

This action, like the Falkland Islands battle of 1914, was hailed as a great victory in Britain. It had a salutary effect in the United States, although there were diplomatic reservations in that country. The USA and the Central and South American republics had declared a 300-mile non-combatant zone around their coasts. Clearly, both Britain and Germany had penetrated this zone during the naval action, and additionally, Britain had intercepted a number of German supply ships within it.

Back in September, the American President, Franklin D. Roosevelt, had written to Winston to congratulate him on his appointment, adding, 'What I want you and the Prime Minister to know is that I shall at all times welcome it if you will keep me in touch personally with anything you want me to know about . . .'

With the approval of the Foreign Secretary and the War Cabinet, Winston seized this invitation with both hands. It was the beginning of a correspondence and a relationship that was to have the most profound consequences for the progress and outcome of the Second World War. Now Winston sought to reply to complaints from Latin American countries that were supported by the United States. In mitigation, Winston pleaded by telegram, dated 25 December, personally to the President:

> As a result of action off Plate whole South Atlantic is now clear . . . This must be a blessing to South American Republics whose trade was hampered by activities of raider and whose ports were used for his supply ships and information centres. In fact we have rescued all this vast area from war disturbances.

Winston then promised to despatch by air the fullest possible account of the action, with details of the damage to the British cruisers. He ended the telegram: 'Permit me to send you, Sir, all the compliments of the season.'

That first Christmas of war brought most of Winston and Clementine's children – and grandchildren – together for what was, effectively and for most people, the last Christmas of peace. In this period of 'phony war', the RAF had experienced little action, and that mostly a matter of dropping leaflets over Germany, and the Army in France was constrained by the French from doing anything offensive that might upset the Germans. Only the Navy was fully engaged, as it always must be, on convoy duties and in hunting U-boats.

In October, Winston and Clementine had seen their third child married. Randolph was now 28, stoutish, still exceedingly handsome, his looks somewhat marred by spots. His name and his charm (when he applied it) got him most of the things he wanted, except a seat in Parliament. He had a reputation for drunkenness and boorishness and treated most people with the utmost contempt. But to those he loved, like the vivid Laura Charteris, the aged, eccentric millionairess Lady Houston, Nancy Mitford and his sisters (most of the time), he could be angelic. He shared his mother's dislike for Brendan Bracken, and there were always storms when they met. Clementine cared no more for him now than when he was a boy. Winston still worshipped him, though he could give him the rough edge of his tongue, especially over his extravagance and gambling debts. Randolph made a spasmodic and rather scrappy living by journalism and lecturing, until he joined the Army.

Randolph's regiment, to emulate his father, had to be the 4th Hussars. He found the discipline of an officer's training hard to bear and when commissioned threw his weight about noisily in the mess. On leave he met, and immediately became engaged to, a jolly, plump, red-haired 19-year-old country girl, Pamela Digby, the daughter of an eleventh baron. They married three days later, making the war an excuse for haste, though there was not much going on with the 4th Hussars.

The wedding reception took place at Admiralty House, and Winston and Clementine were delighted, hoping that this pretty, giggly girl could 'settle him down'. The newlyweds joined the parents for Christmas, and so did Diana and Duncan Sandys, who was also in the Army, with their children Julian and Edwina. These were looked after by Cousin Moppet at the Chartwell cottage, their mother having joined the WRNS.

Sarah and her husband, Vic Oliver, were working in

London, Vic with Pat Kirkwood in *Black Velvet* at the Hippodrome. They joined the Christmas party, too, from their flat in Westminster. All theatres and other places of entertainment had been closed from fear of bombing at the outbreak of war, but they had now reopened, and these two were back earning their living on the stage. As for Mary, 'I was 17 and, having just left school, was revelling in my first taste of London and "grown-up" life.' She was also 'doing her bit', in that awful contemporary phrase, by working in a canteen and a Red Cross workroom and helping Clementine with the relatively modest entertaining that went on at Admiralty House. As the only two non-family members of the party, Brendan Bracken and 'the Prof' turned up on Christmas morning to join the festivities. Clementine's dislike for Bracken was, as usual, made more starkly obvious by the friendliness shown to him by everyone else, especially Winston.

Winston, still glowing over the *Graf Spee* victory, had predicted to Roosevelt that the real war would soon begin. He was also plotting a new Gallipoli, a pre-emptive strike at Hitler's supplies of iron ore from Sweden.

For the democracies of Western Europe, the winter of 1939–40 was one of frozen fear. The weather was paralysingly cold, the French government remained throughout fearful of stirring up the hornets' nest of German militarism, cravenly thankful that the Wehrmacht remained behind the Siegfried Line. In London, Chamberlain and his Foreign Secretary, Lord (Edward) Halifax, remained equally thankful to sustain the status quo. It was, altogether, like the deadlock of the winter of 1914–15, without the fighting and bloodshed. And it seemed that it was again only the First Lord of the Admiralty who showed any urgent desire to take the offensive.

Now that he was back on the Admiralty's bridge, conducting affairs with the energy of youth tamed by the wisdom of his 65 years, Winston's influence went far beyond the Fleet. The *Graf Spee* victory, which had done Winston and the Navy such a power of good, had an aftermath that was equally satisfactory. The *Altmark*, a German naval auxiliary store ship and tanker that had accompanied the battleship and taken on board some three hundred prisoners from the ships she had sunk, was attempting to break through the British blockade back to Germany.

The *Altmark* had almost reached neutral Norwegian waters when she was sighted from the air, and the destroyer *Cossack* was sent in to discuss the release of the prisoners with the Norwegian authorities. The Norwegians said they had searched the ship and found no prisoners on board. When the British captain, Philip Vian, pressed the point his ship was threatened by two Norwegian gunboats.

Vian signalled the Admiralty for instructions. Winston, relishing his role and without consulting anyone, sent orders to his latter-day Francis Drake: free the prisoners, and reply in kind to any serious interference by the Norwegians. Vian acted in the Elizabethan tradition: he boarded the German vessel, killing a number of Germans in doing so, and opened the hatches – and there were the three hundred British sailors, cheering and waving their hats in the dark confines of the hold.

The *Altmark* affair was militarily insignificant, but it lifted people's hearts and proved that the Navy was *doing something*. But time and again, when he proposed something positive, Winston was put down. Halifax would certainly have rejected the *Altmark* boarding if he had been consulted. When Winston proposed dropping mines in the upper reaches of the Rhine to float down to the Ruhr in retaliation for indiscriminate German mining round the British coast, the French government, fearing reprisals, refused their consent. More seriously, another mining offensive off the Norwegian coast was for a time unsupported by the British War Cabinet.

One door in the blockade of Germany that had not been sealed allowed into Germany Swedish iron ore, upon which the German war machine largely depended. The ore came from mines in the far north of Sweden and then went by rail to

Narvik, in northern Norway. From this port within the Arctic Circle the ore was shipped down the serrated Norwegian coast, within territorial waters and therefore immune from British interference, to the Baltic.

Winston proposed to mine these Norwegian waters, forcing the traffic into the open sea, where the freighters could be intercepted. This was later enlarged into an altogether more dramatic operation: lay minefields and then land forces at Norwegian ports and occupy the Swedish iron-ore mines. The cover and justification was to be military support for the Finns, who had been invaded by the Soviet Union. These two linked proposals were debated to and fro in the War Cabinet for week after week, with Halifax and Chamberlain procrastinating and sounding warnings, particularly of critical reaction in the United States, while the Labour leaders opposed the whole thing.

Winston became more and more exasperated by this temporizing. On 14 March he wrote to Halifax a long and angry letter, including:

> *I feel I ought to let you know that I am vy deeply concerned about the way the war is going . . . There is no sort of action in view except to wait on events. These I fear are taking an increasingly adverse turn . . . We have never done anything but follow the line of least resistance . . . Considering the discomfort & sacrifice imposed upon the nation, public men charged with the conduct of the war sh'd live in a continual stress of soul . . .*

The only 'stress of soul' Halifax and his number one, R. A. Butler, were suffering was concern for securing a truce – a truce, and peace, contrived through the good offices of the Pope, Benito Mussolini (Italy was not yet in the war) and Franklin D. Roosevelt. So, it seemed, Poland was to be sold down the river, too, and Germany allowed to range over Europe again!

After more exhausting and exasperating delays, the Norwegian operation, including minelaying and the landing of a force on Norwegian soil, was authorized by the War Cabinet. The mining was to take place on 5 April. Then suddenly, like an echo of the voice of Kitchener in 1915, the French war cabinet demanded a postponement. Three days later the mining was carried out, and the troops were about to embark . . .

The Norwegian authorities were busily engaged in drafting protests at the British action when they were diverted by the prospect of rather more serious and imminent action against their country. Off Oslo, on the morning of 9 April, there suddenly appeared a German invasion force of warships, shortly followed by the thunder of aircraft. Five more Norwegian ports, including Narvik, were attacked and taken simultaneously. It was a brilliant operation in which the Luftwaffe gained almost complete control of the air while the German navy was putting ashore the occupying troops. The fact that the navy lost a great many modern and valuable warships was of trivial importance in German reckoning. Air power was what mattered, after the occupying force had been landed.

'We have been completely outwitted,' Winston noted. 'The Germans have succeeded in occupying all the ports on the Norwegian coast, including Narvik, and large scale operations will be required to turn them out of any of them.' They were indeed! After a closely fought battle, Narvik eventually fell to Allied troops, but only for the purpose of destroying installations, and they soon had to be withdrawn – just as, on a much larger scale, Allied troops had had to be evacuated from Gallipoli.

Too late, too late – always too late. But for those three lost days, British forces instead of the Germans would now have been in Narvik. Although Euripedes was not Winston's favourite writer – especially not in the original Greek, when he had been at Harrow – he would have agreed that 'the god of war hates those who hesitate.'

*

The failure in Norway and the related failure of Winston in relation to it might well have had fatal consequences for his future. The parallel with Gallipoli was too close for comfort. In both campaigns the Navy had taken on a task that was beyond its capacity. In 1915 it was the minefields and shore batteries that proved fatal; in 1940 it was air power. Peacetime planning should have revealed the truth. Winston may have been wrongly advised, but he should have questioned that advice. If he had not read it himself, Winston's attention should have been drawn to the documented fact that the German planning staff advocated the conquest of Norway and considered it feasible. This information was freely available before the war, but Admiralty staff either had never heard of it or simply wrote it off as impossible in view of the great superiority of the Royal Navy. But it was the Luftwaffe that made the conquest of Norway possible. Winston, who had been warning the nation of the growing strength of the German air force, failed to recognize its influence on sea power.

Was April 1940 going to be another May 1915 for Winston? There were many in the House who thought he ought to go. Chips Channon was among those who were disappointed by his 'long winded dull statement' on Norway to the Commons on 11 April:

> It pleased no-one, and he looked tired and ill, and made little attempt to touch the real point; why did we allow Narvik to be captured and where was the fleet, could we not have stopped the Germans, if their invasion had been so long and elaborately planned? Why did we not know about it? Is our Naval Intelligence so weak? He spoke for an hour and his speech was a flop . . .

While one considerable group of members, mainly the older generation, regarded the disaster of Norway as a repeat of the Dardanelles, another equally vehement group thought that Winston had lost his fire and instinct for the positive as a reaction against the reputation he had acquired at the Dardanelles. (The general public knew nothing of Winston's efforts to act before the Germans. They only saw the failure of the Navy.) Roger Keyes, a one-time friend and stout supporter, was of this second group. Harold Nicolson recorded meeting him in the Lobby on 30 April, when gloom and defeatism were rife in the House:

> [Keyes] is in despair. He says that if only we had struck quickly with the Navy all would have been well. He says that the Admiralty Board refused to take naval risks since they were frightened by the possible attitude of Italy. He says that we have been outmanoeuvred and beaten because we were too afraid. He says that Winston's drive and initiative have been undermined by the legend of his recklessness. Today he cannot dare to do the things he could have dared in 1915.

How could Winston be 'disentangled from the ruins'? asked another member, Harold Macmillan. Clementine was beside herself with anxiety about Winston's position. She always believed afterwards that Norway 'might well have ruined you'. Only his rearmament campaign and warnings before the outbreak of war saved him in the eyes of many people. General Sir Edmund Ironside ruefully noted Winston's state of mind and guilt after a meeting on 4 May. 'We found him very tired and sleepy and he hardly did anything at all. He took quietly what we said without demur . . . Winston seems to me to be a little weighed down by the cares of being solely responsible for Narvik.'

On 7 May a critical debate on the conduct of the war opened in the Commons, with the defeat in Norway as the chief subject for discussion. Later the debate developed into a censure motion. The first day was also the most sensational. Roger Keyes arrived in the uniform of an admiral of the fleet, with six rows of ribbons to confirm his authority on naval affairs. He was the most famous living admiral. If his arrival was spectacular, his attack on the Government was 'devastating', according to Harold Nicolson, and when he sat down there was 'thunderous applause'.

Later on this epochal day in the Commons, Leo Amery, addressing Chamberlain, quoted Cromwell's words to another patriotic parliamentarian, John Hampden: 'Your troops are most of them old, decayed serving men and tapsters, and such kind of fellows.' Amery then continued, glaring at the Prime Minister:

> I have quoted certain words of Oliver Cromwell. I will quote certain other words. I do it with great reluctance, because I am speaking of those who are old friends and associates of mine, but they are words which, I think, are applicable to the present situation. This is what Cromwell said to the Long Parliament when he thought it was no longer fit to conduct the affairs of the nation: 'You have sat too long for any good you have been doing. Depart, I say, and let us have done with you. In the name of God, go!'

On the second day of the debate, 8 May, Lloyd George arose like some ghost from the past and hammered home the attack on Chamberlain with some of the old fire that had many times set the chamber alight with its Welsh eloquence, ending with the demand that Chamberlain 'should sacrifice the seals of office'. He had earlier remarked that he did not think 'that the First Lord was entirely responsible for all the things which happened in Norway', at which Winston immediately arose and declared, 'I take complete responsibility for everything that has been done by the Admiralty, and I take my full share of the burden.'

Winston was fully aware of the growing body of support he was drawing with every passing day and every new revelation of the incapacity of the present administration to cope with the rising tide of war, even though he was associated with it. He was also aware that he could afford to take responsibility for any failure on his part. Finally, and above all, he was fully aware that no chink in his loyalty to his chief – to Chamberlain – must be discernible. For this reason, when the Prime Minister asked him to wind up the debate for the Government, he agreed at once.

Before Winston delivered his defence of Chamberlain's administration, he saw Harold Macmillan in the smoking room and invited him to sit beside him. Harold Macmillan wished him luck in his task, but added that he hoped his case would not be too convincing.

'Why not?' Winston demanded.

'Because we must have a new Prime Minister, and it must be you.'

Later, 'Winston finally rose', recorded one eyewitness:

> and one saw at once that he was in bellicose mood, alive and enjoying himself, relishing the ironical position in which he found himself: i.e. that of defending his enemies, and a cause in which he did not believe. He made a slashing vigorous speech, a magnificent piece of oratory. I was in the gallery behind him, with Rab [R. A. Butler] who was, several times, convulsed with laughter. Winston told the story of the Norwegian campaign, justified it, and trounced the Opposition, demolishing Roger Keyes, etc. How much of the fire was real, how much ersatz, we shall never know, but he amused and dazzled everyone with his virtuosity . . .

Never had there been stronger proof of Winston's ability, at least equal to F. E. Smith's, to be a top advocate if he had chosen the law rather than politics.

When the vote came to be taken, there was complete confusion in the House, with speculation on how many Conservatives might vote against their chief. There was a three-line whip, and if all Conservatives obeyed it as was expected of them, Chamberlain would get a majority of 213 votes. In the event, some sixty Conservatives abstained and thirty-three voted against, giving the Government a meagre and quite inadequate (under the circumstances) majority of eighty-one.

It was clear now that Chamberlain could no longer continue as Prime Minister without resorting to a coalition, as Asquith had found necessary in May 1915. But it also became increasingly clear that neither the Labour Party nor the Liberal Party would serve under him, and this was the problem discussed between Chamberlain, Halifax and Winston after they had failed to persuade the Labour leaders to serve in a coalition – though they might be prepared to serve under someone other than Chamberlain.

The critical conversation that followed was recalled by both Halifax and Winston, with small divergences. But both agreed that it had become evident that Chamberlain was now prepared to go, that Halifax was favoured by him as a successor, but that Halifax thought Chamberlain should recommend to the King that he should send for Winston to attempt to form a government.

While this conversation was going on at 10 Downing Street, the rebel Conservatives who had voted against Chamberlain had been involved intermittently in their own debate about the way out of the current stalemate. On the evening of this day, 9 May, when Winston was 'in heavy business' at the Admiralty, he received a letter by messenger from Bob Boothby, summing up the rebels' position, their names, and their beliefs. 'I find a gathering consensus of opinion,' he concluded, 'in all quarters that you are the necessary and inevitable Prime Minister . . . God knows it is a terrible prospect for you. But I don't see how you can avoid it.'

29

'This Frightful and Brutal Onslaught'

At 4.30 a.m. on 10 May, General Heinz Guderian, a notable German tank specialist, crossed the Luxembourg frontier, leading the 1st Panzer Division. To the north, at precisely the same time, General Erwin Rommel led his 7th Panzer Division across the Belgian frontier.

> Still further north, along the Dutch frontier facing Maastricht [as one noted historian related], German storm-troopers had nestled right up to the Dutch customs post. As the first light of dawn emerged, the Dutch could hear the rumble of approaching tanks; the tension grew unbearable, but still the frontier guards continued to stroll quietly up and down, apparently noticing nothing. Then the rumbling grew louder and louder as squadron after squadron of Ju-52s, containing the whole of the German 22nd Airborne Division, plus some 4,000 paratroopers, passed overhead . . .

Winston worked far into the night of 9 May and the early hours of 10 May. Shortly after he fell asleep in his bedroom in Admiralty House, and one hour after the German tanks crossed the frontiers of Luxembourg, Belgium and Holland, Winston was awakened with the news of the onslaught against the West. We can see him then, immediately alert, eyes shining, already savouring the action and decision-making of the day that lay ahead. He orders the curtains to be drawn back, revealing another sunny day, and reaches across for his silk vest. (He has sometimes embarrassed servants who see him wandering the corridors stark naked.)

He next reaches for the telephone and dials the private numbers of Oliver Stanley, War Minister, and Sam Hoare, Secretary of State for Air. They have both heard the news. 'Come over here for breakfast,' Winston invites them, though it sounds more like an order.

By six o'clock both men have arrived with their private secretaries, all of them smart in black pinstripe suits, as if for a Cabinet meeting. They note that Winston has already an enormous cigar alight *and* is tucking into bacon and eggs, with toast and marmalade to follow. Hoare, a tall, bald man with a long, lugubrious face, notes that Winston looks as if he might have just returned from a refreshing early morning ride instead of suffering an almost sleepless night.

'Well, this is bad news, Winston, what do you think?' Hoare asks, sitting down at one of the two places laid for the guests.

'It is certainly inevitable news, Sam, and scarcely surprising.' Winston pushes aside his empty plate and relights his cigar, smiling puckishly. 'At least we can say that there will be no more talk about our criminal ineptitude in Norway.'

All the while the boxes are coming in, Admiralty boxes, War Office boxes, Foreign Office boxes, but there is no time to deal with them now. While Hoare and Stanley are finishing their breakfast, a call comes in from Randolph, who is in camp with his regiment.

'I've just heard the wireless news – what's happening?' he asks.

'Well, the German hordes are pouring into the Low Countries,' Winston tells his son. 'But the British and French armies are advancing to meet them, and in a day or two there will be a head-on collision.'

Randolph follows with another question. 'What about what you told me last night about you becoming Prime Minister today?'

Winston, hoping that his two guests did not hear Randolph's booming voice, replies discreetly, 'Oh, I don't know about that. Nothing matters now except beating the enemy.'

Winston turns to his guests. 'Gentlemen, I propose now to

dress and hope to meet you again in the Upper War Room shortly.' Assisted by his valet, Sawyers, Winston dresses rapidly and, with a second cigar glowing satisfactorily, makes his way from Admiralty House into the main Admiralty building. Eric Seal, small, bald and as bright as a morning sparrow, joins him.

Some weeks earlier, Chamberlain had set up the Military Co-ordination Committee and appointed Winston its chairman. It is this body that is now assembled in the Upper War Room; it consists of most of those who will be responsible for meeting the German onslaught on the Continent – and no doubt on England, too.

Winston opens the meeting by informing the dozen or so men present that they have only some forty-five minutes because he has been told that there is a War Cabinet meeting at 10 Downing Street at 8 a.m. He continues:

> We may have to meet again later. Meanwhile, I must tell you that I have just heard that the Governments of Belgium and Holland have appealed to the Foreign Office for help. We have also learned that the German Air Force is bombing aerodromes in Belgium and northern France, and German parachute troops have been dropped into Belgium. At the same time, our troops and our French allies have begun their march into Belgium, and all British shipping has been ordered to leave Belgian and Dutch ports. Finally, in accordance with our pre-arranged plan, two of our fighter aircraft squadrons have been ordered to France . . .

The discussion that follows is brief. It is decided to send two further fighter squadrons to France and at last to authorize the long-delayed operation of mining the River Rhine, on the assumption that any French objections must now have been overtaken by events.

'Thank you, gentlemen. Mark my words, I think we may

501

be seeing more of each other henceforward . . .' Winston's parting raises smiles as he strides to the door, followed by Hoare and Stanley. There are still few people about as they walk across the Horse Guards Parade to Downing Street – only some soldiers on guard, their rifles with fixed bayonets, the crew of the balloon barrage unit busy inflating their great charge, one or two early strollers in St James's Park feeding the ducks, and their own private detectives at a discreet distance behind.

How often Winston has made this journey, to visit, or return from, the Prime Minister – Asquith in the last great war, Chamberlain in this new and already terrible conflict! Was this the last time? It would seem so if today he was installed in 10 Downing Street.

Clementine was away from London during the days of the long parliamentary debate and vote of censure on the Government. She had missed all the drama of the attack by Amery and the defence by Winston of the Norwegian campaign, and the final humiliating vote. She longed to be at his side at this time, but an appeal by her sister Nellie to join her was too strong.

Bertram Romilly was dying – dying from the effects of the wounds he had received at the height of the Great War just as the fires of the Second World War were blasting into flames. Bertram and Nellie had led a demanding life. He was rarely out of pain, and their two boys, Giles and Esmond, with their unsuitable joint nickname, 'the Lambs', had been exceedingly troublesome. Any woman but Nellie would have succumbed to the burden, made heavier by constant penury. Bertram's own father had died at the age of 90 earlier in the year, when it was already clear that Bertram did not himself have long to live. Nellie and Bertram spent their last days together at the family seat, Huntington Park, in the Welsh Marches near Kington in Herefordshire.

The funeral at the village church in this beautiful setting was on 8 May, and on the following evening Winston telephoned asking if Clementine could return to London as events were moving fast. Should he be asked by the King to form a government, he would like her to be at his side. Clementine took the earliest train the following morning, 10 May. She could not know, as her train followed the peaceful Wye River, that once again the guns were thundering across the Channel and the Germans were on the rampage.

For Winston, the morning's events tumble one upon another with bewildering speed, with two full War Cabinet meetings before noon, and an unceasing succession of telephone calls, messages and meetings at the Admiralty. On one occasion as he sweeps back into his office, 'The Dutch Ministers were in my room,' he recalled. 'Haggard and worn, with horror in their eyes, they had just flown over from Amsterdam . . .* The avalanche of fire and steel had rolled across the frontiers, and when . . . the Dutch frontier guards fired, an overwhelming onslaught was made from the air . . .'

At around ten o'clock, another visitor is Sir Kingsley Wood, who has just come from a meeting with Chamberlain. The Prime Minister, it seems, is inclined to dig his heels in, on the pretext that a crisis like this is no time to change Government or Prime Minister. On the contrary, Wood told him, it makes it all the more necessary for him to resign and for the formation of a coalition national government, which cannot now be formed with him as leader. Labour would not permit any such thing.

People come and go. Telephones ring like a background chorus to some anarchic opera. Admirals, messengers, secretaries and ministers swarm everywhere, as if the Admiralty is some anthill. Then there is the news, the news by day

---

*Their seaplane had been hit by German gunfire and had force-landed off Brighton. Their rescue had been followed by brief incarceration as enemy aliens.

'fitting to the night
Black, fearful, comfortless and horrible . . .'

Paris bombed, Lyons bombed, the Swiss mobilizing, paratroopers dressed as nuns dropped behind the fighting, Brussels captured . . . Most of the distant news is inaccurate scaremongering, but close to home there is no doubt that Chamberlain has gone to the palace for an audience with the King, and that can only mean his resignation. In neat, comforting juxtaposition, almost immediately a message arrives on Winston's desk: 'Your wife is safely home.'

A dozen more people come and go. A dozen more telephone calls. A note that HMS *Kelly*, Commander Lord Louis Mountbatten, has been torpedoed but is being towed home . . . Then, with priority above all others, a note: 'His Majesty the King wishes to see you at 6 p.m.'

Winston brushed aside everything and, with apologies, everyone else and headed for Admiralty House. Clementine was there, in the drawing room, still wearing her hat.

· 'Clemmie, my dear, I knew you would arrive in time.' He embraced her. 'You could not have missed this historical moment. My poor darling – what a rush, what sadness for you!'

'Yes, I have heard the war news,' Clementine said. 'Oh, the wickedness and sadness, and now this excitement. It is all too much for one day.' She was already fretting. 'Have you been called to the Palace, my dear?'

Winston's face was aglow, with no trace of weariness, no evidence of sleeplessness. His cigar was out. 'I must leave now. Be here when I return.'

'Oh, my dear, what a lot of work for you!'

The Admiralty car collected Winston and his private detective, W. H. Thompson, at ten minutes to six and swept across Horse Guards Parade. The barbed-wire barrier was opened by two soldiers, the corporal in charge presenting arms as the big black limousine emerged into St James's Park. There was little traffic down the Mall. Although it was rush hour

504

no public transport used this route, and because of petrol rationing few people drove to work. The sun was still high in the early summer sky, and the leaves were fresh on the plane trees.

It was nearly a year since Buckingham Palace, royal standard flying above, had assumed its war guise, with sandbags and drawn curtains or shutters on the ground floor. There were no sightseers, no curious members of the public to watch the comings and goings. Everyone had news of the assault on the West, but no member of the public was aware of the political upheaval.

King George was in his small study on the first floor, dressed for the occasion in his uniform of admiral of the fleet. He had served in the Navy in the Great War, had fought at Jutland, was proud of the fact, and wore the appropriate war ribbons; a pale figure of medium height, he had a pleasing vulnerable face.

George VI did not approve of Winston. Unlike his grandfather, Edward VII, who had loved dash, flash, and eccentricity, 'Bertie' had inherited his father's suspicion of the irregular and had an earnest desire to follow the qualities of the traditional Conservatives. The Hanoverian anxiety to conform and show suspicion of the decadent aristocracy (as they saw it) had somehow missed out Edward VII, but was bred strongly in his son and grandson. George VI regarded Winston as a bit of a cad and an ambitious turncoat who would go to undue lengths to achieve his ambitions. Winston had supported Bertie's elder brother, David, when he wanted to marry an American divorcée, something that his wife, dear Elizabeth, found especially hard to forgive. Winston had also savagely attacked the saintly Neville Chamberlain, who was a gentleman and had fought so selflessly for peace in our time.

In fact, George VI so admired the arch-appeaser Chamberlain that he had wanted to go to the airport to meet and congratulate his Prime Minister when he returned from Munich in 1938 with his hollow promises from Hitler. This would have been political intervention on a highly controversial issue, as he was warned. But he still insisted on inviting

Chamberlain on to the Buckingham Palace balcony to receive the plaudits of the crowds. Winston, and all those opposed to the Munich Agreement and fighting for greater preparations for war, had been appalled.

Now, for King George, the thought of Winston as Prime Minister was distinctly unsavoury. Moreover, he would be seeing him several times a week. Never for one moment would the King oppose Chamberlain's choice of a successor, but how he would have preferred Lord Halifax. Edward Halifax was a gentleman, too, and a friend who had a special dispensation to walk through the gardens of Buckingham Palace on his way to the Foreign Office every morning. 'I met Halifax in the garden,' the King wrote in his diary the next day, '& I told him I was sorry not to have him as P.M.'

Anyway, here was Winston, dressed correctly (something George VI always noticed) in morning coat, pinstriped dark grey trousers, polka-dot bow tie – something else he would have to get used to – bowing deeply before him.

'Sit down, Mr Churchill,' George VI said, offering him a cigar, which he lit for him, and taking a cigarette himself. 'I suppose you don't know why I have sent for you?' he asked quizzically, with a half smile.

Winston matched the tone. 'Sir, I simply cannot imagine why.'

The King laughed. 'I want to ask you to form a Government. Will you do that, Mr Churchill?'

Seriously now, Winston answered, 'Yes, I will certainly do so.'

There followed a short discussion on the military scene, and it was clear that the King had as full and up-to-date news as Winston. Then, before taking his leave, Winston said, 'I propose to form a Government of national character under the circumstances. We need the best men from all the parties for the struggle that lies ahead. The first thing I shall do is to send for the leaders of the Labour and Liberal parties, and then form a War Cabinet of five or six ministers. I will, sir, hope to let you have at least five names before midnight.'

The King rose from his chair. 'You will have a busy evening, Mr Churchill.'

Winston smiled. 'Yes, sir.' He bowed his head and strode for the door, which was opened for him. Once outside, he replaced the cigar in his mouth, although it had gone out. There was still no-one but police at the gates. History had been made without a witness. 'I felt as if I were walking with destiny,' he later wrote of that evening, 'and that all my past life had been but a preparation for this hour and for this trial . . . There remained for me only to vindicate my father's memory.'

He did not exchange a word with Thompson on the way back. But at the end of the brief journey, while he was descending from the car, he said, 'You know why I have been to Buckingham Palace, Thompson?'

'Yes, sir. And I hope I may be allowed to congratulate you. I only wish,' he continued, 'that the position had come your way in better times for you have an enormous task.'

Thompson noticed that there were tears in Winston's eyes as he replied: 'God alone knows how great it is. I hope that it is not too late. I am very much afraid that it is. We can only do our best.'

Winston formed his administration with the speed that the situation demanded, bringing in leading Labour and Liberal figures. Significantly, the Government did not include his old friend who had led the nation to victory in 1918, David Lloyd George, although, to Clementine's horror, he was offered, but declined, Agriculture. It did include the pliant Labour member A. V. Alexander as First Lord of the Admiralty, which Winston proposed largely to run himself. Halifax remained for the time being at the Foreign Office. Max Beaverbrook (against the King's advice and to Clementine's distress) became Minister of Aircraft Production. The King was informed of the names of five of the leading ministers, as promised, that same evening of 10 May, and three days later the Government was complete.

Winston's accession to power was not universally welcomed. From the hard core of pro-Chamberlain back benchers there was great dismay, and when, in turn, Chamberlain and Winston entered the House, it was the ex-Prime Minister who received the greater accolade. Chips Channon, with his little group of loyalists, drinking on the evening of Chamberlain's resignation, confided to his diary: 'We were all sad, angry and felt cheated and outwitted.' Another of the group, which included R. A. Butler and a future Prime Minister (as Lord Home), was Jock Colville, one of the Prime Minister's secretariat and, at 24, the youngest, who said: 'Everybody here is in despair at the prospect of Winston as Prime Minister.' And on the following day, clutching at any straw, Colville added, 'There seems to be some inclination in Whitehall to believe that Winston will be a complete failure and that Neville will return.'

If Winston had been made aware of this puny cavilling he would have brushed it aside as beneath contempt; as it was, he was busier than ever before in his life, with scarcely time to look at a few (selected from hundreds by his secretarial staff) of the congratulatory letters and telegrams that poured into his office. But there was one from Pamela Lytton that he did not miss. She was now in her sixties, still happily married to Victor, with two daughters and a son,* and still a close friend of Winston's. 'All my life I have known you would become P.M.,' she wrote, 'ever since Hansom Cab days! Yet, now that you *are*, the news sets one's heart beating like a sudden surprise.'

'Thank you so much dear Pamela,' Winston telegraphed back.

'Thank heaven that you are there, and at the helm of our destiny,' wrote Violet Bonham Carter '– and may the nation's spirit be kindled by your own.'

---

*This son was later killed in action, his brother having been killed in a flying accident in 1933.

Winston's power was now absolute. To make this abundantly clear – as if it were necessary! – he created a new 'supremo' post, Minister of Defence, and added it to his prime ministerial duties. His confidence in his own genius was limitless, his power of application and dedication unsurpassed, his attention to the smallest detail exceeded only by his talent for encompassing, like the sweep of a radar aerial, a complete strategic concept. His sheer physical endurance, remarkable for a man of 65, was quite as great as when he had been at the Admiralty twenty-six years earlier.

Winston had always been convinced that the failure of operations for which he had been responsible, from Gallipoli to Norway, was caused by his lack of supreme power and control over events. He knew, and told the people of Britain and the Commonwealth, and those who had fled here to continue the fight, that defeats and setbacks were inevitable, that 'blood, toil, tears and sweat' were all that he could offer for the present, but that the righteous cause must prevail.

> We have before us an ordeal of the most grievous kind [he told the Commons on Monday 13 May, as the German armies swept into France]. We have before us many, many long months of struggle and suffering. You ask us what is our policy? I will say: it is to wage war, by sea, land and air, with all our might and with all the strength that God can give us: to wage war against a monstrous tyranny, never surpassed in the dark lamentable catalogue of human crime. That is our policy. You ask, What is our aim? I can answer in one word: Victory – victory at all costs, victory in spite of all terror, victory, however long and hard the road may be; for without victory there is no survival. . . . I take up my task with buoyancy and hope. I feel sure that our cause will not be suffered to fail among men. At this time I feel entitled to claim the aid of all, and I say, 'Come, then, let us go forward together with our united strength.'

The first evidence of the rigours and intensity of the new regime was in the retention of an office at the Admiralty for Winston's night work, in addition to the establishment at 10 Downing Street. Some of Chamberlain's staff were peremptorily sacked, and Colville might well have been among them if his antagonism towards Winston had been known. Eric Seal was retained as Winston's Principal Private Secretary and also John Peck, both of whom made it amply clear that the survivors of Chamberlain's staff would now be expected to work at least twice as hard and through a good part of the night. Anthony Bevir, who had been gassed in the Great War, also joined the Downing Street staff at this time, along with the able, witty, but shy John Martin.

All these, and many more of Winston's close staff, including Miss Kathleen Hill, his chief shorthand taker, typist and secretary throughout the war, and her staff, by day and by night, formed a team that worked together compatibly while learning much about one another and even more about their master. They learned of Winston's demanding nature, which took little or no interest in their convenience or comfort but much interest in their welfare if illness or personal distress was drawn to his attention. He was quite likely to interrupt them in the middle of a much-delayed meal or sleep or bath. He himself hated to have a meal or afternoon sleep cut short, but he would often summon a secretary to his bath or while he was dressing.

They learned that Winston expected things to be done, memoranda or letters typed, immediately and often at a speed beyond human contrivance; and that it was a crime in his eyes for his staff to forget something or, worse still, for him to suspect that one of his staff clearly hoped he would fail to remember some oversight. His anger was appalling to witness and unforgettable. But it was brief, and the occasion was never again referred to. If anger was unjustly applied, there would be no apology, but the sunshine following the storm was the more radiant.

On what she called her 'baptism of fire', Marian Holmes

510

was taking dictation directly on to the silent typewriter he always insisted should be used. She misunderstood a long pause as the completion of her duty. 'Dammit, don't go,' Winston called out loudly. 'I've only just started.'

> He then looked up. 'I'm so sorry. I thought it was Miss Layton. What is your name?' 'Miss Holmes.' 'Miss Hope?' 'Miss Holmes.' 'Oh.' He then carried on dictating directives and comments on various documents from his box, every so often glancing at me over his spectacles. 'That is all for the moment. You know you must never be frightened of me when I snap. I'm not snapping at you but thinking of the work.' This was said with a cherubic smile.

Winston's secretariat basked as much in his loyalty to them as in the team solidarity and loyalty he aroused in them. One and all were treated exactly as if they were part of his family. Their loyalty not only survived his awkwardness and peremptoriness, his thoughtlessness and black storms, but actually thrived and flourished on these demerits. For he held no grudges and was rich in magnanimity and poor in vindictiveness. At the same time, his staff had to admit that his sentimental loyalty to old friends, especially old *brave* friends, like the egocentric Roger Keyes and Sir Archibald Sinclair, could be excessive. Keyes at Combined Operations was not a success, and although Sinclair survived the entire war at the Air Ministry it might have been better if he had not done so. Sinclair's relations with Beaverbrook were especially bad.

This secretariat rapidly adjusted themselves to a working routine that could hardly be more different from Chamberlain's. First, there was Winston's capacity to deal with several subjects and several of his staff at the same time, delegating decisions to others if they did not interest him, like home affairs, and dictating answers and orders with extraordinary speed – 'Pray, let me have on a single sheet

511

by . . .' Winston's 'prayers' rapidly became notorious to the wide range of authorities who received them, and down to their lowest subordinates.

Second, there were his working hours. He would usually awake at 8 a.m., when a large cooked breakfast would arrive with the boxes and, almost immediately, Miss Hill. Work would begin at once, his bed a desk, punctuated frequently by telephone calls and by arrivals and departures. The cat, Nelson, was usually at hand, stroked and murmured to when Winston was teasing a problem. At ten o'clock his valet would arrive, draw his bath and lay out his clothes. Miss Hill would leave, with enough typing to keep most secretaries busy for a week. Much of it would be passed out to the typing pool for retyping.

The remainder of the morning might be occupied with a meeting of the chiefs of staff or of the War Cabinet, although he might also have brief meetings with individuals after midday. The remarkable General Hastings ('Pug') Ismay, a fine, honourable, loyal, dedicated soldier who was Winston's chief of staff and his forceful but discreet link between the armed services and the politicians, was almost always at hand, as were Ismay's equally efficient assistants, General Sir Ian Jacob and Sir Leslie Hollis.

After a good lunch with Clementine – often their first meeting of the day – and one or more members of his secretariat and perhaps Sinclair and one or two others, he would return to his bedroom and have not merely a nap but a deep sleep for an hour, sometimes longer, followed by another bath. Later in the afternoon he would go to the House when it was sitting, and if he was not answering questions at question time or making a speech, his cronies would gather around him in the Smoking Room and begin drinking and listening, often before six o'clock.

Back at Downing Street, always with Thompson alert at his side on every journey, there might be more meetings and telephoning, sometimes to Roosevelt, especially after the United States became an ally. Miss Hill might be called in for a few last letters before Winston changed for dinner.

Dinner, in peace or war, tended to be the longest single event of the day, accompanied by vintage Pol Roger champagne and fine claret or burgundy. Jack and Goonie might be there and perhaps the Portals,* Jock Colville and another couple – around twelve in all unless there was a visiting dignitary, when there would be more. The quality of the food was superb and virtually unaffected by rationing, which might not have existed as far as 10 Downing Street and Chequers (the Prime Minister's country retreat) were concerned. Mrs Georgina Landemare was an exceptional cook and could, when required (which was quite often), put back the time of a meal at short notice.

The women would retire in due course, and in the dining room the brandy and cigars would go round and Winston would continue to hold the conversation over a vast range of topics, sinking into a glum silence in the rare event of a debate between two of the guests.

Jock Colville once stated that Winston's after-dinner conversation was often a monologue, interspersed with comments from those who knew him well enough to risk it.

But in fact he welcomed interruptions, however contradictory or irreverent, provided they were short, witty and did not stem the flow or divert the theme. Sometimes, when he was tired, he used his audience as a waste-paper basket, or repeated long stories they had all heard before, but when he did this it was frequently because his thoughts were on something else, and the surface talk was an automatic exercise. I remember on one occasion he saw us yawn, and he looked benignly at Commander Thompson, the 'Flag Commander', saying: 'You must admit, Tommy, that

---

*Air Marshal Sir Charles (Peter) Portal, Chief of Air Staff from October 1940, and his wife, Joan, much loved by Clementine.

at least I do not repeat my stories as frequently as our dear friend, the President of the United States.'

The men might rejoin the ladies at around 11 p.m., but at this time Winston would disappear into his office for the long night session with his night staff.

The large desk does not have on it the neat piles of papers specially selected for formal photographs, but is covered with a great many knick-knacks, mostly of a sentimental nature, gold medals (which he favours as paperweights), toothpicks, and common clerks' sleeve cuffs. Beside the desk is a table on which sit bottles of whisky (single malt and blends), glasses, and several soda syphons, and a box of Havana cigars. One of the night secretary's duties is to ensure that a tumbler of whisky and soda is constantly on hand. A great deal of it will be drunk during the night, but woe betide the secretary who puts in more than half a finger of whisky to a near half pint of soda – without ice of course.

This night session will probably continue until 3.30 or even 4 a.m., when Winston will suddenly retire, saying good night as he goes through the door. In less than five minutes he is in a deep sleep.

Winston's instructions were to awaken him early only on the most urgent need. Five mornings after the pre-dawn news of the invasion from Germany, Paul Reynaud, the French Prime Minister, telephoned at 7 a.m. in a great state of anxiety, demanding to be put through to Winston. It was 15 May, another brilliant summer early morning. The secretary on duty decided that the call should be put through. Winston listened in alarm and disbelief to Reynaud's halting English, reporting catastrophe and breakthrough. 'The battle is lost, Monsieur Churchill. We shall be giving up the struggle . . .'

'Surely, Mr Reynaud, it cannot have happened so soon?'

'The front is broken near Sedan. The Germans are pouring through in great numbers.' The Frenchman was in a state of total despair.

Winston tried to rally him. 'All experience shows that the

offensive will come to an end after a while. I remember 21 March 1918. After five or six days they have to halt for supplies, and the opportunity for counter-attack is presented.' To impress Reynaud, he added. 'All this I learned from the lips of Marshal Foch himself.'

There was silence at the other end of the line. Then, in the same broken voice: 'We are defeated; we have lost the battle.'

Winston, recalling that visit to France in March 1918, when 700,000 German infantry burst through the massive British defence line, indicated that he would come over himself. By the time Winston's plane flew off from Croydon the following afternoon, with an escort of Spitfire fighters, the Dutch forces had capitulated, Belgium was overrun, and the penetrations into France were so deep that the Germans were expected in Paris in about three days. With Pug Ismay and his staff, Winston hastened from Le Bourget to the Quai d'Orsay in the centre of the city. There were bonfires of confidential documents, the rising grey smoke staining the blue sky with shame.

Winston has written of his reception:

> *Reynaud was there, Daladier, Minister of National Defence and War, and General Gamelin. Everybody was standing. At no time did we sit down round a table. Utter dejection was written on every face. In front of Gamelin on a student's easel was a map. . . . The Commander-in-Chief briefly explained what had happened. North and south of Sedan, on a front of fifty or sixty miles, the Germans had broken through . . .*

A few minutes later the explanation, such as it was, concluded. Winston broke the silence with the question, 'Where is the strategic reserve?' and then repeated his question in his execrable French, '*Où est la masse de manoeuvre?*'

Gamelin shook his head sadly, and shrugged his shoulders. '*Aucune.*'

None? No reserve? Winston could not believe his ears. 'What were we to think of the great French army and its highest chiefs?'

Criticism was futile at this stage: besides, the French could point to the fact that the puny British Expeditionary Force (BEF) could not boast a single armoured division or claim it had been in any way reinforced since the outbreak of war. What the French needed above everything was the RAF. Their own air force, such as it was, had been already all but wiped out. But Fighter Command at home was the first line of the nation's defence in the event of a German invasion. In the end Winston telegraphed London to despatch six more fighter squadrons, above the four already promised, leaving Fighter Command with the rock-bottom minimum for home defence. The long telegram to the Cabinet was dictated in the simplest code by Ismay in Hindustani, in which he was fluent, to an Indian officer standing by in London.

Surely this would cheer the French and relieve some of the gloom and despondency in which they were immersed. The news was given to Daladier and Reynaud (in pyjamas) in the early hours. 'Daladier never spoke a word. He rose slowly from his chair and wrung my hand,' Winston recounted.

In less than ten days from the first breakthrough, Lord Gort, the British Commander in Chief in France, was engaged in contingency planning for 'a possible withdrawal towards Dunkirk'. The following afternoon 'the emergency evacuation across the Channel of very large forces' was under discussion at Dover, and the excellent Admiral Sir Bertram Ramsay was put in operational control if it became necessary to withdraw the BEF.

Meanwhile, the German armoured columns swept forward as if on manoeuvres. Little or no attempt was made to halt them. They just followed the roads, and when they ran short of fuel they simply filled up, like summer tourists, at the filling stations. Great numbers of utterly demoralized and leaderless French troops surrendered with their arms. When they had time the Germans smashed the French rifles by running over them with tanks.

Winston flew to Paris again on 22 May, in another attempt to put steel into the French government, leaving his deputy, the Labour leader Clement Attlee, to see through a parliamentary bill which gave the Government such wide powers that Britain was converted overnight into a parliamentary near-dictatorship. Reynaud had assumed the roles of Prime Minister and War Minister and was endeavouring to form a new French army from reserves in Alsace and North Africa.

As the last days of May ticked away, Belgium surrendered and the BEF was forced, along with great numbers of French soldiers, back to the Channel ports, and the ultimate defeat of France became inevitable. Armoured enemy columns coming up from the south were already closing on Boulogne, which was evacuated by sea after a stiff fight. Winston gave orders that Calais should be defended to the death, however. 'Every hour you continue to exist is of the greatest help to the BEF,' he signalled the brigadier commanding the defence. 'Have greatest possible admiration for your splendid stand . . .'

These defenders of Calais, and a tremendous defence put up by five French divisions over three days, when hopelessly outnumbered, made it possible for half the French First Army and the greater part of the BEF to fall back on Dunkirk, where their evacuation had been urgently organized.

'The House,' Winston announced solemnly, 'should prepare itself for hard and heavy tidings.' 'The deliverance of Dunkirk', as he called it, began at 6.57 a.m. on 26 May. All that was left as a toehold for the British and French troops was the port of Dunkirk and the open beaches to the east. Two days later, 50,000 men had been evacuated safely by some 40 destroyers, 36 minesweepers, 77 trawlers and drifters, personnel ships, and, later, many other vessels, down to scores of private motor yachts, ketches, cutters, cockle bawleys, Thames ferryboats and barges, and even lifeboats purloined from docked liners. These 'little ships', which were to become a part of the legend of Dunkirk, were

517

used to ferry the troops out to the larger vessels; and it was, improbably, thanks to Jack Churchill's artist son, Johnny, that they were present in their hundreds and saved so many soldiers from death or capture.

The evacuation was already under way when Lord Gort recognized that it could be much speeded up by using small boats from the beaches. The matter was one of the utmost urgency, and it was decided that the one soldier Winston would listen to was his nephew, a corps camouflage officer. He was instantly despatched to London, and arrived at Admiralty House, soaked through, to be greeted by his uncle and Clementine, still in their dressing gowns.

'I see you have come straight from battle,' Winston declared delightedly.

Johnny explained the purpose of his mission, and within minutes orders were despatched to requisition boats and recruit crews. Within twenty-four hours they were being towed in convoy across the Channel or proceeding under their own power. Meanwhile, the larger vessels plied to and fro across the Channel, by day under almost constant shelling and bombing and machine-gunning from the air, while French and British troops fought gallantly to hold the perimeter and keep the German vanguard at bay. Casualties were grievous, and 243 vessels in all, including 9 destroyers and more than one hundred 'little ships', were sunk. But over three hundred and thirty eight thousand troops had been landed safely in Britain when the evacuation had finally to be concluded on 4 June. Some had their rifles, but most had lost their arms, and all the tanks, armoured carriers, trucks and artillery were lost to the enemy.

Parliament assembled on the same day, and Winston made one of his most notable and memorable speeches of the war. In it he sounded a note of thankfulness and relief at the massive escape from the enemy, with special credit to the RAF. Few RAF fighters were seen over the bridgehead, but they were out every day, in great numbers and inflicting savage losses on the Luftwaffe. Unfortunately, much of the fighting was above cloud or out of sight of the beleaguered troops, and bad feeling had been aroused between the two services.

Winston warned, 'We must be very careful not to assign to this deliverance the attributes of a victory. Wars are not won by evacuations. But there was a victory inside this deliverance, which should be noted. It was gained by the Air Force.' And he ended his long, uplifting speech, heavy with rhetoric and facts, with a clarion call and an important reference to the United States, which would ensure that it was widely reported across the Atlantic.

> Even though large tracts of Europe and many old and famous States have fallen or may fall into the grip of the Gestapo and all the odious apparatus of Nazi rule, we shall not flag or fail. We shall go on to the end, we shall fight in France, we shall fight on the seas and oceans, we shall fight with growing confidence and growing strength in the air, we shall defend our island, whatever the cost may be, we shall fight on the beaches, we shall fight on the landing grounds, we shall fight in the fields and in the streets, we shall fight in the hills; we shall never surrender, and even if, which I do not for a moment believe, this island or a large part of it were subjugated and starving, then our Empire beyond the seas, armed and guarded by the British Fleet, would carry on the struggle, until, in God's good time, the new world, with all its power and might, steps forth to the rescue and the liberation of the old.

In the thick of the French fighting, on 15 May, Winston had found time to send a long telegram to Roosevelt, defining the extremity of the situation. 'We expect to be attacked here ourselves,' he told the President, '. . . and are getting ready for them. If necessary, we shall continue the war alone and we are not afraid of that. But I trust you realize, Mr President, that the voice and force of the United States may count for nothing if they are withheld too long . . .'

Winston then continued with a long shopping list of 'immediate needs', including several hundred of the latest types of aircraft, a loan of forty or fifty destroyers, steel, anti-aircraft guns and ammunition. After Dunkirk, Winston reiterated the items he wanted most urgently, but whatever the personal feelings of the President might be, he was governed by Congress, the mood of the American people was certainly not for military intervention, and Joseph Kennedy was sounding ever louder his defeatist message from the American Embassy in London. Winston knew that he had a long haul ahead in persuading the United States to become involved in the European war, but he kept hammering away, repeating his appeal for the loan of destroyers and the transfer of fighters from the US army to Britain. When he passed the draft to Jock Colville, he said sharply, 'Here's a telegram for those bloody Yankees. Send it off tonight.'

Winston did not get either destroyers or fighters immediately, but he was greatly encouraged by Roosevelt's 'magnificent speech, instinct with passion and carrying us a message of hope' when Italy entered the war on the German side and attacked France in the south – 'the hand that held the dagger has struck it into the back of its neighbour.' He was also encouraged – excited even – by a report from the British Embassy in Washington that Roosevelt was prepared to go far beyond lending some destroyers if Britain was really *in extremis*. Yes, telegraphed Lord Lothian, the Ambassador, in that event the United States would come in, suggesting that with the additional resources of the British and French empires – Canada, North Africa, Australia, New Zealand, South Africa and the French possessions in the Far East – and on the assumption that the Royal Navy survived, the war could be carried on from Canada. Roosevelt added what Lothian called 'the curious suggestion that the seat of Government should be Bermuda and not Ottawa, as the American republics would dislike the idea of a monarchy functioning on the American Continent!'

*

After the deliverance of Dunkirk, the battle for France continued, the French having some success against the incompetent and over-confident Italians. But the pressure was too great, and although the pace of the retreat slackened, by the time Winston agreed to make a fourth flying visit from London the rendezvous with the French leaders could no longer be Paris. The Government had moved to Tours, and Winston's escorted aircraft made a landing on a small airfield there. He was met by glum faces, and it was typical of the state of morale and disorganization that the meeting was held in a château with one lavatory and one telephone, which was almost unserviceable anyway.

Every argument Winston and Ismay put forward for holding the German advance was countered by excuses – the roads were crowded with refugees, there were no reserves, there was no point in fighting for Paris. 'Making Paris into a ruin would not affect the final event.' All they wanted was the RAF – every single fighter squadron: that was where their hope lay. 'Now is the decisive moment,' Weygand appealed. No, argued Winston, this is not the decisive moment. 'The moment will come when Hitler hurls his Luftwaffe against Great Britain. If we can keep command of the air, and if we can keep the seas open, as we shall certainly keep them open, we will win it all back for you.'

There was only one new, and impressive, figure at the meeting – Charles de Gaulle, a junior general recently appointed Undersecretary for National Defence. Winston eyed him with some favour in the midst of what he called 'this miserable discussion'. The complete and utter debasement of France, from the civilian level to the military high command and the Prime Minister, was etched with memorable precision on his mind when a message came through from the RAF. A bombing force in the south of France was about to take off to bomb Italy, but the local authorities refused to allow them to do so. After a difficult discussion Reynaud agreed to overrule these local authorities. But by then it was too late. The citizenry, it was learned, fearful of reprisals, had obstructed the runway with trucks and carts. This one minor event seemed to reflect the complete demoralization of the French people.

On the way back home, without escort because of inclement weather, Winston's pilot spotted German fighters below. They were attacking fishing vessels. There was fatter game above for them, but mercifully the pilot, responsible for the heart of Britain's war machine, succeeded in evading them and was soon met by a force of British fighters – fighters that the French were still crying out for even as they were suing for an armistice with Adolf Hitler.

For the first time in some 125 years, Britain was threatened by invasion by a great Continental land power. The people were bewildered by the speed of events and the imminence of the danger. But they were also in a prime condition for rallying, in spirit, determination and industry. From supine pacifism to a pacific war, they had now been dragged, willy-nilly, to the reality of a militarized and conquered Europe, 23 miles distant at the nearest point.

The British people had watched nation after nation succumb pacifically or violently to German power and wicked tyranny. They were ready to be organized, ordered and raised in spirit to meet this menace. They were ready to put everything on a secondary basis to military readiness and, above all, to be inspired by a great leader. The gods of fate had given them Winston Churchill, and for him it was – as he was to remind an audience later – 'the nation and the race dwelling all round the globe that had the lion's heart. I had the luck to be called upon to give the roar.'

During the critical weeks between Winston's accession to the premiership and the air offensive against Britain after the defeat of France, Clementine and her entourage and Mary continued to live in Admiralty House. They finally moved to 10 Downing Street on 14 June, while an additional flat, the Annexe, was converted and used domestically nearby above Storey's Gate. Besides Mary, Jack was another member of the family who had to be accommodated. Goonie's health was precarious; she was suffering from cancer and had to live in the country. Jack had made for himself a job in Winston's entourage that carried no title, or definition even, but he was a sort of aide-de-camp. 'Self-effacing and discreet,' Mary described him, 'Jack was the most loyal of brothers and was always there when he was needed.'

Grace Hamblin, or 'Hambone', as the children still called her, Clementine's private secretary at Chartwell, where she used to live out with her parents, now came to live permanently with Clementine in London, a priceless asset and a much-loved woman.

Besides all the service chiefs and senior officers of the armed forces, there came to number 10 the ministers of the day – Beaverbrook and Sinclair most frequently, but *not* together – and the leaders of the expatriate occupied nations, such as General Sikorsky, from Poland, and General de Gaulle, leading the Free French. Then there were the children. Randolph had returned with his regiment from abroad, sought a seat in Parliament, and been returned unopposed for the totally safe Conservative seat of Preston, and thus he became a soldier-statesman in somewhat muted emulation of his father.

Randolph was generally loathed by his father's secretariat. 'I thought Randolph one of the most objectionable people I had ever met,' Jock Colville recalled. 'Noisy, self-assertive, whining, and frankly unpleasant. He did not strike me as intelligent.' Pamela was with child, and the present Winston Spencer Churchill, MP, was born on 10 October. Diana's life was relatively straightforward at this time, although, with everything in turmoil, each day could bring more bedlam and the closer imminence of catastrophe. Julian and Edwina were still at the Chartwell cottage; Duncan had just got back from Norway, where he had been with his anti-aircraft regiment. Later, the children had to be retrieved from the Kent cottage for safety; Duncan was invalided out of the Army after a crippling accident; and Diana herself, who enjoyed her time in the WRNS, had to resign her commission for family reasons.

While Diana's second marriage endured happily, the marriage of Sarah and Vic Oliver was soon breaking up, as Clementine had feared it would. Of Winston and Clementine's children, Sarah was the most unbalanced and the most affected by the Marlborough–Ogilvy strain of unsteadiness and tendency to hysteria. But when she had a part on the stage she was determinedly professional and, in that summer of 1940, was much admired in Ivor Novello's *Murder in Mayfair* – a somewhat questionable title with the bombs falling freely and killing many in the West End of London. After the break-up of her marriage, Sarah packed in her acting career and joined the Air Force as a lowly WAAF. She was later commissioned and did useful service in photographic intelligence.

Soon after Dunkirk, Mary, not yet 18, went to stay with Venetia Montagu (née Stanley) in Norfolk. Edwin had died young, leaving Venetia with a daughter, Judy, one of Mary's closest friends. When the German bombing became serious Mary was prohibited from London and lived at Chequers for the time being.

With her husband as Prime Minister, Clementine's strictures and complaints, and her own nagging anxieties, increased rather than diminished. The detested Birkenhead was long since dead, but war brought the equally detested Beaverbrook and Brendan Bracken more than ever into the bounds of their household. And Sir John Anderson, Home Secretary, was only one of a number of her new enemies. Beaverbrook and Bracken, so important in Winston's close team, put up philosophically with Clementine's all-too-evident antagonism.

As for Winston's secretariat, at one time or another Clementine succeeded in making herself a nuisance with all of them. Like a very bad queen, she would be friendly – almost too friendly – at times, especially when circumstances were relatively relaxed, and then jump on them if they did not toe the line when it suited her that they should. Jock Colville, who was with her a great deal and used to play bézique, tennis and croquet with her and travel long distances at her side in motor cars and trains, would suddenly find himself severely dealt with.

When Clementine had to go to Glasgow on 24 October, she ordered Colville to make the necessary arrangements. As he was extremely busy on his official work he delegated the task to Miss Hamblin – whose job it was anyway. When Clementine learned of this she was furious with him, accusing him of giving himself airs. Her tirade was listened to with great amusement by Brendan Bracken: 'Mrs C considers it one of her missions in life to put people in their place and prides herself on being outspoken.' Colville also found her perversity trying: 'She can never resist an opportunity of taking the opposite view.' And she was all too ready to take offence.

Jock Colville, a highly intelligent observer and judge, also found Clementine unsound in her views. 'We talked a good deal of politics,' he wrote of one car journey, 'about which her views are as ill-judged as they are decisive.' She was certainly, as so often in the past, unsound in her judgement of Winston and his style of leadership. Rough as he could be with his colleagues, they were well used to his outspokenness or, if new to the job, soon would become so. At the very height of the post-Dunkirk, invasion-risk period, when a thousand problems had to be faced and decisions made daily, Clementine wrote a letter of warning to him:

> *My Darling,*
> *I hope you will forgive me if I tell you something I feel you ought to know.*
> *One of the men in your entourage (a devoted friend) has been to me & told me that there is a danger of your being generally disliked by your colleagues and subordinates because of your rough sarcastic & overbearing manner – It seems your Private Secretaries have agreed to behave like school boys & 'take what's coming to them' & then escape out of your presence . . . My darling Winston, I must confess that I have noticed a deterioration in your manner; &*

you are not as kind as you used to be . . . you must
combine urbanity, kindness and if possible Olympic
calm . . . Besides you won't get the best results by
irascibility & rudeness . . .

Clementine could not have been referring to Seal, Winston's
Principal Private Secretary, who represented the general view
of the secretariat, as her informant. He confided in Colville
his belief that Winston had changed so much since becoming
Prime Minister: 'He has sobered down, become less violent,
less wild, less impetuous.' No other great leader, in a time of
national crisis, was served by a more loyal, dedicated and, if
occasionally exhausted and exasperated, ardently admiring –
even loving – staff.

30

'America on the Brink'

A telegram to the British Ambassador in Washington, Lord Lothian, summed up Winston's views on the United States while instructing Lothian about the attitude this influential, intelligent and well-informed diplomat should take up. Only the force of events, Winston believed, could govern United States opinion. 'Up till April they were so sure the Allies would win that they did not think help necessary. Now they are so sure we shall lose that they do not think it possible.' Roosevelt was facing his third presidential election, and the American political scene was swiftly developing its usual sensitive condition at this time.

Winston concluded his telegram:

> *We know President is our best friend, but it is no use trying to dance attendance upon Republican and Democratic Conventions. What really matters is whether Hitler is master of Britain in three months or not. I think not. But this is a matter which cannot be argued beforehand. Your mood should be bland and phlegmatic. No one is down-hearted here.*

At this time, the end of June, almost no munitions had arrived from the United States. A trickle of American aid began in the following month and later rose to a flood. The first need was for rifles and ammunition. Tens of thousands of rifles had been lost in France, and reserves were limited. The civilian Home Guard, part-time civilian volunteers, were drilling with pikes and broomsticks. Fast freighters, heavily escorted, were commissioned to bring in the first 100,000 American rifles, and special trains were ready at the ports to distribute them to troops and Home Guards awaiting the threatened German invasion of the southern and south-eastern coasts.

Winston did not, in his heart of hearts, believe that the Wehrmacht would attempt an invasion. The German army was still stunned by the swiftness of France's collapse and was quite unprepared for the enormous planning and logistical effort an invasion would entail. No landing craft were even under construction, and the Luftwaffe had not yet occupied, or built, the necessary airfields. The German navy had been crippled in the Norwegian campaign. Yet contingency plans to meet the threat had to be made with the utmost urgency, and Winston was shrewd enough to recognize the immense patriotic rallying effect on the people that these preparations would inspire.

The communal digging of tank traps and filling of sandbags by the million; the overnight construction of concrete pillboxes all over the southern counties; the equally swift appearance of barbed-wire defences and mine warning signs along the beaches; stout stakes and old vehicles in the fields to prohibit landings from the air; the removal of all road signs, even railway-station signs; the order to immobilize cars when parked: all this had an extraordinary stiffening effect on a people who, twenty months earlier, had been cheering Neville Chamberlain as he returned from a meeting with Hitler with a piece of paper in hand, saying, 'Peace in our time.'

> *We are greatly concerned* [Winston wrote to Ismay] *– and it is certainly wise to be so – with the danger of the Germans landing in England in spite of our possessing the command of the seas and having very strong defence by fighters in the air. Every creek, every beach, every harbour has become to us a source of anxiety . . .*

Winston also believed in seeing for himself and making his presence felt, so he toured risk areas, firing questions at local commanders and private soldiers alike. On 3 July, accompanied by Clementine, he visited the headquarters of the 3rd Division and met its commanding officer, General Bernard Montgomery, for the first time. Here he witnessed an exercise featuring all seven of the division's light tanks, each armed with a single Bren gun.

The party then drove into Brighton from the west, Winston pointing out the road where his school, run by the Misses Thompson, had been, and the pier on which he had played as a boy. In a kiosk where he had once admired the performing fleas a platoon of the Grenadier Guards was making a sandbag machine-gun post. Open-top buses still cruised up and down the Marine Parade between the barbed-wire sea defences and the hotels, which had mostly closed down due to the fear of invasion. Later, Winston issued orders to Montgomery to commandeer as many buses as he needed to provide his division with greater mobility.

'I was disturbed to find the 3rd Division spread along thirty miles of coast,' Winston minuted later, 'instead of being, as I had imagined, held back concentrated in reserve, ready to move against any serious head of invasion.'

Soon after this visit, General Ironside was replaced as Commander in Chief Home Command and in charge of all counter-invasion measures, by General Alan Brooke. 'Brookie' was already well known to Winston through his two elder brothers, whom he had known as young fellow officers, and a strong and invaluable mutual respect grew between the two men. On 17 July Winston was collected by the General from Gosport, and together they inspected the defences along the Hampshire and Dorset coasts. 'He was in wonderful spirits,' Brooke noted in his diary, 'and full of offensive plans for next summer. We had a long talk together, mostly about old days.'

It was especially heartening for Brooke, the tough professional soldier, to hear 'offensive' talk from Winston. Just twenty-three years earlier to the day, Winston had prepared a scheme for the capture of the enemy-held islands of Borkum and Sylt, close to the west German coast. The plan included the use not only of tanks but also of tank-landing craft and specially constructed 'bullet-proof lighters', both of them theoretical forerunners of the landing craft used in vast numbers in amphibious operations in the Pacific, the Mediterranean and the English Channel in 1942–45.

This 1917 plan had never been made public, but even before the last troops had been evacuated from Dunkirk, Winston was minuting Pug Ismay:

> . . . Enterprises must be prepared, with specially-trained troops of the hunter class, who can develop a reign of terror down [the enemy] coasts, first of all on the 'butcher and bolt' policy: but later on . . . we could surprise Calais or Boulogne, kill and capture the Hun garrison. . . . The passive resistance war, in which we have acquitted ourselves so well, must come to an end . . .

Commandos, or 'Leopards', were first proposed by Winston a week or so later, and a combined operations command in mid-July.

By agreement, neither France nor Britain could sue for peace without the consent of the other. When it was clear that the French were determined to reach an agreement for an armistice, Winston intimated that the Government might give this consent 'provided . . . that the French Fleet is sailed forthwith for British harbours pending negotiations'. Winston's one great fear was that Germany would make it a condition of French surrender that its fleet would be included. The French had a powerful fleet with many modern, fast and excellent cruisers, a carrier and four battleships of the most modern type, as well as earlier Dreadnoughts. In the event, the French fleet was scattered at the time of the French peace negotiations. Those ships at Plymouth were forcibly taken under British control, and many of the officers and men volunteered to serve with their former allies.

But the most powerful and potentially dangerous concentration of French warships was at Oran in the western Mediterranean on the North African coast. If these vessels fell into enemy hands they would provide a fearful threat to British naval power.

Winston decided, with a heavy heart, to take positive action against this fleet. Early on 1 July, an overwhelming force, including the biggest warship in the world, two more battleships and a modern carrier, as well as thirteen smaller craft, sailed from Gibraltar and on the following morning was off Oran. Now the Commander in Chief despatched an ultimatum to the French admiral that explained their presence and offered three 'fair offers': to join him and continue the fight against Germany, to sail under British control to a British port, or to sail with skeleton crews to a French port in the West Indies, 'where they can be demilitarized' or entrusted to the neutral care of the United States. Failing a reply within six hours, the ultimatum concluded, 'force may be necessary to prevent your ships from falling into German or Italian hands'.

There then followed a most miserable business. 'I sat all the afternoon in the Cabinet Room,' recalled Winston, 'in frequent contact . . .'

'You are charged with one of the most disagreeable and difficult tasks that a British Admiral has ever been faced with,' the admiral on the spot was signalled. And so it was. The French admiral, while claiming that he would not surrender his ships to the Germans, refused to give them up. A ten-minutes-long bombardment, followed by air attack, resulted in the crippling of all the big ships except one, which escaped, at a cost of more than 1,250 French lives. Winston wept while announcing the attack in the House of Commons, and 'the fatal stroke', as he called it, embittered Anglo-French relations for many years.

Step by rapid step, with the priceless aid of her dominions, Britain was securing herself under Winston's steady and dauntless leadership. By August, two months after the fall of France, the defences against invasion had been immeasurably strengthened, and the spirit of the people could now be compared to the image of the bulldog that Winston was satisfied to assume. The only weapon that could still cause the immediate defeat of Britain was air power. 'Our fate now depended upon victory in the air,' Winston stated baldly. In effect this meant that Britain's survival lay in the hands of a few hundred fighter pilots and in the construction, repair and maintenance of their machines.

Reichsmarschall Hermann Goering, the commander of the Luftwaffe, entered the conflict with the RAF in absolute confidence of swift victory, forgetting that Britain had had almost twenty-five years – since those Gotha attacks that had led to the Churchill children's evacuation to Lullenden – to perfect a command and co-ordinated communications system and radar chain. The Luftwaffe, on the other hand, had had no preparation or training for a sustained bombing attack against the airfields and air defences of an island power. Their bombers were ill protected and of modest size; their fighters, though quite as lethal as the RAF's, had been primarily designed to act with an advancing army, as in Poland, Norway, Belgium, Holland and France.

The odds were heavily loaded in favour of the Luftwaffe in numbers and in battle experience (many of the leading pilots had fought in Spain and learned much), but the RAF was fighting over its own territory, which had moral and practical advantages: many shot-down RAF fighter pilots were flying again in a few hours; most shot-down German airmen went either into the Channel or into a prisoner-of-war camp.

The bombing attacks against shipping and RAF airfields increased through the month of July. Day after day the formations of bombers came over, escorted by great numbers of fighters. The climax was reached in the middle of August, when many of the best pilots on both sides had been lost, their places taken by raw youngsters. By the end of this month the key British airfields had been devastated and the vital co-ordination of communications sorely damaged.

Winston and Clementine were able to see for themselves the importance and effectiveness of this control structure. On Sunday 15 September, they were at Chequers for the weekend when Winston decided that the early-morning weather suggested a big day for air battles. A telephone call was put through to RAF 11 Group Headquarters, at Uxbridge, in north-west London, where Air Vice-Marshal Keith Park was told that the Prime Minister would like to come over.

On arrival, they were taken straight down to the underground bomb-proof operations room, where Keith Park met them. He was a tall, narrow-faced New Zealander – with characteristic 'Kiwi' chin – who had fought in the RFC as a pilot in the Great War and remained in the service, achieving this high command early in this war. He was a man who believed in keeping in close touch with his men, flying in his own Hurricane to forward airfields to give advice and listen to problems. His group, with its twenty-five squadrons, covered the critical area of central south and south-east England, where the heaviest fighting had taken place. Already some two-thirds of the Hurricane and Spitfire pilots who had been under Park's command in early July were now dead or so grievously wounded that they were unlikely to return to their squadrons.

Park now returned to his seat with his staff high above the large-scale map-table, surrounded by WAAF and RAF plotters who took in the messages from the radar stations and, through 'tellers', translated them into numbered plots, showing the height, strength and direction of incoming raids. The controller's task, supervised by Park, was to issue orders to the Group's six sector stations and thence to the squadrons, to take off and climb on a given bearing to meet the enemy.

On that day it became increasingly clear that the Germans were coming in in greater numbers than ever before and that 11 Group was being stretched to the utmost. One by one, the big illuminated wall board showed squadrons being scrambled, and Park explained that they were calling on 10 Group to the west and 12 Group based in East Anglia and the Midlands for support. Yet still the enemy plots – forty, fifty, sixty – marched implacably across the table towards London.

533

'What other reserves have we?' Winston asked.

'There are none,' Park crisply replied.*

Winston, according to Park, 'looked grave' at this news. Winston later wrote of this moment: 'The odds were great; our margins small; the stakes infinite.' After the day's fighting appeared to be over, with record German losses, Winston and Clementine climbed up the steps from the underground bunker, blinking in the bright sunlight.

'We are very glad, sir, you have seen this,' Park remarked. 'Of course, during the last twenty minutes we were so choked with information that we couldn't handle it. This shows you the limitation of our present resources. They have been strained far beyond their limits today.'

'Have any results come to hand yet?' Winston asked. 'We appear to have repelled the attack satisfactorily.'

'I am not satisfied, sir, that we have intercepted as many raiders as I had hoped.'

What has now come to be known as 'Battle of Britain' day, 15 September, was clearly a disappointment to this commander.

Winston and Clementine motored straight back to Chequers. Sawyers met them at the door and enquired about the day's events. Winston did not give him a full account because he was intent on getting to his bed for his much-delayed sleep. He did not wake up until 8 p.m. and at once rang John Martin, asking for the day's news. Winston recalled:

It was repellent. This had gone wrong here; that had been delayed there; an unsatisfactory answer had been received from so-and-so; there had been sinkings in the Atlantic. 'However,' said Martin, as

---

*This was not strictly true, as there were several squadrons outside 11 Group that could still be called upon, but Park's assertion certainly added to the drama of the occasion.

he finished this account, 'all is redeemed by the air. We have shot down 183 for a loss of under forty.'*

Two days after this tremendous fight, Hitler gave the order to postpone the threatened invasion of Britain, but this was not known until much later, and Winston continued his frequent trips, in a train specially equipped with full office facilities, to the 'front line' towns and villages of Kent. Here he talked to the authorities about their problems and to those who had suffered from the bombing and the shellfire from Cap Gris Nez.

Winston also several times visited the much-bombed airfields and their pilots and ground staff. We can see him then, arriving, usually without notice, at a flight dispersal. All the glass has long since been blasted from the hut's windows, and fresh circles in the grass of the airfield indicate filled-in bomb craters – though these are almost indistinguishable from the simulated ones, to deceive the enemy that the damage is worse than it really is.

The scattered Hurricanes, some in the open, others in blast bays, are being worked on by the riggers and fitters, instrument fitters, electricians, and armourers – the last sprawled across the wings with long snakes of linked 0.303 ammunition, which they feed into the ammunition boxes beside the wing guns. Winston remarks at the number of dogs about. 'Can they *all* be mascots?' he might ask the flight commander as he greets him at the entrance to the hut.

'Well, no, sir. Just pets. A lot of the lads are fond of them. And they make wizard guards.'

'How many Huns have you brought down, Flight-Lieutenant?'

---

*This figure, and many others, was exaggerated for a number of mainly innocent reasons. German claims were even more unrealistic.

'Three, or maybe four, sir. Not many.'

'You will, no doubt, add substantially to your tally. May I come in?'

Inside, the word has spread and all the pilots – sergeants and commissioned officers – are standing, some with unfinished games of draughts and cards beside them. Winston casts his eye round, missing nothing, pausing at each face. They look ridiculously young and rather tired. Some have shaved. None wear ties: the word had soon got round that the standard Van Heusen collars shrink in seawater, causing several pilots to strangle after bailing out into the sea or crash-landing on it. Many wear silk scarves. There is a strong smell of cigarette smoke and sweat in the air, with a slight aroma of cordite (Winston is quick to recognize that), aviation fuel and glycol: the concentrated scent of air battle.

Winston sits down in one of the battered bamboo armchairs and indicates to the pilots that they should gather round him. The flight commander offers him a mug of tea, which he refuses with an expression of distaste. 'I was always being offered tea on the Western Front in the Army. I have never found it a congenial drink.' A pilot officer, in intelligent anticipation, had already ordered an aircraftsman to bicycle 'like a bat out of hell' for the officers' mess – 'Tell the steward to hand over a bottle of whisky for Christ's sake!'

'Have you been in action today, Sergeant?' Winston asks a pilot with a DFM ribbon beneath his wings.

'No, sir. A Flight did the early patrol and we've not had much trade since.'

Winston has them all at ease, joking about Goering getting stuck in the narrow cockpit of a Messerschmitt 109 while showing off to some pilots. 'Vy do you not shoot down all zee Hurricanes?' he mimics, and then answers the question, 'Ve already haff – zee RAF just send up dummies, Reichsmarschall!'

For some five minutes the conversation becomes more serious, and Winston, encouraging complaints, hears the flight commander ask if 12 Group can reinforce them more swiftly, and when can they have twenty-millimetre cannon because the Germans are armouring their bombers, making them very difficult to shoot down with machine guns. Everyone is smoking, and Winston's cigar has been relit with a Ronson lighter by a flying officer.

Then suddenly the telephone rings – a clamorous, urgent ring – and the duty corporal grabs the receiver. Almost at the same moment he shouts, 'Scramble! Angels Twelve over Ashford!'

Those pilots not wearing their yellow Mae Wests grab them, and all those who are scheduled to fly run for the door, any remaining formality scattering like the dominoes and the mugs of tea. The flight commander, the last to leave the hut, cries, 'Excuse us, sir. I hope you'll be here when we get back.'

'Good luck, young man.' And a second later, recalling the cry: 'Tally ho!'

The aircraftman arrives with a bottle of Haig whisky from the mess. Flight (the flight-sergeant in charge of the servicing crew) grabs it and searches for an empty mug. Winston walks to the door and witnesses, not for the first time, the Hurricanes scrambling: the mobile starter being unplugged as the Merlin engine bursts into life, and rushed to the next fighter; the pilots pulling on their helmets and plugging in radio plug and oxygen tube as they gather speed, tightening their straps; the riggers running and ducking against the whipped-up slipstream dust. The heavy rhythmic murmur of the engines builds towards a climax, and then – bumping on the rough grass – the fighters lift off in turn, wheels at once retracting as the machines climb away . . . Winston glances again at his big fob watch. It has taken a few seconds over two minutes.

Another two weeks or so of concentrated attack on the airfields would have turned the tide in favour of the Germans. But then, mercifully for Britain and the democratic world, Goering, in his fury and frustration, and because British bombers were penetrating German defences and bombing Berlin, ordered the attacks to turn on London itself. Great damage was done to the capital, but it was of no consequence compared with the opportunity given to the airfields to recover. The ground crews and supporting WAAFs worked tirelessly, and the factories redoubled their efforts, under the inspired leadership of Max Beaverbrook, to produce planes.

By the end of September, the tide had turned. The Germans had withdrawn, first their vulnerable dive bombers, and then their high-level bombers. The vaunted Luftwaffe was reduced to night bombing, though all through that autumn and winter London and many other cities were subjected to savage attack from the skies. From 7 September to 3 November an average of two hundred German bombers attacked London every night. At first there was some pretence of attacking military or industrial targets, and for night after night the great oil tanks at Thameshaven blazed, lighting up the river. But soon the bombing became indiscriminate, and in the West End of London people no longer stood in the streets to watch the fires, and ceased to go to the theatre and dine out.

In the late 1930s the Government had had constructed a bomb-proof Cabinet retreat – a series of war rooms with domestic accommodation – beneath the solid Whitehall building at Storey's Gate. Winston hated it. He referred to himself as a 'Troglodyte' or 'Trog' when, following severe damage to 10 Downing Street, he was persuaded to resort to an underground existence, at least when the bombing was particularly heavy. It was a miniature subterranean replica of number 10, with its own map room and Cabinet room, accommodation for the secretariat, typists, and so on – even a little telephone office for making transatlantic calls to Roosevelt.*

In the event, Winston spent only three nights as a bed 'Trog' and had an office and domestic accommodation for

---

*The Cabinet War Rooms have been preserved exactly as they were and are open to the public.

himself and Clementine built over the Cabinet War Rooms aboveground but protected by steel shutters.

London's long ordeal – the bombing continued far into 1941 and was renewed intermittently – was also a marvellous opportunity for Winston to show himself to the people and sustain their spirits. He was often out on the streets after a severe bombing. One night he found the scene of a catastrophe in south London, where twenty or thirty poor people's houses had been destroyed or gutted.

> Already little pathetic Union Jacks had been stuck up amid the ruins. When my car was recognized the people came running from all quarters, and a crowd of more than a thousand was soon gathered . . . They crowded round us, cheering and manifesting every sign of lively affection, wanting to touch and stroke my clothes. One would have thought I had brought them some fine substantial benefit which would improve their lot in life.

On another visit, with Ismay at his side, he was mobbed as he got out of his car. 'Good old Winnie . . . We thought you'd come and see us. We can take it. Give it 'em back!' When Winston could contain himself no longer, he burst into tears. 'You see, he really cares; he's crying.'

> Having pulled himself together [General Ismay recalled], he proceeded to march through dockland at breakneck speed. I could never understand how he managed it. He was no longer a young man, and normally he never took any exercise at all. If he had been asked to walk from Downing Street to the House of Commons, he would have refused indignantly.
> On and on we went until darkness began to fall . . . he wanted to see everything. Consequently, we were still within the brightly lit target when the Luftwaffe arrived on the scene and the fireworks started. It was difficult to get a large car out of the area, owing

539

to many of the streets being completely blocked by fallen houses.

Incendiary bombs fell round the car: 'We were evidently in the middle of the bull's-eye!' There was great anxiety at number 10, with ministers, secretaries, policemen and orderlies waiting in the long passage. Winston strode past them without a word, leaving Ismay to take the brunt of the blame for hazarding the Premier's life. He told them, 'in the language of the barrack-room, that anybody who imagined that he could control the Prime Minister on jaunts of this kind was welcome to try his hand on the next occasion'.

An even greater fear for Winston's life was felt at weekends, when he went to Chequers. It was known that the Luftwaffe had photographed it and bombs had fallen nearby during the daylight phase of the Battle of Britain. The chiefs of staff advised him that it could no longer be considered a safe retreat, especially on moonlit nights.

Winston had met and knew slightly Ronald Tree, a rich Anglo-American with a charming wife, Nancy, who had a large house called Ditchley near Oxford and only five miles from Blenheim. Tree was a backbench Conservative MP, and it was a great surprise to him when he was told that the Prime Minister wanted to see him urgently in his room at the House.

'Would it be possible for you to offer me accommodation at Ditchley for certain weekends – when the moon is high?' Winston asked without any preliminaries – but with a touch of mystery and poetry invested in the last phrase, as Tree recalled.

'Of course we would be delighted,' Tree replied. 'When will you be coming?'

'Would Friday be all right?' Winston asked, to Tree's dismay, for it was Tuesday. 'I'll be bringing down a full staff of secretaries,' Winston added, 'and special telephones with the scrambling system will be installed. Then there will be a company of infantry, with machine-guns for posting around the house. Do you have room to billet them, too?'

Thus ended for some time the certainty of quiet weekends at Ditchley for Ronald and Nancy Tree, and the beginning of a period when the centre of the nation's power from time to time accommodated itself in the living rooms and bedrooms of the house. Cases of Pol Roger champagne were acquired, along with a projector and pre-release films, like Chaplin's *The Great Dictator* (much laughter) and *Lady Hamilton*, with Vivien Leigh in the title role and Laurence Olivier as Admiral Nelson. The second of these had to be shown time and again, to the boredom of everyone except Winston, who wept copiously every time Nelson died.

The visitors' book had never been so freely used or the names been so exalted. Generals, air marshals and admirals arrived in droves. Lord Lothian turned up from Washington to discuss the preliminaries to the Lend-Lease Agreement, which made it possible for Britain to continue buying arms from America even though all dollars had been exhausted. Averell Harriman spent weekends at Ditchley at one time or another. Lindemann ('the Prof') always motored over from Oxford in an ancient Rolls-Royce on Sundays.

German bombing soon began concentrating on provincial industrial cities and towns. Winston was at Ditchley on the night of 14 November, when over five hundred German bombers almost completely destroyed the centre of Coventry. The bombers could be heard passing overhead for most of the night. Nancy Tree, who ran a team of mobile canteens for disasters like this, was called soon after midnight. When she returned she told Winston of a city in ruins, with thousands of people roaming the countryside, as in H. G. Wells's *The Shape of Things to Come*, and hundreds of corpses lying amidst the rubble. Winston at once ordered his car and drove to the city, hoping to give comfort to the survivors by his presence.

The turn of the year 1940–1 marked the warming of relations between the USA and Britain. Joe Kennedy had at last been recalled, to be replaced by the wise, sympathetic and altogether more suitable Gilbert ('Gil') Winant. He was a slow speaker, appeared deceptively dreamy and enjoyed a wonderful relationship with Winston, as well as his own President. He also fell head over heels in love with Sarah, whose marriage to Vic Oliver was finished, but they never married and the relationship was believed to be an innocent one.

Roosevelt had also concluded a deal over the destroyers Britain had so sorely needed, which involved leasing British bases on the western Atlantic in exchange for them. This was politically acceptable to the American people – as it might well be – and politically rather more than materially gratifying to Britain, for the destroyers were terrible sea boats and potentially sea coffins. In addition, a bill passed by the American Congress in January 1941 allowed British warships the use of American ports, and it was not long before American warships were making themselves responsible for escorting Allied convoys on the first leg of the Atlantic crossing.

Also in January 1941, Roosevelt sent his special envoy, Harry Hopkins, to London in order to sound out the spirit of the nation and report on Britain's most urgent needs. Hopkins was a frail, untidy idealist whose fine mind and saintliness had especially appealed to the President. It appeared on the face of it unlikely that Hopkins, with his sensitivity and egalitarian principles, would appeal to Winston, or he to this seemingly unpositive man of delicate health and socialist views. But to everyone's delight – not least their own – the envoy and Premier had struck an instant chord, and after talking for hours on end at Downing Street, Winston invited him to Ditchley.

Hopkins's nominal host, Ronald Tree, was greatly intrigued to meet the American and was as amazed as everyone else how well he got on with Winston:

> Hopkins, frail, hollow-cheeked, untidily dressed, so thin that he seemed to be kept alive only by some flame burning invisibly, but palpably, inside . . . Churchill and Hopkins were complete opposites in every respect – background, training and human

understanding – Churchill a rumbustious and argumentative extrovert . . . [Hopkins] was intensely loyal to Roosevelt, and a most faithful and accurate transmitter of his master's views. . . . Churchill recognized this at once. The two men, from their first meeting, developed a mutual admiration that was later to play a great part in the rapport between Churchill and Roosevelt which counted much in the winning of the war.

Conversation at dinner on 11 January ranged far and wide, with special emphasis on the American President and American policy. Over the brandy, Winston, with a cigar well alight, was in jubilant flow and said he considerered the new American presidential bill tantamount to a declaration of war by America – or if not, at least an American challenge to Germany to declare war if she dared.

Hopkins was full of praise for Winston's speeches, which, he said, produced the most stirring and revolutionary effect on all classes. Winston was intrigued to hear that at one American Cabinet meeting Roosevelt had insisted on a radio being brought in so that all could hear one of the Prime Minister's powerful speeches.

Although there were frequent visits to Ditchley, each one memorable to the Trees, Chequers still remained the first choice for weekend visits, except 'when the moon was high' and the night blitz was at its worst. And it was at Chequers that the 'new' Winston Spencer Churchill was christened on the day following 'old' Winston's sixty-sixth birthday, 1 December 1940. The event had been preceded some weeks earlier by a family row, caused by the fact that the Duke of Marlborough, Sunny's eldest son, and his wife, Mary (Cadogan), who had recently given birth to a son, announced that he was to be named Winston. Pamela's protests were ignored, and she was reduced to appealing, in floods of tears, to Winston to intervene. He did so, but the Duchess demanded to know how Pamela knew she was going to give birth to a boy. 'If it isn't this time it will be next time,'

Winston argued with shaky logic but absolute firmness. In the end, the Marlborough child was named Charles, leaving Randolph and Pamela triumphant.

The christening ceremony was performed at the parish church of Ellesborough, near to Chequers, with Max Beaverbrook, Brendan Bracken and Lord Brownlow (at one time equerry to the Duke of Windsor) as godfathers, and the American journalist, and friend of Randolph, Virginia Cowles, as godmother. Winston wept throughout, the tears streaming down his cheeks, murmuring from time to time, 'Poor infant, to be born into such a world as this.'

Pamela and the baby were able to leave Chequers soon after the christening. Randolph had found and leased a one-time rectory at Hitchin, north of London, and the family moved in before Christmas. Randolph was not with them for long. He had earlier volunteered to join one of the first commandos. This required the permission of his commanding officer in the 4th Hussars, who was delighted at the news. 'What a shock it was to be told that the other officers disliked him, they were fed up with his diatribes and could hardly wait for him to get some job elsewhere,' according to his cousin Anita Leslie. 'Randolph, who had thought he was well regarded, burst into tears. That was one of his endearing traits,' she added defensively, '– his honest childlike desire to be loved and his amazement when he discovered that he wasn't.'

Randolph continued the tough training on the Western Isles of Scotland that had been interrupted by his son's christening. No. 8 Commando consisted of ten troops, each of fifty men. Randolph's troop included the 'White's Club brigade', made up of the most raffish young members of that club, heavy drinkers and heavy gamblers all, including Evelyn Waugh and Admiral Beatty's son, Peter. As soldiers they were totally undisciplined and totally incompetent, spending much of the day telephoning their (race horse) trainers and bookies. They were loathed by everybody, especially the naval officers, with whom they had to work on landing exercises, and the regular officers, who had already seen

544

service in Norway but were looked down upon as common by the nobs from White's.

Randolph attracted further odium when the 4th Hussars were sent overseas, being accused by officers' wives of taking advantage of prior knowledge through his connections. They were, moreover, almost wiped out in the Crete operations. But in February 1941, No. 8 Commando itself was sent overseas, to Egypt via the Cape. Randolph spent much of the voyage gambling.

Before completing his 'training' in Scotland, Randolph contrived to join the family Christmas at Chequers. In spite of the evident strain in relations between Sarah and Vic Oliver, it was a happy time. When Randolph left in his troopship, Pamela invited Diana and her children to live with her and her baby. This could have been a happy and economical ménage, and was until Pamela received a letter from Cape Town. Randolph confessed to losing a fortune gambling on the voyage. She was on no account to let Winston know, but was to arrange to pay off the debts over a period – then Randolph listed those who should be sent £10 a month, an impossible task for this innocent 20-year-old who had never known of gambling in her family.

This was worse than anything Clementine had suffered. Pamela was forced to sell off all she had, jewellery, wedding presents, everything. She called on Beaverbrook, who continued to pay Randolph's salary of £1,500 a year as a journalist, and asked, in tears, if it could be advanced. Beaverbrook refused but presented her with a cheque strictly as a present and agreed that young Winston and her nursemaid could live at his house, Cherkley, when Pamela said she would have to give up her house and take a job in London. All this marked the end of Randolph's first marriage.

Mary was feeling penurious, too, but on a different scale and for more worthy reasons. She and Judy Montagu had now joined the ATS, the women's army, specializing in anti-aircraft gunnery and earning 1s 8d a day. They were also suffering the first rigours of army food. But it was not as bad as all that. Venetia and Clementine

545

visited them at weekends when they could, laden with 'vast and delicious picnic lunches'. As soon as they had completed their training, the two girls were sent to a mixed heavy battery to the north-east of London. Later, Mary was posted to Hyde Park, less than a mile from Downing Street, where she was visited by Winston, anxious to learn the wonders of modern radar-directed anti-aircraft gunnery.

31

'The Outwitted Bunglers'

Winston's reign as solitary leader in the struggle against tyranny ended on 22 June 1941, with the German attack on Russia. It was a Sunday, the day of the week on which Britain and Germany had gone to war nearly two years earlier.

Saturday 21 June was a burning hot day in London. Winston had awakened as usual at 8 a.m. and worked in bed, dressed in a silk vest and with Kathleen Hill at her regular post, 'silent' typewriter before her. She took his dictation straight on to the machine and never queried a word, typing 'blind' and very swiftly, her eyes on him all the time. Winston looked up from his boxes and papers only when Clementine came in, stroked Nelson, and asked who was coming to luncheon.

'Dickie Mountbatten, my dear. Hot from Egypt and the sinking of his ship.'

Mountbatten arrived shortly before 1 p.m., debonair as ever, wearing the four rings of a captain in the Royal Navy, with the DSO heading three rows of ribbons. Winston greeted him: 'My boy,' he said warmly, a hand on each shoulder. 'I can't tell you how glad I am to see you back safely.'

They went into the dining room, where Clementine, too, greeted him like a long-lost son. 'What a ghastly experience for you!' she exclaimed. 'Did you lose many of your crew, Dickie?'

Note: 'So far as strategy, policy, foresight, competence are arbiters, Stalin and his commissars showed themselves at this moment the most completely outwitted bunglers of the Second World War.' – Winston on Russian blindness to the imminent German attack.

'Yes, I'm afraid so. More than half.'

Jock Colville joined them for coffee. He had been to Waterloo Station on behalf of Winston to greet the Prime Minister of New Zealand, Peter Fraser. The talk had moved to wider issues, but Colville pressed Mountbatten to describe again the sinking of his destroyer, the *Kelly*. He did so, adding, 'We weren't safe from the bombers even when we got most of the survivors on to Carley Floats. They came down low over us and we could see their faces as they opened fire with their machine-guns.' He laughed as if this were some sort of a joke. 'Funny thing was, the day before, we sank a couple of caiques jam-full of German infantry heading for Crete. We could have killed hundreds of them in the water . . .'

After his sleep that afternoon Winston drove down to Chequers with Clementine, Mary and Judy Montagu. Dinner that night included Gil Winant and his wife, Connie, the Foreign Secretary, Anthony Eden, and his wife, Beatrice (neither marriage very happy), Secretary to the Cabinet Edward Bridges (son of the one-time Poet Laureate Robert Bridges), and 'Tommy' Thompson, the naval commander who was distrusted and disliked by everyone except Winston, for whom he prepared all his movements as aide-de-camp.

Halfway through dinner, Winston caused the Americans great surprise by saying, 'A German attack on Russia is now certain, and Russia will assuredly be defeated.' He allowed the news to sink in and then added: 'Hitler is counting on enlisting capitalist and right-wing sympathies here and in America – splitting opinion. He is quite wrong. I will go all out to help Russia.'

Winant pulled himself together. 'My country will do the same, I can assure you.'

Winston nodded approval. 'It will be a very bloody and bitter fight.'

After dinner, because the night was so warm, it was decided that they might walk in the garden for a while. The party broke up spontaneously into groups, Jock Colville and Winston strolling together. Colville could not recall any precedent for this walking, something that Winston rarely indulged in and certainly not at the end of dinner, with good brandy unconsumed on the table, and in the dark – so pitch dark that elsewhere on the lawn Eden stepped backwards and fell head over heels into a deep ditch and a barbed-wire fence.

Winston at once began elaborating on the theme of arms for Russia, and at one point Colville could not resist saying, 'For you, sir, the arch anticommunist, this is bowing down to the House of Rimmon.'*

'Not in the least. I have only one single purpose – the destruction of Hitler – and my life is much simplified by this single aim. If Hitler invaded Hell I would at least make a favourable reference to the Devil in the House of Commons!'

Colville laughed: how he now loved this man – especially in this mood after a good dinner! Ruminatively, Winston suddenly said, after a brief silence, 'You will live through many wars, but you will never have such an interesting time as you are having now.' Colville had suggested several times that he would like to join the RAF and be a fighter pilot, but Winston, who hated changes and new faces, always blocked him. But now, to Colville's excitement, Winston added, 'And you may get some fighting later on.'

The next time the private secretary and his master met was early the following morning, Sunday 22 June. Colville had been telephoned in the early hours to be told that the Germans had indeed invaded again – this time to the east. Colville sat on the news for four hours and then awoke Winston, Eden and Winant at 8 a.m., knocking on each door and passing the news verbally. To the Englishmen it was no surprise at all. Thanks to British ability to read the German codes they knew almost to the day when the

---

*A phrase meaning to compromise one's conscience. (II Kings V, 18.)

invasion would take place, though Joseph Stalin had ignored all the warnings and had made no special plans to counter it. Winston merely grunted. 'Tell the BBC I will broadcast at 9 p.m.' Winant was pleased, but inclined to interpret it all as a put-up job between Hitler and Stalin: after all, he declared with wonderful innocence, a pact of friendship was in force between the two great powers.

Winston worked all that Sunday on his speech, and it was ready only twenty minutes before it was to be broadcast, unread by anyone except Miss Hill. It was heard by, or reported to, millions throughout the free world and, at great risk, many more in the conquered nations. Its message was clear, its construction, its language, its sentiment perfect for the new and breathtaking turn in the events of this war.

> The Nazi régime is indistinguishable from the worst features of Communism [it began emphatically]. It is devoid of all theme and principle except appetite and racial domination. It excels all forms of human wickedness in the efficiency of its cruelty and ferocious aggression. No-one has been a more consistent opponent of Communism than I have for the last twenty-five years. I will un-say no word that I have spoken about it. But all this fades away before the spectacle which is now unfolding. The past, with its crimes, its follies, and its tragedies, flashes away . . .
>
> We are resolved to destroy Hitler and every vestige of the Nazi régime. From this nothing will turn us – nothing . . . We shall fight him by land, we shall fight him by sea, we shall fight him in the air, until, with God's help, we have rid the earth of his shadow and liberated its peoples from his yoke. Any man or state who fights on against Nazidom will have our aid. Any man or state who marches with Hitler is our foe . . . It follows therefore that we shall give whatever help we can to Russia and the Russian people . . .

Overnight, Britain had a new ally of some two hundred million people. Suddenly, the bogey of the Russian bear that had so recently crushed half of Poland to death and had invaded Finland, was transformed into a brave, patriotic defender of his territory. Suddenly, Stalin, who only months earlier had signed a pact of friendship with the arch-enemy Adolf Hitler and had beamed at his side in every newspaper in the world, became good old Uncle Joe. For all but a small group of right-wing Conservatives, the dramatic *volte-face* was accomplished with wonderful ease, subtly assisted by the Ministry of Information.

Now began four years of sacrifice by the West on behalf of Soviet Russia, of the painful and expensive delivery of great masses of war material – all received without thanks or grace, only with demands for more and more, and complaints that the West was not pulling its weight and was content to watch the Soviets taking the brunt of the fighting. Forgotten were the two years when Soviet Russia had given important economic aid to Nazi Germany, supporting Hitler in all his depredations, blindly indifferent to the fate of the nation that had fought on alone. Now this Bolshevik dictatorship stridently demanded every sort of support, including raids on the Continent of Europe to divert some of the weight off themselves, and within a very few weeks, an invasion – a second front.

At the time of the German invasion of Russia, Winston was feeling increasingly confident that before too long Britain would have an ally in the West – and a great deal more compatible ally than Russia, too. The American President, now firmly in the saddle for his third term of office, felt able to show, privately and publicly, more support for Britain and antagonism towards Germany and Italy. In the first half of 1941, great quantities of tanks and military aircraft had been shipped to Egypt for the North African campaign, and long-range American aircraft were contributing to the Battle of the Atlantic, with American flying instructors teaching British cadet-pilots both in Britain and in American flying schools.

By April, American naval escorts were working with North Atlantic convoys, and by September they had shoot-on-sight orders. And right at the start of the year delegates from the British chiefs of staff secretly visited Washington to discuss war plans.

Most important of all these promising developments was a planned meeting between the two leaders for August. Late on the evening of Thursday, 24 July, Winston, Harry Hopkins and Jock Colville were closeted in the inner sanctum of number 10 awaiting a telephone call from President Roosevelt. Harriman was shortly to leave by flying boat from Lisbon to report his findings on the war in Britain and the Middle East to the President, and Hopkins was expected to fly off in the opposite direction to Moscow in a day or two. Hopkins was looking tired but alert, a small pile of cigarette butts in the brass ashtray at his elbow.

When the black telephone rang soon after eleven o'clock, Colville glanced questioningly at Winston, who indicated by a nod that Hopkins should be the first to speak. Hopkins reached forward and took the instrument from Winston's secretary. His voice at once assumed a tone appropriate to a long friendship. 'Yes, Mr President, it is good to talk with you. Yes, yes, I am very much better. The Prime Minister feeds me well and the weather is beautiful . . . No, sir, Mr Churchill remains very obdurate about the Middle East. It is, he says, the one place where he can *fight* the enemy – otherwise only bombing . . .' Roosevelt's voice rang out clearly in the small room, accepting what Hopkins had been saying. 'We shall be talking about that and much else soon.'

Hopkins handed the telephone to Winston, who talked vehemently and optimistically to the American President for some minutes, concluding, 'I am greatly looking forward to our meeting, too, Mr President, and your Newfoundland rendezvous is admirable – admirable.'

The two leaders said goodbye, and Colville took the telephone, murmuring discreetly, 'That was *not* the scrambler, sir.'

Winston stared bleakly at the black telephone and then at the red one beside it, his face assuming an expression of anger. 'What idiocy! – what a *fool* I am!' Characteristically, he had no intention of blaming anyone but himself for this breach of security, and there was nothing that displeased him more than his own mistakes. Mercifully, they were very rare.

'Surely, sir, the chances of the Germans picking up those few words are one in a million,' Hopkins said consolingly.

Winston rose from his chair. 'I am very fierce about security, Mr Hopkins. We'll just have to alert our intelligence services to the situation.' He turned to his secretary. 'Jock, drinks are called for. Can you please arrange?'

The two men talked of the American President, the state of his health, the triumphant manner in which he had sailed through his third term re-election the previous autumn, and how he would be hating the advent of the hot and sticky season in Washington.

Nothing could appeal more to Winston's adventurous and romantic nature than to embark on board a battleship to speed across the U-boat-ridden North Atlantic to a secret meeting with the man who could save the cause of democracy in the West. An alliance, an Atlantic alliance, was Winston's ambition, and he hoped to draw up and sign a charter as a preliminary to this aim. For two years the two great leaders had been exchanging communications. Both believed they knew the other very much better for all these letters, telegrams and telephone calls. Both men had roots deep in Europe and North America. Both men were sentimentally and historically attached to their navy, which each had led in the Great War. In 1938, when Winston's biography of *Marlborough* had been completed, he sent Roosevelt a complete signed set. Roosevelt said how much he enjoyed reading them, though it is extremely doubtful that he did more than glance through this immense work, which he referred to as *Marlboro*, like the American cigarette.

On 3 August 1941, at noon, a special train pulled out of Marylebone Station in north-west London, bound for Scotland. The passengers included the entire hierarchy of Britain's war machine – chiefs of staff, and their staff, consultant admirals, generals and air marshals, a diplomatic staff and a solid slice of Winston's secretariat, along with their secretaries and stenographers – 'a retinue which Cardinal Wolsey might have envied'.

This train stopped at the little wayside halt of Wendover, which, being the nearest to Chequers, had acquired a new importance. Winston and Sawyers and one or two others were waiting on the 'down' platform, Winston in a blue suit, a yachting cap signifying he was seaward bound. He was in fine form, bubbling with expectation at the adventure ahead. With cigar firmly in his mouth, unlit, he did what was expected of him and gave the 'V' sign to the scattering of passengers on the opposite platform. Within a few minutes of boarding his train, he had settled down to a substantial lunch of tomato soup, sirloin of beef and raspberry and currant tart. Its passage was eased by a steady flow of champagne. The Prof, who normally refused to sleep in any other bed but his own, had surprised everyone by agreeing to come, and a more austere and strictly vegetarian meal was prepared for him.

The Scottish train, with a change of crew, steamed through the night, arriving at Thurso in the far north early in the morning. Here, after breakfast, Winston left the train and transferred to a destroyer for the short crossing of the Pentland Firth to Scapa Flow.

Battleships anchored in the mist of this northern anchorage were as familiar as the shallow undulation of the surrounding heather-clad island hills: it all reminded Winston of 1914, when the Grand Fleet had begun its four-and-a-half-year vigil, challenging for twenty-four hours a day the German High Seas Fleet to come out and dispute Britannia's rule of the seas. He still became romantic when he contemplated British sea power, ready as always to drop a tear if anyone were to quote Henry Newbolt.

The battleship towards which the destroyer was taking the Premier's party still carried the scars of battle, the evidence of Germany's most recent unsuccessful challenge. The *Prince of Wales* had been badly hit by the giant German battleship *Bismarck* at the same time as the battle-cruiser *Hood* had been blown up, but the hits she had made in reply led to the destruction of the *Bismarck* a few days later.

One of the first of his fellow passengers who greeted Winston was Hopkins. He had just returned from Moscow, where he had conferred with Stalin and Russian supply staff on the nature of the aid the USA might supply to the beleaguered empire. He arrived by bomber at Scapa Flow on 2 August, exhausted and ill, his frail constitution tested beyond bearing. Gil Winant came up from London to check his condition, and ordered him to bed. Hopkins had slept for eighteen hours and had recovered somewhat when Winston arrived.

Winston saw his American friend step forth from the shadow of the after fourteen-inch quadruple gun turret. He was wearing a tweed overcoat and holding down his wide-brim felt hat, and Winston thought he looked close to death. (Later he signalled Roosevelt: 'Harry returned dead-beat from Russia.') But his gaunt smile and mellow voice, with its east-coast American accent, were reassuring.

'Ah, my dear friend,' Winston greeted him. 'How are you? And how did you find Marshal Stalin?'

'I must tell you all about it.'

The two men, one so slight, the other rotund and shorter, linked arms and went below, chattering like two schoolboys after a keen game. Captain John Leach, RN, had given the admiral's cabins aft to Winston, but a great Atlantic gale got up that first night of the crossing, and to everyone's inconvenience Winston insisted on moving, lock, stock and barrel, at 4 a.m. to the admiral's sea cabin on the bridge, where the degree of movement and the noise of the propellers of the 35,000-ton vessel were much reduced. During the day, Winston and Hopkins spent many hours together, much of the talk being about Roosevelt, his character and career, and – above all – his desire to bring the USA into the war.

'Do you play backgammon, Mr Hopkins?'

'Yes, a little, sir. Would you like a game?'

So they whiled away a few hours playing for low stakes. 'The Prime Minister's backgammon game is not of the best,' Hopkins told Roosevelt later. 'He likes to play what is known to all backgammon addicts as a "back game". As a matter of fact, he won two or three very exciting games from me by these tactics. He approaches the game with great zest, doubling and redoubling freely.' Hopkins won seven guineas – or about thirty-five dollars – off the Prime Minister in one session, which pleased him. Clementine's severe injunction to 'often sip the air on the Bridge' was somehow forgotten. Winston still hated the sea. More to his liking was a pot of caviar, a gift from Stalin. He opened it at dinner. 'Ah, Mr Hopkins, it is good to have such a treat, even if it means fighting on the side of the Russians to get it.' Later at dinner, with the cheese removed, Winston noticed that Hopkins passed by the second brandy. 'I hope you're not going to become more temperate as you get closer to home.'

Then there was the evening film. *Saps at Sea* was a curious choice under the circumstances – 'A gay but inconsequent entertainment,' Winston thought it. More to his liking and a more judicious choice was *Lady Hamilton*, and once again Winston had to reach for his handkerchief as Nelson lay dying in the *Victory*'s cockpit. When the lights went up he stood and turned, wiping his eyes, to the audience, who had all lost shipmates in the *Bismarck* action not three months earlier. 'I thought this would interest you, gentlemen, who have been recently engaged with the enemy in matters of equal importance. Good night!' And he stomped off to his cabin, dead cigar in his mouth.

For Winston, these five days at sea were the nearest he came to enjoying a holiday. The storm of the first day had caused them to lose their destroyer escort, and the *Prince of Wales* steamed on alone at high speed, altering course to avoid a U-boat that had been identified and located, thanks to the decrypts of the German code signals. But this meant total radio silence, and for the first time in the war, Winston was unable to issue orders or ask for information. 'A comparatively idle day,' John Martin noted of 5 August. And Winston commented, 'For the first time for many months I could read a book for pleasure.' *Captain Hornblower RN*, by C. S. Forester, he found 'vastly entertaining'. When security allowed, he signalled the colleague in Egypt who had sent the novel, 'Hornblower admirable.' This caused great confusion at General Headquarters, where the code word was sought in vain.

On the morning of 9 August, a grey, faintly misty day, the *Prince of Wales* was approaching Newfoundland, escorted by two US destroyers, their snow-white paint contrasting with the dun camouflage paint of the battleship. Winston signalled the King, 'With humble duty, I have arrived safely and am visiting the President this morning.' After a rather sticky start, when Winston would rather cavalierly postpone meetings with the King at very short notice, Sovereign and Prime Minister were getting on better, and Winston did his utmost to keep him well informed. For his part, George VI had written the American President a message that he had asked Winston to hand to Roosevelt:

> *This is just a note to bring you my best wishes, and to say how glad I am that you have an opportunity at last of getting to know my Prime Minister. I am sure that you will agree that he is a very remarkable man, and I have no doubt that your meeting will prove a great benefit to our two countries in the pursuit of our common goal.*

Placentia Bay was like an enlarged version of Scapa Flow, the surrounding hills higher, with spruce forests in place of heather. As the *Prince of Wales* and her escort rounded Cape St Mary's headland, first charted by John Cabot in

1497, Winston was greeted by a sight of great splendour and reassurance, a fleet of shining warships, flags flying, bands playing, the seamen lined up and cheering. Here was the manifest evidence at last that Britain had friends on this side of the Atlantic.

The *Prince of Wales*'s band was playing, too, a Royal Marines detachment standing by to present arms. 'The cable ran out . . . the one note on the bugle – the "G" – rang out mournfully, the booms swung out, gangways went down and the Jack was hoisted at the bows.'

Franklin D. Roosevelt is sitting in his wheelchair on the upper deck of the heavy cruiser *Augusta* beneath an awning. He is dressed in a single-breasted, tan Palm Beach suit and wears a trilby hat. At his side is his son Elliot, a tall figure like his father, but in uniform. Roosevelt exchanges words with him from time to time as they watch the dark battleship, which dwarfs all other warships in the bay, drop anchor and go through the formalities prior to the disembarkation of his guest. He sees the admiral's barge with the British party and Harry Hopkins on board leave the battleship's side and cut through the still water towards them. His sight of it is cut off as the barge slows down alongside the *Augusta*, and Roosevelt is helped to his feet by Elliot, and the father and son, arm in arm, stand against the rail and a stanchion securing the awning.

The band is playing 'God Save the King', which changes to 'The Star-Spangled Banner' as Winston, in the uniform of Warden of the Cinque Ports,* steps on to the teak deck of the American ship. He is smiling – grinning, according to some accounts – and is holding a letter in his hand. He bows perceptibly, says, 'Good morning, Mr President,' and hands

---

*An honorary, distinguished title referring to the five original Anglo-Saxon defence ports in south-east England. Winston had been recently appointed.

him the letter. 'This is from His Majesty, King George. He asked me to be messenger.'

'Welcome to the New World, Mr Churchill,' says Roosevelt, taking the letter and handing it to Elliot. Then occurs an embarrassing moment.

As they shake hands, Winston remarks, 'I am so happy to meet at last the man with whom I have corresponded and talked on the transatlantic telephone so often.'

Roosevelt reminds Winston that this is not their first meeting. 'It was in the summer of 1918 at a dinner at Gray's Inn, where I also met your King's father. I made a speech as Assistant Secretary of the Navy – I think all your War Cabinet were there . . .'

'Of course, of course,' Winston chips in, trying to cover the gaffe, although he has no memory at all of the occasion.

'Would you care to look over the ship, Mr Churchill?' Winston tactfully agrees, recognizing that this will allow the crippled President to descend, unembarrassed, to their first meeting by the special means provided.

Later the two leaders have a brief talk alone in the captain's cabin assigned to the President. It is no more than an extended introduction, to accustom themselves to each other's company, to smoke, and to discuss the state of the world. Then Roosevelt asks, as if family host at a party, 'Would you care to meet the others?' He manoeuvres his wheelchair deftly towards the door, where an aide takes over. Winston has been wondering, briefly and mournfully, whether the 'dry' US Navy would make an exception for this occasion, but in the wardroom where the service chiefs of both nations have paired off for first informal discussions, the dry martinis and whisky sours are going down freely.

Roosevelt, with Winston at his side like a male nurse, soon leave for their tête-à-tête lunch in the captain's day cabin. They talk 'navy' most of the time, sometimes historically, more often about the U-boat war and the *Bismarck* fight, which had been followed so eagerly in America. Winston had once mused somewhat anxiously to Averell Harriman, 'I wonder if he will like me.' All doubts, on both sides, are rapidly eliminated, and the guard outside the door often hears the sound of laughter. The steward brings in a decanter of brandy – refused by the President – along with cigars and cigarettes. Roosevelt slips a cigarette into a holder without looking down, the steward clips a cigar, hands it on a salver to Winston and lights it. The steward is nonplussed to see the guest rolling the cigar to and fro across his coffee cup with the flat of his hand – a practice he had acquired many years before.

That evening, Winston returned to the *Augusta* to dine. The menu was vegetable soup, broiled chicken, spinach omelette, lettuce and tomato salad, and chocolate ice cream. Both leaders made speeches, and there were several rather long ones from the American chiefs of staff. But, as at any dinner back home, Winston did most of the talking. 'Winston Churchill held every one of us that night,' the President's son Elliot recorded, 'and was conscious every second of the time he was holding us. All that Father did was to throw in an occasional question – just drawing him on, drawing him out . . . Churchill reared back in his chair, he slewed his cigar round from cheek to cheek and always at a jaunty angle, he hunched his shoulders forward like a bull, his hands slashed the air expressively, his eyes flashed . . .'

It had been agreed that on the following day, Sunday 10 August, there should be a joint service on board the *Prince of Wales*. Winston gave much thought to the preparations, determined that the occasion should have a high emotional content – 'fully choral and fully photographic', as John Martin noted. The hymns were 'Onward Christian Soldiers', 'Oh God Our Help in Ages Past', 'Eternal Father', and, in culmination, 'For Those in Peril on the Sea'. Moreover there were to be no more than 250 hymn sheets for the congregation of 500, to ensure Anglo-American sharing. The pulpit on the quarterdeck was draped with the Stars and Stripes and Union Jack, and British and American chaplains were to share in the reading of prayers.

The service took place on the battleship's quarterdeck, in

the shadow of heavy guns. Voices were raised in a mighty chorus, the sun shone, the cameras clicked and whirred. It all gave the impression that Britain and the United States were already allies, fighting together the good fight against tyranny . . . just as Winston had intended. 'I shall never forget it,' Roosevelt told George VI in a return letter. '. . . I hope you will see the movies of it.' (He did.)

Two more full days of consultations and meetings took place, concluding with the drawing up of the Atlantic Charter, a series of resolutions agreed between the two nations, including Clause Six: 'After the final destruction of Nazi tyranny, they hope to see established a peace which will afford to all nations the means of dwelling in safety within their own boundaries . . .' It was never intended to amount to much more than a series of fine clichés, but it made an excellent form of propaganda to the uncommitted world. But the real work of the meeting was done privately between the service chiefs and their staffs, mostly on a contingency basis.

There was no hint of any sort of commitment to a more belligerent national stance beyond help with Atlantic convoys. 'Not a single American officer,' Ian Jacob noted in his diary, 'has shown the slightest keenness to be in the war on our side,' disregarding the likelihood of their being briefed to be discreet. 'They are a charming lot of individuals but they appear to be living in a different world from ourselves.'

It was all very cordial, and any criticism was very mild, though the American air chiefs, with half an eye on the future of the aircraft industry and future American airliners, thought Britain should not give such high priority to heavy bomber construction. Winston extemporized an office in order to carry on working when other engagements permitted. Kathleen Hill had not been invited into the all-masculine world of a battleship, but an army sergeant clerk was conscripted to take down shorthand, and Winston became so used to him that he became a permanent member of Winston's personal staff.

Winston could not bear to leave Placentia Bay without feeling American soil under his feet, even if it was an island off Canada, and he proposed a boating party and picnic tea one afternoon. Wearing his one-piece boiler suit, a favourite garment originally conceived for air-raid shelter use, and accompanied by the Prof, John Martin, Alexander Cadogan (Permanent Undersecretary at the Foreign Office), Tommy Thompson, and – representing the United States – Averell Harriman, they landed from their launch on to a shingly bay. 'We clambered over some rocks, the PM like a schoolboy,' wrote Cadogan, 'getting a great kick out of rolling boulders down a cliff.' Winston picked some wild flowers, and the group found the perfect spot for their picnic, but clouds suddenly rolled up and they were caught in a very violent shower. They returned to their launch soaked through.

Of the American army, Jacob had noted that it 'sees no prospect of being able to do anything for a year or two, and is thus completely taken up with equipment problems'. That was in mid-August 1941. Early in December it was obliged to reconsider this policy urgently, for war came to the United States with a swiftness and inevitability that surprised both leaders, although – as with the Russians – the warning signs were there. These signs were too obvious and too dire to be ignored by the end of November. On Winston's sixty-seventh birthday, 30 November, a message from Tokyo to the Japanese Ambassador in Berlin with instructions to address the German leaders was intercepted and at once decoded. Its warning note was all too clear. '. . . there is extreme danger that war may suddenly break out between the Anglo-Saxon nations and Japan through some clash of arms, and add that the time of the breaking out of this war may come sooner than anyone dreams.' In fact, the Japanese fleet was already at sea, with almost the entire naval air force, and Japanese troops were embarking in transports for the invasion of Siam, Malaya, the Philippines and the Dutch East Indies.

On the evening of Sunday 7 December, Winston had two American friends and colleagues at Chequers for dinner, Winant and Harriman, but he was not a very genial host. 'The Prime Minister seemed tired and depressed,' Harriman recalled. 'He didn't have much to say throughout dinner and was immersed in his thoughts with his head in his hands part of the time.'

Outside in the pantry Sawyers was waiting to bring in the cheese and brandy. It was just before nine o'clock, and like almost everyone else in the country he switched on the evening news bulletin. It contained items about the fighting in Russia and in Libya, where a real breakthrough against General Rommel had recently been accomplished. Then, as if the news had only just been received in Broadcasting House, there were references to Japanese attacks on American shipping at Hawaii and on British ships in the Dutch East Indies. Suddenly realizing the implications of this news, and uncertain in his mind whether his master might have forgotten to switch on the little portable set he kept at hand, Sawyers entered the dining room.

Sawyers's intuition was confirmed. Winston had forgotten to switch on his set, and the three men had only picked up the tail end of the bulletin and were only half listening anyway. 'Wasn't there something about the Japanese attacking the Americans?' Harriman suddenly asked. 'In spite of being tired and resting, we all sat up,' Winston remembered.

Sawyers entered at that moment, sized up the situation, and said, 'It's quite true, we heard it ourselves outside. The Japanese have attacked the Americans.'

Winant recalled that they looked at one another incredulously, and Winston, suddenly transformed from deep gloom and introspection to feverish activity, sprang to his feet and exclaimed, 'We shall declare war on Japan.' Winant followed him out of the room, half protestingly, half laughingly declaring, 'Good God, you can't declare war on a radio announcement.'

Winant later recalled, 'He stopped and looked at me . . . and then said quietly, "What shall I do?" The question was asked not because he needed me to tell him what to do, but as a courtesy to the representative of the country attacked.'

Winston said, 'I shall speak to your President.' Winant followed him through to his office, where John Martin was on duty with the staff. 'I want a call to the White House,' he ordered.

It came through in two or three minutes. 'Mr President, what's this about Japan?' he asked without ceremony.

'It's quite true,' Roosevelt replied. 'They have attacked us at Pearl Harbor. We are all in the same boat now.'

Winston handed the instrument to Winant. They exchanged a few words, and then Winant exclaimed, 'That's fine, Mr President, that's fine.' A strange comment! But for security reasons, Roosevelt had been unable to define the details of the catastrophe. Winston took the telephone again. 'This certainly simplifies things,' he said. 'God be with you!'

Winston and his two guests retired to the hall in a state of mixed emotions. It had been inevitable, but now that it had happened they all felt constrained while they searched for the right words. The two Americans understood clearly the sense of relief and elation their host must be experiencing; Winston understood in what poor taste it would be to expose his real feelings.

'Being saturated and satiated with emotion and sensation,' Winston wrote of that epochal evening, 'I went to bed and slept the sleep of the saved and thankful.'

The Doctor's Prescription

On Pearl Harbor evening, Clementine had dined alone upstairs. She was, she said, quite worn out. She was very bound up with her fund for the relief of suffering among Russian civilians. The invasion of Russia by the Germans had brought out all her latent natural sympathy with the Soviets in accordance with the middle-class liberal idealism of the period. It offered her the chance to compensate for Winston's hostility towards everything Russian and his attempts to reverse the course of Bolshevism at the time of the revolution and its aftermath. No-one was a greater admirer of 'Uncle Joe' Stalin than the Prime Minister's wife. Her Russian Fund had already reached its target of £1,000,000.

It was not until the next morning that she learned from Winston of the Japanese attack on the United States and on the Dutch and British in south-east Asia.

'I shall have to go to see Roosevelt again,' he told her.

'When, my dear?' she asked anxiously.

'Very soon. Perhaps later this week or next week.'

'You will take Charlie with you this time, won't you?'

Clementine had tried unsuccessfully to persuade Winston to take his doctor, Sir Charles Wilson, to Newfoundland. Winston took an idiosyncratic attitude towards his health. He liked to pretend, and give the impression, that he was above such petty considerations as the well-being of his body. In truth, he was deeply interested. When Charles Wilson had been appointed his personal doctor by direction of the Cabinet (and warm approval of Clementine) in May 1940, Winston appeared to be coldly disapproving of the whole business, and he treated check-ups with disdain as time wasting.

Winston's relationship with Wilson fluctuated from almost pathetic dependency to serious respect to affectionate chaffing. Sir Alexander Cadogan, Permanent Undersecretary at the Foreign Office, recounted in a letter home from Cairo how Wilson himself fell ill with a slight stomach upset, and the delight that this caused Winston.

> Winston now goes about saying to everyone 'Sir Charles has been a terrible anxiety to us the whole time, but I hope we'll get him through!' Last night at dinner Winston held forth to the whole table on medicine, psychology & etc. (all Sir Charles's subjects) and worked himself up to a terrific disquisition. I suspect (and I inferred from Sir Charles's expression) that it was pretty good nonsense. And I think Winston must have had an inkling of that too, as he ended up 'My God! I do have to work hard to teach that chap his job!'

Winston yielded to Clementine on this occasion and took Charles Wilson with him, as he was to on all future long trips. Clementine remained in London for Christmas, reflecting on all that had happened since Christmas 1940, when the family had been with her. Now, with the world turned upside down – 'Europe over-run by the Nazi hogs & the Far East by yellow Japanese lice', as she put it in a letter to Winston – she spent Christmas alone with Cousin Moppett in London. A few days earlier, she had driven Mary to her new camp in north-east London, and Sarah and Diana were both away. As for Randolph, he was in Cairo stirring up things, making enemies among the 'brass', but doing useful work in keeping the troops fed with information from home and setting up a magazine for them. He was finding life as a staff officer very tame. The commandos had proved disappointing, and when he heard of the formation of a special parachute unit, he cabled Pamela that he was going to join the SAS – Special Air Service, as it came to be known.

The news sent Clementine into a state of frenzied concern. How *could* he do such a thing, adding to everyone's worry? She saw it as typically selfish and 'sensational'. 'Surely there is a half-way house between being a Staff-Officer and a Parachute Jumper,' she exclaimed to Winston. What with having a young wife with a baby, and a father with all the burdens he was carrying, it was hardly dignified. She proposed sending her son 'an affectionate cable begging him on *your* account to re-join his Regiment & give up this scheme'. But Winston wholly approved of his son's volunteering for hazardous duties and was proud of his decision. No cable was ever sent and Randolph became a parachutist.

The early part of 1942 was a bad period for Clementine. Every new failure and defeat in the Far East and in the western Sahara, too, where Rommel was on the rampage again, struck deep in her heart. She always tended to regard any setback in the war as a personal affront to her husband and herself. Her anguish was genuine enough, but she greatly overestimated the hurt that bad news did to Winston. Winston was indeed cast down by the sinking in the South China Sea of the *Prince of Wales* and *Repulse*, which he had despatched – against Admiralty advice – to deter the Japanese from attacking Malaya and Singapore. But he was much too busy organizing counter-measures for the pain to linger. He had the professional military mind that accepts defeats and losses as inevitable, while correcting and minimizing the damage and organizing counter-measures.

'These were dark and perplexing days indeed,' Mary wrote of her mother at this time. 'Clementine hated to see Winston so beset on all sides.' Clementine was, as so often in the past, adding measurably to the pressure in her usual way.

Clementine's great 'hate' remained Max Beaverbrook. In all the years of peace and war that she had known this Canadian genius, she had never been able to reconcile herself to him, and even now believed he could be the Jacky Fisher of this new war and bring her husband down. Beaverbrook, now Minister of Supply, had been an essential

567

colleague for Winston to take to Washington; besides, he was a constantly stimulating companion. The two men understood one another completely, so that when they had a tiff in Washington and Beaverbrook announced his resignation, Winston was soon able to talk him out of it.

While Winston discussed strategy with Roosevelt and the American chiefs of staff in Washington, Beaverbrook discussed production and supply with Harry Hopkins and the man in charge of American war production, Donald M. Nelson. Beaverbrook stood high in the estimate of American opinion, and they listened to his advice. He was the man who had revolutionized fighter-aircraft production to keep the RAF supplied during the Battle of Britain. He compared US output unfavourably with Canada's and generally chivvied the Americans along. It worked wonders. Beaverbrook also got on famously – almost too well for Winston's comfort – with Roosevelt.

On Winston's return from the Arcadia Conference in Washington, which also took in an important visit to Ottawa, he demanded from the House of Commons a vote of confidence in view of the new expansion of the war and the problems it had brought. He received it by 464 votes to one. But there remained a restlessness, which was understandable considering that over sixty thousand troops had been lost in the fall of Malaya and Singapore alone.

Clementine, who looked at the world in simple and unchanging black and white, judged that Beaverbrook was behind all the trouble with the imminent reconstruction of Winston's War Cabinet. She never hesitated to comment firmly on her husband's appointments, and now she was determined that Beaverbrook should be sacked once and for all. 'She became very heated and expressed herself in violent and immoderate terms,' according to Mary, who was still at Enfield but heard about the row.

'I don't argue with Winston, he shouts me down,' Clementine once claimed disingenuously. 'So when I have anything important to say I write a note to him.' On this occasion, she did both. She apologized, as well she might. 'I am ashamed that by my violent attitude I should just now have added to your agonizing anxieties – Please forgive me.' She persisted, nonetheless, unable to recognize that now was the time to ease off. 'I do beg of you to reflect, whether it would not be best to leave Lord B entirely out of your reconstruction.' She wrote of his 'intrigue & treachery & rattledom . . . Try ridding yourself of this microbe which some people fear is in your blood – Exorcise this bottle Imp & see if the air is not clearer & purer . . .'

At this time, Beaverbrook, who never recognized Clementine's hostility, wrote to a friend of the 'excellence' of the Churchills' 'home life'. 'His relationship with Mrs Churchill might be told in story form as an example of a life-time of domestic content.'

By contrast with Max Beaverbrook, Dickie Mountbatten could do no wrong in the eyes of Clementine, and they were 'Clemmie' and 'Dickie' from the beginning. Clementine thought him charming, brave, well bred, decent and British, though in truth he was almost completely German, like his beloved nephew, Midshipman Prince Philip. She encouraged and applauded every promotion contrived by Winston, and these were numerous.

Winston's warm regard for Captain Lord Louis Mountbatten stemmed from a variety of factors. First, there was the link through the father. Winston had held Prince Louis of Battenberg in great esteem, but later it became conditioned by guilt. Under the circumstances of the time, Winston had had to sack him in 1914, and he knew, from his father's similar experience, what this had done to a man of such sensitivity and pride. This guilt was compounded by the fact that he had promised to ensure that Prince Louis would be reinstated and given a command after the war. In the hurly-burly of 1918 this had slipped his memory, or perhaps had been conveniently forgotten, and it had been beneath the Admiral's dignity to remind him. He had heard later that Prince Louis (now the Marquis of

Milford Haven*) had, moreover, been deeply offended at not being invited to the surrender ceremony of the German High Seas Fleet.

So Winston knew from powerful personal experience how deep was Mountbatten's desire to right a great wrong and reinstate family pride and achievement, for what else had Winston himself been striving to do since his father's downfall and death? Nothing, Winston knew, could be more praiseworthy, and of course Dickie must be helped on his way.

That Mountbatten qualified for any support Winston could give him had been proved long ago. Polo told a lot about a man; they had played together many times. Moreover, the positivism and grit Mountbatten had shown on the polo field was matched by all Winston had heard of his naval career. In parallel with Winston's experience in the Army, and regardless of any unpopularity he might attract, Mountbatten gained promotion and forged links with the powerful – Mountbatten was a commander in the Royal Navy at 32, and a captain commanding a flotilla of the newest and most powerful destroyers before he was 40.

Both men were grade-one egocentrics and, like many egocentrics, were accident-prone. As motorists they had numerous road accidents because they drove fast and badly, like many with a good conceit of themselves and not much regard for other people. As for flying, it was almost certain death as soon as they got their hands on the controls of an aeroplane. Both men liked ceremony and ceremonials, colour and tradition; both were fiercely patriotic and concerned for the poor and underprivileged. They shared a warm interest in genealogy, almost exclusively their own. They also

---

*It was another awful blow when he had to drop the name Battenberg as being too German. But then the King had been obliged, at the same time in 1917, to assume the wholesome name Windsor.

570

shared a complete fearlessness in face of the enemy, and men who ducked from bullets were, to them, incomprehensible; yet they had their little weaknesses of nerve, Mountbatten for heights, Winston for flying and assassination.

Finally, but in quite different ways, they had grave difficulties with their wives. Mountbatten's wife had brought him untold wealth to match the royal connection that he offered her. But Edwina, Sir Ernest Cassel's granddaughter, while encouraging his career, was almost impossible to live with and possessed a sexual appetite as insatiable as her husband's was negligible. Although both men greatly enjoyed being with young pretty women, lust was sublimated to the achievement of ambition. There was, quite simply, no time for sex. For the same reason, children interested them only as objects of pride and sentimental attachment, to be spoilt and indulged rather than loved and cherished. Perhaps only by odd chance, both men had one daughter who turned into a tough, sensible, practical and well-balanced woman: the survivor.

After losing his ship off Crete and recounting his experience to Winston and Clementine, Mountbatten had been appointed to command an aircraft carrier, which had been badly damaged and was being repaired in the USA. He was there when Harry Hopkins received an unexpected cable from Winston: 'We want Mountbatten here for a very active and urgent job.'

The Great War hero Admiral Keyes had been a flop at Combined Operations, by no means lacking in fire but totally devoid of the ability to get on with anyone else, megalomania having long since taken over. So the 68-year-old Admiral of the Fleet handed over command to the 41-year-old Captain, now promoted Commodore, who was instructed by Winston, 'I want you to turn the south coast of England from a bastion of defence into a springboard of attack.'

Mountbatten had the sparkle and zest, and certainly the self-confidence, for this task. He was also a great charmer and got on well with colleagues with whom Keyes had not been on speaking terms for months. It was a brilliant appointment. Later, this golden son of the poor wronged Prince Louis was further promoted to the supreme command in south-east Asia, where Mountbatten held the three ranks of Admiral, General and Air Marshal: some promotion for a man of 43! After all, Winston had been only a struggling, penurious politician at this age.

On 27 December 1941, when Winston was in Washington and a guest of Roosevelt's, a disquieting and significant mishap occurred that made him thankful that he had yielded to Clementine and brought Charles Wilson along. Winston was a deep and steady sleeper, but on this night he found his bedroom too warm and got up to let in some air. He found the sash window stiff and had to use a lot of strength to move it. This effort caused him unusual breathlessness, and at the same time he experienced a dull pain over his heart and down his left arm. He considered calling for his doctor, but the pain disappeared and he went back to sleep. The next morning, he thought about this experience, which left him feeling faintly uneasy. So he called Wilson, who came at once by taxi from his nearby hotel.

'I am glad you have come,' Winston greeted him, and he recounted his nocturnal experience. 'What is it? Is my heart all right?'

Wilson slipped on his stethoscope and examined Winston's chest thoroughly. Everything pointed to a coronary insufficiency, for which the usual treatment was six weeks in bed. But as Wilson recognized, if the Prime Minister followed that course the whole world would know that Winston had a crippled heart, and the effect would be devastating. 'I knew, too, the consequences to one of his imaginative temperament of the feeling that his heart was affected.' On the other hand if Wilson did nothing and a more severe, even fatal, heart attack followed, he would bear the responsibility and it would lead to the ruin of his career.

Wilson stalled for time by continuing to use his stethoscope; then he decided that he must procrastinate and hope for the best.

'Well, is my heart all right?' Winston demanded at length.

'There is nothing serious. You have been overdoing things.'

Winston protested, as Wilson knew he would. 'Now, Charles, you're not going to tell me to rest. I can't. I won't. Nobody else can do this job. I must.'

At the end of the consultation Winston had convinced himself that he had simply strained one of his heart muscles; and Wilson, without refuting this diagnosis, warned him that his circulation was a bit sluggish and that he must do all he could not to over-exert himself.

But that night at the White House marked the end of a period when Winston could test himself to the uttermost without thought for his health.

This same visit marked the end of another era for Winston and the nation he led. Until this time – until the blessed catastrophe of Pearl Harbor and the entry of the United States into the war – Britain was the sole arbiter of the conduct of the war in the West. Winston and the War Cabinet made decisions without reference to any other government, except, where appropriate, the governments of the dominions. It made for simplicity and speed. Winston judged it to be helpful to the cause to keep Roosevelt *au courant* with events, and several hundred letters and cables, as well as telephone calls, had been exchanged by the time of Pearl Harbor. But the course of events was shaped in London. Now the relationship was quite different. At the first meeting of the British chiefs of staff after the American declaration of war on Japan, one of the members suggested a line of action towards some matter connected with the United States to conform with the soft approach with which they were all familiar. Winston broke in 'with a wicked leer in his eye', according to Brooke. 'Oh! that is the way we talked to her while we were wooing her; now that she is in the harem, we talk to her quite differently.'

The soft pedal was now redundant in the war concerto. From now on it was to be straight talk and hard bargaining. Friendships would be forged in the alliance, but so would

573

enemies be made. The conflict between, say, Generals Montgomery and Bradley was still far ahead; but Admiral King in Washington was already forming an antagonistic approach to Britain, and conflicts of interest soon led to disputes between the joint chiefs of staff. At a lower level, war-hardened British and dominion troops were inclined to assume a patronizing attitude towards the rookies with dollars in their pockets and medal ribbons on their chests before they had seen the enemy.

All this was inevitable and rarely very serious. What was much more fundamental was the switch of control of the course of the war from Britain to the United States. This did not happen at once or even swiftly. For a time, Britain's war machine was a great deal more powerful than America's, as well as experienced in battle. But as the war industry and the armed forces of the richest nation on earth grew, so its influence and power increasingly dominated the counsels of war. Winston and the British War Cabinet and the chiefs of staff had all anticipated this, and by the end of 1942, when American troops had landed in North Africa to collaborate with the British 8th Army in driving out General Rommel and his Afrika Corps, and American forces in the Pacific were beginning to hold the onrushing Japanese, the United States was starting to 'call the shots'.

Britain and her Commonwealth could not conceivably have defeated Nazi Germany alone. As soon as the giants of East and West entered the conflict, Britain, and the leader responsible for her survival, suffered declining importance and influence. And after Winston's Christmas visit to the White House at the end of 1941, his health was never to be as strong again, either.

Five days for Winston in Florida gave Roosevelt a rest from being host to a demanding guest, and the guest a rest in the winter sun. 'The blue ocean is so warm that Winston basks half-submerged in the water like a hippopotamus in a swamp,' his doctor recorded. The few days away also did no harm to Winston's 'pump', as he called what had become for him a disconcerting preoccupation.

Consuelo Balsan, driven from her French homes by the Germans, was living in equally luxurious style in Florida, and Winston lunched with her one day, reminding him of those happy days at Blenheim two wars ago. But now, as he remarked of her lavish home afterwards, 'Wealth, taste and leisure can do these things, but they do not bring happiness.'

Winston came back home by flying boat from Bermuda. Poor navigation led to their almost overflying France and the formidable anti-aircraft batteries of Brest. Shortly after, another error, this time of RAF misidentification, led to fighters being scrambled to intercept. Winston and flying once again appeared incompatible. And much more flying lay ahead. 'The P.M. is always a little apprehensive in the air,' Wilson recorded. On another flight, in a converted bomber equipped with some mattresses and a makeshift heating system, Winston burnt his feet against some pipes and complained, in the depth of the night, 'They are red hot. We shall have the petrol fumes bursting into flames. There'll be an explosion soon.'

The transatlantic flying boats were as luxurious as the converted bombers were cold and primitive. Oxygen was impractical and they were not pressurized, so they flew at moderate heights, usually at about eight thousand feet. Moreover, there was no escort on these long flights to North Africa and Russia, and there was a real risk of being shot down. In August 1942, soon after Winston landed at Cairo, a plane following the route Winston's plane had taken two days earlier was shot down. Its passenger was General W. H. E. Gott, whom Winston had just appointed to lead the 8th Army.

Winston's practice of seeing things, and people, for himself certainly multiplied many times over the risk element. He knew it himself, and before one long flight he wrote to George VI recommending Anthony Eden as his successor if he failed to return. We see him at Marrakesh in January 1943 seeing off Roosevelt who has flown over for talks. Because it is early in the morning – by Winston's reckoning – he leaves himself no time to dress and hastens to join the President in his car 'in his most flamboyant dressing-gown, covered with red dragons'. We can see him, too, landing at Moscow airport in a machine that has flown at great risk all the way from Cairo, greeted by the Russian Foreign Minister, Molotov, before racing off through the centre of the besieged city to a dacha in a pine wood. He has come to transmit to the Soviet leader the discomfiting news that there can be no question of a second front that year. Stalin is not pleased.

At the end of 1943, Winston confessed that he was 'at the end of my tether'. Not a day passed throughout the year when he did not face some new anxiety and make some important decision. The culmination was the summit meeting at Teheran with Roosevelt and Stalin. Here he had been made to feel, as never before, the second fiddler. While not quite ganging up with Stalin against Winston, Roosevelt was making it almost too clear that he did not wish the Russians to get the impression that the West spoke with one voice.

Winston took the near-snubs, the private meeting between the Russian and the American, and other disagreeable events philosophically, but Charles Wilson – now elevated to the peerage as Lord Moran – was increasingly concerned about Winston's health. The party returned to Cairo for further meetings. Winston lunched with Brooke on 9 December. Brooke thought he looked awful; the previous evening, when dining with Smuts at the Embassy, the South African leader had drawn Brooke aside and said he doubted 'whether he [Winston] would stay the course'.

> I shall always remember that lunch as a bad nightmare [Brooke continued]. He was dressed in a grey zip-suit, with zip-shoes, and his vast Mexican hat. We sat among the flower beds at a small card-table . . . He held a fly-whisk in his hand. After two spoonfuls of soup he started discussing the question of the Command of the Mediterranean and said, 'It is all quite simple, there are . . .' then down came the

fly-whisk with a crash, and a fly corpse was collected
and placed in a fly mortuary near the corner of the
table. He then had two more spoonfuls of soup and
said: 'This is the most *dee*licious soup,' followed by
another spoonful . . .

More fly murders continued throughout the meal, and almost
nothing was said, 'and I began to wonder how near he was to
a crash'.

Next stop on the way to visit the troops fighting in Italy was
(or should have been) Carthage, where he was to meet General Dwight D. Eisenhower, Roosevelt's choice for supreme
commander for the Channel assault on France. Unfortunately, the pilot landed on the wrong airfield and no-one
seemed able to make up his mind whether they should take
off again or order some cars to take them the rest of the way.
Winston disembarked from the Skymaster and sat down on
his boxes. A cold wind whipped up the dust of the wilderness
to which they had descended. No human or habitation could
at first be seen. Then his daughter Sarah, the airwoman,
who had been Winston's constant support and companion
on this journey, spotted some aircraft on the ground being
serviced. The Prime Minister, his hat in his hand, surveyed
the landscape gloomily. When it was decided to re-embark
and fly on to their destination, he was reluctant to bestir
himself and then walked very slowly back to the aircraft,
not noticing the distant, waving airmen.

Soon they were at Eisenhower's villa, and Winston slumped
into the first chair. To Charles Wilson's deep anxiety, the
Prime Minister did nothing for the rest of the day, not even
glancing at the telegrams, which were, as always, piling up for
attention. That night, Wilson was awakened by the presence
of Winston at the end of his bed.

'I've got a pain in my throat, here.' He pointed to his collar
bone. 'It's pretty bad. Do you think it's anything? What can
it be due to?'

Wilson attempted to reassure him. On the one hand, his
charge was becoming increasingly hypochondriacal; on the

other, he was overworking and looked awful and had been beset by numerous minor ailments for weeks past. The next morning, 12 December, Wilson went to Winston's room. Winston had a temperature, and it remained up all day. John Martin was told to tell the Cabinet in London. As a precaution, two nurses and a pathologist were summoned from Cairo. An X-ray revealed congestion in the left lung. It was pneumonia. At least Charles Wilson had a clear diagnosis and could start him on antibiotics, and as a precaution a cardiologist was also summoned from Cairo.

The climax then came rapidly. At 6 p.m. on 14 December, Wilson was called to Winston's bedside.

'I don't feel well,' he said. 'My heart is doing something funny – it feels to be bumping all over the place.'

> He was very breathless and anxious-looking [Wilson recorded]. I felt his pulse: it was racing and very irregular. The bases of his lungs were congested and the edge of his liver could be felt below the ribs. I had taken the precaution this morning to send to Tunis for digitalis, and now I gave it to him. As I sat by his bedside listening to his quick breathing, I knew that we were at last right up against things . . .

Sarah spent endless hours at her father's bedside. 'Once he opened his eyes,' she recalled, 'and must have caught my troubled look before I had time to mask it. He looked at me without speaking for a moment, then said, "Don't worry, it doesn't matter if I die now, the plans of victory have been laid, it is only a matter of time," and fell into a deep sleep once more.'

Clementine, 'blackout & winter wearied', had begun worrying about Winston's health and safety well before the North Africa crisis. She fussed about his 'gyppie tummy' and about his means of travelling home. '*Please please* don't fly home,' she appealed to him, and recommended instead 'a perfectly good cruiser'. As soon as the Carthage bulletins began arriving, she very quickly decided to fly out to see him. For support on the journey, she took the ubiquitous Grace Hamblin and Jock Colville, just back from his sojourn with the RAF.

All the London and home counties airfields were clamped with fog on 16 December, so the party, with Mary, made their fumbling journey to Lyneham in Wiltshire by two cars. They had what Colville called 'a rather sticky dinner' before embarking, in full flying kit, in an unheated Liberator bomber with a mattress each. Clementine, alarmed at the whole business, sat up most of the night, talking and drinking coffee. 'The journey out was *horrible*,' she complained. 'Icy cold . . . After saying we were going straight thro' we came down *in the dark* at Gibraltar – oh Wow – your cowardly old Mother's knees knocked together,' she told Mary . . . 'Jock was such a comfort.'

On arrival at the villa, Clementine was taken straight into Winston's room. The crisis was now over, but she was appalled at his appearance. Wilson commented that if she had seen him forty-eight hours earlier she would indeed have been shocked. But when Colville was called in later in the afternoon he 'found instead of a recumbent invalid a cheerful figure with a large cigar and a whisky and soda in his hand'.

General Eisenhower's villa had become a convalescent home. Charles Wilson would have preferred more peace and quiet for his patient, but Winston thrived on people and their coming and going. The villa was also the scene of a family gathering. Randolph had been in Cairo, all keyed up to parachute into Yugoslavia with Evelyn Waugh. Now he boomed about the place being rude, but cheering up his father with endless games of bézique at huge odds; while Sarah – always her father's favourite – hovered about ready to take on small tasks or run errands.

On 25 December Eisenhower's villa filled with more generals, admirals and air marshals than anyone believed were operating in North Africa. And they had not come to wish Winston a happy Christmas, either. Winston had summoned them to discuss a further landing in Italy, at Anzio, in the expectation of capturing Rome and winding up the Italian campaign before the Overlord invasion of northern France.

However, there were fun and festivities later. Christmas lunch was the first meal Winston had taken outside his bedroom. He was in tremendous form, quite his old self, putting down turkey and plum pudding and proposing numerous toasts, and smoking several giant cigars. He was dressed in a padded silk Chinese dressing gown, looking (according to Harold Macmillan) 'rather like a figure in a Russian ballet'. But he was dead beat by 5.30 p.m., when he returned to his bed, knowing that he had some way to go before he was fully recovered. So between them Clementine and Charles Wilson were successful in persuading him to convalesce at Marrakesh in the New Year instead of coming straight home.

New Year's Eve dinner was the last of the Carthage celebrity celebrations, and it was another of those evenings notable for Clementine's shrill interventions. Eisenhower was invited, which was only civil as it was his villa, and General Montgomery and his aide-de-camp, Noel Chevasse, were invited for the night. In the early evening, as everyone dispersed to change, Montgomery overheard Clementine call out to Chevasse, 'I look forward to seeing you in half an hour.'

According to Jock Colville, who was also present, Monty intervened tartly, 'My ADCs don't dine with the Prime Minister.'

With a withering expression on her face, Clementine said, 'In my house, General Montgomery, I invite who I wish and I don't require your advice.'

Montgomery was never Clementine's favourite general, although perhaps she loathed de Gaulle more. On another occasion, when Monty was a guest at Chartwell and they were playing croquet (not a game to soothe relations), he declared that all politicians were dishonest.

'If that is your view, General Montgomery, I wish you to leave at once. I will arrange to have your bags packed.'

Only profuse apologies saved him from that counter-attack.

When Winston had completed his convalescence at Marrakesh, he was taken home in a battleship by the Royal Navy.

Winston was at sea again five months later, on 12 June 1944. It would have been six days earlier if he had had his way. On 30 May, at one of his last luncheon audiences with the King before the invasion of Europe, this conversation took place:

George VI: Where will you be on D-Day, Mr Churchill?

Winston: Well, sir, I hope to watch the initial attack from one of the bombarding ships. As long as a month ago I asked Admiral Ramsay to work out a plan for me.

George VI: Perhaps I should come, too.

Winston: A splendid idea, sir. Perhaps we could both talk over the idea with Admiral Ramsay. Would the day after tomorrow be convenient?

Later, the King wrote in his diary, 'It is a big decision to take on one's own responsibility. W. cannot say no if he goes himself, & I don't want to tell him he cannot. So? I told Elizabeth about the idea & she was wonderful as always & encouraged me to do it.'

But that was as far as the proposed expedition went. Sir Alan Lascelles, the King's stuffy and humourless private secretary and adviser on all things, put his foot down on the grounds that it would place too great a burden on the commander of the ship, and asked what would happen if both King and Prime Minister were killed by a bomb. 'Are you, sir, prepared to advise Princess Elizabeth on the choice of her first Prime Minister?'

Winston went ahead with his own plans, however, and a further meeting with the King, a verbal appeal from him not

581

to embark on so hazardous a passage, and two letters and a telephone call were needed to persuade him, almost at the last moment, to agree to remain ashore. The Normandy landings, unwitnessed by Sovereign or Premier, took place on 6 June, a vast operation, Winston told the House of Commons, 'undoubtedly the most complicated and difficult that has ever taken place'. Thousands of tons of bombs, and shells and rockets from bombarding men of war, had fallen on the German defences. Glider troops and parachutists seized the key points inside France before troops of the 2nd British and Canadian Army and 1st United States Army were put ashore along the selected line of Normandy beaches. By brilliant deception the Allies had given the enemy the firm impression that the landings would be in the Pas de Calais, and complete surprise gave the assaulting forces a great advantage.

Winston spent the morning in the map room, where the progress of the landings was minutely plotted. Only on one beach, Omaha, had the V American Corps been held up by furious resistance. After midday, he was able to telegraph Stalin: 'Everything has started well. The mines, obstacles and land batteries have been largely overcome. The air landings were very successful, and on a large scale. Infantry landings are proceeding rapidly, and many tanks and self-propelled guns are already ashore.' Almost total control of the sea and the air had made all this possible.

For Winston, lunch with the King on D-Day was followed by his statement to the House of Commons on the mighty operations. He was able to add to the tension and excitement by first announcing the liberation of Rome . . . Everything seemed to be falling into place. But as always, Winston still wanted to be there, a witness to the assault on 'fortress Europe'.

Five days after the first landings, Montgomery was able to signal Winston that it was safe for him to land and visit his headquarters. Late on the evening of 11 June, then, with Smuts, Brooke, and the American chiefs of staff who had come over to visit the American forces ashore, Winston took his own special train out of London for Portsmouth, consuming a considerable and agreeable dinner on the way. As always, Generals Marshall and Arnold and Admiral King were astonished at the amount of Pol Roger and brandy that Winston drank, but it was a friendly occasion for all, with a scarcely disguised triumphant note to the conversation. The party broke up soon after 11 p.m., leaving Winston a further two hours to work on his papers before turning in.

The dawn of 12 June broke bright and calm after the uncertain weather that had led first to the postponement of the original attack by twenty-four hours and then to some difficulties with the delivery of supplies and reinforcements. The destroyer *Kelvin* awaited the British party, and a similar destroyer was ready for the American top brass. Both vessels had a smooth crossing, passing between convoys of empty and packed landing craft, minesweepers and sections of floating breakwaters and piers for erection off the French beaches. Above, the air was filled with the sound of aircraft.

Brooke described the extraordinary scene as the *Kelvin* approached the beaches.

> Everywhere the sea was covered with ships of all sizes and shapes, and was a scene of continuous activity. We passed through rows and rows of tank landing-ships and finally came to a 'Gooseberry', namely a row of ships sunk in a half crescent to form a sort of harbour and provide protection from the sea. Here we were met by Admiral Vian [hero of the *Altmark* rescue in Norway before France was even conquered], who took us in his Admiral's barge from which we changed into a 'DUKW'.

This amphibious vehicle drove the party straight up the beach and on to a road, where General Montgomery, dressed in non-uniform casual leather wool-lined jacket and black beret, and his staff awaited them with a veritable swarm of jeeps.

Winston climbed into the front seat of one of them, and

583

the whole party raced away to Monty's headquarters. It was four years since Winston had been in France, a country he had always loved. 'There was very little firing or activity,' he noted. 'The weather was brilliant. We drove through our limited but fertile domain in Normandy. It was pleasant to see the prosperity of the countryside. The fields were full of lovely red and white cows basking or parading in the sunshine. The inhabitants seemed quite buoyant and well nourished and waved enthusiastically.' It was different from what he had imagined it would be, and very different from the French battlefields of 1916. Yet they were only some three miles from the German line when they halted five miles inland at a beautiful château with lawns and lakes – and a few bomb craters.

Lunch had been laid out for them in a large tent facing inland, and the enemy. Winston asked the General, 'What is there to prevent an incursion of German armour breaking up our luncheon?'

Montgomery replied that he did not think that they would come, and Winston followed up with sage military advice. 'Anything can be done once or for a short time, but custom, repetition, prolongation, is always to be avoided when possible in war.' He thought Monty was taking too much of a risk if he made a habit of proceedings like this. But the only excitement, and mild at that, was in the air, where occasional tip-and-run German fighter-bombers flashed overhead and were heavily engaged by anti-aircraft fire.

In the afternoon, Winston and his party toured the area like holiday tourists and even visited the nearest little French harbours, which were doing exceptionally good trade. Then Monty, still in wool-lined leather jacket in spite of the heat, bade them all goodbye, and off they went in the DUKW again and back to the *Kelvin*. Vian asked, 'Would you like to see a big bombardment of German positions by some battleships and cruisers?'

It seemed the only means of witnessing some action, so they steamed fast between two battleships making a fearful noise with their heavy guns at a target 20,000 yards distant and then approached some cruisers firing at a shorter range. The *Kelvin* headed towards the shore again, and Winston said to Vian, 'Since we're so near why shouldn't we have a plug at them ourselves before we go home.'

'Certainly, sir,' Vian replied, and in the shortest time all the destroyer's guns opened fire, to Winston's undisguised delight. But Vian was not going to risk return fire from the German positions; the *Kelvin*'s helm was put over, and they raced for the open sea. Winston went down to his tiny cabin. There he lay down and went straight off and remained sound asleep for the four-hour-long passage home to Portsmouth.

Arnold, King and Marshall were all waiting for them when at length the British party returned to Winston's train, and there was continuous chat, broken by food and drink, on the return journey to London. Winston began a message to Roosevelt: 'I had a jolly day on Monday on the beaches . . .' It might have been a postcard from Coney Island or Clacton, and even ended, 'How I wish you were here!'

But the Normandy visit gave a false impression of what was to come, and tens of thousands of young men were to die before Paris was relieved, then Brussels and Antwerp, and the Rhine reached. Six weeks before the Rhine was finally crossed and the Russians began their assault on Berlin, the original 'Big Three' met for the last time, at Yalta in the Crimea. Here, with the comfort of Sarah in the immense British contingent, Winston was a sad witness to Roosevelt's failing capacities and the opportunistic tactics employed by Stalin in dividing the two Western leaders – one so personally weak and sick, the other impotent in his relative lack of power. The peace was turning sour even before victory had been achieved.

Clementine was given the opportunity to observe the more agreeable and non-political aspect of the Soviet people. The Russian Red Cross were anxious to acknowledge the great support they had received from the British people and especially her own work, over almost four years of war, and invited her to Moscow and a number of provincial cities. As she was taken from one hospital to another and travelled vast distances through towns and cities – like Stalingrad – virtually destroyed by the war, she found herself admiring and liking her resilient and kindly hostesses. At the same time, she was followed everywhere by news of success after success claimed by the Allied and Russian armies.

> *I have just heard the glorious news of the meeting of the Red Army with the Allies and by your statement on the wireless it seems the end is near* [she cabled Winston]. *I long to be with you in these tremendous days and I think of you constantly.*
> *All my love Clemmie*

But Winston and Clementine were still separated by a thousand miles when Hitler committed suicide and the wretched tattered remnants of a squalid regime pleaded for peace.

'All Our Enemies
Having Surrendered Unconditionally . . .'

Five years – short of two days – from the time when he assumed control of the British war effort, on 10 May 1940, Winston woke up on VE (Victory in Europe) Day at his customary hour of eight o'clock after over four hours of sleep. He had determined to spend the greater part of this fine morning of 8 May 1945 in bed working on the speech he was to broadcast at 3 p.m. John Martin and John Peck were on duty that morning from the secretariat; Elizabeth Layton, a bright secretary since 1941, sat before the typewriter. John Peck came in at one moment with a message from the King, asking if Winston (as he had offered the previous day) would redraft the last paragraph of the speech he was to broadcast, and a messenger brought in a cable from Clementine in Moscow: 'All my thoughts are with you on this supreme day my darling. It could not have happened without you.'

There was only one other interruption to the morning's work, and that was self-imposed. The staff of the map room, led for most of the war by Captain Richard Pim, RNVR, had been unfailingly efficient and obliging. They had been on shift duty round the clock, so that at any eccentric hour Winston could stroll in – in uniform, lurid silk dressing gown, boiler suit or tails – and learn how things were going, down to the smallest detail. This time there were no urgent enquiries. Instead, Sawyers marched in behind the dressing-gowned stout figure, holding in his arms a reward in the form of bottles of champagne and a large Gruyère cheese. 'For Captain Pim and his officers with the Prime Minister's compliments on Victory Day in Europe,' ran the accompanying card.

Shortly before noon, Winston dressed in morning coat,

Sawyers brushed his top hat, and he went downstairs where his car awaited him. Last time, on 11 November 1918, his victory day destination had been Downing Street: this time it was the Palace. The crowds were out in as great numbers, cheering and waving flags all down the Mall. The sky was clear of balloons, the anti-aircraft guns had gone from the parks, the blackout had been lifted, and tonight many buildings would be floodlit: Winston had already given instructions that there should be no shortage of beer in the pubs, a small, human detail that no-one (except John Martin) knew about at the time.

It was a few minutes after 1 p.m. when the car swept into the Buckingham Palace forecourt, watched by thousands at the railings and perched about the Victoria Monument. It was a Tuesday, the regular day for lunch with the King; but this was the first when there were no setbacks to report, and no military successes to report either, except that the war was won. After four years, the monarch and his first minister had long since reached a complete understanding, and there was genuine mutual affection, which was shared with Queen Elizabeth.

The King and Queen came forward to greet him in the small drawing room, the King in naval uniform of admiral of the fleet with six rows of ribbons and the 'wings'* of the Fleet Air Arm on his sleeve; the Queen in a simple three-quarter-length yellow and white summer dress, smiling a welcome. Winston responded to their presence with his familiar little respectful nod of the head to them both.

'Well, Mr Churchill, a great day for you – the end of the European war. Allow me to congratulate you,' said the King.

'And you, sir. It has been a long haul.'

They helped themselves to the proffered glasses of champagne and raised their glasses to toast victory and then all

---

*He and Winston were the only officers who sported wings when, strictly speaking, neither was entitled to wear them.

those who had lost their lives in the fighting and in the bombing of the cities.

As the Queen led the way in to luncheon, flanked by her husband and Winston, she remarked what a pity it was that Clementine was in Russia and could not be here to share the celebrations. This was, indeed, a sore subject for Winston.

'Yes, ma'am, I am most disappointed,' Winston said from his heart. He had hoped that she would return early, even if it meant giving small offence to her Russian hosts. On 4 May he had telegraphed her at length, asking her to come home – she had after all been away for some six weeks – but she claimed she still had 'some necessary engagements to fulfil and some loose ends to tidy up' and extended her timetable.

'Were the crowds very thick between here and Whitehall?' the Queen asked.

'Much revelry, ma'am, much picnic-ing.' Winston addressed the King. 'It seems such a short time ago since your father and mother were at the balcony here responding to the cheers of the crowds. Where were you, sir, on Armistice Day in 1918?'

'I was at Cambrai, Mr Churchill, a Staff Officer in the RAF under Major-General Sir John Salmond – still with us, still in harness, I'm glad to say . . .'

After luncheon, Winston left the Palace through the little back gate, where the car awaited him, avoiding the worst of the crowds and returning swiftly to Whitehall. As painstaking as ever with the text of his speeches, he went once more through the script of his broadcast, which Elizabeth Layton had retyped. Since he had left for luncheon, numerous messages had arrived from all over the world. John Martin picked out one or two that he knew he would wish to see, with number one priority being a further cable from Clementine, distance lending no enchantment to her bossy instruction: 'Please be sure and keep official and popular rejoicings going tomorrow at the same pitch as today with special reference to Russia. This is important.' Winston had no misgivings that the rejoicing would be sustained and cabled back reassurance to his wife, but the special reference to Russia was more difficult to control. His personal feelings towards this ally were daily becoming colder, as Clementine's warmed, and he had no intention of doing anything whatever.

The second cable was more straightforward. It was from President Harry Truman, whom Winston held in high regard: 'With warm affection, we hail our comrade-in-arms across the Atlantic.' But in America, the celebrations were more muted, the Japanese war being a greater consideration with the people there than in Britain. In Washington any flags that were flown were at half-mast out of respect for the late President Roosevelt. While in New York, 'There were celebrations, but they were generally restrained.'

Winston then made his way to the Cabinet room to make the broadcast that, perhaps above all others, would be most listened to throughout the world. Certainly another record was being broken at number 10 – the depth of organized chaos and the number of people, mostly spilling over from the Annexe, milling around. Marian Holmes had been working since March 1943 as one of the four secretaries under Kathleen Hill, who operated on a roster basis from 8.30 a.m. to the early hours of the following day. She recalled the attempt at a trial run, with Winston bawling into the microphone, 'What you doing?' and John Martin replying, 'They are just fixing the microphone, sir.' Next there was heard by all a 'terrific trumpet', which turned out to be Winston blowing his nose, followed by the snapped order, 'Pull those blinds down. Can't see what I'm doing.'

At 3 p.m. precisely, the intent familiar voice, still with the slight lisp that he had once feared might cripple his career in politics, sounded out from London:

> Yesterday morning [he began] at 2:41 a.m. at General Eisenhower's headquarters, General Jodl, the representative of the German High Command, and Grand-Admiral Doenitz, the designated head of the German State, signed the act of unconditional surrender of all German land, sea and air forces . . . The German war is therefore at an end . . .

Winston went on to recount how 'almost the whole world was combined against the evil-doers, who are now prostrate before us.'

> We may allow ourselves [he concluded] a brief period of rejoicing; but let us not forget for a moment the toil and efforts that lie ahead. Japan, with all her treachery and greed, remains unsubdued . . . We must now devote all our strength and resources to the completion of our task, both at home and abroad. Advance, Britannia! Long live the cause of freedom! God save the King!

In many parts of London and elsewhere, and in White-hall, the speech had been carried by loudspeakers. Harold Nicolson, unable to force his way through the crowds packing Parliament Square in time to hear the speech inside the Palace of Westminster, listened to it packed tight among the people. 'There followed the Last Post,' he wrote of this day, 'and *God Save the King* which we all sang very loud indeed. And then cheer upon cheer.'

> I dashed back into the House and into the Chamber . . . Cool and hushed . . . The clock reached 3:15, which is the moment Questions automatically close. We knew that it would take Winston some time to get to the House from Downing Street in such a crowd . . . Then a slight stir was observed behind the Speaker's chair, and Winston, looking coy and cheerful, came in. The House rose as a man, and yelled and yelled and waved their Order papers. He responded, not with a bow exactly, but with an odd shy jerk of the head and with a wide grin.

Winston repeated the statement he had just broadcast, and then he thanked and blessed the House for 'all its noble support of him throughout the years'. He proposed that 'this House do now attend at the Church of

591

St Margaret's, Westminster, to give humble and reverend thanks to Almighty God for our deliverance from the threat of German domination'.

Both on the outward walk to the church and on the return, the crowds cheered and threatened to mob the long line of MPs. Passing through Central Hall before re-entering the House, a small boy slipped out of the crowd and presented his autograph album to Winston. Quite slowly, Winston felt for his glasses, gave them a clean, took the pencil, and signed his name. Then he ruffled the boy's hair and remarked, 'That will remind you of a glorious day.' It was a vintage little performance by a man who knew his public. Renewed cheers!

The stupendous day of victory was not yet over; indeed, it had hardly begun. There was a (for him) brief interval in the Smoking Room for champagne with cronies, then back through the crowds to the Annexe, and in a few minutes, off again to the Palace with the entire War Cabinet and the chiefs of staff for a celebratory meeting with the King and Queen, and photographs. Back to the Annexe then, and up and on to a balcony overlooking Whitehall where the crowds had been told he might appear and address them.

'God bless you all! This is your victory!'

'No, it's yours!' yelled the crowd.

'It is the victory of the cause of freedom in every land. In all our long history we have never seen a greater day than this . . .'

The evening sun shone. The crowds were briefly silent, smiling, with none of the hysteria of 1918 and no sign of drunkenness. 'God bless you all!' he concluded, taking off his hat and waving it.

Winston returned once more to the Annexe. Winant was there, and before Winston changed into his boiler suit for the evening, the American Ambassador – a dear friend of the family now – introduced him to his son, who had just been released from a prisoner-of-war camp. Then dinner at 8.30 p.m., a mainly family occasion with his two elder daughters, Duncan Sandys and Winston's old newspaper friend William Berry, Lord Camrose, editor in chief of the *Daily Telegraph*.

Shortly before 10.30 p.m., Winston was told that there was a great milling crowd in Parliament Street, calling for a speech. 'I will go up in five minutes,' he told Desmond Morton crisply.

'Will you be changing, sir?' Morton asked.

'Certainly not.' This was no time for formal attire when the British people had associated him affectionately with his boiler suit ever since the Blitz.

He took with him his grandson, Julian Sandys, and when the pair appeared on the balcony, the reception was louder than any he had heard all day.

All the diners except Camrose left soon after Winston's return. Now, surely, it was time to relax and reflect, Camrose judged. Not a bit of it. Leslie Rowan was on duty now and was frequently called in with recently received telegrams, the next morning's newspapers, and a copy of the text for Clementine's broadcast in Russia, on Winston's behalf, for the following day. It began:

> It is my firm belief that on the friendship and under-standing between the British and Russian peoples depends the future of mankind. Here in our island home we are thinking today very often about you all, and we send you from the bottom of our hearts our wishes for your happiness and wellbeing . . .

But one of the telegrams was from the British chargé d'affaires in Moscow, which informed him that the Soviet government took exception to a British complaint concerning the seizure by the Russians of sixteen Polish emissaries and their confinement to prison: just one more piece of evidence of Soviet hostility and cupidity. All the goodwill built up from four years of fighting in a great common cause was being dissipated. Almost every solemn commitment made by Stalin at Yalta had been broken, and all Winston's fears for the future were being realized. He dictated a sharp reply to Moscow, in stark contrast with his message to the common people who had fought so bravely and suffered so terribly. It finished:

'It is no longer desired by us to maintain detailed arguments with the Soviet Government about their views and actions.'

Camrose left at 1.15 a.m. Winston had a pile of papers still in front of him. 'You won't be dealing with them tonight,' remarked Camrose before departing.

'Certainly I shall,' Winston told him. 'There is much still to study and settle. Goodnight, Bill.'

He was already planning the next day. The Lord Mayor of London was very anxious for him to make a visit, and he thought it proper – and told Rowan to make the necessary arrangements – to call on the American, Soviet and French ambassadors.

Besides the triumphs and happiness of the day just ended, there were other, smaller elements of satisfaction, and he allowed his mind to play over one or two of them before heading for his bed. Both were from the United States, which added a touch of gilt and were in quaint contrast while saying the same thing.

The first, only just arrived from Eden, who was in San Francisco, was a telegram that ran: 'All my thoughts are with you on this day which is so essentially your day. It is you who have led, uplifted and inspired us through the worst days. Without you this day could not have been.'

The second had caught his eye after he had read *The Times* leader when Camrose had still been with him. It was a letter, prominently displayed, from a Mr Wellesley Atkinson, who lived at the southern end of the same state of California, in San Diego:

> *In the late summer of 1940 I was mining gold in a remote section of northern California. Each noon we left off work in the river bottom and we walked up to our cabin on the hillside above for lunch and to listen to the news. It got so we took a long time to walk up to the cabin. We did not want to hear the news. . . . We knew our freedom was no longer secure . . . Then we heard that voice throwing back defiance into the teeth of the enemy, rallying the nation and the world. There*

594

*was anger in that voice, and measured fury but no
despair. It was the calm voice of a courageous leader
pleading for unity.*

*We opened our cabin door and let that voice ring
out into the stillness . . . Let the world hear it . . . It
seemed like Sunday and that we had been to church.
That, Mr Editor, is what we really think of Winston
Churchill.*

Early morning, Saturday 12 May, and Winston – never good
at early rising – is fretting in the back seat of his car. They
are speeding along the Oxford road, the same road on which
he had driven in his red Napier, Clementine at his side, to
Asquith at Sutton Courtenay, in a last effort to save his
job at the Admiralty back in 1915 and two wars ago. Now
Clementine is somewhere up there in the sky; at least, he
hopes she is. Sawyers had told him flatly that he would be
late, and certainly his watch suggests that his butler-valet is,
once again, right.

The big Skymaster had left Moscow the evening before,
with a single refuelling stop at Malta. As Winston's car turns
off the road, slowing at the main entrance to Northolt, the
gates are flung open and the four guards stand to attention
and salute. Winston swiftly leaves the car at the control
tower. Above, the four-engine Douglas machine can be
seen circling the airfield. So he is just in time, and Sawyers
is wrong, which gives the Prime Minister great satisfaction.
(What he does not know, and will not be told, is that he is
indeed late and the Skymaster has been circling the airfield
awaiting his arrival.)

On the journey back to London, it is family news first.
And first of the family news is about Jack. Winston had kept
from Clementine in her absence the news that his brother
had suffered a heart attack and was in University College
Hospital; now he could lighten it by telling her he was on
the slow road to recovery. Sarah's divorce had at last come
through, and Nellie's son Giles had been released from his
prisoner-of-war camp. He and a number of other notables,

595

including the King's cousin, Lord Lascelles, had been taken by their guards to a hiding place as potential hostages before their camp was overrun.

'And now, my dear,' Clementine asks, 'what have you decided about an election?'

'I've not yet settled between June and October. If it is to be June, then we have only a few days to announce it. I have cabled Anthony in San Francisco to see what he thinks. In the glow of victory it is too easy to forget that we still have a mighty foe in the East, and that the Russians become daily more intractable and dangerous.'

'But, my dear, they were so charming, so grateful for what we have done . . .' Winston makes no further comment.

Polling Day was finally fixed for 5–12 July, and while the war in the Pacific and South-East Asia continued as fiercely as ever, and massive British and Commonwealth naval, air, and military forces had been despatched in support of the Americans, party politics returned to Britain. Clementine was miserable about it. All she wanted was for Winston to leave the political arena altogether and remain the national hero. She wanted Chartwell to become a great national Churchill museum, while they built a nice economical-to-run small house nearby and lived there modestly with a few friends and their family coming to call. 'Having led a Coalition Government and a united nation,' Mary has written, 'Clementine felt very strongly that he should retire rather than become the leader of one half of the nation against the other.' Winston retorted to all this that he was not yet ready to be put on a pedestal. To Clementine's dismay, he was soon conspiring privately with Max Beaverbrook and Brendan Bracken again.

Clementine loyally went canvassing and speechmaking in Woodford (Epping) on his behalf. She had always hated it, never more so than now, while Winston stomped the country electioneering and making broadcasts – in one of which he made reference to the recently, and thankfully, dead German Gestapo. 'No Socialist Government conducting the entire life

596

and industry of the country,' he said, 'could afford to allow free, sharp, or violently-worded expressions of public discontent. They would have to fall back on some form of Gestapo, no doubt very humanely directed in the first instance . . .'

Mary claimed that Clementine begged him to omit that word; however that may be, the effect was devastating. Not that it could be claimed to have lost the Conservative Party the election. That was settled long before the campaign began, and largely by the three and a half million servicemen and women who had had enough of authority bearing down upon them and judged that they would enjoy greater benefit and liberty and suffer less unemployment from a socialist welfare state than under continued Tory control.

At 2.45 p.m. on July 25, some two and a half months after Clementine's return from Moscow, Winston, in reverse role and with Mary beside him, landed at Northolt to be greeted by Clementine. Also in the welcome-home party were Jack (quite recovered, but looking gaunt), Jock Colville and Edwina Mountbatten. Winston had broken off in the middle of the Potsdam Conference in Berlin, where Truman let it be known that he would shortly be dropping a new type of ultra-destructive bomb – an atomic bomb – upon Japanese cities. Progress on negotiations about Persia, Turkish frontiers and the occupation of Vienna had been made, but none on Poland, when Winston had to leave his fellow delegates in order to be present at the result of the British general election. Stalin and Truman expected him back in twenty-four hours, Stalin because he thought Winston would have fixed the results, Truman because he could not entertain the idea of the British electorate rejecting their leader after winning the war against Germany.

In the afternoon, Winston went to see the King to report on the 'Big Three' conference and then returned to the Annexe. That evening he dined with Clementine, Jack, Randolph and Mary. Optimism was in the air. It appeared inconceivable to everyone – including the Labour leader, Clement Attlee – that the people would ungratefully turn out the man who was

597

the greatest national hero since Wellington; the echoes of the cheering of 8 May had scarcely faded away in Whitehall, and the embers of the victory bonfires were scarcely cool.

After dinner, Diana and Duncan Sandys joined them following a visit to Duncan's constituency. Their unfavourable report tempered the optimism, but Winston went to bed 'in the belief that the British people would wish me to continue my work'. The map room, still with Captain Pim in command, had been converted from fighting war to political war, with elaborate communications to constituencies throughout the land instead of military headquarters. Before he fell asleep, Winston imagined himself in his usual map-room chair, watching the results flashing on to the screen, a seat lost here – like a torpedoed ship in the Atlantic – a minor victory there, but on the whole a favourable campaign, like the one so recently concluded.

'Thus slumber,' he wrote. 'However, just before dawn I woke suddenly with a sharp stab of almost physical pain. A hitherto subconscious conviction that we were beaten broke forth and dominated my mind . . . The power to shape the future would be denied me. The knowledge and experience I had gathered, the authority and goodwill I had gained in so many countries, would vanish. I was discontented at the prospect, and turned over at once to sleep again.'

Winston finally woke up at 9 a.m., before any results could have come in, worked for an hour, and then took his bath. He was in it when there was a knock on the door. 'Captain Pim, sir.'

It could mean only catastrophe. 'Come in – hand me that towel, Dick – what is it?'

'The first results are in, sir.'

Winston had wrapped his big white body in the enormous towel and was drying himself vigorously. 'What do they show?'

'The first ten results all show Labour gains,' declared the captain. Winston grunted, made his way swiftly to his bedroom, and dressed in his blue boiler suit. He was, in turn, joined in the map room by Sarah and Jack, his old colleague David Margesson, Max Beaverbrook, Brendan Bracken and

Jock Colville. By midday it was clearly a landslide to the left. Pim was offered a brandy by Winston every time there was a Conservative gain; he claimed he only got three balloons all day.

They all retired for a gloomy luncheon. Clementine was silently hugging the prospect of Winston's retiring from politics. 'It may well be a blessing in disguise,' she said, attempting to sound solemn rather than triumphant.

Winston replied, 'At the moment it seems quite effectively disguised.'

He had retained his own seat, which Labour had not opposed, with a majority of 17,000. But a rather crank independent had taken over ten thousand votes from him, and that in itself was something of a humiliation. Randolph and his friend Julian Amery, absolutely confident of victory, had both lost at Preston. As the day wore on, the gloom became more and more intense. Captain Pim's flashing panels showed one friend and colleague after another disappearing from the political scene. Mary dropped into Mrs Landemare's kitchen, and heard her exclaim, 'I don't know *what* the world's coming to, but I thought I might make some tea.'

Winston's courage and resolution in the face of such a massive defeat brought forth the admiration of everyone that day. When Charles Wilson arrived later, he found him 'lost in a brown study. He looked up. "Well, you know what has happened?" I spoke of the ingratitude of the people. "Oh, no," he answered at once. "I wouldn't call it that. They have had a very hard time."'

Winston could, if he wished, have remained Prime Minister until Parliament met, and with the imminent dropping of the atomic bombs and the Japanese surrender he could have announced the end of the Japanese war, too, before accepting the adverse vote. But, as he was to write, 'The verdict of the electors had been so overwhelmingly expressed that I did not wish to remain even for an hour responsible for their affairs.'

He therefore made arrangements to see the King at 7 p.m. to hand in his resignation.

599

It was a very sad meeting [George VI noted in his diary]. I told him I thought the people were very ungrateful after the way they had been led in the War. He was very calm & said that with the majority the Socialists had got over the other parties (153) & with careful management they could remain in power for years.

The King then offered to appoint Winston a Knight of the Garter, the highest order of chivalry, but he declined, for the present, though accepting later, deciding that it might be improper when he intended to lead the opposition in Parliament. Half an hour later, the King was offering the premiership to the less substantial figure of Mr Clement Attlee, who was to preside over the affairs of the nation for six years and five months.

That evening, Winston broadcast to the nation a message of thanks to the people for their 'unflinching, unswerving support which they have given me during my task, and for the many expressions of kindness which they have shown towards their servant'.

At the time, Winston wisely and successfully concealed the bitterness of rejection and defeat, which emerged publicly only some three years later with the publication of the first volume of his history of the Second World War. Writing of the night of 10 May 1940, 'at the outset of this mighty battle':

> I acquired the chief power in the State, which henceforth I wielded in ever-growing measure for five years and three months of world war, at the end of which time, all our enemies having surrendered unconditionally or being about to do so, I was immediately dismissed by the British electorate from all further conduct of their affairs.

As so often in their married life, Clementine's logic was to prove superior to her imagination. Certainly, it would have been more comfortable for her and greatly more beneficial to Winston's historical reputation if he had resigned from politics at the peak of his world renown. But to everyone who knew him well the thought that he would not re-enter the political arena never occurred. He was, after all, only just 70, and politics had been his life for forty-five years. It is hard to understand why Clementine, of all people, believed it possible that her husband would now sink into a world of lifelong fame, painting and bricklaying. That she should advocate this, vehemently and none too privately either, shows how unyielding and imprudent she could be.

Winston's mistakes and misjudgements began long before the election results were known. *The Times* described his conduct during the election campaign as 'one of the strangest episodes of his career . . . He could have emerged from the election with his reputation untarnished. Instead he indulged in accusations, imputations and even personal abuse against his wartime colleagues which shocked his hearers – even his friends – and embittered his opponents.'

As wartime prime minister of a coalition government, Winston had had to defend his administration and his personal conduct of the war on many occasions, but he always spoke from a position of such authority that his attackers never came near to untoppling him, even after grave defeats in Greece, the Sahara and the Far East. Now he found the adjustment to leading the Conservative Party in opposition at first beyond his powers. As one of the chief founders of the welfare state in Asquith's time before the Great War, he now indulged in attacking its dramatic extension, which was the Labour Party's first concern. He appeared to carry on a personal vendetta against Herbert Morrison, the much-respected Leader of the House, and their weekly duels were named after a popular radio programme of the time, *Children's Hour*.

It had become quite clear that even if Britain had wished to do so, she could not afford to continue her rule over India and Burma, as well as many of the African colonies.

Winston's views on India were still coloured by his soldiering days out there and by his romantic vision of the White Raj governing while protecting the brown millions – the Disraelian philosophy inherited from his father. He fought tooth and nail against the manner and speed with which the Attlee government proposed to liberate India from British rule. He was also horrified when it was announced that his old friend Dickie Mountbatten was to preside, as the last viceroy, over the transfer of power. 'Everyone knows that the fourteen months' time limit is fatal to any orderly transference of power,' he told the House, 'and I am bound to say that the whole thing wears the aspect of an attempt by the Government to make use of brilliant war figures in order to cover up a melancholy and disastrous transaction.' In the event, Mountbatten speeded up the process even further, was obliged to partition the subcontinent because of Hindu-Moslem hostility, and was a helpless witness to the inevitable communal strife that resulted in millions of deaths. Mountbatten received almost nothing but praise, Winston almost no credit, over the transfer of power in India, an ironic reversal of fortune by contrast with 1914. It was five years before Winston forgave his old friend.

Winston's reputation abroad after the war, especially in the United States, France and the old dominions, stood and remained pinnacle high, however, and during his 'victory' tours of the liberated European nations every kind of honour was heaped upon him. In March 1946 he visited the United States and with President Truman at his side made a speech of such historical importance that, certainly in America, it was the single act in peacetime for which he will be best remembered.

He delivered it at Fulton, Missouri, at Westminster College, and used it as a masterly survey of 'this still agitated and un-united world', with particular reference to the threat of the Soviet Union.

From Stettin in the Baltic to Trieste in the Adriatic, an iron curtain has descended across the Continent.

Behind that line lie all the capitals of the ancient states of Central and Eastern Europe. Warsaw, Berlin, Prague, Vienna, Budapest, Belgrade, Bucharest and Sofia, all these famous cities and the populations around them lie in what I must call the Soviet Sphere, and all are subject in one form or another, not only to Soviet influence but to a very high and, in many cases, increasing measure of control from Moscow.

At a time of gigantic Russian rearmament accompanied by paranoia and threats, 'our supreme task,' said Winston, 'is to guard the homes of the common people from the horrors and miseries of another war.' He called for greater strength and purpose in the United Nations and a 'a new unity in Europe', and he deplored the 'shadow which has fallen upon the scenes so lately lighted by the Allied victory'.

The speech had a largely hostile reception in the United States and not an entirely favourable one at home. Both isolationist and idealist opinion, of the kind that had inspired Roosevelt to yield to Russian pressure at Teheran and Yalta and 'give' half of central and eastern Europe to the Soviet Union, still prevailed. But disillusionment soon set in, and Winston's warnings would be seen in a new light as the cold war began. Already, only a few days before the Fulton speech, George Kennan, the American chargé d'affaires in Moscow, had despatched a long warning telegram of the attempted Russian extension of the limits of Soviet power. Worse, much worse, was to come . . .

With the single exception of his blind spot over India, Winston's foreign policy and speeches were sound, just as his parliamentary performance on home affairs was gravely flawed.

He made a series of speeches which were as important as statements by a Sovereign government [*The Times* commented]. They had a world-wide influence. They were creative. They helped to form the policies not only of Britain but of the whole free world. Yet when he made them he was out of office and speaking only for himself.

When Winston returned to Downing Street as Premier again in 1951 his own performance and that of the Government were unsensational. The nation's finances needed serious attention, food rationing was still in force, the armed services had been dangerously run down, and union and social strife needed to be reduced, industry modernized, and numerous but unspectacular steps taken. Winston took relatively little part in parliamentary debate, seeing himself on the world's stage rather than as a lead actor in the Commons.

For Winston, the immediate post-war years were unsatisfactory or disastrous. The first great sadness, and a loss from which he never really recovered, was the death of his brother. Jack had always been a self-effacing, undemonstrative, but cheerful and quietly amusing figure, without an enemy in the world. Except for his lifelong love of the Army, and his courage in battle, he was the opposite of Winston in almost every respect.

To the end of his days, Jack retained his soldier's stance, tall and handsome and with the military moustache he had worn since he left school. Rebecca West once commented of Jack that 'it was an experience to see [Winston] with his brother who had none of Winston's spectacular animation, but who caught the eye with a ruddy handsomeness such as King David might have had.' Winston was admiring not just of his serenity and quiet good humour but also of his looks. Winston never thought of himself as handsome, but at one time in his early forties he had astonished his family by starting to grow a moustache. It turned out so fair and wispy and thin that it was shaved off, without a word to anyone or by anyone, and never referred to.

Jack acted as a sounding board during his brother's wartime premiership and came to live in the number 10 Annexe after his Regent's Park house was bombed, when Goonie retired to the country. He was always ready with steadying advice, and he and Goonie, before she died, acted as a joint calming influence at tempestuous times in Winston's marriage. They were both so nice and so kind that their presence was a deterrent to the worst outbreaks of rows and rudeness between Winston and Clementine.

Jack remained in the Oxford Yeomanry (as a reservist) from 1908 until 1921, and in addition to his medals won in the Boer War, he was mentioned in despatches in the Great War and earned the DSO in June 1918. His heart never fully recovered from the attack it suffered in 1945, and he was taken ill again at the end of 1946. Winston visited him at least once a day when he was in University College Hospital, where he died peacefully on 26 February 1947. There was a memorial service in St Martin's Church, Bladon, the following day, and he was buried next to Jennie and his father. Among numerous tributes, *The Times* stressed how he had 'remained throughout his life on the closest terms with his elder brother'.

Clementine had loved Jack, too, and was to miss him greatly. But with Winston's re-entry into peacetime politics, depression and nervousness soon overcame her. She remained unstable for many months, turning domestic life into 'a series of scenes', as their youngest daughter described conditions at home. They were now extremely well off from bequests and his commissioned history of the Second World War, but as always during Clementine's black periods, she fretted more than ever about extravagance. To Clementine's dismay, Winston had insisted on keeping and reinstating Chartwell after the years of neglect. How could they afford it? How was she to find, keep and *pay* the servants?

Winston deftly stemmed the assault by recruiting German prisoners of war as gardeners and then – the master stroke – negotiated the sale of Chartwell to the National Trust. The property was paid for by 'Winston's friends, who chose to remain anonymous', although everyone knew they were led by Lord Camrose, with the proviso that he and Clementine could live there for the rest of their lives at a nominal rent of £350 a year. Still discontented, Clementine complained about the way Winston side-tracked the gardeners from their real work of tidying the borders and keeping the lawns like velvet, to the more robust business of felling trees and keeping the hedges in order. Winston's fascination with landscape gardening had not diminished with the years.

For a town house during the years out of office, Winston bought 28 Hyde Park Gate, on the opposite side of the park from Sussex Square. It looked capacious enough, but as soon as peacetime political life got into its stride and Winston began busying himself again with war memoirs and took up again the writing of his *History of the English-Speaking Peoples*, the number of secretarial staff alone demanded expansion. Clementine worried herself sick. 'She felt desperate,' according to Mary, 'and at a loss to know how to solve this knotty and urgent problem.' The house next door, number 27, was put on the market at that time. To most women with plenty of money, here would have been the solution, but to Clementine, 'it seemed a monstrously extravagant way to acquire more office space.' In the end she salved her conscience by allowing Winston to buy it and converting the top two floors into a maisonette to rent.

After that, Clementine suffered nervous collapse and was ordered to take a complete rest. This seemed, to Winston, the right time to put into effect a plan he had privately conceived for some time. In spite of the farming disasters between the wars, he had always fancied developing Chartwell into a proper estate with a home farm. Two farms adjoining Chartwell were on the market, and he made offers, which were accepted, for both of them in December 1946 at a total cost of almost £33,000.

The single completely happy family event after the war was the marriage of satisfactory Mary to a professional soldier, Christopher Soames, who was two years older than her. They were married, as Winston and Clementine had been, at St Margaret's, Westminster, and left for their honeymoon in Switzerland. Unlike those of Mary's brother and her two

606

older sisters, her marriage was a great success, and they had three sons and two daughters.

Randolph was in America lecturing at the time of Mary's wedding. She wrote of him after the war:

> Randolph led his own rampaging existence: lecturer, journalist, author and politician – he always had lances to break, and hares to start. Although blazingly loyal and demonstratively affectionate, he was not a 'comfortable' person to have around, and too often was in the mood when he would – all else failing – pick a quarrel with a chair.

He had proved his courage many times during the war, and was to do so again as a war reporter in Korea, where he was shot in the leg. His capacity for drink remained prodigious, and he was embittered by his father's evident lack of enthusiasm for his company, the rows that marked his presence becoming increasingly exhausting for the older man with the passing years. And yet there remained a deep affection between them.

Randolph's long-delayed divorce came through a few months after the end of the war, and in November 1948 he married June Osborne. It was inevitably a tempestuous relationship, held together only by their beautiful daughter, Arabella, although finally ending in divorce in 1961. In the previous year Randolph had been entrusted with the writing of Winston's biography, incontrovertibly the single most important and worthwhile task of his life. He went about it with professional zeal, surrounding himself with a team of researchers and secretaries at his place at Stour. His health, alas, was already failing. His prodigious cigarette smoking was taking its toll. In a life touched by tragedy, insecurity and loneliness, the worst blow was that he was able to complete only the first two volumes of a biography that gave strong evidence of matching its subject in its quality and understanding. He died on 6 June 1968.

Winston himself had been dead for more than three years

when Randolph died. But he was not spared the death, by her own hand, of his eldest child. Diana, another heavy drinker, had also inherited her mother's lack of mental steadiness, and as Mary noted, 'The misery her bouts of nervous ill-health had caused her had been accentuated by the break-up of her marriage.' Announcing that she wished to be known simply as 'Mrs Diana Churchill' in future, she lived in a pleasant home in Belgravia, deriving pleasure from very little except her children, one of whom married in 1962. After her divorce, she saw more of her mother, though they were never to achieve an intimate relationship. Ironically, Clementine was in hospital, suffering again from 'nervous exhaustion', when life seems suddenly to have become intolerable for Diana, and on the night of 19–20 October 1963, she took an overdose of tablets and was found dead in the morning. Winston, approaching his eighty-ninth birthday, found the news hard to accept, and did so very slowly, before he 'withdrew into a great and distant silence'.

And then there was Sarah, 'the Mule', as Winston affectionately called her. Of all his children, he was closest to her, though she also exasperated him with her numerous men friends and marriages. She was just as liable to nervous breakdowns as her elder sister and her mother, but in between she was bright and cheerful and a little ray of sunshine by contrast with the shadow cast by Diana – 'a joy to all' as Winston described her: 'Sarah has been a great joy and gets on with everybody,' he wrote to Clementine from the south of France.

Sarah picked up her acting career again after she left the RAF, and was often in America, notably playing the lead in a touring version of *The Philadelphia Story* in 1949. She was being courted at this time by a photographer and war artist, Anthony Beauchamp. Winston and Clementine had both met him and had not cared much for him. On 18 October 1949, Beauchamp at last persuaded Sarah to marry him, and they did so after sending cables home to tell of their decision. Unfortunately, the newspapers published the news before any of the family heard, and her parents were outraged, especially Clementine. For several months there was an almost total estrangement. Relations were slowly rebuilt, but as Clementine had predicted, the marriage soon broke up. Misery followed misery. Beauchamp took an overdose of sleeping pills and died. Sarah was not only struck down with shame and misery; she became the subject of a much publicized case of drunkenness in America, widely reported with many photographs in England, and in 1959 she was found 'slightly distracted' after a stage performance in Liverpool, calling for the police instead of a taxi, and confusing the name of her hotel. She was taken to court and fined, amidst another welter of publicity.

This pathetic, mercurial, nerve-wracked but sweet-natured woman at last found happiness in a kind (twenty-third) baron, Henry Audley, like Sarah 49 years old, but in frail health. Alas, they enjoyed little more than one year's happiness before he died of a massive coronary on 3 July 1963. She lived nearly twenty years longer, dying on 24 February 1982.

All three of Jack's more stable and robust children were still alive and enjoying good health when the last of Winston's first three children died. Johnny has been an artist all his life, a sculptor, townscape and landscape painter, lecturer and writer, and divides his time between France, Britain and the United States. His younger brother, Peregrine, after taking an honours degree at Cambridge, later formed a construction company overseas, with a consultancy in London. He is married to a charming French-born woman, Yvonne, and lives deep in the heart of Hampshire. Jack's only daughter, Clarissa, surprised – but greatly pleased – both families when in the late summer of 1952 she announced her engagement to Anthony Eden. Eden had been a close friend and colleague of Winston's and Clementine's for so many years that the announcement was all the more surprising. Eden had been alone since his marriage had been dissolved in 1950, and after their wedding from number 10 Downing Street a new and happier era opened for him. Clarissa saw him through

609

a serious illness and a series of operations a year after their marriage, and saw him become Prime Minister in April 1955 and suffer the agonies of the aborted Suez operation the following year. He was created an earl in 1961, and the marriage remained full, rich and happy until Eden's death early in 1977.

Winston resigned as Prime Minister in 1955, four years after the death of George VI, the sovereign who had so reluctantly accepted him as his Prime Minister in 1940. His handing over to Eden had been delicate to engineer by his friends and colleagues. It was generally expected that he would follow this with the resignation of the parliamentary seat he had held for forty years. His own feeling about this fluctuated with the state of his health. As it happened, the year 1959 marked an improvement in his health and also in his spirits. On 20 April he told his constituents that he would be prepared to serve them again if they so wished. Wild applause! He was 84, his hearing was negligible, and his voice was scarcely audible.

The mishaps and setbacks of old age were increasingly incapacitating him. A fall in Hyde Park in 1960 was followed by another more serious one in the Hotel de Paris, in Monte Carlo, in the summer of 1962, when he broke his hip and had to spend weeks in hospital. The French Riviera continued to hold its magic for Winston after his resignation as Premier. He had at one time contemplated buying a villa there, to Clementine's consternation. 'Winston pooh-poohed Clementine's prudent and practical objections which greatly irritated her and the "Villa" discussions could become explosive,' Mary recalled. Even in their seventies and eighties these two could each spark up a row in no time. Until Max Beaverbrook had to give up his villa, La Capponcina, Winston loved best to stay there, where the staff welcomed him alone or with their master.

Almost to his last visits to the sun, staying mostly at the Hotel de Paris, Winston continued to paint, though with less dash and speed than he used to. He was immensely proud of his painting and touchingly immodest and anxious for praise. Peter Quennell remembers an occasion in 1952 at La Capponcina when Winston was showing him his paintings. 'He made us stop at each one, and demanded our comment. He was quite implacable about it.' And in an autobiographical volume, Quennell noted, 'Like all artists, good or bad, I suspected, he was sometimes plagued by doubts, and felt the sad discrepancy between what he had envisaged and the results he had produced. So splendidly confident in everything else he did, here he needed our support, and hovered about us almost anxiously . . . while he awaited the words of appreciation that were often difficult to find.'

A visit to the Riviera early in 1956 also led to an enduring friendship with Aristotle and Tina Onassis. Writing to Clementine (in hospital again), Winston described his first impression of the Greek shipping millionaire: 'He is a vy able and masterful man & told me a lot about Whales. He kissed my hand!' This led to many cruises aboard Onassis's giant yacht, the *Christina*. When Winston was very old and sometimes very silent, Onassis had a way of charming and provoking him back to the present. He would ask him, perhaps, 'Why were you so unfair to Lloyd George? He was a good friend and you didn't treat him very well.' If this did not arouse him, Onassis would try another tack, always rather close to home. 'My God, that was dishonourable, the way you treated FDR.' Sooner or later, Winston would be aroused from his lair and come roaring out, refuting angrily all his host's accusations. 'No, no, you've got it quite wrong.' The table would go quiet, and eventually Winston would sink back into apathy. Then Onassis would call out, 'It was really bloody the way you let Stalin down . . .'

Julian Amery also recalls the 90-year-old Winston's last visit to The Other Club, founded by Winston and F. E. Smith in 1911:

> He sat opposite me, very deaf now, so I sent written messages to him across the table. To the first and second there was no response, but the third suddenly aroused him and led him to make a five-minute

611

speech, just like the old days. Offered six oysters, he finished them, and the second lot that were put in front of him. The sole was consumed, followed by beef, then a *bombe* of some kind, along with champagne and plenty of brandy. Then he wouldn't go. He just sat there and wouldn't go, and we had to sit there with him.

Randolph's son, Winston, who had been born in the hectic, dangerous days of 1940, married in his grandfather's last year of life, in 1964. His bride was Mary ('Minnie') d'Erlanger. Old Winston was especially fond of the young man, who so closely resembled him and who, early in life, loved flying and had shown an adventurous spirit and had acted, as he had, as a correspondent at minor wars about the world.

Much was made of Winston's eightieth birthday, including the presentation by both Houses of Parliament of a portrait commissioned by Graham Sutherland, an artist much admired by Winston. In mid-August 1954, Graham Sutherland and his charming wife, Kathy, were invited to Chartwell for the weekend so that the artist could do some preliminary sketches and subject and sitter could get acquainted. It all went off very well. Winston and Clementine liked them both. 'He really is a most attractive man,' Clementine commented. The only difference between artist and sitter was about Winston's clothes. Winston had wanted to be painted in his robes of the Garter, which he had accepted in 1953, but Sutherland insisted on his politician's working day wear of black coat, striped trousers and bow tie.

'Are you going to paint me as a cherub or a bulldog?' Winston asked puckishly.

'It depends on what you show me.'

Later, Sutherland reported, 'He showed me a bulldog so I painted a bulldog.'

Winston gave three sittings and pronounced himself 'much struck by the power of the drawing'. Mary claimed that no-one else followed the progress of the portrait and that both

Winston and Clementine were outraged when they first saw it. Winston 'took an instant loathing. He felt he had been betrayed by the artist . . . Clementine too was shocked by it – she thought it was a cruel and gross travesty.'

A certain amount of confusion occurs here, for it is quite clear that Sutherland took the finished portrait down to Saltwood Castle in Kent, the home of Lord (Kenneth) Clark, the distinguished art historian and a man of boundless probity. 'Mr Sutherland showed me the portrait,' Lord Clark recorded. 'Maurice Bowra [warden of Wadham College, Oxford] was there.' It seemed that Clark had asked Clementine and Mary over to see it. 'At that time they were not upset at all, in fact they both admired it very much indeed.'

The Sutherland portrait showed a bowed, belligerent figure, deeply lined and aged, lower lip thrust forward – a real warrior and a brilliant rendering of the man as the public knew him best. Winston was at first deeply impressed, like Clementine. He was more familiar with Sutherland's earlier portrait of Max Beaverbrook than was Clementine. Again, compromise was not a notable feature, and Winston was sufficient of an artist himself to understand Sutherland's interpretation. He alone had been privileged with glimpses of it as it progressed.

The presentation of this portrait, marking the culmination of a day of birthday tributes from all over the world, took place on the morning of 30 November. In Winston's speech of thanks to the House in reply to a fulsome speech of praise by Clement Attlee, he referred to the portrait as 'a remarkable example of modern art. It certainly combines force with candour . . .'

When it was that Clementine took against the portrait remains uncertain. Perhaps on a more leisurely examination back at Chartwell she decided it was not sufficiently flattering. Perhaps one of the family commented that it was malignant, concealing all his qualities of kindness. But suddenly she could not bear it, and when Clementine took against something or someone, there was no limit to her execration. She judged it quite differently than she had on

613

her first view of it. She now believed that it sought to reduce Winston's standing and reputation in the eyes of the world. Her taste in art, such as it was, was strictly traditionalist. She was, for example, suspicious of and even hostile to the taste of Clarissa Eden, who was deeply intellectual. She could now see nothing but malignity in Sutherland's interpretation of Winston. By chance, Eden's Parliamentary Private Secretary Evelyn Shuckburgh a few weeks later was present at Buckingham Palace when Winston was lunching, and Prince Charles and Princess Anne were brought in to meet the guests. 'The little princess was fascinated by Winston,' he wrote in his diary, 'who sat slumped in his chair, looking just like the Sutherland portrait.'

Clementine stuck rigidly to her view that it was horrible, and Winston recognized how upset she was and agreed, with some regret, that it should not be hung at Chartwell. Later, Sutherland commented mildly, 'I felt that his wife disliked it more than he did.' At the same time, she let it be widely known how outraged Winston had been when he had first seen it. 'It caused him great pain,' she wrote to Max Beaverbrook, a friend and admirer of the artist, '& it all but ruined his eightieth birthday . . . It will never see the light of day.'

She never wrote truer words than these, for at some time in 1955 or 1956 – date uncertain – she had the portrait destroyed. She told no-one for about ten years, and then she divulged the truth to Mary and her husband, Christopher, that 'the Graham Sutherland portrait of my father was no longer in existence. We were both flabbergasted,' Mary recalled. Another decade passed. After Clementine's death her executors, including Mary, announced the truth. As Mary was to write, she was thankful that this act of vandalism was kept so confidential, for the outrage at this revelation was loud and universal.

The Times, in a leader, commented, 'A portrait of the greatest Englishman of his time by an artist who is arguably the best English portraitist is an object of outstanding historical importance . . . It was a work of honesty and force, a portrait of a warrior in his old age. Its destruction is a great misfortune.'

The artist himself merely commented (speaking for countless British people), 'It was an act of vandalism.' But added, 'I am not distressed. I think it is an odd sort of thing to happen.' Honor Balfour suggested that, 'Maybe the Churchills would not have destroyed Sutherland's masterpiece had he painted a poetic conception.' A correspondent to *The Times* wrote, 'To me the picture simply shows a proud, defiant and slightly belligerent old man. Surely not a bad description of Sir Winston.' And that, in essence, seemed to be the general view.

A weighty point, which Clementine had not perhaps considered, was raised by a distinguished Member of Parliament, and amateur artist, who recalled that the portrait was, ultimately, not to hang at Chartwell at all after Winston's death. 'I have consulted a number of my parliamentary colleagues who were involved in the painting of Sir Winston's portrait,' he wrote, '. . . and they all endorse my conviction that the picture was intended to be a tribute to him . . . and as such . . . hung in the Palace of Westminster.'

The depth of emotion suffered by Clementine over portraits of Winston was brought to the public's attention a few weeks after her death by David McFall, the distinguished sculptor and Royal Academician, who had been commissioned to sculpt a bronze figure of Winston to stand in his constituency:

> On the subject of portraits of Sir Winston she became transported into a screaming dervish. Conducting me around the gallery of 'acceptable' portraits at Chartwell, 'Not one had a single sitting,' she declared. 'Madam, it is self-evident,' I replied. 'And there will be no more,' she continued, 'you are the very last.'

Clementine later visited McFall's studio in Chelsea, where she announced in defiant tones that 'the Sutherland picture will never be seen again,' and that 'she had seen to it' – 'Adding to my consternation, that "Accidents could be arranged to sculpture as well."'

615

34

'I Lived in Churchill's Time . . .'

On 12 September 1958, when Winston was 83 and Clementine 73, they celebrated their golden wedding anniversary. They were staying with Max Beaverbrook at La Capponcina, not such an unsuitable venue for Clementine as it once was, for the fire had gone out of her dislike of the newspaper tycoon and statesman and she now got on quite well with him. She had not become 'calm of mind all passion spent', but she was certainly more comfortable company and had become quite a friend of Field Marshal Montgomery, with whom she used to scrap so violently.

It was a quiet, happy day, the only interruptions being telephone calls and numerous visits by the postman with messages from family, friends and strangers all over the world. In the afternoon, Winston learned that his horse, Welsh Abbot, had won a race at Doncaster. His son-in-law, Christopher Soames, had introduced him to the delights and excitement of racing ten years earlier, and he had made a lot of money out of it and been elected a member of the Jockey Club.

But truth to tell, the last decade of Winston's life was not much fun for him. A series of minor accidents and falls, a touch of pneumonia here, a dose of pleurisy there, conjunctivitis, an intractable skin trouble and a couple of operations, 'one of which found the abdomen full of adhesions', had all been faced with an odd mixture of almost morbid interest and insouciance.

Charles Wilson, his doctor to the end, wrote of Winston at 80:

A fine disregard for common sense has marked his earthly pilgrimage. What he wanted to do he has always done without a thought for the consequences. And now he can say that he has had his cake and eaten it too . . . fatigue of mind and body he hardly knew until he was 70; while whatever may happen overnight in the way of revelry, he wakes with a song in his heart and a zest for breakfast.

But as his eighties wore on, the zest diminished and then quite disappeared. Disability followed disability, deprivation followed deprivation. There were minor strokes, and each time he recovered less, until he became deaf and then almost speechless. It was a sad decline. At 90, he had wanted to die ten years earlier. He had long since ceased to paint, and he could not read. Old age had become 'a dreary solitude', and almost the only emotion he could express was distaste for being alone.

Poor Winston, who had spent the greater part of his professional life hurrying and impatient with the tardiness of others, spent most of January 1965 dying. He had a further stroke on 11 January and asked his doctor, 'Is this it?'

'I'm afraid so,' Wilson replied.

Christopher Soames, who had grown close to his father-in-law, was the last member of the family to exchange coherent words with him.

'Wouldn't you like a glass of champagne?'

'I'm so bored with it all.'

Day after day passed, the press jamming the street, cameras poised, and the family gathered, and then dispersed and gathered again as one crisis followed another. Clementine declined into a trance, from which she raised herself to go for walks with Mary – who only once heard her close to breaking down: 'I don't know where all my tears have gone.'

Suddenly, like a flash of glorious light in the chill January gloom, a message arrived: young Winston's wife, Minnie, has given birth to a son and both are doing well . . . Grandfather Randolph left a note with the news for Clementine, adding '. . . in the midst of death, we are in life'.

Two days later, early on Sunday morning, 24 January, the

duty nurse woke up the members of the family in the house to tell them that the end was near. All gathered round the bed, Clementine holding Winston's right hand, Randolph and his son by the pillow, Sarah and Mary at the foot of the bed, and others elsewhere in the lamp-lit room. Even now, he did not go quickly. But at length, Winston's deep breathing changed its rhythm; then came several long sighs – and silence.

'Has he gone?' Clementine asked. And the doctor confirmed that this was so.

A few minutes later the press were told: 'Shortly after 8 a.m. this morning, Sunday January 24th, Sir Winston Churchill died at his London Home.'

His father, Lord Randolph, had died on 24 January, too, exactly seventy years earlier.

Winston had remained a commoner to the end. He had accepted the Garter, the Order of Merit, a knighthood and much else, but when Queen Elizabeth II had asked him if he would like a dukedom, 'or anything like that', he had declined. He recalled all too vividly how near he had come to inheriting the Marlborough dukedom, and he was not now intending to deprive his male heirs of a political career where it matters, in the House of Commons. His funeral, however, was not only the most lavish and solemn, glorious and reverential, of any ever enjoyed by a commoner; it was the most triumphal funeral since that of Horatio Nelson, in 1806, after his victory at Trafalgar had saved the nation from an earlier tyrant at the cost of his own life.

During the lying in state in Westminster Hall, thousands upon thousands – four thousand an hour – paid their last respects. On the day of the funeral, Saturday 30 January, kings and queens, heads of state of many lands, old colleagues in war like Generals Eisenhower and de Gaulle who later had become leaders of their own nations, old colleagues in politics like Attlee and Macmillan, all made their way to St Paul's Cathedral. It was a bitter, grey day, 'the wind full of daggers of ice'.

From Westminster Hall, the coffin draped with the Union

Flag and resting on a gun carriage was drawn by sailors from the service he had led in two world wars the length of Whitehall, the Strand, Fleet Street, and up Ludgate Hill to the entrance of St Paul's Cathedral, the pavements tightly packed with citizens all the way, every flag at half-mast. At the bottom of the wide steps leading to the west door, the family mourners, Clementine heavily veiled, watched the coffin being carried inside.

The catafalque stood beneath the dome, flanked by candles burning in great sticks unused since the funeral of the Duke of Wellington more than one hundred years earlier.

> Queen Elizabeth arrived with her husband and son. The subdued hum of conversation died away. In the stillness that preceded the sweet singing in the choir as the procession moved up the aisle towards the catafalque, heraldic tabards moving out of the Middle Ages, in that moment there could have been no-one who did not feel himself in the presence of history . . .

The coffin, carrying Winston's decorations, orders and achievements, was placed upon the catafalque, and the service began. Afterwards, it was a long journey, with several stages, for the coffin and family mourners – to Tower Pier, and thence upriver in a launch, the south-bank dockyard cranes dipping in honour like serried lines of giraffes, while a flight of jet fighters roared overhead, in a formation as immaculate as all the proceedings of this day. But for Clementine, in her eightieth year, it was all proving a great strain, on her legs alone, and she was thankful to fall back in her seat in the train carriage at Waterloo Station. The steam locomotive was the *Winston Churchill* of the 'Battle of Britain' class, and the television picture of it from the air, streaming smoke as it cut its way through the English winter countryside, was for many the most memorable sight of a day rich in ceremony and solemn mass movement.

The final burial in a commonplace churchyard at Bladon, with only the family mourners present, was sublimely simple after the public extravagances of the earlier part of the day in the capital. The committal and the lowering of the coffin took only a few minutes, and then the family filed past Winston's grave, which was close to those of his brother and mother and father. There were only two wreaths and cards – 'To my darling Winston, Clemmie' and 'From the Nation and Commonwealth, Elizabeth R.'

Then everyone climbed thankfully into the twelve limousines, which drove them at a discreet pace through the village, only the urgently erected seven telephone kiosks outside the White Horse pub providing a hint that this had not been the burial of one of Bladon's four hundred villagers. A few minutes later, Clementine was back in the train to return home. Only a handful of villagers could now remember that day in 1908 when she had stepped from the special train and had made her way here, just married to the man she had now buried.

The tributes to Winston from all over the world, on radio and television and in the press, for which he had always held such respect and affection and occasional contempt, were countless. None was more moving than that of Anne Sharpley in the London *Evening Standard*. On the day of the funeral she wrote:

On such a day, when half of England's history and all her glories seem to lie in a single oaken coffin, to us who remain the past is noble, the present sorrowful, the future full of anti-climax. And yet no mood could be more at odds with the spirit of the man we mourn.

All his long life, Winston Churchill looked to a future more generous, more just and more abundant than all that had gone before. Where it was menacing, he faced it with an historian's mind and a warrior's courage. When the darkness fell on Europe

620

and millions lay beneath the laws of servitude and murder, he was freedom's beacon.

He had seen the marauders making ready, and warned his country to make ready too.

To his rare blend of shrewdness and romanticism, the partnership between this country and America was a unique alliance of age and wisdom with youth and power. Joined in a relationship so intimate and firm, defending the simple and honourable principles for which the free world fought, then peace could not become simply a shield for the strong and a mockery for the weak.

Twenty-five years later, Julian Amery, who knew him so well and whose father thought so well of him, too, but was often a stern critic (especially over India), remarked spontaneously, 'I don't know of any richer personality in history – as orator, author, man of action in war, statesman in peace. As a conversationalist he was continually original, with the marvellous ability to change gear so swiftly that he was a constant surprise.'

Although this biographer saw him only once, distantly across a dull, grey airfield, his inspiration in war and peace (and in completing this book about him) has been as infinite as it has been for so many millions. 'Some day, some year,' the Prime Minister of Australia, Sir Robert Menzies, remarked on the day of Winston's funeral, 'there will be old men and women whose pride it will be to say "I lived in Churchill's time . . ."'

Clementine lived even longer than Winston, and she suffered fewer physical disabilities and enjoyed a slower rate of decline in spirit and body. The Ogilvy stock proved more physically robust in her case, though her sister Nellie died of cancer at the age of 66, in 1955. It was Clementine's nervous system that was frail, not her physique. Released of her worries over Winston, after his death she briskly set about a programme of new economies. Both the Hyde Park

Gate houses were sold, and she acquired a lease on a flat at 7 Princes Gate, not far away. Here she settled with a staff of two, a secretary-chauffeuse-companion and cook, and lived very modestly. Chartwell was ready for the public the following year. The Queen had conferred a life peerage on her, and she opened their old home as Lady Spencer-Churchill. She attended several debates at the House of Lords but never voted because her hearing was so bad that she could not follow what was happening.

With the death of Randolph on 6 June 1968, little more than three years after Winston's, Clementine was left with only her two youngest girls, and when Christopher Soames was appointed Ambassador in Paris, Mary went to live there and seldom came home. Meanwhile, the older and more disabled Clementine became, the more she worried about money and the more she contrived further economies. Unfortunately, when she decided to put several of her pictures up for auction, including two of Winston's, she did not do so anonymously, and the news that she was in financial trouble was taken up by the press. A national appeal was proposed in *The Times*, and gifts of money poured in with letters of sympathy. All this was very unfortunate and embarrassing for her and the family, and a statement had to be issued and the money sent back. And then the pictures fetched a price far exceeding what she had been led to expect, with the result that even her imagined financial insecurity was cured overnight.

Clementine died peacefully in her flat on 12 December 1977, aged 91 years and 8 months. She had acquired a degree of serenity in her old age that she had never known before. Her last great campaign had been against Winston's old doctor. Charles Wilson, Lord Moran, had published in 1966 a brilliant, revealing and highly readable account of Winston's health record (and much else) from the time he was appointed his personal physician in 1940 until his death. He claimed that Winston had authorized him, even encouraged him, to write this book. But of course there was no proof of that, and Clementine and her family and friends claimed that Wilson had not only broken the Hippocratic oath of patient confidentiality but – like the unfortunate Graham Sutherland – had painted a false picture of the man. She could not have the book banned or destroyed, however, and the publicity aroused by the controversy ensured that it sold like hot cakes.

There were a few indignant letters from her in *The Times* on other controversial subjects after this, and she remained discomfortingly forthright on a wide range of topics privately. But year by year the fuse lengthened, and the charge when fired became less lethal. She ceased to travel, liked to be read to (a tiring business because of her deafness), played cards, and was curious to know what was in the newspapers, which she read (while she still could) wearing cotton gloves against the stain of newsprint ink. From her later eighties, her life became as circumscribed as Winston's had been at this age, but her forthrightness, lack of introspection and attachment to stoicism almost as a cult got her through these last years with much less misery.

On 24 January 1977, the anniversary of Winston's death, a service of thanksgiving for Clementine's life was held in Westminster Abbey. It was a very grand and very solemn occasion, with one brilliant touch: young Winston, soon to become a Member of Parliament himself, read from the sermon Welldon had given at the marriage of Winston and Clementine almost seventy years earlier:

> The sun shines upon your union today; the happy faces of your friends surround you; good wishes are lavished upon you; many prayers ascend to Heaven on your behalf. Will you suffer me to remind you how much you may be to the other in the coming days? There must be in the statesman's life many times when he depends upon the love, the insight, the penetrating sympathy and devotion of his wife . . .

How far did Clementine match up to the good Welldon's expectations? What can be said incontrovertibly of Clementine's record is that she did for Winston, and her country, what she believed to be for the best. It is futile to speculate what might have been. She remained for all her life the woman whom Winston married as a young statesman, a woman of numerous contradictions of character, steel-willed, sharp-tempered, sentimental, dogmatic, argumentative, yet undeviatingly loyal, fierce in her hates and unforgiving, intractable, high-principled, a possessor of great moral courage, but so exhausting to live with that neither she nor Winston would have survived without the long breaks in one another's company.

Appendix

Winston's father, Lord Randolph Churchill, was a figure who readily attracted enemies, socially and politically. Malicious rumours about him, all without any substantiation, began to circulate, even before his death, that he had contracted syphilis early in the course of his marriage. On discovering his affliction, he abstained from intercourse with Jennie – so the story went – which was the reason for the difference in personalities of her two boys.

The notorious Frank Harris seized upon this and included it in his *My Life & Loves*, a scurrilous book banned in Britain but freely available on the Continent. This grossly defamatory story was used time and again to depreciate the political reputation of Winston, implying that he had inherited the irrational, unstable and immoral tendencies of his father. It was immensely damaging, especially in the early 1920s and the 1930s when he was embarrassing the Government over rearmament, India and the abdication crisis. The Conservative Central Office justified his omission from the Cabinet by repeating the rumours that he was an unbalanced alcoholic. To compound this insult to the Churchill reputation, it has been repeated in recent biographies, especially in America, as if it were the historical truth.

Chronology of the Life of
Winston Spencer Churchill 1874–1965

1874	30 November	Born at Blenheim Palace
1880	4 February	His brother, John Strange (Jack), born
1882	November	To St George's School
1884	September	To the Misses Thomsons' school
1885	1 April	Clementine Hozier (future wife) born
1888	April	To Harrow School
1893	September	To Sandhurst Military College
1894	December	Passes out of Sandhurst
1895	24 January	Lord Randolph Churchill (father) dies
	20 February	Commissioned in 4th Hussars regiment
	9 November	Arrived in New York City and thence to the Cuban war of liberation
	27 December	Returns to London
1896	February	First earnings from journalism
	September	Soldiering in India
1897	September	Malakand campaign in India
1898	9 July	Returns to London
1898	26 July	Embarks for Egypt and the Sudan to join General Kitchener
	2 September	Cavalry charge at the Battle of Omdurman
	27 September	Returns to London
	2 December	Rejoins his regiment in India
1899	April	Returns to London via Cairo
	3 May	Resigns his army commission

	14 October	Commissioned in the Royal Bucks Hussars and embarks for South Africa and the Boer War as a correspondent for the *Morning Post*
	7 November	Publishes *The River War*
	15 November	Made prisoner of war by the Boers
	23 December	Returns to Durban after escaping from Pretoria
1900	28 February	At the relief of Ladysmith
	20 July	Lands back in England
	1 October	Elected to Parliament as MP for Oldham
1904	31 May	'Crosses the floor' to join the Liberals
1905	10 December	Appointed Undersecretary at the Colonial Office after winning the seat at North-West Manchester
1906	2 January	Publishes *Lord Randolph Churchill*
	13 January	Liberal landslide victory in general election
	August	To German army manoeuvres as a guest of Kaiser Wilhelm II
1907	August	To French army manoeuvres
	October to January 1908	Tour on behalf of the Colonial Office to Malta, Cyprus, Egypt, East Africa and the Sudan
1908	12 September	Marries Clementine Hozier
1909	11 July	Daughter Diana born
1910	February	Appointed Home Secretary
1911	28 May	Son Randolph born
	September	Appointed First Lord of the Admiralty
1914	4 August	Britain declares war on Germany
	24 August	Battle of Heligoland Bight
	7 October	Daughter Sarah born
	29 October	Prince Louis of Battenberg resigns

		as First Sea Lord and is replaced by Admiral Lord ('Jacky') Fisher
1914	1 November	Battle of Coronel
	8 December	Battle of Falkland Islands
1915	8 March	Gallipoli naval bombardment
	25 April	Gallipoli landings
	17 May	Is informed by Asquith that he must resign as First Lord
	November	Volunteers for active service in France
1916	February	Appointed Battalion Colonel at the Front
	2 March	Returns to London
	7 March	Makes ill-considered speech on naval estimates
	7 May	Returns to parliamentary duties
1917	July	Appointed by Lloyd George as Minister of Munitions
1918	15 November	Daughter Marigold born
	December	'Khaki' general election in which he retains his seat
1919	January	Appointed Secretary of State for Army and RAF
1921	January	Inherits a substantial Irish fortune
	February	Appointed Secretary of State for the Colonies
	April	Moves house to Sussex Square in London
	29 June	Jennie Churchill (mother) dies
	23 August	Marigold (daughter) dies
1921–1922		Works to achieve Irish and Middle East settlements
1922	15 September	Daughter Mary born
	15 September	Chartwell Manor bought
	15 November	Fails re-election as MP for Dundee
1923	10 April	Publishes the first volume of *The World Crisis*

	6 December	Fails to re-enter Parliament
1924	29 October	Elected to Parliament as MP for Epping, as a Conservative; Conservative government returned
	6 November	Appointed Chancellor of the Exchequer
1925		Returns Britain to the gold standard
1926	4 May	Organizes the production of the *British Gazette* for the duration of the general strike
1929	9 August to 5 November	Visits Canada and the USA
1929–1939		Backbench MP opposing government policy on India and rearmament (the 'wilderness years')
1939	3 September	Appointed First Lord of the Admiralty for the second time
1940	10 May	Appointed Prime Minister
1941	9–12 August	Atlantic Alliance meeting with Franklin D. Roosevelt at Placentia Bay, Newfoundland
	December	Arcadia Conference, Washington, DC
	27 December	Suffers first heart trouble
1943	28 November to 1 December	Teheran Conference with Roosevelt and Joseph Stalin
	12 December	Seriously ill at Carthage, North Africa
1944	12 June	Visits Normandy six days after D-Day invasion
1945	4–11 February	Yalta Conference with Roosevelt and Stalin
	8 May	Celebration of Victory in Europe (VE) Day
	26 July	Resigns as Prime Minister on defeat of Conservatives by Labour

1946	5 March	Fulton, Missouri, speech warning of Soviet designs
1951	27 October	On Conservative election victory, again becomes Prime Minister
1955	5 April	Resigns as Prime Minister
1964	27 July	Last appearance in the House of Commons
1965	24 January	Dies at the age of 90
	30 January	State funeral
1977	12 December	Clementine dies at the age of 91

Source Notes

In any dual biography of Winston Churchill and Clementine Churchill, the author must rely on the eight volumes of Martin Gilbert's majesterial biography, the first two of which were written by Winston and Clementine's son, Randolph. The standard biography of Clementine is her daughter Mary's *Clementine Churchill*. Both these works are quoted extensively, as are the thirteen companion volumes of correspondence and papers, the first five of which (1874–1914) are edited by Randolph Churchill and the remainder (1914–1939) by Martin Gilbert.

Other works upon which I have relied and quoted from are Churchill's own books (listed in the copyright acknowledgements), Violet Bonham Carter's *Winston Churchill as I Knew Him* (1966), John Colville's *The Fringes of Power: Downing Street Diaries 1939–1955*, Peter de Mendelssohn's undeservedly neglected *The Age of Churchill: Heritage and Adventure 1874–1911* (1961), Lord Moran's highly controversial and revealing *Winston Churchill: The Struggle for Survival 1940–1965* (1966), and Anita Leslie's *Cousin Randolph* (1985).

A number of significant sources only are indicated below:

Chapter 1
Page 10. The description of Clementine at the age of 23 comes from Lady Cynthia Asquith *Diaries* (1968).

Chapter 2
Page 11. Winston's account of his mother is taken from *My Early Life* (paperback edition) and Anita Leslie in *The Fabulous Leonard Jerome* provides the second description.

Pages 14–15. This material on the first Duke of Marlborough is drawn largely from Winston's standard biography of his ancestor.

Pages 18–19. Jennie's description of Blenheim is from Winston's *Lord Randolph Churchill Vol 1*.

Page 37. The account of Winston's journey home is built up from railway timetables, contemporary weather reports, Kelly's *London Directory* and a close examination of 2 Connaught Place today (unchanged externally but now an office).

Chapter 4

Page 40. Material on the Miss Thomsons' school at Hove is derived from local records and examination today, again unchanged but now an old people's home.

Page 41. The *Eurydice* disaster account is compiled from contemporary reports.

Page 42. 15 *lines up*. Drawn from Robert Rhodes James's *Lord Randolph Churchill* (1969), p. 255.

Pages 46–7. Reported in Winston's *My Early Life*, and discussed at a meeting with Amery's son Julian, 25 July 1989.

Chapter 5

All quotes in this chapter are from the official biography, *My Early Life* and companion volumes. The quotation 15 lines from the end, page 69, is from *Two Gentlemen of Verona*, Act 1.

Chapter 6

This account of Winston's Cuba campaign is drawn largely from his own writings and several accounts of the insurrection from Spanish sources.

Chapter 7

Page 81. 15 *lines up*. Shane Leslie, *The End of a Chapter* (1916), p. 117.

Page 96. *line* 1. Bindon Blood, *Four Score Years and Ten* (1933), p. 303.

Chapter 8

Page 116. *line* 18. R. Hough, *Former Naval Person* (1985), p. 21.

The other quotes in this chapter stem mainly from *Companion*, Vol 1, pp. 839–86, and *My Early Life* pp. 171–200.

Chapters 9 and 10

Besides the standard works on the Boer War (e.g. Byron Farwell, *The Great Boer War* [1976]), much valuable detail acquired from retracing Winston's journey from Durban to Estcourt, Ladysmith and Pretoria; and also the scenes of battle like Spion Kop. Also useful was Ian Hamilton's *Listening for the Drums* (1944), quoted at length, p. 149.

Chapter 11

The quotations from Winston's maiden speech in Parliament are reported in *Hansard*, the parliamentary record, for 13 May 1901.

Chapter 12

Page 171. The quotations on or by Marsh are from Christopher Hassall, *Edward Marsh* (1959), p. ix, and Edward Marsh, *A Number of People* (1939), p. 154.

Pages 178–9. Travels in East Africa in 1989 were of assistance in writing of this area.

Chapter 13

Page 182. A great deal of family detail on Jack Churchill and his wife Gwendeline ('Goonie') is derived from conversations with their children, Peregrine Churchill who controls many of the family papers, and the Countess of Avon.

Chapter 14

Page 195 (*and over*). This exquisite quote on Winston's underwear comes from *Winston Churchill as I Knew Him* by Violet Bonham Carter, p. 216, the most revealing single volume about him at this time.

Chapter 15

Page 214. *last line*. W. S. Blunt, *Diaries* (1920), Vol II, p. 271. Three volumes concerning Jacky Fisher relate to this chapter: his *Records* of 1919, a most idiosyncratic book of memoirs; Winston's *World Crisis*, Vol I (1923), p. 155, and A. J. Marder (ed.), *Fear God & Dread Nought: The Letters of John Arbuthnot Fisher*, Vol II (1956), p. 155.

Page 224 (*and later*), *line* 20. Viscount Haldane, *Autobiography* (1929), p. 230. Violet Bonham Carter's account of these negotiations at Archerfield are fascinating.

Chapter 16

Page 235. The long quote by Admiral James is from C. Eade (ed.), *Churchill by his Contemporaries* (1953), p. 139.

Page 242. This long quote on Beatty's exasperation is from a letter to his wife, Beatty Papers.

Page 245. *Belfast Weekly Newsletter*, 15 February 1912.

Page 247. 10 *lines up*. Broadlands archives.

Page 250. *line* 20. W. Raleigh, *The War in the Air*, Vol I (1922), p. 265.

Chapter 17

Page 255. *line* 2. R. H. Bacon, *The Life of John Rushworth Jellicoe* (1936), p. 183.

Page 259. *line* 2. To Lord George Hamilton, 7 August 1914. Hamilton MSS.

Page 265. *line* 7. Asquith MSS; line 24. Royal Archives, Windsor.

Chapter 18

Page 287. *last lines*. This is the first of a number of extracts from M. & E. Brock (eds.), *H. H. Asquith: Letters to Venetia Stanley* (1982), a revealing and totally indiscreet correspondence between the Prime Minister and his love.

Page 291. *line* 9. Commodore Tyrwhitt to his wife. Tyrwhitt Papers.

Page 298. *line* 21. To Lady Beatty 30 October 1914. Beatty Papers.

Page 299. 3 *lines up*. Princess Louis of Battenberg to her lady-in-waiting, 30 October 1914. Broadlands Archives.

Chapter 19
Page 306. 11 *lines up*. Fisher Papers, Kilverstone.
Page 313. *last line*. Lord Hankey, *Supreme Command 1914–18*, Vol I (1961), p. 265.

Chapter 20
The main sources of reference in this 'Dardanelles' chapter are the Fisher Papers at Lennoxlove and Kilverstone, and the Lloyd George *Memoirs*, e.g.:
Page 332. 13 *lines up*. D. Lloyd George, *Memoirs*, Vol I (1933), pp. 225–6.

Chapter 21
Page 347. *line 9*. *The National Review*, Vol 65, p. 623.
Most quotes thereafter, except for those from the official Winston biography and papers, are from Violet Bonham Carter and the Cynthia Asquith diaries.

Chapter 22
Page 366. 5 *lines up*. Winston's *Thoughts and Adventures*, p. 110.
Page 380. 13 *lines up*. A. D. Grigg, *With Winston Churchill at the Front* (1924), p. 59.

Chapter 23
Apart from (credited) magazine and newspaper comments, most quotes are from the Fisher Papers.

Chapter 24
Page 408. 15 *lines up*. Hansard.
Page 409. This vivid account of the lull before the storm is from Winston's *The World Crisis*, Vol IV (1927), p. 410.

Chapter 25
Page 418. *last line*. Andrew Boyle, *Trenchard* (1962), p. 237.

Chapter 26

Apart from credited quotes from magazines and newspapers, the quotes are mainly from Gilbert and Soames.

Chapter 27

Page 459. *line* 6. Sarah Churchill, *A Thread in the Tapestry* (1967), pp. 36–7.

Page 460. 7 *lines up*. Anita Leslie, *Cousin Randolph* (1985), p. 13.

Page 470. 4 *lines up*. J. Campbell, *F. E. Smith, 1st Earl of Birkenhead* (1983), p. 712.

Chapter 28

Page 479. *last lines*. Nigel Nicolson (ed.), *Harold Nicolson Diaries & Letters 1930–39* (1966), p. 403.

Page 485. *line* 10. Conversation with Sir Clifford Jarrett, 25 June 1984.

Page 488. *line* 19. W. F. Kimball (ed.), *Churchill & Roosevelt: the Complete Correspondence*, Vol I (1984), p. 24.

Page 497. *line* 14. Channon diaries, p. 302.

Chapter 29

Page 499. *line* 6. Alastair Horne, *To Lose a Battle* (1969), pp. 180–1.

Page 504. *line* 1. *King John*, Act V.

Much other material in this chapter stems from the Colville diaries and *Hansard*.

Chapter 30

Page 539. *line* 10. Hastings Ismay, *Memoirs* (1960), p. 184.

Page 539. *line* 24. R. Tree, *When the Moon was High* (1975), p. 130.

Chapter 31

The opening pages originate from Colville and conversations with Mountbatten, July 1972.

Page 555. *line* 27. G. McJimsey, *Harry Hopkins* (1987), p. 174.

Other material in this chapter originates in the Roosevelt Papers, Winston's *History of the Second World War*, Vol III (1950), Eleanor Roosevelt's *As He Saw It* (1946), p. 29, Colville diaries and Harriman & Abel's *Special Envoy to Churchill and Stalin 1941–6*, (1976).

Chapter 32
By the nature of this chapter, the Moran diaries figure strongly, for example, p. 572.
Page 566. *line* 7. D. Dilke (ed.), *The Diaries of Sir Alexander Cadogan*, 1938–45, pp. 475–6.
Page 569. *line* 12. 3 March 1942, Beaverbrook Papers.
Page 581. *line* 9. J. Wheeler-Bennett, *King George VI* (1958), p. 601.

Chapter 33
Wheeler-Bennett's life of George VI, and conversations with Peter Quennell, Peregrine Churchill, Lord Mountbatten and Julian Amery all contributed to this chapter. A number of people including Kathleen Sutherland contributed usefully to the passage on the destruction of Graham Sutherland's portrait of Winston.
Page 600. Wheeler-Bennett, p. 636. Memories of Winston's last years have been provided by Moran (especially), Winston's son-in-law Christopher Soames, and, among others, recent conversations with the Right Hon. Julian Amery, MP, and the present Winston S. Churchill, MP, and fellow writers who covered Winston's funeral.

Recommended Reading

Winston's early life, including his soldiering:

Winston Churchill, *My Early Life* (1930)
Peter de Mendelssohn, *The Age of Churchill* (1961)
Randolph S. Churchill, *Winston S. Churchill*. Vol I Youth 1874–1900 (1966)
Winston S. Churchill, *Frontiers & Wars*: his four early books covering his life as soldier and war correspondent (1962)
Mrs George Cornwallis-West, *The Reminiscences of Lady Randolph Churchill* (1908)

Clementine's antecedents and early life:

Mary Soames, *Clementine Churchill* (1979)
Mabel, Countess of Airlie, *Thatched with Gold* (1962)
Wilfrid Scawen Blunt, *My Diaries* (Vol I 1912, Vol 2 1920)
Jonathan Guinness, *The House of Mitford* (1984)

Winston and Clementine, from marriage to 1919:

Violet Bonham Carter, *Winston Churchill as I Knew Him* (1965)
Cynthia Asquith, *Diaries 1915–18* (1968)
Kenneth Rose, *King George V* (1983)
H. H. Asquith, *Letters to Venetia Stanley* (Selected and edited by M. and E. Brock) (1982)
R. Hough, *First Sea Lord*, an authorized biography of Admiral Lord Fisher (1969)
R. Hough, *Former Naval Person: Churchill & the Wars at Sea* (1985)
Randolph S. Churchill, *Winston S. Churchill*. Vol II Young Statesman 1901–14 (1967)

Martin Gilbert, *Winston S. Churchill*. Vol III 1914–16 (1971)
Martin Gilbert, *Winston S. Churchill*. Vol IV 1916–22 (1975)
Martin Gilbert, *Winston S. Churchill*. Vol V 1922–39 (1976)

Winston and Clementine, 1919–1939:

Mary Soames, *Clementine Churchill* (1979)
Chips: The Diaries of Sir Henry Channon (edited by Robert Rhodes James) (1967)
Frances Donaldson, *Edward VIII* (1974)
Frances Stevenson, *Lloyd George*: A Diary by Frances Stevenson (edited by A.J.P. Taylor) (1971)
Earl of Birkenhead, *F. E.* (1960)
Consuelo Vanderbilt Balsan, *The Glitter & the Gold* (1925)
Andrew Boyle, *Poor Dear Brendan* (1974)
Martin Gilbert, *Winston S. Churchill*. Vol V 1922–39 (1976)

Winston and Clementine, from 1939:

Mary Soames, *Clementine Churchill* (1979)
Martin Gilbert, *Winston S. Churchill* Vol VI 1939–41 (1983)
Martin Gilbert, *Winston S. Churchill* Vol VII 1941–45 (1986)
Ronald Lewin, *Churchill as Warlord* (1973)
John Colville, *The Fringes of Power: Downing Street Diaries 1939–55* (1985)
Ronald Tree, *When the Moon was High: Memoirs of Peace and War 1897–1942* (1975)
Lord Moran, *Winston Churchill: the Struggle for Survival 1940–65* (1966)

(For Winston Churchill's interpretations of the history of the two world wars, readers are also directed towards the volumes of *The World Crisis* and *The Second World War*, the second being less tendentious than the first.)

Index

Note: Ranks and titles are generally the latest given in the text

Earl): WSC dines with, 120;
in 1900 election, 153; leads
divided party, 162, 170; resigns
leadership, 170; in 'Souls', 191;
criticizes WSC's presence at
Sidney Street, 208–9; succeeds
WSC as First Lord, 345, 347;
appoints Fisher to chair Board
of Inventions, 357; presents
1916 Naval Estimates, 382,
385, 387; and WSC's criticisms,
389–90, 398; writes on golf,
424; and WSC's Abbey Division
defeat, 449

Balfour, Honor, 615

Ballin, Albert, 273–7

Balmoral, 222

Balsan, Consuelo (formerly Duchess
of Marlborough), 447, 482, 575

Balsan, Jacques, 447, 482

Baltic Project, 305, 314

Bangalore (India), 85–6

Baring, Hugo, 83

Barnes, Reginald, 74–7, 83, 87,
91–3, 126, 404

Barrymore, Ethel, 181

Baruch, Bernard, 462, 465–6

Bath, 89

Battenberg, Admiral Prince
Henry, 274

Battenberg, Admiral Prince Louis
of (later Marquess of Milford
Haven): accompanies Prince
of Wales to India, 23; child by
Lillie Langtry, 159–60; Fisher
recommends, 236; as Second
Sea Lord, 237; on Enchantress
tour, 238; and WSC's warship
names, 247; on WSC's row
with Poore, 254; as First Sea
Lord, 255–7; and Callaghan
dismissal, 258; and Fleet
Reserve, 268–9; and outbreak
of First War, 273–4, 276–9;
concurs with WSC in war, 295;
resignation, 296–9; death 438;
and Mountbatten, 569

Beatty, Admiral David (later 1st

Earl): in Sudan, 110; appointed
WSC's Naval Secretary, 237; on
Enchantress cruise, 239–40, 242;
and Bridgeman, 258; supports
Jellicoe over Callaghan, 258;
commands battle-cruisers, 280;
on Battle of Coronel, 296; on
dismissal of Battenberg, 298;
on appointment of Fisher, 299,
334; and Falklands Battle, 306;
attacks German battle-cruisers,
307; opposes Dardanelles
campaign, 324; and Fisher's
resignation, 336; as First Sea
Lord, 455

Beatty, Ethel, Countess, 240

Beatty, Peter (son of above), 544

Beauchamp, Anthony, 608–9

Beaverbrook, William Maxwell
Aitken, 1st Baron: and WSC's
dismissal as First Lord, 349;
parliamentary career, 416;
relations with WSC, 416;
Clementine's attitude to, 448,
524, 567–9, 616; at Chartwell,
459; as Minister of Aircraft
Production, 507, 523, 538;
relations with Sinclair, 511,
523; godfather to young
Winston, 544; helps Pamela,
545; accompanies WSC to
Washington, 568; and 1945
election, 596, 598; Riviera
home, 610, 616; Sutherland
portrait of, 613; and portrait of
WSC, 614

Beit, Alfred, 124

Belgium: in First War, 287–90;
Second War, 499–501, 515, 517

Bell, Gertrude, 427

Beresford, Admiral Lord Charles,
23, 297, 299

Beresford, Lord William, VC, 72–3,
80, 90–91

Berkhamsted, 9

Bevir, Anthony, 510

Birkenhead, Frederick Edward
Smith, 1st Earl of: friendship

Churchill, Lord Randolph (WSC's father): courtship and marriage, 14, 15–19, 184; qualities and character, 15; elected to parliament, 17, 20; and birth of WSC, 22; and brother George's Aylesford affair, 23–5, 56; social ostracism, 25, 32; in Ireland, 27–9, 56; Irish policy, 29; political career, 29, 34, 42–4, 56, 192; relations with WSC, 32, 39, 43, 51, 63, 66; and WSC's pneumonia, 40; and WSC at Harrow, 45, 53–4, 58–9; marriage relations, 55; gambling, 43, 56; ill-health, 56–7, 63, 66; and WSC's boyhood injury, 59–61; critical letter to WSC on entry into Sandhurst, 63, 67; financial economies, 64–5; decline and death, 67–9, 71, 379, 618; and WSC's parliamentary performances, 159; and WSC's change of party, 165; WSC's biography of, 173–4, 424; and Margot Asquith, 192; syphilis rumours, 468, 625

Churchill, Randolph (WSC's son): born, 215; at Overstrand, 271, 275; at Hoe Farm, 354; letter from WSC in France, 379; at Blenheim, 399; and First War air raids, 401; at Lullenden Farm, 402; dominance in family, 402; relations with mother, 411, 460–61; character and behaviour, 411, 428, 461–2, 489, 523, 607; Frinton holiday, 439; influenza, 448; on WSC's appointment as Chancellor, 452; at Eton, 452; relations with father, 462–3, 464, 489, 607; gambling, 462, 489, 544; accompanies WSC to North America, 464–5; drinking, 464, 489, 607; marriage, 489; war service, 489, 500, 523, 544–5,

566–7; elected to parliament, 523; in Carthage with WSC, 579; loses seat in 1945 election, 597, 599; post-war career, 607; divorce and remarriage, 607; death, 607–8, 622; at WSC's death, 617

Churchill, Sarah (WSC's daughter): born, 290; at Hoe Farm, 354; on family in First War, 399; steals chocolate, 402; on Lindemann, 459; on Johnny and Randolph, 463; relations with father, 464, 608; first marriage, 464; drinking, 464, 609; stage career, 489–90, 524, 608; marriage breakdown, 524, 542, 545; unbalance, 524; in WAAF, 524; and Winant, 541–2; in North Africa with WSC, 577–8; at Yalta, 585; divorce, 595; later marriages, 608–9; death, 609; at WSC's death, 618

Churchill, Winston (father of 1st Duke of Marlborough), 14

Churchill, Winston Leonard Spencer: born, 11, 21–2; in Ireland, 25, 27–8; and Mrs Everest, 25–6, 72; appearance, 26–7, 80, 225, 267, 415; attitude to learning, 31; friendship with brother Jack, 31, 34, 36–7, 45, 237, 461; relations with father, 32, 42, 43, 51, 63, 66; schooling, 32–5, 39; relations with mother, 38, 39; boyhood interest in soldiering, 45–6; pneumonia, 39–40; holidays in Isle of Wight, 40–42; joins Primrose League, 44; at Harrow, 44–51, 53–5, 58; memorizes poetry and plays, 48 & n; ambitions, 51–2, 79, 87; lisp, 51–2; fencing, 54; pets, 54–5, 58, 82; fails Sandhurst Further entry, 58; youthful injury, 59–61; gains entry to Sandhurst, 62; Swiss holiday,

651

657

659

Mussolini, Benito, 492

314–15, 320, 322,
325, 333
Quennell, Peter, 611
Quick Luncheon Club, 407
Quilter, Colonel, 318–19

radar, 477, 486–7
Ramsay, Admiral Sir Bertram,
516, 581
Rawlinson, General Sir Henry, 412
Reading, Rufus Isaacs, 1st Marquess
of, 266n
Redesdale, Bertram Mitford, 1st
Baron: fathers Blanche Hozier's
children, 5
Redesdale, Clementine, Lady, 5
Redmond, John, 362
Reitz, Francis, 134–5
Repulse, HMS (battle-cruiser), 567
Reynaud, Paul, 514–17, 521
Rhine, River: mining of, 501
Rhodes, Cecil, 122
Ritchie, Sir George, 416–17
Roberts, Field-Marshal Frederick
Sleigh, 1st Earl, 66, 100,
147–9, 163
Robertson (servant), 37
Robinson, Geoffrey *see* Dawson,
Geoffrey
Rodd, Sir Rennell, 227
Roden, John Strange Jocelyn, 5th
Earl of, 30
Romilly, Bertram, 369, 502
Romilly, Esmond, 502
Romilly, Giles, 502, 595
Romilly, Nellie (*née* Hozier;
Clementine's sister): born, 5;
at Blenheim, 200; Clementine
recuperates with, 214; on
Enchantress cruise, 238; visits
mother in Dieppe, 270; brings
mother to England in war,
284–5; nursing in war, 285–6;
and WSC's departure for
Western Front, 360; marriage,
369; WSC helps financially, 426;
and brother's death, 433; and
husband's death, 502; death, 621

Rommel, General Erwin, 499,
567, 574
Roose, Dr Robson, 35, 39–40, 57–8,
61, 68–9
Roosevelt, Elliot, 558–9
Roosevelt, Franklin Delano:
wartime relations with WSC,
488, 512, 519–20, 527, 538,
542, 551–2, 573; and Halifax's
hope for truce, 492; wartime
aid for Britain, 542; wins third
presidential term, 551; meets
WSC in Newfoundland, 552–3,
555, 557–61; and Japanese
attack on Pearl Harbor, 563,
573; WSC visits in Washington,
565–8, 572–3, 574–5; at
Marrakesh meeting, 575–6; at
Teheran Conference, 576; and
WSC's visit to Normandy, 585;
at Yalta, 585; death, 590
Rosaura (yacht), 472–3
Rose, Mlle (governess), 435–6
Rosebery, Archibald Philip
Primrose, 5th Earl of, 66,
152–3, 154, 159
Ross, Robert, 260
Rothermere, Harold Sidney
Harmsworth, 1st Viscount,
416, 478
Rothschild, Nathan, Baron, 168
Rothschild, Nathaniel, 58
Rowan, Leslie, 593–4
Rowntree, Seebohm: *Poverty*, 160
Royal Air Force: formed, 418;
pre-war strength, 475–7; early
wartime actions, 488; fighters
in France, 501, 516; wins
Battle of Britain, 532–7; WSC
visits, 532–7
Royal Bucks Hussars, 124
Royal Fleet Reserve ('The Third
Fleet'), 268–70, 274, 277
Royal Military College *see* Sandhurst
Royal Naval Air Service, 244,
250, 418
Royal Navy: Fisher reforms, 216–18,
221; pre-1914 disposition,

662

White, General Sir George, 126, 142, 145–7
White, Luke, 46
Whyte, Maryott ('Moppett'; 'Nana'), 448 & n, 459, 489, 566
Wigram, Ralph, 475
Wildman-Lushington, Captain Gilbert, 251
Wilhelm II, Kaiser, 56, 176, 264, 273, 291
Williams, Colonel Owen, 23
Wilson, Sir Arthur ('Tug'), 219–20, 236, 255, 302, 305, 314, 339, 348
Wilson, Sir Charles see Moran, Charles, 1st Baron
Wilson, George, 67
Wilson, Colonel Gordon, 177–8
Wilson, Field-Marshal Sir Henry, 431
Wilson, Muriel, 181, 188, 203
Wimborne, Cornelia, Lady (née Spencer-Churchill; WSC's aunt), 196, 266, 403, 404, 437
Wimborne, Ivor Bertie, 1st Baron, 196, 200

Winant, Connie, 548
Winant, J. Gilbert, 541, 548, 555, 562–3, 592
Windsor, Edward, Duke of (formerly Prince of Wales; then King Edward VIII), 468–9, 505
Windsor, Duchess of (formerly Mrs Wallis Simpson), 468–9, 505
Wolff, Sir Henry Drummond, 74
Wolseley, Field-Marshal Garnet, Viscount, 122, 142
Wood, Sir Evelyn, 2, 100, 103, 122
Wood, Sir Kingsley, 503
Woodford (Epping), 596
Workers' Weekly, 450
Wylie, Captain James, 134
Wyndham, George, 152

Yalta Conference, 1945, 585, 593
Yule, Revd Henry, 22

Zeebrugge, 316
Zinoviev, G., 450